THE ECONOMICS OF WOMEN, MEN, AND WORK

PRENTICE HALL SERIES IN ECONOMICS

Adams/Brock, *The Structure of American Industry,* Tenth Edition
Blanchard, *Macroeconomics,* Second Edition
Blau/Ferber/Winkler, *The Economics of Women, Men, and Work,* Fourth Edition
Boardman/Greenberg/Vining/Weimer, *Cost Benefit Analysis: Concepts and Practice,* Second Edition
Bogart, *The Economics of Cities and Suburbs*
Case/Fair, *Principles of Economics,* Sixth Edition
Case/Fair, *Principles of Macroeconomics,* Sixth Edition
Case/Fair, *Principles of Microeconomics,* Sixth Edition
Caves, *American Industry: Structure, Conduct, Performance,* Seventh Edition
Colander/Gamber, *Macroeconomics*
Collinge/Ayers, *Economics by Design: Principles and Issues,* Second Edition
DiPasquale/Wheaton, *Urban Economics and Real Estate Markets*
Eaton/Eaton/Allen, *Microeconomics,* Fourth Edition
Folland/Goodman/Stano, *Economics of Health and Health Care,* Third Edition
Froyen, *Macroeconomics: Theories and Policies,* Seventh Edition
Greene, *Econometric Analysis,* Fourth Edition
Heilbroner/Milberg, *The Making of Economic Society,* Eleventh Edition
Hess, *Using Mathematics in Economic Analysis*
Heyne, *The Economic Way of Thinking,* Ninth Edition
Hirshleifer/Hirshleifer, *Price Theory and Applications,* Sixth Edition
Keat/Young, *Managerial Economics,* Third Edition
Lynn, *Economic Development: Theory and Policy*
Milgrom/Roberts, *Economics, Organization, and Management*
O'Sullivan/Sheffrin, *Economics: Principles and Tools,* Second Edition
O'Sullivan/Sheffrin, *Macroeconomics: Principles and Tools,* Second Edition
O'Sullivan/Sheffrin, *Microeconomics: Principles and Tools,* Second Edition
O'Sullivan/Sheffrin, *Survey of Economics*
Petersen/Lewis, *Managerial Economics,* Fifth Edition
Pindyck/Rubinfeld, *Microeconomics,* Fifth Edition
Reynolds/Masters/Moser, *Labor Economics and Labor Relations,* Eleventh Edition
Roberts, *The Choice: A Fable of Free Trade and Protectionism,* Revised
Schiller, *The Economics of Poverty and Discrimination,* Eighth Edition
Weidenbaum, *Business and Government in the Global Marketplace,* Sixth Edition

FOURTH EDITION

THE ECONOMICS OF WOMEN, MEN, AND WORK

Francine D. Blau

Cornell University

Marianne A. Ferber

University of Illinois at Urbana-Champaign

Anne E. Winkler

University of Missouri-St. Louis

Prentice
Hall

Upper Saddle River, New Jersey 07458

Library of Congress Cataloging-in-Publication Data

Blau, Francine D.
   The economics of women, men, and work / Francine D. Blau, Marianne A.
Ferber, Anne E. Winkler.—4th ed.
     p.   cm.
   Includes bibliographical references and index.
   ISBN 0-13-090922-X
   1. Women—United States—Economic conditions. 2. Feminist Economics—
United States. 3. Women—Employment—United States. 4. Sexual division of
labor—United States. 5. Labor market—United States. 6. Women—United
States—Social conditions. I. Ferber, Marianne A., [date]– II. Winkler, Anne E.,
[date]– III. Title.

HQ1421 .B56 2001
305.42′0973—dc21

Executive Editor: *Rod Banister*
Editor-in-Chief: *P. J. Boardman*
Managing Editor: *Gladys Soto*
Assistant Editor: *Marie McHale*
Media Project Manager: *Bill Minick*
Marketing Manager: *Joshua P. McClary*
Marketing Assistant: *Christopher Bath*
Production Managers: *Gail Steier de Acevedo and John Roberts*
Production Coordinator: *Kelly Warsak*
Permissions Coordinator: *Suzanne Grappi*
Associate Director, Manufacturing: *Vincent Scelta*
Manufacturing Buyer: *Natacha St. Hill Moore*
Composition: *Impressions Book and Journal Services Inc.*
Full-Service Project Management: *Impressions Book and Journal Services Inc.*
Printer/Binder: *RRD/Harrisonburg*
Cover Printer: *Phoenix Color Corp.*

10 9 8 7 6 5 4 3 2 1
ISBN 0-13-090922-X

For

Lawrence M. Kahn
Daniel Blau Kahn
Lisa Blau Kahn

and

Bob Ferber
Don Ferber
Ellen Ferber Rogalin

and

Michael Joseph Kowalkowski
Henrik Francis Kowalkowski
Andrew Joseph Kowalkowski

With love

BRIEF CONTENTS

CONTENTS

PREFACE

We wrote *The Economics of Women, Men, and Work* because we saw a need for a text that would acquaint students with the findings of research on women, men, and work in the labor market and the household. We are extremely gratified on the publication of the 4th edition to reflect that this belief was justified, and hope that this expanded and updated new edition will serve as effectively as the first three.

OVERVIEW OF THE TEXT

The book is written at a level that should both utilize and enhance students' knowledge of economic concepts and analysis but do so in terms intelligible to those not versed in advanced theory. Even though we assume a knowledge of introductory economics on the part of the reader, an interested and determined individual wanting to learn more about the economic status of women as compared to men could benefit considerably from the material offered here. The book also draws upon research in the other social sciences. The text, used in its entirety, is primarily intended for courses specifically concerned with the economic status of women. However, this book could be used to good advantage in interdisciplinary women's studies courses, as well as introductory-level courses in economic problems. Selected readings would also make a useful supplement to round out a general labor economics course. In addition, it would also serve as a useful reference work for those not familiar with the rapidly growing body of literature on women, men, and work as well as for practicing economists looking for a single volume on this topic.

SIGNIFICANT FEATURES OF THE 4TH EDITION

The 4th edition has been thoroughly revised to reflect the numerous changes in the labor market and in the family that have occurred in recent years. All data and references have been updated to take into account the most recent research on each subject covered. Questions have been added at the end of each chapter to provide for review of major concepts and to stimulate further discussion among students and instructors. The other new features of the 4th edition as well as some of the changes previously incorporated in the 3rd edition are summarized here.

- As in the past, we thoroughly review trends in the labor supply of women and men to the market. In Chapter 4, we summarize these trends and provide some analysis of important recent developments including the large increase in labor force participation of single mothers in the late 1990s.

- Our consideration of the role of labor market discrimination in explaining gender differences in labor market outcomes in Chapter 7 now includes a more detailed discussion of issues surrounding the notion of a "glass ceiling."

- We highlight important recent developments in the labor market and their consequences for women and men. These include the decrease in the gender wage gap, as well as the declining employment prospects of less-educated men, growing wage inequality, the rise of nonstandard employment arrangements such as temporary and on-call workers and consultants, and changes in welfare policy that have moved greater numbers of welfare recipients, largely single mothers, into the labor force. Each chapter has been modified to some extent to reflect these changes as relevant, and Chapter 8, "Recent Development in the Labor Market," and Chapter 10, "Policies Affecting Paid Work and Family," focus specifically on these developments.

- We devote considerable attention to changes within married-couple families as well as to changing family structure and the implications of these shifts for labor market outcomes. Chapter 3, which focuses on nonmarket work, introduces a new discussion of trends in time spent with children, which is of interest, both in terms of its implications for time spent in nonmarket work and its potential implications for children's development. Further, this chapter takes a much closer look at alternatives to the standard economic approach, including the transaction cost approach and bargaining models, as well as an expanded discussion of the radical feminist and Marxist feminist views of decision making in the family.

- In keeping with the times, the discussion in Chapter 9 examines trends in marriage, divorce, and overall fertility, along with trends in births to unmarried mothers, teen births, and cohabitation. The discussion of cohabitation has been further expanded to include gay and lesbian couples. Chapter 9 also devotes considerable attention to the implications of the large increases in the number of dual-earner, married-couple families and single-parent families for children's outcomes.

- All discussions concerning policy have been thoroughly revised. In Chapter 7, we discuss affirmative action and findings regarding the effectiveness of antidiscrimination legislation. Discussions of policies that affect paid work and family have been updated, expanded, and consolidated into a single chapter, Chapter 10. This chapter focuses on three broad policy areas: (1) policies to alleviate poverty, including the Temporary Assistance for Needy Families (TANF) program, the Earned Income Tax Credit (EITC), and child support enforcement; (2) government tax policies; and (3) policies that should better help workers and their families balance the dual demands of paid work and family responsibilities. Among the changes, the section on welfare has been revised to reflect recent evidence on the effect of the 1996 welfare legislation (TANF) on welfare caseloads and economic well-being. The discussion on child support has been considerably expanded, and now includes more information on the success of child support enforcement, as well as the particular difficulties of this policy for what have been termed "deadbroke" dads. The section on family leave has been expanded to consider recent findings regarding the effect of the 1993 federal family leave legislation and discusses related leave policies. The section on income tax policy now includes a more detailed discussion of how taxes affect women's labor force participation and how the so-called marriage penalty arises, along with a fuller discussion of available policy options.

• Finally, Chapter 11, which examines gender differences from an international perspective, has been completely updated. As in the 3rd edition, after considering differences in women's status across broad regions of the world, it compares the United States with a number of other economically advanced nations, especially Sweden and Japan, with respect to labor force participation, the gender pay gap, occupations, sharing of housework, and demographic trends. This chapter also specifically examines the situation of women in developing countries, highlighting the difficulties they face as well as the progress that they have made, and briefly considers the problems of women living in countries that were formerly part of the Soviet bloc.

ACKNOWLEDGEMENTS

Since all of us have taught a course on women in the labor market for some time, we wish to acknowledge that the book has benefited from the experience and the insights we have gained from our students. We are also greatly indebted to a rather large and diverse group of colleagues, from a number of disciplines, whose comments on the various editions were often voluminous and always extremely valuable:

Deborah Anderson, University of New Mexico, Albuquerque
Orley C. Ashenfelter, Princeton University
Nancy S. Barrett, Western Michigan University, Kalamazoo
Andrea H. Beller, University of Illinois, Urbana-Champaign
Lourdes Beneria, Cornell University
Barbara R. Bergmann, American University
Jewell Ray Bowen II, University of Missouri-St. Louis
Charles Brown, University of Michigan
Clair Brown, University of California, Berkeley
Greg J. Duncan, Northwestern University
Margaret C. Dunkle, American Association of University Women,
    Educational Foundation
Cristina Echevarria, University of Saskatchewan
Paula England, University of Pennsylvania
Belton M. Fleisher, Ohio State University
Claudia D. Goldin, Harvard University
Janet Gornick, Baruch College, City University of New York
Ulla Grapard, Colgate University
Shoshana Grossbard-Schechtman, San Diego State University

Daniel S. Hamermesh, University of Texas, Austin
Michele Hoyman, University of North Carolina-Chapel Hill
Joan A. Huber, Ohio State University
John Johnson IV, University of Illinois, Urbana-Champaign
Heather Joshi, City University, London
Joan R. Kahn, University of Maryland
Lawrence M. Kahn, Cornell University
Kristen Keith, University of Toledo
Mark R. Killingsworth, Rutgers University
Pareena Lawrence, University of Minnesota
Phil Levine, Wellesley College
Shelly J. Lundberg, University of Washington, Seattle
Julie A. Matthaei, Wellesley College
Joan Moriarty, Cornell University
Janet Norwood, Urban Institute
Elizabeth Peters, Cornell University
Leila Pratt, University of Tennessee at Chattanooga
Harriet B. Presser, University of Maryland
Barbara B. Reagan, Southern Methodist University
Barbara F. Reskin, Harvard University
Patricia A. Roos, State University of New York, Stony Brook
Elaina Rose, University of Washington, Seattle
Steven H. Sandell, U.S. Department of Health and Human Services
Lisa Saunders, University of Massachusetts, Amherst
Richard Stratton, University of Akron
Myra H. Strober, Stanford University
Louise A. Tilly, New School University
Donald J. Treiman, University of California, Los Angeles
Jane Waldfogel, Columbia University
Alison Wellington, The Naval Post-Graduate School
Herbert D. Werner, University of Missouri-St. Louis
H. F. (Bill) Williamson, University of Illinois, Urbana-Champaign
Frances Woolley, Carleton University, Ottawa

Without their help, this book would have had many more deficiencies. For those that remain, as well as for all opinions expressed, we, of course, take complete responsibility. This list of acknowledgments would be incomplete if we did not also thank Joan Moriarty, Abhijay Prakash, Nantaporn Plurphanswat, Nathan Forck, Jeremy Bixby, Maria Tiratsuyan, and Lisa Blau Kahn, the research assistants who helped us track down sources and references and prepare tables and graphs for this edition. Finally, we are immensely grateful to the exceptionally helpful team at Prentice Hall that worked with us on this edition: Rod Banister, economics executive editor; Gladys Soto, managing editor; Marie McHale, assistant editor; Kelly Warsak, production coordinator; and Sarah Brown, copyeditor.

F. D. B.
M. A. F.
A. E. W.

CHAPTER 1

INTRODUCTION

Chapter Highlights

- What Economics Is About
- Uses of Economic Theory
- The Scope of Economics
- Individuals, Families, and Households
- Outline of the Book
- Appendix: A Review of Supply and Demand in the Labor Market

Courses in economics abound at universities and colleges, and there is an ample supply of texts focusing on the many facets of this discipline. These courses and books increasingly recognize that women play an important role in the economy as workers and consumers and that in many ways their behavior and their problems differ from those of men. However, male patterns often receive the major emphasis and gender differences are, at best, just one of many topics covered. For example, workers are often assumed to enter the labor market after completing their education and to remain until their retirement. Similarly, institutions studied are mainly those involved in traditional labor markets, from businesses to labor unions and relevant government agencies. Although women in growing numbers are spending an increasing proportion of their time working for pay, their lives and their world continue to be significantly different from those of men, and much of their time continues to be spent in nonmarket activities.

In recent years, much attention has been focused on the rising labor force participation rates of women and particularly on the changing economic roles of married women. Much has been made, especially in the popular media, of the often large percentage increases in the number of women in nontraditional occupations, not to mention the publicity received by "the first woman" in a given field, whether it be stockbroker, jockey, or prime minister. All this tends to obscure both the continued responsibility of most women for the bulk of nonmarket work and the large occupational differences between men and women that remain, despite considerable progress. As long as this situation persists, there is a need to address these issues in depth, as is done in this book.

Although economic behavior is clearly not isolated from the remainder of human existence, the primary focus of this book is on the economic behavior of women and men, on economic institutions, and on economic outcomes. To refresh the memory of students who have some acquaintance with economics, and to provide a minimal background for those who do not, we begin with a brief introduction to the tools of this discipline. Neoclassical or mainstream economic theory provides the major emphasis of this book. But students should be aware that we have endeavored to constantly stretch and challenge the existing theories to shed light on issues related to gender and work. Further, in addition to presenting conventional analyses, we sometimes offer critiques of existing approaches. We also tend to emphasize the importance and implications of gender inequities in the labor market and in the household to a greater extent than some of our colleagues might. Finally, we have attempted to take account of institutional factors, alternative perspectives, and the insights of other disciplines where relevant.[1]

Throughout this book, but especially in those segments where we deal with policy, we are confronted by a dilemma common to the social sciences. On the one hand, much of what we present is positive, rather than normative, in the sense that we present facts and research results as we find them. Furthermore, we try to avoid value judgments and prescriptive attitudes, for personal values should not be permitted to intrude upon objective analysis. On the other hand, it is unrealistic to claim that the choice of topics, the emphasis in discussions, and the references provided are, or even can be, entirely value free. A reasonable solution is to try to present various sides of controversial questions, while making clear that different premises will lead to different conclusions and that the policies one should adopt depend on the goals one wants to reach. This is the approach we attempt to follow.

At the same time, the tenor of this book is undoubtedly colored to some extent by our feminist perspective. Thus, we recognize, for instance, the extent to which persons of the same sex may differ, and persons of the opposite sex may be similar. And, like other feminists, in considering gender differences, we have become increasingly aware of how these differences vary by race and ethnicity. Our feminist perspective also means we believe that, as much as possible, individuals should have the opportunity to live up to their potential, rather than be forced to conform to stereotypical roles. Most of all, it means that, while recognizing differences between women and men, some possibly caused by biological factors and others by the way girls and boys are reared in our society, we are less inclined to emphasize the differences between them than the common humanity that unites them.

WHAT ECONOMICS IS ABOUT

Neoclassical economics is concerned with decision making under conditions of **scarcity.** This means that there are not enough resources to satisfy everyone's wants, and choices have to be made about their use. Given this constraint, it is crucial to recognize that using labor, capital, and land to produce one good means that fewer of these inputs will be available for producing other goods. Hence, the real cost of having more of one good is forgoing the opportunity of having more of another.

This concept of **opportunity cost** is fundamental to an understanding of the central economic problem—how to allocate scarce resources so as to maximize well-being. In

---

[1]   For a feminist critique of neoclassical economics, see Julie A. Nelson, *Feminism, Objectivity and Economics* (London: Routledge, 1996).

order to make a rational decision whether to spend money to buy a new suit or whether to spend time going for a hike, it is not sufficient to know how much utility or satisfaction will be derived from each. Because the amount of money and time is limited, and we cannot buy and do everything, it is crucial also to be aware of how much satisfaction is lost by giving up desirable alternatives. **Rationality,** as economists use the term, involves some knowledge of available opportunities and the terms on which they are available. Only on the basis of such information is it possible to weigh the alternatives and choose those that provide more utility than any others.

It is one of the most fundamental assumptions in traditional economics that people may be expected to behave rationally in this sense. This does not mean, as critics have occasionally suggested, that only monetary costs and benefits are considered. It is entirely rational to take into account nonpecuniary factors since *satisfaction,* not, say, money income, is to be maximized. This definition is so broad that almost everyone might be expected to behave this way. Nonetheless, rationality cannot be taken for granted. It is not satisfactory simply to argue that whatever a person does must provide more satisfaction than any alternative course of action because he or she would otherwise have made a different choice. Such an argument amounts to a mere tautology. An individual who blindly follows the traditional course of action without considering costs and benefits, or who fails to consider long-run implications or indirect effects is not necessarily rational. Nor is it uncommon to find persons who, with surprising regularity, make choices that they presently appear to regret. Most of us have probably known someone whose behavior fits one or more of these patterns.

These facts should be kept in mind, lest we accept too readily that whatever people do must be for the best. On the other hand, as a first approximation it is probably more realistic to assume that people tend to try to maximize their well-being rather than that they are indifferent to it. We shall, for the most part, accept this as a reasonable generalization, while recognizing that it is not necessarily appropriate in every instance. Specifically, it must be kept in mind that the knowledge needed to make optimal decisions is often difficult and costly to obtain. When this cost is likely to exceed the gain derived, it is rational to *satisfice* rather than to insist on maximization.[2] By the same token, however, when additional information can be provided relatively cheaply and easily, it is likely to be useful in improving decision making.

USES OF ECONOMIC THEORY

Assuming that individuals are rational is only one of the many simplifying assumptions economists tend to make in formulating **theories** and building **models.** The justification for making such assumptions is that, much like laboratory experiments in the biological and physical sciences, these abstractions help to focus attention on the particular issue we are attempting to clarify and on the main relationships we want to understand.

In many instances, the approach is explicitly to examine the effects of changes in a single variable, say, price or income, while assuming that all else remains the same. This is not to suggest that economists believe that this ever happens in the real world. An aerospace engineer finds it useful to test a plane in a tunnel where everything except wind speed is

---

[2]   This concept was first proposed by Herbert Simon in *Models of Man* (New York: Wiley, 1957). He argued that when the knowledge needed to make optimal decisions is difficult and costly to obtain, an individual may be content with selecting a "satisfactory" alternative—one that meets a minimum standard of acceptability.

artificially stabilized, even though the vehicle will later have to fly in an environment where temperature, atmospheric pressure, and humidity will vary. Simi-larly, the social scientist finds it helpful to begin by abstracting from numerous complications.

A theory is not intended to be a full description of the underlying reality. A description is like a photograph, which shows reality in all its details. A theory may be likened to a modern painting, which at most shows the broad outlines of its subject but may provide deeper insight than a more realistic picture would. Hence, a theory or model should not be judged primarily on its detailed resemblance to reality, but rather in terms of the extent to which it enables us to grasp the salient features of that reality. Thus, economic theory, at its best, can help us to understand the present and to correctly predict the future.

Economists should not, therefore, be faulted for making simplifying assumptions or using abstractions, as long as they are aware of what they are doing and test their conclusions against empirical evidence, which is drawn from the real world with all its complexities. Unfortunately, such testing is not always easy to do. Computers now enable us to process vast amounts of information, and econometricians have made substantial progress in developing better methods for doing so. The availability, timeliness, and quality of the data, however, often still leave much to be desired.

Collecting data is a slow, expensive, and generally unglamorous undertaking. The U.S. government does more and better work in this respect than governments of many other countries. Even so, collecting, compiling, and publishing the information may take quite some time. Some data are, in any case, collected only intermittently, other data not at all. For a variety of reasons, including the government's appropriate reluctance to invade certain areas, as well as lack of interest in pursuing topics with no strong political constituency, there are some substantial gaps in official data collection. Private research organizations have endeavored to fill these to a degree, but they are even more likely to be constrained by lack of necessary funds. The data from such special surveys are particularly likely to be collected sporadically or at lengthy intervals. In spite of these difficulties, the possibilities for empirical work have improved beyond the wildest dreams of economists of even one or two generations ago.

When suitable data are available, evidence for some relationships can be obtained using such simple devices as averages and cross tabulations. In other instances, however, very sophisticated statistical methods are required to analyze the data. Such studies are time consuming, and rarely are conclusions from any one study regarded as final. At times there are ambiguities, with different sets of data or various approaches producing inconsistent results. Even so, such studies enhance the progress of science, for they help us to identify important areas for future research.

Because of these difficulties of data collection and analysis, timely and definitive answers are simply not available for every question. We have, however, done our best to summarize existing knowledge on each topic considered in this book.

THE SCOPE OF ECONOMICS

Traditionally, and for the most part even today, economics has focused on the market and on the government. In the market, goods and services are sold. Government is itself a major buyer and seller of goods and services and is also an agent that regulates and otherwise influences the economy. Only in recent decades have mainstream economists devoted any significant attention to the allocation of time within the household itself, and even now such material is not always included in general economics courses. Also, for the most part, the value of nonmarket household production is ignored when aggregate indicators of economic welfare, such as gross domestic product (GDP), are computed. This is a matter for concern, in part because women play the dominant role in the nonmarket sector. Recently, however, researchers in a number of countries, including the United States, have been devoting attention to this issue. In Canada, for instance, the government has been collecting relevant data and providing estimates of the value of goods and services produced in the household. The U.S. government is also planning to undertake a national survey for the same purpose. In the meantime, it has made use of existing time-use data from nongovernmental surveys to adjust the U.S. GDP figures for nonmarket production in satellite GDP accounts, which can be compared alongside the standard national accounts.

In its microeconomics section, the typical introductory economics course puts primary emphasis on the analysis of product market transactions with the firm as seller, concerned with maximizing profits, and the household as buyer, concerned with maximizing satisfaction or utility. Later it introduces markets for factors of production, specifically labor, in which the household is generally the supplier and the firm the purchaser. As a rule, however, this discussion is a brief portion in the section on factors of production, and most students may well come away with a view of the market as chiefly an institution where goods and services are supplied by businesses, and the demand for them comes from the household.

In this book, our interest is most specifically in women and men, their work in the labor market and in the household, and the interdependence among individuals within the household and between the household and the market. Therefore, we briefly review supply and demand in this context in the appendix to this chapter.

In a market economy, the forces of supply and demand for labor determine both the jobs that will be available and how much workers will be paid for doing them. Much of our analysis throughout this book will be concerned with the determinants of the supply of labor. We shall examine how individuals and their families decide to allocate their time between housework and market work and how women's changing roles in this regard are affecting their own well-being and that of their families.

Demand is essentially determined by the behavior of employers, who are in turn influenced by the business climate in which they operate. In the simplest case, their goal is to maximize profits, and their demand for labor is related to its productivity in making the goods or producing the services sold by the firm. Thus, the firm's demand for labor is *derived* from the demand of consumers for its final product. It is, however, possible that employers depart from the dictates of profit maximization and consider aspects of workers that are not directly related to their productivity. Discrimination against women in the labor market and its role in producing wage and occupational differences between women and men is another topic that we shall explore in some depth. At the same time, we also take note of the fact that there are differences within each of these groups, most notably by race and ethnicity.

On the supply side, workers may influence their productivity by attending school or getting training on the job. We shall also consider the determinants of such human capital investment decisions and their role in producing differences in labor market outcomes.

INDIVIDUALS, FAMILIES, AND HOUSEHOLDS

Throughout this book, we shall at times focus on the behavior of families and, at other times, on that of individuals. A **family** is officially defined as consisting of two or more persons, related by blood, marriage, or adoption, living in the same household.[3] It is, of course, the individual that in the last analysis consumes commodities and supplies labor. Nonetheless, it is often appropriate to treat the family as the relevant economic unit because decisions of various members within a family are interdependent, much of their consumption is joint, and it is common for them to pool income. At the same time, it is important not to lose sight of the fact that the composition of families changes as individuals move in and out and that the interests of family members may diverge to a greater or lesser extent. We shall return to these issues throughout this book as we discuss the status of women and men within the family and in the labor market.

The broader concept of the **household** is also relevant to economic decision making and is becoming increasingly more so. A household consists of one or more persons living in one dwelling unit and sharing living expenses. Thus, all families are households, but one-person households, or those composed of unrelated individuals, are not families. The term *household* is more general than *family* and does greater justice to the increasing prevalence of alternative living arrangements; however, since families still constitute a substantial majority of households that include more than one person, and since the term *family* is more familiar and connotes a more uniform set of relationships, we have chosen to use it primarily in this book.

A NOTE ON TERMINOLOGY

Traditionally the terms *sex* and *gender* were used interchangeably to refer to the biological and social differences between women and men. More recently, it has become increasingly common to use the term *sex* to refer to the biological differences between males and females, and *gender* to encompass the distinctions society has erected on this biological base.[4] Thus, *gender* connotes a cultural construct, including distinctions in roles and behaviors as well as mental and emotional characteristics.[5] We see enough merit in this distinction between *sex* and *gender* that we have generally observed it in writing this book.

The question of appropriate language also arises with respect to racial and ethnic groups. Historically, people of African origin in the United States were generally called Negroes. Several decades ago the term *black* came into use, followed more recently by *African American.* For purposes of this book, we generally use black, mainly because *black* is the term that continues to be used in the official government statistics on

---

[3] This is the official definition used in government statistics. The typical **nuclear family** is composed of married parents and children, but single-parent families are becoming more common. An **extended family,** a type of unit more common in some other societies, may include grandparents, uncles, aunts, and other relatives. Cohabiting couples, who are also growing more prevalent, are not included in the official definition of a family. In addition, as of 2000, same sex couples are not permitted to legally marry and hence are also not recognized as a family. They are, however, permitted to form legal unions in Vermont and it may well be that other states will follow suit in the future.

[4] Francine D. Blau, "Gender," in *The New Palgrave: A Dictionary of Economic Theory and Doctrine,* vol. 2, ed. John Eatwell, Murray Milgate, and Peter Newman (London: MacMillan Press, 1987), p. 492.

[5] Helen Tierney, ed., *Women's Studies Encyclopedia* (New York: Greenwood Press, 1989), p. 153.

which we frequently rely. Similarly, because *Hispanic origin* is used in government statistics and is more widely used than the alternatives such as *Spanish origin, Latin American,* or *Latino,* we use it exclusively throughout the text.

OUTLINE OF THE BOOK

As suggested earlier, the primary focus of this book is on "economic woman," as she interacts and competes with "economic man." Economic behavior is not, however, treated in isolation from the remainder of human existence. To provide a more comprehensive picture, subsequent chapters will reflect insights from other social sciences, which enhance our understanding of a variety of factors. Such noneconomic factors help to determine economic behavior and how that behavior, in turn, helps to shape other aspects of life.

Chapter 2 deals with the historical evolution of the roles of women and men, focusing particularly on the United States. Chapter 3 considers the gender division of labor within the family, with special attention paid to the allocation of household tasks among men and women, as well as to new approaches to family decision making such as bargaining models. Chapter 4 analyzes the individual's decision about how to allocate his or her time between the household and the labor market, with emphasis placed on explaining the factors behind recent trends in women's and men's labor force participation.

The next four chapters deal specifically with women's position in the labor market as compared to that of men, beginning with an overview of gender differences in occupations and earnings in Chapter 5, followed by an in-depth examination of the various explanations of the existing situation. Specifically, Chapter 6 reviews the human capital approach, and Chapter 7 concentrates on discrimination as a cause of women's less favorable labor market outcomes. Chapter 8 rounds out the picture by considering the effects of recent developments in the labor market on women and men, including trends in real wages and growing wage inequality, the decrease in the gender pay gap, the increasing payoff to education, corporate restructuring, the growth of the nonstandard work force, the rising self-employment of women, and changes in unions.

In Chapters 9 and 10 we return to the family. Chapter 9 examines the impact of women's employment on family structure and on the well-being of family members, with special attention paid to the growing number of dual-earner and single-parent families. Chapter 10 looks at a variety of policies affecting paid work and families, including those designed to alleviate poverty, government tax policies, and the growing number of "family friendly" policies that can reduce the burden faced by the increasing number of individuals who have to juggle paid work and family responsibilities. We examine both those family friendly policies that are currently widely available and those that may be emerging.

Finally, in Chapter 11, we compare the economic status of women relative to men throughout the world, with special emphasis on similarities and differences between the United States and other economically advanced nations. We also consider the particular problems and issues facing women in developing nations and in the countries of the former Soviet bloc. Substantial differences in the behaviors and economic status of men and women across countries suggest that particular outcomes are not inevitable but rather are subject to choice by each society. In instances where a country appears to have impressive achievements in gender equality to its credit, we may be able to learn from the experiences there.

================

A P P E N D I X

A Review of Supply and Demand in the Labor Market

As we explained in Chapter 1, supply and demand provide economists with a framework for analyzing labor markets. We briefly review these concepts here in the context of a particular type of labor, clerical workers.

Curve *DD* in Figure 1.1 shows the typical downward-sloping **demand curve.** Wage rate (price) is on the vertical axis, and quantity (number of workers) is on the horizontal axis. The demand curve represents the various amounts of labor that would be hired at various prices by firms in this labor market over a given period of time. Everything else remaining the same, including methods of production and prices of other inputs, changes in the wage rate cause movements along this curve. There is a change in the *quantity demanded,* but demand (that is, the demand curve) remains the same. If, on the other hand, other factors do not remain the same, the entire demand curve may be shifted.

Demand curves are normally expected to slope downward to the right, which means that the firm will hire more workers at a lower wage rate and fewer at a higher wage rate. There are several reasons for this. The first is that in the short run there is **diminishing marginal productivity** of labor, meaning that additional units of labor provide progressively less additional output when combined with fixed amounts of capital (plant and equipment). Capital can only be expanded or contracted over a longer pe-riod of time, which means that if, for instance, output of a factory is to be increased almost immediately, the only way to do this would be to hire additional workers or have workers put in longer hours. The second is the **substitution effect.** When the price of a particular input changes, while prices of potential substitutes remain the same, there will be a tendency for profit-maximizing employers to use more of the one that is now relatively cheaper and less of the one that is now relatively more expensive. In the short run, for example, less skilled labor may be substituted for skilled workers. In the long run, it may be possible to substitute capital for labor. Last, there is the **scale effect,** which may also operate in both the short and long run. As wages increase, the price of the product will go up, less of it will be purchased, and fewer workers will be employed. The scale effect is likely to be especially large when wages constitute a substantial part of the costs of production. This is usually the case for services, for example. These are the factors that cause the quantity of labor hired to decrease as the wage rate increases, but the movements are along the given demand curve and do not involve a shift of the demand curve.

The **supply curve,** shown by *SS* in Figure 1.1, slopes upward and to the right. It shows the number of workers who would be willing to do clerical work at all possible prices. The supply curve is upward sloping because, if rewards for one type of job increase while those for all others remain the same, additional workers will be attracted from related occupations. So, for example, an increase in the wages of clerical workers may induce individuals who are currently employed in other jobs to improve their clerical skills and compete for clerical positions. Similarly, if pay for clerical work declines relative to others, the quantity of labor supplied to clerical jobs is expected to decline as workers move to other sectors.

It is important to emphasize that the supply curve depicted in Figure 1.1 represents the number of individuals available for a particular line of work. As we shall see in greater detail in Chapter 4, the number of hours supplied to the market by any particular individual may not increase when wages rise. This may happen because, at a higher wage rate, an individual who participates in the labor market may choose to allocate more of his or her time to nonmarket activities and the satisfactions they bring.

The intersection of the supply and demand curves shown in Figure 1.1 represents a **stable equilibrium.** An equilibrium exists when all persons willing to work at the going rate are able to find employment and all employers willing to hire someone at the going rate are able to find workers. In other words, the quantity demanded and

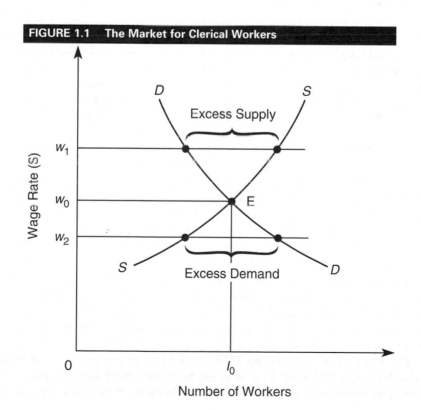

FIGURE 1.1   The Market for Clerical Workers

the quantity supplied are equal at E, so there are no forces causing the wage to move from its pres-ent level as long as there are no external shocks. In this case, the equilibrium wage is w_0, and the equilibrium quantity of labor employed is l_0. To illustrate why point E represents a *stable* equilibrium, let us assume that, for whatever reason, the wage rate is initially set higher than w_0, say at w_1. At this point, the quantity of labor supplied would exceed the quantity of labor demanded and push wages down toward E. Conversely, if wages were initially set at w_2, the opposite would be true. In short, we have a stable equilibrium where there is no tendency to move away from E. If an external shock were to cause a deviation, there would be a tendency to return toward that point.

External shocks may, of course, also cause shifts in demand, supply, or both, leading to a new equilibrium. Such shocks may come from changes in markets for goods, for nonlabor inputs, or for other types of labor, and they are extremely common. Therefore, a stable equilibrium is not necessarily one that remains fixed for any length of time. It merely means that at any given time there is a tendency toward convergence at the point where the quantity of labor supplied equals the quantity of labor demanded, until conditions cause this point to shift.

It may be instructive to consider a couple of examples in which there are shifts in the supply or demand curves. These sample situations can help to clarify the difference between factors that cause a movement along an existing supply or demand curve and those that cause a shift in the entire curve. We shall also be able to see how the new equilibrium position is established.

Suppose that the government issues a report on the dangers of credit spending and that it is effective enough to cause a reduction in the demand for such services provided by the banking industry. That is, at any given price of these services, consumers demand less of them. Since this industry employs a substantial number of clerical workers, such a change would cause a marked inward shift in the marketwide demand curve for clerical workers, from DD to $D'D'$ in Figure 1.2a. That is, at any given wage rate, firms are willing to hire fewer clerical workers. This illustrates that the demand for labor is a *derived* demand: It is derived from consumer demand for the goods and services that the workers produce. A new equilibrium will occur at E_1, where the quantity of labor supplied again equals the (new) quantity of labor demanded. At E_1, fewer individuals are employed as clerical workers and a lower wage rate is determined for that occupation.

Shifts in supply curves can also alter the market equilibrium, as shown in Figure 1.2b. For instance, suppose that the government's antidiscrimination policies increase opportunities for women in managerial jobs, raising their wages and making it easier for them to obtain such employment. This will result in a reduction in the supply (inward shift in the supply curve) of clerical workers, an occupation staffed primarily by women. At any given wage, fewer women would be available to work in clerical jobs than previously. At the new equilibrium (E_1), the wages are higher, and the number of workers employed is lower than in the initial situation (E_0). This illustrates that improved opportunities for women in traditionally male jobs can potentially improve the economic welfare even of those women who remain in traditionally female pursuits.

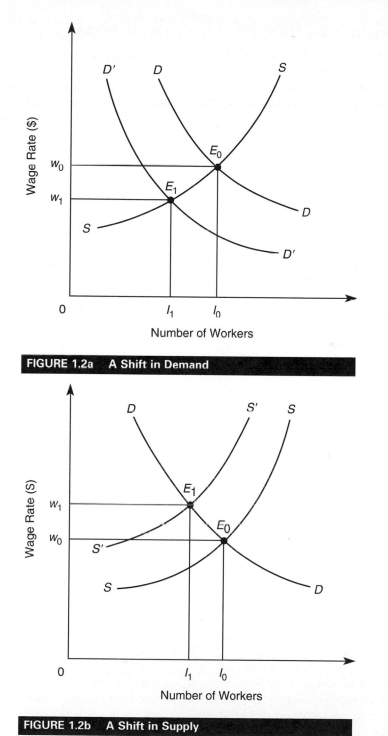

FIGURE 1.2a   A Shift in Demand

FIGURE 1.2b   A Shift in Supply

QUESTIONS FOR REVIEW AND DISCUSSION

1. Define scarcity and explain why the concept is so central to neoclassical economics.

2. In everyday language "cost" generally means the amount of money it takes to purchase a commodity. Can this be tied to the concept of opportunity cost and if so how?

3. Discuss the uses and abuses of simplifying assumptions in economic models.

4. Using a graph, show how each of the following labor markets (assumed to be competitive and initially in equilibrium) is affected by the following changes. Clearly explain your reasoning.

   a. Labor market for math and science teachers.
      Wages available in private industries utilizing these skills rise.

   b. Labor market for university professors.
      College enrollments expand.

   c. Labor market for low-skilled workers.
      The 1996 federal welfare legislation requires that a much larger fraction of welfare recipients work than in the past.

   d. Labor market for workers who completed high school only.
      The workplace becomes more computerized and technically sophisticated.

   e. Labor market for workers who completed college or more.
      The workplace becomes more computerized and technically sophisticated.

CHAPTER 2

WOMEN AND MEN: CHANGING ROLES IN A CHANGING ECONOMY

Chapter Highlights

- The Nature of Males and Females
- The Role of Sociobiology in Explaining Gender Differences
- Factors Influencing Women's Relative Status
- Women's Roles and Economic Development
- The U.S. Experience

It seems to me that an economic interpretation of history is an indispensable element in the study of society, but it is only one element. In layers below it lie geography, biology and psychology, and in layers above it the investigation of social and political relationships and the history of culture, law and religion.

—JOAN ROBINSON
*Freedom and Necessity**

We are constantly told today that we live in an era of rapid change—change in economic conditions, in economic and social institutions, in mores and beliefs. And so we do. Changes in the roles of women and men, their relations to each other, and the nature of the families in which most of them continue to live have been taking place at a speed that is quite possibly unprecedented. This situation has inevitably created stresses and strains. Not surprisingly, people who feel insecure in a world of shifting boundaries and values are prone to look back with nostalgia to the "good old days" when women were women and men were men, and both knew their proper place.

---

* Joan Robinson, *Freedom and Necessity: An Introduction to the Study of Society* (London: George Allen and Unwin, 1970), p. 5.

How realistic is this picture some hold of traditional gender roles, unchanging for all time and pervasive for all places, which is supposed to have existed before the recent era of turmoil and upheaval? The answer to this question has substantial practical implications. If the same roles of women and men have existed always and everywhere, some may conclude that these roles are biologically determined and that they probably cannot, and perhaps should not, be changed. If, on the other hand, there has been a good deal of variation in the roles of men and women over time, it is likely that there is also room for flexibility now and in the future.

For this reason, it is particularly important to gain some insight into the nature of gender roles through the course of human development. There are, of course, other reasons as well. Some awareness of the complexities of history is indispensable for an understanding of the present. It is also crucial if we are to make any progress toward correctly anticipating the future. In our brief historical review, we shall find that, although the rate may have been a great deal slower in the past, there has always been change. Furthermore, societies throughout time have been characterized by a diversity of economic and social institutions.

We begin by briefly considering the biological and anthropological evidence about the nature of males and females and the sociobiologist's explanation for gender differences. This takes us somewhat far afield from traditional economics but provides valuable background for the historical analysis that follows. Here we consider the changing roles of men and women in the household and in the economy, and the evolution of the family, in the course of economic development into the period of industrialization in the nineteenth and twentieth centuries. Although other factors are not ignored, economic causation is assigned the predominant role in shaping these changes. The focus during the most recent periods is on the United States.

THE NATURE OF MALES AND FEMALES

As recently as the 1970s, a common interpretation of the behavior of, and relation between, men and women emphasized the importance of "man the hunter" and of the biological maternal function of the female in determining the nature and content of her being.[1] In this view, a woman's early life is a preparation for becoming, and her later life is devoted to being, a successful wife and mother. Accordingly, her nature is compliant, not competitive; nurturant, not instrumental. Her activities, though not necessarily confined to the home, at least center around it, for her primary mission is to be a helpmate to her husband and to provide a warm and safe haven for her family. If she does work for pay, she will do best in jobs compatible with her household responsibilities and her "feminine" personality. Men, on the other hand, are not constrained by their paternal function from fully entering the world outside the home. On the contrary, their natural role as provider and protector spurs them on to greater efforts.

Based on this earlier work,[2] the popular perception was often that investigations of male and female roles among nonhuman species provided support for the view that

---
[1] See, for example, Lionel Tiger, *Men in Groups* (New York: Random House, 1969).

[2] Foremost among these have been Robert Ardrey, *The Territorial Imperative* (New York: Atheneum Press, 1966); Desmond Morris, *The Human Zoo* (New York: McGraw-Hill, 1969); and Lionel Tiger and Robin Fox, *The Imperial Animal* (New York: Holt, Rinehart & Winston, 1971).

biology is destiny. Therefore, we begin with a brief look at animals and their behavior, although this subject is receiving much less attention now. The reason is that more recent research suggests that no generalization holds for all species and that extrapolation from animal studies does not support the traditional view. Before summarizing this evidence, we consider the question of why researchers' perceptions of animal behavior have changed over time.

In this area, as in others, the problem has been that the subjective expectations of scientists tend to influence how they interpret particular situations and what they notice about them.[3] For example, one male with a group of females is traditionally viewed as the ruler of a dependent harem. From another point of view, it may be a group of dominant females who have no use for more than one male for breeding purposes. Similarly, while attention is frequently focused on individual males who play a dominant role, it goes unnoticed that even the highest-ranking ones may be routed by a group of females who gang up to chase them away if they, for instance, disturb the young.

When most researchers were male and, whether male or female, held traditional views of appropriate gender roles among humans, they tended to see confirmation of these views in their observations of animal behavior. As more women joined the ranks of researchers, and as both men and women were influenced by changing gender roles in human society, perceptions of animal behavior were accordingly revised. The new view that emerged in the 1970s, reflecting as it does a process of reexamination and more careful scrutiny of the evidence, probably can be given more credence than earlier ones.

As anthropologists reconsidered the evidence from studies of animals about the nature of females and males, a number of correctives to anthropomorphic models of male dominance and aggressiveness, and of female passivity and nurturance, have emerged.[4] Many of the new studies of various animal groups show evidence of "female dominance, autonomy, and power; of male nurturance and cooperation; and of monogamous behavior as well as promiscuity in both males and females."[5]

Much of the research on sex roles among animals focused specifically on primates because they are closer to human beings than are other animals. Even there, however, sweeping generalizations are rarely justified. The behavior of these animals is typically dimorphic (that is, certain types of behavior are more typical of one sex than the other). But these differences are generally a matter of degree, not of kind, and there is much overlap. Only among some species such as rhesus monkeys are males far more aggressive and belligerent than females. Nor do differences in behavior necessarily mean that females are socially inferior. Only among some species, especially baboons and rhesus monkeys, is there a rigidly hierarchical social structure dominated by highly aggressive males. It is particularly interesting that among chimpanzees, the most

---

[3] As Joyce M. Nielsen says in *Sex and Gender in Society: Perspectives and Stratification,* 2nd ed. (Prospect Heights, IL: Waveland Press, Inc., 1990), "The pattern, then, is that most of what sociobiologists say about humans is based on anthropomorphized versions of animal behavior, which are then used to 'explain' the human pattern that the anthropomorphizing was based on" (p. 157).

[4] Some information on various animal species was provided, for instance, in Janet Chafetz, *Masculine, Feminine, or Human?* (Itasca, IL: Peacock Publishers, 1978); as well as, more recently, by Jane B. Lancaster, "Introduction," in *Female Primates: Studies by Women Primatologists,* ed. Meredith F. Small (New York: Alan R. Liss, 1984), pp. 1–8; and Doane Quiatt and Vernon Reynolds, *Primate Behavior* (Cambridge: Cambridge University Press, 1993).

[5] Cynthia F. Epstein, *Deceptive Distinctions: Sex, Gender, and the Social Order* (New Haven, CT: Yale University Press, 1988), p. 59.

socially advanced nonhuman primates, females do not appear to occupy a subordinate position. Haremlike groups with dominant males are entirely unknown.[6]

These examples should suffice to make anyone cautious about the argument that any attribute or behavior is always male or female, even if generalizing from animals to humans were otherwise acceptable. But such a generalization is itself debatable. An alternative approach suggests that what distinguishes Homo sapiens from other species is that, for humans, it is primarily the norms and expectations of their societies, not blind animal instincts, that are important in shaping their actions and their relations. In this view, biology constrains, but does not determine, human behavior. Human gender roles are no more limited to those of animals than is human behavior otherwise limited to that of animals.[7]

There are, to be sure, physiological and psychological differences between men and women, but, it is argued, they do not adequately explain all existing variations in behavior or why female traits are so often viewed as socially inferior to male traits. Biological nature, which determines the difference between the sexes, is seen as a broad base upon which a variety of structures, with respect to socially determined gender differences, can be built. This hypothesis is consistent with the diverse male and female roles that sprang up under varying conditions in early societies, in spite of the fact that some differentiation of the work and roles of men and women seems to have been present in all known instances. Anthropologists of this school have pointed out that women vary in their social roles and powers, their public status, and their cultural definitions and that the nature, quantity, and social significance of women's activities are far more varied and interesting than has often been assumed. At the same time, there are also many scientists who emphasize biology, and particularly the biological origin of differences between men and women, and nature as well as nurture. As a result, sociobiology is once again enjoying a great deal of attention.

THE ROLE OF SOCIOBIOLOGY IN EXPLAINING GENDER DIFFERENCES

From Edward O. Wilson's *Sociobiology: The New Synthesis* on, sociobiologists have followed Darwin's theory of natural selection and have argued that genes determine human as well as animal traits and hence have been called "genetic determinists."[8] Their views created a good deal of uneasiness among social scientists, because, in the past, social Darwinism had been used to justify such causes as colonialism, imperialism, racism, sexism and, at its worst, mass murder.[9] Selective criteria were frequently

---

[6] Edward O. Wilson, *Sociobiology: The New Synthesis* (Cambridge, MA: Belknap Press of Harvard University Press, 1975).

[7] This was first emphasized by anthropologists such as Ernestine Friedl, *Women and Men: An Anthropologist's View* (New York: Holt, Rinehart & Winston, 1975); and Michelle Z. Rosaldo and Louise Lamphere, eds., *Women, Culture and Society* (Stanford: Stanford University Press, 1974).

[8] See, for instance, Betty Rosoff and Ethel Tobach, "Introduction," in *Challenging Racism and Sexism: Alternatives to Genetic Explanations,* ed. Ethel Tobach and Betty Rosoff (New York: Feminist Press of the City University of New York, 1994), pp. 1–30.

[9] Melvin Konner, "Darwin's Truth, Jefferson's Vision: Sociobiology and the Politics of Human Nature," *American Prospect* 45 (July 1999): 30–38.

employed to indicate superiority and inferiority in order to justify the exploitation and subjection of particular groups. For instance, it was after Africans were enslaved to further the economic well-being of their owners that criteria such as skull volume and brain size were constructed to rationalize and justify this practice, while criteria that did not favor white men were discarded.[10] Further, the contention that the deficiencies of the "downtrodden" were simply part of the human condition rather than outcomes of social inequities was enthusiastically accepted by the ruling class.[11]

All this has been changing in recent decades. On the one hand, sociobiology today has come a long way from the social Darwinism of the nineteenth century. On the other hand, social scientists who long were reluctant to incorporate biological variables in their models are increasingly ready to embrace the notion that many patterns of human behavior have a basis in evolution. They also make room for the possibility that male and female brains, although similar, may function differently.[12] Similarly, they recognize that although measured attributes of individual boys and girls reveal few consistent sex differences, there is a powerful tendency for children to seek out playmates of the same sex, and groups of boys and of girls are very different from each other. Further, they accept that this greatly influences their development.[13] Nonetheless, significant unresolved questions remain. The sociobiological explanation of existing differences between women and men in preferences for mates provides a good example.

Research in the 1960s and 1970s showed that women placed considerable emphasis on finding good providers, while men were looking for relatively young women who would bear children and be good homemakers. This is seen as the result of differential selection pressures experienced by ancestral humans. Women needed mates who were able and willing to support them and their children, while men wanted partners who would bear and nurture their children, as well as tend home and hearth. By virtue of their youth, women at the beginning of their childbearing age were also likely to possess physical characteristics that came to be accepted as standards of beauty. Women who conformed to these standards tended to experience greater reproductive success than those who did not and passed their genes on to their offspring. Similarly, intelligence, aggression, and territoriality, "all characteristics of the stereotypical male of Western capitalist society,"[14] were qualities that enabled the men that possessed them to leave more offspring than others. Hence these attributes, inherited by sons from their fathers who were more successful at surviving and reproducing, increased in frequency during subsequent generations.

---

[10] Ruth Hubbard, "Race and Sex as Biological Categories," in *Challenging Racism and Sexism: Alternatives to Genetic Explanations,* ed. Ethel Tobach and Betty Rosoff (New York: Feminist Press of the City University of New York, 1994), pp. 11–21.

[11] Val Woodward, "Can We Draw Conclusions About Human Societal Behavior from Population Genetics?" in *Challenging Racism and Sexism: Alternatives to Genetic Explanations,* ed. Ethel Tobach and Betty Rosoff (New York: Feminist Press of the City University of New York, 1994), pp. 35–65.

[12] Deborah Blum, *Sex on the Brain: The Biological Differences Between Men and Women* (New York: Viking Penguin, 1997).

[13] Eleanor Maccoby, *The Two Sexes: Growing Up Apart, Coming Together* (Cambridge, MA: Harvard University Press, 1998), p. 287.

[14] Gisela Kaplan and Lesley J. Rogers, "Race and Gender Fallacies: The Paucity of Biological Determinist Explanations of Difference," in *Challenging Racism and Sexism: Alternatives to Genetic Explanations,* ed. Ethel Tobach and Betty Rosoff (New York: Feminist Press of the City University of New York, 1994), p. 76.

Thus, preferences that served their purpose well in the past have presumably become part of men's and women's sexual nature and are maintained throughout the world to this day. Therefore, while fully recognizing the complex interaction between biology and voluntarily chosen behavior,[15] sociobiologists generally conclude that, in spite of some psychological differences among individuals, the basic characteristics of the sexes are extremely difficult to change. This view is supported by the finding of one study that women who are financially independent are as likely as those who are not to have a preference for good providers.[16] This would clearly not be expected if women were merely motivated by rational economic concerns. At the same time, men particularly value physical appearance and prefer mates who are a few years younger than they are, while women seek somewhat older men who are reliable providers.

This sociobiological view of differences between the sexes does shed a good deal of light on the behavior and social organization of animals—including humans. Hence it is not surprising that it has been widely accepted not only among researchers in natural history and animal behavior, but also among many psychologists and other social scientists. Even so, there are critical reservations about this interpretation that deserve to be taken seriously. Further, neo-Darwinist theory, accepted by Wilson and his followers, often leads to oversimplifications. That is most likely a major reason why it has not replaced other behavioral sciences, but has rather become a small, albeit significant, part of the whole field.

One of the objections to this explanation of human behavior is that it views gene replication as the main or even sole purpose of life,[17] with reproduction taking precedence even over survival.[18] Another problematic assumption is that characteristics of parents are inherited only by children of the same sex. It is argued that because strong, aggressive men and attractive, maternal women are more likely to find mates and have children, their sons will be strong and aggressive and their daughters attractive and maternal. This proposition has little scientific support. Finally, as a number of authors have pointed out,[19] there is a tendency to exaggerate biological differences between women and men, to emphasize distinctions rather than to recognize the many similarities, and to ignore the great diversities within each group. It is, for example, common to stress the difference in means of height, strength, math SATs, and so forth, rather than the fact that the range for each substantially overlaps. The same attitude is indicated by use of the phrase "the opposite sex" rather than "the other sex."

An alternative to the uncritical acceptance or rejection of sociobiology is a middle course. This new approach embraces many elements of evolutionary theory, but no longer imposes rigid limits on social change as early theories did;[20] it accepts the

---

[15] Maccoby, *Two Sexes.*

[16] Michael W. Wiederman and Elizabeth Rice Allgeier, "Mate Selection," in *Human Sexuality: An Encyclopedia,* ed. Vern L. Bullough and Bonnie Bullough (Buffalo, NY: Garland Publishing, 1994), pp. 386–90.

[17] Kaplan and Rogers, "Race and Gender Fallacies."

[18] Konner, "Darwin's Truth."

[19] Hubbard, "Race and Sex"; and Blum, *Sex on the Brain.*

[20] Discussed in Cynthia Russett, *Sexual Science: The Victorian Construction of Womanhood* (Cambridge, MA: Harvard University Press, 1989).

importance of biology without ignoring the possibility that function may to some extent influence structure.[21] This leaves room for adaptation in behavior to changing circumstances. For instance, in earlier days men may have looked for women who would make good mothers, while women generally looked for men who would make good providers, but this does not preclude the possibility that men today increasingly prefer women able to share in supporting the family, and women search for men who are likely to become nurturing fathers and partners in homemaking. This view is supported by findings that male and female preferences for characteristics of mates are slowly becoming more similar.[22]

In sum, all differences in the roles of men and women are not likely to disappear. Certainly, this is suggested by the evidence that women tend to spend a significantly larger share of their time and income on their children,[23] and that it is mothers who tend to put far more effort into raising the quality of children.[24] Importantly, however, recognition of differences need not mean that superiority and dominance is assigned to characteristics of one sex, and inferiority and submissiveness to those of the other. It is, for instance, now acknowledged that among primates there are species where males are dominant by virtue of their strength and aggressiveness, and other species where females dominate over individualistic males by virtue of having formed strong group bonds.[25] Nor is there any reason to accept traits of males as the standard and the traits of women as deviant. For example, devoting time to care of the young and the old at the expense of maximizing earnings in the labor market need not be viewed as aberrant behavior. In other words, the most realistic and also the most constructive approach is likely to be one that recognizes the role of both biology and of the environment, of limitations imposed by heredity and the opportunities for overcoming them, and of the importance of history as well as the possibility for progress.

FACTORS INFLUENCING WOMEN'S RELATIVE STATUS

In their studies of human societies, anthropologists, particularly women anthropologists who began to focus on this issue in the 1970s, agree that the relative status of women has varied over time and across societies. There is less agreement on the factors determining their relative position. Although it may not be possible to definitively answer this question at present, some important insights can be gained by considering existing theories.

---

[21] Blum, *Sex on the Brain,* p. 41.

[22] Wiederman and Allgeier, "Mate Selection."

[23] Rae L. Blumberg, "Income Under Female Versus Male Control: Hypotheses from a Theory of Gender Stratification and Data from the Third World," *Journal of Family Issues* 9, no. 1 (March 1988): 51–84; and Shelly J. Lundberg, Robert A. Pollak, and Thomas J. Wales, "Do Husbands and Wives Pool Their Resources? Evidence from the U.K. Child Benefit," *Journal of Human Resources* 32, no. 3 (summer 1997): 463–80.

[24] Kathleen Cloud, "What Every Woman Knows: Women's Preference for Quality in Human Capital Investments" (paper presented at the Conference of the International Association for Feminist Economics, Washington, DC, June 1996).

[25] Blum, *Sex on the Brain,* p. 73.

Ernestine Friedl was one of the first anthropologists to emphasize the importance of environmental constraints in shaping human organization.[26] She argues that the technology employed by a society to produce the necessities of life has tended, in the past, to determine the division of labor on the basis of gender. She also believes that the more important women's role is in production and in controlling distribution outside the family, the higher their status compared to men. Friedl and others espousing this view point to the relatively egalitarian situation in primitive societies where men and women shared in providing food, clothing, and shelter for their families or, in modern days, when both earn an income. In contrast, the status of men and women was very unequal in societies where men provided all the needed resources and women devoted themselves to transforming these resources into usable form and creating a pleasant atmosphere in which they could be used.

Others tend to disagree, at least with the emphasis on the importance of production roles in determining status. In past epochs, slaves did a great deal of productive work without achieving correspondingly high status, and members of the upper class derived their power and prestige from ownership of wealth rather than from any work they did. There is little dispute, however, about the fact that property gives owners power over distribution and that this helps to determine status.

We are inclined toward the view that the structure of social relationships and participation in productive work both play a role. Specifically, in the case of women, it appears that sharing in the provision for the family's needs is a necessary, though not a sufficient, ingredient in achieving a greater degree of equality.[27] Clearly, the extent to which women's activities are confined to the home, while men monopolize the public sphere, also plays an important role.[28]

In the remainder of this chapter, we explore the effect that changing technology and changing property relations have had on the nature and perception of gender roles, focusing primarily on the United States. First, however, we briefly consider the issue of the relationship between women's roles and economic development in more general terms.

WOMEN'S ROLES AND ECONOMIC DEVELOPMENT

In technologically primitive **hunting and gathering societies,** men and women shared in providing food, clothing, and shelter for their families. Men hunted large animals and defended the tribe, whereas women gathered a variety of vegetable foods, occasionally hunted small animals,[29] and had the main responsibility for food preparation and care of children. Such a division of labor was undoubtedly expedient when women were

---

[26] Friedl, *Women and Men.* See also Joan Huber and Glenna Spitze, *Sex Stratification: Children, Housework, and Jobs* (New York: Academic Press, 1983).

[27] Nielsen, *Sex and Gender in Society.*

[28] Michelle Z. Rosaldo, "Women, Culture, and Society: A Theoretical Overview," in *Women, Culture, and Society,* ed. Michelle Z. Rosaldo and Louise Lamphere (Stanford: Stanford University Press, 1974). See also Julie A. Matthaei, *An Economic History of Women in America* (New York: Schocken Books, 1982).

[29] Some evidence suggests that women may have participated in hunting more than was acknowledged earlier, especially in tribes where group hunting was common. See, for instance, Agnes Estioko-Griffin and P. Bion Griffin, "Woman the Hunter: The Agta," in *Woman the Gatherer,* ed. Frances Dahlberg (New Haven, CT: Yale University Press, 1981), pp. 121–52.

pregnant or nursing most of their adult lives, and thus could not participate in activities that would have taken them far from home. The greater strength of men also gave them a considerable advantage for such activities as hunting large animals and fighting.

The extent to which men and women contributed to the necessities of life was determined by the availability of various resources, and women's status appeared to vary accordingly. In general, the fact that men provided for the safety of the tribe and furnished most of the meat, always regarded as the prestige food, gave them the advantage. Nonetheless, the common payment of the bride price suggests that women were also valued for their contributions.

In the somewhat more advanced **horticultural societies,** plants were cultivated in small plots located near the home. Men continued to conduct warfare and also prepared the ground by slashing and burning; women prepared the food and cared for infants. But virtually all other activities were shared. Accordingly, men and women tended to be considerably more equal during this stage than in the agricultural societies that would follow.

In **pastoral societies,** on the other hand, men tended to monopolize the herding of large animals, an activity that often took them far from home. Herding provided the bulk of what was needed for subsistence. Women's contributions were largely confined to tending the primitive equivalent of hearth and home, and females never reached more than a subservient status.

The situation changed radically when horticultural societies were superseded by **agricultural societies,** which arrived with the introduction of the plow. Although women "helped" in the fields,[30] looked after small animals and gardens, and worked in the now permanent homes taking care of large families, only men owned and worked the land, and the disparity in power and influence became great indeed. The **dowry,** paid by the father of the bride to the groom, who henceforth undertakes her support, and **purdah,** the practice of hiding women from the sight of men, came into use during that period in some of these societies. Both may be viewed as ways of subordinating women as well as signs of their subjugation.

There was one factor that helped to offset this lowly position for at least a small minority of women. As ownership of land and other assets created an upper class of landed gentry, membership in that class entailed great wealth and power. Under these conditions, birth in the right family conferred status even on women. Property was generally owned and inherited by men, but in the absence of a male heir in a ruling family, a woman might even become head of state.[31] Hence, there were ruling queens, Elizabeth I of England being the best known. In general, however, while upper-class females enjoyed a rather luxurious lifestyle, they were mainly seen as producers of children, rarely had influence except as behind-the-scenes manipulators, and were typically used as pawns in political and economic alliances. Only in exceptional cases did women achieve important roles

---

[30] Very poor women also worked as hired laborers and domestic servants.

[31] Only recently have any women become heads of state who were not born into the position, and even today they tend to come from the upper classes. The proposition that women were always relegated to a more or less inferior status in all primitive societies, and that at least a few attained power and prestige when class structure developed, is in sharp contrast to the views propounded by Friedrich Engels in *The Origin of the Family, Private Property, and the State* (New York: International Publishers, 1884; reprint, 1972). His contention was that women were powerful matriarchs during the earlier stages of development (primitive communism) and that it was the development of private property that was the root of the subjugation of women.

in the economy and in the development of culture, aided by achieving high rank in religious orders in some instances or by the extended absence of fighting men in others.

Women were also more likely to be partners, though not equal ones, among the growing class of merchants and artisans in the urban centers that began to grow along with developing agriculture. They participated in what were, in those early days, truly family enterprises, generally took charge when the men traveled on business, and often continued to be in charge after the husband died. Household and workplace were not rigidly separated, nor were consumption and production. Father, mother, children, perhaps other relatives, and often apprentices lived and worked together. Yet their tasks and responsibilities were determined by their age and by their sex. Whenever the father was present, he was the head of the family enterprise.

As we have seen, women tended to have a higher status in horticultural societies than in agricultural ones, in which women's activities came to be increasingly centered within the home. Nonetheless, since much production was concentrated in the household, and since women were active participants, they continued to be perceived as productive members of the family, albeit not equal partners.[32] During the early stages of **industrialization,** on the other hand, much of the production previously concentrated in the household was shifted from the home to the factory and the office. This shift reduced the burden of housekeeping but did little to advance the status of women, who, for the most part, continued to center their activities around the home. Indeed, the perceived importance of their productive role initially tended to decline, as did their relative status. In time, however, continued industrialization began to draw ever-increasing numbers of women into the paid labor force, paving the way for a "subtle revolution" in gender roles.[33] In the following sections, we review this process in greater detail, focusing upon the situation in the United States.

The case of the United States is in some respects unique, even in comparison to other economically advanced countries. In particular, the frontier experience was shared by only a few of these countries, such as Canada and Australia. Nonetheless, the broad contours of the shifts outlined here are to some extent applicable to many of them. Indeed, the alteration of men's and women's work roles occurring in the United States today may be seen as part of a transformation taking place in much of the industrialized world. (Recent developments in other countries are discussed in greater detail in Chapter 11.)

THE U.S. EXPERIENCE

THE PREINDUSTRIAL PERIOD

In colonial America, as in other preindustrial economies, the family enterprise was the dominant economic unit, and production was the major function of the family.[34] Most of the necessities for survival were produced in the household, though some goods

---

[32] Nancy Folbre, *Who Pays for the Kids?* (London: Routledge, 1994), p. 135.

[33] Ralph E. Smith, "The Movement of Women into the Labor Force," in *The Subtle Revolution: Women at Work,* ed. Ralph E. Smith (Washington, DC: Urban Institute, 1979), pp. 1–29.

[34] A more detailed account of the position of women during the colonial era and the early years of the Republic may be found in Alice Kessler-Harris, *Out to Work: A History of America's Wage Earning Women* (New York: Oxford University Press, 1982), pp. 3–45.

were generally produced for sale, the proceeds of which were used to purchase some market goods and to accumulate wealth. Cooking; cleaning; care of the young, the old, and the infirm; spinning; weaving; sewing; knitting; soap and candle making; and simple carpentry were carried on in the home. Much of the food and other raw materials were grown on the farm. All members of the family capable of making any contribution participated in production, but there was always some specialization and division of labor.

Among the nonslave population, men were primarily responsible for agriculture and occasionally trade, whereas women did much of the rest of the work, including what would today be characterized as "light manufacturing" activity. But gender-role specialization was by no means complete. Slave women were used to work in the fields. Widows tended to take over the family enterprise when the need arose, and in very early days, single women were on occasion given "maidplots." Even though men and women often had different tasks, and men were more often involved in production for the market and generally owned all property, everyone participated in productive activity. Even aged grandparents would help with tasks that required responsibility and judgment and would perhaps also supervise children in carrying out small chores they could adequately perform from a very early age.

All family members, except for infants, had essentially the same economic role. They either contributed goods and services directly or earned money by selling some of these in the market. The important economic role of children, as well as the plentiful availability of land, encouraged large families. High infant mortality rates provided a further incentive to bear many children. In the eighteenth century, completed fertility may have averaged as many as 8 to 10 births per woman.[35]

Wealthy women were primarily managers, not workers, within the household. This was, no doubt, a less arduous and possibly a more rewarding level of task but one no less absorbing. For most women, regardless of their affluence, there was little role conflict. The ideal of the frugal, industrious housewife working alongside her family corresponded closely to reality. The only women for whom this was not true were very poor women, who often became indentured servants, and, of course, black women, who were generally slaves. The former were, as a rule, not permitted to marry during their years of servitude; the latter might potentially have their family entirely disrupted by their owners' choice. Both had to work very hard, and slaves did not even have the modest legal protection of rights that indentured servants enjoyed.

The one thing all these diverse groups had in common was that they were productive members of nearly self-sufficient households. Government played a very small role, and although there was some exchange of goods and services, chiefly barter, it was not until well into the nineteenth century that production outside the home, for sale rather than for direct use, came to dominate the economy.

---

[35] For a description of demographic trends during this period, see Karl E. Taeuber and James A. Sweet, "Family and Work: The Social Life Cycle of Women," in *Women and the American Economy: A Look to the 1980s,* ed. Juanita M. Kreps (Englewood Cliffs, NJ: Prentice Hall, 1976), pp. 31–60.

INDUSTRIALIZATION

During the early period of industrialization in the late eighteenth and early nineteenth centuries, women (and children) in the United States, as elsewhere, worked in the textile mills and other industries that sprang up in the East. Initially, primarily young farm girls were employed in the factories, often contributing part of their pay to supplement family income and using some to accumulate a "dowry" that would make them more desirable marriage partners. The employment of these young women in factories may have appeared quite natural to observers at the time. They were doing much the same type of work they had done in the home, only in a new location and under the supervision of a foreman rather than the head of the household.[36] Once married, women generally left their jobs to look after their own households, which would soon include children.

The earliest available data show that at the end of the nineteenth century, when the labor force participation rate for men was 84 percent, only 18 percent of all women were in the paid labor force, and the percentage of married women who worked outside the home was only 5 percent.[37] The situation was different for black women. Around 23 percent of black wives were employed. Most of these women worked either as domestics or in agriculture in the rural South. Although such early industries as textiles, millinery, and cigars did employ women, mainly young single ones, the new, rapidly growing sophisticated industries relied from the beginning almost entirely on male workers.

Among some immigrant groups, however, who in the course of the nineteenth century increasingly replaced American-born workers in factories, it was not uncommon even for married women to be employed.[38] Most of these people came to the New World determined to improve their economic condition and particularly to make sure that their children would get a better start than they did. At times, the whole family worked. Often if a choice needed to be made between the children leaving school to supplement family income or the mother seeking employment, the latter choice was made even among groups traditionally reluctant to have women work outside the home. By the same token, maternal employment was associated with dire need and was viewed as a temporary expedient to give the family a better start. Few wives remained in the labor force once the husband earned enough for an adequate living. The immigrants' goal of achieving the desired standard of living included what by then was widely considered the American ideal of the family—the male breadwinner who supported his family and the female homemaker who cared for his domestic needs.

---

[36] This was pointed out by Edith Abbott, *Women in Industry* (New York: Appleton and Company, 1910). For a recent discussion, see Dora L. Costa, "From Mill Town to Board Room: The Rise of Women's Paid Labor," *Journal of Economic Perspectives* 14, no. 4 (fall 2000): 101–22.

[37] All labor force participation figures cited here and below are from Claudia Goldin, *Understanding the Gender Gap: An Economic History of American Women* (New York: Oxford University Press, 1990), with the exception of the overall male and female participation rates, which are from U.S. Census Bureau, *Historical Statistics of the United States: Colonial Times to 1970,* part 1 (1975), pp. 131–32. As discussed later, official figures undoubtedly underestimate the proportion of women who worked for pay. Not only was seasonal work frequently ignored, but work done in the home, such as taking in boarders and bringing home piecework, was often overlooked as well.

[38] Milton Cantor and Bruce Laurie, eds., *Class, Sex and the Woman Worker* (Westport, CT: Greenwood Press, 1977) contains a great deal of interesting information on immigrant women during the early years.

INDUSTRIALIZATION AND THE EVOLUTION OF THE FAMILY

As an increasingly larger segment of the population began living in urban centers rather than on farms, and family shops were replaced by factories, women found that their household work increasingly came to be confined to the care of children, the nurturing of the husband, and the maintenance of the home. There was no longer a garden or farm animals to take care of, no need for seasonal help with the crops, and no opportunity to participate in a family business. As husbands left the home to earn the income needed to support their families, a more rigid division developed between the female domestic sphere and the male public sphere.

Thus, along with industrialization in the nineteenth century arose the concept of the **traditional family,** which lingered to a greater or lesser degree well into the twentieth century.[39] The family shifted from a production unit to a consumption unit, and the responsibility for earning a living came to rest squarely on the shoulders of the husband. Wives (and children) grew to be dependent on his income. Redistribution became an important function of the family, as it provided a mechanism for the transfer of income from the market-productive husband to his dependent wife and children. Not only did specific *tasks* differ between men and women, as was always the case, but men and women now had different *economic roles* as well. Many workers and social reformers explicitly advocated that a man should be paid a "family wage," adequate to support not only him but also his wife and children.

As we have seen, among the poor, particularly blacks and immigrants, it was often necessary for wives to enter the labor market. But for the middle-class white wife, and even for the working-class wife whose husband had a steady income, holding a job was frowned upon as inconsistent with her social status. If the wife entered the labor market, it was assumed that she was either compensating for her husband's inadequacy as a breadwinner or that she was selfishly pursuing a career at the expense of her household responsibilities.

The status of children also changed. Only in very poor families would they be expected to help to raise the family's standard of living, though some might work to earn spending money or because their parents thought it would be good for their moral fiber. Furthermore, the age when children came to be considered young adults and were supposed to become productive members of the family increased considerably. By the end of the nineteenth century, child labor laws were passed that prohibited employment of "minors."

As a consequence of industrialization and urbanization, more and more goods and services used by households came to be produced outside the home. Nonetheless, much time and effort were still expended to purchase and maintain these commodities and to use them to attain the desired standard of living. With soap and bleach purchased at the store, and the washing machine doing the scrubbing, laundry became far

---

[39] Historian Carl N. Degler has termed this the "first transformation." In his view, the second transformation came in the 1940s, when married women began to enter the labor market in large numbers. See his *At Odds: Women and the Family in America from the Revolution to the Present* (New York: Oxford University Press, 1980). It was also during this period that women's work in the household came to be officially classified as unproductive, as pointed out by Nancy Folbre, "The Unproductive Housewife: Her Evolution in Nineteenth-Century Economic Thought," *Signs: Journal of Women in Culture and Society* 16, no. 3 (spring 1991): 463–84.

less of a chore, but it was done far more frequently, and housewives came to take pride in making it "whiter than white." Groceries bought at the supermarket and a gas or electric range made cooking much easier, but homemakers would now serve elaborate meals rather than a pot of stew. To do otherwise would not be consistent with the role of dedicated mother and wife, whose every thought was for the well-being of her family. The husband might help her, but this was never to interfere with his "work." The children, too, particularly girls, might be expected to assist their mothers, but the basic responsibility for the household rested with the wife.

The net result of these developments was that the number of hours that full-time homemakers devoted to housework, over 50 a week, did not change from the beginning of the century to the 1960s.[40] Two additional trends contributed to this. One was the decline in the number of household servants, whose presence was not uncommon in middle-class households in the nineteenth and early twentieth centuries. Probably more important was the tendency to use the time no longer needed to produce essentials to raise the standard of comfort the family could enjoy, not to increase the wife's leisure time.[41]

Fertility declined with industrialization, in part because of the diminished economic value of children. There was far less opportunity for children to participate in production in urban households, and with growing immigration, hired workers were more readily available as a source of farm labor.[42] Further, the number of years of schooling grew in both towns and rural areas, so that children remained dependent for a longer period of time. Consequently, women born in the early nineteenth century averaged somewhat less than five births, considerably below the rate of their eighteenth-century predecessors, and those born toward the end of the century averaged only about three births. But as the number of children declined, the amount of maternal care per child increased greatly, and the number of years of such care was extended substantially.

Responsibility for spending the family's money and for determining the amount to be saved was not as clear, but there were certain generally accepted norms. The wife made most of the everyday purchases but was expected to comply with her husband's wishes and to try to please her family. Thus, to some extent, she might be viewed as the purchasing agent rather than an independent decision maker when she did the shopping. The husband generally determined where the family would live and what major items should be bought, such as larger durables and, particularly, the house.

---

[40] Joann Vanek found that even as late as 1966, full-time homemakers were devoting as much time to their work as their grandmothers had in the 1920s. See Vanek, "Time Spent in Housework," *Scientific American* 231, no. 5 (November 1974): 116–20. It was not until the late seventies that this situation changed; see our discussion in Chapter 3 and also Joseph H. Pleck, "Husband's Paid Work and Family Roles: Current Research Issues," in *Research in the Interweave of Social Roles: Families and Jobs,* ed. Helena Lopata and Joseph H. Pleck (Greenwich, CT: JAI Press, 1983), pp. 251–333.

[41] Bonnie J. Fox points out that advertisements tended to emphasize improved housekeeping standards and better service to the family rather than liberation from household chores; see "Selling the Mechanized Household: 70 Years of Ads in the *Ladies Home Journal,*" *Gender and Society* 4, no. 1 (March 1990): 25–40.

[42] Improved methods of birth control are often credited for the declining birth rate. But significant decreases occurred in much of the industrialized world before any major breakthroughs in contraceptive techniques. See Joan Huber, "Toward a Sociotechnological Theory of the Women's Movement," *Social Problems* 23, no. 4 (April 1976): 371–88.

The man's authority as "head of the household" was supposed to be absolute in all important matters, for he basically determined the family's lifestyle by providing the money income on which it so crucially depended.[43] Further, the husband's decisions defined the parameters within which the other family members had to operate. Thus, he was dominant within the household as well as in the outside world. It was, however, generally assumed that, within the family, he would see to it that benefits were distributed equally or according to need, as deemed appropriate.

As the economic role of women changed within the family, so too did the image of the ideal wife. Whereas the colonial wife was valued for her industriousness, the growing **cult of true womanhood** that developed with industrialization in the nineteenth century equated piety, purity, domesticity, and submissiveness with the femininity to which all women were expected to aspire.[44] Their role was in the now consumption-oriented home—as daughter, sister, but most of all as wife and mother. This ideal particularly extolled the lifestyle of affluent middle- and upper-class women, who were to a great extent freed even from their domestic chores by the servants their husbands' ample incomes could provide. Understandably, overburdened working-class women, who often contributed to family income, if not through wage labor then by taking in boarders or doing piecework at home, might come to look longingly at such a more leisurely existence as something to hope for and strive toward. For men of all social classes, it came to be a mark of success to be the sole wage earner in the family.

This image of the family was fostered not only by the example of the middle and upper middle classes, which was the envy of the poor woman bearing the double burden of paid and unpaid work or toiling at home to make ends meet on a limited budget,[45] but also by male workers and their trade unions. Initially, the availability of women and children for work in industry was welcomed by national leaders because they provided cheap, competitive labor, while agricultural production could be maintained by men.[46] However, attitudes changed as workers became more plentiful with the growing influx of immigrants. Working men were particularly eager to get married women out of the labor force entirely and women out of all but the lowest-paid jobs.

---

[43] See, for instance, Janet R. Wilkie, "Marriage, Family Life, and Women's Employment," in *Women Working,* ed. Ann H. Stromberg and Shirley Harkess (Mountain View, CA: Mayfield Publishing Company, 1988), pp. 149–66. She suggests that "the husband's occupation affected where the family lived, whether they moved, how they spent disposable income, whether the wife worked, and so forth. In fact, the husband's primacy went well beyond this. Men enjoyed greater power in other non-job related spheres of the marital relationship" (p. 151).

[44] This subject is explored in depth by Barbara Easton, "Industrialization and Femininity: A Case Study of Nineteenth Century New England," *Social Problems* 23, no. 4 (April 1976): 389–401; and Barbara Welter, "The Cult of True Womanhood, 1820–1860," in *The American Family in Social-Historical Perspective,* ed. Michael Gordon (New York: St. Martin's Press, 1978), pp. 313–33. This attitude was by no means confined to the United States. The German equivalent was *Küche, Kirche, Kinder:* kitchen, church, and children.

[45] As Louise Tilly and Joan Scott, *Women, Work and Family* (New York: Holt, Rinehart & Winston, 1978) forcefully point out, mothers found it very difficult to combine employment outside the home with housework and child care.

[46] George Washington is quoted as writing to Lafayette, "I conceive much might be done in the way of women, children and others [producing yarn and cloth] without taking one really necessary hand from tilling the earth." Cited in Alice Kessler-Harris, *Women Have Always Worked* (New York: McGraw-Hill, 1981), p. 8.

Their goals were to reserve the better positions for themselves, make sure they would not be underbid, and give greater force to the argument that a "living wage" for a man had to be sufficient to support a dependent wife and children. Thus, women received little, if any, support from organized labor in trying to improve their own working conditions and rewards.[47]

This was the genesis of the traditional family, once accepted as the backbone of American society. As we have seen, it is in fact comparatively recent in origin, dating back only to the mid-nineteenth and early twentieth centuries. Even in its heyday, it was never entirely universal. Many poor, black, and immigrant married women worked outside their homes; in addition, many others earned income at home, taking in boarders or doing piecework. Moreover, the historical record indicates that single-parent families were not all that uncommon; in 1900, 9 percent of children lived in such families, in most cases with a widowed parent. As a point of comparison, the same proportion of children lived with a single parent in 1960.[48]

Throughout this period, market work was quite common among single women, and a relatively small number of women, particularly college graduates, chose careers over marriage as a lifelong vocation. Nonetheless, exclusive dedication to the role of mother and wife was widely accepted as the only proper and fulfilling life for a woman. It was not long, however, before this orthodoxy was challenged. Progressive modernization brought about dramatic changes in conditions of production and in the economic roles of men and women, followed by changes in ideas and aspirations that made rigid differentiation, let alone ranking of the roles of the sexes, increasingly less appropriate.

As family size continued to shrink, the amount of time and energy needed for childbearing and childrearing declined. At the same time, women were living longer. Although, as previously noted, full-time homemakers continued to work long hours, thus achieving ever higher standards of homemaking, women had the choice of devoting time to other activities, especially during the years after their children grew up. More and more of the goods and services that were previously provided within the household for its own use were now mass-produced and available for purchase. New appliances facilitated faster and easier production of many of the others. Increasingly, the market also provided many new goods and services desired by consumers that could not readily be produced in the home. This undoubtedly was one of the reasons why increasing numbers of women and men decided that a second paycheck would make a greater contribution to the family's standard of living than additional time devoted to upgrading the quality of homemaking. Other factors, to be discussed in Chapter 4, such as increased education and changes in the demand for labor, were important in facilitating the influx of women into the labor market. However, the shrinking household and household sphere were among the basic developments that made it possible.

---

[47] Alice Kessler-Harris, "Organizing the Unorganizable: Three Jewish Women and Their Union," in *Class, Sex and the Woman Worker,* ed. Milton Cantor and Bruce Laurie (Westport, CT: Greenwood Press, 1977) is very eloquent on this point.

[48] For an interesting historical perspective on the family, see Linda Gordon and Sara McLanahan, "Single Parenthood in 1900," *Journal of Family History* 16, no. 2 (April 1991): 97–116.

WOMEN IN THE LABOR MARKET

As suggested previously, there were always women who were economically active beyond taking care of family and home.[49] Official statistics cited earlier indicate that 84 percent of men, but only 18 percent of women and less than 5 percent of married women, were in the labor force in 1890. It has, however, been suggested that, although the census did not severely undercount the paid work of married women outside the home in the early years of collecting separate data for men and women, it did considerably understate paid work in the home (such as taking in boarders or doing piecework) and on the farm.[50] It has been estimated that women's labor force participation, more broadly defined to include paid work done within the household, was as high as 26 percent in 1890, but decreased thereafter with the decline in the family farm and in paid work done at home, not to reach the previous high again until around 1940.[51] Interestingly, these trends are consistent with the notion, discussed earlier in this chapter, that women's participation in productive activity is likely first to decline, but to rise once more as the economy moves from one dominated by agriculture through early, and then advanced, industrialization.

Each of the two definitions of labor force participation has merit, depending on whether one is primarily interested in the extent to which women are independent wage carners or in their productive contributions to the household. The issue is mainly relevant for wives because, throughout the period for which data have been available, single women were considerably more likely to be gainfully employed outside the home. As late as 1940, the labor force participation of married women was only 14 percent, while it was 46 percent for single women. One reason for the low rates for married women was the so-called *marriage bar* prohibiting the employment of married women that began to come into use in the late 1800s and lasted into the mid-1900s. Marriage bars were particularly prevalent in teaching and clerical work, two occupations that were to become among the most common for married women in later years. Another obstacle to married women's employment outside the home was the lack of availability of part-time work at a time when women's household responsibilities were quite demanding.[52]

Not only were relatively few women employed during the early years of the twentieth century, but they also tended to work in different occupations than men and were concentrated in a relatively few jobs. As shown in Table 2.1, at the turn of the century, 42 percent of men were in agricultural jobs and 38 percent were in manufacturing jobs.

[49] Much useful information on the economic status of women in the United States prior to World War II is found in Goldin, *Understanding the Gender Gap;* Matthaei, *Economic History;* and Costa, "From Mill Town to Board Room."

[50] For an interesting paper on how families made ends meet, see Robert V. Robinson, "Family Economic Strategies in Nineteenth and Early Twentieth-Century Indianapolis," *Journal of Family History,* no. 1 (January 1995): 1–22.

[51] This figure reflects Goldin's estimate that including undercounted workers would lead to a seven percentage point increase in her calculation of the overall labor force participation rate for women. For white married women, in particular, including such workers would raise their rate by as much as 10 percentage points, from 2.5 to 12.5 percent. See Goldin, *Understanding the Gender Gap,* pp. 44–45. See also Claudia Goldin, "The U-Shaped Female Labor Force Function in Economic Development and Economic History," in *Investments in Women's Human Capital,* ed. T. Paul Schultz (Chicago: University of Chicago, 1995), pp. 61–90.

[52] Goldin, *Understanding the Gender Gap,* chap. 6, pp. 159–84.

TABLE 2.1   Distribution of Workers by Occupation, Race, and Gender, 1890/1900

	Men	Women		
	Total (%)	Total (%)	White (%)	Nonwhite (%)
Professional	10.2	9.6	12.5	0.9
Clerical	2.8	4.0	5.2	0.4
Sales	4.6	4.3	5.7	0.1
Service	3.1	35.5	31.3	48.2
Manufacturing	37.6	27.7	34.7	6.4
Agricultural	41.7	19.0	10.8	44.0
Total Employed	100.0	100.0	100.0	100.0

Source: From *Understanding the Gender Gap: An Economic History of American Women,* by Claudia Dale Goldin, Tables 3.2 and 3.3. Copyright © 1990 by Claudia Dale Goldin. Used by permission of Oxford University Press, Inc.

Of the 18 percent in white-collar jobs, the largest share was in the professional category (which included managers and proprietors) followed by sales and clerical occupations. Relatively few men, 3 percent, were in service jobs (for instance, waiter or barber).

In contrast, among women nearly 36 percent were in the service sector, the majority employed in domestic service. As many as 28 percent were in manufacturing, virtually all in textiles, clothing, and tobacco. Another 19 percent were in agriculture. Table 2.1 further shows that over 90 percent of black women worked as either domestic servants or as farm laborers, as compared with only 42 percent of white women. It was also the case that foreign-born white women were overrepresented in manufacturing and domestic service, as compared with U.S.-born white women, though these figures are not shown separately here.

Another 10 percent of all women were in professional positions; almost all were schoolteachers or nurses. These professions, like domestic service, may be regarded as extensions of women's domestic role, though initially almost all schoolteachers were men. The remainder of women workers were in clerical work and sales occupations. Like teaching, clerical work was originally a primarily male occupation. As late as the turn of the century, 85 percent of clerical workers were men. It was not until after 1900, when such positions gradually ceased to be viewed as apprenticeships, that women entered this field to any significant extent; in time, as more women entered the labor market, clerical work became predominantly female and absorbed a substantial proportion of employed women.

A wide variety of factors undoubtedly contributed to the rapid growth of clerical jobs. Among these was the growth of large corporations, which greatly increased the volume of paperwork. The large proportion of women with a high school education who needed little or no on-the-job training to perform such work provided an inexpensive labor pool to satisfy the expanding demand. Employers were willing to hire these women, even when they were not expected to stay for a long time; this became all the more common after the separation of purely clerical from apprenticeship functions.

Women, in turn, were likely to find these jobs attractive because relevant skills did not tend to depreciate much during periods out of the labor force and reentry was relatively easy. It is also possible that many preferred clean white-collar jobs to the dirtier, noisier, and at times more physically demanding blue-collar jobs, and they had few other such alternatives.[53]

Women's labor force participation has been rising ever since the 1890s, the first year for which official data are available. However, while it rose only from about 18 percent to 28 percent over the next 50 years until 1940, between then and 1999 it increased considerably more rapidly to 60 percent.[54] The causes of this increase are considered in greater detail in Chapter 4, however, the growth in the demand for clerical workers undoubtedly facilitated the rapid influx of women into the labor force that began in the 1940s. Beyond that, it is very likely that the steady increase in women's earnings, both in absolute terms and relative to men's, was a contributing factor. Recent research provides evidence on the historical trend in women's earnings relative to men's. Available data from the manufacturing as well as the agricultural sector indicate that the gender earnings ratio rose from 1815, around the start of early industrialization, through the turn of the century. Later data, which are available for the economy as a whole, indicate that the ratio increased from .46 in 1890 to .56 by 1930. The trend over these 40 years was largely due to an increase in the relative earnings of women within broad occupations, though there was also some movement of women into higher paying sectors.[55] Subsequently, there was little change until about 1980, but since then the ratio has risen to well over .70. We present recent trends in the gender earnings ratio in greater detail in Chapter 5.

Nonwage benefits, on the other hand, provided little incentive for women to enter the labor force. Because the foundations of the modern welfare state were laid during the time when the traditional family was still accepted as the norm, these programs generally addressed the needs of traditional families rather than those of two-earner or one-adult households. This was true both for the benefits employers began to provide early in the century, including health insurance, disability coverage, and pensions, and for those introduced by government in the 1930s, most notably Social Security. Both types of programs were expanded further during World War II, when wage increases were severely restricted by government controls, but it was not until considerably later that attention turned to benefits required particularly by families without full-time homemakers. This subject will be discussed at greater length in Chapter 10.

How much families and their needs have changed becomes clear when it is recognized that by the late 1990s, three-fourths of all employed married men and over 90 percent of employed married women had a spouse in the labor force. In addition, over 13 per-

---

[53] For analyses of women's occupational choices and of their entry into clerical work, see Claudia Goldin, "Historical Evolution of Female Earnings Functions and Occupations," *Explorations in Economic History* 21, no. 1 (January 1984): 1–27; and Margery Davies, "Woman's Place Is at the Typewriter: The Feminization of the Clerical Labor Force," in *Labor Market Segmentation,* ed. Richard C. Edwards, Michael Reich, and David M. Gordon (Lexington, MA: D.C. Health, 1975), pp. 279–96.

[54] For more detailed data, including differences by race and marital status, see Goldin, *Understanding the Gender Gap,* chap. 2.

[55] Goldin, *Understanding the Gender Gap,* p. 58–63.

cent of employed women maintained families (with no husband present).[56] These changes reflect the rapidly rising labor force participation of women, which had reached 60 percent by 1999, as well as the much higher divorce and nonmarital birth rates of recent decades. These developments will be discussed in greater detail in following chapters.

CONCLUSION

The overview provided here, though very general, permits us to draw some conclusions. The roles of men and women and the social rules that prescribe appropriate behavior for each are not shaped by biology alone. Rather, they are determined by the interaction of technology, the role of women in production, and a variety of social and political factors. There is some reason to believe that women are less likely to be seen as dependents, defined solely in terms of their maternal and family role, when they participate in "productive" work.

It is also likely that the roles of men and women that may have initially developed as a rational response to conditions that existed at one time in the course of economic development continue their hold long after they have ceased to be functional.[57] Thus, the view that women should devote themselves to homemaking, once a full-time occupation when life was short, families were large, and housekeeping was laborious, lingered long after these conditions had changed substantially. Jobs originally allocated to men because they required great physical strength often continued as male preserves when mechanization did away with the need for muscle power. The possibility that such lags in adjustment are not uncommon should be kept in mind when we come to analyze the current situation.

Our review also suggests that neither the role of housewife nor that of working woman is without significant problems for women. Men's work in the public sphere (that is, outside the family) has usually enjoyed higher status than women's domestic work within the family circle. But even when women have succeeded in entering the world beyond the household to a greater or lesser extent, men have not shown much inclination to share in household work.[58] This, in turn, has made it difficult for women to achieve substantial equality in the public sphere. Many of those who *have* tried have been confronted by the problem of "the double burden" of responsibility for home and market work, or have had to make a choice between a career and marriage.[59] In mod-

---

[56] U.S. Census Bureau, "Historical Income Tables–Families," www.census.gov; and Bureau of Labor Statistics, *The Employment Situation: January 2001.*

[57] "Although stereotypes are often initially based on fact, they are seldom revised as quickly as the facts change." Smith, "The Movement of Women," p. 3.

[58] It is interesting to note that even Marx, who extolled the virtues of not specializing in just one type of work but rather of participating in a variety of different activities, never included "woman's work" among them. Thus, he suggests that under the ideal conditions of full communism, man will be able to hunt in the morning, fish in the afternoon, raise cattle in the evening, and criticize after dinner. (Karl Marx and Friedrich Engels, *The German Ideology,* trans. W. Loach and C. P. Magill [London: Lawrence and Wishart, 1938].) Nowhere does he suggest that man might also share in cleaning the house, preparing dinner, or putting the children to bed.

[59] Not only does the woman who is employed and retains the primary responsibility as homemaker work long hours, but she is also confronted by a substantially different set of values in the two spheres. In the home, there is emphasis on nurturing, mutual aid, and service to others. In the marketplace, competitive,

ern times, machines have largely done away with the need for muscle, and physical strength is no longer required for the most highly valued work. At the same time, child-bearing absorbs an increasingly smaller proportion of a woman's adult life and can, for the most part, be timed at will. It is entirely possible that, under these conditions, it is the unequal distribution of labor in the home rather than women's lesser ability to perform other types of work that is the main obstacle to equality.

QUESTIONS FOR REVIEW AND DISCUSSION

1. Explain how women's and men's roles in production changed between the colonial period and early industrialization.
2. From a historical perspective, how has the labor market experience of black and white women differed?
3. Compare and contrast the role of women in the following stages:
   a. hunting and gathering
   b. horticulture
   c. agriculture
   d. early industrialization
   e. today
4. In view of what we have learned from sociobiologists, to what extent can traditional roles of men and women be expected to change with changing economic conditions?

Suggested Readings

Blum, Deborah. *Sex on the Brain: The Biological Differences Between Men and Women.* New York: Viking Penguin, 1997.

Costa, Dora L. "From Mill Town to Board Room: The Rise of Women's Paid Labor," *Journal of Economic Perspectives* 14, no. 4 (fall 2000): 101–22.

Friedl, Ernestine. *Women and Men: An Anthropological View.* New York: Holt, Rinehart & Winston, 1975.

Goldin, Claudia. *Understanding the Gender Gap: An Economic History of American Women.* New York: Oxford University Press, 1990.

———. "The U-Shaped Female Labor Force Function in Economic Development and Economic History." In *Investments in Women's Human Capital,* edited by T. Paul Schultz, pp. 61–90. Chicago: University of Chicago, 1995.

Matthaei, Julie A. *An Economic History of Women in America.* New York: Schocken Books, 1982.

Nielsen, Joyce M. *Sex and Gender in Society: Perspectives and Stratification,* 2nd ed. Prospect Heights, IL: Waveland Press, Inc., 1990.

O'Kelly, Charlotte G. *Women and Men in Society.* New York: D. Van Nostrand Co., 1980.

---

individualistic behavior is rewarded. Thus, the person whose identity is grounded in the family, who tends to give priority to cooperation and seek approval rather than gain, may well be at a disadvantage. See Clair (Vickery) Brown, "Home Production for Use in a Market Economy," in *Rethinking the Family: Some Feminist Questions,* ed. Barrie Thorne (New York: Longman, 1981), pp. 151–67.

Rosaldo, Michelle Z., and Louise Lamphere eds. *Women, Culture and Society.* Stanford: Stanford University Press, 1974.

Tiger, Lionel, and Robin Fox. *The Imperial Animal.* New York: Holt, Rinehart & Winston, 1971.

Tilly, Louise, and Joan Scott. *Women, Work and Family.* New York: Holt, Rinehart & Winston, 1978.

Welter, Barbara. "The Cult of True Womanhood, 1820–1860." In *The American Family in Social-Historical Perspective,* edited by Michael Gordon, pp. 313–33. New York: St. Martin's Press, 1978.

Wilson, Edward O. *Sociobiology: The New Synthesis.* Cambridge, MA: Belknap Press of Harvard University Press, 1975

CHAPTER 3

THE FAMILY AS
AN ECONOMIC UNIT

Chapter Highlights

- The Simple Neoclassical Model: Specialization and Exchange
- Other Advantages of Families
- The Disadvantages of Specialization
- Transaction Cost and Bargaining Approaches
- Marxist and Radical Feminist Views of the Family
- Nonmarket Work
- The American Family at the Threshold of the Twenty-First Century

For a long time, neoclassical economics, the dominant school of economics in the United States and most of the rest of the world today, and the approach we primarily draw on in this text, concerned itself largely with the behavior of "economic man." It was, of course, acknowledged that this man interacted with others, in competition or in cooperation, but it was his individual well-being that he would attempt to maximize. Consumer economics had long recognized the existence of the family and its importance as a unit of consumption. However, it was not until the 1960s, with the path-breaking work of Gary Becker and Jacob Mincer, that mainstream economists began to concern themselves with the issues confronted by men and women in allocating their time and wealth so as to maximize family well-being.[1]

---

[1] See Gary S. Becker, "A Theory of the Allocation of Time," *Economic Journal* 75, no. 299 (September 1965): 493–517; and Jacob Mincer, "Labor Force Participation of Married Women," in *Aspects of Labor Economics,* ed. H. Gregg Lewis, Universities National Bureau of Economic Research Conference Series, no. 14 (Princeton, NJ: Princeton University Press, 1962), pp. 63–97. An early pioneer was Margaret G. Reid, *Economics of Household Production* (New York: Wiley, 1934), but her interesting ideas had little impact on economists before they were revived in the 1960s, a time when large numbers of women were entering the labor market. Home economists were influenced to a greater extent. A large number of authors have contributed to the growing literature of the "New Home Economics" in recent decades, but much of this work has been conveniently summarized by Gary S. Becker in *A Treatise on the Family*

Since then using sophisticated theory and advanced econometric methods, models have been developed and tested that have produced important insights in this area. Yet, many of these models are not altogether satisfactory, for there is still a tendency to treat even this multiperson family as a single-minded, indivisible, utility-maximizing unit.

In this chapter, we draw heavily upon neoclassical economic analysis, with appropriate simplifying assumptions, to better understand the determinants of the division of labor in the family. Because a substantial majority of people continues to live in married-couple families, we focus largely on the division of labor between husbands and wives. At the same time, it would be a mistake to overlook the fact that the number of cohabiting heterosexual couples has increased considerably, and that there are gay and lesbian couples, as well. While recent research has paid increasing attention to cohabiting couples, gay and lesbian couples have received scant attention.[2] We shall examine both of these types of couples in Chapter 9.

Our focus on economic analysis does not mean that we believe families are established or dissolved entirely, or even primarily, for economic reasons. On the contrary, human need for companionship, sexual attraction, affection, and the desire to have children all play a substantial part in family formation. Human need for independence and privacy, incompatibilities, preference for a variety of partners, and disappointment when children do not live up to expectations all play a large part in family breakups. Nonetheless, it is our belief that economic factors are important and that focusing upon them considerably enhances our understanding of the determinants of the division of labor in the family.

After presenting the neoclassical model of the family, we provide an evaluation and critique of this approach and introduce a more complex reality. In particular, the simple neoclassical model suggests that there are considerable efficiency gains to the traditional division of labor in which the husband specializes in market work and the wife specializes in home work. Though this may be true under certain circumstances, it is also the case that such an arrangement has become less and less prevalent. Moreover, individuals continue to form families despite this decrease in specialization. We shed light on the reasons for these developments by extending the simple model in two ways.[3]

- We point out that there are other types of economic benefits to forming families besides specialization. Thus, couples may discard specialization and still reap economic gains from living in families.
- We examine the disadvantages of the traditional division of labor, particularly for women, which are not considered in the simple neoclassical model. This helps to explain why the traditional division of labor has declined.

(Cambridge, MA: Harvard University Press, 1981, enlarged edition, 1991). For theoretical extensions, see Robert A. Pollak, "Allocating Time," unpublished working paper, Washington University (September 1999).

[2] M. V. Lee Badgett, "Gender, Sexuality, and Sexual Orientation: All in the Feminist Family," *Feminist Economics* 1, no. 1 (spring 1995): 121–39.

[3] Much of this material was first developed in Marianne A. Ferber and Bonnie G. Birnbaum, "The New Home Economics: Retrospect and Prospects," *Journal of Consumer Research* 4, no. 4 (June 1977): 19–28.

We then briefly discuss alternative neoclassical approaches of transaction costs and bargaining models, as well as the radical feminist and Marxist feminist approaches.[4]

Next, we examine available evidence on the allocation of time to market work, housework, and volunteer work by men and women, as well as changes in this allocation during recent decades. This will provide some indication as to the extent that husbands and wives specialize and to what extent we are moving toward more egalitarian marriages, in which both spouses equally share the responsibility for earning a living and for homemaking. Here we focus on trends in nonmarket work and in Chapter 4 we examine trends in female labor force participation.

Finally, the chapter concludes by looking at the American family at the threshold of the twenty-first century. As we shall see, married couples, who are the focus of this chapter, have been declining as a share of all households. We briefly summarize the changes that have occurred and point to the increasing complexity of families in the United States and elsewhere. More detailed analyses of these trends are provided in Chapter 9.

THE SIMPLE NEOCLASSICAL MODEL: SPECIALIZATION AND EXCHANGE

The basic underlying assumption of the neoclassical analysis of the family is that it is a unit whose adult members make informed and rational decisions that result in maximizing the utility or well-being of the family. Beginning with this premise, economists have applied the tools of their discipline to the analysis of the division of labor within the family. Models employing these basic economic concepts have also been used to explain women's increasing labor force participation rates, growing divorce rates and declining fertility, the family's greater emphasis on education of children, and a number of other aspects of human behavior.

As noted earlier, the simplest model of the family assumes that the family's goal is to maximize its utility or satisfaction by selecting the combination of **commodities** from which it derives the greatest possible amount of utility. These commodities are produced by combining the home time of family members with goods and services purchased in the market, using labor market earnings.

Virtually all market-purchased goods and services require an infusion of home time to transform them into the commodities from which we may derive utility—from food that needs to be bought and prepared and furniture that needs to be purchased, arranged in the home, and maintained, to day care centers, which must be carefully chosen and where children must be dropped off and picked up. Similarly, even time spent

---

[4] See Heidi I. Hartmann, "Capitalism, Patriarchy, and Job Segregation by Sex," *Signs: Journal of Women in Culture and Society* 1, no. 3 (spring 1976, pt. 2): 137–70; Heidi I. Hartmann, "The Family as the Locus of Gender, Class and Political Struggle: The Example of Housework," *Signs: Journal of Women in Culture and Society* 6, no. 3 (spring 1981): 366–94; and Nancy Folbre, *Who Pays for the Kids? Gender and the Structures of Constraint* (London: Routledge, 1994). For an institutional approach to the family, see Clair Brown, "Consumption Norms, Work Roles, and Economic Growth," in *Gender in the Workplace,* ed. Clair Brown and Joseph A. Pechman (Washington, DC: Brookings Institution, 1987); and Daphne Greenwood, "The Economic Significance of 'Women's Place' in Society: A New-Institutionalist View," *Journal of Economic Issues* 18, no. 3 (September 1984): 663–80.

in leisure generally requires the input of market goods and services to be enjoyable—from television sets and CD players to concerts and baseball games. Thus, time spent on paid work produces the income necessary to purchase market goods, which in turn are needed together with home time to produce commodities. A crucial question for the family is how time should be allocated between home and market most efficiently in order to maximize satisfaction.

COMPARATIVE ADVANTAGE

Under certain conditions, commodity production is carried out most efficiently if one member of the family specializes, at least to some extent, in market production while the other specializes, at least to some extent, in home production. They may then exchange their output or pool the fruits of their labor to achieve their utility-maximizing combination of market-purchased goods and home-produced goods. In order for this to be true, it is necessary only for the two individuals to have differing **comparative advantages** for home and market production. That is to say, the ratio of the value of time spent at home to the value of time spent in the market must be higher for one individual than the other.[5]

Is it generally the case that women are relatively more productive in the home and men are relatively more productive in the market? Whether or not one assumes that women are biologically better suited for housework because they are the ones who bear children, it will frequently be the case that women have a comparative advantage in household production and that men have a comparative advantage in market work. This can be true because men and women are traditionally raised with different expectations and receive different education and training. It may also be the case that women have been discriminated against in the labor market, lowering their market earnings. Moreover, the traditional division of labor itself is likely to magnify differences in the household and market skills of men and women because both types of skills tend to increase with experience "on the job." Thus, even a small initial gender difference in comparative advantage may increase considerably over time.

Although each of the preceding factors tends to produce gender differences in comparative advantage for homemaking as compared to market work, it is not necessarily the case that the traditional division of labor is the optimal arrangement. Treating children according to gender rather than individual talents and discriminating against women workers in the labor market clearly introduce distortions. Even more obvious is the fact that circular reasoning is involved when women supposedly specialize in housework because they do it better, but, in fact, they do it better because they specialize in it. To the extent that women's relative advantage for homemaking is socially determined and reflects unequal access to market opportunities, the traditional

---

[5] The case for specialization as a way to maximize the well-being of the family is very similar to that for international trade, where each country specializes in production for which it has a relative advantage. There are, however, also important differences between the two situations. A particularly important one is that countries generally need not rely on a single trading partner, so that there is somewhat less opportunity for the stronger partner to take advantage of the weaker one. Another difference is that couples, unlike countries, must also share a good deal of consumption.

division of labor is not always efficient, let alone desirable, particularly when, as we shall see, it entails many disadvantages for women.

In the following discussion we assume that women have a comparative advantage in housework relative to men because the reality that we seek to explain is one in which women generally have primary responsibility for homemaking. We do not mean to imply, however, that the traditional division of labor is inevitable or that it will persist indefinitely into the future. Indeed, we are also concerned with better understanding the reasons why traditional patterns are changing.

SPECIALIZATION AND EXCHANGE: NUMERICAL EXAMPLES

Two simple examples will help to clarify the notion of comparative advantage and to illustrate the efficiency of specialization and exchange. The analysis is analogous to the standard proof of gains from international trade and is illustrated in Tables 3.1a and 3.1b.

TABLE 3.1   An Illustration of the Gains from Specialization and Exchange

(a) CASE 1: ABSOLUTE ADVANTAGE

Separate Production

	Value of Market Goods	*Value of Home Cooking*	*Total Income*
John	(6 hrs. × $10) $60	(2 hrs. × $5) + $10	= $70
Jane	(7 hrs. × $5) $35	(1 hr. × $10) + $10	= $45
Total (John and Jane)	$95	$20	$115

Specialization and Exchange

	Value of Market Goods	*Value of Home Cooking*	*Total Income*
John	(8 hrs. × $10) $80	(0 hrs. × $5) + $0	= $80
Jane	(5 hrs. × $5) $25	(3 hrs. × $10) + $30	= $55
Total (John and Jane)	$105	$30	$135

(b) CASE 2: COMPARATIVE ADVANTAGE

Separate Production

	Value of Market Goods	*Value of Home Cooking*	*Total Income*
Dave	(6 hrs. × $10) $60	(2 hrs. × $5) + $10	= $70
Diane	(7 hrs. × $15) $105	(1 hr. × $15) + $15	= $120
Total (Dave and Diane)	$165	$25	$190

Specialization and Exchange

	Value of Market Goods	*Value of Home Cooking*	*Total Income*
Dave	(8 hrs. × $10) $80	(0 hrs. × $5) + $0	= $80
Diane	(6 hrs. × $15) $90	(2 hrs. × $15) + $30	= $120
Total (Dave and Diane)	$170	$30	$200

Absolute Advantage   The simplest case is when one individual has an absolute advantage in market work while the other individual has an absolute advantage in household production. Suppose John could earn $10 for working one hour in the labor market or could produce a mediocre dinner worth about $5 at home during the same period of time. A second individual, Jane, would earn only $5 an hour in the labor market but is able to prepare an excellent dinner at home worth about $10 in one hour. In this case, it is clear that John and Jane's combined level of economic well-being can be increased if they each specialize. John, who has an absolute advantage in market work, can spend all his time in the labor market earning money while Jane, who has an absolute advantage in cooking, prepares the dinners.

This is illustrated in the top section of Table 3.1a. Initially, John and Jane are each self-sufficient and both allocate some time to market work and some time to the preparation of home-cooked meals. John devotes six hours to earning income and two hours to cooking. His total income (including the value of home-cooked meals) is $70. Jane spends seven hours in the market and one hour on cooking. Her total income is $45. The sum of their two incomes (although they are not necessarily sharing at this point) is $115. If they collaborate, they have the option of each specializing to a greater extent in the activity they do better and exchanging (or pooling) their output, as shown in the bottom section of Table 3.1a.

Through specialization and exchange, John and Jane can produce a higher value of both market goods and home-cooked meals and, thus, increase their total income. The concept of opportunity cost is useful in understanding this. As we explained in Chapter 1, opportunity cost is the benefit forgone in the next best alternative. John's opportunity cost of obtaining $10 worth of market goods in terms of the value of meals forgone ($5) is lower than Jane's ($20). On the other hand, a home-cooked meal valued at $10 is cheaper for Jane to produce in terms of the value of market goods forgone ($5) than it is for John ($20). Suppose John decides to devote all his time to the market, and Jane transfers two additional hours from market work to cooking. By reallocating their time, the couple is able to raise their total income from $115 to $135.

Comparative Advantage   Less obvious is the fact that specialization can also raise the income of the couple when one individual not only earns more in the labor market but is also a better cook. In other words, one individual has an absolute advantage in both types of work. In this situation, the crucial question is whether each has a *comparative advantage* for doing one type of work.

This is illustrated in Table 3.1b. Dave earns $10 per hour for time spent in the labor market or can produce a meal worth, say, $5 for an hour spent cooking. Diane is more efficient than Dave in both activities. Her market wage is $15, while she can produce a meal worth $15 in an hour's time. The important point here is that, although Diane is a bit more efficient than Dave in the labor market, she is a far better cook than he is. The opportunity cost (in terms of market goods forgone) of a home-cooked meal worth $10 is lower when Diane produces it than when Dave does. It takes Dave two hours (valued at $20) to produce such a meal, and Diane can do so in 40 minutes (valued at $10). Table 3.1b shows that through specialization and exchange, the couple can increase their total output of both market goods and home-cooked meals and raise their total income from $190 to $200.

GAINS TO SPECIALIZATION AND EXCHANGE

These examples serve to illustrate the potential gain in output of specialization and exchange. They do not, however, in themselves tell us how much time John and Jane will spend on each type of work. The goal of the family is to maximize utility or satisfaction. Thus, the value attached to various commodities and the time allocation actually chosen by each couple will depend on their preferences for market- versus home-produced goods. Many outcomes are possible. For example, it might be that Jane and John would have such a strong preference for market goods that their well-being would be maximized by both of them only working for pay and purchasing all the goods and services they consume rather than producing any at home. Or Diane and Dave might have such a strong preference for home production that she would entirely specialize in housework, and he would divide his time between market and home. In the appendix to this chapter, we present a fuller treatment of the decision-making process that explicitly takes into account both the production possibilities available to the couple and their preferences for each type of good.

In any case, however, each couple will seek to produce their desired combination of market and home goods in the most efficient way. Thus, as long as they produce some of each type of good, if the wife has a comparative advantage in housework (relative to the husband) and the husband has a comparative advantage in market work (relative to the wife), the analysis suggests that they will choose to specialize at least to some extent in the activities generally associated with women and men.

It would appear, then, that this analysis provides a perfect explanation for the traditional family with a male breadwinner and a female homemaker. Each may help the other if demand is high for the production he or she is not particularly qualified for, but each has a clearly defined sphere of primary responsibility. For whenever such specialization does not take place, the couple will fail to maximize their output and, potentially, their well-being. Of course, if both spouses happened to have the same comparative advantages, this conclusion no longer follows. It is then not clear within the framework of this simple analysis what the couple gains from collaborating, for their pooled income will presumably be no greater than the sum of their separate incomes. However, specialization and exchange is not the only economic rationale for families to form and stay together. There are likely to be other economic gains as well, in addition to important noneconomic advantages. Furthermore, the traditional division of labor results in a number of disadvantages, particularly for women, that are not considered in this simple model. We now examine each of these points in turn.

OTHER ADVANTAGES OF FAMILIES

When husbands and wives do not differ in their relative abilities in the market and in the household or do not differ significantly, there are nonetheless reasons why they may still find it in their economic self-interest to form families. These include economies of scale, externalities in consumption, public goods, the opportunity to make marriage-specific investments, risk pooling, as well as institutional factors. Arguably, these benefits do not necessarily require a husband–wife family per se, but they are likely to be enhanced when individuals expect to have a long-term relationship with a strong degree of commitment.

ECONOMIES OF SCALE

Economies of scale exist when an increase in the scale of operation of a productive unit can result in increased output at decreasing incremental cost. To the extent that a couple is able to benefit from such economies of scale, both in the production of some home goods and in purchasing market goods and services, there are economic gains when they live together. For example, ample housing for two is likely to cost less than the combined amount each would pay for their housing separately. Meals for two generally take less than twice as much time to prepare as meals for one, and so forth.[6]

PUBLIC GOODS

A public good has the unique characteristic that the consumption or enjoyment of the item by one person does not diminish the consumption or enjoyment of the same item by others. Within the family, this is likely to be the case with many goods. For example, one partner's enjoyment of a television program is unlikely to be reduced at all by the fact that the other partner is also watching. Similarly, the delight of a parent in his or her child's adorable antics is not apt to be diminished by the other parent's pleasure. Many aspects of housing—the views from the windows, the decoration of the rooms— also have public goods aspects. In fact, the enjoyment of these goods by one partner may even enhance that of the other. To the extent that public goods are important, the gains from joint consumption are increased. This is because two individuals derive more total satisfaction from sharing a given stock of public goods and services by living together than they would by living separately.

EXTERNALITIES IN CONSUMPTION

Externalities in consumption occur when the consumption of a good or service by one of the partners has an impact on the well-being of the other. To the extent that these externalities are positive—one person derives enjoyment from the other's consumption—gains will be greater than indicated by the simple model. For example, a husband's purchase of a new suit may increase his wife's utility as well as his own. Both members of a couple may enjoy their summer vacation more because they are traveling together than they would if each were traveling alone. When two people care for one another, one partner may even derive satisfaction simply from the enjoyment and happiness of the other. This also greatly enhances the gains from joint consumption.

MARRIAGE-SPECIFIC INVESTMENTS

Marriage-specific investments refer to skills and knowledge developed in marriage and other investments made during a marriage that are worth far more within the marriage than they would be if the marriage were terminated.[7] Examples of such investments include learning to cook each other's favorite meals or learning to do the

---

[6] Economies of scale also explain the advantages of larger groups living together. The fact that such arrangements are not common in affluent societies suggests that most people value additional privacy highly once they can afford it.

[7] See Becker, *A Treatise on the Family;* and Robert A. Pollak, "A Transaction Cost Approach to Families and Households," *Journal of Economic Literature* 23, no. 2 (June 1985): 581–608.

same recreational activities, such as skiing or rock climbing. Perhaps the prime example of a marriage-specific investment is the rearing of children. Parents devote considerable time and energy to nurturing their children and fostering the same values that they themselves have. Thus, children generally provide considerable satisfaction to parents within the marriage. They may, however, be an obstacle to forming and maintaining a successful relationship with a different partner.

RISK POOLING

Married-couple families, particularly those in which there are two earners, have the added advantage that if one of the spouses becomes unemployed, they may be able to rely on the earning power of the other partner to cover at least part, if not all, of their family's expenses. In bad economic times, if the husband loses his job or his earnings decline, even a traditional homemaker may enter the labor market to maintain family income. This is the "added worker" effect, which will be discussed in Chapter 4. In addition, couples have much greater flexibility to switch jobs, change careers, or pursue additional education or job training because they can rely on the other spouse's earning power, whether or not she or he is already in the labor market.

INSTITUTIONAL ADVANTAGES

In the United States today, married couples also frequently enjoy institutional advantages including, for instance, coverage by a spouse's health insurance, pension rights, and Social Security benefits. Some employers have extended benefits such as health insurance to the live-in partners of unmarried heterosexual workers, as well as gay and lesbian workers, but to date this is far from universal.[8]

THE DISADVANTAGES OF SPECIALIZATION

As we have just seen, there are significant economic advantages to forming families, even in the case of couples whose comparative advantage in market work and home production is similar, so that they have little to gain from specialization and exchange. We now return to the issue of specialization and exchange itself, which the simple model suggests is the economic foundation of marriage. Here we consider the possibility that such specialization and a gender-based division of labor may not always be desirable, particularly for women, even when specialization and exchange does yield some economic gains to the family. The potential disadvantages of specialization are generally not discussed in the standard models but are nonetheless important.

SHARING OF HOUSEWORK

One correct prediction of the simple model is that, given gender differences in comparative advantage, women's employment outside the home is not necessarily accompanied by an increase in the amount of housework done by her husband. A fuller consid-

---

[8] Also, in July 2000, the state of Vermont became the first state to extend a wide range of legal protections to gay and lesbian couples.

eration of the issues, however, suggests a number of reasons why a couple might often find it desirable to share the housework rather than for each spouse to specialize.

First, the sweeping assumption that women have a comparative advantage in all household tasks is unrealistic. The problem is that the simple model assumes there is only one type of home good. In our numerical example, it was home-cooked meals; more generally it is an aggregate category of home goods. In fact, tasks typically performed within the household vary from child care, house cleaning, cooking, and shopping to gardening, home repairs, car maintenance, and taking care of the family finances. It is not particularly likely that the wife will have a relative advantage in performing all of these tasks as compared to the husband; rather it is likely that he will have a comparative advantage in at least some of them, even taking his larger market earnings into account. Of course, once the wife is at home because she is better at some, or many, of the household tasks, it may be more efficient for her to undertake other related work as well. But the husband also spends a good bit of time in the home, and not all household tasks are performed in or around the house (for example, shopping, dropping off a child at day care, or going to the bank). This explains why even a traditional family will generally find it efficient for the husband to do a bit more housework than suggested by the simple model.

Second, it is worthwhile to consider the utility or disutility that people derive from work itself. The simple model considers only the utility derived from the consumption of market-produced and home-produced goods. Yet most people spend much of their time working, and their well-being is very much influenced by the satisfaction or dissatisfaction associated directly with their work. If everyone always enjoyed more (or disliked less) the kind of work they do more efficiently, the gains from specialization would be even greater than indicated by the simple model; and that may to a degree be the case. But this line of reasoning ignores the possibility that how we feel about doing particular tasks depends on how much time we have to spend on them. Persons who dislike market or home work to begin with are likely to hate additional time spent on it even more as they do increasingly more of it. And even those who like what they do are, nonetheless, likely to become less enthusiastic.[9] The stronger this effect, the less likely that there will be the gains in utility from specialization suggested by the simple model.

A similar issue arises with respect to the utility each individual derives from leisure. The model fails to consider adequately that leisure is likely to be more highly valued by the partner who has less of it and that the one who has a great deal of leisure may become bored and also come to feel useless. Thus, the situation in which the wife works in the market and retains full responsibility for housework is not likely to be optimal if it results in considerably less leisure for her than for her husband; this is especially likely to occur during the childrearing years. Alternatively, when the husband has a demanding full-time position, while the responsibilities of the full-time homemaker have become rather modest because the children are growing up or have left home, he will be very short of leisure, whereas the wife may have more of it than she finds desirable.

---

[9] The reasoning is analogous to diminishing marginal utility as additional units of the same good are consumed.

Finally, some tasks are more efficiently performed by two people together, and many people may enjoy housework more when they do not have to do it alone. Frequently, homemakers spend much of their time isolated and have little possibility for interaction with other adults.

For all these reasons, complete specialization by the husband in market work, whether or not the wife specializes completely in housework, may not maximize utility for the family. Nonetheless, the simple model does seem to square with reality to the extent that, on average, husbands devote substantially less time to housework.

LIFE CYCLE CHANGES

A serious shortcoming of the simple model is that it ignores the fact that the comparative advantage of an individual does not necessarily remain the same over the life cycle. The value of home production for women peaks during the childrearing years and then declines as children grow up and become more self-sufficient. At the same time, labor market earnings tend to increase with experience and decline while a person is not employed. If a woman withdraws from the labor force for a considerable period of time for childrearing, she is likely to pay a high price in terms of career advancement and earnings when she reenters the labor market. Hence, specializing in home work may not be advantageous to the wife or even to her family in the long run, even if it maximizes family well-being in the short run. Couples who are aware of this may decide it is worthwhile for the family to make some sacrifices of utility during the early years to keep the wife in the labor market in order to improve her long-run career prospects and enhance her lifetime earnings. As women increasingly value career achievement as an end in itself, the costs of work disruptions are apt to loom even larger. These issues are considered in greater detail in Chapter 6.

It might be argued that offsetting these disadvantages for the wife's career and the lifetime income of the family is the higher quality of children produced when the mother is at home full-time. However, recent research concerning the effects of alternative ways of caring for children on their well-being and achievement levels shows that adequate out-of-home care generally does not have negative effects. The effect of maternal employment on children is considered further in Chapter 9.

COSTS OF INTERDEPENDENCE

Whatever the probability that the well-being of husband and wife will be maximized by specialization under existing circumstances, they will be less well prepared to deal with unforeseen developments. When each spouse is able to manage a household and to earn a living if the need arises, the family will not be devastated if the husband is laid off or does not get a promotion or if the wife becomes ill and needs care instead of providing it for the rest of the family. Each will also be better equipped to manage alone if the need arises, whether because of divorce, separation, or death.

The difficulties encountered by the wife who has specialized in housework are related to her financial dependency and the negative effect on her potential earnings of time spent out of the labor force. As long as the relationship lasts, both husband and wife may gain from the greater proficiency each acquires in the area in which he or she specializes. However, their skills in the other area are likely to deteriorate or, at best, may fail to improve.

This problem will be especially serious for the homemaker. The husband who has concentrated on market work may be seriously inconvenienced by a lack of household skills, but his market earnings may be used to purchase household services. The woman who has specialized in household production, on the other hand, is left with no earnings and market skills that may be obsolete. In view of the high divorce rate and the substantially higher life expectancy of women than men, the risk of becoming a displaced homemaker is serious. The special problems of female-headed families are discussed more fully in Chapter 9.

There are also potential difficulties for a full-time homemaker even if the partnership lasts until her death or until a time when she is adequately taken care of by a pension or inheritance. As pointed out earlier, the value of the homemaker's contribution to the family is greatest while the children are young. Now that the average number of children is about two and female life expectancy is 79, this period would be relatively early in a woman's life. After that the value of her contribution at home, assuming traditional childbearing patterns, would decline. Because her earning ability (generally lower than her husband's to begin with) would also decline during the time she was out of the labor market, her contribution during the latter part of her life would be considerably smaller than her partner's.

One way of looking at this is that the husband's increasing earnings in the market compensate for her declining productivity, so that she can now enjoy her share of the family's total income and a good deal of leisure. Yet, even if her partner is very fond of her, is happy to share his largesse, and is grateful to her for the considerable contributions she made earlier, she may come to wonder about her present worth to the family. That is the reason we used to hear so much about the empty nest syndrome. But she may not be so lucky. Her spouse may ask what she has done for him lately; he may take advantage of his increasingly greater bargaining power by appropriating a larger share of family income for commodities only he uses or only he wants and, in general, by adopting a lifestyle that conforms to his, but not necessarily to her, preferences.

TASTES AND BARGAINING POWER

In our development of the simple model, we did not consider how the couple determines the allocation of income and of time to various commodities the family would enjoy. The decision will be relatively easy to make if they both have the same tastes and preferences. Then they will each opt for the same combination of goods and services to be shared. However, if their tastes differ significantly, the question arises as to how they will decide on the combination of commodities to be produced and consumed. Putting the matter somewhat differently, whose preferences (husband's or wife's) will receive greater weight? These issues are first considered here in general terms and then, in the next section, are examined in light of alternative approaches to analyzing family decision making that have been developed more recently: transaction cost and bargaining models.

Considerable flexibility exists in the case where the partners may pool production but then each can choose different bundles of commodities for individual consumption, although even here the share of the total going to each partner could be a matter of dispute. In fact, as we shall see, the assumption of income pooling within the household is not entirely realistic. But more difficult problems arise in the case of public goods or for commodities that have significant externalities. We saw earlier that for people with similar tastes, public goods and positive externalities increase the gains from joint consumption and collaboration. However, where one person's public good is another's public "bad" or where negative externalities in consumption exist, consumption of the commodity by one individual may reduce the well-being of the other. For example, one partner may derive enormous satisfaction from the presence of children, whereas the other may dislike having them around. Or one individual listening to loud music may have a negative effect on the enjoyment of the evening for the other.

These difficulties are relevant to the conclusions we derived from the simple model regarding the benefits of specialization. They suggest that conflicts of interest may arise between husband and wife and that relative bargaining power would be likely to play a role in resolving these conflicts.

Because in the traditional family the husband earns the money, he may be viewed as having the "power of the purse" and, therefore, be accorded a greater say in spending decisions. However, as might be expected, this is less likely to be the case when wives are employed.[10] A number of sociologists also suggest that decision making and allocation of responsibilities are built into the traditional husband–wife roles based on cultural norms and are unrelated to individual skills and interests. Accordingly, it is still often the case that the husband makes the important decisions. For instance, he may determine what car they will buy, although the wife may decide on the color. On the other hand, in families in which husbands and wives are both highly educated with similar earning power, they tend to make decisions concerning purchases of large-ticket items jointly, including the purchase of cars.[11]

Further, in a money economy, adherence to the traditional division of labor results in the wife being financially dependent on her husband. Since she has more to lose if the marriage breaks up, she is likely to be under greater pressure to subordinate her wishes to her husband's than vice versa. Finally, the lesser outside contacts of the full-time homemaker in comparison to her employed husband may make her more dependent on his counsel and judgment than he is on hers. In fact, as noted earlier, a number of studies tend to confirm the dominance of the husband in decision making in marriages with the traditional division of labor.

DOMESTIC VIOLENCE

While domestic violence is the exception rather than the rule, an additional disadvantage of specialization is that it will tend to limit opportunities for women who are in abusive, harmful situations to get out.[12] This issue gained substantial attention following the arrest in 1994 of O. J. Simpson, a well-known media figure and former star foot-

---

[10] For studies of allocation and decision making within marriage, see Philip Blumstein and Pepper Schwartz, *American Couples* (New York: William Morrow, 1983); and Edward P. Lazear and Robert T. Michael, *Allocation of Income Within the Household* (Chicago: University of Chicago Press, 1988). See also Marianne A. Ferber, "Labor Market Participation of Young Married Women: Causes and Effects," *Journal of Marriage and Family* 44, no. 2 (May 1982): 457–68.

[11] See, for instance, Philip Blumstein and Pepper Schwartz, "Money and Ideology: Their Impact on Power and the Division of Household Labor," in *Gender, Family, and the Economy: The Triple Overlap,* ed. Rae L. Blumberg (Newbury Park, CA: Sage, 1991), pp. 261–88; and Diane Crispell, "Dual-Earner Diversity," *American Demographics* 17, no. 7 (July 1995): 32–37.

[12] For a discussion on trends in domestic violence, see Francine D. Blau, "Trends in the Well-Being of American Women, 1970–1995," *Journal of Economic Literature* 36, no. 1 (March 1998): 112–65.

ball player, who was accused of murdering his ex-wife, Nicole Brown Simpson, following a pattern of domestic abuse. While he was acquitted of the murder charge in criminal court, he was later convicted in civil court. In any case, Simpson's case served to focus considerable attention on the issue of domestic violence and on the question of why abused spouses so often stay in such situations. It has been suggested that Nicole Brown Simpson felt trapped because her opportunities outside of marriage would not be good enough to enable her to maintain the lifestyle she had been accustomed to while she was married.[13] If that was the case for Nicole Brown Simpson, it would be all the more true for women with considerably worse prospects than hers. This is also what bargaining models of economic behavior predict.[14] That is, women who are not employed themselves are less likely to have the financial means to leave an abusive relationship or to effectively persuade their husbands to stop the battering while still remaining in the marriage. Therefore it is not surprising that research has identified a link between improvements in women's economic status and reduced domestic violence.[15] Services for victims of domestic violence such as shelters, counseling, and legal advice would also be expected to improve their bargaining position in the family.

Dealing with spousal abuse, whether the aggressor be a husband or occasionally a wife, is often made more difficult by the ambivalent attitudes of society. Many believe that such battering is a "family matter" and should stay outside the realm of the legal system or suggest that the victim might have "asked for it" in some way. Another complication is that there may be children in the household, further adding to the emotional as well as the financial difficulty of leaving.

The consequences of domestic violence likely vary, depending on the length and severity of the abuse, but may include both psychological difficulties and physical injuries. Domestic violence may also affect employment and earnings. Interestingly, it has been found that labor force participation rates of women who are victims of domestic violence are the same or even higher than of otherwise similar women who are not victims. This could be because battered women seek employment outside the home as a refuge or as a means to achieving economic independence (in preparation for leaving). On the other hand, there is some evidence that battering negatively affects women's job performance and may consequently lower their wages.[16]

DISADVANTAGES OF SPECIALIZATION: A SUMMARY

Thus, we find that the traditional family, in which husband and wife each specialize in a separate sphere, is not as advantageous as the simple economic model presented at the beginning of this chapter suggests. Specializing in homemaking is a particularly

---

[13] Michele Ingrassia and Melinda Beck, "Patterns of Abuse," *Newsweek,* July 4, 1994.

[14] For sociological theories regarding domestic violence, see Murray A. Strauss and Richard J. Gelles, *Physical Violence in American Families* (New Brunswick, NJ: Transaction Publishers, 1990). An economist, Robert Pollak, formalizes the notion of an intergenerational cycle of domestic violence in "An Intergenerational Model of Domestic Violence," unpublished working paper, Washington University (May 2000).

[15] Amy Farmer and Jill Tiefenthaler, "An Economic Analysis of Domestic Violence," *Review of Social Economy* 55, no. 3 (fall 1997): 337–58; and Helen V. Tauchen, Ann Dryden Witte, and Sharon K. Long, "Domestic Violence: A Nonrandom Affair," *International Economic Review* 32, no. 2 (May 1991): 491–521.

[16] Amy Farmer and Jill Tiefenthaler, "The Employment Effects of Domestic Violence," unpublished working paper, University of Arkansas and Colgate University (January 2000).

high-risk undertaking, for the value of home production peaks early in the life cycle; market skills tend to decline when a person is out of the labor market; and the woman is often socially isolated in the home. Therefore, the homemaker's bargaining power within the family is likely to decline over time, and she will find it difficult to manage on her own if the need arises. There are, however, risks for the wage earner as well. If the marriage breaks up, he may be confronted with the need to pay alimony or face the problem of avoiding it. Also, he may lack even the minimal skills to keep house for himself. Last, but not least, children of divorced parents may have to live in poverty with a mother unable to earn a decent living or, in some cases, with a father relatively inexperienced in child care.

One may speculate as to why so many couples opted for so long for a lifestyle that raises so many potential problems, even as conditions grew less favorable for traditional marriages. A number of obvious answers come to mind. First, there can be little doubt that many young people, fully aware of a rising divorce rate, nonetheless expected their own marriages to succeed. This is not so different from the person who starts a small business, fully expecting to make a go of it in spite of the formidable bankruptcy rate. Second, important initial decisions were made at a relatively young age, when concerns for well-being in middle and old age generally do not loom very large. Third, pressures from relatives and peers toward adoption of traditional family arrangements likely played a role. Among some groups it may still take a strong-willed, confident, young person to withstand these pressures. There is, however, no doubt that all this has changed considerably and that surely helps to account for the rising proportion of couples who are rejecting the old breadwinner–homemaker dichotomy.

Before leaving the subject of the disadvantages of specialization, it is also worth noting that public policies, some of them the subject of lively public debate, can have considerable influence on the decision as to whether or not the wife should be a full-time homemaker. These include tax and Social Security provisions that favor one-earner as opposed to two-earner couples, which are discussed in some detail in Chapter 10, as well as divorce laws that may or may not adequately protect the interests of partners with little or no labor market experience in cases of marital dissolution.

TRANSACTION COST AND BARGAINING APPROACHES

One of the shortcomings of the neoclassical model of the family highlighted by the preceding discussion is that it ignores the internal decision-making structure of the family. It simply assumes that the family operates efficiently and frictionlessly either because there is a consensus on preferences within the family or because decisions are made by an altruistic family head and accepted by all other members.[17] In this view of the family, power has no relevance.

However, more recently, alternative approaches, emphasizing transaction costs and bargaining, have been developed that unlock the "black box" of the family and look

---

[17] The consensus model was proposed by Paul Samuelson, "Social Indifference Curves," *Quarterly Journal of Economics* 70, no. 1 (February 1956): 1–22. The altruist model was introduced by Gary S. Becker, "A Theory of Marriage: Part II," *Journal of Political Economy* 82, no. 2 (March/April 1974): 11–26.

more deeply into how families are organized and make decisions.[18] The transaction cost approach, for instance, focuses on the role of institutions in structuring complex, long-term relationships so as to minimize transaction costs. That is, just as a merger between firms eliminates the costs of negotiating repeated contracts and ensures that the initially separate firms will do business together for years to come, a marriage fosters a long-term relationship between partners. Marriage incorporates both rules about the nature of the ongoing relationship and about the rights of each individual should the union break up. Hence, it might be seen as a contractual affiliation that is "flexible enough to allow adaptive sequential decision making in the face of unfolding events."[19]

Marriage as an implicit contract provides incentives for couples to make substantial marriage-specific investments. Hence, they are likely to invest more time and effort in activities that produce "commodities" more highly valued within the marriage than they would be otherwise. Most importantly, they often devote much effort to raising their children, who are likely to be particularly valued by their own parents, but may be a liability in the search for a new spouse.[20] Since women, especially traditional homemakers, are more likely than men to make such marriage-specific investments, this puts them at a greater disadvantage if the marriage should end.

Because marriage is intended to be a long-term relationship, it is not realistic to specify everything in advance, that is, to provide for all possible contingencies.[21] At the same time, it is quite unlikely that husbands and wives share the same preferences regarding all consumption and production decisions. These factors serve to make bargaining between the partners very important. A class of models has been developed that allows for husbands and wives to have different preferences with outcomes determined through a process of bargaining.[22]

In these models, the bargaining power of each spouse is determined by his or her *threat point*—the level of well-being that each would attain if they cannot reach a cooperative solution within the marriage. In the most common type of family bargaining model, termed *divorce-threat* bargaining models, the threat point depends on the

---

[18] While this section focuses on decision making among spouses, bargaining models have been applied to decisions made by a parent and an adult child as well. See, for instance, Lilliana E. Pezzin and Barbara Steinberg Schone, "Intergenerational Household Formation, Female Labor Supply and Informal Caregiving: A Bargaining Approach," *Journal of Human Resources* 34, no. 3 (summer 1999): 475–503.

[19] For a discussion of the transaction cost approach, see Pollak, "A Transaction Cost Approach"; quote is from p. 595.

[20] For instance, see Evelyn Lehrer, "On Marriage-Specific Human Capital: Its Role as a Determinant of Remarriage," *Journal of Population Economics* 3, no. 3 (October 1990): 193–213.

[21] For a discussion, see Paula England and George Farkas, *Households, Employment and Gender* (New York: Aldine Publishing Co., 1986).

[22] For reviews of the literature, see Shelly J. Lundberg and Robert A. Pollak, "Bargaining and Distribution in Marriage," *Journal of Economic Perspectives* 10, no. 4 (fall 1996): 139–58; Bina Agarwal, " 'Bargaining' and Gender Relations: Within and Beyond the Household," *Feminist Economics* 3, no. 1 (March 1997): 1–51; and Theodore Bergstrom, "Economics in a Family Way," *Journal of Economic Literature* 34, no. 4 (December 1996): 1903–34. For early work in this area, see Mary Jean Horney and Marjorie B. McElroy, "Nash-Bargained Household Decisions: Toward a Generalization of the Theory of Demand," *International Economic Review* 22, no. 2 (June 1981): 333–49; and Marilyn Manser and Murray Brown, "Marriage and Household Decisionmaking," *International Economic Review* 21, no. 1 (February 1980): 31–44. In related work, Pierre-Andre Chiappori has developed a "collective" model that nests the cooperative bargaining model and common preference model within it as special cases in "Collective Labor Supply and Welfare," *Journal of Political Economy* 100, no. 3 (June 1992): 437–67.

amount of income controlled by each party if the marriage were to terminate.[23] As in the case of negotiations between a vendor and a customer, the final solution is likely to more closely reflect the preferences of the party with the stronger threat effect, who is better able to "walk away" from the deal. Apart from each individual's control of resources outside the marriage, factors external to the family may also affect one or both of the partners' threat points. Such factors might include laws defining the division of marital property, the probability of remarriage, as well as eligibility rules for and benefit levels under welfare.[24]

To make the discussion concrete, let's reconsider the example of John and Jane, one of the married couples discussed earlier. They maximized total family income by specializing; Jane split her time between home production and market work while John did only market work, with no time spent in home production. Once total income is maximized, the next issue is to decide how to allocate this joint income among different commodities the family might use. For instance, even if parents agree on a basic level of support for their children, they may differ on the amount and quality of items like children's clothing or "extras" like music lessons and gymnastics classes. As another example, one spouse may prefer to spend discretionary income on expensive cars, while the other may prefer travel. The simple model assumes either that John and Jane have the same preferences or that John is an altruistic head and so only his preferences matter.

While in some instances one of these assumptions may be reasonable, bargaining models more realistically allow for the possibility that John's and Jane's preferences may differ, and that both matter. In this view, whether the amount spent, say, on their children's clothing ultimately favors John's or Jane's preferences depends, in large part, on their relative bargaining power. Assuming a traditional division of labor, Jane is expected to have less power because she has a weaker threat point. That is, if the couple were to divorce, she would probably not fare as well as John; for even if she were to receive child support and perhaps a small divorce settlement, she would likely have more difficulty supporting herself (and their children) because she has mainly invested in marriage-specific rather than market skills. Other factors that affect her relative bargaining power would be the level of welfare benefits and food stamps available to her if she were divorced, her labor market opportunities, and her chances for remarriage. John, on the other hand, is likely to be in a much stronger bargaining position because, during the marriage, he remained fully attached to the labor market. However, it is also the case that once divorced, he may have considerably less contact with his children, depending in part on the provisions of the child custody agreement. John may also need to pay alimony and child support. In addition, he is likely to have to purchase some household services formerly obtained from his wife, and it may be difficult, for instance, to find restaurants and caterers willing and able to provide meals equally convenient and suited to his personal tastes.

---

[23] As an alternative, Shelly J. Lundberg and Robert A. Pollak suggest a noncooperative threat point within the marriage itself, in which the partners fully specialize in the provision of public goods according to traditional gender roles; thus, the wife may provide all the child care, while the husband may do all the outdoor work. In this scenario, an individual has a stronger threat point if the noncooperative solution is closer to his or her desired level of public goods. See "Separate Spheres Bargaining and the Marriage Market," *Journal of Political Economy* 101, no. 6 (December 1993): 988–1010.

[24] Marjorie B. McElroy, "The Empirical Content of Nash-Bargained Household Behavior," *Journal of Human Resources* 25, no. 4 (fall 1990): 559–83.

One way of determining whether husbands' and wives' preferences differ significantly is to see whether they spend their personal income in the same way. A good deal of research shows that they generally do not. One study specifically examined the effect of a policy change in the United Kingdom in the 1970s that transferred receipt of income, in the form of a child benefit, from the father to the mother. It found that this led to an *increase* in expenditures on children's clothing.[25] This study, among others, suggests that the "common preference" assumption of the simple model does not hold up. Indeed, consistent with bargaining models, there is mounting evidence that who controls family resources affects a wide array of outcomes beyond consumption expenditures, including decisions as to how couples allocate their time, as well as how much they give to charities and who should receive these donations.[26] In addition, as discussed earlier, women who have greater economic resources tend to experience lower levels of domestic violence, again showing that the distribution of resources in a marriage affects family outcomes. These findings do not directly prove that bargaining takes place, nor indicate what specific form it might take, but they are consistent with a bargaining framework rather than either the consensus or altruist models.

In our preceding discussion, we focused on expenditures on children's clothing as an illustrative example of a case in which husbands and wives may disagree about expenditures on children. In fact, a growing body of research suggests that mothers allocate more resources and place greater emphasis on their children's well-being than do fathers. Notably, in developing countries where resources are scarce, children's health and survival probabilities have been found to improve when mothers have greater control over family resources.[27]

The research evidence reviewed also suggests that government has the *potential* to promote certain outcomes, to the extent that its policies and laws affect the distribution of resources between men and women both inside and outside of marriage.[28] For instance, in the United Kingdom, when the government paid the child benefit to mothers rather than fathers, it was found to improve children's well-being. Another way that government may affect families is through laws that govern the distribution of marital assets in case of divorce. For example, adopting community property law (which man-

---

[25] Shelly J. Lundberg, Robert. A. Pollak, and Terence J. Wales, "Do Husbands and Wives Pool Their Resources? Evidence From the U.K. Child Benefit," *Journal of Human Resources* 32, no. 3 (summer 1997): 463–80. Similarly, Shelley A. Phipps and Peter S. Burton find that expenditures on child care increase with women's but not men's incomes in "What's Mine is Yours? The Influence of Male and Female Incomes on Patterns of Household Expenditure," *Economica* 65, no. 260 (November 1998): 599–613.

[26] Regarding married couple labor supply, see Paul Schultz, "Testing the Neoclassical Model of Family Labor Supply and Fertility," *Journal of Human Resources* 25, no. 4 (fall 1990): 599–634; and for cohabitors see Anne E. Winkler, "Economic Decisionmaking Among Cohabitors: Findings Regarding Income Pooling," *Applied Economics* 29, no. 8 (August 1997): 1079–90. Regarding charitable contributions, see James Andreoni, Eleanor Brown, and Isaac Rischall, "Charitable Giving by Married Couples: Who Decides and Why Does it Matter?" unpublished working paper, University of Wisconsin-Madison (December 1998).

[27] See, for instance, Duncan Thomas, "Intra-Household Resource Allocation: An Inferential Approach," *Journal of Human Resources* 25, no. 4 (fall 1990): 635–64; Duncan Thomas, "Like Father, Like Son: Like Mother, Like Daughter: Parental Resources and Child Height," *Journal of Human Resources* 29, no. 4 (fall 1994): 950–88; and Rae L. Blumberg, "Income Under Female Versus Male Control: Hypotheses From a Theory of Gender Stratification and Data from the Third World," *Journal of Family Issues* 9, no. 1 (March 1988): 51–84.

[28] Agarwal, " 'Bargaining' and Gender Relations."

dates equal division of property) would give the wife a larger share of marital assets and hence increase her bargaining power within marriage. Interestingly, a recent study found that marital property laws that favor women are associated with increased labor supply of wives, largely reflecting their decision to reduce time spent in home production.[29]

MARXIST AND RADICAL FEMINIST VIEWS OF THE FAMILY

Up to now we have focused on the mainstream neoclassical model of the family, first developed by Gary S. Becker, followed by a brief discussion of the transaction cost and bargaining variations of the neoclassical model. Now we turn to the so-called heterodox views of Marxists and radical feminists, who offer substantially different interpretations of the division of labor within the family and of its relation to the position of women and men in the family and in the labor market.[30] Like proponents of bargaining models, adherents of both these schools of thought emphasize the role of power relationships and the potential for exploitation. Beyond that, however, their views differ fundamentally from each other. Marxists focus on the role of class and capitalism, while radical feminists focus on the role of gender and patriarchy. [31]

Capitalism describes an economy where the preponderance of capital is privately owned and controlled, even though government may also play a large part, as is the case in the United States and other capitalist countries. Marxists see such an economy as one in which capitalists wield power over workers who do not own the means of production and are therefore forced to sell their labor for low wages, while women are doubly exploited because they supply unpaid reproductive services in the family that enable capitalists to pay workers such low wages. Marxists maintain that women had not been oppressed before capitalism, and that their emancipation will inevitably come about as a result of a successful resolution of the class struggle. Meanwhile, they believe that under capitalism the working class family is a haven from the cruel world, entirely unified by mutual benevolence.

In addition, Marxists have always claimed that once socialism has been achieved women should fully participate in the labor market and housework will be socialized. One reason they favored this is because they believed that "petty housework crushes, strangles, stultifies and degrades her, chains her to the kitchen and the nursery, and . . . wastes her labour on barbarously unproductive, petty nerve-racking, stultifying and crushing drudgery."[32] In practice, however, the goal of socializing housework was never

---

[29] Jeffrey S. Gray, "Divorce-Law Changes and Married Women's Labor Supply," *American Economic Review* 88, no. 3 (June 1998): 628–51.

[30] See, for example, Hartmann, "Capitalism, Patriarchy, and Job Segregation"; Heidi I. Hartmann, "The Family as the Locus of Gender, Class and Political Struggle: The Example of Housework," *Signs: Journal of Women in Culture and Society* 6, no. 3 (spring 1981): 366–94; and Folbre, *Who Pays for the Kids?*

[31] The following analysis draws freely on the explications of Nancy Folbre, "Socialism, Feminist and Scientific," in *Beyond Economic Man,* ed. Marianne A. Ferber and Julie A. Nelson (Chicago: University of Chicago Press, 1993), pp. 94–110; and Julie A. Nelson, "The Study of Choice or the Study of Provisioning? Gender and the Definition of Economics," in *Beyond Economic Man,* ed. Marianne A. Ferber and Julie A. Nelson (Chicago: University of Chicago Press, 1993), pp. 23–36.

[32] Vladimir I. Lenin, "A Great Beginning. On the Heroism of Workers in the Rear," reprinted in Robert C. Tucker, *The Lenin Anthology* (New York: W. W. Norton & Company, Inc., 1975).

given high priority by the avowedly Marxist governments of the Soviet bloc countries. Nor is there any evidence that men were encouraged to participate in the housework that still had to be done,[33] or to perform the services in the labor market that women had previously performed in the household.

Other socialists have often been more sympathetic to women's concerns and their views are much closer to those of feminists than are those of doctrinaire Marxists. For instance, one of the best-known early British socialists, Robert Owen, wanted to eliminate the rigid boundary drawn by both neoclassical and Marxist economists between the dog-eat-dog economy where all people single-mindedly pursue their own self interest, and the family, where everyone is dedicated to the common good. Owen further viewed allegiance to family as basically another version of self-interest.[34] Or again, the early German socialist August Bebel provided an extensive account of legal injustices, with emphasis on women's lack of control over their own lives.[35] These authors, while sharing Marxists' concern with class, were clearly concerned with patriarchy as well.

Patriarchy refers to a system where men's dominance as a group over women as a group is the real source of gender inequality.[36] Radical feminists generally see the family as the true locus of women's oppression. In addition, although they recognize both the existence of emotional ties and of some unified interests within the family, they nonetheless see the family as the locus of struggle. Radical feminists were also the ones who originated the slogan "the personal is political." In this view, when Jane is responsible for taking care of the household and the children, while John "helps her" by clearing the table, taking out the garbage, and putting the children to bed, this is not merely the result of a private decision of these individuals, but is to a considerable extent influenced by patriarchal tradition. Adherence to this patriarchal tradition serves in turn to perpetuate it. Further, radical feminists assert that the patriarchal tradition existed long before capitalism and would, absent other changes, continue even if capitalism disappeared. In fact, they believe that the particular economic system is largely irrelevant to their concern with patriarchy, just as Marxists believe that patriarchy is irrelevant to their concern with the economic system.

The Marxist feminist interpretation of the situation is somewhat different from either of the other two. Adherents of this view believe that the present status of women is the result of a long process of interaction between patriarchy and capitalism. They argue that patriarchy preceded capitalism and helped to shape its present form, but that capitalism in turn has helped to shape patriarchy as it exists today. Specifically, they claim that the primary mechanism for maintaining male superiority in the capi-

---

[33] This is not particularly surprising given the views of the founders of Marxism. Marx, for instance, always disparaged American feminist socialists for giving precedence to the "woman question" over the problems of labor and even suggested that they be expelled. Similarly, the leader of the Communist revolution in Russia, Vladimir Lenin, argued that issues such as marriage and divorce were diversionary because they were not class based. Earlier, Marx's collaborator, Friedrich Engels, had written with great concern about unemployed men "who are condemned to perform household duties. One may well imagine the righteous indignation of the workers at being virtually turned into eunuchs." See Friedrich Engels, *The Condition of the Working Class in England,* trans. and ed. W. O Henderson and W. H. Chaloner (Stanford: Stanford University Press, 1958), p. 162.

[34] Robert Owen, *Lectures on the Marriages of the Priesthood of the Old Immoral World . . . with an Appendix containing the Marriage System of the New Moral World* (Leeds: J. Hobson, 1840).

[35] August Bebel, *Women and Socialism* (New York: Schocken Books, 1971).

[36] Folbre also suggests that it is based on age and sexual preference in *Who Pays for the Kids?*

talistic economy has been occupational segregation, the restriction of women in the labor market to a relatively small number of predominantly female jobs.[37] This job segregation, caused and perpetuated not only by capitalists but also by male workers and their unions, depresses wages for women and thus makes them economically dependent on men. At the same time, the traditional division of labor in the home reinforces occupational segregation in the labor market. Therefore, Marxist feminists argue that if women's subordination is to end, and if working men are to escape class oppression, occupational segregation and the traditional division of labor in the household will both have to end. In their view, in order to achieve freedom for everyone, men must be persuaded, or forced if need be, to join with women in the struggles against patriarchal capitalism, the embodiment of the stratified society par excellence.

NONMARKET WORK

Economists have traditionally focused their analyses and interests on market work; however, much work is performed outside the market, both in the household and in the voluntary sector. Such unpaid work substantially contributes to the well-being of individuals, their families, and society at large.[38] In this section we consider both types of nonmarket work and how women's and men's involvement in these activities has changed with women's rising labor force participation. By examining the available evidence, it is possible to estimate how much time husbands and wives spend on market work, home production, and volunteer work, and the extent to which changes have taken place in recent decades in the allocation of time to each of them.

HOUSEWORK

Estimates of hours spent in housework vary considerably. A review of the individual studies suggests why this is the case. They are based on different samples, drawn from different populations, the information is collected in different ways, and definitions of housework are not always the same.[39] For instance, some studies collect information based on retrospective questions about particular activities such as "how many hours did you spend doing laundry last week?" while other studies ask respondents to record in a "time diary" what they do during specific blocks of time. It turns out that estimates of hours spent in housework obtained from retrospective reports tend to be quite a bit higher than those recorded in time diaries, even when the same set of activities is con-

---

[37] Some Marxist feminists go so far as to analyze the household itself in class terms, seeing the husband as the capitalist who appropriates the surplus value of the worker–wife. See, for instance, Harriet Fraad, Stephen Resnick, and Richard Wolff, *Bringing It All Back Home: Class, Gender and Power in the Modern Household* (London: Pluto Press, 1994).

[38] As will be discussed in Chapter 4, one recent estimate suggests that GDP would increase by 24 percent if the value of nonmarket work in the household were included; see J. Steven Landefeld and Stephanie H. McCulla, "Accounting for Nonmarket Household Production Within a National Account Framework," *Review of Income and Wealth* Series 46, no. 3 (September 2000): 289–307.

[39] For a discussion of methodological issues, see National Research Council, *Time-Use Measurement and Research* (Washington, DC: National Academy Press, 2000); Pollak, "Allocating Time"; and Beth Anne Shelton and Daphne John, "The Division of Household Labor," *Annual Review of Sociology* 22, no. 1 (1996): 299–322. Nancy Folbre and Julie A. Nelson emphasize that nonmarket work reflects household production "intertwined" with caring activities in "For Love or Money—Or Both?" *Journal of Economic Perspectives* 14, no. 4 (fall 2000): 123–40.

sidered.[40] In terms of definitions, some studies explicitly include child care, others do not; some include only work done around the house, while others include household-related activities performed elsewhere. Notably, despite these types of differences, the available data indicate similar trends in time spent in housework. They show for the 1970s that wives, both employed and nonemployed, did substantially less housework than was the case in the 1960s, but time spent by husbands in housework did not change very much.[41]

Table 3.2, which provides data for more recent years, also shows that while the division of labor remained quite unequal in the late 1980s, the difference in the allocation of time to market work and nonmarket work between husbands and wives nonetheless narrowed considerably throughout the decade.[42] These data have the important advantage that they show trends in paid work and housework disaggregated by marital status and by employment status of the wife. Regrettably, no such data are available through the 1990s. Where possible, we compensate for this deficiency by supplementing these data with other more recent evidence.

On average, for women, hours of market work increased and hours of housework decreased considerably, while hours of both market work and housework increased somewhat for men. For women, time spent in housework declined by 5.4 hours from the late 1970s to late 1980s, somewhat more so for married women than unmarried women, and surprisingly, more for nonemployed than for employed wives. The increase in wives' market work of 6.6 hours was the result, in part, of the rise in the proportion of married women who were in the labor force, and, in part, the result of an increase in hours of paid work among employed wives. In contrast to the experience of wives, hours of housework increased by 1.7 hours among married men, whether their wives were employed or not. Housework declined (by 1.2 hours), however, for men who were not married.

Overall, women's time spent in housework decreased from about four times to three times that of men from the late 1970s to the late 1980s alone. This substantial change is mainly due to the sizable reduction in housework done by women and to a much lesser extent to the small increase in housework by men. Even so, the increase in housework for married men is in stark contrast to the decline for all women and for unmarried men. The trend toward smaller families, changes in household technology, and the availability of market substitutes probably help to explain the decline for other groups. Therefore, absent some reallocation between husbands and wives, we would have expected husbands' housework to have declined also. The fact that it increased instead suggests that there was indeed some reallocation of tasks. The rise in real wages for women over this period, which increased the opportunity cost of time spent in non-market activities, was likely one of the factors that contributed to the decrease in the

---

[40] See, for instance, Suzanne Bianchi, Melissa A. Milkie, Liana C. Sayer, and John P. Robinson, "Is Anyone Doing the Housework? Trends in the Gender Division of Household Labor," *Social Forces* 79, no. 1 (September 2000): 1–39.

[41] See Joseph H. Pleck, "Husband's Paid Work and Family Roles: Current Research Issues*," Research in the Interweave of Social Roles: Jobs and Families,* ed. Helena Lopata and Joseph H. Pleck (Greenwich, CT: JAI Press, 1983), pp. 251–333; and Francine D. Blau, Anne E. Winkler, and Marianne A. Ferber, *The Economics of Women, Men, and Work,* 3rd ed. (Upper Saddle River, NJ: Prentice Hall, 1998), table 3.2, p. 52.

[42] The table and discussion here draw on Blau, "Trends in the Well-Being of American Women." See also John P. Robinson and Geoffrey Godbey, *Time for Life: The Surprising Ways Americans Use Their Time,* 2nd ed. (University Park: Pennsylvania State University Press, 1999).

TABLE 3.2   Average Weekly Hours of Housework and Market Work, 1978 and 1988

	1978			*1988*		
	Market Work	*House- work*	*Total*	*Market Work*	*House- work*	*Total*
Women	20.1	26.7	46.8	26.4	21.3	47.7
Nonmarried	27.2	17.2	44.4	32.1	13.4	45.5
Married	18.3	29.1	47.4	24.9	23.6	48.5
Not employed	0.3	37.1	37.4	0.3	33.0	33.3
Employed	29.3	24.3	53.6	32.2	20.8	53.0
Men	42.5	6.1	48.6	43.3	7.4	50.7
Nonmarried	38.3	8.2	46.5	41.2	7.0	48.2
Married	43.1	5.8	48.9	43.7	7.5	51.2
Wife not employed	42.5	5.0	47.5	41.3	6.4	47.7
Wife employed	43.5	6.4	49.9	44.4	7.8	52.2

Note: Time spent on housework may be understated because respondents were not specifically queried about child care or time spent on household chores away from home (e.g., shopping). This would imply a corresponding under-statement of total work time. Data are drawn from the Panel Study of Income Dynamics.

Source: Adapted from Francine D. Blau, "Trends in the Well-Being of American Women: 1970–1995," *Journal of Economic Literature* 36, no. 1 (March 1998): 112–65. Reprinted by permission of American Economic Association.

time they spend on housework. A dynamic process may be going on in which rising market wages induce women to allocate more time to market work and less time to housework. As they do so, they accumulate more labor market experience, further enhancing their market wages and resulting in further decreases in their housework time.

Data available from other sources indicate that, more recently, from the mid-1980s to the mid-1990s, women's time spent in housework has continued its steady decline. On the other hand, the amount of time married men spent on housework does not appear to have increased any further.[43] It is not yet clear why this is the case and whether this finding portends a long-term change.

Two developments documented in Table 3.2 are particularly striking. One is that although nonemployed wives continue to do more housework than employed wives, the time they spend on it decreased somewhat more than for employed wives. This is particularly notable in light of the fact that, during the first half of the twentieth century, the amount of time that full-time homemakers spent on housework remained virtually unchanged.[44] Equally notable is that time spent on housework increased not only for husbands with employed wives but also for those whose wives were not employed. A possible explanation is that women's rising earnings opportunities may have altered the balance of bargaining power in the household whether or not the wife actually worked outside the home, and that wives may have used their increased bargaining power to insist on a reallocation of housework.

---

[43] Robinson and Godbey, *Time for Life,* chap. 22; and Bianchi et al., "Is Anyone Doing the Housework?"

[44] As noted in chapter 2, until the mid-1960s housewives continued to spend as many hours on housework as their grandmothers had at around the turn of the century. See Joann Vanek, "Time Spent in Housework," *Scientific American* 231, no. 5 (November 1974): 116–20.

In any case, the net result of these changes is that total work time (including both market work and housework) increased slightly for both women and men from 1978 to 1988, but men's total work time increased a bit more. Therefore the modest changes in leisure time over this period tended to favor women over men.[45]

As might be expected, time spent in housework varies not only by the employment status of the wife but also depends on the presence and ages of children. Men tend to do the most housework in families with young children, though not necessarily child care, and do far less when their children are older, especially if there is a daughter age 12 or older. While this suggests that the presence of older children provides a certain amount of relief for parents, particularly for fathers, there is also evidence from other sources that busy parents, especially those with a college education, are not taking the time to teach their children household skills.[46]

There are also interesting differences in the allocation of housework between married couples and cohabiting men and women. In both types of living arrangements, women do considerably more housework than men, but the gender gap is wider among married couples. On average, cohabiting men spend 7 percent more time in housework than married men, while cohabiting women spend 18 percent less time on housework than married women.[47] These findings are consistent with Becker's theory of specialization. Cohabitation, by definition, involves fewer legal protections. Consequently, specialization is particularly risky. It is also expected that there would be less specialization among partners in gay and lesbian couples for this reason, among others.[48]

A serious limitation of the data presented in Table 3.2 is that respondents were not specifically asked about time spent on child care or on household chores away from home. Child care in any case raises measurement problems because it is not clear which child care activities should be included. In many cases, such as going for a walk with a child, it is difficult to separate nonmarket work from leisure. In addition, counting time spent with children accurately is complicated by the fact that parents are often in close proximity to children while, say, cleaning house or reading the newspaper although they are not directly engaged in one-to-one interaction. Bearing these difficulties in mind, given the considerable interest in how much time parents and children spend together, and in trends in nonmarket time, we review recent trends in child care time.

It should come as no surprise that nonemployed mothers spend more time with their children than employed mothers do. One study, which defined time spent with mothers quite broadly to include time directly engaged with them or when a mother is just present, found that, in 1997, children of employed mothers spent around 83 percent as much time with their mothers as did children of nonemployed mothers. This fig-

---

[45] Similar results are reported by Beth Anne Shelton, *Women, Men and Time: Gender Differences in Paid Work, Housework and Leisure* (New York: Greenwood Press, 1992), who finds little difference between women and men in total leisure in 1975 or 1981.

[46] Frances K. Goldscheider and Linda J. Waite, *New Families, No Families* (Berkeley: University of California Press, 1991); and Sue Shellenbarger, "Busy Parents Let Kids Off the Hook When Assigning Chores," *Wall Street Journal,* 17 April 1996, sec. B, p. 1.

[47] Scott J. South and Glenna Spitze, "Housework in Marital and Nonmarital Households," *American Sociological Review* 59 (June 1994): 327–47.

[48] Lisa A. Giddings, "Political Economy and the Construction of Gender: The Example of Housework within Same-Sex Households," *Feminist Economics* 4, no. 2 (summer 1998): 97–106.

ure is down somewhat from 86 percent in 1981, not because employed mothers and their children are now spending less time together, but because time spent with non-employed mothers increased by somewhat more than did time spent with employed mothers.[49] The relative time spent by employed compared to nonemployed mothers may sound higher than one might have expected. However, it is important to keep in mind that a considerable fraction of employed women work less than full-time, full year and so have a fair amount of time available to be with their children. In addition, those who are able may juggle their schedules to make as much time for their children as possible.

In drawing comparisons between the time that employed and nonemployed women spend with their children, it should also be remembered that nonemployed women engage in a variety of nonmarket activities, albeit often in the home, which limit the time that they engage in direct activities with their children such as playing with them or helping them with their homework. Of course, employed mothers engage in nonmarket activities in the home as well, though often to a lesser degree. Hence, drawing meaningful comparisons about "quality time" with children is extremely difficult using data of this type. In addition, there may be substantial value to simply having a mother in close proximity, even if she is, say, busy with housework. [50]

Some recent research also indicates that, despite concerns about maternal employment, whether children live with two parents or only one of them is a more important determinant of time spent with their mother than whether their mother is employed. This is in large part because two parents can often coordinate their schedules to allow for more time with their children. There is evidence that the amount of time that mothers and children spend together in two-parent families increased from 1981 to 1997, while there was virtually no change for single mother families. Regarding fathers, while they continue to spend considerably less time with children than mothers, it appears that in recent decades those in two-parent families substantially increased the amount of time spent with their children, both in absolute terms and relative to mothers, whether time spent with children is limited to direct activities with children or is more broadly defined. Although data on such trends are not available for divorced and never-married fathers, their average level of involvement with their children tends to be much lower.[51]

While recent trends regarding the allocation of work and child care in two-parent families are generally heartening, more egalitarian families face many challenges, including determining what is a fair share of housework for each partner and how specific housework tasks are to be allocated. In addition, there are still many men who were raised in traditional homes where boys only did "male chores" like raking leaves or shoveling snow and resisted doing the laundry and cooking dinner. Two-earner couples, who often face a "time squeeze," must also learn how to "make do" and be will-

---

[49] These estimates, which are based on children's time use data, are from John F. Sandberg and Sandra L. Hofferth, "Changes in Children's Time with Parents, U.S. 1981–1997," unpublished working paper, University of Michigan (April 2000), figure 4.

[50] See Suzanne M. Bianchi, "Maternal Employment and Time with Children: Dramatic Change or Surprising Continuity?" *Demography* 37, no. 4 (November 2000): 401–14.

[51] This paragraph draws from Sandberg and Hofferth, "Changes in Children's Time"; Bianchi, "Maternal Employment"; and Joseph H. Pleck, "Balancing Work and Family," *Scientific American Presents* 10, no. 2 (summer 1999): 38–43.

ing to accept less than perfection from each other when it comes to housekeeping and taking care of children.[52]

As for the problems of women, it is important to note that the data we have examined tend to underestimate the difficulties of both nonemployed and employed women. Full-time homemakers may have a great deal more leisure than either other women or men, but as we have seen, it is unequally distributed over the life cycle. In addition, they tend to have less bargaining power within the family and, most seriously, they will often be in dire straits if the need arises, for whatever reason, for them to manage on their own. As for employed women, the problems they face differ greatly, depending on whether they are part-time or full-time workers, a fact that cannot be readily discerned from data on "employed" women. Those employed part-time, often because they have primary responsibility for their family, are likely to confront a smaller and less attractive choice of jobs, frequently lower earnings, very scant fringe benefits, and fewer opportunities for promotion, while those who work full-time must deal with a considerably heavier workload. Finally, employed women who are responsible for very young children or other family members who need personal care are likely to confront particular problems. The difficulties of mothers of infants and toddlers are particularly serious because many are also at the age when workers need to prove themselves on the job and to begin to show that they are upwardly mobile if they are to make much progress. Their extra responsibilities are apt to make it more difficult for them to compete with their male counterparts. Thus, whatever route employed wives choose, the unequal division of labor in the home is likely to adversely affect their success in the labor market.[53]

On the other hand, it has been argued that the unequal division of household and market labor is in some ways less of a problem for women than it superficially seems to be. First, many tasks women perform are no longer as physically exacting as those their grandmothers did. Second, as discussed earlier, such activities as shopping and, to a considerable extent, child care, may be enjoyable enough to be regarded as quasi-leisure. However, much of paid work has also become less onerous, and such time on the job as interacting with fellow workers and entertaining clients is as likely to be quasi-leisure as any family work. In fact, an extensive study of people's preferences indicates that, on the whole, they enjoy child care more than any other activities included in a comprehensive list, but enjoy their jobs far more than any other types of housework and considerably more than many leisure activities.[54]

The question also arises as to what has happened to all of the housework that used to be done in past years.[55] In part, "norms" about how much time should be devoted to housework as well as what sort of housework needs to be done have changed. For instance, one study finds that while women's overall satisfaction with the cleanliness of their homes has changed little during the past two decades, sales have declined for

---

[52] Sue Shellenbarger, "More Men Move Past Incompetence Defense to Share Housework," *Wall Street Journal,* 21 February 1996, sec. B, p. 1.

[53] For further discussion, see Barbara R. Bergmann, *The Economic Emergence of Women* (New York: Basic Books, 1986).

[54] F. Thomas Juster, "Preferences for Work and Leisure," in *Time, Goods and Well-Being,* ed. F. Thomas Juster and Frank P. Stafford (Ann Arbor: Institute for Social Research, University of Michigan, 1985).

[55] Bianchi et al., "Is Anyone Doing the Housework?"

products like furniture polish and carpet cleaner, indicating that individuals are spending less time on "discretionary" cleaning.[56] Another part of the answer is that homemakers have taken advantage of conveniences such as washing machines and dishwashers, microwaves and food processors. These appliances have considerably reduced the effort required for many basic housekeeping activities, though not necessarily the time. Further, many items that were previously produced at home are now often purchased, including frozen dinners, restaurant meals, clothing, and child care. As might be expected, two earner families spend more on items that are frequently job related such as clothing and meals away from home, as well as on services including child care and housecleaning. Of course, to what extent such goods and services are purchased also depends on whether the wife is employed full- or part-time.[57] Another important related factor is income, which tends to be higher for two-earner families.

In spite of the many changes, it is likely that for the foreseeable future, the ultimate locus of responsibility for homemaking in most instances will continue to rest with women. So, when unexpected problems and small emergencies come up, it will still be women who are expected to give family needs greater priority relative to market work than men do. Part of the explanation for the slow pace of change is that the role of homemaker continues to be associated with femininity but is seen as in conflict with masculinity.[58] To the extent that this remains true, it is also likely that even wives who are employed full-time will continue to do a considerable amount of housework. Conversely, the conflict between housework and masculinity most likely helps to explain why housework hours have risen only modestly for men. Further, one study finds that nonemployed men tend to spend little time on housework, perhaps because they are likely to be particularly anxious not to damage their masculine image.[59] Nevertheless, as men assume more homemaking responsibilities, these cultural definitions may be expected to erode further and hasten the decline in the traditional gender division of labor.

VOLUNTEER WORK

In addition to market work and housework, many people also spend an appreciable amount of time on volunteer work. Before examining trends in volunteer work for men and women, such activities must be distinguished from other work. Volunteer activities are defined as tasks performed without direct reward in money or in kind that mainly benefit others rather than the individuals themselves or their immediate family.

Thus, volunteer work is neither a way of earning a living nor an integral part of homemaking.[60] Nevertheless, much business is transacted, and many profitable con-

---

[56] John P. Robinson and Melissa Milkie, "Dances with Dust Bunnies: Housecleaning in America," *American Demographics* 19, no. 1 (January 1997): 37–59.

[57] See, for example, Horacio Soberon-Ferrer and Rachel Dardis, "Determinants of Household Expenditures for Services," *Journal of Consumer Research* 17, no. 4 (March 1991): 385–97; and R. S. Oropesa, "Using the Service Economy to Relieve the Double Burden: Female Labor Force Participation and the Service Purchases," *Journal of Family Issues* 14, no. 4 (September 1993): 438–73.

[58] Julie Brines, "Economic Dependency, Gender, and the Division of Labor at Home," *American Journal of Sociology* 100, no. 3 (November 1994): 652–88; and Pollak, "Allocating Time."

[59] Brines, "Economic Dependency."

[60] For women, it may be thought of as "social homemaking" or women extending the services they generally perform for their own families to the community. See, for instance, Julie A. Matthaei, "Capitalism and Sexual Division of Labor: An Essay in U.S. Economic History," *Social Concepts* 1, no. 2 (September 1983): 13–35.

tacts are made, at the meetings of the Rotarians. People participate in labor unions at least in part to improve their own working conditions, and in the symphony guild so that they will be able to attend concerts. They are also more likely to participate in the PTA or scouting when they have children who are involved. Further, anything that enhances life in the community influences the well-being of the family at least indirectly, and often the connection is a fairly close one. In principle, the distinction is made in terms of which is the dominant purpose, but in practice it is by no means easy to decide where the line should be drawn.

The issue also arises as to how to distinguish volunteer work from leisure activities individuals undertake simply because they derive gratification or enjoyment from doing them. One such example might be bringing over meals to a sick neighbor. Another might be taking a Brownie troop on a museum outing. This problem is sometimes solved by including only services rendered as part of an organized program. However, in that case, valid volunteer activities may be excluded. Given these ambiguities, it is not surprising that estimates of the amount of volunteer work done vary widely, depending on the definition used, the questions asked, and the respondent who answers the questions.

An alternative view of volunteer work is that, rather than indirectly enhancing either the income or direct enjoyment of the participants, it is mainly a "conscience good." This interpretation is based on the finding that people most often do volunteer work in response to a request, rather than of their own accord.[61] To the extent that this view is realistic, volunteer work is distinct both from other work and from recreation.

In any case, there is no doubt that much valuable volunteer work is performed in this country, though the fraction of the population that does so has varied somewhat over time. As shown in Table 3.3, a recent survey found that nearly 56 percent of adults did some type of volunteer work in 1998, a figure marginally higher than the most recent high of 54 percent in 1989.[62] Volunteer work is defined quite broadly in this survey and includes helping out others on an informal basis, as well as doing work for religious and nonprofit organizations, whether it be serving food at a shelter, counseling youth, or serving as a board member.

In terms of gender differences, in all years for which data are available, women volunteered at higher rates than men. In 1998, for instance, the rates were 62 percent for women as compared to just 49 percent for men. Part of the explanation for this difference is that women are more likely to be part-time workers, who are much more likely to be volunteers than full-time workers. On the other hand, the nonemployed are less likely to do volunteer work than people who are employed either full-time or part-time, most likely because they tend to be considerably older. Table 3.3 also shows that women's rate of participation in volunteer activities has increased more than men's over time, which is rather surprising in light of the fact

---

[61] Richard B. Freeman, "Working for Nothing: The Supply of Volunteer Labor," *Journal of Labor Economics* 15, no. 1, pt. 2 (January 1997): S140–66.

[62] It should be noted that other estimates for volunteering have been far lower, with the variation depending in part on whether or not volunteering on an informal basis, such as helping out neighbors, is included. See, for instance, Howard V. Hayghe, "Volunteers in the U.S.: Who Donates the Time?" *Monthly Labor Review* 114, no. 2 (February 1991): 17–23.

TABLE 3.3 Trends in Time Spent Volunteering, Selected Years		
	Percentage Volunteering	*Average Weekly Hours of Volunteers*
Women		
1987	46.7	4.7
1993	51.2	4.2
1998	61.7	3.4
Men		
1987	43.8	4.8
1993	43.9	4.3
1998	49.4	3.6
Total		
1987	45.3	4.7
1993	47.7	4.2
1998	55.5	3.5

Note: Figures are computed for individuals age 18 and over.
Source: Adapted from Independent Sector, *Giving and Volunteering in the United States: Findings From a National Survey* (Washington, DC, 1988, 1994, 2000).

that women's labor force participation also increased during the same years. On the other hand, there has been a decline in average hours spent volunteering for both women and men, leading to an overall decrease from 4.7 to 3.5 hours per week between 1987 and 1998. Thus the picture is rather complex and does not fully bear out the concern that women's entry into the labor market has caused a decline in volunteerism.

Women and men also differ in the kinds of volunteer work they do. Women have been found to contribute more time to health organizations and educational institutions, while men have been found to do more voluntary work for civic and political organizations, as well as sport and recreational organizations. There do not appear to be substantial differences in the proportions of women and men involved in social welfare organizations and religious institutions.[63]

Rates of volunteerism also differ by race and ethnicity, among other factors. While the participation rate for the population as a whole was 56 percent, it was only 47 percent for African Americans (up from 35 percent in 1995) and 46 percent for Hispanics (up from 40 percent in 1995). The lower figures for these groups are likely explained by the fact that volunteerism is greater among higher-income individuals.[64]

In sum, there are many reasons why people do work that, by definition, brings few or no direct material rewards. True altruism (or conscience), contact with congenial people, dedication to a particular cause, desire for recognition, furthering business, and advancing one's own or a spouse's career or the well-being of one's children all may

---

[63] "A Vast Empirical Record Refutes the Idea of Civic Decline," Special issue of *Public Perspective* 7, no. 4 (June/July 1996); and Hayghe, "Volunteers in the U.S."

[64] Figures are from Independent Sector, *Giving and Volunteering in the United States: Findings from a National Survey* (Washington, DC, 2000).

play a part to a greater or lesser extent.[65] Research also suggests that unpaid work in the community provides more psychological benefits than unpaid work at home,[66] and that volunteer activities may help women who are out of the labor force get better jobs when they reenter. Indeed, one recent study finds that volunteer work increases future paid earnings, perhaps by providing the individual with valuable human capital or by providing networking opportunities that the individual would otherwise not have. Although experience gained in volunteer work is probably not as valuable, in general, as that acquired on the job, women with demanding family responsibilities, such as caring for young children or elderly relatives, will often value the more flexible schedule, and others may enjoy the greater ability to choose the type of work they do.[67] Finally, experience in volunteer work is particularly useful for persons interested in running for political office, both because of the skills acquired and the valuable contacts often made.

From the point of view of society, voluntary organizations also serve a number of useful functions. They offer the opportunity for mediation, integration of subgroups, affirmation of values, and distribution of power. All of these are important, especially in a democratic society. Beyond this, volunteers provide free services. It is frequently argued that as more and more women enter the labor market and have less time to spend on unpaid work, their contributions to worthy causes will be greatly missed. However, while women's average hours of volunteerism have declined, along with those of men, the data also show that a greater fraction of women are participating in volunteer work than in the past. Further, it must not be overlooked that an increasing number of women now earn an income. They are, therefore, able to contribute more money to worthy causes. Employed women also pay taxes, thus making additional expenditures on public services possible. Hence, workers could be hired to do much of what was earlier done by volunteers.

THE AMERICAN FAMILY AT THE THRESHOLD OF THE TWENTY-FIRST CENTURY

While this chapter has focused on married-couple families, it is important to discuss to what extent this is still the predominant type of family in the United States, to what extent even this type of family has changed in recent decades, and what the increasingly common alternatives are. These changes have, of course, not occurred in isolation, but rather are part of a wave of changes that have also taken place in other economically advanced nations to a greater or lesser extent. Here we provide an overview of the developments in the United States, with a more detailed examina-

[65] Notably, Richard Freeman finds that the opportunity cost of time as reflected by the wage, an important determinant of labor force participation, explains only a very minor part of the decision to volunteer in "Working for Nothing."

[66] Chloe Bird and Catherine Ross, "Houseworkers and Paid Workers: Qualities of the Work and Effects on Personal Control," *Journal of Marriage and Family* 55, no. 4 (November 1993): 913–25.

[67] See, for instance, Kathleen M. Day and Rose Anne Devlin, "The Payoff to Work Without Pay: Volunteer Work as an Investment in Human Capital," *Canadian Journal of Economics* 31, no. 5 (November 1998): 1179–91; Marnie W. Mueller, "Economic Determinants of Volunteer Work by Women," *Signs: Journal of Women in Culture and Society* 1, no. 2 (winter 1975): 325–38; and Francine D. Blau, "How Voluntary Is Volunteer Work? Comment on 'Economic Determinants of Volunteer Work by Women'," *Signs: Journal of Women in Culture and Society* 21, no. 1 (autumn 1976): 251–54.

tion reserved for Chapter 9, and some discussion of demographic trends in other countries in Chapter 11. Demographic changes are both a cause and a consequence of changes in labor force activity among women. Chapter 4 considers the substantial impact that changes in the family have had on women's labor market activity and outcomes. Chapter 9 then "turns the tables" and explores the economic factors, including women's rising labor force participation, that have led to changes in the American family.[68]

The most fundamental shift in the family in recent years relates to the "declining significance of marriage."[69] The once strong ties between marriage, sexual activity, and childbearing have become substantially weaker. This can be seen in falling marriage rates and increases in unmarried, opposite-sex couples, often termed *cohabitors*. As of 1995, 41 percent of women age 15 to 44 had cohabited with a person of the opposite sex at some time in their lives and this figure was as high as 50 percent for women in their thirties.[70] There has also been a substantial increase in the proportion of births to unmarried mothers, from slightly more than 1 in 10 births in 1970 to 1 in 3 in 1999.[71] Furthermore, the divorce rate rose considerably from the 1970s until the 1980s, although it then leveled off and has since declined somewhat.

Table 3.4 provides a snapshot of family structure in 1998 and also shows evidence of considerable differences by race. Marriage is much less common among blacks than whites. In 1998, only 42 percent of black adults were married as compared with 62 percent of whites. This race difference in marriage rates is reflected in the much higher proportion of births to unmarried women among blacks as well as in the much higher proportion of black families maintained by mothers. Similar differences in family structure are found between whites and Hispanics, although they are not nearly as large. These demographic patterns can be seen in children's living arrangements. As shown in Table 3.4, in 1998, only 68 percent of all children were living with two married parents and this figure was as low as 36 percent for black children. The majority of the remaining children were living with a single parent, while a much smaller fraction were living in households with cohabiting parents, or with a grandparent, other relative, or nonrelative. Even two-parent families have changed over time, with many more children today living in a blended (or step) parent family rather than in a traditional nuclear family.[72]

The U.S. Census Bureau has lagged behind in documenting a number of recent changes in family structure. For instance, until the mid-1980s, single mother families that live as subfamilies in the households of the children's grandparents, of other relatives, or

---

[68] Who should be defined as a family is increasingly complex. Teresa J. Rothausen further argues that the current notion of "family" may be biased toward a "white middle-class" reality in " 'Family' in Organizational Research: A Review and Comparison of Definitions and Measures," *Journal of Organizational Behavior* 20, no. 6 (November 1999): 817–36.

[69] Larry Bumpass, "The Declining Significance of Marriage," Changing Family Life in the U.S." NSFH Working Paper No. 66 (University of Wisconsin-Madison, Center for Demography and Ecology, 1995).

[70] U.S. Census Bureau, *Statistical Abstract of the United States: 1999* (Washington, DC: GPO, 2000), table 66.

[71] Source is in table 9.3.

[72] Stacy Furakawa, "The Diverse Living Arrangements of Children: Summer 1991," Bureau of the Census, *Current Population Reports* P70–38, September 1994; and Lynne M. Casper and Kenneth R. Bryson, "Co-resident Grandparents and Their Grandchildren: Grandparent Maintained Families," Population Division Working Paper No. 26 (Washington, DC: U.S. Census Bureau, March 1998).

TABLE 3.4   Family Structure by Race and Hispanic Origin, 1998

	All Races	Whites	Blacks	Hispanic Origin
Unmarried births as percentage of all births	32.8	26.3	69.1	41.6
Percentage of children under age 18 living with two married parents	68.1	74.0	36.2	63.6
Percentage of married adults	59.7	62.1	41.8	58.9
Mother-only families with children under age 18 as percentage of all families with children under age 18[a]	26.1	20.9	57.3	29.9
Percentage where mother is never married	42.2	31.6	63.7	44.3

[a] Includes female-headed families living independently and those living in the household of others (subfamilies).

Note: Persons of Hispanic origin can be of any race.

Source: U.S. Department of Health and Human Services, "Births: Final Data for 1998," *National Vital Statistics Reports*, Report 48, no. 3 (March 28, 2000) (unmarried birth statistics); U.S. Census Bureau, "Family and Household Characteristics, March 1998 (Update)," *Current Population Reports* P20-515, Table 11 (mother-only families); U.S. Census Bureau, "Marital Status and Living Arrangements: March 1998 (Update)," *Current Population Reports* P20–514, Tables 1, 4 and 5 (marriage and two-parent data).

of nonrelatives were not properly counted.[73] Cohabitors were not officially counted before 1990 and could only be crudely identified in government statistics by counting households with unrelated adults of the opposite sex. Since then, respondents are asked about "live-in partners," but official statistics on families and fertility have not been modified accordingly.[74] Similarly, official data on stepparent families count only those in which the adults are married, but not those in which the adults are cohabiting.[75] One consequence of these deficiencies is that a household consisting of a mother and one or more children living with the children's father may be counted as a single-parent family. Therefore, as rates of cohabitation have risen, government statistics have become increasingly misleading regarding the extent to which children live with one parent or both. Indeed, one recent study finds that nearly 40 percent of all children born to unmarried mothers in the early 1990s went home to households that included both parents. In the case of white and Hispanic children, this figure was 50 percent or higher, as compared with just over 20 percent for African American children. All told, it is estimated that about 40 percent of all children will spend some time in a cohabiting family before they reach age 16.[76]

[73] Rebecca A. London, "Trends in Single Mothers' Living Arrangements from 1970 to 1995: Correcting the Current Population Survey," *Demography* 35, no. 1 (February 1998): 125–31.

[74] Anne E. Winkler, "The Living Arrangements of Single Mothers: An Added Perspective," *American Journal of Economics and Sociology* 52, no. 1 (January 1993): 1–18; and Larry Bumpass and R. Kelly Raley, "Redefining Single-Parent Families: Cohabitation and Changing Family Reality," *Demography* 32, no. 1 (February 1995): 97–110.

[75] Larry L. Bumpass, R. Kelly Raley, and James A. Sweet, "The Changing Character of Stepfamilies: Implications of Cohabitation and Nonmarital Childbearing," *Demography* 32, no. 3 (August 1995): 425–36.

[76] Larry Bumpass and H.-H. Lu, "Trends in Cohabitation and Implications for Children's Family Context in the United States," *Population Studies* 54, no. 1 (March 2000): 29–41.

How to classify cohabitors, whether to include them in the definition of family or as a separate category, is a difficult issue for both philosophical and conceptual reasons. First, who is considered to be a family is a subject of considerable debate (see the inset that follows on defining a family). The Census Bureau's official definition is any two or more individuals living together related by blood, marriage, or adoption, thereby excluding cohabitors. Second, even among researchers, the issue of whether cohabitors behave more like married couples or single persons who happen to live together for a time is unresolved. Nevertheless, it is important to accurately quantify these living arrangements in some way, so that we have as much information as possible about a variety of characteristics of these households.

Along with and related to changing family structure, the demographic "mix" of the U.S. population has been changing. Changes in race and ethnicity have been a consequence of shifts in immigration, both in terms of source countries and absolute numbers, as well as of differences in birthrates among various groups in the U.S.-born population. The largest increase is projected among Hispanics, both white and black, from 9 percent of the population in 1990 to 16.3 percent by 2020. The non-Hispanic black population is also expected to increase over the same period, but only from 11.8 percent to 12.9 percent, while it is anticipated that the share of the non-Hispanic white population will decrease from 75.6 percent to 64.3 percent of the total population.[77]

How to classify individuals of mixed races and ethnicities is another issue that remains to be resolved. Regarding race, individuals have generally been limited to choosing a single category in government surveys. For the 2000 U.S. census, five major race groups were identified: black or African American, white, American Indian or Alaska native, Asian, and Native Hawaiian or Other Pacific Islander. One significant difference between the 2000 census and earlier ones is that individuals were allowed to select as many of these categories as apply, rather than being restricted to choosing a single race. Notably, intermarriage among race and ethnic groups is becoming more common. Of new marriages involving at least one African American, 12.1 percent were with a white partner in 1993, compared to only 2.6 percent in 1970, and the rates were even higher among Asians and Native Americans.[78]

The information provided above suggests that the American family at the start of the twenty-first century is quite different from that of the 1950s' characterization of an invariably white family, comprised of a homemaker wife and breadwinner husband with two or three children and a dog, that has been immortalized in television, movies, and American lore. A historical perspective indicates that this family was, to some extent, a demographic aberration. In fact, fertility rates were lower and the average age of marriage was higher in earlier times than in the 1950s, and divorce was, even then, by no means unheard of.[79] And, of course, considerable racial and ethnic diversity existed at that time as well. Nonetheless, without a doubt, the changes that have occurred since then have had a major impact both on how people live and on how they make a living. These issues will be discussed further in subsequent chapters.

---

[77] U.S. Census Bureau, "Population Projections of the U.S. by Age, Sex, Race and Hispanic Origin: 1995–2050," *Current Population Reports* P25–1130 (February 1996).

[78] Douglas J. Besharov and Timothy S. Sullivan, "One Flesh," *New Democrat* 8, no. 4 (July/August 1996): 19–21. See also Zhenchao Qian, "Breaking the Racial Barriers: Variations in Interracial Marriage Between 1980 and 1990," *Demography* 34, no. 2 (May 1997): 263–76.

[79] Julie DaVanzo and M. Omar Rahman, "American Families: Trends and Correlates," *Population Index* 59, no. 3 (fall 1993): 350–86.

Who Is a Family?

In order to have an accurate picture of the circumstances in which Americans live, and to make decisions about insurance, benefits, and pensions, the government and private employers alike must decide what constitutes a family. The Bureau of the Census officially defines a family as any two or more persons related by blood, marriage, or adoption living together. However, as the results of a Roper survey* that follow indicate, there remains substantial diversity of opinion as to whether other groupings, such as unmarried, opposite-sex adults or same-sex couples living together should also be regarded as a family.

Question: You hear a lot today about the changing American family. I'd like to know your opinion on what a "family" is (Card shown respondent). For each of the following types of living arrangements, please tell me whether you definitely would call it a family, you definitely would not call it a family, or if you aren't sure.

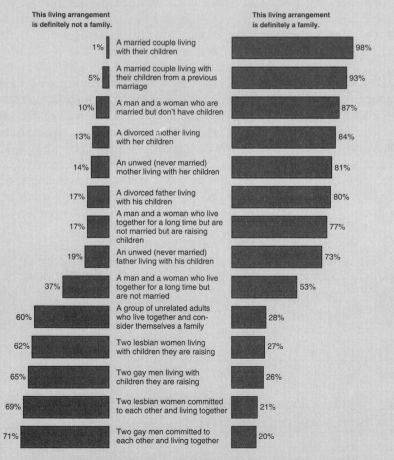

This living arrangement is definitely not a family.		This living arrangement is definitely a family.
1%	A married couple living with their children	98%
5%	A married couple living with their children from a previous marriage	93%
10%	A man and a woman who are married but don't have children	87%
13%	A divorced mother living with her children	84%
14%	An unwed (never married) mother living with her children	81%
17%	A divorced father living with his children	80%
17%	A man and a woman who live together for a long time but are not married but are raising children	77%
19%	An unwed (never married) father living with his children	73%
37%	A man and a woman who live together for a long time but are not married	53%
60%	A group of unrelated adults who live together and consider themselves a family	28%
62%	Two lesbian women living with children they are raising	27%
65%	Two gay men living with children they are raising	26%
69%	Two lesbian women committed to each other and living together	21%
71%	Two gay men committed to each other and living together	20%

* "What Constitutes a Family," Public Opinion and Demographic Report, *American Enterprise* (July/August 1992), p. 101. Reprinted by permission from *The American Enterprise*, a Washington-based magazine of politics, business, and culture (614) 375-2323.

CONCLUSION

We saw in Chapter 2 how the concept of the traditional family evolved with the man as the breadwinner and the woman as the homemaker, combining her time and the goods and services purchased with the husband's earnings to satisfy the family's needs and wants. The simple neoclassical model explains how such a division of labor may be advantageous under appropriate conditions. But as we have seen, it cannot be taken for granted that these conditions are satisfied at any given point in time, let alone that they will be for the rest of each person's life.

The traditional specialization came about during a time when cloth was spun, bread was baked, and soap was produced at home, the family was large, and market wages in jobs available to women were low, so that her relative advantage for home work was great. With many children and a shorter life expectancy, the problem of the decline in the value of housework after the children grew up was far less serious. Also, with severe social and religious sanctions against divorce, women were less likely to find themselves and their children dependent on a recalcitrant ex-husband for a living. However, as these factors have changed, the advantages of the traditional division of labor have decreased and the costs associated with it, particularly for women, have increased.

Growing recognition of the drawbacks of the traditional division of responsibilities between husband and wife may be one of the factors that has contributed to the increase in women's labor force participation and the decline of the married-couple family comprised of a homemaker wife and breadwinner husband. Furthermore, the lessening economic gains from marriage, women's increasing awareness of the risks associated with full specialization in the home, and improvements in women's labor market opportunities are also likely related to the decline in marriage, the increase in divorce, and the rise in cohabitation. Related to these changes, there has been a noticeable, though modest, reallocation of household tasks between married men and women and it appears that the gender difference in housework among married couples is likely to continue to narrow. Even so, unless there are major changes in the availability and affordability of day care and elder care, and in the attitudes of men and women, women are likely to continue to shoulder the lion's share of home responsibilities for quite some time to come.

A P P E N D I X

Specialization and Exchange: A Graphical Analysis

As discussed in Chapter 3, a complete analysis of the division of labor between the individuals who make up a couple takes into account both their production possibilities and their preferences. In this appendix, we do this by providing a fuller examination of the simple neoclassical model in the context of a graphical analysis. The same conclusions are reached as to the value of specialization and exchange as those based on the examples presented in Tables 3.1a and 3.1b.

For simplicity, we assume that individuals derive utility from only two types of goods—home goods, produced with inputs of home time, and market goods, purchased with market income. In Figure 3.1, H and M measure the dollar value of household output and market goods, respectively. Two persons, Kathy and Jim, each allocate their time between market work (M production) and housework (H production).[80]

If Kathy and Jim are each dependent on their own output, their consumption opportunities are limited to their individual *production possibility frontiers*. The production possibility frontier shows the largest feasible combinations of the two outputs that can be produced with given resources (in this case, time inputs) and know-how. M_1H_1 indicates the combinations of household and market outputs available to Jim, while M_2H_2 shows the options from which Kathy can choose. For example, if Jim devotes full time to market work (M production), he can produce a maximum of $80 worth of market goods. If he spends all his time on household activities, he can produce $30 worth of home goods.

The slope of the line M_1H_1 tells us the money value of the market goods Jim must give up to get an additional dollar of home goods. The fact that M_1H_1 is more steeply sloped than M_2H_2 means that Jim must give up more market goods to get an additional dollar of home goods than Kathy. Specifically, Jim must give up $2.67 of market goods to get an additional dollar of home goods ($80/$30), whereas Kathy needs to give up only $.56 of market goods to get an additional dollar of home goods ($50/$90). Viewing the matter somewhat differently, Kathy must forgo more home goods to get an additional dollar of market goods than Jim. Kathy would have to give up $1.80 worth of home goods to get an additional dollar of market goods ($90/$50), while Jim needs to give up only $.38 worth of home goods to get an additional dollar of market goods ($30/$80). Thus, Jim has a comparative advantage in market work and Kathy has a comparative advantage in home production.

If Jim and Kathy decide to collaborate, their combined production possibility curve will be MYH, as shown in panel c. At point M both Jim and Kathy specialize entirely in market work, producing $130 ($80 + $50) of market goods. If they prefer to

---

[80] We also assume fixed proportions production functions for H and M for each individual. This means, for example, that an additional hour spent on the production of H by Kathy increases output by the same amount, regardless of how much H she has already produced. This simplifying assumption results in the straight-line production possibility frontiers shown in Figure 3.1. For a discussion of this point, along with a consideration of other ways in which the standard theoretical model might be broadened, see Pollak, "Allocating Time."

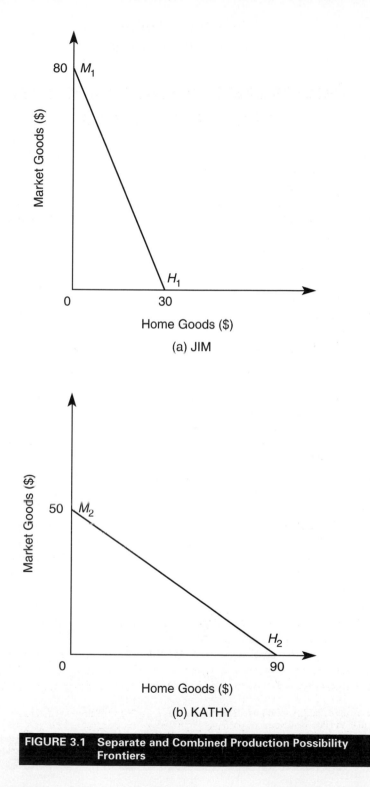

FIGURE 3.1   Separate and Combined Production Possibility Frontiers

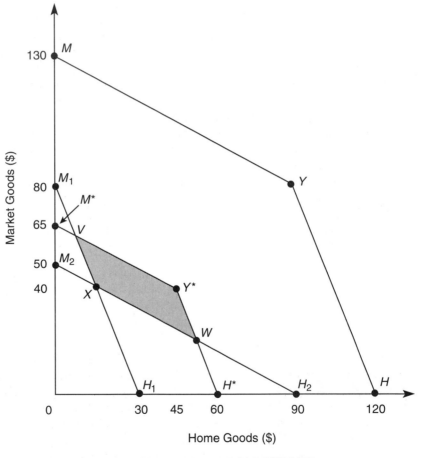

(c) JIM AND KATHY COMBINED

FIGURE 3.1   Separate and Combined Production Possibility Frontiers (continued)

have some home goods, it will pay for only Kathy to do housework, up to the point where she does no market work at all (point *Y*), because she adds more to home production ($1.80) for every dollar of market goods given up than Jim would add ($.38). Therefore, the segment *MY* has the same slope as M_2H_2, showing that as long as only Kathy is dividing her time between market and home, it is Kathy's slope that is relevant. Jim will do some housework only if a mix of more household production and fewer market goods are desired than segment *MY* represents. Beyond that point, the slope of M_1H_1 becomes relevant, as it is only Jim who is dividing his time between home and market. At the extreme, at point *H,* both Jim and Kathy work only in the home, producing $120 ($30 + $90) of home goods.

The combined production possibility frontier (*MYH*) makes feasible some combinations of *M* and *H* that would not be attainable by Kathy and Jim on their separate production possibility frontiers. These gains from specialization and exchange may be illustrated by putting the output combinations represented by production possibility frontier *MYH* on a per capita or per person basis. This is shown by production possibility frontier M*Y*H* which is obtained by dividing MYH by two. (For instance, point Y reflects $90 worth of home goods and $80 worth of market goods, while point Y* reflects $45 worth of home goods and $40 worth of market goods). M*Y*H* may be compared to the options represented by Jim and Kathy's individual production possibility frontiers, M_1H_1 and M_2H_2 (panel c). The shaded area *WXVY** represents the increased per capita output that is now available. This gain in output may potentially be distributed between Jim and Kathy so as to make them both better off than they would have been separately. To obtain the gains represented by *WXVY**, the couple must produce a nontrivial amount of both market and home goods, for it is the production of both commodities that gives each of them the opportunity to specialize in the area of their comparative advantage.

This analysis also illustrates that the gains from specialization will be larger the more the two individuals differ in their comparative advantages. To see this, imagine the extreme case in which Kathy and Jim both have the same production possibility frontier, say M_1H_1. The combined production possibility frontier would then be $2 \times M_1H_1$. On a per capita basis (dividing the combined production possibility frontier in half), we would simply be left with M_1H_1. Kathy and Jim would do no better combining forces than they would each do separately. Based on this simple analysis alone, it is not clear what the economic gains to collaborating are for such a couple. However, as we saw in Chapter 3, there are likely to be economic gains even in this case, mainly because two people can use many goods and services more efficiently than a single person can. Here, however, we focus on a couple that can potentially increase its income through joint production.

To provide a link between the potential increase in output due to collaboration and the goal of maximizing satisfaction, we need to introduce an additional tool of economic analysis and pursue our inquiry one step further. So far we have only established the various combinations of the two types of outputs that Kathy and Jim could produce. Which of these they would choose depends on their tastes, that is to say, on their preferences for market goods compared to home goods. To considerably simplify the analysis, we will assume that they have identical tastes. If home goods are valued more highly than market goods, the couple will be willing to give up a considerable amount of market goods in order to get an additional dollar of home goods, and vice versa if market goods are valued more highly. This relationship can be illustrated using indifference curves, as seen in Figure 3.2.

Let us assume that Kathy and Jim have been told that they could have the combination of market and home goods represented by point *A* in panel a. They are then asked to find various other combinations of *H* and *M* from which they would derive exactly the same amount of satisfaction or utility. These other points can all be connected into one indifference curve, U_2, called that because the couple is indifferent about being at various points on the curve. The U_2 curve is *negatively sloped*. This means that if the amount of market or home goods is decreased, the amount of the other good must be increased for the couple to remain equally well off.

Notice too that indifference curve U_2 is convex to the origin. That is, it gets steeper as we move to the left and flatter as we move to the right. What this means is that at a point like *C*, where *M* goods are relatively plentiful and *H* goods are relatively scarce, it takes a fairly large amount of *M* ($15 worth) to induce the couple to give up a fairly small amount of *H* ($5 worth) and still remain equally well off. On the other hand, at a point like *E*, where *M* goods are relatively scarce and *H* goods are relatively plentiful, the couple is willing to give up a fairly large amount of *H* ($20 worth) to get even a small additional amount of scarce *M* ($2 worth). This is generally realistic to the extent that relatively scarce goods are valued more highly.

However, Kathy and Jim do not have just one indifference curve, but rather a whole family of higher or lower indifference curves. For it is possible to choose a point like *G* on curve U_3 that offers more of both *M* and *H* and is therefore clearly preferable to point *A* on curve U_2. Hence, all points on curve U_3 will, by extension, be preferable to (give more satisfaction than) all points on curve U_2. Similarly, it is possible to choose a point like *J* on curve U_1 that offers less of both *M* and *H* than at point *A*. Point *J* is clearly less desirable than point *A* and, by extension, all points on curve U_1 are less desirable (give less satisfaction) than all points on curve U_2. It should be clear that indifference curves can never intersect. All points on any one curve represent an equal amount of utility, while any point above (below) represents a larger (smaller) amount of utility. At the point where two curves intersect, they clearly represent the same amount of utility, yet at all other points they do not. This is a logical impossibility.

On the other hand, another couple's preferences might look like those depicted in panel b of Figure 3.2. These indifference curves are steeper and show that this couple places a relatively higher value on home goods, compared with market goods, than Kathy and Jim do. In general, it would take a larger amount of market goods to induce them to give up a dollar's worth of home goods while remaining equally well off.

To determine the division of labor (or time allocation) a couple will actually choose, we must consider both their production possibilities and their tastes or preferences. In Figure 3.3, we superimpose the couple's hypothetical indifference map on the production possibility frontier shown in Figure 3.1, panel c. It is then readily possible to determine the combination of home-produced and market-produced goods that a rational couple with those tastes (indifference curves) will choose. It will always be the point where the production possibility curve just touches the highest indifference curve it reaches. The reason is simple—the couple always prefers to be on a higher indifference curve (by definition, as we have seen), but since they are constrained to the possible combinations of output represented by the production possibility frontier, there is no realistic way they can reach an indifference curve that at all points lies above the frontier.

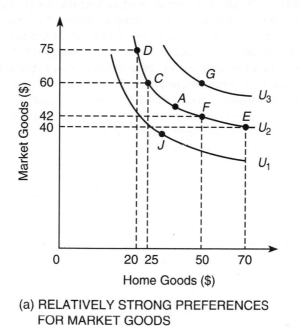

(a) RELATIVELY STRONG PREFERENCES
   FOR MARKET GOODS

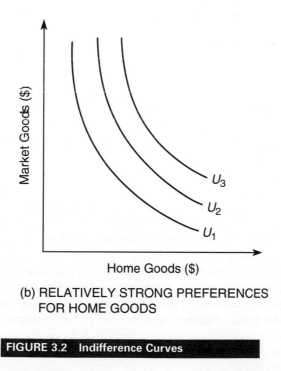

(b) RELATIVELY STRONG PREFERENCES
   FOR HOME GOODS

FIGURE 3.2   Indifference Curves

In Figure 3.3, we illustrate the impact of the couple's preferences on their time allocation. The combined production possibility curve for the couple, MYH, shows the various combinations of H and M the couple can produce while taking full advantage of their combined resources and the comparative advantage each has in producing one of the goods. Let us continue to assume that the wife has a comparative advantage in home production and that the husband has a comparative advantage in market work.

As may be seen in panel a, a couple with relatively strong preferences for market goods will maximize satisfaction at point A along segment MY. The husband will specialize entirely in market production and the wife will do all the housework and also supply some time to the market. They will consume M_a dollars of market goods and H_a dollars of home goods.

Panel b shows a couple with stronger preferences for home-produced goods. They will maximize utility at point B. The wife will devote herself entirely to household production, while the husband will do some housework as well as supplying time to the market. Such a couple will consume fewer market goods (M_b) and more home goods (H_b) than a couple with stronger preferences for market goods.

Finally, panel c shows a couple with intermediate tastes. They will maximize utility at point Y. Both wife and husband will each fully specialize in home and market production, respectively, and will consume M_c dollars of market goods and H_c dollars of home goods.

Couples may differ in their allocation of tasks within the family, not solely due to differences in tastes. The relative productivity of each member of the family in the production of market and home goods will also be an important factor. We have already noted that if both husband and wife are equally productive in each endeavor, there will be no gains to specialization or division of labor within the family. However, even if we assume that the wife has a comparative advantage in household production and that the husband has a comparative advantage in market work, the relative productivities of each individual in home and market production are still relevant. This is illustrated in Figure 3.4.

Panel a shows two hypothetical production possibility frontiers. In MYH, the segment corresponding to the wife's frontier (MY) is relatively flat, indicating that she is considerably more productive in the home than in the market. For given tastes (represented by indifference curve U), the couple maximizes utility at point Y, where the wife specializes entirely in home production and the husband specializes completely in market work. However, if the couple's production possibility frontier were $M'Y'H'$, even with the same tastes (indifference curve), they would choose point A along segment $M'Y'$. Here the wife will continue to do all the housework but will do some market work as well. This is because $M'Y'$ is steeper than MY, indicating a higher ratio of the wife's market productivity relative to her home productivity. The opportunity cost of home goods in terms of market goods forgone has increased and as a result the family consumes less home goods.

Similarly, as shown in panel b, the couple's time allocation may also depend on the husband's relative productivity in the home and the market. For given tastes (represented by indifference curve U), the couple will choose point Y when the husband's productivity in the home is extremely low relative to his market productivity. (This is

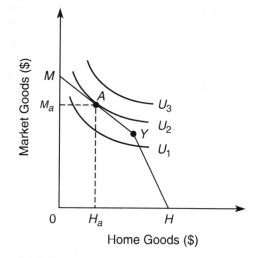

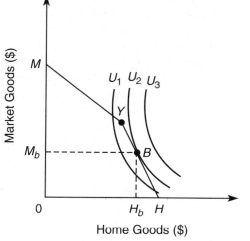

(a) RELATIVELY STRONG PREFERENCES
   FOR MARKET GOODS

(b) RELATIVELY STRONG PREFERENCES
   FOR HOME GOODS

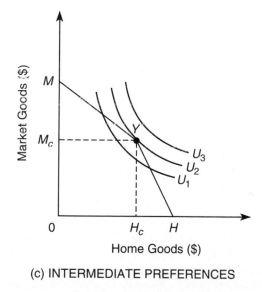

(c) INTERMEDIATE PREFERENCES

FIGURE 3.3   The Role of Tastes in Determining the Household Division of Labor

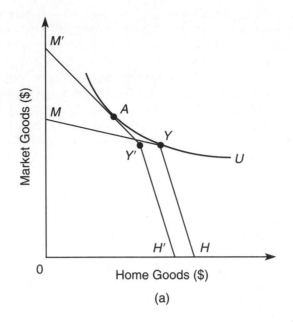

(a)

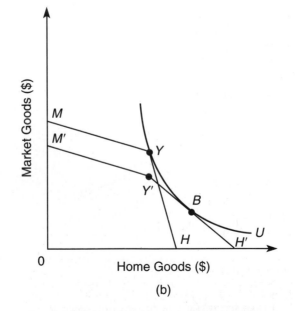

(b)

FIGURE 3.4 The Role of the Production Possibility Frontier in Determining the Household Division of Labor

indicated by the relatively steep slope of segment *YH* on frontier *MYH.*) They are more likely to choose a point like *B* along the flatter segment *Y'H'* on frontier *M'Y'H'*, where the husband does some housework as well as market work, when his market productivity is lower relative to his home productivity. At *B,* the couple consumes more of the now relatively cheaper home-produced goods than at *Y.*

Figure 3.4 shows how the relative productivity of the husband and the wife in the home and the market influence the division of labor in the family and the combination of home- and market-produced goods that they choose to consume. Nonetheless, as long as the comparative advantages of husband and wife differ in this simple model, specialization will be efficient. As we have seen, the greater the difference between the two in their comparative advantage, the greater the gains to specialization and exchange.

Thus, the fuller analysis presented here supports the conclusions reached on the basis of the numerical example provided in Chapter 3. In this case too, however, the same qualifications hold. First, there are other potential economic benefits to marriage besides specialization and exchange, and, second, there are disadvantages, particularly for women, to the traditional division of labor.

QUESTIONS FOR REVIEW AND DISCUSSION

1. Explain why husbands and wives benefit from specialization and exchange. Under what conditions are these benefits likely to be large?

2. Jason and Jennifer are married. If Jason works in the labor market, he can earn a wage of $20 per hour, while Jennifer can earn a wage of $10 per hour.

   a. Who has an absolute advantage in the labor market? How do you know?

   b. Suppose we want to know who has a comparative advantage in the labor market. What specific information do we need to know? Discuss.

3. In view of the advantages of specialization and exchange pointed out by Becker, why are families increasingly moving away from the traditional division of labor?

4. To what extent is the presumption that women have a comparative advantage in housework justified?

5. Explain under what conditions it would be rational for a woman who could earn more than her husband in the labor market to specialize in housework.

6. For a long time, economists did not include housework in their analyses. In what respect was this omission justified or not?

7. Why have women been so eager to increase their participation in the labor market and why have men been so reluctant to increase their participation in housework?

8. What is a "bargaining approach" to decision making? What are the benefits of this approach as compared with the standard neoclassical model?

9. Suggest some factors that would improve the bargaining power of married women.

Suggested Readings

Becker, Gary S. *A Treatise on the Family.* Cambridge, MA: Harvard University Press, 1981, enlarged edition, 1991.

Bianchi, Suzanne. "Maternal Employment and Time with Children: Dramatic Change or Surprising Continuity?" *Demography* 37, no. 4 (November 2000): 401–14.

Blau, Francine D. "Trends in the Well-Being of American Women, 1970–1995." *Journal of Economic Literature* 36, no. 1 (March 1998): 112–65.

Ferber, Marianne A., and Bonnie G. Birnbaum. "The New Home Economics: Retrospects and Prospects." *Journal of Consumer Research* 4, no. 1 (June 1977): 19–28.

Ferber, Marianne A., and Julie A. Nelson, eds. *Beyond Economic Man.* Chicago: University of Chicago Press, 1993.

Folbre, Nancy. *Who Pays for the Kids? Gender and the Structures of Constraint.* London: Routledge, 1994.

Folbre, Nancy, and Julie A. Nelson. "For Love or Money—Or Both?" *Journal of Economic Perspectives* 14, no. 4 (fall 2000): 123–40.

Fuchs, Victor R. *Women's Quest for Economic Equality.* Cambridge, MA: Harvard University Press, 1988.

Hartmann, Heidi I. "The Family as the Locus of Gender, Class and Political Struggle: The Example of Housework." *Signs: Journal of Women in Culture and Society* 6, no. 3 (spring 1981): 366–94.

Juster, F. Thomas, and Frank P. Stafford. "The Allocation of Time: Empirical Findings, Behavioral Models, and Problems of Measurement." *Journal of Economic Literature* 29, no. 2 (June 1991): 471–522.

Lazear, Edward P., and Robert T. Michael. *Allocation of Income Within the Household.* Chicago: University of Chicago Press, 1988.

Lundberg, Shelly, and Robert A. Pollak. "Bargaining and Distribution in Marriage." *Journal of Economic Perspectives* 10, no. 4 (fall 1996): 139–58.

Robinson, John P., and Geoffrey Godbey. *Time for Life: The Surprising Ways Americans Use Their Time*, 2nd ed. University Park: Pennsylvania State University Press, 1999.

CHAPTER 4

THE ALLOCATION OF TIME BETWEEN THE HOUSEHOLD AND THE LABOR MARKET

Chapter Highlights

- Labor Force Participation and Attachment: Definitions and Trends
- The Labor Supply Decision
- Analyzing Trends in Women's Participation: An Overview
- The World War II Experience
- The Post–World War II Baby Boom
- The 1960s to the 1980s: Increased Participation of Married Mothers
- The 1990s: Increased Participation of Single Mothers
- Analyzing Trends in Men's Participation
- Black and White Participation Differentials: A Closer Look

The rapid growth in women's labor force participation has been one of the most significant economic and social developments in the post–World War II period, in this country and elsewhere. One reason for our interest in women's participation trends is that they underlie the transformation in gender roles that has occurred in the United States in recent years. However, there are also other reasons for examining women's labor force participation.

First, the economic well-being of women and their families is obviously significantly influenced by whether or not they participate in the labor force and their earnings levels, given participation. Such issues have gained in importance with the increase in the incidence of female-headed families and the growing dependence of married-couple families on the contributions of working wives. Second, the family bargaining models that we reviewed in Chapter 3 suggest that, in married-couple families, women's participation in the labor force and their level of earnings while employed may affect the distribution of resources within marriage. According to these models, a woman who works outside the home will have a higher utility at the threat point and, hence, a more favorable distribution within marriage. Third, shifts in participation are of importance for women's wages in that they influence the average levels of labor market experience of women and, as we shall see in Chapter 6, experience is an important determinant of wages.

In this chapter, we first review the definition of the labor force and summarize trends over time in female and male labor force participation. We shall see that, while female participation rates have been increasing, male rates have been declining, albeit not as dramatically. As a consequence of both types of changes, men's and women's labor force participation rates and their patterns of involvement in market work over the life cycle are becoming increasingly similar. We then turn to the development of some economic concepts for analyzing these trends and use them to provide a better understanding of the reasons for the remarkable influx of women into the labor market. Next we use economic theory to analyze the decrease in male labor force participation and conclude with an examination of factors contributing to differences in labor force participation trends between blacks and whites.

THE LABOR FORCE: SOME DEFINITIONS

Each month, the U.S. Census Bureau conducts a survey to gather statistics on the labor force. According to the official definition, the **labor force** includes all those individuals 16 years of age and over who worked for pay or profit during the reference week or actively sought paid employment during the four weeks prior to the reference week. That is, the labor force is comprised of both the **employed** and the **unemployed.**

The **employed** group includes all those who worked one hour per week or more as paid employees or were self-employed in their own business or profession or on their own farm. This includes part-time workers who worked less than 35 hours per week, as well as those who worked full-time, 35 hours or more. It also includes all those temporarily absent from paid employment because of bad weather, vacation, family leave, labor–management disputes, or personal reasons, whether or not they were paid. An exception to the emphasis on paid employment is that those who worked at least 15 hours as unpaid workers in an enterprise operated by a family member are also included.[1] The **unemployed** include those who do not have a job but who have made specific efforts to find a job within the past four weeks, as well as those not working but waiting to be called back to work or to report for a new job within 30 days. The relationships among these labor force concepts are illustrated in Figure 4.1.

The **labor force participation rate** of a particular group is equal to the number of its members who are in the labor force divided by the total number of the group in the population. Thus, for example, a labor force participation rate of 60 percent for women means that 60 percent of women 16 years of age and over are labor force participants.

---

[1] The labor force excludes people engaged in illegal activities such as prostitution and drug trafficking. Furthermore, employment ranging from baby-sitting to yard work, which is paid for in cash and not reported for tax purposes (the so-called "underground economy"), is likely to be underreported in labor force statistics.

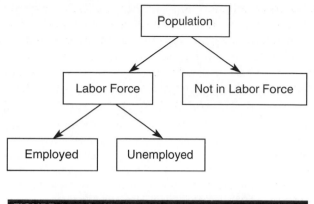

FIGURE 4.1   An Illustration of Labor Force Definitions

A careful reading of the definition of the labor force makes it clear that being in the labor force is not synonymous with working. Individuals who work less than 15 hours a week as unpaid family workers, and those who only do unpaid work in the household or as volunteer workers, no matter how many hours, are excluded. On the other hand, persons temporarily not working, or unemployed, are included. In large part, this results from the emphasis in the official definition of the labor force on being employed in or seeking *market* work. Because women have tended to have primary responsibility for nonmarket work, they constitute a high proportion in the categories that are left out. Thus, their share of the labor force considerably understates their share of work. This was particularly true in earlier days when family enterprises were more common and when most married women were homemakers.[2] In fact, as discussed in the following inset, until surprisingly recently the official definitions were not even applied in the same way to men and women. In spite of these reservations, women's labor force participation rate is considered to be an important indicator of their status in a market economy, for work done outside the labor market seldom offers as much prestige, let alone money income, and is sometimes not even viewed as real "work."

Other aspects of the official definition of the labor force have also been the object of criticism at various times. For example, the definition of the unemployed excludes those who would like a job but who have given up searching because they believe no work is available, so-called discouraged workers. Although no definition is likely to be equally satisfactory to all, adherence to a reasonably consistent definition over a long period of time provides useful data for analyzing trends. In some cases, criticism has been accommodated by providing additional data that may be used to construct labor force measures based on different definitions. We take advantage of such data in our discussion of discouraged workers in Chapter 8.

---

[2] It has been suggested that, historically, such activities of married women as taking in boarders, piecework done at home, and even seasonal work done in factories frequently went unreported, especially when it was the husband who was interviewed. (See, for instance, Milton Cantor and Bruce Laurie, eds., *Class, Sex, and the Woman Worker* [Westport, CT: Greenwood Press, 1977].) How important this undercount may have been is suggested by the fact that when, in 1910, census enumerators were given instructions to take special care not to overlook women workers, especially unpaid family workers, the participation rate was found to be about 4 percentage points higher than would be expected based on earlier and immediately subsequent decades. It is due to this incomparability that 1910 is normally omitted from historical series on women's labor force participation. We follow this practice in Table 4.1.

No More Guessing About Who Is a Homemaker

It has only been since January 1994 that the Bureau of Labor Statistics, which collects data on work activity in the home and in the labor market, has been asking men and women the same questions regarding their activity in the previous week. Prior to this time, if an adult woman opened the door, it was assumed that she might well be a homemaker. Accordingly, she was asked the question, "What were you doing most of last week—working, keeping house, or something else?" If an adult man opened the door, he was asked about "working, or something else?" As a consequence of this type of stereotyping, women were more likely to be classified as out of the labor force (that is, keeping house) rather than as unemployed (currently without a job, but searching). In the new survey, all individuals are asked the same questions, thus avoiding any potential bias from this source.

The survey was also reworded to distinguish hours spent at home-based work for pay from hours spent doing unpaid work around the house. Specifically, the question asking "Did you do any work at all last week, not counting work around the house?" was changed to "Last week did you do any work **for pay**?"

Because the revised survey better captures women's full range of paid work activities and their unemployment, these changes have led to higher estimates of women's labor force activity than found with the previous survey. During a test period in 1993 when the old and new sets of questions were used, the estimate of women's employment-to-population rate (that is, the number of women who were employed as a share of the female population) was 54.2 percent based on the old questions, and 54.9 percent using the new set. This might seem like a small difference, but it translates into thousands of women who were previously uncounted.

Source: U.S. Department of Labor, Bureau of Labor Statistics, "Revisions in the Current Population Survey Effective January 1994," *Employment and Earnings* (February 1994).

TRENDS IN LABOR FORCE PARTICIPATION

The purpose of this section is to briefly review the trends in female and male labor force participation. The reasons for the observed changes are considered later, but here we may obtain an overview of how substantial these changes have been. Labor force participation rates for selected years since 1890 are shown in Table 4.1.[3] The figures indicate a relatively slow rate of increase in the labor force participation rates of women in the pre-1940 period. Since then, however, considerably larger changes have occurred. In 1940, 28 percent of women were in the labor force; by 1999, the figure had risen to 60 percent of women 16 years of age and over, and more than three-quarters (77 percent) of women between the ages of 25 and 54 were labor force participants. During this time, women workers increased from 25 to 47 percent of the labor force.

---

[3] Until 1890, published census volumes contained few tabulations of the labor force participation and occupations of women; see Claudia Goldin, *Understanding the Gender Gap: An Economic History of American Women* (New York: Oxford University Press, 1990), p. 186.

TABLE 4.1 Labor Force Participation Rates of Men and Women, 1890–1999		
Year	*Percent of Men in the Labor Force*	*Percent of Women in the Labor Force*
1890	84.3	18.2
1900	85.7	20.0
1920	84.6	22.7
1930	82.1	23.6
1940	82.5	27.9
1945	87.6	35.8
1947	86.8	31.5
1950	86.4	33.9
1960	83.3	37.7
1970	79.9	43.3
1980	77.4	51.5
1990	76.4	57.5
1999	74.7	60.0

Notes: Based on the total population prior to 1950 and the civilian population thereafter. Rates are computed for individuals 14 years of age and over before 1947, and 16 years and over thereafter.

Sources: U.S. Department of Commerce, Bureau of the Census, *Historical Statistics of the United States Colonial Times to 1970,* Bicentennial Edition, Part 1, 1975, pp. 131–32; and *Employment and Earnings,* various issues.

Table 4.1 also indicates the sizable effect that the mobilization for World War II had on female labor force participation. As males left their civilian jobs to join the armed forces, women entered the labor force in unprecedented numbers. Between 1940 and 1945, the female participation rate increased from 28 to 36 percent. As suggested by the 1947 figures, some decline occurred in the immediate post–World War II period, but the upward trend in female participation quickly resumed and has continued to the present. As may be seen in Figure 4.2, however, the steep rise in female participation rates has slowed in the 1990s, with the pace of growth declining to slightly less than half the rate of earlier decades.[4]

In contrast to the situation for women, male labor force participation rates began to decline in the 1950s, from 86 percent in 1950 to 75 percent in 1999. As a consequence of these opposing trends, the *difference* between the male and female participation rates has declined sharply from 55 percentage points in 1940 to 15 percentage points in 1999. This growing convergence is also illustrated in Figure 4.2.

We gain a fuller picture of the trends in labor force participation by examining them separately for different subgroups. Table 4.2 shows trends in labor force participation since 1955 by race and Hispanic origin. The participation rate has declined for all groups of men but much more so for blacks, who have now fallen considerably behind. Hispanic men, however, are more likely to be in the labor force than white or black males.

---

[4] The female participation rate increased at an average annual rate of .3 percentage points in the 1990s compared to .7 points in the 1980s and .8 points in the 1970s.

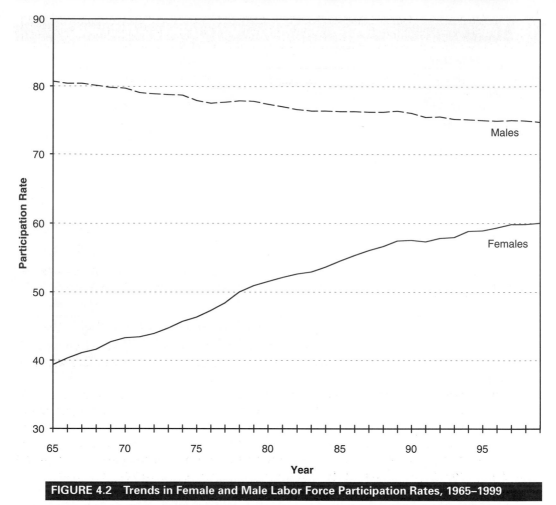

FIGURE 4.2 **Trends in Female and Male Labor Force Participation Rates, 1965–1999**

The rate has risen for all groups of women but substantially more so for whites and Hispanics. Black women have traditionally had far higher labor force participation rates than white women. While this race gap in participation had virtually closed by the mid-1980s, it reopened again in the late 1990s, due to a substantial increase in black women's participation rates. Hispanic women continue to have a lower labor force participation rate than white or black women.

The growth in female labor force participation that has occurred since World War II has been accompanied by pronounced changes in the patterns of women's employment over the life cycle. Before 1940, the typical female worker was young and single, since most women tended to leave the labor force permanently upon marriage and child-bearing. As Figure 4.3 shows, at that time, the peak age-specific participation rate occurred among women 20 to 24 years of age and declined for each successive age group

TABLE 4.2   Labor Force Participation Rates of Men and Women by Race and Hispanic Origin, 1955–1999 (percent)

	Males			*Females*		
Year	*Whites*	*Blacks*	*Hispanics*	*Whites*	*Blacks*	*Hispanics*
1955	85.4	85.0	n.a.	34.5	46.1	n.a.
1965	80.8	79.6	n.a.	38.1	48.6	n.a.
1975	78.7	70.9	80.7	45.9	48.8	43.1
1985	77.0	70.8	80.3	54.1	53.1	49.3
1990	76.9	70.1	81.2	57.5	57.8	53.0
1995	75.7	69.0	79.1	59.0	59.5	52.6
1999	75.6	68.7	79.8	59.6	63.5	55.9

Notes: Civilian labor force; includes population aged 16 and over. Prior to 1975, other nonwhites are included with blacks. Hispanics are also included under the relevant racial category.

n.a. Not available.

Sources: U.S. Department of Labor, Bureau of Labor Statistics, *Working Women: A Databook,* 1977, pp. 44–45; U.S. Department of Labor, *Handbook of Labor Statistics* (August 1989), pp. 25–30; and U.S. Department of Labor, *Employment and Earnings* (various issues).

after that.[5] Over the next 20 years, older married women with school-age or grown children entered or reentered the labor force in increasing numbers, while there was little change in the labor force participation rates of women between the ages of 20 and 34. The proportion of women workers who were married increased from 30 percent in 1940 to 54 percent in 1960. The World War II experience may have played some part in encouraging this shift in the behavior of married women, since it was during the war that, for the first time, large numbers of older married women worked outside the home.

Since 1960, there has been a sizable increase in the participation rates of all women under age 55, but particularly among women ages 25 to 44. This increase in part reflects declines in the birthrate and increases in the divorce rate over this period. Most notable, however, has been the large increase in the participation rates of married women with small children. Among those with children less than six years old, only 19 percent worked outside the home in 1960, compared to 61 percent in 1999. And over half (56 percent) of married mothers who had a child in the last year were in the labor force.

As a result of these changes, the pattern of age-specific participation rates among women has come to more closely resemble the male pattern shown in Figure 4.4. This figure also shows that the decline in male labor force participation rates that occurred during the post–World War II period was concentrated among younger men, those under 20, and among older men, aged 55 and over. Since the 1960s, there have also been smaller but notable decreases in the participation rates of men in the so-called prime

---

[5] Note that when labor force participation rates are changing, cross-sectional data on participation rates by age, as shown in Figure 4.3, may give a misleading impression of the actual experiences of individual women over the life cycle. For a fuller explanation of this issue, as well as an interesting analysis of cohort patterns of married women's participation, see Goldin, *Understanding the Gender Gap,* pp. 21–23.

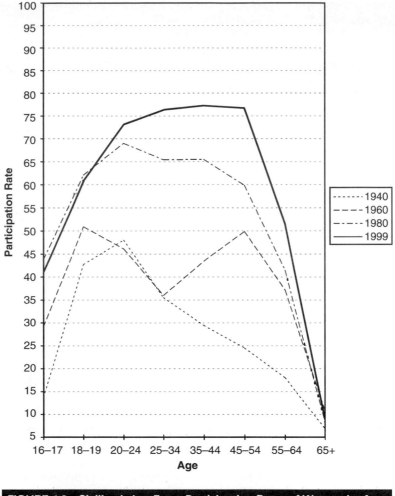

FIGURE 4.3   Civilian Labor Force Participation Rates of Women by Age

working ages, not only those 45 to 54 but even those 25 to 44. Participation rates for these age groups remain relatively high, however, with over 90 percent of 25- to 44-year-olds, and 89 percent of 45- to 54-year-olds in the labor force.

TRENDS IN LABOR FORCE ATTACHMENT

The changes in the pattern of women's labor force participation by age that have occurred since 1940 suggest that rising female participation rates have been associated with an increase in the labor force attachment of women over the life cycle. That is, women are tending to remain in the labor force more consistently over a period of time.

Some indication of women's increasing labor force attachment is provided in Table 4.3. This table shows the **labor force participation rate,** which, it may be recalled, is the

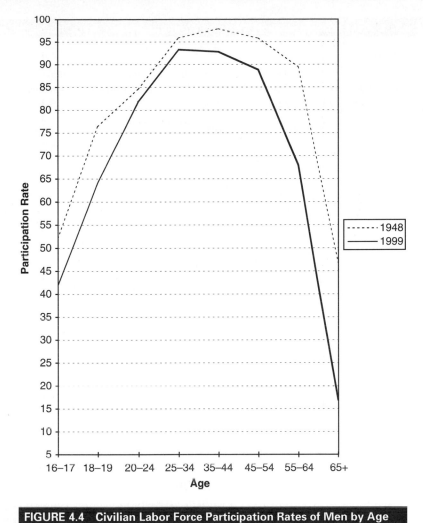

FIGURE 4.4   Civilian Labor Force Participation Rates of Men by Age

percentage of a particular group (say, women) who are in the labor force *at a point in time*. It also shows the **labor force experience rate,** which is the percentage of women who are in the labor force *at some time during the year.* If the same group of women was in the labor force consistently over the year, the labor force participation rate would exactly equal the labor force experience rate, and there would be no *turnover* of the labor force group. Alternatively, if women tended to move into and out of the labor force over the year, the labor force experience rate would exceed the labor force participation rate. In this case, the group of labor force participants would include some different individuals at different points in time (that is, there would be *turnover* in the labor force group).

The **labor force turnover rate** is an indicator of labor force attachment and tells us the extent to which the composition of the labor force group *turns over* during the year. It is equal to the difference between the labor force experience rate and the labor force

TABLE 4.3 Labor Force Turnover of Men and Women Selected Years, 1957–1998 (percent)

	Males			Females		
Year	Labor Force Participation Rate	Labor Force Experience Rate	Labor Force Turnover Rate	Labor Force Participation Rate	Labor Force Experience Rate	Labor Force Turnover Rate
1957	81.9	88.2	7.8	35.8	47.3	32.1
1967	80.4	86.7	7.8	41.1	53.1	29.2
1977	77.7	83.4	7.4	48.4	58.2	20.1
1987	76.2	79.8	4.7	56.0	62.3	11.3
1998	74.9	77.5	3.5	59.8	64.6	8.0

Notes: Civilian labor force. The labor force participation rate is the proportion of individuals in the labor force during the reference week (annual averages). The labor force experience rate is the proportion of individuals in the labor force at some time during the year. The labor force turnover rate is the difference between the labor force experience rate and the labor force participation rate divided by the labor force participation rate.

Sources: 1957–1977 data are from Cynthia B. Lloyd and Beth T. Niemi, *The Economics of Sex Differentials* (New York: Columbia University Press, 1979), Table 2.6, p. 71. Copyright 1980 by Columbia University Press. Reprinted with permission of the publisher. Later data are from U.S. Department of Labor, Bureau of Labor Statistics, "Working-Age Population with Some Employment Rose to New High in 1987," News (August 22, 1988); and "Work Experience of the Population in 1998," News (January 31, 2000).

participation rate divided by the labor force participation rate.[6] Now to get a better idea of what the labor force turnover rate measures, let's consider a couple of examples. At one extreme, suppose that 50 percent of women participate in the labor force at any point in time (LFP = 50) and that all of them stay in the labor force throughout the year (LFE = 50). Then the labor force turnover rate would be zero. There is no turnover in the group of women who are in the labor force. Toward the other extreme, now suppose that all women are in the labor force at some point during the year (LFE = 100), but that at any particular point in time only 50 percent of women are observed in the labor force (LFP = 50). The labor force turnover rate would now be 100 percent: (100–50)/50 = 1 and we then multiply by 100 to express the turnover rate as a percentage. This means that the labor force group turns over completely over the course of the year as each woman works about half a year on average.

As may be seen in Table 4.3, in 1957, the labor force turnover rate of women was nearly one third, considerably higher than the male rate of 7.8 percent. The female rate has declined considerably since then, indicating that women are becoming more firmly attached to the labor market. Although the female turnover rate is still higher than the male rate, the gender differential has fallen considerably. By 1998, the female rate was 8.0 percent compared to a male rate of 3.5 percent. A further indication of women's increasing labor force attachment is that the percentage of women workers who are employed full-time, year-round has been increasing steadily since the mid-1960s, from 37

---

[6] It may be clearer to consider the formula for the labor force turnover rate as follows:
LF Turnover Rate = (LFE – LFP)/LFP, where LFE is the labor force experience rate and LFP is the labor force participation rate. Generally LFE and LFP are both expressed as percentages and the labor force turnover rate would be multiplied by 100 so as to express it as a percentage as well.

percent in 1963 to 58 percent in 1999. Seventy-four percent of male workers worked full-time, year-round in 1999.

This growing labor force attachment of women has contributed to the rise in their labor force participation rate. The labor force group is increased by entries into the labor force and decreased by exits from the labor force. When the number of entrants exceeds the number of those who leave the labor force, the size of the labor force is increased. Thus, both *increases* in flows of *entrants* and *decreases* in flows of *exits* potentially contribute to the growth of the female labor force. The data in Table 4.3 suggest that both of these factors have played a role in increasing the female participation rate. Labor force experience rates have risen, indicating that entries have increased. However, at the same time, participation rates have risen by *more than* experience rates, indicating that women are remaining in the labor force more continuously (that is, exits from the labor force have decreased).

As we shall see in greater detail in Chapter 6, work experience is an important determinant of labor market earnings. The lesser amount of work experience of women relative to men has traditionally been cited as an important reason for their lower earnings. It is not immediately obvious, however, whether or not recent increases in women's labor force participation have been associated with increases or decreases in the *average* amount of work experience of the female labor force. Two changes that would tend to have opposite effects are going on here. On the one hand, the growing number of new entrants, who have worked only a short time, has a negative effect on the average labor market experience of women workers. On the other hand, the growing tendency for women to remain in the labor force for longer periods of time has a positive effect.

Unfortunately, the usual published statistics on labor force participation do not help to answer the question of what the net effect of women's increased labor force participation on their average experience has been because data on work experience are not collected. However, from time to time, estimates have been made from special surveys that explicitly ask respondents about their labor market experience, as well as less directly from information on labor force entry and exit rates. The evidence suggests that before the late 1960s, rising female labor force participation rates were associated with constant or slowly increasing average levels of work experience among women workers, but in recent years, notable gains in women's average experience levels have occurred.[7] Again, these trends are discussed in greater detail in Chapter 6.

THE LABOR SUPPLY DECISION

In Chapter 3, we examined the division of housework and market work between husband and wife. Here we focus upon the closely related question of how an individual, whether a wife, husband, or single individual, decides on the allocation of his or her

---

[7] Goldin, *Understanding the Gender Gap,* pp. 37–41; James P. Smith and Michael P. Ward, "Time Series Changes in the Female Labor Force," *Journal of Labor Economics* (January 1985, supp.); June O'Neill and Solomon Polachek, "Why the Gender Gap in Wages Narrowed in the 1980s," *Journal of Labor Economics* 11, no. 1, pt. 1 (January 1993): 205–28; and Francine D. Blau and Lawrence M. Kahn, "Swimming Upstream: Trends in the Gender Wage Differential in the 1980s," *Journal of Labor Economics* 15, no. 1, pt. 1 (January 1997): 1–42.

time between the home and the labor market. We again use a neoclassical model and assume that the individual's goal is to maximize utility or satisfaction.[8] A brief preview of our conclusions may be helpful in following the more detailed analysis presented below. The economic model suggests that individuals decide whether or not to participate in the labor force by comparing the value of their time in the market given by their hourly wage rate (w) to the value they place on their time spent at home (w^*). If the value of time in the market is greater than the value of time spent at home ($w > w^*$), they choose to participate in the labor force. Alternatively, if the value of home time is greater than or equal to the value of market time ($w^* \geq w$), they choose to remain out of the labor force. After tracing out the reasoning behind this decision rule in this section, in the next section we analyze the long-run increase in women's labor force participation in terms of factors that have increased the value of their market time and lowered the value of their home time.

Individuals are viewed as deriving utility from the consumption of *commodities* (goods and services) that are produced using inputs of market goods and nonmarket time.[9] For example, the commodity, a family dinner, is produced using inputs of market goods (like groceries, cooking equipment, etc.) and the individual's own time in preparing the meal. In order to keep this model reasonably simple, we make the following three additional assumptions.

First, we assume that all income earned in the labor market is spent on market goods. This avoids the need to consider the determinants of savings and also means that we may use the terms *market income* and (the money value of) *market goods* interchangeably.

Second, we assume that all nonmarket time is spent in the production of commodities, whether the output is a loaf of bread, a clean house, a healthy child, or a game of golf. This approach not only avoids the need for analyzing a three-way choice among market work, housework, and leisure but also makes the often difficult distinction between nonmarket work (including volunteer work) and leisure unnecessary.[10] We do not wish to suggest, however, that in reality there is no difference between the two. Indeed, one of the concerns about the impact of married women's increased labor force participation on their welfare is that it has not been accompanied by a comparable reallocation of household chores. As a result, women are often saddled with the "double burden" of home and market work. This may reduce the leisure time available to them,

---

[8] As before, the underpinnings of the analysis are derived from the work of Gary S. Becker; see "A Theory of the Allocation of Time," *Economic Journal* 75, no. 299 (September 1965): 493–517; and Jacob Mincer, "Labor Force Participation of Married Women," in *Aspects of Labor Economics,* ed. H. Gregg Lewis, Universities National Bureau of Economic Research Conference Studies, no. 14 (Princeton, NJ: Princeton University Press, 1962), pp. 63–97. James Heckman and Reuben Gronau, among others, have made significant contributions to the development of statistical techniques for estimating the theoretical relationships; for an excellent review, see Mark R. Killingsworth, *Labor Supply* (Cambridge: Cambridge University Press, 1983).

[9] Students who have read the appendix to Chapter 3, where a graphical analysis of specialization and exchange was presented, will recognize that the basic approach employed here is quite similar. However, in this analysis, we do not need to make the rigid distinction between home goods (produced exclusively with inputs of home time) and market goods (produced entirely with market-purchased goods) that was used to simplify the analysis in the appendix to Chapter 3. Indeed, not only can we recognize that market goods and nonmarket time are both inputs into the production of commodities, but also that there may be more than one way to produce the same commodity.

[10] Market work is relatively easy to distinguish as any activity for which there is material, usually monetary, reward. But it is quite problematic to determine whether preparation of a gourmet meal, going to a League of Women Voters meeting, growing flowers, or taking a child for a walk is work or leisure.

impede their ability to compete with men in the labor market, or both. These issues were examined in Chapter 3.

Third, and perhaps even more crucially, we focus here on the individual rather than on the family as a whole. This is quite realistic when the individual is the only adult in the family. However, as we saw in Chapter 3, where more than one adult is present, the division of labor among them, and thus the labor supply decision of each, is reasonably expected to be a family decision. We do not introduce all the complexities of family decision making here for that would cause the exposition to become unduly complex. We do, however, view the individual in a family context by taking into account the impact of the earnings of other family members on each person's labor supply decision, but the labor supply of other members of the household is taken as given and is assumed not to be influenced by the individual's own choice. This assumption is probably less unreasonable when we consider women's labor supply decisions since, in most American families, husbands are still likely to remain in the labor market full-time regardless of their wives' participation decision. However, some research suggests that the husband's labor supply does respond to the wife's decision under certain circumstances and it is of course possible that this responsiveness has increased in recent years as the two-earner family has become increasingly the norm.[11]

Now that we have reviewed some of the assumptions of the model, we are ready to turn to analysis of the labor supply decision itself. In this model, as we have seen, both market goods and nonmarket time are used in the production of the commodities from which the individual derives satisfaction. Thus, the goal of the individual is to select the utility-maximizing combination of market goods and nonmarket time. Since market goods are purchased with income earned through market work, and all time available is spent either on market work or nonmarket activities, this is the basis of the labor supply decision. In making this choice, the individual must take into account both the options that are open to him or her, given by the *budget constraint* shown in panel a of Figure 4.5, and his or her tastes or preferences expressed in the family of *indifference curves* shown in panel b of Figure 4.5. Let us trace out this decision for the hypothetical case of a married woman named Mary.

THE BUDGET CONSTRAINT

The budget constraint shown in panel a gives the various combinations of nonmarket time and market goods from which Mary can choose, given her market wage rate and the nonlabor income available to her. The **wage** is the amount of money an individual earns for each hour he or she works; the wage is an hourly rate of pay. **Nonlabor income** is any income an individual receives, apart from his or her own labor market earnings. The amount of nonlabor income is thus unrelated to the amount of time the individual devotes to the labor market. Nonlabor income may include the earnings of a spouse, as

---

[11] The empirical evidence regarding the dependence of husbands' labor supply decisions and earnings on the decisions of their wives is mixed. For example, a study by Thomas Mroz found no evidence of such dependence; see "The Sensitivity of an Empirical Model of Married Women's Hours of Work to Economic and Statistical Assumptions," *Econometrica* 55, no. 4 (July 1987): 765–800. On the other hand, Shelly J. Lundberg finds that the presence of children is a crucial variable, with each spouse acting independently of the other's decision except when young children are present; see "Labor Supply of Husbands and Wives: A Simultaneous Equations Approach," *Review of Economics and Statistics* 70, no. 2 (May 1988): 224–35.

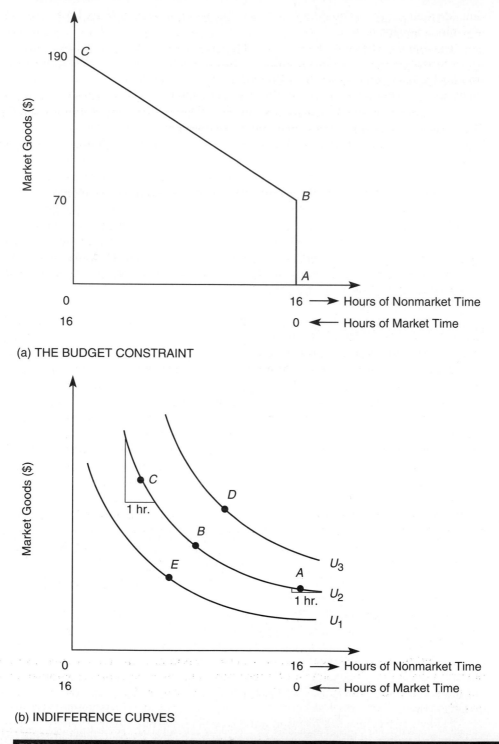

(a) THE BUDGET CONSTRAINT

(b) INDIFFERENCE CURVES

FIGURE 4.5 The Budget Constraint and the Indifference Curves

well as any income received from interest, dividends, or rental property. Government transfer payments, such as welfare or unemployment insurance, may also be considered nonlabor income, although the amount of income received from such sources is influenced by the amount of time a person supplies to the labor market. Hours of *nonmarket time* are measured from left to right along the horizontal axis.

We assume that Mary has a total of 16 hours available to her in a day to allocate between market and nonmarket activities (allowing 8 hours for nondiscretionary activities like sleeping). Since any of this time that Mary does not spend in nonmarket activities is spent in the market, hours of *market time* are measured from right to left along the horizontal axis.

Mary's nonlabor income is $70 a day. The vertical segment *BA* of the budget constraint shows that Mary has this income available to her even if she supplies no time to the labor market. She may further increase her money income by participating in the labor force. For each additional hour she supplies to the market, she must give up an hour of nonmarket time. In return she receives $7.50, her hourly market wage (*w*). Thus, segment *CB* is negatively sloped. Its slope is equal to –7.50 or –*w*. If Mary devotes all her time to the market, her total earnings will be $120 ($7.5 × 16). Her total daily income, including her nonlabor income, will be $190 ($120 + $70).

INDIFFERENCE CURVES

Mary's preferences for market goods and nonmarket time are represented by her indifference map, shown in panel b. As discussed previously, we can incorporate the family context of decision making into the budget constraint by including the income of other family members as part of the individual's nonlabor income. This issue is more difficult when we consider the indifference curves. One possibility would be to view the indifference curves in Figure 4.5 as representing the family's preferences for various combinations of market goods and Mary's nonmarket time. We do not adopt this approach because, as we saw in Chapter 3, preferences among family members may differ, and the process of arriving at family decisions is complex. However, it is important to recognize that our discussion of indifference curves as representing the individual's preferences is only an approximation. In fact, we expect that the individual's decisions are made in the context of the family and that the preferences of other family members have been taken into account in the decision-making process. Bearing this in mind, we now take a closer look at the indifference curves.

Suppose Mary is told that she could have the combination of market goods and nonmarket time represented by point *B*. She is then asked to find various other combinations of market goods and nonmarket time from which she would get exactly the same amount of satisfaction or utility and identifies the combinations represented by points *A* and *C*. These and other points, which represent equal satisfaction, can all be connected into one indifference curve, called that because she is indifferent about being at various points on the curve. Thus, each indifference curve indicates the various combinations of market goods and nonmarket time that provide Mary with the same amount of utility or satisfaction.

However, Mary has not just one indifference curve, but a whole family of higher and lower curves. A point like *D* on indifference curve U_3 is clearly preferable to *B* since it offers more of both market goods and nonmarket time. Thus, by extension, all points on U_3 are preferred to all points on U_2. Similarly, B is preferred to E and, thus, all the points on U_2 are preferred to all the points on U_1.[12] As we move out from the origin in a northeasterly direction, consumption possibilities, and thus potential satisfaction, increase.

Indifference curves are generally assumed to be convex to the origin. That is, they become flatter as we move from left to right and steeper as we move from right to left. This is the case because it is believed that individuals generally value relatively scarcer commodities more highly than relatively more plentiful ones. At point A, where nonmarket time is relatively plentiful and market goods are relatively scarce, Mary would be willing to exchange an hour of nonmarket time for a relatively small amount of income (market goods) and still feel equally well off. However, at a point like C, where market goods are relatively plentiful and nonmarket time is relatively scarce, it would take a lot of income (market goods) to induce her to give up an additional hour of scarce nonmarket time.

It is interesting to consider more closely the way in which an individual like Mary may substitute market goods for nonmarket time (or vice versa) along an indifference curve while still remaining equally well off. It is important to recognize that we assume she does not derive satisfaction directly from market goods and nonmarket time. Rather, she values them only insofar as they can be used to produce commodities.[13] Thus, broadly speaking, two types of substitution are involved.

Substitution in Consumption   Some commodities are relatively *goods intensive* to produce. That is, they are produced using relatively large amounts of market goods and relatively little nonmarket time. Examples of these include buying expensive antiques, furniture, and clothing or recreational activities such as dining out at an elegant restaurant or flying to the Caribbean for a short vacation.

Other commodities are relatively *time intensive*. That is, they are produced using relatively large inputs of nonmarket time and relatively fewer inputs of market goods. Examples of these include recreational activities like hiking, bird watching, going to a baseball game, or taking a cycling trip. Also, as anyone who has spent time caring for youngsters can attest, small children are a relatively time-intensive "commodity."

Substitution in consumption involves choosing among commodities so as to substitute goods-intensive commodities for time-intensive ones or time-intensive commodities for goods-intensive ones. When such substitutions are made along a given indifference curve, the implication is that the individual is indifferent between the two alternatives. So, for example, an individual may be indifferent between a goods-intensive vacation like staying for short time at a very expensive resort or a more time-intensive one of spending an extensive period hiking and backpacking. Or, more broadly, an individual might be indifferent between having a large family of time-intensive children and spending more time in recreational activities that are more goods intensive.

---

[12]   As noted in the appendix to Chapter 3, it should be clear that indifference curves can never intersect. All points on any one curve represent an equal amount of utility, while any point above (below) represents a larger (smaller) amount of utility. At the point where two curves intersect, they represent the same utility. Yet at all other points they do not. This is a logical impossibility.

[13]   The indifference curves used in this chapter are a graphical representation of what has been termed the individual's *indirect utility function;* see Becker, "A Theory of the Allocation of Time." Students who read the appendix to Chapter 3 will recognize that we took a different approach in the analysis presented there and simply assumed that families derive utility *directly* from market and home goods.

Substitution in Production   In many instances, the same commodity can be produced using a relatively time-intensive technique or a relatively goods-intensive technique. For example, a meal may be prepared from scratch at home, made with the use of convenience foods, or purchased at a restaurant. A clean house may be produced by an individual doing the work himself or herself or by hiring cleaning help. A small child may be cared for entirely by a parent, have a baby-sitter for a few hours a day, or spend all day at a child care center.

Substitution in production involves choosing among various ways of producing the same commodity so as to substitute goods-intensive production techniques for time-intensive ones or time-intensive production techniques for goods-intensive ones. Again, when such substitutions are made along a given indifference curve, the implication is that the individual is indifferent between the two alternatives. Examples here include those described above: preparing a meal at home versus eating out, hiring cleaning help versus doing it oneself, taking a child to a child care center versus taking care of the child oneself.

Substitution between Market Goods and Nonmarket Time   As an individual like Mary moves from point A to point B to point C along indifference curve U_2 in Figure 4.5, she is likely to exploit opportunities for substitution in both consumption and production. That is, she will substitute goods-intensive commodities for time-intensive commodities in consumption, and goods-intensive for time-intensive production techniques. As she continues to do so, she will exhaust many of the obvious possibilities. It will take larger increments of market goods to induce her to part with her scarcer nonmarket time. This is why the indifference curves are believed to get steeper as we move from right to left.

Comparing across individuals, the steepness of the indifference curve is influenced by how difficult or easy it is for them to substitute market goods for nonmarket time while remaining equally well off. This, in turn, will depend on their opportunities for substituting one for the other in production or consumption or both. For example, those who enjoy hiking very much will not easily be induced to decrease the time they spend on it. They will have steeper indifference curves, reflecting that they have greater difficulty in substituting market goods for nonmarket time in consumption than those who care less for such time-intensive activities.

Similarly, we would expect those whose services are in greater demand in the home (say, because small children are present) to have steeper indifference curves, reflecting their greater difficulty in substituting market goods for nonmarket time in production. Tastes and preferences will be a factor here, too. People who feel very strongly that children should be cared for full-time by their own parent and that alternative care is an extremely poor substitute will have steeper indifference curves than those who believe that adequate alternative care can be provided.

This analysis assumes that there is some degree of substitutability between market goods and nonmarket time. However, it has been pointed out, quite correctly, that there are some commodities that cannot be purchased in the market. Various personal services and management tasks provided in the home may be of this nature. Similarly, there are some commodities available in the market that cannot be produced at home. Examples of this range from sophisticated medical care and advanced education to means of transportation and communication, insurance, and many consumer durables.[14] Nonetheless, it is highly likely that when all commodities are aggregated together (as in the indifference curves shown in Figure 4.5) some substitution possibilities between market goods and nonmarket time exist. Given that, the ease or difficulty of substitution is represented by the steepness of the indifference curves.

Tastes   Beyond considerations of this kind, economists generally do not analyze the determinants of individuals' preferences for income (market goods) versus nonmarket time. However, it is important to point out that individuals do not operate in a social vacuum. Their tastes and behavior are undoubtedly influenced by social attitudes and norms.[15] For example, the willingness of a woman to substitute purchased services for her own time in child care is undoubtedly influenced by the social acceptability of doing so. Yet it is probably true that attitudes follow behavior to some extent, as well. Thus, it is likely, for example, that it has become more acceptable for mothers of small children to work outside the home in part because it has become more common for them to do so.

A woman's relative preference for income (market goods) versus nonmarket time also reflects a variety of other factors not generally emphasized by economists. As we saw in Chapter 3, women may value earning their own income for the economic independence it brings and to enhance their relative power position in the family. An increasing number of women value career success in much the same way their male counterparts do, which also affects the shape of their indifference curves.

Although such considerations do not invalidate the use of this model in analyzing women's labor supply decisions, they do serve to make us aware that the term *tastes* (or *preferences*), as economists use it, covers a lot of ground. This is particularly important as we attempt to explain women's rising labor force participation over time.

THE PARTICIPATION DECISION

Let's suppose that Mary's indifference curves and her budget constraint are those shown in panel a of Figure 4.6. Mary will maximize utility or satisfaction at point Y where the budget constraint just touches the highest attainable indifference curve, U_2. At Y, the amount of income needed to induce her to give up an additional hour of nonmarket time, given by the slope of the indifference curve at Y, exactly equals the market wage she is offered for that hour, given by the slope of the budget constraint. That is, the budget constraint is tangent to the indifference curve at Y. Mary, therefore, supplies 8 hours per day to the market and spends 8 hours on nonmarket activities. Her daily earnings of $60 ($7.50 × 8) plus her daily nonlabor income of $70 give her (and her family) a total income of $130 per day.

It is interesting to consider in greater detail why Mary does not select point A, where she would supply no time to the labor market. At A, where indifference curve U_1 intersects the budget constraint, it is *flatter* than the negatively sloped portion of the budget constraint (which passes through point A and point 190 on the market goods axis). This means that, at point A, Mary values her nonmarket time *less* than the wage the market is willing to pay her for it. Thus, she will certainly choose to supply some time to the market.

---

[14]   Nancy Folbre and Julie A. Nelson, "For Love or Money—Or Both?" *Journal of Economic Perspectives* 14, no. 4 (fall 2000): 123–40; and Clair (Vickery) Brown, "Home Production for Use in a Market Economy," in *Rethinking the Family: Some Feminist Questions,* ed. Barrie Thorne (New York: Longman, Inc., 1981).

[15]   The importance of social norms is particularly emphasized by Clair Brown, "An Institutional Model of Wives' Work Decisions," *Industrial Relations* 24, no. 2 (spring 1985): 182–204.

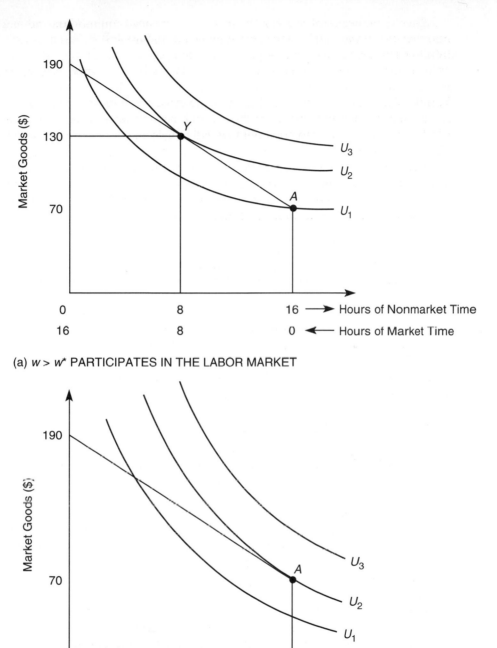

(a) $w > w^*$ PARTICIPATES IN THE LABOR MARKET

(b) $w < w^*$ DOES NOT PARTICIPATE IN THE LABOR MARKET

FIGURE 4.6   The Labor Force Participation Decision

Another woman, Joyce, faces the same budget constraint as Mary but has steeper indifference curves (shown in panel b of Figure 4.6). Perhaps she has more young children to care for than Mary. In Joyce's case, the budget constraint touches the highest attainable indifference curve at point A. At A, the indifference curve is steeper than the budget constraint. This means that Joyce sets a *higher* value on her nonmarket time than the wage rate she is offered in the market. She will maximize her utility by remaining out of the labor force, spending all 16 hours available to her on nonmarket activities. Her consumption of market goods will be limited to her nonlabor income of $70 per day.

The slope of the indifference curve at zero hours of market work (point A in panels a and b of Figure 4.6) is termed the **reservation wage** (w^*). It is equal to the value the woman places on her time at home. If the market wage is greater than the reservation wage (that is, $w > w^*$), as in panel a, the individual will choose to participate in the labor market. If the reservation wage is greater than or equal to the market wage (that is, $w^* \geq w$), as in panel b, the individual will choose not to participate. This decision rule can be summarized by the following simple equations:

$w > w^* \Rightarrow$ in the labor force
$w^* \geq w \Rightarrow$ out of the labor force

This economic analysis suggests that factors that increase the value of market time (w) tend to increase the probability that the individual will choose to participate in the labor force, all else equal. That is, labor force participation is *positively related* to the wage or the value of market time. On the other hand, factors that increase the value of nonmarket time (w^*) tend to lower the probability of labor force participation, other things being equal. That is, labor force participation is *negatively related* to the reservation wage or the value of nonmarket time.

THE VALUE OF NONMARKET TIME (w^*)

As our previous discussion suggests, the value of nonmarket time is influenced by tastes and preferences and also by the demands placed on an individual's nonmarket time. Given the traditional division of labor in most families, the presence of small children, and other circumstances that increase the need for housework, particularly influence women's participation decisions.

Another factor that influences the value placed on nonmarket time is the availability of income from sources other than the individual's own work efforts. Figure 4.7 shows the impact of changes in nonlabor income on the labor force participation decision. Let's suppose that the figure represents the budget constraint and indifference curves for Susan, a married woman with two small children. Suppose that her husband is unemployed and that initially her budget constraint is *ABC*. This represents $30 of nonlabor income (from interest on some bonds the family owns) and her market wage of $7.50. She maximizes utility at point *D*, where she supplies five hours a day to the market and earns $37.50. This brings the family's total daily income to $67.50. Now suppose Susan's husband finds a job. When his earnings ($50) are added to the interest received from the bonds ($30), her nonlabor income becomes $80. Her new budget constraint is *AB'C'*. Note that segment *B'C'* is parallel to segment *BC*. This is because Susan's market wage rate, which is the slope of segment *BC*, remains unchanged at $7.50.

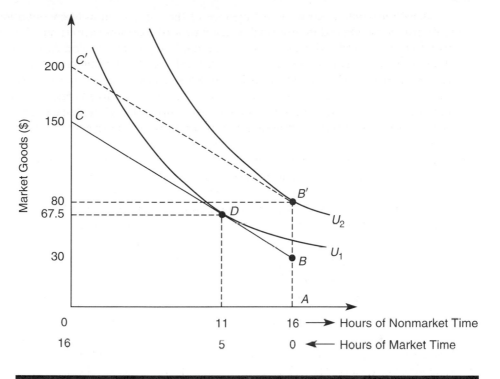

FIGURE 4.7   The Impact of Nonlabor Income on Labor Force Participation

At the higher income level, Susan's consumption possibilities have increased, and she is able to reach a higher indifference curve. She maximizes utility at B' where she has more of both market goods and nonmarket time, and supplies less time to the market; in fact, in this example, she withdraws from the labor force entirely. This represents the impact of the **income effect.** Ordinarily, when individuals' incomes go up, they demand more of all commodities from which they derive utility. To the extent that nonmarket time is used to produce these commodities, an increase in income will increase the value of nonmarket time and result in less time spent in the labor market. The income effect will be relatively large when the demand for time-intensive commodities increases sharply with income. The individual then needs to transfer more time from market to nonmarket activities in order to produce them. This is likely to occur when market goods are not considered to be very good substitutes for home-produced items. So Susan, whose wage rate has not changed while her income increased, may choose to consume more recreation or spend more time caring for her children.

Table 4.4 illustrates the impact of the value of nonmarket time (w^*) on women's labor force participation decisions, using actual data on female participation rates by marital status and presence and age of children. Marital status reflects in part the availability and level of alternative sources of income. Thus, we see that, in 1999, within children's age categories, women who are married, spouse present, are generally less likely to work outside the home than never-married women and other ever-married women. The latter includes women who are separated from their husbands, divorced, or widowed. Further evidence for the importance of the value of home time is provided by studies that have found that, among married women, labor force participation is negatively related to husband's income, all else equal.[16] It may be recalled that we expect an increase in the wife's nonlabor income to raise the value of her nonmarket time ($w*$).

The impact of children on women's labor force participation may be discerned by comparing the participation rates of women with small children (children under 6) to the rates for women with school-age children (children 6–17), within each marital status category. We see that the presence of small children has a negative effect on women's participation, no doubt because they greatly increase the value of time spent at home. Of course, the causation may, to some extent, run in the opposite direction. That is, women who are more committed to the labor market or who face more attractive labor market opportunities may choose to have fewer children. It is very difficult to distinguish between these two possible explanations for the association between women's labor force participation and the presence and age of children.[17]

TABLE 4.4 Labor Force Participation Rates of Women by Marital Status and Presence and Age of Youngest Child, 1966, 1988, and 1999

Marital Status	*Total*	*No Children Under 18*	*Children 6–17*	*Children 3–5*	*Children Under 3*
1966					
Never married	40.8	n.a.	n.a.	n.a.	n.a.
Married, husband present	35.4	38.4	43.7	29.1	21.2
Other ever married	39.5	34.7	65.9	57.5	38.6
1988					
Never married	65.2	67.3	67.1	53.9	40.1
Married, husband present	56.5	48.9	72.5	61.2	54.5
Other ever married	46.1	38.1	77.5	67.0	52.4
1999					
Never married	68.1	67.1	82.7	77.5	62.3
Married, husband present	61.6	54.4	77.1	65.7	59.2
Other ever married	49.4	40.9	81.8	79.1	73.8

Notes: Data are for March of each year and include women 16 years of age and over in 1999 and 1988, and 14 years of age and over in 1966.

n.a. Not available.

Sources: U.S. Department of Labor, Bureau of Labor Statistics, *Special Labor Force Report,* no. 2163, Table B-5, p. 16; U.S. Department of Labor, Bureau of Labor Statistics, Bulletin 2340 (August 1989), Tables 55–57, pp. 35–44; and unpublished data from U.S. Department of Labor, Bureau of Labor Statistics.

---

[16] See, for example, the studies reported in James P. Smith, ed., *Female Labor Supply: Theory and Estimation* (Princeton, NJ: Princeton University Press, 1980).

[17] See, for example, Robert Willis, "What Have We Learned from the Economics of the Family?" *American Economic Review* 77, no. 2 (May 1987): 68–81; and Martin Browning, "Children and Household Economic Behavior," *Journal of Economic Literature* 30, no. 3 (September 1992): 1432–75. The statistical problem in identifying the causal effect of children on labor supply is that, as in any problem of this type, it is necessary to find a variable that determines the number of children but does not directly influence labor supply. For an interesting new approach using variation in the sex mix of the first two children as well as

Within each marital status category, participation rates among women with no children under 18 tend to be low compared to those with children present. In each case, this represents the age structure of the women in this category. Married and other ever-married women with no children under 18 tend to be older women whose children have left home. This is particularly true of other ever-married women, since this marital status category includes widows. This also explains the extremely low participation rate of other ever-married women overall. The relatively low participation rate of never-married women with no children under 18 is due to this being a younger group, on average. It thus includes many young women who are still completing their education and who may be out of the labor force for this reason.

The data in the table also illustrate some interesting trends in the impact of marital status and the presence of children on labor force participation. Although the presence of small children was an important determinant of women's labor force participation throughout this period, women with small children were considerably more likely to work outside the home in the 1990s than in the 1960s. For example, in 1999, 59 percent of married women with children under three years old were in the labor force, compared to only 21 percent in 1966. Similarly, 66 percent of married women with children between the ages of three and five were labor force participants in 1999, compared to 29 percent in 1966.[18]

The differences in participation rates by marital status are also considerably smaller today than they were 30 years ago. In addition, within the group of married women, wives' participation decisions have become less sensitive to their husbands' income in recent years and more sensitive to their own market opportunities, that is, to the wage they can earn in the market.[19] In this way too, married women's behavior has become more similar to that of their nonmarried counterparts.

Table 4.4 also suggests some interesting differences in trends between the mid-1960s and the late 1980s, on the one hand, and the late 1980s and late 1990s on the other. The 1966 to 1988 period was characterized by especially large increases in the labor force participation rates of married women. In 1966 the participation rate of married mothers was 17 to 28 percentage points lower than that of other ever-married mothers, depending on the age of their children. By the late 1980s, among women with children aged 3 or more, the participation rates of married women were only 5–6 percentage points lower, and, among women with children under 3, married women were actually somewhat more likely to be in the labor force. And, while data on the participation rates of never-married mothers are not available for 1966, in 1988 married mothers were *more* likely to be in the labor force than never-married mothers with children in the same age category.

---

twin births as predictors of fertility, see Joshua D. Angrist and William N. Evans, "Children and Their Parents' Labor Supply: Evidence from Exogenous Variation in Family Size," *American Economic Review* 88, no. 3 (June 1998): 450–77; see also Joyce P. Jacobsen, James Wishart Pearce III, and Joshua L. Rosenbloom, "The Effects of Childbearing on Married Women's Labor Supply and Earnings: Using Twin Births as a Natural Experiment," *Journal of Human Resources* 34, no. 3 (summer 1999): 449–74.

[18] Statistical analyses controlling for other factors affecting the labor force participation of wives, including husband's income and education, confirm that very young children exert a smaller negative influence on wives' participation than formerly; see, for example, Arleen Leibowitz and Jacob Klerman, "Explaining Changes in Married Mothers' Employment Over Time," *Demography* 32, no. 3 (August 1995): 365–78.

[19] Chinhui Juhn and Kevin M. Murphy, "Wage Inequality and Family Labor Supply," *Journal of Labor Economics* 15, no. 1, pt. 1 (January 1997): 72–97.

In contrast, since the late 1980s, growth in labor force participation of married mothers has slowed and their participation rates actually leveled off in the late 1990s. At the same time participation rates have grown especially rapidly among single mothers with small children, particularly since the mid-1990s.[20] As a consequence, never-married mothers are now more likely to be in the labor force than married mothers with children in the same age category. Further, the gap in participation rates between married mothers and other ever-married mothers has widened.

THE VALUE OF MARKET TIME (*w*)

In addition to the impact of the value of nonmarket time, the labor force participation decision is influenced by the labor market opportunities an individual faces, particularly the wage rate available in the labor market. To see this in greater detail, let us consider the case of Ellen, who initially faces the budget constraint, *ABC,* shown in Figure 4.8. Her potential market wage is $8.00 per hour, while her nonlabor income (say, equal to her husband's earnings) is $100 per day. Given her tastes (represented by her indifference map), she maximizes utility at point *B* where she devotes all her time to nonmarket activities. Note that at point *B* the indifference curve (U_1) is steeper than the budget line (*BC*)—Ellen's reservation wage (*w**) is higher than the wage rate offered to her by the market (*w*).

Now suppose that Ellen's market opportunities improve and her potential market wage increases to $12.00. Her new budget constraint is *ABC'*. Segment *BA* of her budget constraint remains unchanged because it is still the case that if she remains out of the labor market entirely, she (and her family) will receive $100 a day of nonlabor income. However, *BC'* is steeper than *BC* because she now receives $12.00 for each hour she supplies to the market rather than $8.00. Another way to see this is to realize that *C'* must lie above *C* because, if Ellen devotes all her time to market work, her total income at a wage of $12.00 per hour ($292) will be higher than it would have been at a wage of $8.00 per hour ($228).

At the higher wage, the budget constraint (*BC'*) is now steeper than the indifference curve at point *B*—the market wage (*w*) is greater than the reservation wage (*w**), and Ellen maximizes her utility at point *E* on indifference curve U_2, where she supplies five hours to the market. Thus, Ellen now chooses to participate in the labor force.

This example illustrates the **substitution effect.** An increase in the wage rate, all else being equal, raises the opportunity cost of time spent in nonmarket activities and, hence, the "price" of nonmarket time. Individuals are expected to respond by supplying more time to the market and substituting market goods for nonmarket time in consumption or production. Since the wage increase has clearly enabled Ellen to reach a higher indifference curve, we may conclude that she feels better off with the combination of commodities represented by point *E,* even though she has less nonmarket time available at *E* than at *B*.

---

[20] Rebecca M. Blank, "Distinguished Lecture on Economics in Government—Fighting Poverty: Lessons from Recent U.S. History," *Journal of Economic Perspectives* 14, no. 2 (spring 2000): 3–19; and Bruce D. Meyer and Dan T. Rosenbaum, "Making Single Mothers Work: Recent Tax and Welfare Policy and Its Effects," National Bureau of Economic Research Working Paper No. 7491 (January 2000).

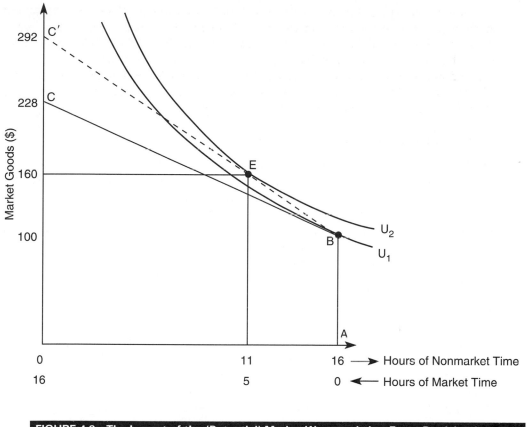

Published data are not readily available on participation rates of individuals by the wage they could potentially earn in the labor market. However, some indication of the impact of the potential market wage on labor force participation may be gained by examining the association between educational attainment and labor force participation. This is because, as we shall see in greater detail in Chapter 6, education is strongly positively associated with labor market earnings. A common interpretation of this empirical relationship is that education increases market productivity and hence market earnings. This would lead us to expect that education would be positively associated with labor force participation. One qualification worth noting, however, is that, especially for women, the positive effect of education on labor force participation may be reduced to the extent that additional education also raises the productivity of women's nonmarket time. This would be the case if, for example, the time that more-educated women spend with their children contributed more to their children's achievement levels than time spent by less-educated women.

Nonetheless, as may be seen in panel a of Figure 4.9, there is a positive relationship between education and labor force participation among women. Those with higher levels of education are more likely to be in the labor force. This implies that the impact of

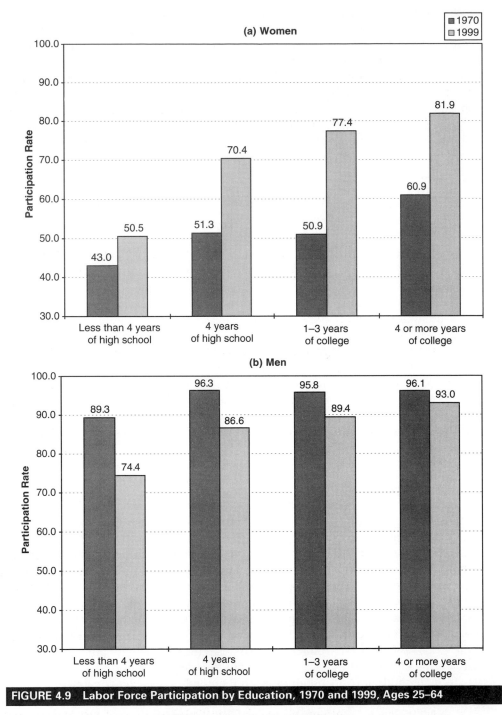

FIGURE 4.9   Labor Force Participation by Education, 1970 and 1999, Ages 25–64

Note: Educational categories are defined somewhat differently in 1999.

Source: U.S. Dept. of Labor, *Handbook of Labor Statistics,* 1989, and author's tabulations from the 1999 microdata file of the March *Current Population Survey.*

education on labor market earnings is greater than its impact on the value of home time and that we may interpret this positive relationship between education and labor force participation as reflecting a positive relationship between wages and labor force participation. However, it should be noted that the positive relationship between education and participation may also reflect self-selection: Women who plan to spend a relatively high proportion of their adult years in the labor force are more likely to invest in education. Finally, we may note that the jobs held by more educated individuals usually have greater nonpecuniary (or nonmonetary) attractions—such as a more pleasant environment, more challenging work, and so on—as well as higher wages. This calls attention to the fact that the value of market work should ideally take into account not only pecuniary benefits but also other aspects of the job.

Panel a of Figure 4.9 also shows that while education was a determinant of labor force participation in both 1970 and 1999, participation rates of high school graduates and of college-educated women increased substantially more over the period than they did for women who did not complete high school. This has resulted in a stronger relationship between participation and education in 1999 than existed in 1970. Panel b of Figure 4.9 indicates that a similar trend occurred among men. Although participation fell for all education groups, it decreased more for less-educated men.

At the same time that the participation of less-educated men and women decreased relative to their more educated counterparts over the past 25 years, their relative labor market wages were also falling. A trend toward widening wage inequality in the United States and to a lesser extent in many other economically advanced nations has resulted in widening wage differentials between more skilled and less-skilled workers. There is some evidence that the declining relative labor force participation of less-educated women and men is due at least in part to their declining market wage opportunities.[21] The trend toward rising wage inequality is considered in more detail in Chapter 8, where we review recent labor market developments. In addition to declining relative participation and wages, the economic status of less-educated women has also been adversely affected by a considerably faster increase in single headship among them than among their more highly educated counterparts.[22] As we shall see in Chapter 9, such families face considerable economic disadvantages.

THE HOURS DECISION

The impact of a change in the wage rate on the number of *hours* supplied to the market by those who are already labor force participants is a bit more complex than the impact of a wage change on *labor force participation*. This is illustrated in Figure 4.10. As we saw in Figure 4.8, an increase in the wage rate corresponds to an outward rotation of the budget constraint, since more market goods can now be purchased for every hour worked. This is shown in Figure 4.10 as a rotation from CD to CD'. In both panels a and b, the in-

---

[21]   Chinhui Juhn, "Decline of Male Labor Market Participation: The Role of Declining Market Opportunities," *Quarterly Journal of Economics* 107, no. 1 (February 1992): 79–121; and Juhn and Murphy, "Wage Inequality."

[22]   Francine D. Blau, "Trends in the Well-Being of American Women: 1970–1995," *Journal of Economic Literature* 36, no. 1 (March 1998): 112–165.

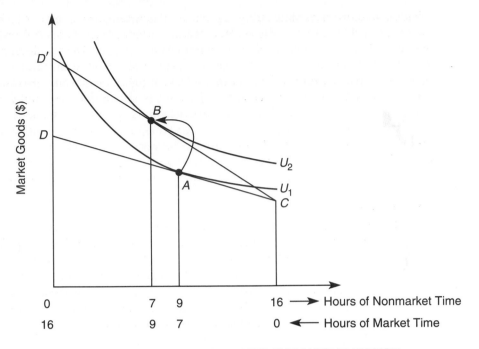

(a) THE SUBSTITUTION EFFECT DOMINATES THE INCOME EFFECT

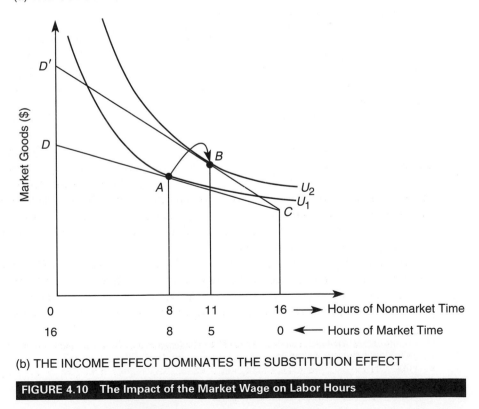

(b) THE INCOME EFFECT DOMINATES THE SUBSTITUTION EFFECT

FIGURE 4.10   The Impact of the Market Wage on Labor Hours

dividual initially maximizes utility at point *A* on indifference curve U_1. At a higher wage, he or she is able to reach a higher indifference curve and selects point *B* on indifference curve U_2. This may result in either an increase (shown in panel a) or a decrease (shown in panel b) in hours supplied to the market.[23] This is the case because, for those who are labor force participants, an increase in the wage rate has two distinct effects.

On the one hand, the increase in the wage is like an increase in income. For any given amount of time supplied to the market *greater than 0 hours,* income is higher along *CD'* than along *CD*. This gives rise to an *income effect* that, other things being the same, increases the demand not only for most market goods, but also for nonmarket time, and hence lowers hours supplied to the market. On the other hand, the increase in the wage also raises the opportunity cost of nonmarket time. This results in a *substitution effect* that, all else equal, causes a reduction in nonmarket time and an increase in the supply of hours to the market.

Thus, when the wage rate rises, the substitution effect operates to increase labor hours supplied, but the income effect operates to reduce labor hours supplied. The net effect is theoretically indeterminate. If the substitution effect dominates the income effect, work hours are increased (panel a). If the income effect dominates the substitution effect, work hours are reduced (panel b). Again, recall that a wage increase unambiguously raises the probability of labor force participation because, in this case, there is no offsetting income effect, only a positive substitution effect.

EMPIRICAL EVIDENCE ON INCOME AND SUBSTITUTION EFFECTS

Our analysis of the labor force participation decision and the hours of work decision of participants suggests the importance of distinguishing between these two types of decisions. In recent years economists have found that this distinction is indeed quite important empirically. For both men and women, the participation decision is much more responsive to income and wages than the hours of work decision of labor force participants. Early studies of labor force participation suggested that married women's labor supply was much more sensitive to wages and income than men's labor supply. Economists now realize that this impression arose in good part because the responsiveness of women's *participation* decisions, which tends to be rather large, was being compared to the responsiveness of men's *hours of work* decisions, which tends to be rather small. Women's overall labor supply response is influenced by their participation decisions to a greater extent than men's because a considerably higher fraction of women than men are out of the labor force.[24] It is, however, also true that even for the hours of work decision, married women's responsiveness to wages and income tends to exceed men's.[25]

Traditional gender roles may be one reason for the gender difference in the responsiveness to wage changes. As a group, men have traditionally worked full-time in the market and devoted most of their nonmarket time to recreation rather than household production. Although it is possible to substitute market goods for nonmarket time in

---

[23]   The diagrammatic representation of the effect of a wage change on work hours is shown in greater detail in the appendix to this chapter.

[24]   James J. Heckman, "What Has Been Learned About Labor Supply in the Past Twenty Years," *American Economic Review* 83, no. 2 (May 1993): 116–21.

[25]   See the survey in Killingsworth, *Labor Supply.*

recreational activities, these possibilities are necessarily limited. The situation is quite different for women, most of whom spend a great deal of nonmarket time doing housework. Since purchased goods and services are in many cases useful substitutes for nonmarket time in producing the commodities the family wants, the substitution effect is more likely to dominate the income effect for women than for men.[26]

As noted above, an interesting development for married women in recent years is that the positive relationship between employment and their own wages appears to have grown stronger over time while the negative relationship between employment and husband's earnings appears to have grown weaker. This suggests that married women's labor supply decisions are becoming more responsive to their own opportunities rather than to their family situation.

ECONOMIC CONDITIONS

Fluctuations in economic conditions also affect labor force participation. These effects are likely to be largest among demographic groups that contain a relatively high proportion of individuals who are loosely attached to the labor force. This would include teenagers and older individuals of both sexes and adult women in the so-called prime working ages. Economists view the response of labor force participation to the changes in the level of economic activity as being the net result of two opposing effects.

The **added worker effect** predicts that during economic downturns, if the primary earner becomes unemployed, other family members may enter (or postpone their exit from) the labor force in order to maintain family income. The decline in their nonlabor income due to the unemployment of the primary earner lowers the value of other family members' nonmarket time (w^*). (This is shown as a movement from point B' to point D in Figure 4.7.) Such individuals may leave the labor force when economic conditions improve and the primary earner is again employed on a regular basis.

At the same time, the **discouraged worker effect** holds that during times of high unemployment, when individuals lose their jobs, they may become discouraged and drop out of the labor force after a fruitless period of job search. Others who are outside the labor market may postpone labor force entry until economic conditions improve. Discouragement is due to the decline in the perceived reward to market work (w) because of the difficulty of locating an acceptable job. (This is shown as a movement from point E to point B in Figure 4.8.) As economic conditions improve, previously discouraged workers may renew their job search and enter the labor force.

Both these effects can operate at the same time for different households. The *net* effect of economic conditions on labor force participation depends on whether the discouraged or added worker effect predominates in the aggregate. This is an empirical question. The data suggest that for the labor force as a whole the discouraged worker effect is dominant. Thus, the labor force tends to shrink or grow less rapidly in recessions and to expand or grow more rapidly during upturns in the economy. One study finds that cyclical sensitivity is particularly pronounced for teenagers, older men, and women under 35.[27]

---

[26] This difference was first emphasized by Mincer, "Labor Force Participation of Married Women."

[27] Kim B. Clark and Lawrence H. Summers, "Demographic Differences in Cyclical Employment Variation," *Journal of Human Resources* 16, no. 1 (winter 1981): 61–79. There is evidence that the added worker effect also exists, though it is small; see Shelly Lundberg, "The Added Worker Effect," *Journal of Labor Economics* 3, no. 1 (January 1985): 11–37. Recent work suggests that one reason the added worker

SOME APPLICATIONS OF THE THEORY: TAXES, CHILD CARE COSTS, AND LABOR SUPPLY

Taxes and the Decision to Work   Not all money earned is actually at the disposal of the worker. Some of it has to be paid out in taxes. Because earnings are taxed and the value of home production is not, labor force participation among married women is discouraged. This effect is increased by the progressive nature of the tax system. Because the family (rather than the individual) is the tax unit, married women, often regarded as secondary earners within the family, face relatively high tax rates on the first dollar of their labor market earnings. In general, we expect that the higher the tax rate (the lower the after-tax wage), the more likely a woman is to decide not to participate in the labor force.

These points may be illustrated by Figure 4.8. Suppose Joan earns $12.00 per hour and faces budget constraint ABC'. If she has to pay out, say, one-third (33.3 percent) of her income in taxes, her after-tax wage (or hourly take-home pay) will be only $8.00. This situation is represented by budget constraint ABC. At this lower wage, Joan chooses to stay out of the labor market.[28]

One recent study used the reduction in the top marginal tax rates under the Tax Reform Act of 1986 to obtain empirical evidence about the labor supply response of married women to changes in the tax rate. In that legislation, the top rate was lowered from 50 to 28 percent. It was found that the reduction in the tax rate increased the labor supply of married women from very high-income families (who were most affected by the change) relative to women from less-affluent families (whose marginal tax rates were not affected). The reduction in taxes was estimated to have increased the participation rates of the high-income women by 8.4 percent.[29] Further consideration of the impact of the federal income tax on the labor supply of wives is provided in Chapter 10.

Government Subsidies of Child Care and Women's Labor Force Participation   As we have seen, young children are still a significant deterrent to the entry of their mothers into the labor market. Child care subsidies by the government could lower the cost of child care. What would be the expected effect on women's labor supply? We can use economic theory to see that a reduction in child care costs is expected to increase women's labor force participation.

Recall that so far we have assumed that individuals do not value market goods and nonmarket time in themselves, but rather because they can be used to produce commodities. This framework yields valuable insights into the possibilities of substitution in

---

effect has been found to be so small empirically is that receipt of unemployment insurance helps to counteract the negative effect on family income that would otherwise occur when the primary breadwinner becomes unemployed. See Jonathan Gruber and Julie Berry Cullen, "Does Unemployment Insurance Crowd out Spousal Labor Supply?" *Journal of Labor Economics* 18, no. 3 (July 2000): 546–72.

[28]   We have simplified the representation of a progressive tax in Figure 4.8 in that we show only one tax rate—the one Joan faces given her level of family income—and assume that additional hours worked do not push her into a higher tax bracket. In fact, as long as individuals are below the maximum rate, it is possible that as they work more hours their higher total income will push them into a higher tax bracket. Thus, the after-tax budget constraint may be "kinked," its slope becoming flatter each time the individual enters a higher tax bracket.

[29]   Nada Eissa, "Taxation and Labor Supply of Married Women: The Tax Reform Act of 1986 as a Natural Experiment," National Bureau of Economic Research Working Paper No. 5023 (February 1995).

consumption and in production, which help determine the steepness of the indifference curves. However, to examine the impact of the cost of child care explicitly, it will be more convenient to simply assume that the indifference curves represent the individual's preferences for market goods (income) versus nonmarket time.

Suppose Figure 4.8 represents the situation of Nancy, a woman with small children. To examine the impact of child care costs, we may view the hourly cost of child care that Nancy must pay if she works as a "tax" on her market earnings. If the budget constraint shows the wage Nancy receives after child care costs are subtracted out, it is clear that a decrease in child care costs is equivalent to an increase in the wage rate. For example, suppose Nancy can earn $14.00 an hour but must pay $6.00 an hour in child care costs. This results in a *net* wage of $8.00 per hour ($14.00 − $6.00 = $8.00), given by segment *BC*. At this wage, she chooses not to participate in the labor market. However, if her child care costs were to fall to $2.00 per hour, her net wage rises to $12.00 per hour ($14.00 − $2.00 = $12.00), given by segment *BC′*, and she would participate.

In this example, the decrease in child care costs results in Nancy deciding to enter the labor force. In general, we would expect the availability of child care at a lower price to increase the labor force participation rate of women with small children. The empirical evidence supports this expectation. For example, one study using data from the mid-1980s found that, for married mothers with children under 13, participation would increase from 58.8 percent to 64.0 percent if child care were subsidized by 50 percent. If universal no-cost child care were available, the participation rate of this group would rise to 68.7 percent.[30] A recent study using data from the early to mid-1990s sheds further light on this relationship. This study found that the labor force participation of the least skilled women is most responsive to the market price of child care, suggesting that the price of child care is a particularly strong determinant of labor force participation for this group.[31]

A decline in child care costs is also likely to have long-run effects on women's labor supply and wages. Because women would experience shorter (and possibly fewer) labor force interruptions, they would accumulate longer and more continuous labor market experience. This would be expected to have a favorable effect on the types of jobs they are able to obtain and on their earnings, and would in turn further reinforce the tendency toward spending more time in the labor market.[32] Therefore, in the long run, a reduction in child care costs is likely not only to raise women's labor force participation, but also to enhance their occupational attainment and earnings. Thus, child care subsidies could contribute to a reduction in labor market inequality between men and women. Whether or not such subsidies are desirable on other grounds is considered in greater detail in Chapter 10.

[30] Rachel Connelly, "The Effect of Child Care Costs on Married Women's Labor Force Participation," *Review of Economics and Statistics* 74, no. 1 (February 1992): 83–90. See also David M. Blau and Philip K. Robins, "Child-Care Costs and Family Labor Supply," *Review of Economics and Statistics* 70, no. 3 (August 1988): 374–81; and Jean Kimmel, "The Effectiveness of Child-Care Subsidies in Encouraging the Welfare-to-Work Transition of Low-Income Single Mothers," *American Economic Review* 85, no. 2 (May 1995): 271–75. For further analyses of the impact of child care costs on women, see James J. Heckman, "Effects of Child Care Programs on Women's Work Effort," *Journal of Political Economy* 82, no. 2 (March/April 1974, supp.): S136–63; and Myra H. Strober, "Formal Extra Family Child Care—Some Economic Observations," in *Sex, Discrimination, and the Division of Labor,* ed. Cynthia B. Lloyd (New York: Columbia University Press, 1975).

[31] Patricia M. Anderson and Phillip B. Levine, "Child Care and Mothers' Employment Decisions," National Bureau of Economic Research Working Paper No. 7058 (March 1999).

[32] For evidence that current work experience increases the probability of future participation due to its effect on wages, see Zvi Eckstein and Kenneth I. Wolpin, "Dynamic Labour Force Participation of Married Women and Endogenous Work Experience," *Review of Economic Studies* 56, no. 3 (July 1989): 375–90.

The Contribution of Nonmarket Production to Gross Domestic Product

Gross domestic product (GDP) is the total money value of all the goods and services produced by factors of production located within a country over a one-year period. No one doubts that unpaid activities like housework and volunteer work are valuable to households and to the community, but at present these contributions are not included in GDP estimates. The results of this omission are potentially serious. GDP is considerably underestimated. Comparisons of GDP between countries are distorted to the extent that the relative sizes of household and market sectors differ. Finally, within a country, the growth in GDP is overstated if women reduce home production as they work more in the labor market.

A major obstacle to including these contributions in GDP is lack of agreement on an acceptable way to estimate the value of time spent in nonmarket production.[*] There are two fundamentally different methods, each with its own strengths and drawbacks. Economists, for the most part, tend to use the **opportunity cost approach,** which sets the value of unpaid work equal to the income the person could earn in the labor market. It meshes well with the theory of labor supply in which individuals who participate in the labor force equate the value of nonmarket time to the market wage rate. For individuals who do not participate in the labor market, the value of nonmarket time must be at least as great as the potential market wage.

However, despite its theoretical appeal, there are a number of difficulties with this approach. First, for those who are out of the labor force, we have the nontrivial problem of estimating their potential market earnings. Second, although the market wage is known for those who are employed, the presumption that it accurately represents the value of nonmarket time may not be correct. Many workers do not have the option of working precisely as long as they wish but must work a specified number of hours or forgo an otherwise desirable job. Hence, they may not be able to divide their time so that the value of the last hour spent at home is exactly equal to their wage rate.

In addition to these problems, while correct application of the opportunity cost approach may identify the value of the nonmarket production to individuals and their families, it results in a higher value being placed on the nonmarket production of those whose (potential) market productivity is higher. So, for example, an hour spent scrubbing floors by a college graduate is valued more highly than an hour spent by a high school graduate in the same activity. This is the case even if the quantity and quality of their nonmarket production is identical.

The main alternative to the opportunity cost approach is the so-called **market cost approach,** which sets the value of nonmarket production equal to the cost of hiring someone to do it. This method is not free of difficulties either. The main one is the need to make sure that the purchased item is of equal quality and, for that matter, that it is possible to purchase it. What qualifications must a housecleaner, a cook, a gardener, and a baby-sitter have to adequately replace the services of a homemaker and parent? Is it possible to delegate

---

[*] See, for instance, Barnet Wagman and Nancy Folbre, "Household Services and Economic Growth in the U.S., 1870–1930," *Feminist Economics* no. 1 (spring 1996): 43–66; Carmel U. Chiswick, "The Value of a Housewife's Time," *Journal of Human Resources* 17, no. 3 (summer 1982): 413–25; and Martin Murphy, "The Value of Nonmarket Household Production: Opportunity Cost Versus Market Cost Estimates," *Review of Income and Wealth* 24, no. 3 (September 1978): 243–55.

such tasks as directing children's upbringing and planning and budgeting for the household?

One approach to estimating market value is to first determine how much time is spent on each individual activity, itself a very difficult task, and then to use the wages of such specialists as cooks, home decorators, chauffeurs, and even child psychologists to estimate the value of nonmarket time. This may be unrealistic in that it is unlikely that the typical homemaker has all these skills to the same extent that such specialists do. Another alternative is to value unpaid home work at the wage of a domestic worker. However, there are elements of "personal and emotional care" in much nonmarket work, such as caring for one's own children, that would not be fully captured in such market-based estimates, suggesting that estimates for some types of activities might be too low.[†]

The arguments presented here suggest that obtaining estimates of the value of unpaid work, while difficult, would be useful. Clearly, a first step in measuring the value of unpaid work is to collect data on time spent in such activities including unpaid housework, yard work, child care, and elder care. Unfortunately, the major government survey on work in the United States, the *Current Population Survey,* does not specifically ask about time spent in unpaid activities, though a national time-use survey is currently being planned. In the meantime, the U.S. government has made use of existing time-use data from nongovernmental surveys to adjust the GDP figures for nonmarket production in satellite GDP accounts, which can be compared alongside the standard national accounts.[‡] Based on this work, it is estimated that by ignoring nonmarket output GDP was underestimated by 24 percent in 1997. Estimates for earlier years are even higher because a larger fraction of women were full-time homemakers and household technology was less advanced.[§] Such measures could be used to supplement existing data on GDP, or GDP could even be redefined to include the value of unpaid work, though this might raise comparability issues with past GDP data. Thus, this remains a controversial issue.

Another question that might be raised about including the value of unpaid work in GDP is whether it would affect the status of women as a group, since they are of course disproportionately involved in this activity. Here too, there is some considerable controversy. Some argue that the exclusion of unpaid work from GDP in some sense brands it as "unproductive." In this view, assigning money value to housework would favorably affect women's status because it would gain recognition for the activities of women in the home and validate their economic contributions.[‖] Others dispute this contention and believe that the inclusion of housework in GDP would not fundamentally affect the status of women since it would not make housewives more independent, nor raise the wages of women who perform these services for pay.[#]

[†] Folbre and Nelson, "For Love or Money."

[‡] National Research Council, *Time-Use Measurement and Research* (Washington, DC: National Academy Press, 2000). A similar effort to collect time use data is also underway in Canada, Australia, and several of the Scandinavian countries.

[§] J. Steven Landefeld and Stephanie H. McCulla, "Accounting for Nonmarket Household Production Within a National Account Framework," *Review of Income and Wealth* Series 46, no. 3 (September 2000): 289–307.

[‖] See Susan Himmelweit, "The Discovery of 'Unpaid Work': The Social Consequences of the Expansion of 'Work,' " *Feminist Economics* 1, no. 2 (summer 1995): 1–19; and Nancy Folbre, *Who Pays for the Kids? Gender and the Structures of Constraint.* London: Routledge, 1994.

[#] Barbara R. Bergmann, "The Economic Risks of Being a Housewife," *American Economic Review* 71, no. 2 (May 1981): 81–86.

ANALYZING TRENDS IN WOMEN'S PARTICIPATION: AN OVERVIEW

In the remaining sections of this chapter we apply the theoretical model of labor supply to analyze some of the major trends in labor force participation described at the beginning of this chapter. In this section, we provide an overview of the factors responsible for the long-term increase in women's labor force participation over the course of the twentieth century. In the following sections, we take a closer look at a number of subperiods of particular interest. We first consider explanations for the dramatic rise in female labor force participation during World War II and the further increase that occurred during the post–World War II baby boom. We then analyze the period of the 1960s to the 1980s when there were especially sharp increases in the labor force participation rates of married mothers of young children and then the 1990s when growth in the participation rates of this group slowed but that of single mothers with young children increased substantially. Next, we consider explanations for the long term decrease in men's labor force participation rates and conclude with an examination of the reasons for differences in labor force participation trends of blacks and whites.

Why did female labor force participation rise over the course of the twentieth century? Drawing upon the analysis presented earlier in this chapter, the obvious answer to this question is that a shift toward more market work by women can be explained by a rise in the wage rate (w), a decrease in the value of time spent in the home (w^*), or both. There is considerable evidence of developments that would be expected to have each of these effects and also of complex interactions, reinforcing the original results.[33]

FACTORS INFLUENCING THE VALUE OF MARKET TIME (w)

A variety of factors caused the real (inflation-adjusted) wages of women to increase over time. The result was an outward rotation of the budget constraint, as shown in Figure 4.8. Under these circumstances, more women are expected to find that the wage offered them by the market exceeds their reservation wage and to choose to enter the labor force. This process does not require that women's wages increase relative to men's wages. During the 1950s and 1960s both men's and women's real wages were rising and the gender gap remained roughly constant. For much of the period since 1970, men's real wages were stagnant or declining, while women's real wages increased overall and rose particularly sharply in the 1980s. During this time the gender pay gap narrowed.

Rising Qualifications: Education and Experience   As young women received more education, the wage rate they were able to earn by working in the market went up and they were more likely to work outside the home. At the same time, once women were more inclined to work for pay, they would want to obtain more market-oriented schooling in order to be able to obtain better-paying jobs.

---

[33] See Goldin, *Understanding the Gender Gap,* for an interesting econometric analysis of these trends in labor force participation.

The magnitude of this phenomenon can be gauged by the enormous increases in the proportion of the population that has graduated from high school or obtained college degrees. Between 1940 and 1998, the proportion of women who had completed at least four years of high school increased from 26 to 83 percent. The increase for men was even greater, from 23 to 83 percent, since initially women were more likely to graduate high school than men.[34] During this same period, the proportion of women who completed four or more years of college increased from 3.8 to 22.4 percent, whereas for men the proportion rose from 5.5 to 26.5 percent.

The statistics for higher education reflect the fact that traditionally more young men than young women completed college and pursued graduate study. However, this gender differential has declined since the late 1960s. Women have been increasing their share of college, graduate, and professional degrees, as well as their representation in traditionally male fields of study. (Data on this are presented in Chapter 6.) Hence, although men's educational attainment has also increased over time, gender differences in educational attainment have narrowed substantially.

Women's increased expectation of participating in the labor force over the life cycle increased their incentives to invest in education and helped to narrow the gender gap in educational attainment at the college and graduate level. An additional factor increasing the returns to education was the growing number of years women could expect to live. Life expectancy at birth for women went up from 48 years around 1900 to 79 years toward the end of the century. Though most individuals retire by age 65, this increase in life expectancy meant that women were able to reap considerably higher rewards from education and on-the-job training over their lifetime, even if they took some time out for homemaking.

As women accumulated more labor force experience and responded to the increased incentives to invest in market-related education and on-the-job training, their potential market wages were further increased, raising the opportunity cost of nonmarket activities and, thus, further increasing their labor force participation.

The Demand for Female Labor   It is also frequently suggested that, first with industrialization and then with the movement to the postindustrial economy, the demand for workers in traditionally female clerical and service jobs increased and caused their wages to be higher than they otherwise would have been. The fact that women's occupations, and more recently sex-integrated occupations, have expanded more rapidly than male occupations tends to support this view.[35] Since, as discussed in Chapter 2, married women were barred from clerical employment by many large firms in the 1920s and 1930s, they did not fully benefit from this expansion in demand until marriage bars were abandoned in the 1950s.[36]

---

[34] There was a pronounced gender difference earlier in the century. In 1900 only two-thirds as many boys as girls graduated from high school. Note that the statistics presented on educational attainment here, which are from the *Statistical Abstract of the United States,* differ somewhat from those presented in Chapter 6. This is due to the age range, which is 25 years or over here, but 25–64 in Chapter 6.

[35] Valerie Oppenheimer, *The Female Labor Force in the United States: Demographic and Economic Factors Governing Its Growth and Changing Composition* (Westport, CT: Greenwood Press, 1976; originally published 1970), was the first to emphasize the expansion of female occupations.

[36] Goldin, *Understanding the Gender Gap.* Both Oppenheimer and Goldin attribute the increased willingness of employers to hire older married women in the 1950s to a decrease in the supply of young, single female workers. This was due to the small size of the cohort born during the 1930s coupled with the decline in the marriage age that occurred during the 1950s.

It is also quite likely that antidiscrimination legislation has increased the demand for women in traditionally male jobs since its passage in the mid-1960s.

Overall Productivity Increases   Women, like male workers, have benefited from increases in labor productivity due to growth over time in the capital stock and technological change, which exerted upward pressure on wages, all else equal.

FACTORS INFLUENCING THE VALUE
OF NONMARKET TIME ($w*$)

It would be a mistake, however, to ascribe the impetus for the persistent influx of women into the labor market solely to higher wage rates and to overlook those changes that influenced the relative value of nonmarket time. While changes in $w*$ are not directly measurable, our review of the changes in the various factors influencing $w*$ below suggests that their net effect was to decrease the value of nonmarket time. In any case it seems clear the value of nonmarket time did decline *relative to* market time and, thus, the proportion of women working for pay increased.

Availability of Market Substitutes and Technological Change   Among the most obvious changes was the increase in the availability of goods and services that had previously been produced in the home but that became increasingly available for purchase in the market. Not only did fruits and vegetables, in earlier days grown in the family garden, come to be available at the grocery, but in time they were cleaned, canned, frozen, and eventually often included in prepared dishes or even meals. First yarn, earlier spun at home, became commonly available; next it was cloth, and then ready-made clothing, now most often of the easy-care variety. Schools extended the hours and years of care provided for older children. For young children, nursery schools and, more recently, day care centers became more prevalent, while hospitals increasingly cared for the sick, and various types of care for the infirm and aged became more common. These are only a few examples of commodities that in earlier days were produced with large inputs of home time but that today require mainly expenditures of money.

At the same time, technological changes made housework easier and less time consuming. This includes important innovations like indoor plumbing and electrification of houses, as well as appliances, from sewing machines, vacuum cleaners, washing machines, and refrigerators to dishwashers and microwave ovens, which became increasingly common in U.S. households.

To be sure, some changes did have the opposite effect, such as the considerably higher cost and greater difficulty of finding domestic help. But by and large, market goods have become more substitutable for nonmarket time and technological change has made doing housework less taxing. As a result, women would be expected to be more willing to give up time at home in order to be able to do more market work, a change illustrated in Figure 4.6 by the flatter indifference curves shown in panel a as compared to the steeper indifference curves shown in panel b.

Thus, we see that the greater availability of goods and services for purchase as well as labor-saving technological change in the home have resulted in a decrease in the value of women's nonmarket time ($w*$) and caused their labor force participation to increase. At the same time, women's rising labor force participation tended to increase the demand for market goods and services that substitute for their time in the home or make house-work tasks easier, further encouraging development and production of such products.

Demographic Trends   Another important change that influenced relative preferences for home versus market time was the long-run decline in the birthrate, from 30.1 births per 1,000 population in 1910 to 14.6 per 1,000 by 1997. Because the rearing of young children, generally considered to be women's responsibility, is very time intensive, especially in the absence of adequate provision for their care outside the home, their presence used to be one of the strongest barriers to women's entry into the labor market. As we have seen, it is only since the 1960s that mothers of preschoolers are working outside the home to any significant extent, and even now their participation is lower than that of mothers with school-age children.

Not only is the period during which there are young children in the home more protracted as their numbers rise, but the longer the woman is at home, the less favorable the terms she is likely to encounter in the labor market upon her return, and the more likely she is to remain out permanently. As we have noted, women are, of course, aware of this and to some extent adjust family size to their work plans, as well as vice versa.

Just as women's labor force participation is influenced by, and in turn influences, their fertility, the same is true of marital stability. The divorce rate per 1,000 population per year went from 0.9 in 1910 to 4.3 in 1997. The divorce rate influences women's labor force participation in part due to its impact on the composition of the female population: Divorced women have considerably less nonlabor income than married women and are thus more likely to participate in the labor force. However, married women's behavior is affected by rising divorce rates as well. As they have become aware of the increasing probability of divorce, their participation has increased as a means of safeguarding their standard of living in case of a marital breakup.[37] The other side of the coin is that a two-earner couple can more readily afford to get divorced. The woman can count on her own income, rather than being completely dependent on the often grudging and uncertain support of an ex-husband; the man need not spend resources to fully support, or to avoid support of, an ex-wife.

Rising Husband's Income   Not all changes operated in the direction of lowering the value of nonmarket time. In particular, earnings of men increased more rapidly than the cost of living for most of the twentieth century. As their husband's real income goes up, all else equal, married women's labor force participation is reduced due to the income effect (Figure 4.7). As we have seen, however, for women, the positive substitution effect of their own rising real wages tends to more than offset the negative income effect due to the increasing real incomes of their husbands.[38] And, perhaps due to changing

---

[37]   William R. Johnson and Jonathan Skinner, "Labor Supply and Marital Separation," *American Economic Review* 76, no. 3 (June 1986): 455–69. The terms under which divorce is available can also affect the labor supply of married women; see, for example, Elizabeth H. Peters, "Marriage and Divorce: Informational Constraints and Private Contracting," *American Economic Review* 76, no. 3 (June 1986): 437–54; and Jeffrey S. Gray, "Divorce-Law Changes, Household Bargaining, and Married Women's Labor Supply," *American Economic Review* 88, no. 3 (June 1998): 628–42.

[38]   This was first pointed out by Mincer in "Labor Force Participation of Married Women." Claudia Goldin, *Understanding the Gender Gap,* presents evidence of a declining income elasticity of married women's labor supply over the twentieth century.

gender roles, married women's participation has become increasingly sensitive to their own wages and less sensitive to their husband's income in recent years. Finally, since the 1970s, men's real wages in general have been stagnating, and those of the less educated and unskilled have been declining in real terms.[39]

Tastes   Over time, the development of many desirable market products that could not be produced in the home, like automobiles, air conditioning, television, CD players, and personal computers, increased people's preferences for market-produced goods and reduced the relative value placed on nonmarket time.[40] Such changes in tastes may be related to broader trends like the growing urbanization of the population. The movement from country to city reduced the opportunity for household production (say, growing and processing vegetables) and increased the convenience of market purchases as well as access to market work. Even leisure activities changed from those that mainly required time—hiking, swimming in the waterhole, and chatting on the front porch—to others that required substantial expenditures—going to the theater, concerts, and sporting events, watching television, listening to CDs, and surfing the Web.

It is also entirely possible that the trend toward rising female participation rates itself was responsible for further changes in tastes. It was probably far more difficult for women to enter the labor force in the past when it was the exception than today when it has almost become the rule. Shifting cultural norms, encouraged in part by the example of more women working in the market, have led women to place a higher value on the independence and autonomy that their own earnings bring, and, increasingly, many value career success in much the same way as their male counterparts. In addition, to the extent that people want to keep up with the Joneses in their consumption standards, it takes two paychecks to keep up with the two-earner families of today.

THE WORLD WAR II EXPERIENCE

As we saw in Table 4.1, there was a sharp rise in the female labor force participation rate during World War II, particularly among married women. The rate declined sharply in the immediate post–World War II period, although it remained above prewar levels and began its long-term rise shortly after that. In this section we explain these changes by considering factors influencing the value of market time (w) and nonmarket time (w^*). Overall, the World War II experience illustrates the importance of both economic and social factors in causing changes in female labor force participation.

As men were mobilized for the armed forces and the need for workers rose at the same time, there was a large increase in demand for women to fill the available positions. This increase in labor market opportunities, which included relatively high-paying, traditionally male jobs, increased the potential market wages of women. At the same time, married women were urged to work outside the home to contribute to the war effort. This raised the nonpecuniary benefits of market work for women and lowered their

---

[39]   See, for example, Chinhui Juhn, Kevin M. Murphy, and Brooks Pierce, "Wage Inequality and the Rise in Returns to Skill," *Journal of Political Economy* 101, no. 3 (June 1993): 410–42; and Lawrence F. Katz and Kevin M. Murphy, "Changes in Relative Wages, 1963–87: Supply and Demand Factors," *Quarterly Journal of Economics* 107, no. 1 (February 1992): 35–78.

[40]   This factor is particularly emphasized by Brown, "An Institutional Model of Wives' Work Decisions."

subjective assessment of the value of nonmarket time. In addition, the birthrate, already relatively low in the Depression years of the 1930s, remained low during the war because many young men were away in the armed forces. And, many of the women whose husbands joined the military experienced a decrease in their nonlabor income, since "Uncle Sam" did not pay as much as civilian employment.

A further factor that worked to lower the value of home time for married women was that the government and some employers opened day care centers for children of employed mothers.[41] Even though there were not enough places for all such youngsters, this action increased both the supply, and the acceptability, of alternative care of children, at least for the duration of the war. Thus, the combination of an increase in the value of market time and a reduction in the value of nonmarket time induced a large increase in the proportion of employed women working outside the home.

In the immediate postwar period, each of these factors was reversed, helping to bring about the observed decline in women's participation rates. As men returned to the civilian labor force, many were able to reclaim their former jobs from the women who had held them during the war. This was the case because many union contracts reserved their former jobs for men who had left them for military service. Even in the absence of union agreements, some employers may have voluntarily done this because they felt it was the appropriate recompense for the veteran's wartime contribution. Moreover, whether or not a returning veteran claimed a specific job that had been held by a woman, the influx of returning males into the labor market certainly lowered the demand for women workers. And, husbands' earnings rose as they resumed civilian employment, increasing wives' nonlabor income.

In addition, social values changed and the employment of married women outside the home was once again frowned upon, now that the wartime emergency was over. Indeed, after enduring the major dislocations of the Great Depression of the 1930s followed by a world war of unprecedented proportions, there may understandably have been a desire to return to "normalcy," including traditional gender roles. This swing in attitudes likely also played a part in producing the upsurge in birthrates during the postwar period, discussed in the next section. Finally, when the wartime labor shortage was over, day care centers were perceived to be no longer needed and were closed. These changes combined to lower the benefits of market work relative to the value of home time and to reduce women's labor force participation rate in the immediate post–World War II period.

The operation of the long-term factors discussed in the preceding section meant that the postwar participation rate, while lower than the wartime peak, exceeded prewar levels. And we see the continued rise in participation rates that followed the war as being primarily due to fundamental economic and social factors. Yet the wartime experience may have hastened this process by helping to break down the attitudinal barriers to married women's employment outside the home and giving many women a taste of earning their own income. For example, historian William H. Chafe argues that the notion that woman's appropriate sphere was in the home was so deeply embedded that it took a cataclysmic

---

[41] Given public concern, both about stimulating maternal employment in war industries and about possible neglect of children, during the 1941–1943 period the federal government provided matching funds to induce states to provide day care centers. It has been estimated that 1.6 million children attended these programs. The best-known centers established by large private employers were those by Curtiss-Wright in Buffalo and by Kaiser in Portland. See Bernard Greenblatt, *The Changing Role of Family and State in Child Development* (San Francisco: Jossey Bass, 1977), pp. 58–60.

event like World War II to break down this normative barrier.[42] On the other hand, economic historian Claudia Goldin gives less weight to the influence of World War II on later trends, presenting evidence that the war had little *direct* effect on women's participation in the postwar years. Goldin found that more than half of the women working in 1950 had been employed in 1940 (that is, before the United States entered the war). Just 20 percent of those working in 1950 had entered the labor force during the war, and about half of the wartime entrants left the labor force sometime after December 1944. However, Goldin acknowledges that this evidence does not rule out *indirect* effects of the war, such as on views of women's roles or on the subsequent behavior of young women who were employed during the war and later returned to the labor force after dropping out for a time.[43]

THE POST–WORLD WAR II BABY BOOM

As noted previously, the long-run downward trend in birthrates was interrupted by the post–World War II baby boom. From 1946 to the mid-1950s, birthrates rose steadily, and they remained at relatively high levels until the early 1960s. Although some of this rise in birthrates was simply a result of the postponement of childbearing that had occurred during the Depression and the war years, much of it did indeed reflect an increase in family size in comparison to earlier periods. At the height of the baby boom, women averaged three births, considerably more than the replacement-level fertility rates of their Depression-era mothers. This means that the decline in the birthrate, which contributed to the rise in female labor force participation over the long run, does not help to explain it during the baby boom era.

How did participation rates increase in the face of the negative effect of high birthrates? The first point to be made is that the increase in birthrates would principally affect younger women (under age 35) in the prime childbearing ages, who would be most likely to have small children present. Recall that this was precisely the group for whom labor force participation rates did *not* increase over the 1940–1960 period (Figure 4.3). Rising participation rates were primarily due to the entry of older women (over age 35) with school-age or grown children. They were desirable workers from the employer's perspective, since they were from a generation that benefited from considerably more education than their elders had received: The rate of high school completion increased from 29 percent in 1930 to 49 percent in 1940.[44] Further, while the baby boom meant that young children would cause mothers to stay home, this was not so as the children grew older and more self-sufficient. Indeed, it might be argued that teenagers, and especially college students, need more money rather than time, especially now that young people tend to stay in school so much longer.

---

[42]   William H. Chafe, *The American Woman: Her Changing Social, Economic, and Political Role, 1920–1970* (Oxford: Oxford University Press, 1972). Similarly, Dorothy Sue Cobble emphasizes the dramatic impact the war years had on the attitudes of women workers, particularly the emergence of a new consensus on equal pay and a breakdown of the formerly near-universal consensus in favor of protective legislation for women; see Dorothy Sue Cobble, "Recapturing Working-Class Feminism: Union Women in the Postwar Era," in *Not June Cleaver: Women and Gender in Postwar America, 1945–1960,* ed. Joanne Meyerowitz, (Philadelphia: Temple University Press, 1994), pp. 57–83.

[43]   Claudia Goldin, "The Role of World War II in the Rise of Women's Work," *American Economic Review* 81, no. 4 (September 1991).

[44]   Goldin, *Understanding the Gender Gap.*

Second, during this period, economic factors were particularly favorable for rising female participation rates. Real wages were steadily increasing and economic conditions were relatively good.[45] Thus, both the continued rise in participation rates in this period and its concentration among older women can be explained in significant part by economic and demographic factors.

THE 1960S TO THE 1980S: INCREASED PARTICIPATION OF MARRIED MOTHERS

As we have seen, female labor force participation rates rose sharply from the 1960s to the 1980s, and the increases in participation were especially large for married mothers, including those with small children. In this section, we again use the tools of economic analysis to understand the factors responsible for this increase.

We begin by considering demographic factors that are expected to affect the value of home time (w^*). The post–World War II baby boom was followed by a baby bust, during which birthrates fell. By the late 1970s, total fertility rates had fallen below the replacement level and relatively low rates have continued since that time. This decrease in fertility would be expected to lower w^* and thus increase the labor force participation of women. In addition, increasing numbers of women began to postpone marriage and childbirth into their late twenties, thirties, or even early forties. This pattern of childbearing appears to be associated with stronger attachment to the labor market and a reduction in time spent out of the labor force for childrearing. A further demographic trend that encouraged rising participation rates was the sharp increase in the divorce rate, since divorced women are more likely to be in the labor force than married women. This trend may also have contributed to the increase in married women's participation as they sought to protect their family income in the face of a rising probability of a marital breakup. Although the divorce rate began to level off and even to fall slightly in the 1980s, it remains at a high level.

These demographic shifts, particularly the decline in fertility, would have most affected the labor force participation of younger women, and it may be recalled that it was exactly this group, women under age 45, who posted the largest gains in participation rates over this period.[46] Nonetheless, while these demographic factors have undoubtedly been important,[47] as we have seen, a major factor contributing to rising female labor force participation rates during this period was the increase in participation rates among married mothers, including those with small children present.

---

[45]   Goldin, *Understanding the Gender Gap,* finds that demand factors, in conjunction with the particularly large wage elasticity of supply that prevailed at that time for married women, largely account for the increase in participation that occurred during this period.

[46]   One reason for the decline in marriage rates for the baby boom cohort was the so-called "marriage squeeze." During the early part of the baby boom, from 1946 to 1955, the birthrate for each successive year was higher than the previous year's. This meant that women born during this period faced a worse "marriage market," that is, a shortage of men two years older who they would traditionally marry. Some evidence suggesting that this development contributed to the rise in female participation is presented in Shoshana Grossbard-Schechtman and Clive W. Granger, "Women's Jobs and Marriage, Baby-Boom Versus Baby-Bust," *Population* 53 (September 1998): 731–52 (in French).

[47]   Jacobsen, Pearce, and Rosenbaum, "The Effects of Childbearing," estimate that declining fertility explains between 6 and 13 percent of the increase in married women's labor supply between 1970 and 1980.

Economic conditions are a possible factor contributing to the rising labor force attachment of married mothers during this period, but here the picture is mixed. During much of the 1960s, real wages were rising and unemployment was relatively low, favorable conditions for increases in female labor force participation rates. However, during the 1970s and the early 1980s, the situation was more complex. A stagnating economy resulted in frequent bouts of high unemployment and little increase in real wages.[48] Moreover, while the economy expanded during the mid- to late 1980s, overall real wages did not increase. This raises the question of why married women's participation rates continued to rise despite these unfavorable economic conditions.

One obvious explanation is that, although real wages were not rising overall, they were increasing for women, particularly well-educated women. This may help to explain not only rising participation rates for women as a group, but also why participation rates have increased more slowly for less-educated women whose real wages have lagged. It further points to rising educational attainment of women as an additional factor increasing the wages they could earn in the labor market and hence their labor force participation. It is also possible that stagnating male incomes increased the impetus of married women to enter the labor force. However, recent research suggests that, just as rising real incomes of husbands did not forestall the rise in participation of their wives during earlier, more prosperous, times, the poor income performance of husbands does not explain much of the increase in wives' participation during the 1970s and 1980s. In both cases, the dominant factor was women's own labor market prospects.[49]

Rising real wages for a large proportion of women in conjunction with the demographic factors discussed above and the continued increase in women's educational attainment all contributed to the rise in participation rates over this period. However, a number of studies suggest that the increase in married women's participation during this time cannot be fully explained by changes in such measurable factors. It also reflects, in part, changes in women's responses to these factors, perhaps due to changing social attitudes, as women's participation has become less sensitive to the presence of small children and to their husband's income and more responsive to their own market opportunities (wages).[50]

One may speculate that changes in the work expectations of younger women help to explain some portion of the participation increase not due to changes in measurable factors. It may be recalled that prior to World War II, most women left the labor force permanently upon marriage and childbearing. It is quite likely that the older married women who entered or reentered the labor force during World War II and the early postwar period had not anticipated working during this stage of the life cycle but were drawn into the labor market by prevailing economic and social conditions.

---

[48]   The unstable economic conditions of the 1970s and early 1980s may, however, have contributed to the growth in participation by giving married women an incentive to enter the labor market as soon as possible rather than waiting to supply labor in a more uncertain future; see Francine D. Blau and Adam J. Grossberg, "Wage and Employment Uncertainty and the Labor Force Participation Decisions of Married Women," *Economic Inquiry* 29, no. 4 (October 1991): 678–95.

[49]   Juhn and Murphy, "Wage Inequality and Family Labor Supply."

[50]   See Goldin, *Understanding the Gender Gap;* David Shapiro and Lois Shaw, "Growth in the Labor Force Attachment of Married Women: Accounting for Changes in the 1970s," *Southern Economic Journal* 50, no. 2 (October 1983): 461–73; Juhn and Murphy, "Wage Inequality and Family Labor Supply"; and Leibowitz and Klerman, "Explaining Changes."

As the reentry pattern became firmly established, younger women could increasingly anticipate spending a substantial portion of their mature years in the labor force. They must also have learned, by observing the experiences of older women, that time spent out of the labor force was costly in terms of career advancement and earnings. To maximize their labor market earnings and to secure the more attractive jobs that were increasingly becoming available to women, they would have to increase their investment in market-oriented human capital and keep work force interruptions to a minimum. The development and dissemination of more effective contraceptive techniques, most importantly the birth control pill, was undoubtedly important in enabling women to achieve these goals.[51] As young women entered the labor force with greater training and higher work expectations, they were more likely to remain employed after the birth of a child or to return shortly thereafter. Further, once it had become socially acceptable for mothers of older children to work outside the home, it was not long before it was socially permissible for women with increasingly younger children to do so as well.

THE 1990S: INCREASED PARTICIPATION OF SINGLE MOTHERS

As we have seen, trends in the labor force participation rates of single and married mothers of small children diverged over the 1990s. Participation rates of single mothers expanded particularly rapidly during the 1990s, especially during the latter part of the decade. At the same time, growth in the participation rate of married mothers slowed, and participation rates of this group leveled off in the late 1990s. How do we explain these trends?

Starting with the trends for single mothers of small children, empirical analyses indicate that the increasing participation of this group reflects the impact of some important changes in government policy combined with a buoyant economy.[52] As of February 2000, the record U.S. economic expansion of the 1990s had lasted nearly nine years. Single female family heads are disproportionately low skilled, and an expanding economy disproportionately benefits less-skilled individuals. However, it is unlikely that economic expansion alone can fully account for the participation gains of single mothers over the past decade. Shifts in government policies that occurred at the same time reinforced the positive effects of the booming economy on the employment of this group.

As explained in greater detail in Chapter 10, welfare policies changed in the 1990s so as to provide greater incentives for individuals on welfare to be employed, as well as to leave the welfare rolls altogether. In addition, the Earned Income Tax Credit (EITC) was expanded several times in the 1990s. This raised the subsidy received by low income families with a working adult, and thus increased the incentive of single mothers to work outside the home.

The reasons for the slowing growth in the participation rates of married mothers with small children during the 1990s have not yet been analyzed. It would be tempting

---

[51] An especially interesting analysis is provided in Claudia Goldin and Lawrence F. Katz, "Career and Marriage in the Age of the Pill," *American Economic Review* 90, no. 2 (May 2000): 461–75.

[52] This section draws heavily on Blank, "Fighting Poverty." See also Meyer and Rosenbaum, "Making Single Mothers Work"; and Nada Eissa and Jeffrey B. Liebman, "Labor Supply Response to the Earned Income Tax Credit," *Quarterly Journal of Economics* 111, no. 2 (May 1996): 605–37.

to attribute this development, at least in part, to favorable economic conditions as well. That is, given better employment prospects for their husbands, some women who might otherwise have entered the labor force may have chosen not to do so. However, during the 1970s and 1980s, the dominant economic factor explaining the increase in women's labor force participation was their *own* labor market opportunities. Moreover, empirical studies suggest that married women's participation behavior has been getting more sensitive to their own opportunities and less sensitive to their husbands' incomes over time. This makes it unlikely that husbands' employment prospects would provide the entire explanation for the slowing growth in married mothers' participation, but we must await empirical studies of the 1990s to resolve this issue. In any case, it is perhaps not surprising that growth in the participation rates of married mothers would eventually taper off as those women who could most readily participate in the labor force, and had the greatest incentives to do so, had already entered.

ANALYZING TRENDS IN MEN'S PARTICIPATION

The changes in men's labor force participation patterns, while less dramatic than women's, are nonetheless quite significant. The decline in the participation rates of younger men (Figure 4.4) is mainly due to their tendency to remain in school longer. This in turn reflects the ever-increasing skills demanded by our advanced economy. Expenditures on education are more profitable to the individual when they are made relatively early in the life cycle, since this results in a longer period over which to reap the returns to this investment in the form of higher earnings. Finally, with rising real incomes, families were better able to keep their children in school longer because they could afford to pay the bills and also to forgo the contribution their children might otherwise have made to family income.

The declining participation rates of older males are often viewed as evidence of the dominance of the income effect over the substitution effect. As real wages have risen over the course of the century, men's demand for nonmarket time appears to have increased. One indicator of this is that the full-time workweek declined from 60 hours at the turn of the century to about 40 hours in the 1940s and remains at about that level today. Further, *annual hours* of full-time workers have declined as paid vacations, holidays, and sick leave have become more prevalent.[53] The increased propensity of men to retire at earlier ages is seen as part of this pattern. In addition, the provision of Social Security and the growing coverage of private pension schemes, while in part a transfer of income from earlier to later years, also created an income effect that encouraged older males to retire.[54]

We may note that the same factors that have influenced the labor force participation of younger and older men have also impacted the participation of women in these

---

[53] For an analysis of these trends, see Thomas J. Kniesner, "The Full-Time Work Week in the U.S.: 1900–1970," *Industrial and Labor Relations Review* 30, no. 1 (October 1976): 3–15. Since 1940, trends in work hours of both men and women have diverged between the more and less educated, with rising annual hours worked for well-educated workers and decreasing annual hours among the less educated; see Mary T. Coleman and John Pencavel, "Changes in Work Hours of Male Employees, 1940–1988," *Industrial and Labor Relations Review* 46, no. 2 (January 1993): 262–83; and Mary T. Coleman and John Pencavel, "Trends in Market Work Behavior of Women Since 1940," *Industrial and Labor Relations Review* 46, no. 4 (July 1993): 653–76.

[54] See Patricia M. Anderson, Alan L. Gustman and Thomas L. Steinmeier, "Trends in Male Labor Force Participation and Retirement: Some Evidence on the Role of Pensions and Social Security in the 1970s and 1980s," *Journal of Labor Economics* 17, no. 4, pt. 1 (October 1999): 757–83.

age groups. As may be seen in Figure 4.3, the long-term increases in the participation rates of women over 65 have been quite modest. In addition, the participation of younger women has recently declined somewhat as more of them are remaining in school for longer periods.

Figure 4.4 also shows a decline in the participation rate of prime-age males, which is smaller than that for younger and older men, but is nonetheless significant. This development appears closely connected to the declining relative demand for less-skilled workers, which has depressed their relative wages.[55] This is suggested by Figure 4.9b, which shows that participation rates have dropped most markedly for less-educated males. The decrease in participation of prime-age males may also reflect the greater provision in recent decades of disability income under government programs to older men below conventional retirement age. In the absence of such programs, more men with disabilities would probably have been forced to seek work.[56] Less-skilled men are disproportionately affected by the provision of disability income because the opportunity cost to leaving the labor force is less for low-wage workers. The empirical evidence suggests that the availability of disability income was more important in the 1960s and 1970s than for the more recent period when declining market wages were the dominant influence. Since black males are a less-educated and less-skilled group, on average, they would be particularly affected by these developments. This, in addition to their high unemployment rates, which tend to discourage labor force participation, may help to explain why the participation rates of black males have been declining at a faster pace than those of white males.

The decline in male labor force participation in the prime working years may also, to some extent, reflect the impact of the increased employment of women outside the home. As the two-earner family has become the norm, the additional income may induce some (still relatively few) males to leave the labor force for periods of time, say, to retool for a midlife career change.

BLACK AND WHITE PARTICIPATION DIFFERENTIALS: A CLOSER LOOK

Since the 1950s, black male participation rates have declined faster than those of white males, while black female participation rates have increased at a slower pace than those of white females (though the period from 1995 to 1999 is a recent exception). As a result, black male participation rates are now considerably below those of white males, while black female participation rates are now only a few percentage points higher than those of white females.

We have seen previously that, among both men and women, the participation of less-educated individuals has been declining relative to the participation of the more highly educated. Since blacks have less education, on average, and are more likely to have dropped out of high school than whites, they would be disproportionately affected by the overall trends toward lower participation among this group. This possibility is examined more closely in Table 4.5, which gives white and black participation rates separately by educational category for 1970 and 1999.

---

[55] Juhn, "Decline of Male Labor Market Participation."

[56] Donald Parsons, "The Decline in Male Labor Force Participation," *Journal of Political Economy* 88, no. 1 (February 1980): 117–34.

In the case of males, black rates were lower than white rates in all education categories except college graduates in 1970, and declined relative to the white rates in each category over the 29 years. However, the decrease was largest among dropouts, where the race gap increased from 3.1 percentage points in 1970 to 21.4 points in 1999. This is especially striking in that the white decrease in participation was largest for this group.

Thus, the data in Table 4.5 indicate that participation trends for poorly educated males have been even more unfavorable for blacks than whites. This suggests that declining labor market opportunities for the less educated in general may explain a portion of the race trends in participation among men, but do not appear to fully account for them.[57] Moreover, this situation for less-educated males in general, and especially blacks, is even worse than the figures in Table 4.5 suggest. The data presented in the table, as well as the other data presented in this chapter, focus on the civilian, noninstitutional population. Not included in such tabulations are those in institutions, including the incarcerated. The fraction of the population that is institutionalized has been increasing among blacks, especially less-educated blacks, but has been fairly stable among whites. In 1990, fully 7.4 percent of black men who had not completed high school were institutionalized, compared to 1.9 percent of less-educated white men.[58]

The reasons for the especially poor employment outcomes of blacks compared to whites with similar educational attainment have not been fully identified. However, the disadvantaged economic status of blacks undoubtedly plays a role. The black unem-

TABLE 4.5   Participation Rates by Race and Education, 1970 and 1999, Ages 25–64

	1970			*1999*		
	Whites	*Blacks*	*Difference*	*Whites*	*Blacks*	*Difference*
			WOMEN			
I. Total	47.9	59.0	−11.1	72.7	75.1	−2.4
II. By Education						
less than 12 years	41.6	51.3	−9.7	49.2	54.1	−4.9
12 years	50.3	65.8	−15.5	70.2	73.6	−3.4
13 to 15 years	49.3	75.8	−26.5	76.9	81.5	−4.6
16 or more years	59.0	92.0	−33.0	81.8	88.0	−6.2
			MEN			
I. Total	94.0	89.4	4.6	88.8	78.2	10.5
II. By Education						
less than 12 years	89.8	86.7	3.1	77.8	56.4	21.4
12 years	96.6	94.0	2.6	87.6	79.7	7.8
13 to 15 years	96.0	92.2	3.8	90.4	84.8	5.5
16 or more years	96.4	97.0	−0.6	93.5	89.5	4.0

Source: Authors' tabulations from the 1970 and 1999 March *Current Population Surveys*.

---

[57]   Juhn, "Decline of Male Labor Market Participation"; and Chinhui Juhn, "Black-White Employment Differential in a Tight Labor Market," in *Prosperity for All? The Economic Boom and African Americans,* ed. Robert Cherry and William M. Rodgers III (New York: Russell Sage Foundation, 2000), pp. 88–109.

[58]   Amitabh Chandra, "Labor-Market Dropouts and the Racial Wage Gap: 1940–1990," *American Economic Review* 90, no. 2 (May 2000): 333–338.

ployment rate is considerably higher than the white rate: Even in the midst of a boom year like 1999, when the white unemployment rate stood at 3.7 percent, the black rate was 8.0 percent. As we saw earlier, the net effect of high unemployment rates is to discourage labor force participation.

Among women, blacks had higher participation rates than whites in all education categories in 1970. This was still the case in 1999, although their participation advantage had declined considerably in all education groups. Thus, the relative participation picture for black women was more favorable than that for black men. This more favorable picture for black women reflected the considerable increase in their participation rates between the mid-1990s and the end of the decade, which we noted earlier. In 1995, white women had somewhat higher participation rates than black women overall and among the less educated. The relative participation gains for black women in the late 1990s reflect sizable increases in the participation of less-educated black women. For example, the participation rate of black women with less than a high school education increased from 45.9 percent in 1995 to 54.1 percent in 1999; the increase was from 67.8 percent to 73.6 for black women with 12 years of education. These may be compared to increases from 47.7 percent to 49.2 percent for white women with less than a high school education and from 69.2 to 70.2 percent for white women with 12 years of education.[59] These trends are likely tied to the growth in participation rates of single mothers during this period that we discussed previously, since, within each education category, black women are more likely to be single-family heads than are white women.[60] In addition, given their extremely high unemployment rates, blacks as a group are likely to have benefited disproportionately from the decline in unemployment that occurred over the late 1990s.

CONCLUSION

We began by reviewing the trends in male and female participation rates. We found that while female labor force participation rates increased over the course of the last century—from 20 percent in 1900 to 28 percent in 1940 and 60 percent in 1999—male participation rates declined from 87 percent in 1950 to 75 percent in 1999. We then turned to the economic theory of labor supply to gain insight into the determinants of labor force participation in order to better understand these trends, as well as differences in participation across various groups.

We conclude this chapter with a consideration of the outlook for the future. Predictions are always hazardous, and the past record of economists and demographers in this respect is not entirely encouraging. Nonetheless, the fundamental importance of the growth in women's labor force participation for the transformation in gender roles that has occurred in recent years calls for some comment about reasonable expectations for the future.

Some guidance about the future can be obtained by a careful scrutiny of the past; recent developments may be particularly instructive. As we have seen, the steep increase in female participation rates slowed in the 1990s, with the pace of growth declining to somewhat less than half the rate of earlier decades. Indeed, as may be seen

---

[59] See Table 4.5 and comparable data from Francine D. Blau, Marianne A. Ferber, and E. Winkler, *The Economics of Women, Men, and Work,* 3rd ed. (Upper Saddle River, NJ: Prentice Hall, 1998), p. 117.

[60] Blau, "Trends in the Well-Being of American Women."

in Figure 4.2, the long-term upward trend was actually interrupted between 1989 and 1991, when no growth in female participation rates occurred. While this "pause" might reasonably be attributed to the recession, it is also true that participation increases were somewhat fitful over the rest of the decade, with years of rising participation alternating with years of stability. What does all this mean for the long run?

First, and most importantly, there is no indication that women are increasingly forsaking market work for traditional homemaking roles. Of course, some women have always chosen that option, at least for a period of time, and that continues to be true. However, there is no sign of an upsurge in such behavior, despite the leveling off of participation rates of married mothers with small children that occurred in the late 1990s.

Second, now that 77 percent of women in the prime working ages (25–54) are labor force participants, it is perhaps to be expected that the female labor force will grow more slowly. However, we consider it extremely unlikely that women's participation rate will decline in the foreseeable future. At a minimum, we would expect the proportion of women in the labor force to continue at the present level. Even that seems unlikely, as women continue to accumulate more market-oriented education and increasingly enter nontraditional fields with higher returns. In addition, today's young women who have far higher labor force participation during their childrearing years than earlier cohorts are more likely to remain employed continuously up to retirement age. Thus, the Bureau of Labor Statistics (BLS) projection that 62 percent of adult women will be in the labor force by the year 2008, an increase of 2 percentage points over the 1999 level of 60 percent, appears quite reasonable.[61]

As for the labor force participation of men, one factor influencing future trends is retirement behavior. Participation rates of males over 65 are already quite low, so there is not too much room for additional large decreases there, although there is scope for further substantial declines in the participation rates of men ages 55–64. However, fiscal problems with the Social Security system have resulted in legislation to gradually increase the age when full benefits become available, which might be expected to offset the trend toward early retirement somewhat. On the other hand, the worsening job market for less-skilled men has produced increasing labor force withdrawals of prime-age males, as well as less-educated older men, and it is not clear whether or not this trend will abate in the foreseeable future. Weighing these considerations, we would expect men's labor force participation to decline somewhat further. The BLS projects an additional decrease of 1 percentage point in the male participation rate, from 75 percent in 1999 to 74 percent in 2008, and this too seems reasonable. Should there be a dramatic shift toward acceptance of men and women as equally responsible for earning income and homemaking, there could be a larger decline, but we do not anticipate such a change.

Combining the two projections, we expect a further reduction in the differential in labor force participation between men and women, though we do not expect it to disappear entirely for a long time to come. Under the BLS projections, the gap between the male and female participation rates would decline from 15 percentage points in 1999 to 12 percentage points in 2008. The full magnitude of the change becomes clear when we remember that this differential was 66 percentage points at the turn of the century.

---

[61] See Howard N. Fullerton Jr., "The Labor Force: Steady Growth, Changing Composition," *Monthly Labor Review* 122, no. 11 (November 1999): 19–32.

APPENDIX

The Income and Substitution Effects: A Closer Look

As discussed in Chapter 4, for labor force participants, an increase in the wage rate has an uncertain effect on hours supplied, all else equal. This is illustrated in greater detail in Figure 4.11. The *overall* effect of the wage change is shown (in panels a and b) by the move from point *A* to point *C*. It may be broken down into two distinct components, attributable to the income and substitution effects.

The income effect is represented by a hypothetical increase in income just large enough to get the individual to the higher indifference curve, U_2, leaving the wage rate unchanged. This would result in a move from point *A* to point *B*. For the reasons discussed earlier, the effect of the increase in income, all else equal, is unambiguously to reduce labor hours supplied to the market. The substitution effect is given by the impact of a hypothetical change in the wage (the slope of the budget constraint) along a given indifference curve, U_2. This results in a move from *B* to *C*. The substitution effect of an increase in the opportunity cost (or price) of nonmarket time, all else being equal, is unambiguously to increase labor hours supplied.

As may be seen in panel a, if the substitution effect is large relative to the income effect, *the substitution effect dominates the income effect* and the wage increase results in an *increase* in hours worked. Alternatively, as seen in panel b, if the income effect is large relative to the substitution effect, *the income effect dominates the substitution effect* and the wage increase results in a *decrease* in hours worked.

QUESTIONS FOR REVIEW AND DISCUSSION

* Indicates that question can be answered using an indifference curve framework as well as verbally. Consult with your instructor about the appropriate approach for your class.

1. Suppose that you have the following information for Country X.

Population:	100,000
Employed:	60,000
Unemployed:	3,000
Not in labor force:	37,000

    a. Calculate the size of the labor force, the labor force participation rate, and the unemployment rate.

    b. Provide examples of individuals who would be classified as "not in the labor force."

    c. What economic factors might shift a woman from "not in the labor force" to in the labor force? Discuss.

    d. Suppose there was an economic downturn. How would you expect this to affect the number employed, the number of unemployed, and the number classified as "not in the labor force"? Explain.

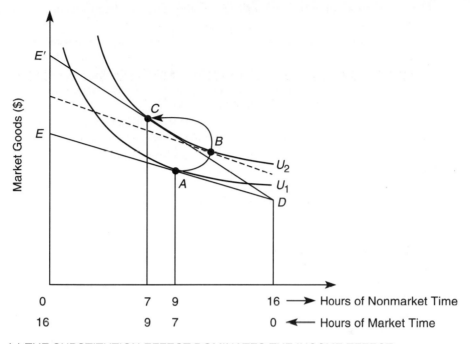

0   7   9   16 ⟶ Hours of Nonmarket Time

16   9   7   0 ⟵ Hours of Market Time

(a) THE SUBSTITUTION EFFECT DOMINATES THE INCOME EFFECT

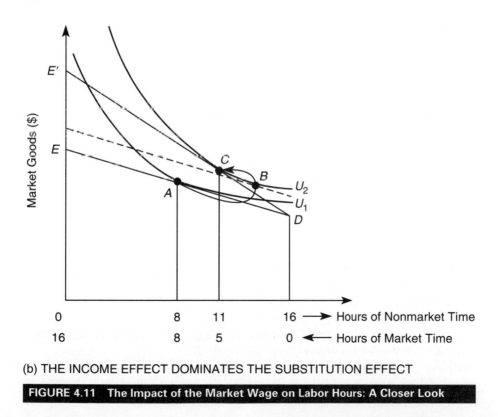

0   8   11   16 ⟶ Hours of Nonmarket Time

16   8   5   0 ⟵ Hours of Market Time

(b) THE INCOME EFFECT DOMINATES THE SUBSTITUTION EFFECT

FIGURE 4.11   The Impact of the Market Wage on Labor Hours: A Closer Look

2. Clearly nonmarket production has some value. Discuss the merits of estimating its value.

3. It is frequently pointed out that each method of valuing nonmarket production is far from perfect. Explain what their main advantages and deficiencies are.

4. Explain the reasons why men's labor force participation has been declining. Why have these same factors not caused women's labor force participation to decline as well?

5. Use economic reasoning (economic theory) to explain why the labor force participation rate for married women and never-married women might differ.*

6. Suppose the government were to provide a $2-per-hour subsidy for families with an employed mother who purchases child care.
   a. Consider a mother with a preschool-age child who is currently not employed. How would this affect her decision to work, all else equal?*
   b. Consider a mother with a preschool-age child who is currently employed. How would this affect the number of hours that she chooses to work (assuming she can vary them), all else equal?*

7. Now suppose that the government provides a subsidy of $300 per month for all families with children. Answer part a and part b of question 6 again under this scenario. How would your answers to question 6 change? Explain fully.*

8. Do you expect that sometime in the future labor force participation rates for men and women will be equal? Discuss.

Suggested Readings

Becker, Gary S. "A Theory of the Allocation of Time." *Economic Journal* 75, no. 299 (September 1965): 493–517.

Blank, Rebecca M. "Distinguished Lecture on Economics in Government—Fighting Poverty: Lessons from Recent U.S. History." *Journal of Economic Perspectives* 14, no. 2 (spring 2000): 3–19.

Brown, Clair. "An Institutional Model of Wives' Work Decisions." *Industrial Relations* 24, no. 2 (spring 1985): 182–204.

Goldin, Claudia. *Understanding the Gender Gap: An Economic History of American Women.* New York: Oxford University Press, 1990.

Heckman, James J. "What Has Been Learned About Labor Supply in the Past Twenty Years." *American Economic Review* 83, no. 2 (May 1993): 116–21.

Juhn, Chinhui. "Decline of Male Labor Market Participation: The Role of Declining Market Opportunities." *Quarterly Journal of Economics* 107, no. 1 (February 1992): 79–121.

Juhn, Chinhui, and Kevin M. Murphy. "Wage Inequality and Family Labor Supply." *Journal of Labor Economics* 15, no. 1, pt. 1 (January 1997): 72–97.

Killingsworth, Mark R. *Labor Supply.* Cambridge: Cambridge University Press, 1983.

Leibowitz, Arleen, and Jacob Klerman. "Explaining Changes in Married Mothers' Employment Over Time." *Demography* 32, no. 3 (August 1995): 365–78.

Mincer, Jacob. "Labor Force Participation of Married Women." In *Aspects of Labor Economics,* edited by H. Greg Lewis. Universities National Bureau of Economic Research Conference Studies, no. 14. Princeton, NJ: Princeton University Press, 1962, pp. 63–97.

Smith, James P., ed. *Female Labor Supply: Theory and Estimation.* Princeton, NJ: Princeton University Press, 1980.

CHAPTER 5

DIFFERENCES IN OCCUPATIONS AND EARNINGS: OVERVIEW

Chapter Highlights

- Occupational Differences
- Trends in Occupational Segregation
- Female–Male Earnings Ratio

Chapter 4 reviewed the large increase in women's labor force participation that has occurred since World War II. This increase, in conjunction with a decline in male labor force participation rates, has resulted in a steady narrowing of gender differentials in involvement in work outside the home. Further, as women have become more committed to market work, their labor force attachment has increased and they have been employed more continuously over the life cycle. We now shift to the question of how women fare in the labor market. In this chapter, we review the extent of gender differences in the two main indicators of labor market status—occupational attainment and earnings. As we shall see, although there have been important recent gains, substantial differences between men and women remain.

In Chapters 6 and 7, we consider alternative theoretical explanations for the observed differences in outcomes between men and women. In Chapter 6, we focus on supply-side explanations, particularly the human capital model, which emphasizes the role of women's preferences and the choices that they may make to invest less in job-related education and training, as well as to spend a smaller share of their adult years in the labor force. These explanations can also include premarket discrimination, or societal discrimination, in which various types of social pressures influence women's choices adversely.

In Chapter 7, we consider demand-side explanations of the gender differences in outcomes. Emphasis will be on the results of gender discrimination in the labor market, which occurs when men and women with equal qualifications are treated differently. We also point out that labor market discrimination can indirectly lower women's earnings and occupational attainment by reducing their incentives and opportunities to acquire education and training.

In Chapter 8, we use what we have learned from Chapters 6 and 7, as well as some additional insights, to explain the reasons for the narrowing of the gender earnings gap in recent years. This trend is considered in the context of other recent changes that have profoundly affected the labor market.

OCCUPATIONAL DIFFERENCES

We can get a general idea of the differences in occupations between men and women by comparing the distribution of male and female workers across the nine broad categories shown in Table 5.1. Because of their breadth, these are referred to as major occupational classifications and many specific detailed occupations are included in each of them.[1] The distributions are shown for 1972 and 1999. In both years, women tended to be concentrated in **administrative support** and **service** occupations. In 1999, 41 percent of all women workers were in these two categories, compared to only 15 percent of men. Administrative support occupations include clerical jobs like secretary, file clerk, data-entry keyer, and bookkeeper, as well as other support jobs such as teacher's aide, computer operator, postal clerk, and messenger. Examples of service occupations include child care workers, firefighters and police, waiters and waitresses, hairdressers, cooks, maids, and a variety of private household workers. Women were also somewhat more highly represented than men in **professional** jobs. Examples of jobs in this category are architects, engineers, lawyers, physicians, teachers, registered nurses, pharmacists, and social workers. Men, on the other hand, were considerably more likely than women to be in blue-collar jobs, with 38 percent of male workers employed in such jobs in 1999, as compared to 9 percent of women. These include semiskilled and unskilled **operator and laborer** occupations such as typesetters and compositors; assemblers, truck, taxicab, and bus drivers; construction helpers; and garage and service station attendants, as well as **precision production, craft, and repair** jobs, which are the strongholds of skilled blue-collar workers, like automobile mechanics, data processing equipment repairers, telephone installers and repairers, and electricians, carpenters, and plumbers.

Although in broad outlines the situation was fairly similar in both 1972 and 1999, some notable changes occurred between those years. Women were substantially less concentrated in administrative support and service occupations in 1999 than they had been in 1972, when 53 percent held such jobs. Women were also much more likely to hold **executive, administrative,** and **managerial** jobs; the proportion of workers in these jobs who were women rose from 20 to 45 percent. Examples of such jobs include ad-

---

[1] A listing of most of the detailed categories included in each major occupation is provided in Francine D. Blau, Patricia Simpson, and Deborah Anderson, "Continuing Progress? Trends in Occupational Segregation over the 1970s and 1980s," Feminist Economics 4, no. 3 (fall 1998): 29–71, appendix table A-1.

TABLE 5.1   Distribution of Men and Women by Major Occupation, 1972 and 1999[a]

Occupation	1972 Men (%)	1972 Women (%)	1999 Men (%)	1999 Women (%)
Executive, administrative, and managerial	11.5	4.6	15.0	14.2
Professional specialty	9.7	12.4	13.6	18.0
Technicians and related support	2.3	2.4	2.9	3.6
Sales occupations	10.0	11.1	11.3	13.0
Administrative support, including clerical	6.4	31.5	5.5	23.4
Service occupations	8.3	21.2	9.9	17.5
Precision production, craft, and repair	19.4	1.6	18.6	2.1
Operators, fabricators, and laborers	25.9	13.4	19.3	7.1
Farming, forestry, and fishing	6.4	1.9	3.8	1.1
Total employed	100.0	100.0	100.0	100.0
Segregation index	41.8		32.3	

[a] Data refer to civilian workers 16 years of age and over.

Sources: Department of Labor, Bureau of Labor Statistics, *Employment and Earnings* (January 1984 and 1999), Table 9.

ministrators in public administration and education, financial managers, personnel and labor relations managers, and a large group of managers "not elsewhere classified," as well as a variety of "management related occupations," like accountant and auditor, purchasing agent and buyer, management analyst and underwriter.

OCCUPATIONAL SEGREGATION

One way to assess the magnitude of differences in the distribution of women and men across occupational categories is the **index of segregation.**[2] It gives the percentage of female (or male) workers who would have to change jobs in order for the occupational distribution of the two groups to be the same. The index would equal zero if the distribution of men and women across occupational categories were identical; it would equal 100 if all occupations were either completely male or female. As can be seen in the last row of Table 5.1, for these major occupational categories, the index of segregation by gender was 32.3 in 1999, down from 41.8 in 1972.

The industries in which men and women work also differ considerably. As may be seen in Table 5.2, in 1999, men were more heavily concentrated in construction, manufacturing, and transportation and utilities—40 percent of men worked in those industries, as compared to 16 percent of women. In contrast, women were considerably more

---

[2] Otis Dudley Duncan and Beverly Duncan, "A Methodological Analysis of Segregation Indexes," *American Sociological Review* 20, no. 2 (1955): 210–17. The index of occupational segregation by sex is defined as:

$$\text{Segregation index} = 1/2 \, \Sigma_i \, |M_i - F_i|$$

where M_i = the percentage of males in the labor force employed in occupation i, and F_i = the percentage of females in the labor force employed in occupation i.

TABLE 5.2 Distribution of Men and Women by Major Industry, 1972 and 1999[a]

| | 1972 | | 1999 | |
| | Men (%) | Women (%) | Men (%) | Women (%) |
Industry				
Agriculture	5.8	2.1	3.4	1.4
Mining	1.1	0.1	0.7	0.1
Construction	9.8	0.9	11.3	1.4
Manufacturing	28.2	17.9	19.1	10.4
Transportation and public utilities	8.6	3.6	9.5	4.4
Wholesale and retail trade	18.9	22.2	20.2	21.2
Finance, insurance, and real estate	4.3	6.9	5.2	8.2
Services	17.2	41.9	25.9	48.6
Public administration	6.1	4.2	4.6	4.3
Total employed	100.0	100.0	100.0	100.0
Segregation index	30.7		26.7	

[a] Data refer to civilian workers 16 years of age and over.

Sources: U.S. Department of Commerce, Bureau of the Census, *Current Population Reports,* Series P-23, "A Statistical Portrait of Women in the United States: 1978"; and Department of Labor, Bureau of Labor Statistics, *Employment and Earnings* (January 1999), Table 17.

likely to be employed in services and in finance, insurance, and real estate—57 percent of women were in these industries, compared to 31 percent of men. To some extent, these differences in distribution by industry simply reflect gender differences in occupations. For example, we have seen that men are more likely to work as blue-collar workers than women, and a high proportion of such workers is employed in construction and manufacturing. However, there can also be substantial differences in the employment of men and women by firm or industry *within* occupational categories,[3] further contributing to the observed industry differences by gender.

The index of segregation can also be calculated for gender differences in industry distribution and is shown in the bottom row of Table 5.2. It indicates that segregation by major industry category is substantial but is less pronounced than segregation by major occupation. The extent of industry differences between men and women has also declined since the early 1970s, chiefly as men's concentration in manufacturing has declined and their employment in services has increased. However, gender differences in distribution by industry have decreased much less than gender differences in occupations.

In order to examine occupational differences by race and ethnicity as well as by gender, Table 5.3 provides data separately for black, white, and Hispanic workers. Black and Hispanic men and women were less likely than whites of the same sex to be employed in

---

[3] See, for example, Francine D. Blau, *Equal Pay in the Office* (Lexington, MA: Lexington Books, 1977); Erica L. Groshen, "The Structure of the Female/Male Wage Differential: Is It Who You Are, What You Do, or Where You Work?" *Journal of Human Resources* 26, no. 3 (summer 1991): 457–72; and Kimberly Bayard, Judith Hellerstein, David Newmark, and Kenneth Troske, "New Evidence on Sex Segregation and Sex Difference in Wages from Matched Employee–Employer Data," NBER Working Paper No. 7003 (March 1999). For historical evidence, see Claudia Goldin, *Understanding the Gender Gap: An Economic History of American Women* (New York: Oxford University Press, 1990).

TABLE 5.3   Distribution of Workers by Occupation, Race, Hispanic Origin, and Gender, 1999

| | *Whites* | | *Blacks* | | *Hispanics* | |
| | *Men (%)* | *Women (%)* | *Men (%)* | *Women (%)* | *Men (%)* | *Women (%)* |
Occupation						
Executive, administrative, and managerial	15.9	14.7	8.5	11.1	7.3	9.0
Professional specialty	13.6	18.7	9.5	13.5	5.3	9.1
Technicians and related support	2.9	3.6	2.7	3.5	1.7	2.5
Sales occupations	11.7	13.3	7.6	10.8	7.5	11.7
Administrative support, including clerical	5.1	23.6	8.1	23.9	5.7	22.6
Service occupations	8.9	16.2	17.4	25.6	14.9	26.7
Precision production, craft, and repair	19.4	2.1	14.3	2.1	21.2	2.8
Operators, fabricators, and laborers	18.3	6.5	29.8	9.4	27.8	13.6
Farming, forestry, and fishing	4.1	1.2	2.2	0.2	8.6	1.8
Total employed	100.0	100.0	100.0	100.0	100.0	100.0
Segregation indexes						
By sex	33.2		34.6		39.3	
By race or ethnicity (compared to whites)	n.a.	n.a.	23.1	13.3	21.7	17.9

Notes: Data refer to civilian workers 16 years of age and older. Hispanics may be of any race.

n.a. Not applicable.

Source: U.S. Department of Labor, *Employment and Earnings* (January 1999), Table 10; and unpublished data from the U.S. Department of Labor, Bureau of Labor Statistics.

higher-paying managerial and professional positions. At the other end of the scale, they were overrepresented in service occupations, as well as among operators and laborers.

Within each race or ethnic group, however, the patterns of occupational differences by gender showed considerable similarities. Women were heavily overrepresented in administrative support and service occupations and, especially among minority workers, more likely than men to be in professional and sales jobs. At the same time, women were underrepresented in blue-collar occupations. However, in contrast to the case among whites, minority women were more likely than minority men to be managerial workers. Overall, as indicated by the segregation indexes displayed in the last two rows of Table 5.3, gender differences in occupations within race and ethnic groups were larger than occupational differences by race or ethnicity.[4]

So far we have discussed gender differences in occupational distributions for broadly defined occupational categories, but data on these major occupations do not

---

[4] Even when more detailed occupational categories are considered, it is found that occupational segregation by race is considerably less pronounced than by sex. It has also declined more rapidly since 1960. See Victor Fuchs, Women's Quest for Economic Equality (Cambridge, MA: Harvard University Press, 1988); and Joyce P. Jacobsen, "Trends in Work Force Sex Segregation, 1960–90," Social Science Quarterly 75, no. 1 (March 1994): 204–11.

TABLE 5.4 Percent Female in Selected Professional Specialty Occupations, 1970 and 1999[a]

Occupations	1970	1999
Architects	4.0	15.7
Biological and life scientists	37.8	43.8
Chemists, except biochemists	11.7	27.4
Clergy	2.9	14.2
Computer systems analysts and scientists	13.6	28.5
Dentists	3.5	16.5
Dieticians	92.0	84.0
Economists	15.9	51.2
Editors and reporters	41.6	49.8
Engineers	1.7	10.6
Lawyers	4.9	28.8
Librarians	82.1	83.7
Operations and systems researchers and analysts	11.1	46.6
Pharmacists	12.1	49.0
Physicians	9.7	24.5
Psychologists	38.8	64.9
Public relations specialists	26.6	61.0
Registered nurses	97.3	92.9
Social workers	63.3	71.4
Teachers, except college and university		
Prekindergarten and kindergarten	97.9	98.4
Elementary school	83.9	83.8
Secondary school	49.6	57.5
Teachers, college and university	29.1	42.4

[a] 1970 data are from the 1970 census and are for the experienced civilian labor force aged 16 and over. 1999 data are annual averages from the *Current Population Surveys* and are for employed civilians aged 16 and over.

Sources: U.S. Census Bureau, *Detailed Occupation of the Experienced Civilian Labor Force by Sex for the United States and Regions: 1980 and 1970,* Supplementary Report PC80-S1-15 (March 1984); and U.S. Department of Labor, *Employment and Earnings* (January 1999), Table 11.

reveal the full extent of occupational segregation by sex. For example, among sales workers, women tend to be employed as retail sales clerks, whereas men are more likely to be manufacturing sales representatives. Information is available on a far larger set of detailed occupations. The precise number has varied over time but is generally well in excess of 400. The proportion women comprise of workers in these more narrowly defined occupations within the broader groupings does indeed tend to vary considerably. This is illustrated in more detail in Table 5.4, which shows a selection of professional occupations, chosen because we tend to be familiar with the nature and function of the various professions and because both men and women are substantially represented in the category as a whole.

As may be seen in the table, many of the jobs in the professional category are either predominantly female or predominantly male. Indeed, the most segregated jobs account for a substantial share of male and female workers. In 1999, 41 percent of all women professionals were in the five professions shown in the table where women comprised 80 percent or more of workers—dietician, librarian, nurse, prekindergarten and kindergarten teacher, and elementary schoolteacher. This does, however, represent a considerable decrease since 1970, when 59 percent were in these jobs. Men comprised over 80 percent of the workers in four of the professions listed—architect, clergy, dentist, and engineer. Together, these jobs accounted for over one-quarter of male professional workers. While there is still considerable segregation by sex within the professional category, it is important to note that women have made considerable inroads into traditionally male professions since 1970. By 1999, women constituted more than 20 percent of workers in such formerly predominantly male occupations as chemists, computer systems analysts and scientists, lawyers, operations researchers, pharmacists, and physicians.

A number of studies have calculated the index of occupational segregation for various years using the detailed breakdown of all occupations. For much of the twentieth century, these studies have shown levels of occupational segregation well in excess of 60 percent. Significant declines in the index began in the 1970s, and we shall consider this important trend in greater detail later. Nonetheless, the extent of occupational segregation remains substantial. Moreover, measures like the segregation index we have been discussing likely underestimate the full extent of employment segregation by sex. Job categories used by employers are far more detailed than the census occupational categories, and researchers have found that particular firms often employ mostly men or mostly women, even in occupations where both sexes are substantially represented. Restaurants, for instance, commonly employ only waiters or waitresses, but not both.[5]

HIERARCHIES WITHIN OCCUPATIONS

Not only do men and women tend to work in different occupations, they also tend to be employed at different levels of the hierarchy within occupations. No adequate data are available that would enable us to construct economy-wide quantitative measures, but there can be little doubt that such hierarchical differences are substantial.

A good example of this is the hierarchy on university faculties because universities generally use a clear and widely understood set of titles. Despite considerable growth in the ranks of academic women over the past 25 years, in academic year 1998–1999, women constituted 58.6 percent of instructors and 46.8 percent of assistant professors (the lowest ranks), compared to 34.6 percent of associate and 18.7 percent of full professors at the upper ranks. The academic case is not unique. Although, as we have seen, women have markedly increased their share of managerial jobs, their representation in top positions is still extremely sparse. According to a report by Catalyst on Fortune 500 companies, only 11.9 percent of all corporate officers and 5.1 percent of top-level executives were women in 1999; and women held just 3.3 percent of top-earner spots comprised of the five highest-paid executives in the company. This did, however, represent a substantial increase from 8.7 percent of officers, 2.4 percent of top-level executives, and 1.2

---

[5] Blau, *Equal Pay*; Groshen, "The Stucture of the Female/Male Wage Differential"; and Bayard et al., "New Evidence on Sex Segregation."

percent of top earners in 1995.[6] These types of disparities have given rise to the claim that women face a "glass ceiling," or a set of subtle barriers impeding them in their attempts to move up the hierarchy. We return to this issue in Chapter 7, where we more closely examine the evidence on women's representation at the upper levels of industry, government, and academia, as well as possible explanations for the observed gender differences.

EVALUATING THE EXTENT OF OCCUPATIONAL SEGREGATION

However segregation is measured, and whatever the numerical value of the index arrived at, how can it be determined whether any figure in excess of zero and short of 100 is modest or excessive? The answer depends in large part on one's perception of how great the differences are in men's and women's talents, tastes, and motivations and how relevant these are to their occupational distribution and achievements.

On one side are those who argue that occupational segregation is natural and appropriate. In this view, efforts to change the existing situation will merely lead to economic inefficiency and personal frustration. Its proponents emphasize the similarities among individuals within each sex and the differences between the two groups. Those who emphasize the similarities between men and women and the variations among individuals within each sex group are on the other side. In this view, if men and women were not constrained by gender stereotyping and various barriers to individual choice but were free to follow their own inclinations, they would be far less concentrated in separate occupations. The fact that there are occupations that are predominantly male in some countries but female in others lends support to the view that socially imposed restrictions play a role in the sex typing of jobs.[7] In this case, removing existing barriers would presumably increase efficiency and decrease frustration, since individuals could seek work suited to their particular aptitudes.

It should be emphasized that even if the present level of occupational segregation is deemed excessive, it would be unreasonable to conclude that the optimal situation would necessarily be a precisely proportional distribution of men and women. Apart from whatever innate differences there may be, past socialization and the prevalent allocation of household responsibilities would make such an outcome unlikely for some time to come.

In addition, the rate of change is limited by the time it takes for new people to be trained and hired. Large numbers of people cannot be expected to change jobs on short notice, as the computation of the segregation index perhaps implies. The most that could reasonably be expected is that the underrepresented group would be more highly represented among new hires, to the extent that they are qualified for the available positions, than among those presently employed in the occupation. This may be, at best, a very slow process.

---

[6] Top-level or "clout" positions include CEO, chair, vice-chair, president, COO, senior VP, and executive VP; see, Catalyst, *Fact Sheet: 1999 Catalyst Census of Women Corporate Officers and Top Earners* (New York).

[7] This subject will be discussed at greater length in Chapter 11.

TRENDS IN OCCUPATIONAL SEGREGATION

The same issues confronted in measuring current occupational segregation arise in determining the precise extent to which it has changed over time. However, in addition to the concern over how detailed the categories are, or whether or not women are included in the upper ranks of occupational hierarchies, there is also the question of whether or not the same occupational definitions have been used for the various periods to be compared. The main difficulty is that the definition and number of occupational categories often undergo significant changes. Given constant flux in the economy, this is inevitable. For example, had the Census Bureau rigidly adhered to the occupational categories of an earlier era, jobs such as computer systems analyst and programmer, as well as computer operator and data-entry keyer, would not be included. Thus, regardless of the best efforts of the people who compile the data and the researchers who use them, data are not entirely comparable over the years and are less so as the years get farther apart.

In spite of these limitations, there is no reason to question the unanimous findings of numerous studies that point to little change in the degree of segregation over a number of decades prior to 1960. The index of segregation by detailed occupation was actually reported to have increased by 1.1 percentage points between 1950 and 1960, as predominantly female clerical and professional jobs grew in relative size. Between 1960 and 1970, however, an inflow of men into female professions and of women into male sales and clerical jobs produced a modest drop in the segregation index of 3.1 percentage points.[8]

Larger declines in the index were found for the 1970s and 1980s. Estimates based on detailed census data indicate that the index fell by 6 to 8 percentage points in each decade, declining from 67.7 in 1970 to 59.3 in 1980 and 52.0 in 1990.[9] While the level of segregation that remains is considerable, the cumulative reduction of nearly 16 percentage points over the two decades is substantial. This is especially true when considered in light of the previous stability of the index in earlier decades. Some indication of trends over the 1990s may be obtained using *Current Population Survey* data based on a somewhat different set of occupations and workers. The index of segregation computed from this source decreased from 56.4 in 1990 to 53.9 in 1997,[10] yielding an average annual decrease of .4 percentage points over the 1990s, compared to .8 and .6 percentage points in the 1970s and 1980s, respectively. Thus, the long-term reduction in occupational segregation by sex appears to have continued into the 1990s, but at a slower pace.

---

[8] For the pre-1960 period, see Edward Gross, "Plus Ça Change? The Sexual Structure of Occupations Over Time," *Social Problems* 16, no. 1 (fall 1968): 198–208; for 1950 to 1970, see Francine D. Blau and Wallace E. Hendricks, "Occupational Segregation by Sex: Trends and Prospects," *Journal of Human Resources* 14, no. 2 (spring 1979): 197–210. The changes in the index presented for the 1950s and 1960s are not strictly comparable to those given for later years because of changes in the number and composition of occupational categories that are included.

[9] These figures are for a comparable set of occupations in each of the years. See Blau, Simpson, and Anderson, "Continuing Progress?" See also Andrea H. Beller, "Changes in the Sex Composition of U.S. Occupations, 1960–1981," *Journal of Human Resources* 20, no. 2 (spring 1985) 235–50; Jacobsen, "Trends in Workforce Sex Segregation"; and David A. Macpherson and Barry T. Hirsch, "Wages and Gender Composition: Why Do Women's Jobs Pay Less?" *Journal of Labor Economics* 13, no. 3 (July 1995): 426–71.

[10] Jerry A. Jacobs, "The Sex Segregation of Occupations: Prospects for the 21st Century," in *Handbook of Gender in Organizations,* ed. Gary N. Powell (Newbury Park, CA: Sage Publications, 1999), pp. 125–41.

Changes in the extent of segregation may be due to changes in the sex composition of individual occupations, as a result of the integration of previously male or female jobs, or to shifts in the occupational mix of the economy, through greater employment growth in occupations that are already integrated relative to growth in segregated male and female jobs. Changes in the sex composition of occupations were the principal cause of the reduction in segregation over the 1970s and 1980s, though changing occupational mix also played a role. While such shifts in sex composition could have been due either to women entering formerly male jobs or men entering previously female jobs or a combination of both, it was in fact movements of women into predominantly male jobs that played the major role. As women entered formerly male jobs, these occupations became more integrated and the degree of segregation in the labor market overall was diminished. Women were particularly successful in entering formerly male white-collar jobs, particularly professional and managerial occupations. As we have seen, examples of previously male professional jobs where women made notable progress include architect, engineer, lawyer, computer systems analyst or scientist, and physician (see Table 5.4). There were similar large increases in many executive, administrative, and managerial occupations and management-related jobs. Examples of formerly male occupations in this category that experienced large increases in the representation of women are shown in Table 5.5. The impact of these changes in the sex composition of occupations in reducing occupational segregation during this period was supplemented by some important shifts in the occupational mix of the economy that also decreased segregation. Employment in integrated jobs increased compared to employment in predominately female and predominately male jobs. Examples of segregated jobs that declined in relative importance include a number of female administrative support jobs (like secretary, typist, bookkeeper, and telephone operator) and male farm and blue-collar occupations.[11]

Despite recent gains, many predominantly single-sex occupations remain. This can be seen in Table 5.6, which shows some of the most segregated occupations—those that

TABLE 5.5 **Percent Female in Selected Managerial and Management-Related Occupations, 1970 and 1999[a]**

Occupations	*1970*	*1999*
Marketing, advertising, and public relations managers	7.9	37.6
Purchasing managers	8.5	47.4
Financial managers	19.4	51.1
Personnel and labor relations managers	21.1	60.4
Management analysts	10.3	43.2
Accountants and auditors	24.6	58.6
Buyers, wholesale and retail, except farm	27.8	54.5

[a] 1970 data are from the 1970 census and are for the experienced civilian labor force aged 16 and over. 1999 data are annual averages from the *Current Population Surveys* and are for employed civilians aged 16 and over.

Sources: U.S. Census Bureau, *Detailed Occupation of the Experienced Civilian Labor Force by Sex for the United States and Regions: 1980 and 1970,* Supplementary Report PC80-S1-15 (March 1984); and U.S. Department of Labor, *Employment and Earnings* (January 1996), Table 11.

---

[11] See Blau, Simpson, and Anderson, "Continuing Progress?"

TABLE 5.6   Selected Occupations Less than 10 Percent or More than 90 Percent Female, 1999[a]

Occupations	*Less than 10 Percent Female*
Airplane pilots and navigators	3.1
Construction laborers	4.1
Electricians	2.3
Extractive occupations	0.9
Firefighting and fire prevention occupations	2.8
Garage and service station related occupations	3.8
Geologists and geodesists	4.9
Helpers, construction and extractive occupations	5.5
Material moving equipment operators	5.2
Mechanical engineers	7.1
Mechanics and repairers, except supervisors	4.5
Pest control occupations	2.8
Plant and systems operators	4.0
Plumbers, pipefitters and steamfitters	1.8
Precision metalworking	7.6
Timber cutting and logging occupations	1.3
Transportation occupations, except motor vehicles	2.4
Truck drivers	4.9
Vehicles and mobile equipment mechanics and repairers	1.6
Welders and cutters	5.7

	More than 90 Percent Female
Billing clerks	92.0
Bookkeepers, account and auditing clerks	91.4
Dental hygienists	99.1
Dental assistants	96.1
Early childhood teachers' assistants	95.3
Family child care providers	98.0
Financial records processing	90.8
Hairdressers and cosmetologists	90.8
Licensed practical nurses	95.1
Private household occupations	95.2
Receptionists	95.4
Registered nurses	92.9
Secretaries, stenographers, and typists	97.9
Speech therapists	93.1
Teachers' aides	91.0
Teachers, prekindergarten and kindergarten	98.4

[a] Data are for employed civilians aged 16 and over.

Source: U.S. Department of Labor, *Employment and Earnings* (January 1999), Table 11.

are either less than 10 percent or more than 90 percent female. Many of the predominantly male jobs are blue-collar occupations. The predominantly female categories include, in addition to the traditionally female professions, a number of jobs in the administrative support and service areas.

Overall, the figures indicate that a substantial decline in the amount of segregation has occurred since 1960, with the pace of change accelerating markedly over the 1970s and 1980s and continuing at a slower pace in the 1990s. However, many jobs remain segregated by gender, and the relatively rapid changes in managerial and professional jobs have not been matched in blue-collar occupations. Thus, the magnitude of the segregation index continues to be substantial: As we have seen, 52 percent of women (or men) would have had to change jobs in 1990 in order for the detailed occupational distribution of men and women to be the same.

It is also important to consider whether or not the observed trends reflect real improvements in opportunities for women. In some cases, firms have responded to government pressures by placing women into nominal management positions that involve little responsibility and little contact with higher levels of management. In other instances, jobs have become increasingly female when skill requirements declined because of technological changes. In such cases, integration may turn out to be a short-run phenomenon, as resegregation occurs and women increasingly come to dominate such jobs. One example of this trend is the case of insurance adjusters and examiners. Women increased their share of this occupation from 30 percent in 1970 to 71 percent in 1999. They are, however, employed primarily as "inside adjusters" whose decision making has, to a considerable extent, been computerized and involves little discretion. "Outside adjusters," a better-paid and more prestigious group, remain largely male. In yet other instances, women may gain access to a sector of an occupation that was always low paying. For example, the representation of women among bus drivers increased from 28 percent in 1970 to 51 percent in 1999. But men continue to comprise the majority of full-time workers in metropolitan transportation systems, whereas women are concentrated among part-time school bus drivers.[12]

At the same time, it is important to point out that women are expected to benefit from the increase in the demand for female labor that results when they are able to enter additional occupations from which they were previously excluded, even when the new jobs are qualitatively similar to those formerly available to them. Moreover, it is likely that much of the observed decline in occupational segregation does represent enhanced labor market opportunities for women.

FEMALE–MALE EARNINGS RATIO

For many years, the single best-known statistic relevant to the economic status of women in this country probably was that women who worked full-time, year-round, earned about 59 cents to every dollar earned by men working full-time, year-round.[13]

---

[12]   These examples are from Barbara F. Reskin and Patricia A. Roos, *Job Queues, Gender Queues: Explaining Women's Inroads into Male Occupations* (Philadelphia: Temple University Press, 1990).

[13]   Full time is defined as 35 hours or more per week; year-round is defined as 50 weeks or more per year. The focus on full-time, year-round workers is an effort to adjust published government data on annual

TABLE 5.7 Female-to-Male Earnings Ratios of Full-Time Workers, Selected Years, 1955–1999		
Year	*Annual Earnings of Full-Time Year-Round Workers*[a]	*Usual Weekly Earnings of Full-Time Workers*[b]
1955	63.9	
1960	60.8	
1965	60.0	
1970	59.4	62.3
1975	58.8	62.0
1980	60.2	64.4
1985	64.6	68.2
1990	71.6	71.8
1995	71.4	75.5
1999	72.2	76.5

[a] Workers aged 16 and over. Prior to 1979, workers aged 14 and over.

[b] Workers aged 16 and over.

Sources: U.S. Department of Labor, Women's Bureau, Bulletin 298, *Time of Change: 1984 Handbook on Women Workers;* U.S. Census Bureau, Population Reports, Consumer Income Series P-60, *Money Income of Households, Families, and Persons in the United States,* and U.S. Census Bureau, Population Reports, Consumer Income Series P-60, *Money, Income, and Poverty Status in the United States,* various issues; Earl F. Mellor, Investigating the Differences in Weekly Earnings of Women and Men," *Monthly Labor Review,* 107, no. 6 (June 1984); Bureau of Labor Statistics, *Handbook of Labor Statistics,* Bulletin 2340 (August 1989); Bureau of Labor Statistics, *Employment and Earnings,* various issues.

One reason for the public awareness of this figure was that the same earnings ratio persisted for two decades with only modest fluctuations and no significant trend. Although it was in fact somewhat higher in the 1950s, as may be seen in Table 5.7 and Figure 5.1, the female-to-male earnings ratios based on annual data hovered close to the 59 percent figure throughout the 1960s and 1970s.[14] In the early 1980s, however, the ratio began to rise. Between 1981 and 1998 it increased from 59 percent to 72.2 percent.[15]

---

earnings for gender differences in hours and weeks worked. However, since even women who work full-time work on average 8 to 10 percent fewer hours a week than male full-time workers, a finer adjustment for hours would raise the earnings ratio; see June O'Neill, "Women & Wages," *American Enterprise* 1, no. 6 (November/December 1990): 25–33.

[14]   Median rather than mean earnings are shown because more government data are presented that way. The definition of the median is that half the cases fall above it and half below. In this case, half the individuals have higher earnings and half have lower. The mean, or arithmetic mean, is calculated by adding up the total earnings of all the individuals concerned and dividing by their number. Since there is a relatively small number of persons who have extremely high earnings, the mean tends to be higher than the median.

[15]   Focusing on all workers, rather than simply those employed full-time, year-round, Francine D. Blau and Andrea H. Beller found evidence of some earnings gains for women during the 1970s, after adjustment for hours and weeks worked; see "Trends in Earnings Differentials by Gender, 1971–1981," *Industrial and Labor Relations Review* 41, no. 4 (July 1988): 513–29.

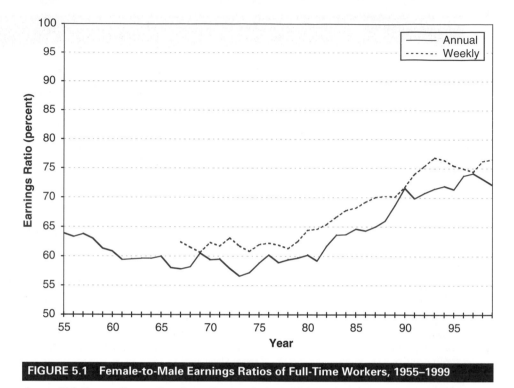

FIGURE 5.1   Female-to-Male Earnings Ratios of Full-Time Workers, 1955–1999

Source: U.S. Census, *Current Population Reports,* Series P-60, various issues; *Employment and Earnings,* various issues; and Census Bureau and Bureau of Labor Statistics web sites.

Table 5.7 and Figure 5.1 also show the female-to-male earnings ratio calculated using data on the usual weekly earnings of full-time workers. For a variety of reasons, the earnings ratio computed on the basis of weekly earnings is generally higher than the annual figure.[16] Of more interest, however, is that the data for weekly earnings also show an upward trend dating from the late 1970s. Between 1978 and 1999, the earnings ratio, defined in these terms, increased from 61 to 77 percent.

Looking more closely at the trends in Figure 5.1, we see that there was substantial and steady narrowing of the gender earnings gap over the 1980s. However, the pace of convergence in both the annual and the weekly earnings series appeared to slow in the 1990s and both series behaved more erratically in that decade.[17] The long-run significance of this recent experience is unclear.

---

[16]   For example, annual earnings include overtime pay and bonuses. Men tend to receive greater amounts of this type of pay; see Nancy Rytina, "Comparing Annual and Weekly Earnings from the Current Population Survey," *Monthly Labor Review* 106 (April 1983): 32–38.

[17]   Between 1980 and 1989, the average annual increase in the ratio was .94 percentage points for annual earnings and .63 percentage points for weekly earnings. In contrast, between 1990 and 1999, the annual average increase in the ratio was .06 percentage points for annual earnings and .53 percentage points for weekly earnings. While the trends in the ratio based on weekly earnings did not differ greatly between the 1980s and the 1990s taken as a whole, there was in fact no evidence of further narrowing of the gender gap for this measure after its 1993 peak.

TABLE 5.8 Female-to-Male Ratios of Mean Earnings for Full-Time, Year-Round Workers by Age, 1960–1999					
Age	*1960*	*1970*	*1980*	*1990*	*1999*
25–34	65.1	64.9	68.5	76.9	76.4
35–44	57.6	53.9	55.3	64.4	65.6
45–54	58.0	56.3	52.0	58.2	59.6
55–64	64.5	60.3	54.9	57.1	58.6

Sources: 1960–1970: June O'Neill, "Women & Wages," *American Enterprise* 1 (November/December 1990), p. 29. Remaining years from U.S. Census Bureau, Consumer Income Series P-60, *Money Income of Households, Families, and Persons in the United States,* 1981, 1991, and 1999.

Evidence on changes in the gender–earnings ratio over the life cycle is shown in Table 5.8 for the 1960 to 1999 period. Data are presented on mean earnings ratios of full-time, year-round workers for four age groups: 25–34, 35–44, 45–54, and 55–64. The age range 25–64 was selected because individuals in this age group have generally completed their formal schooling but have not yet retired from paid employment. The data in the table indicate that women earn less than men in all age categories. However, with the exception of the oldest group, the gap tends to widen with age. This fanning out of the male and female earnings profiles is partially due to women accumulating less work experience than men, on average, as they age. This was particularly true for earlier cohorts. It may also reflect greater barriers to their advancement at higher levels of the job hierarchy, an issue we will discuss further in Chapter 7 when we consider evidence on the glass ceiling.

As was the case for the overall earnings ratio, we see that the gender earnings ratio within age groups also rose substantially in the 1980s; but little further change occurred over the 1990s. Figure 5.2 shows the trends more clearly for those below age 55, where progress has been greatest. The earnings ratio began to rise as early as the 1970s for women under 45, although the gains in the 1980s were considerably larger. Younger women also experienced the largest cumulative increases: Between 1970 and 1999, the earnings ratio rose by about 12 percentage points for 25- to 34-year olds and 35- to 44-year-olds. While the ratio for 45- to 54-year-olds fell between 1970 and 1980, it rose by 8 percentage points between 1980 and 1999.

One question we may address with these data is what happens to the gender ratio as women age. Interestingly, gains in relative earnings of women over the 1980s were large enough so that younger female cohorts did not experience a large decrease in the ratio with age as might be expected based on the data for 1980 or 1990 alone. If we compare the earnings ratio for 25- to 34-year-olds in 1980 to the ratio for 35- to 44-year-olds ten years later in 1990, we find that the ratio fell only slightly from 69 to 64 percent. Further, the earnings ratio of 58 percent for the 45- to 54-year-old age group in 1990 was 3 percentage points greater than that of 35- to 44-year-olds ten years earlier.

This same pattern does not appear to have prevailed over the 1990s. While somewhat less than a full decade of data is available, the 1999 figures strongly suggest a fairly

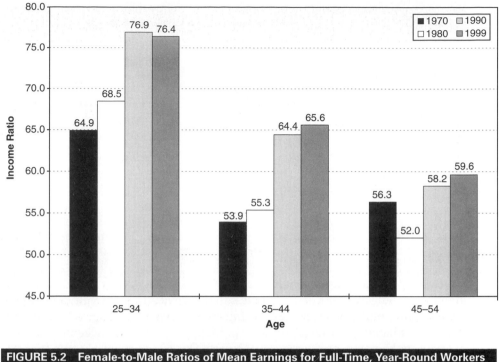

Source: U.S. Census Bureau, *Current Population Reports,* Series P-60, various issues; *Employment and Earnings,* various issues; and Census Bureau and Bureau of Labor Statistics web sites.

substantial fall-off in earnings as women who were 25–34 years old in 1990 aged to 35–44, with the ratio declining from 77 to 66 percent. Similarly, the earnings ratio for 45–54-year-olds in 1999 was four percentage points lower than the figure for 35–44-year-olds in 1990. It is unclear what will happen in the future. However, for now the earnings of younger women appear to be declining relative to men's as they age. In interpreting data like those presented in Table 5.8 it is important to bear in mind that comparisons of this type may be influenced by which men and women choose to seek paid employment in each year, as well as by their success in locating jobs. Due to this problem of "selection bias," we cannot be completely certain that data on those who are employed accurately measure shifts in labor market opportunities for all women.[18]

Table 5.9 provides information on incomes of workers by level of education.[19] Although education has a strong positive effect on the income of both men and

---

[18] Seminal work by Nobel Prize–winning economist James Heckman has greatly increased economists' awareness of this problem; see, for example, James J. Heckman, "Sample Selection Bias as a Specification Error," *Econometrica* 47, no. 1 (January 1979): 153–61.

[19] The reason for using income data is that no comparable earnings data are available for the period examined. Income includes such items as interest, dividends, and transfer payments, as well as earnings. However, because these amounts are relatively small for the great majority of year-round, full-time workers, income ratios tend to be quite similar to earnings ratios.

TABLE 5.9 Median Income of Men and Women by Education for Year-Round, Full-Time Workers, 1967 and 1999 (1999 Dollars)

	1967 Income			1999 Income		
Education	*Men ($)*	*Women ($)*	*Female-to-Male Ratio (%)*	*Men ($)*	*Women ($)*	*Female-to-Male Ratio (%)*
Elementary	24,939	14,107	56.6	20,429	15,098	73.9
High school:						
1–3 years	31,626	17,000	53.8	25,035	17,015	68.0
4 years	35,486	20,648	58.2	33,184	23,061	69.5
College:						
1–3 years	40,461	24,109	59.6	39,971	28,826	72.1
4 or more years	53,105	31,190	58.7	60,201	41,747	69.3

Notes: Data refer to workers 25 years of age and older. Definitions of educational categories are not exactly comparable for the two years. In 1967, mean income for elementary is computed as a weighted average of the medians of "less than 8 years" and "8 years" of schooling. In 1999, median income for 1–3 years of college is computed as a weighted average of the medians for "some college, no degree" and "associate degree."

Sources: U.S. Census Bureau, *Current Population Reports,* Consumer Income Series P-60, various issues.

women, men continue to earn substantially more than women within each educational category. As was the case for the overall earnings gap and the earnings differentials by age, the gender gap within educational categories has also narrowed over time. In 1967 and indeed through much of the 1970s, the gap was so large that it was often noted that women college graduates earned less than male high school dropouts. Now, that is no longer true, and the earnings of women college graduates exceed not only those of male high school graduates but those of males with some college. This reflects not only the narrowing of the gender gap within educational groups but also widening income differentials by education within each gender group. For example, among both men and women, the income of college graduates has increased relative to high school graduates and high school dropouts. In addition, as may be seen in the table, real income has been declining for men in each education category, with the exception of college graduates, and declines have been particularly large for men with less than a high school diploma. In contrast, real incomes have been fairly constant for less educated women and rising for those with at least a high school diploma; gains have been particularly sizable for female college graduates. These trends in real income and income inequality by education are discussed further in Chapter 8.

Table 5.10 reviews the trends in relative income by race and ethnicity as well as by gender. Within each race–ethnic group, women earned less than men in 1999, but the female-to-male income ratio was considerably higher among blacks (83 percent) and Hispanics (86 percent) than among whites (71 percent). Not surprisingly, the trends in income ratios by gender among whites closely mirror the overall trends since they comprise a substantial majority of the population. There was little tendency toward an increase in the gender ratio for this group until the 1980s, and there was little further increase in the ratio in the 1990s. In contrast, the female-to-male income ratio among blacks increased considerably from the mid-1950s, by 27.9 percentage points. A sizable increase in the gender income ratio (17 percentage points) is also apparent among Hispanics since the mid-1970s, when data first became available for this group. Like white women, however, neither black nor Hispanic women have made much progress in closing the pay gap with men of the same race or ethnicity over the 1990s.

In terms of the racial and ethnic differences shown in the table, we see that minority individuals of both sexes earned less than whites in 1999, but the differential was considerably smaller among women than among men. In 1999, the median income of black males was 77 percent of white males' median income, and the figure for Hispanic males was 59 percent. These figures were considerably lower than the income ratios of 90 percent for black women and 72 percent for Hispanic women, both compared to white women. Among women, black-to-white income ratios increased substantially from the mid-1950s, when the ratio was only 51 percent, to the mid-1970s, when it was 96 percent. Black men also gained relative to white men, although not nearly as rapidly, from 63 percent of white men's income in 1965 to 73 percent in 1975. Between 1975 and 1990, however, income differentials between blacks and whites were constant or widening. There were signs of a renewed convergence between black and white men over the 1990s. However, it should be noted that, since there can be year-to-year fluctuations in these data, the exceptionally high value of the ratio in 1999 of 77 percent may possibly overstate the progress of black males. Black women also appear to have gained somewhat since the mid-1990s.

Some caution is warranted in interpreting the trends for black males in Table 5.10. In light of the decrease in the participation and employment rates of black relative to white males since the 1950s, which we reviewed in Chapter 4, the available statistics may overstate the progress of blacks. This is the case because it is likely that it is the blacks with the least favorable labor market opportunities who dropped out of the labor force. The data in Table 5.10 are based on the measured earnings of employed individuals. If the least successful blacks are leaving the labor force at a faster rate than comparable whites, observed black–white earnings ratios may rise, even in the absence of any changes in the relative earnings prospects of all blacks (including both the employed and nonemployed). Putting this somewhat differently, the observed black–white earnings ratio may rise simply because of a change in the composition of employed blacks rather than due to a true improvement in labor market opportunities for blacks. Existing research suggests that this factor is important but the general outlines of the trends remain: The black–white earnings ratio among males increased considerably from the mid-1960s to the late 1970s, but there was little evidence of further increases in the ratio during the 1980s and only moderate signs of further convergence since then.[20] A similar issue potentially affects trends in the

---

[20] This is another example of selection bias and again James Heckman was the first to call it to the attention of economists in his work with Richard Butler, "The Impact of the Economy and State on the Economic Status of Black Americans: A Critical Review," in *Equal Rights and Industrial Relations*, ed. Farrell E. Bloch (Madison, WI: Industrial Relations Research Association, 1977), pp. 235–81. Other work includes Charles Brown, "Black–White Earnings Ratios Since the Civil Rights Act of 1964: The Importance of Labor Market Dropouts," *Quarterly Journal of Economics* 99, no. 1 (February 1984): 31–44; Chinhui Juhn, "Labor Market Dropout, Selection Bias, and Trends in Black and White Wages," Working Paper, University of Houston (1997); James J. Heckman, Thomas M. Lyons, and Petra E. Todd, "Understanding Black–White Wage Differentials, 1960–1990," *American Economic Review* 90, no. 2 (May 2000): 344–49; and Amitabh Chandra, "Labor-Market Dropouts and the Racial Wage Gap: 1940–90," *American Economic Review* 90, no. 2 (May 2000): 333–38.

TABLE 5.10 Ratios of Median Income by Race, Hispanic Origin, and Gender for Full-Time, Year-Round Workers, Selected Years, 1955–1999

Year	Female-to-Male Ratios			Black-to-White Ratios		Hispanic-to-White Ratios	
	Whites	*Blacks*	*Hispanics*	*Males*	*Females*	*Males*	*Females*
1955	65.3	55.1	n.a.	60.9	51.4	n.a.	n.a.
1960	60.6	62.2	n.a.	66.1	67.8	n.a.	n.a.
1965	57.9	62.5	n.a.	62.8	67.9	n.a.	n.a.
1970	58.6	70.5	n.a.	68.1	81.9	n.a.	n.a.
1975	57.5	75.1	68.5	73.2	95.5	71.2	85.0
1980	59.3	78.7	71.7	70.4	93.3	70.0	84.5
1985	64.1	81.2	78.0	70.0	88.5	67.5	82.0
1990	69.0	86.0	83.8	71.4	88.9	64.0	77.7
1995	71.3	83.2	89.6	72.8	85.0	61.2	75.9
1999	71.2	83.0	85.9	77.0	89.7	59.3	71.6

Notes: Prior to 1970, blacks include blacks and other nonwhites; Hispanic individuals may be of any race. Data for 1980–1999 refer to workers 15 years of age and older; and for 1955–1975 to workers 14 years and older.

n.a. Not available

Sources: U.S. Census Bureau, *Current Population Reports, Consumer Income* Series P-60, various issues.

black–white earnings ratio among women, since, although black women have traditionally had higher labor force participation rates than white women, the participation gap has narrowed considerably since the 1950s. However, since the participation decision of women is considerably more complex than men's, researchers have found it more difficult to estimate the likely effects of shifting participation patterns on the black–white earnings ratio for women.[21] Earnings trends by race will be considered further in Chapter 8.

In contrast to the trends for blacks, data on Hispanics show declining income ratios for this group relative to whites since this information first became available in the mid-1970s. Hispanic-to-white income ratios are also considerably lower than black-to-white income ratios for both men and women. One reason for this may be that a large and growing proportion of Hispanics are recent immigrants to the United States. Hence their earnings are reduced because they tend to be relatively young, may not speak English well, and face other difficulties in adjusting to their new environment. Of course discrimination may also play a role in Hispanic–white income differences. Note that the data in the table for whites are presented for all whites (including those of Hispanic origin), rather than for non-Hispanic whites separately because information on the broader group has been available for a longer period of time. Since most Hispanics are white, the inclusion of this growing low income group among whites in Table 5.10 may artificially inflate the progress of blacks in closing the race gap. For example, when income for blacks is compared to that of non-Hispanic whites, the income ratio was 73 percent for men and 86 percent for women in 1999, notably lower than the ratios shown in Table 5.10 of 77 percent for men and 90 percent for women.

The Gender Pay Gap in the News

We are bombarded in the press with a multitude of figures regarding how much women earn relative to men. Compounding this are often inaccurate or misleading interpretations of the data presented. This inset provides a source and context for two figures that have received particular media attention.

The most common figure cited is based on the median earnings of year-round, full-time workers. It is readily available from the Census Bureau web site and is shown in Figure 5.1 and Table 5.7. This figure, which was 72 percent in 1999, pertains to men and women who work full-time and full-year, but may well differ in terms of age, educational attainment, seniority, occupation, industry, and other characteristics related to earnings. Nevertheless, it is frequently misunderstood, as in a recent *Los Angeles Times* article that referred to this ratio as being for men and women "doing the same work."* Indeed, we

---

* Renee Tawa, "Who's In Charge? With More Women Working and Bringing Home Bigger Paychecks, Some Men are Staying Home to Rear the Kids. Now Couples Must Struggle with Touchy Issues of Identity and Balance of Power," *Los Angeles Times*, 27 September 1999, p. E1.

---

21 For a study that does include women, see Francine D. Blau and Andrea H. Beller, "Black-White Earnings over the 1970s and 1980s, Gender Differences in Trends," *Review of Economics and Statistics* 74, no. 2 (May 1992): 276–86.

know that the overall pay ratio for men and women in the same occupation may be considerably higher, though estimates vary.

Another figure that has received substantial attention in the media, for instance by columnist George Will and in a recent book entitled *Women's Figures* by Diane Furchtgott-Roth and Christine Stolba, is the estimate of a 98 percent female–male earnings ratio for women and men ages 27 to 33 who have never had a child.[†] Should we take this statistic to mean that there is virtually no discrimination as these authors do? This is probably not warranted. First, it represents women's and men's earnings at the start of their careers. Hence, it does not reflect later pay differences that arise as a result of differences in promotion; as we saw in Table 5.8, the gender earnings ratio tends to decrease with age. Second, the 98 percent statistic compares men and women who do not have children. As we shall see in Chapters 6 and 9, recent research indicates that mothers incur a wage penalty compared to other women, even when they have the same measured qualifications like education and experience. Researchers have not found a similar wage penalty for fathers, and some have found a wage premium for them. Thus the gender pay gap is smaller when men and women who do not have children are compared.

Based on this evidence, some contend that the gender pay gap is largely due to differences between men and women in "preferences, motivations, and expectations," and "experience, education, and skills."[‡] While these factors may well explain part of the gender pay gap, it is also possible that employers treat women differently. Our extensive review of the evidence in Chapter 7 suggests that discrimination against women in the labor market does exist and, while it may not be as severe as in the past, represents more than an occasional anomaly.

It is also critical to keep in mind the assumptions that are made in interpreting any statistic on the gender pay gap and what can reasonably be concluded based on any particular piece of data. It matters a great deal, for instance, whether we assume that occupation represents solely an individual's choice or that it may be influenced by anticipated or past discrimination; or whether we assume that all mothers tend to prefer less-demanding "mommy-track" positions or that they may sometimes be channeled into them. Similarly, we must be cautious in interpreting an aggregate figure like 72 percent as evidence of discrimination, when it does not take into account valid reasons why male and female pay may differ. At the same time it may not be reasonable to conclude that discrimination has virtually disappeared simply because young women and men at the beginning of their careers have similar starting salaries. Rather, it may be more appropriate to obtain information about a broader and more representative group of workers before reaching such a conclusion. Individuals on both sides of the debate must be careful not to misrepresent reality by oversimplifying complex issues or by stating a statistic without fully explaining its strengths and limitations. The bottom line is that, while pinpointing discrimination is difficult, there is ample evidence that, despite recent progress, it has not gone away.

[†] George Will, "Lies, Damned Lies," *Newsweek,* 29 March 1999, p. 84; Diana Furchtgott-Roth and Christine Stolba, *Women's Figures: An Illustrated Guide to the Economic Progress of Women in America* (Washington DC: AEI Press: 1999); and June O'Neill, "The Shrinking Pay Gap," *Wall Street Journal,* 7 October 1994.

[‡] Furchtgott-Roth and Stolba, *Women's Figures,* p. 4.

CONCLUSION

In this chapter, we presented data on gender differentials in occupations and earnings in general, as well as for various subgroups. Although occupational and earnings differences remain substantial, both have declined significantly over the past 25 years. Reductions in occupational segregation by gender date back to the 1960s, though more rapid progress occurred in subsequent decades. The overall gap in the earnings of male and female full-time workers started to narrow in the late 1970s or early 1980s. These changes have been particularly marked for women under 45. However, the earnings trends appear to have plateaued in the 1990s, and much depends on whether the trend toward convergence is renewed in the early years of the twenty-first century. The next two chapters will thoroughly investigate the possible explanations for the gender differences described here, while Chapter 8 focuses in part on explaining the reasons for the long-term convergence in the gender gap.

QUESTIONS FOR REVIEW AND DISCUSSION

1. Why have women been increasingly eager to move into men's occupations? Why do you think men have generally been less eager to move into women's occupations?

2. Suppose you have the following hypothetical information about the occupational distribution of Country Y. Assume that there are 100 employed men and 100 employed women who either work in Occupation A or Occupation B.

	Employed Women	*Employed Men*
Occupation A	70%	20%
Occupation B	30%	80%
Total	100%	100%

   a. Calculate the index of occupational segregation by sex using the formula given in footnote 2, Chapter 5.
   b. Explain exactly what the number you obtained in (a) means in light of the verbal definition of the sex segregation index.

3. Why is the occupational segregation index lower when you consider the nine major occupational categories than when you consider a large set of detailed occupations?

4. Explain why the female–male earnings ratio is higher for full-time, year-round workers than for all workers.

CHAPTER 6

DIFFERENCES IN OCCUPATIONS AND EARNINGS: THE HUMAN CAPITAL MODEL

Chapter Highlights

- Formal Education
- On-the-Job Training
- Occupations and Earnings
- Other Supply-Side Factors
- The Human Capital Explanation: An Assessment

In this chapter, we present supply-side explanations for the gender differences in occupations and earnings described in Chapter 5. We first summarize the arguments of scholars who emphasize this point of view, beginning with a consideration of the determinants of the decision to invest in formal education and on-the-job training and an analysis of the sources of gender differences in these decisions within the human capital framework. Next we apply these concepts to understanding gender differences in occupations and earnings. We then consider other supply-side factors that may produce gender differences in economic outcomes. We conclude by presenting an evaluation of the contributions of the human capital approach. In Chapter 7 we consider labor market discrimination, which provides an alternative explanation for gender differences in occupations and earnings. It is our view that these two sets of explanations are not mutually exclusive and that both provide valuable insights into the sources of male–female differences in occupations and earnings.

Supply-side explanations focus on the observation that men and women may come to the labor market with different tastes and with different qualifications, such as education, formal training, or experience. Gender differences in tastes might mean, for example, that one group or the other has greater tolerance for an unpleasant, unhealthy, or dangerous environment, for longer work hours or inflexible work schedules, for physical strain, or for repetitive tasks, and is more willing to accept any or all of these in return for higher wages. An example of a gender difference in qualifications would be a woman having a college degree in English and a man having a college degree in engineering. Or, as another example, a woman might move in and out of the labor force as her family situation changes, whereas a man's attachment might be more continuous.

To the extent such differences in men's and women's tastes and qualifications exist, they could cause women to earn less and to be concentrated in different occupations. Little is known about tastes and their effects on occupational choices and rewards; however, there has been a great deal of research on job-related qualifications. Hence, we too shall concentrate on them.

Before considering the effects of gender differences in qualifications on earnings and occupations, one issue that arises is whether they should be viewed as the result of the voluntary choices men and women make or as the outcome of what has been termed *prelabor market* or **societal discrimination.** Societal discrimination denotes the multitude of social influences that cause women to make decisions that adversely influence their status in the labor market. Since we are all products of our environments to a greater or lesser extent, it is often difficult to draw the line between voluntary choice and this type of discrimination.

This distinction may in part reflect disciplinary boundaries. The discipline of economics tends to view individual decision making as determined by economic incentives and individual preferences (or tastes). It does not analyze the formation of preferences, and choices are generally viewed as being at least to some extent voluntary. In contrast, sociologists and social psychologists are more apt to examine the role of socialization and social-structural factors in producing what economists classify as individual preferences.[1] Thus, within the context of sociology or social psychology, individual choices are more likely to be seen as stemming from social conditioning or constraints rather than as voluntary.

The tendency to emphasize the role of choice versus societal discrimination may also reflect an implicit value judgment. Those who are reasonably content with the status quo of gender differences in economic outcomes tend to speak mainly of voluntary choices, whereas those who decry gender inequality in pay and occupations are more likely to focus on societal discrimination.

We tend toward the view that at least some of the gender differences in qualifications that currently exist stem from undesirable societal discrimination, although we acknowledge that, particularly in the past and to a lesser extent today, this type of gender differentiation has often been regarded as perfectly appropriate. The most important point is that even if societal discrimination is a problem, it is essentially different from **labor market discrimination** (which is discussed in Chapter 7), and a different set of policies is required to deal with it.

A second issue that deserves attention is that distinguishing between supply- and demand-side factors is not as easy as it appears at first. Labor market discrimination can affect women's economic status *indirectly* by lowering their incentives to invest in themselves and to acquire particular job qualifications. Thus, gender differences in productivity-related characteristics may reflect not only the voluntary choices of men and

---

[1] Sociologists might question the appropriateness of the term *discrimination* in the context of gender socialization. We use it here only to the extent that the socialization process adversely affects the labor market success of young women.

women and the impact of societal discrimination but also the indirect effects of labor market discrimination. This last point will also be developed further in Chapter 7.

WHAT IS HUMAN CAPITAL?

Within the economics literature, the major supply-side explanation for gender differentials in economic outcomes has been developed within the context of the human capital model. Most of us are familiar with the notion of investments in **physical capital.** For example, businesspeople expend resources today to build new plants or to purchase new machinery. This augments their firms' productive capabilities and increases their output in future years. They make such decisions based upon a comparison of the expected costs and benefits of these investments. Economists like Theodore Schultz, Gary Becker, and Jacob Mincer have pointed out that individuals and their families make analogous decisions regarding **human capital** investments.[2] In this case, resources are invested in an individual today in order to increase his or her future productivity and earnings. Examples of human capital investments include investments in formal education, on-the-job training, job search, and geographic migration.

Although the analogy between physical and human capital is compelling, there are some important differences between the two. Chiefly, an individual's human capital investment decisions will be influenced to a greater extent by nonpecuniary (nonmonetary) considerations than is typically the case for physical capital investment decisions. Some people enjoy going to school; others do not. Some find indoor, white-collar work attractive; others would prefer to do manual work in the fresh air. Another important difference is that it is in general more difficult to borrow to finance human capital investments than to finance physical ones. This is the case because one does not have collateral to offer if the loan is not repaid. These differences between physical and human capital illustrate the general point that although labor markets are similar to other markets, they are not identical to them—in large part because labor services cannot be separated from the individuals who provide them. This does not invalidate the use of economic analysis in the study of labor markets, but it does require us to be aware of some of the differences between labor markets and other markets that can be very important.

We first focus upon the pecuniary aspects of the human capital investment decision and then consider how nonpecuniary factors might influence the analysis. We emphasize two major kinds of human capital investments—formal schooling and on-the-job training. According to the work of Jacob Mincer, Solomon Polachek, and others, gender differences in these areas—in both the amount and type of investments that are made— can produce substantial differences in the pay and occupations of men and women in the labor market.[3]

---

[2] See, for example, Theodore W. Schultz, "Investment in Human Capital," *American Economic Review* 51, no. 1 (March 1960): 1–17; Gary S. Becker, *Human Capital: A Theoretical and Empirical Analysis, With Special Reference to Education,* 3rd ed. (Chicago: University of Chicago Press, 1993); and Jacob Mincer; "On-the-Job Training: Costs, Returns and Some Implications," *Journal of Political Economy* 70, no. 5, pt. 2 (October 1962): 50–79.

[3] Jacob Mincer and Solomon W. Polachek, "Family Investments in Human Capital: Earnings of Women," *Journal of Political Economy* 82, no. 2, pt. 2 (March/April 1974): 76–108; and Solomon W. Polachek, "Occupational Self-Selection: A Human Capital Approach to Sex Differences in Occupational Structure," *Review of Economics and Statistics* 63, no. 1 (February 1981): 60–69.

GENDER DIFFERENCES IN EDUCATIONAL ATTAINMENT

Gender differences in educational attainment in the United States are not large. They are, for example, considerably smaller than minority–white educational differences in the United States or than gender differences in educational attainment in many parts of the developing world. However, there are some significant gender differences in the *pattern* of educational attainment of men and women that are worth noting. Historically, women have been more likely to complete high school than men, but higher proportions of men than women have completed college and gone on to postgraduate education. This is reflected in the data for 1970 and 1999 shown in Table 6.1.

In both years, higher proportions of men than women were high school dropouts, although gender differences were quite small. In 1970, differences between men and women in college completion were considerably larger; men were 1.7 times as likely to have completed four or more years of college than women. However, the gender difference in higher education has declined, as men and women in younger cohorts have acquired more similar educational attainment. By 1999, women were nearly as likely to have completed four or more years of college as men, and, among 25- to 34-year-olds, women were actually slightly more likely to be college graduates than men.

The data in Table 6.1 also show rising educational attainment of both men and women over the period. A typical individual of either sex was much less likely to have dropped out of high school in 1999 than in 1970, and considerably more likely to have had some schooling beyond high school.

Educational attainment is shown separately by race and Hispanic origin in Table 6.2. In all cases, women were less likely to be high school dropouts than men, although these differences are small for all groups. However, while men were more likely to have completed college than women among whites, women were more likely to be college graduates among blacks and Hispanics.

Comparing whites and minorities, we see that both blacks and Hispanics had lower educational attainment than whites. Minorities were more likely than whites to have dropped out of high school and less likely to be college graduates. However, the differences between blacks and whites were considerably smaller than the differences be-

TABLE 6.1 Educational Attainment of the Population by Gender: 1970 and 1999 (Ages 25–64)

	1970		1999	
	Males (%)	*Females (%)*	*Males (%)*	*Females (%)*
Less than 4 years of high school	39.3	38.2	13.6	12.5
4 years of high school only	33.5	42.3	32.2	33.8
Some college	11.9	10.5	25.4	27.5
4 or more years of college	15.3	9.0	28.8	26.2
Total	100.0	100.0	100.0	100.0

Sources: Tabulated from the 1970 and 1999 microdata files of the March *Current Population Survey.*

TABLE 6.2   Educational Attainment of the Population by Gender, Race, and Hispanic Origin, 1999 (Ages 25–64)

	Whites		*Blacks*		*Hispanics*	
	Males (%)	*Females (%)*	*Males (%)*	*Females (%)*	*Males (%)*	*Females (%)*
Less than 4 years of high school	13.0	11.6	18.4	17.5	41.9	40.4
4 years of high school only	31.8	34.1	39.8	35.1	28.2	27.6
Some college	25.3	27.5	26.4	29.5	18.9	20.0
4 or more years of college	29.8	26.8	15.3	18.0	11.0	12.0
Total	100.0	100.0	100.0	100.0	100.0	100.0

Source: Tabulated from the 1999 microdata file of the March *Current Population Survey.*

tween Hispanics and whites, reflecting a considerable increase in the relative educational attainment of blacks since the 1960s. By 1999, the proportion of young non-Hispanic blacks aged 25 to 29 who held high school diplomas, 89 percent, was only slightly less than the figure of 93 percent for non-Hispanic whites in that age group. Hispanics continued to lag behind, however, even in the young age group, where only 62 percent were high school graduates. While the large influx of immigrants with low levels of education may help to explain some of the sizable Hispanic–white difference in educational attainment, the numbers also reflect considerably higher high school dropout rates even of native-born Hispanic students.[4]

The trends in higher education by gender, shown in greater detail in Table 6.3, reinforce our impression of declining differences among younger cohorts. In the early 1960s, women received 39 percent of bachelor's degrees, about the same as their share in 1930. By the late 1990s, 56 percent of bachelor's degrees were awarded to women, as were 57 percent of master's degrees. Similarly, although women received 43 percent of associate degrees in the early 1970s, they received a majority of such degrees by the 1980s and 61 percent by the late 1990s. Women still were awarded only 41 percent of doctorates and 42 percent of first professional degrees in the late 1990s, but this represented a substantial increase in their share since the 1960s. First professional degrees are those awarded in postcollege professional training programs, including those in medicine, law, business, dentistry, pharmacy, veterinary medicine, and theology.

The figures on educational attainment reveal only part of the story of gender differences in formal schooling, however. For, beginning with high school, male and female students have tended to differ in the types of courses they took and their fields of specialization. This was especially true in the past and remains the case to some extent even today.

For example, at the secondary level, girls traditionally took fewer courses in natural sciences and mathematics than boys. Such differences are potentially important. Although differences in the number of courses taken in these fields have been found to

---

4   Steven A. Holmes, "Education Gap Between Races Closes," *New York Times,* 6 September 1996, p. A-18; and George J. Borjas, "Assimilation and Changes in Cohort Quality Revisited: What Happened to Immigrant Earnings in the 1980s?" *Journal of Labor Economics* 13, no. 2 (April 1995): 201–45.

TABLE 6.3 Percentage of Degrees Awarded to Women by Level, 1929–1930 to 1996–1997 (Selected Years)

Years	Associate (%)	Bachelor's (%)	Master's (%)	Doctor's (%)	First Professional (%)
1929–1930	n.a.	39.9[a]	40.4	15.4	n.a.
1960–1961	n.a.	38.5	31.7	10.5	2.7
1970–1971	42.9	43.4	40.1	14.3	6.3
1980–1981	54.7	49.8	50.3	31.1	26.6
1990–1991	58.8	53.9	53.6	37.0	39.1
1992–1993	58.8	54.3	54.2	38.1	40.1
1996-1997	60.8	55.6	56.9	40.8	42.1

[a] Includes first professional degrees.

n.a. Not available.

Source: U.S. Department of Education, National Center for Education Statistics, *Digest of Education Statistics,* 1999.

have little effect on gender differences in pay for high school graduates,[5] taking more high school math has been reported to increase the wages of female college graduates, as well as their likelihood of entering technical and nontraditional fields.[6] Considerable progress has been made in reducing gender differences in high school courses in recent years. However, although the number of years girls study science and math is approaching that of boys, there are still some important differences in the particular courses taken. Girls are more likely than boys to end their high school math careers with algebra, and boys outnumber girls in physics and higher-skill computer courses.[7] Interestingly, boys are no more likely than girls to have a computer at home or to use it. However, girls are considerably more likely than boys to use their household computer for word processing and considerably less likely to use it for playing games. Data on adults indicates that men are very slightly more likely to use a computer at home, although this represents a considerable decrease in the computer use "gender gap" since the mid-1980s when data first became available. At work though, it is women who are more likely to use a computer than men, perhaps in part due to the greater use of word processing in many traditionally female jobs.[8]

---

[5] Charles Brown and Mary Corcoran, "Sex-Based Differences in School Content and the Male/Female Wage Gap," *Journal of Labor Economics* 15, no. 3, pt. 1 (July 1997): 431–65.

[6] Phillip B. Levine and David J. Zimmerman, "The Benefit of Additional High-School Math and Science Classes of Young Men and Women," *Journal of Business and Economic Statistics* 13, no. 2 (April 1995): 137–49.

[7] American Association of University Women *Gender Gaps. Where Schools Still Fail Our Children* (Washington, DC: American Association of University Women, 1998). For analyses of gender differences in mathematics and computer learning, see Sheila Tobias, *Overcoming Math Anxiety* (New York: W. W. Norton, 1993), chap. 3; and Pamela E. Kramer and Sheila Lehman, "Mismeasuring Women: A Critique of Research on Computer Ability and Avoidance," *Signs: Journal of Women in Culture and Society* 16, no. 1 (autumn 1990): 158–72.

[8] Eric C. Newburger, *Computer Use in the United States, 1997: Population Characteristics,* Current Population Reports P20–522, U.S. Census Bureau (September 1999).

Differences between men and women in fields of specialization at the college level are more substantial, as illustrated in Table 6.4. Here too, however, the gender difference has narrowed considerably since the mid-1960s. For example, it has been reported that, in 1964, the index of segregation by college major was 51.4, indicating that over half of college women (or men) would have had to change majors for the distribution of women and men across majors to have been the same. By 1990, this figure had declined substantially to 29.4.[9] Similarly, the considerable increase in the percentage of women receiving first professional degrees, which we saw in Table 6.3, reflected large gains in their representation in traditionally male professions such as medicine, law, and business (a specific breakdown is shown in Table 6.5).

TABLE 6.4   Percentage of Bachelor's Degrees Awarded to Women by Field, 1965–1966, 1996–1997 (Selected Fields)

Discipline	1965–1966 (%)	1996–1997 (%)
Agriculture and natural resources	2.7	39.0
Architecture and related programs	4.0	35.9
Biological sciences/life sciences	28.2	53.9
Business management, administrative sciences, and marketing	8.5	48.6
Computer and information sciences	13.0[a]	27.2
Education	75.3	75.0
Engineering	0.4	16.6
English and English literature	66.2	66.5
Foreign languages	70.7	69.7
Health	76.9	81.5
Home economics	97.5	88.4
Mathematics	33.3	46.1
Physical sciences and science technologies	13.6	37.4
Psychology	41.0	73.9
Social sciences	35.0	48.7
Economics	9.8	30.9
History	34.6	38.4
Sociology	59.6	68.3

[a] Data are for 1969, the earliest year available.

Source: U.S. Department of Health, Education and Welfare, Office of Education, *Earned Degrees Conferred: 1965–66;* U.S. Department of Education, National Center for Education Statistics, *Digest of Education Statistics,* 1999.

---

[9] Jerry A. Jacobs, *Revolving Doors: Sex Segregation and Women's Careers* (Stanford: Stanford University Press, 1989); and Jerry A. Jacobs, "Gender and Academic Specialties: Trends Among Recipients of College Degrees in the 1980s," *Sociology of Education* 68, no. 2 (April 1995): 81–98. Jacobs reports that the trend toward gender integration in fields of study was especially strong in the 1970s and slowed markedly in the late 1980s.

TABLE 6.5   Percentage of First Professional Degrees Awarded to Women by Field, 1966, 1981 and 1997 (Selected Fields)

Field	1966 (%)	1981 (%)	1997 (%)
Business[a]	3.2[b]	23.8	38.9
Dentistry	1.1	14.4	36.9
Medicine	6.7	24.7	41.4
Pharmacy	16.4	42.6	64.5
Veterinary Medicine	8.0[c]	35.2	66.6
Law	3.8	32.4	43.7
Theology	4.1	14.0	26.2

[a] Master's degrees in business administration and management.

[b] Data are for 1964–65.

[c] Data are for 1967–68.

Source: U.S. Department of Health, Education and Welfare, Office of Education, *Earned Degrees Conferred: 1965–66;* U.S. Department of Education, National Center for Educational Statistics, *Digest of Education Statistics,* 1983 and 1999.

In summary, while the educational attainment of men and women is fairly similar, there are still some important gender differences in education that may have an impact on women's earnings and occupational attainment. Historically, women were more likely than men to complete high school, but higher proportions of men than women completed four or more years of college. Further, traditionally women took fewer math and science courses than men in high school, and college men and women tended to differ in their fields of study. However, all these differences have been narrowing in recent years, and the gender difference in the number of years of high school science and math courses has virtually disappeared, although some important differences remain as to the specific courses taken, and among younger people women are actually more likely to graduate college than men.

We now turn to the explanation provided by the human capital model for the historical tendency of men and women to acquire different amounts of education and to specialize in different fields. We then consider some of the other factors that may help to account for these differences.

THE EDUCATIONAL INVESTMENT DECISION

We begin by considering an individual's decision of whether or not to invest in formal education, as illustrated in Figure 6.1. Here we consider Daniel's choice between going to college or ending his formal education with high school. Initially, we focus solely upon the pecuniary costs and benefits of investing in education, although later we consider nonpecuniary costs and benefits as well. This investment decision entails a comparison between the expected **experience–earnings profiles** (the annual earnings at each level of labor market experience) associated with each type of schooling.

In this case, Daniel expects his profile to be *EF* if he enters the labor market after completing high school. Alternatively, if he goes on to college, he will incur out-of-pocket

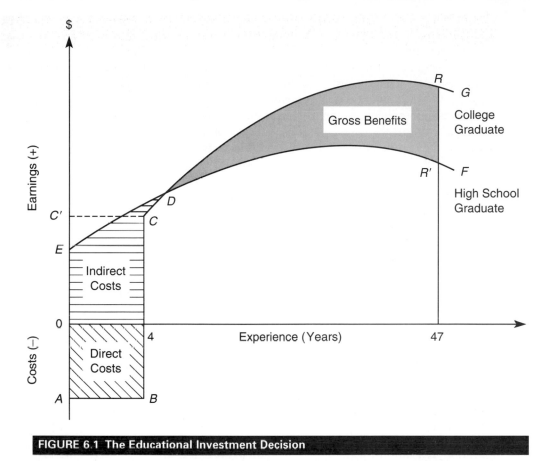

FIGURE 6.1 The Educational Investment Decision

expenses on tuition and books of OA dollars per year (negative "earnings") for the four-year period. (He does not anticipate taking a job while he goes to school.) Upon graduation, he expects to earn OC' dollars. The investment in a college education is believed to increase his productivity and, hence, his earnings above what he could have earned entering the labor force directly after high school (OE). Although, in this hypothetical example, he initially earns less than he could have if he had worked for four years rather than going to college, over his work life his expected earnings are higher. His experience–earnings profile, if he goes to college, is $ABCG$.

As indicated in Figure 6.1, the earnings of both high school and college graduates are expected to increase with labor market experience over much of the individual's work life. Human capital theory attributes this to the productivity-enhancing effects of on-the-job training, which we discuss later in this chapter. Note that Figure 6.1 shows the college graduate's profile as rising more steeply than the high school graduate's. As we shall see later, this has indeed been found to be the case empirically and suggests that college graduates acquire more training informally on the job as well as formally in school.

Now let us consider how Daniel can use the information in Figure 6.1 to make his investment decision. To do so he considers both the incremental costs and the incremental benefits associated with graduating from college. There are two types of costs of schooling that he must take into account. **Direct costs** are expenditures on such items as tuition, fees, and books. Less obvious, but no less important than direct costs, are the earnings forgone during the time an individual is in school. These **indirect costs** correspond to the opportunity costs of schooling. We have assumed that Daniel does not work for pay while attending college, but even if he did, his forgone earnings are still likely to be substantial—college students are seldom employed for as many hours or for as high a wage as workers who are not enrolled in school. The full costs of a college education are equal to the sum of the direct and indirect costs, or area *EABCD*.

The gross benefits of a college education are given by the excess of the expected earnings of a college graduate over those of a high school graduate over the work life. Other things being equal, the size of these benefits depends on the length of the expected work life. If Daniel expects to work 43 years after college until retirement at age 65, his benefits are equal to the shaded area *DRR'*.

For Daniel to decide in favor of a college education (on an economic basis), the *gross benefits* of this investment must exceed the costs; that is, the *net benefits* must be positive. Further, gross benefits must exceed costs by an amount sufficient to give him an adequate return on his investment. Individuals may differ on the rate of return required to induce them to undertake this investment, but all are likely to require a positive rate of return.

For one thing, instead of investing resources in human capital, Daniel could have put his money into a savings bank or invested it in other assets. Those alternatives provide a positive rate of return and, thus, his human capital investment must also do so in order to be competitive. More fundamentally, Daniel, like most people, prefers income (and the opportunity to spend it) now to income (and the opportunity to spend it) later. To induce him to delay his gratification and receive his income later rather than sooner, the labor market has to offer him (and others like him) an inducement in the form of a positive rate of return. In Daniel's case, the investment does appear profitable, although we cannot tell simply by looking at the diagram because while the benefit area appears to exceed the cost area, we do not know what the resulting rate of return is or whether Daniel will find it acceptable. If indeed he deems the investment sufficiently profitable, he is likely to decide to go on to college.[10]

Estimates of the average private rate of return to a college education range from 5 to 15 percent.[11] Interestingly, the rate of return to education tends to be higher than for various types of financial investments. One possible reason for this is that investment in human capital is riskier in that everything depends on how well the specific individual

---

[10] Some additional details may be of interest to advanced students. It is possible to express the **present value** of an income or cost stream today by discounting future income or costs by the interest rate. Based on such a calculation, an individual would undertake the investment in education if the present value of benefits was greater than or at least equal to the present value of the costs. Alternatively, one can solve for the discount rate that exactly equates the present value of costs to the present value of benefits. If this rate, called the **internal rate of return,** represents an adequate rate of return from the individual's perspective, the individual will choose to invest in education.

[11] See, for example, George Psacharopoulos, "Returns to Education: A Further International Update and Implications," *Journal of Human Resources* 20, no. 4 (fall 1985): 583–604. Calculating the rate of return involves estimating the increase in earnings attributable to additional education as well as all the costs involved in acquiring it, including both forgone earnings and out-of-pocket expenses. There are a number of difficulties in statistically estimating the returns to schooling; for a discussion, see David Card, "Earnings, Schooling, and Ability Revisited," *Research in Labor Economics,* ed. Solomon W. Polachek (Greenwich CT: JAI Press, 1995).

fares in the labor market. Numerous studies have confirmed that earnings rise with additional education for both men and women. This is illustrated in Figures 6.2a and 6.2b, which show age–earnings profiles of high school and college graduates for 1974 and 1999. In each year the earnings of college graduates lie above those of high school graduates of the same sex. Moreover, the earnings profiles of college graduates of both sexes are more steeply sloped than those of their high school counterparts, as noted previously.

Despite the general similarity of the profiles in each of the two years, there have been some changes that illustrate important labor market developments over the past 25 years. Earnings are shown in terms of 1999 dollars in both years (that is, they are adjusted for inflation) so levels of earnings and differences across groups are comparable in each year. One striking difference between the mid-1970s and the late 1990s is that, for each sex, the earnings of college graduates have risen relative to high school graduates. This means that the rate of return to education has increased. This is part of a trend toward rising returns to skills over this period.[12] As a consequence, college graduates experienced more favorable trends in real earnings than high school graduates or high school dropouts, with young, less-educated men particularly losing ground in real terms. These recent trends are considered in more detail in Chapter 8.

EDUCATION AND PRODUCTIVITY

Human capital theory postulates that earnings rise with additional education because of the productivity-enhancing effects of education. Intuitively, it seems reasonable that education imparts a variety of skills and knowledge that would potentially be useful on the job, ranging from specific skills like computer programming and accounting to general skills like reasoning ability, writing skills, and proficiency in solving mathematical problems. Educational institutions may also teach certain behaviors that are valued on the job, such as punctuality, following instructions, and habits of predictability and dependability.[13]

Others have suggested an alternative interpretation of the positive relationship between education and earnings in which education functions solely as a **screening device** or a **signal.**[14] In this view, employers have imperfect information on worker productivity and, thus, seek ways to distinguish more productive applicants from less productive applicants before hiring them. At the same time, it is assumed that more able (productive) individuals find the (psychic and monetary) costs of acquiring additional schooling lower than the less able (say, because they find their studies less arduous or because they are awarded scholarships). Since the more able have lower costs, an educational

---

[12]   Rising educational differentials and other increases in the returns to skill over this period have been widely reported in the literature. See, for example, Chinhui Juhn, Kevin M. Murphy, and Brooks Pierce, "Wage Inequality and the Rise in Returns to Skill," *Journal of Political Economy* 101, no. 3 (June 1993): 410–42; and Lawrence F. Katz and Kevin M. Murphy, "Changes in Relative Wages, 1963–87: Supply and Demand Factors," *Quarterly Journal of Economics* 107, no. 1 (February 1992): 35–78. To be fully confident that the return to college has risen, we should also look at trends in out-of-pocket costs, but any changes there are likely to be dwarfed by the large shifts in earnings profiles.

[13]   See, for example, Richard C. Edwards, "Individual Traits and Organizational Incentives: What Makes a 'Good' Worker?" *Journal of Human Resources* 11, no. 1 (winter 1976): 51–68.

[14]   See, especially, Michael Spence, *Market Signalling* (Cambridge, MA: Harvard University Press, 1974).

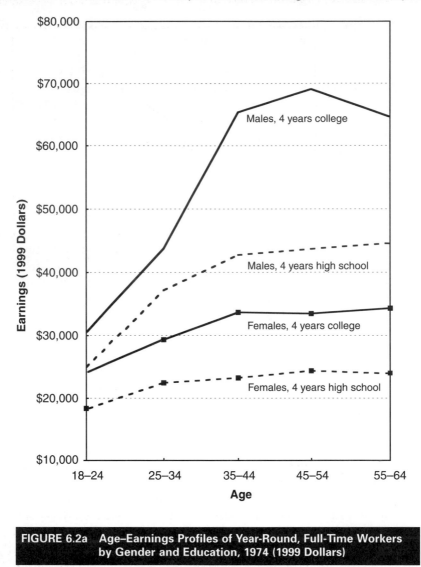

FIGURE 6.2a **Age–Earnings Profiles of Year-Round, Full-Time Workers by Gender and Education, 1974 (1999 Dollars)**

investment may be profitable for them when it would not be for the less able. In an extreme version of the signaling model, education is rewarded *solely* because it *signals* higher productivity to the employer and *not* because of any skills it imparts.

Unfortunately, this theoretical disagreement between the human capital and signaling models has proved difficult to resolve empirically. This is the case because the issue is a particularly thorny one—*not* whether or not more education is correlated with higher productivity and earnings, but *why*. From the individual's perspective, however, it does not matter whether education raises earnings by increasing productivity or by signaling greater ability. Thus, the decision-making process illustrated in Figure 6.1 would be unaffected.

Nonetheless, there is one potential consequence of the signaling model for gender differences in labor market outcomes that is worth noting. If employers believe that a given

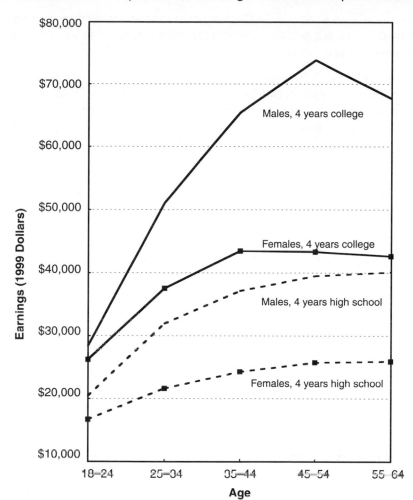

FIGURE 6.2b Age–Earnings Profiles of Year-Round, Full-Time Workers by Gender and Education, 1999 (1999 Dollars)

level of education signals lower productivity for a woman than for a man, women may have to have higher educational credentials than men to obtain the same job. So, for example, suppose an employer who is hiring for entry-level management positions believes that a bachelor's degree signals a lower commitment to the labor market for women than for men. He or she may require a woman to have, say, an MBA degree in order to obtain employment, while being perfectly willing to hire a man with only a bachelor's degree.[15] This is quite similar to the notion of **statistical discrimination** to be discussed in Chapter 7.

---

[15] Such "qualifications" discrimination has been emphasized by Dolores A. Conway and Harry V. Roberts, "Reverse Regression, Fairness and Employment Discrimination," *Journal of Business and Economic Statistics* 1, no. 1 (January 1983): 75–85.

GENDER DIFFERENCES IN EDUCATIONAL INVESTMENT DECISIONS: THE HUMAN CAPITAL ANALYSIS

Does our analysis of the human capital investment decision suggest any reasons why men and women might decide to acquire different amounts or types of formal education? According to the analysis we have presented, the major factors to consider are the expected costs and benefits of the investment. Realistically, the definitions of costs and benefits may be extended to include nonpecuniary, as well as pecuniary, costs and benefits, and we do so later. In addition, because individuals may find it hard to borrow to finance their human capital investments, access to funds is a further consideration of some importance. Thus, we will want to consider why men and women might differ in these respects.

EXPECTED WORK LIFE

The major factor emphasized by human capital theorists as producing gender differences in human capital investments is that, given traditional roles in the family, many women anticipate shorter, more disrupted work lives than men. Such women will reach the point sooner when additional investment is no longer worthwhile. Furthermore, it will not pay for them to make the types of human capital investments that require sustained, high-level commitment to the labor force to make them profitable and that depreciate rapidly during periods of work interruptions.

The impact of these factors is illustrated in Figure 6.3, where we have reproduced the earnings profiles shown in Figure 6.1. Note that the horizontal axis now refers to potential experience or the total time elapsed since completing high school. We have done this in order to be able to represent periods of time out of the labor force on this diagram.

A career-oriented woman who anticipates working the same number of years as Daniel will find it equally profitable to invest in a college education, assuming she faces similar costs and has the opportunity to reap the same returns. However, a woman who expects to spend fewer years in the labor market will find her benefits correspondingly reduced.

For example, suppose Adele plans to be in the labor force for a time—6 years—after college and then to drop out for 10 years, say, for childrearing. If she, like Daniel, expects to retire at age 65, her expected work life is 33 years in comparison to his 43 years. Her shorter work life reduces the benefits of her human capital investment because she does not earn income during the time she spends out of the labor force. Further, it is generally believed that skills depreciate during time spent out of the labor force when they are not used. It is thus expected that, upon her return to the labor force after an interruption of 10 years, Adele's earnings of e_2 will be less in real terms than she was making when she left (e_1) and that she will be faced with profile GH rather than profile CD. We have shown profile GH as approaching CD over time, as Adele retools or becomes less rusty.[16] Nonetheless, the time out of the labor force has cost her a reduction in earnings over the remainder of her working life. In this example, the bene-

---

[16] For evidence that earnings tend to "rebound" after work force interruptions, see Jacob Mincer and Haim Ofek, "Interrupted Work Careers: Depreciation and Restoration of Human Capital," *Journal of Human Resources* 17, no. 1 (winter 1982): 3–24; and Joyce P. Jacobsen and Laurence M. Levin, "Effects of Intermittent Labor Force Attachment on Women's Earnings," *Monthly Labor Review* 118, no. 9 (September 1995): 14–19.

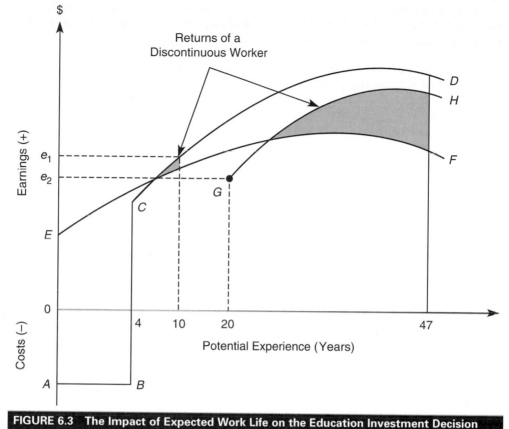

FIGURE 6.3   The Impact of Expected Work Life on the Education Investment Decision

fits of the investment in a college education, the sum of the two shaded areas, may not be large enough to make it worthwhile.

A complication that we have not shown in Figure 6.3 is that a break in experience would also affect EF, the high school earnings profile. Specifically, a portion of the EF line would be shifted down to represent Adele's options after she returns from her work force interruption. Taking this into account is unlikely to affect our conclusion that a work force interruption reduces the returns to investing in a college education, however, because a major factor reducing the returns to the investment in college is simply the interruption itself and the loss of returns for that period. In addition, since the skills of high school graduates are less than those of college graduates, the loss due to depreciation is likely to also be less for them. Thus, we have omitted this shift in EF from Figure 6.3 to keep our diagram as simple as possible while still capturing the major points.

One factor that might somewhat offset the conclusions we arrived at from considering Figure 6.3 is that education may increase productivity in some nonmarket activities as well as in market work. For example, the time that more highly educated parents spend with their children may have a larger positive effect on their offspring's cognitive ability than the time of less well educated parents. Were we to factor in these potential benefits in the home, the loss of returns due to labor force withdrawals would be reduced. However, it is unlikely that our conclusion would be altered: Higher anticipated time spent out of the labor force reduces the amount of educational investments that the individual finds profitable.

Thus, the human capital model shows how an adherence to traditional gender roles in the family can explain why women have traditionally been less likely than men to pursue college and graduate study. It also suggests one reason why gender differences in college attendance have been declining. As we saw in Chapter 4, women have increased their labor force participation. As young women anticipate longer and more continuous working lives, it will be profitable for them to increase their investment in formal education. Furthermore, Figure 6.3 suggests that once women have decided to acquire higher education, for whatever reason, their attachment to the labor force is reinforced because the opportunity cost of time spent out of the labor force is increased.

Although our application of the human capital model suggests a plausible explanation for the historical tendency of men to be more likely to pursue college and graduate study, it does not explain why in the past women were *more* likely than men to complete high school. The gender disparity was quite sizable at one time. For example, in 1900, only two-thirds as many boys as girls graduated from high school. One possible explanation for this difference is that the opportunity cost of remaining in high school was lower for young women than for young men, since their potential labor market earnings were less. As job opportunities for young men who have not finished high school have declined, so too has the gender differential in high school completion.

The human capital model also suggests that discontinuity of expected labor force participation may help to explain gender differences in fields of specialization. In some fields, such as science and engineering, technological change progresses rapidly. A woman returning from a labor force interruption will not only have to contend with her depreciation of skills over the interim but also with the advancement of the field during her absence. On the other hand, in such other fields as teaching history or English, the pace of change is slower. A woman returning from a work force interruption is likely to find that her earnings fall less steeply. Women anticipating traditional roles are, therefore, expected to avoid fields where the rate of technological change is rapid and to concentrate in fields where the cost of work force interruptions is lower.[17] Thus, women's increasing labor force attachment may partially explain their increased representation in traditionally male fields of study.

Gender differences in mathematical ability, as indicated, for example, by differences between young men and women in scores on standardized tests like the SAT, have also been cited as a factor in gender differences in majors.[18] While the gender gap in math scores remains substantial, it has declined in recent years as the high school course work of young men and women has become more similar. In 1977 when the gender difference in SAT math scores was at its highest level in recent years, girls' scores lagged 46 points below boys' scores, on average. By the mid-1990s, the difference was 35 points

[17] Solomon W. Polachek, "Sex Differences in College Major," *Industrial and Labor Relations Review* 31, no. 4 (July 1978): 498–508; and Arthur F. Blakemore and Stuart A. Low, "Sex Differences in Occupational Selection: The Case of College Majors," *Review of Economics and Statistics* 66, no. 1 (February 1984): 157–63. Another issue is that some fields more easily accommodate part-time work, thus facilitating reentry.

[18] Morton Paglin and Anthony M. Rufolo, "Heterogeneous Human Capital, Occupational Choice, and Male–Female Earnings Differences," *Journal of Labor Economics* 8, no. 1, pt. 1 (January 1990): 123–44.

and remained at about that level through 2000 (the most recent year for which this information was available). The SAT verbal scores of boys also exceed those of girls, though these differences (currently 3–4 points) are much smaller and also declined through the mid-1990s.[19]

Whatever their source, gender differences in college major have been found to be strongly related to the gender wage gap among college graduates. One study found that they accounted for 40 to 45 percent of the overall male-female wage differential among this group in the mid-1980s, with about one-third to one-half of this effect due to job characteristics, that is, to the occupational and industrial differences associated with the gender differences in major.[20] It has also been found that the growing similarity in college majors between men and women contributed to a narrowing of the gender wage gap over the 1980s.[21]

Sexism in the Schoolroom

Some authorities have attributed gender differences in academic achievement and later labor market success to differences in the way girls and boys are treated in the classroom. Two studies on this subject received particular attention, one by Myra and David Sadker and a 1992 report by the American Association of University Women entitled *The AAUW Report: How Schools Shortchange Girls*. More recently, several scholars have critiqued these studies, raising questions about the view that girls and women continue to be discriminated against. Christina Sommers and Judith Kleinfeld have been among the most forceful critics.*

In describing how schools shortchanged girls, Sadker and Sadker pointed to research findings indicating that, as early as preschool, teachers spent more time talking to boys, praised them more often, and were far more likely to give them detailed instructions regarding how to do things for themselves. The Sadkers' own research indicated that, although most teachers thought that girls participated in and were called on in class as frequently as boys, boys in fact dominated the classroom vocally. The skewed perceptions of teachers were strikingly revealed when they were shown a film of an eighth grade class and asked who was talking more. The teachers overwhelmingly said the girls were. However, in reality, the boys were out-talking the girls at a ratio of three to one. The teachers

* Myra Sadker and David Sadker, "Sexism in the Schoolroom of the 80's," *Psychology Today* 19 (March 1985): 54–57; American Association of University Women, *The AAUW Report: How Schools Shortchange Girls* (Washington, DC: American Association of University Women Educational Foundation, 1992); Christina Hoff Sommers, *The War Against Boy: How Misguided Feminism is Harming Our Young Men*" (New York: Simon & Schuster, 2000); and Judith Kleinfeld, "Why Smart People Believe that Schools Shortchange Girls: What You See when You Live in a Tail," *Gender Issues* 16, 1/2 (winter/spring 1998): 47–63.

---

[19] "College Board Reports Continuing Upward Trend in Average Scores on SAT 1" Press Release, College Board, August 22, 1996; and the College Board web site (www.collegeboard.org). There was virtually no difference in the mean ACT scores of young men (21.2) and women (20.9) in 2000. The ACT score represents a combined assessment of English, math, reading, and science reasoning; see the ACT web site (www.act.org).

[20] Brown and Corcoran, "Sex-Based Differences." Gender differences in high school courses, however, were found to have little effect on the wage gap.

[21] Eric Eide, "College Major Choice and Changes in the Gender Wage Gap," *Contemporary Economic Policy* 12, no. 2 (April 1994): 55–64.

were convinced only after actually counting the active participants and the passive watchers. Some critics countered that teachers pay more attention to boys simply because boys are more assertive and "grab" teachers' attention. While that may be true, it is not the whole story. The Sadkers found that while teachers accepted answers called out by boys, girls who did the same thing were reprimanded for inappropriate behavior.

Sommers, Kleinfeld, and other critics have criticized reports that girls are at a disadvantage, noting that boys are overrepresented at the bottom as well as at the top of the distribution of students, and that girls do better than boys in terms of lower high school drop out rates and higher grade point averages, as well as college attendance and graduation. A mixed picture of gender differences is also acknowledged by a 1998 report by the American Association of University Women,[†] and the problems boys have in school are certainly a matter for concern. This report also points out that conditions for girls have improved considerably since the earlier studies had found serious problems, but notes that some problems still remain.

On the one hand, girls' high school course enrollment patterns increasingly resemble those of boys. On the other hand, in ninth and tenth grade fewer girls than boys take the advanced algebra and geometry courses that are among the main predictors of students going on to college. The reasons for this difference are not as yet clear, but girls' deficiency in this area surely contributes to their continued underrepresentation in many lucrative fields that require a strong mathematics base.

Another unresolved puzzle is why boys consistently do better than girls on highly selective and competitive tests, such as advanced placement tests, college entrance tests, and the graduate record examination, although they do not get higher grades in courses. One characteristic these tests have in common is their heavy reliance on multiple choice questions, where boys apparently have the advantage. Evidence of this was discovered as long ago as the early 1980s,[‡] but it was not until the second half of the 1990s that efforts were made to address this problem. One was the addition of a writing skills section to the PSAT, which immediately brought about a substantial change. At the same time, the perplexing question as to why boys do better than girls on the various tests mentioned above, while girls generally do better on examinations in all subject areas remains to be determined.

In sum, the early critics of the treatment of girls in the schools discovered very real problems, and their work did much to bring about recent efforts to remedy them, which have turned out to have considerable success. Partly as a result of these developments, considering girls to be disadvantaged in all respects in the educational system is no longer warranted, as Sommers and Kleinfeld point out. On the other hand, the 1998 report by the American Association of University Women emphasizes that it is a mistake to argue that improving the situation for girls is necessarily at the expense of boys. Instead, they suggest that, ideally, equitable education addresses the needs of both girls and boys, rather than seeking to ensure that each receives exactly the same thing.[§] Equally important is the fact that both parties to the dispute agree that the situation is far more complex than merely comparing girls and boys, because such other factors as race, ethnicity, and socioeconomic class also play an important part.

[†] American Association of University Women, *Gender Gaps: Where Schools Still Fail Our Children* (Washington, DC: American Association of University Women, 1998).
[‡] See, for instance, Marianne A. Ferber, Bonnie G. Birnbaum, and Carole A. Green, "Gender Differences in Economic Knowledge: A Reevaluation of the Evidence," *Journal of Economic Education* 1, no. 2 (spring 1983): 24–37.
[§] American Association of University Women, *Gender Gaps.*

GENDER DIFFERENCES IN EDUCATIONAL INVESTMENT DECISIONS: OTHER FACTORS

SOCIETAL DISCRIMINATION

Although expected working life is a factor that has been particularly emphasized by human capital theorists, societal discrimination may also cause gender differences in educational attainment and field of specialization. To see this, we must consider the nonpecuniary as well as the pecuniary costs and benefits of human capital investments. Societal influences may raise the costs of, or lower the returns to, specific types of education for women relative to men. Given these higher costs or lower returns, the investment in education may not prove profitable for many women. This situation is particularly apt to arise in fields that have traditionally been predominantly male.

It is also important to bear in mind that social pressures may help to cause the gender differences in labor force participation patterns, which are identified as being the primary cause of gender differences in educational investment decisions in the human capital model. In addition, women's lower labor force participation may to some extent be due to the discrimination they face in the labor market, which reduces their opportunities and lowers their earnings. Such feedback effects of labor market discrimination are considered in greater detail in Chapter 7.

Socialization Socialization is the name given to the process by which the influence of family, friends, teachers, and the media shapes an individual's attitudes and behavior.[22] The preceding inset illustrates the considerable extent of gender differentiation in the classroom; a later inset points out how even something as seemingly innocuous as children's games can reinforce stereotypical views of appropriate gender roles. As another example, it has been found that male characters have traditionally dominated children's television programming.[23] Moreover, a study analyzing general viewing fare during the 1989–1990 television season concluded that "women are often still depicted on television as half-clad and half-witted, and needing to be rescued by quick-thinking, fully-clothed men."[24] TV programs and movies released in 2000 may signal a change in some respects. As one commentator put it, "This year's heroines of prime time and the big screen are muscular and trained in the martial arts, and they have no compunctions about slapping, immolating and kickboxing their way through life, sometimes with the help of supernatural powers." While conventional beauty and scanty dress generally remain part of the equation, powerful girls and women like the star of *Buffy the Vampire Slayer* or the trio in *Charlie's Angels* have been deemed "strong, athletic women" and "good fantasy images."[25] It will be interesting to see whether this trend continues and what its long-term effects are.

---

[22] See, for example, Cynthia Fuchs Epstein, *Deceptive Distinctions, Sex, Gender, and the Social Order* (New Haven, CT: Yale University Press, 1988); and Margaret M. Marini and Mary C. Brinton, "Sex Stereotyping in Occupational Socialization," in *Sex Segregation in the Work Place: Trends, Explanations, and Remedies,* ed. Barbara Reskin (Washington, DC: National Academy Press, 1984), pp. 192–232.

[23] Bill Carter, "Children's TV, Where Boys Are King," *New York Times,* 1 May 1991, pp. 1, B6.

[24] Andrea Adelson, "Study Attacks Roles of Women in Television," *New York Times,* 19 November 1990, p. B3.

[25] Jennifer Steinhauer, "Ideas & Trends; Pow! Slam! Thank You, Ma'am," *New York Times,* 5 November 2000 (www.nytimes.com).

The socialization process influences the self-esteem of men and women, as well as their perceptions of gender-appropriate competencies and behavior. It also helps to shape the role they expect work to occupy in their lives and the types of jobs to which they aspire. We have already seen how gender differences in the expected importance of market work in their lives may influence men's and women's human capital investment decisions. The consequences of gender differences in occupational orientation are also important. To a great extent in the past, and even today, boys and girls are taught from an early age to aspire to and train for gender-appropriate lines of work. This tends to result in gender differences in fields of specialization. Further, even if, despite these influences, a young woman has an interest in entering a traditionally male field, the disapproval of her family, teachers, or friends is a nonpecuniary cost for her that lowers her subjective evaluation of the net value of this investment.[26] Familial attitudes may also pose practical problems for a young woman, if her family is more reluctant to finance her education than her brother's.[27] While it is likely that these types of problems have diminished with the greater social acceptance of women's employment outside the home and their participation in what were formerly viewed as male occupations, it is unlikely that such gender differences have been entirely eliminated.

Children's Toys: The Selling of Stereotypes

Children's toys expose both boys and girls to gender stereotypes from a very early age,[*] whether as a result of their parents' selection of toys for them; what they see when they go to toy stores, look through catalogs, or watch television; or the kinds of toys that they see at the homes of friends and relatives.

For girls, toy stores, of course, offer ubiquitous dolls. There are babies they can take care of, children they can dress up, and glamorous young women they can try to emulate. And, of course, there is Barbie, the most popular doll ever. While Barbie is now available with wardrobes and accessories for various careers, she still has a body that few girls will ever have; to be exact, only 1 young woman out of 100,000 will have such a shape. Ken's proportions, though also rare in the general population, are more realistic; 1 in 50 young men will have his shape.[†] When it comes

[*] This inset draws on Crispin Sartwell, "The Gender Gap Remains—For Boys," *Baltimore Sun,* 28 May 2000; Megan Rosenfeld, "Games Girls Play: A Toy Chest Full of Stereotypes," *Washington Post,* 22 December 1995, p. A1; and C. Estelle Campenni, "Gender Stereotyping of Children's Toys: A Comparison of Parents and Nonparents," *Sex Roles: A Journal of Research* 40, no. 1 (January 1999): 121–39.
[†] Kevin I. Norton, Timothy S. Olds, Scott Olive, and Stephen Dank, "Ken and Barbie at Life Size," *Sex Roles: A Journal of Research* 34, no. 3–4 (February 1996): 287–94.

---

[26] One study found that women graduate students in the biological and physical sciences received less moral support from either their mothers than either the male students in the same field or students of either sex in education. See Helen M. Berg and Marianne A. Ferber, "Men and Women Graduate Students: Who Succeeds and Why?" *Journal of Higher Education* 54, no. 6 (November/December 1983): 629–48.

[27] There is some evidence that sibling sex composition affects women's but not men's educational attainment. Controlling for household size, women with any sisters have lower educational attainment than women raised only with brothers; see Kristin Butcher and Anne Case, "The Effect of Sibling Sex Composition on Women's Education and Earnings," *Quarterly Journal of Economics* 109, no. 3 (August 1994): 531–65. The authors suggest that their finding is consistent with a "reference group" model in which the presence of a sister affects either parents' educational goals for their daughters or the skills that the young woman develops.

to dress-up for occasions such as Halloween, toy store aisles and catalogs are still replete with ballerina and princess costumes, but there are now also costumes available for girls wanting to be superheroes. This might suggest progress toward gender equity except that they tend to be highly form-fitting feminine outfits, a stark contrast to the macho black ninja costumes marketed for boys. Other toys intended for girls include kitchen accessories and makeup.

The message that comes through loud and clear is that girls want to be pretty, and that they are interested in having boyfriends, even at a very early age. They also want to prepare themselves for a life in which being a good mother and competent household manager is primary. The few toys that do have a connection to careers come in a very poor second. Video games, cartoons, and movies assign girls the same role. For instance, *Powerpuff Girls* on the Cartoon Network has Bubbles, Blossom, and Buttercup who are "cute little pre-schoolers with big eyes and a tendency to play house."[‡] In the *Toy Story* movies, one of the female characters is Bo Peep, who has a sexy voice and bats her eyelashes, while male characters include the action figure Buzz Lightyear. Finally, there are *the* girl toy colors: pink and light purple, strictly off-limits to boys.

Enter a "boy aisle" in the toy store and you will be barraged by light sabers, swords, and the TV and movie action figures that go with them. Traditional superheroes Batman, Superman, and Spiderman have been joined by Teenage Mutant Ninja Turtles, Power Rangers, Star Wars heroes and villains, and others. Watch a cartoon or movie directed at boys and you will see plenty of violence as good battles evil. These are far from the nurturing role models given girls. Moreover, it remains far less socially acceptable for boys to cross the gender barrier in stores and choose a Barbie than it is for a girl to choose a Batman figure.

It is unlikely that sex-stereotyping of toys will abate anytime soon. Toys R Us, for instance, has recently established specific girl and boy zones in their stores, with dolls, homemaking toys, and makeup at one end, and superhero action figures, trucks, train sets, and Lego building kits at the other. There are those who argue that merchants are merely responding to children's preferences, that placing toys for girls and boys in distinct areas is more convenient for shoppers, and that playing with these toys does no real harm to boys and girls. Also, some gender-neutral toys and games such as Monopoly and roller blades are quite popular with children of both sexes. Nonetheless, separate toy aisles for girls and boys help to perpetuate traditional gender roles by limiting children's visions of who they can be and what they should do at a very early age.

[‡] Sartwell, "The Gender Gap Remains."

Gender-Appropriate Traits and Competencies Another way in which social influences may operate to influence women's labor market outcomes is that women may be socialized to emphasize appropriate "feminine" personality traits, such as being subordinate, nurturing, and emotional. Traditionally male fields may be stereotyped as requiring "masculine" personality traits such as dominance, competitiveness, and rationality. Having internalized the idea of what is properly female, women may then avoid male fields because they perceive a nonpecuniary cost in acting in an "unfeminine" manner or because they feel unequipped to do so. In the latter case, they might expect to be less successful in the field, thus lowering their anticipated returns. Similarly, if women are reared to believe they lack competence in "masculine" subjects like math and science, this would raise their perceived costs and lower their perceived returns to entry into fields emphasizing this knowledge. Men may see traditionally female fields as inappropriate for similar reasons.

Biased Evaluations   Even women's possession of "male" traits or competencies and their willingness to display them may not guarantee them equal success. Studies have found that, among both female and male college students, identical papers were given higher ratings on such dimensions as value, persuasiveness, profundity, writing style, and competence when respondents believed the author to be male rather than female. Similar findings have been obtained in studies requiring both women and men to evaluate the qualifications of applicants for employment.[28] The expectation of inferior performance may eventually cause that inferior performance. Even if it does not, it would lower the expected return to investments in educational credentials.

Discrimination by Educational Institutions   Discrimination against women in the course of their studies, particularly in traditionally male fields, may increase the nonpecuniary costs of obtaining education or lower the returns to their investment. It is well to remember that overt discrimination against women in admission to college and professional school was pervasive in the not too distant past. American women were not admitted to higher education until 1837 when Oberlin College opened its doors.[29] Women did not gain entrance to medical school until 1847, and it was not until 1915 that the American Medical Association accepted women members. As late as 1869, the United States Supreme Court upheld the refusal of the Illinois State Bar to admit a woman. One of the justices declared that "the natural and proper timidity and delicacy which belongs to the female sex evidently unfit it for many of the occupations of civil life."[30] Nonetheless, a year later, in 1870, the first woman did succeed in graduating from an American law school.

Even after these "firsts," women were not universally admitted to all institutions of higher education in all fields for a very long time. The prestigious Harvard Medical School did not admit women until 1945, while Harvard Law School excluded women until 1950. Similarly, many highly respected undergraduate institutions, like Princeton and Yale, remained male only until the late 1960s or early 1970s. Others, like Harvard, granted women access to classes and some facilities but officially restricted them to a separate college.

Moreover, the opening of doors to women did not necessarily mean that the doors opened as widely for them as for men. Women continued in many cases to be discriminated against in admissions and financial aid policies long after they gained formal admittance. In some cases, women were held to higher standards than men; in others, overt or informal quotas limited the number of places available to them.[31] Often course requirements for male and female high school students were different, and, at all levels, gender-based counseling was prevalent.

---

[28]   See the studies reviewed in Virginia Valian, *Why So Slow? The Advancement of Women* (Cambridge, MA: MIT Press, 1998), chap. 7, pp. 125–44; and Virginia E. O'Leary and Ranald D. Hansen, "Trying Hurts Women, Helps Men: The Meaning of Effort," in *Women in the Work Force,* ed. H. John Bernardin (New York: Praeger, 1982), pp. 102–4.

[29]   Mount Holyoke was another pioneer in higher education for women. The information on admissions of women is from Michelle Patterson and Laurie Engleberg, "Women in Male-Dominated Professions," in *Women Working: Theories and Facts in Perspective,* ed. Ann H. Stromberg and Shirley Harkess (Mountain View, CA: Mayfield, 1978), pp. 266–92.

[30]   Cited in Patterson and Engleberg, "Women in Male-Dominated Professions," p. 277.

[31]   See, for example, Ann Sutherland Harris, "The Second Sex in Academe," *AAUP Bulletin* 56, no. 3 (fall 1970): 283–95; and Mary Frank Fox, "Women and Higher Education: Gender Differences in the Status of Students and Scholars," in *Women: A Feminist Perspective,* 3rd ed., ed. Jo Freeman (Palo Alto, CA: Mayfield, 1984), pp. 217–35.

Subtle Barriers   Although most of these overt barriers have been removed, it is important to bear in mind that they did place serious limits on the educational options of older women. Thus, their impact continues to be reflected in the *current* occupational distribution of women. Further, subtle barriers to women's success in the study of traditionally male fields remain a problem. In Chapter 7, we shall consider how these types of subtle barriers block women's upward progression in the workplace.

The male dominance of a field can itself discourage young women from attempting to enter. In this way, past discrimination continues to have an impact on younger women. Lacking contact with or firsthand knowledge of successful women, they may assume (quite possibly erroneously) that they too would be unable to succeed. Even if they believe that times have changed and that their prospects for success are greater than indicated by the present low representation of women, the scarcity of women may still pose problems for them, limiting their eventual success and lowering the returns to entering predominantly male fields. For example, without older women to serve as **role models,** female entrants have inadequate information about acceptable (or successful) modes of behavior and dress. They also lack access to the knowledge that older women have acquired about successful strategies for combining work roles and family responsibilities. Thus, they are forced to be pioneers, and blazing a new trail is undoubtedly more difficult than following along a well-established path.

Women students may also be excluded from the informal relationships desirable for eventual career success. Older individuals who are well established in the field (mentors) often take promising young students (protégés) under their wing—informally socializing them into the norms of the field, giving them access to the latest research in the area, and tying them into their network of professional contacts.

The **mentor-protégé system** is generally the result of the older individual identifying with the younger person. Male mentors may simply not identify with young women. Or they may fear that the development of a close relationship with a young woman would be misunderstood by their colleagues or their wives. Thus, women students are likely to be at a disadvantage in predominantly male fields. Their problems will be aggravated if male students neglect to include them in their **informal network.** Such informal contacts among students include study groups and discussions over lunches, sports, coffee breaks, or a Friday afternoon beer, where important information about coursework, the field, and career opportunities may be exchanged.

Thus, women often lack the support, encouragement, and access to information and job opportunities provided by informal contacts between teachers and students and among students, as well as female role models to emulate. This raises the nonpecuniary costs to them in comparison to otherwise similar male students, lowering their incentives to enter traditionally male fields. It also may result in their being less successful than comparable men when they complete their studies. To the extent that they foresee this, their entry into predominantly male fields is further discouraged.

While it is widely believed that a lack of female role models and mentors is a significant problem for women students, quantitative evidence is difficult to gather. One approach uses self-reports and perceptions of young women, often, although not always, finding evidence that female role models and mentors are important.[32] Some interest-

---

[32]   See, for example, Berg and Ferber, "Men and Women Graduate Students"; and Nancy E. Betz and Louise F. Fitzgerald, *The Career Psychology of Women* (Orlando, FL: Academic Press, 1987) and the references therein.

ing recent studies use a different approach, examining the impact of the presence of women faculty on indicators of performance or choices of female students. One study finds that the percentage of female faculty at their undergraduate college or university is positively related to the probability that female students attain an advanced degree.[33] Another reports that while the race, gender, and ethnicity match between high school students and their teachers does not appear to affect how much students learn, it does sometimes positively affect the teacher's subjective evaluation of the students, suggesting, for example, that same-sex teachers might better serve as mentors.[34] On the other hand, for a sample of three schools, no evidence was found that an increase in the proportion of female college or university faculty in a department was associated with an increase in the fraction of majors that were women.[35]

Finally, it should also be pointed out that labor market discrimination itself can adversely affect the incentives of women to invest in formal schooling, insofar as it results in a lower return on their investment. Studies have found that female college seniors expect lower earnings than their male counterparts, even after controlling for any differences in future work expectations.[36] We consider the possibility of discrimination in greater detail in the next chapter.

POLICY ISSUE: THE ROLE OF GOVERNMENT IN COMBATING DISCRIMINATION IN EDUCATIONAL INSTITUTIONS

To remedy discrimination in educational institutions, in 1972 Congress passed Title IX of the Educational Amendments (to the Civil Rights Act of 1964). It prohibits discrimination on the basis of sex in any educational program or activity receiving federal financial assistance and covers admissions, financial aid, and access to programs and activities, as well as employment of teachers and other personnel.

The main provisions relevant at the high school level are that all courses and programs, except sex instruction, chorus, and contact sports, must be available to both males and females. At the university level, the most important provisions are for nondiscrimination in admissions and in faculty hiring, and for equal availability of scholarships and fellowships, assistantships, research opportunities, and housing. Private, single-sex undergraduate schools are exempt from the nondiscrimination in admission requirements; however, once any women (or men) are admitted, no discrimination in admissions is permitted. Even though enforcement has not always been rigorous, it is likely that this legislation has contributed to the substantial changes in the extent and type of participation of women in the educational system that we have described.

---

[33] Donna S. Rothstein, "Do Female Faculty Influence Female Students' Educational and Labor Market Attainments?" *Industrial and Labor Relations Review* 48, no. 3 (April 1995): 515–30.

[34] Ronald G. Ehrenberg, Daniel D. Goldhaber, and Dominic J. Brewer, "Do Teachers' Race, Gender, and Ethnicity Matter? Evidence from NELS," *Industrial and Labor Relations Review* 48, no. 3 (April 1995): 547–61.

[35] Brandice Canes and Harvey Rosen, "Following in Her Footsteps? Women's Choices of College Majors and Faculty Gender Composition," *Industrial and Labor Relations Review* 48, no. 3 (April 1995): 486–504.

[36] Jerry A. Jacobs, "Gender and the Earnings Expectations of College Seniors," Working Paper, University of Pennsylvania (April 2000); and Francine D. Blau and Marianne A. Ferber, "Career Plans and Expectations of Young Men and Women," *Journal of Human Resources* 26, no. 4 (fall 1991): 581–607.

Title IX has had a particularly dramatic impact on high school and collegiate athletics. Since its passage, support and facilities for women athletes have greatly increased, as has women's participation in athletic programs. When the legislation was enacted in 1972, 50 percent of American boys participated in school sports compared to only 4 percent of girls. By the mid-1990s, this was true of a third of girls, and almost one-half of college varsity players were female.[37] The transformation in women's athletics is especially highlighted in the Olympics. In the 1976 Olympics, the first Olympic games after the passage of Title IX, only one out of seven athletes was female. By the 2000 games, 42 percent of the competing athletes were women, and for the first time women competed in the same number of team sports as men.[38] Ironically, the expansion in women's collegiate sports has been accompanied by a decline in the representation of women in coaching and administrative jobs. As the status and importance of female sports has increased, women have faced more competition from men for these positions.[39]

Some research suggests that athletics has a positive effect on girls who participate. They have been found to do better academically and to be less likely to drop out of school, take drugs, or become pregnant, although it is unclear to what extent this might be due to a self-selection of more successful girls into athletics. Leading female athletes can also serve as role models for young women, just as male athletes have long served as role models for young men. In the words of Julie Foudy, member of the 1996 U.S. gold medal soccer team, they are giving the message that "It's O.K. to be successful. It's O.K. to want to be successful." Or, as American swimmer Amy Van Dyken, who overcame severe asthma to become a gold medalist, put it, "It's cool for a woman to be able to bench-press her husband."[40]

A controversial issue that has arisen regarding educational institutions is the desirability and legality of single-sex education. It has been argued that, due to the types of classroom issues that were discussed in an earlier inset, such as the tendency for males to dominate class discussion, women may benefit from single-sex schooling. Similar arguments have been made in favor of predominantly black institutions. At the same time, two elite, state-financed, all-male military schools claimed that the benefits of their educational experience depended on an all-male environment.

From a legal perspective, very different issues are raised depending on whether or not the educational institution involved is publicly funded. As we have seen, single-sex, privately funded institutions are exempt from Title IX's admission requirements. However, constitutional issues are raised about single-sex, publicly funded schools. In 1996,

---

[37] For evidence on the remaining disparities, see Welch Suggs, "Uneven Progress for Women's Sports: A *Chronicle* Survey Finds Gains at Big-Time Football Powers, Struggles at the 'Have-Nots'," *Chronicle of Higher Education,* 7 April 2000, pp. A52–A57.

[38] Frank Deford, "The Women of Atlanta," *Newsweek,* 10 June 1996, pp. 62–83; and Jere Longman, "Women Move Closer to Olympic Equality," *New York Times,* 20 August 2000 (www.nytimes.com). On the other hand, while the overall number of female athletes at the Olympics has increased, a number of countries that exclude female athletes from their delegations have continued to participate. These include, but are not limited to, a number of Moslem countries where the clergy argue that Islam forbids women from displaying their bodies and competing in sports before a male audience. See Haider Rizvi, "Olympics: Women's Rights Groups Seek Ban Against Male-Only Teams," Inter Press Service, 24 July 1996.

[39] Annelies Knoppers, "Gender and the Coaching Profession," in *Women, Sport, and Culture,* ed. Susan Birrell and Cheryl L. Cole (Champaign, IL: Human Kinetics, Inc, 1994), pp. 119–33.

[40] Deford, "The Women of Atlanta"; and Jere Longman, "Atlanta Games, a Celebration for 197 Nations, Close," *New York Times,* 5 August 1996, pp. A1, C5. The quotations are from Longman.

the United States Supreme Court found that the exclusion of qualified women from the Virginia Military Institute (V.M.I.), a state-run, all-male military school, was not permissible. This is an important case and the reasoning behind it is particularly instructive. Writing for the majority, Justice Ruth Bader Ginsburg explained that the state must demonstrate an "exceedingly persuasive justification" for any official action that treats men and women differently. "The justification must be genuine, not hypothesized or invented *post hoc* in response to litigation. . . . And it must not rely on overbroad generalizations about the different talents, capacities, or preferences of males and females." This decision resulted in the admission of women into V.M.I. and a similar institution, the Citadel in South Carolina, which was not explicitly involved in the case.[41]

Private schools were unaffected by the Supreme Court decision. As of the mid-1990s, there were only three all-male private colleges in the United States, with a total enrollment of under 5,000 students. Interestingly, all-female private colleges were much more prevalent; there were 84 of them with 120,000 students. Profiting from the view that women's schools can benefit and motivate female students, and the high-profile success of some of their graduates, enrollments at women's schools rose over the 1990s.[42] However, controversy still surrounds the issue of publicly supported, women-only schools, with some advocating such institutions as a desirable educational experience for young women and others claiming that they discriminate against young men by excluding them. The legal status of such schools has not been resolved by the courts.[43]

EXPLAINING WOMEN'S RISING EDUCATIONAL ATTAINMENT

Whatever the past barriers to women's access to higher education or the remaining gender differences in fields of study and in the acquisition of first professional and Ph.D degrees, the increase in women's representation in college and postgraduate study that we documented earlier has been truly remarkable. How do we explain this change that began in earnest in the 1970s? As we noted above, the human capital model provides one explanation. As women anticipated spending longer periods in the labor market, the return to their investment in higher education increased and with it their motivation to secure more market-oriented education as well. Rising labor market opportunities for women, resulting in part from the passage of antidiscrimination legislation, which we discuss in Chapter 7, undoubtedly also played a role. Shifting social attitudes toward women's work roles and their capabilities likely also played a part. Finally, passage and enforcement of Title IX, which, as discussed above, specifically banned discrimination in educational institutions, led to changes in the admis-

---

[41] Linda Greenhouse, "Military College Can't Bar Women, High Court Rules," *New York Times,* 27 June 1996, pp. A1, B8.

[42] Mike Allen, "Separatism Is In, Except for White Men," *New York Times,* Sunday, 30 June 1996, p. E5. For evidence on the effects of single-sex female schools, see Judith Dobrzynski, "How to Succeed? Go to Wellesley," *New York Times,* Sunday, 29 October 1995, sec. 3, pp. 1, 9; Elizabeth M. Tidball, "Women's Colleges and Women Achievers Revisited," *Signs* 5, no. 3 (spring 1980): 504–17; and Sara J. Solnick, "Changes in Women's Majors from Entrance to Graduation at Women's and Coeducational Colleges," *Industrial and Labor Relations Review* 48, no. 3 (April 1995): 505–14.

[43] See, for example, Jacques Steinberg, "All-Girls Public School to Open Despite Objections," *New York Times,* 14 August 1996 (www.nytimes.com).

sion practices of educational institutions facilitating and reinforcing the impact of these other developments.

A recent study points to an additional factor that may have importantly influenced women's educational decisions and most particularly their increasing participation in professional programs: the development of oral contraception, otherwise known as "the pill," and especially its growing availability to young, unmarried women beginning in the late 1960s and early 1970s.[44] This was associated with and facilitated a delay in marriage and childbearing, which in turn enabled women to pursue professional training after college. The authors argue that the pill had important *direct* and *indirect* effects on women's career investments. The direct effect of the pill was that it increased the reliability of contraception and the ease of using it, thereby enabling women to postpone marrying and starting a family and more confidently embark on a lengthy professional education.[45] The indirect effect of the pill was that, since it encouraged the delay of marriage for *all* young people (not just those acquiring professional training), a woman who postponed marriage to pursue professional studies would have a larger pool of eligible bachelors to choose from. Had this not occurred, a woman who put off marriage for professional studies would have faced a much smaller pool of potential mates and, given this smaller selection, would have had to settle for a lesser match. This would have raised the cost to women of professional study.

ON-THE-JOB TRAINING

One of the major insights of human capital theory is the observation that individuals can increase their productivity not only through their investments in formal education but also by learning important work skills while they are actually on the job.[46] Sometimes they participate in formal training programs sponsored by their employers. More often, they benefit from informal instruction by their supervisors or coworkers and grow proficient at their jobs through repetition and trial and error. Human capital theory suggests that the weaker attachment to the labor force of women who follow traditional gender roles means that they will acquire less of this valuable on-the-job training. As will be discussed in Chapter 7, women may also be denied equal access to on-the-job training due to employer discrimination.

GENDER DIFFERENCES IN LABOR MARKET EXPERIENCE

Before developing these ideas further, let us look at the actual extent of gender differences in work experience. Unfortunately, this information is not collected by government agencies on a regular basis but must be pieced together from various special sur-

---

[44] Claudia Goldin and Lawrence F. Katz, "Career and Marriage in the Age of the Pill," *American Economic Review* 90, no. 2 (May 2000): 461–75.

[45] As the authors point out, in the absence of reliable contraception, a young woman entering a professional program would have had to choose abstinence or cope with considerable uncertainty regarding pregnancy.

[46] See, for example, Becker, *Human Capital;* Mincer, "On-the-Job Training"; and Walter Oi, "Labor as a Quasi-Fixed Factor," *Journal of Political Economy* 70, no. 6 (December 1962): 538–55.

veys. The available data indicate that, on average, women in the labor market have less work experience than men, but that gender differences have been narrowing.

For example, it has been found that employed women in all age groups increased their average labor market experience over the 1950 to 1980 period taken as a whole, with much of the gains occurring in the post-1970 period.[47] Despite an increase in average experience within most age groups over the 1970s, with younger women having less experience than older women, the *average* level of experience for all women workers fell slightly. This is because the large increases in labor force participation of younger women (discussed in Chapter 4) resulted in a decrease in the average age of women workers.[48] Even with women in each age group working more years than previously, this change in age mix resulted in a small decline in average experience for the group as a whole. This is somewhat ironic in that it is precisely this pattern of growing labor force attachment of women during the childbearing years that would increase women's average experience in the long run. By the 1980s, overall female experience levels did unambiguously begin to rise relative to males'. Between 1979 and 1988, for example, the gender gap in full-time experience decreased by nearly three years (from 7.5 to 4.6 years).[49]

Additional evidence indicating a declining experience gap between men and women is presented in Table 6.6, which shows gender differences in job tenure (length of time with the current employer). Between 1966 and 1983, the tenure gap between men and women was reduced by more than 50 percent, from 2.4 years to 1.0 year; it was then reduced in half again to .5 years in 1999. However, it should be noted that the reduction in the sex difference in the latter period reflects not only increases in the labor force attachment of women but also large decreases in the tenure of older men, particularly the less skilled, which may signal a decline in job security for this group.[50] These declines in tenure for older men are part of a larger pattern of deteriorating labor market outcomes for less-skilled Americans that we have already noted in this chapter and in our con-

---

[47] James P. Smith and Michael P. Ward, "Women's Wages and Work in the Twentieth Century," RAND, R-3119-NICHD, 1984. These estimates are based on data on women's labor force participation and labor force turnover (entries and exits) rather than on direct information on actual work experience. However, direct data on experience, where available, suggest these estimates are reasonable. For complementary estimates that also include an earlier period, see Claudia Goldin, Understanding the Gender Gap: An Economic History of American Women (New York: Oxford University Press, 1990), chap. 2.

[48] Goldin, *Understanding the Gender Gap,* p. 41.

[49] The estimated change in the experience gap is from Francine D. Blau and Lawrence M. Kahn, "Swimming Upstream: Trends in the Gender Wage Differential in the 1980s," *Journal of Labor Economics* 15, no. 1, pt. 1 (January 1997): 1–42. A number of other studies also report rising experience levels for women; see June O'Neill and Solomon W. Polachek, "Why the Gender Gap in Wages Narrowed in the 1980s," *Journal of Labor Economics* 11, no. 1, pt. 1 (January 1993): 205–28; Alison J. Wellington, "Changes in the Male/Female Wage Gap, 1976–85," *Journal of Human Resources* 28, no. 2 (spring 1993): 383–411; Elaine Sorensen, *Exploring the Reasons Behind the Narrowing Gender Gap in Earnings* (Washington, DC: Urban Institute Press, 1991); and Audrey Light and Manuelita Ureta, "Gender Differences in Wages and Job Turnover Among Continuously Employed Workers," *American Economic Review* 80, no. 2 (May 1990): 293–97. Another way to look at the experience gap is to cumulate it over the work life. For example, it has been reported that, for a sample of men and women aged 51–61 in 1992, mean labor market experience at age 50 was 9.6 years less for women than for men; see Phillip B. Levine, Olivia S. Mitchell, and John W. Phillips, "Worklife Determinants of Retirement Income Differentials Between Men and Women," National Bureau of Economic Research Working Paper No. 7243 (July 1999). Of course, the lifetime gap would be expected to be smaller for later cohorts of women who have been more consistently attached to the labor force.

[50] Henry S. Farber, "Are Lifetime Jobs Disappearing? Job Duration in the U.S.: 1973–1993," in *Labor Statistics Measurement Issues,* ed. John Haltiwanger, Marilyn Manser, and Robert Topel (Chicago: University of Chicago Press, 1996).

TABLE 6.6 Median Years with Current Employer of Employed Men and Women by Age, 1966, 1983, and 2000

	1966			1983			2000		
	Males	*Females*	*Difference*	*Males*	*Females*	*Difference*	*Males*	*Females*	*Difference*
Total, 16 years and over	5.2	2.8	2.4	4.1	3.1	1.0	3.8	3.3	0.5
25 to 34 years	3.2	1.9	1.3	3.2	2.8	0.4	2.7	2.5	0.2
35 to 44 years	7.8	3.5	4.3	7.3	4.1	3.2	5.4	4.3	1.1
45 to 54 years	11.5	5.7	5.8	12.8	6.3	6.5	9.5	7.3	2.2

Notes: For 1966, totals include all workers 14 years and over. Definitions of job tenure are not exactly comparable across the three years. In 1966 it is median years on the job. In 1983 and 2000, it is median years of tenure with the current employer.

Sources: 1966: U.S. Department of Labor, Bureau of Labor Statistics, "Job Tenure of Workers, January 1966," Special Labor Force Report No. 77 (1967); and U.S. Department of Labor, Bureau of Labor Statistics, Employee Tenure in 2000 Summary. *News* (August 29, 2000).

sideration of labor force participation by education in Chapter 4. We return to this issue again in Chapter 8.

To summarize, the view that women have, on average, less work experience than men is borne out by the evidence. However, the differences between men and women in the extent of involvement in paid employment have been narrowing over time. We examine below how, according to the human capital model, gender differences in labor force attachment and experience could lower women's pay and cause differences in occupational choices between men and women.

THE ON-THE-JOB TRAINING INVESTMENT DECISION

We begin with a general analysis of the training investment decision. On-the-job training may be divided into two types:

- General training
- Firm-specific training

General training increases the individual's productivity to the same extent in all (or a large number of) firms. For example, an individual may learn to operate an office machine that is widely used by many firms in the labor market. On the other hand, **firm-specific** training, as its name implies, increases the individual's productivity only at the firm that provides the training. For example, one may learn how to get things done within a particular bureaucracy or deal with the idiosyncrasies of a particular piece of equipment. Most training probably combines elements of both general and firm-specific training. However, for simplicity we assume that training may be classified as being entirely general or entirely firm specific.

GENERAL TRAINING

General training is, by definition, completely transferable from the firm providing the training to other firms. The employer would presumably not be willing to foot any part of the bill for such training because, in a competitive labor market, there is no way for the employer to collect any of the returns. After obtaining the training, workers have to be paid what they are worth elsewhere, or they would simply leave the firm. Thus, if general training is to occur, the employee must be willing to bear all the costs, since he or she will reap all the returns. As in the case of formal education, an individual decides whether or not to invest in general training by comparing the costs and benefits.

Let us consider Lisa's investment decision, illustrated in Figure 6.4. She will contrast the experience–earnings profile she can expect if she takes a job with no training (UU') to the profile she can expect if she receives general training (GG'). On-the-job training, although often informal, still entails costs just as does formal schooling. Some of these costs may be direct. For example, in the cases where there are formal programs, there may be expenses for instructors or for materials used in the training. Another portion of the costs is indirect, as the worker and his or her coworkers or supervisor transfer their attention from daily production to training activities. Such expenses arise even when, as is frequently the case, there is no formal program. The re-

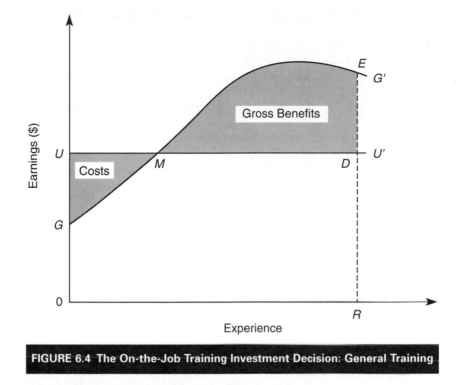

FIGURE 6.4 The On-the-Job Training Investment Decision: General Training

sulting decline in output represents the opportunity cost to the firm of the training activity.

How does Lisa go about "paying" such costs if she decides to invest in general training? She does so by accepting a wage below what she could obtain elsewhere. This lower wage corresponds to her productivity (net of training costs) to the firm during the training period. The costs of the investment in general training are given by the area *UGM*. As Lisa becomes more skilled, her earnings catch up to and eventually surpass what she could have earned without training. Assuming a total of *OR* years of labor market experience over her work life, her gross benefits will be equal to the area *MED*. As in the case of formal schooling, she is likely to undertake the investment if gross benefits exceed costs by a sufficient amount to yield the desired rate of return (as appears to be the case in Figure 6.4).

FIRM-SPECIFIC TRAINING

Figure 6.5 illustrates Don's decision of whether or not to invest in firm-specific training. His productivity on the job is shown by the profile *GG'*. This is also what his earnings profile would be if the training were general. However, since firm-specific training is not transferable, Don will not be willing to bear all the costs of the training, because his ability to reap the returns depends upon continued employment at the firm that initially provided the training. If he were to lose his job,

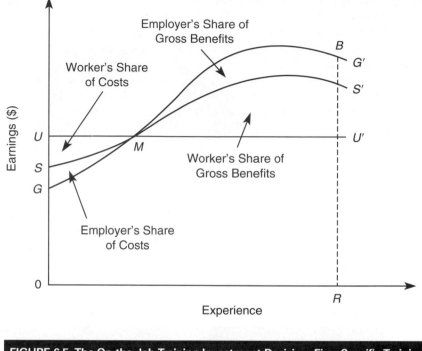

FIGURE 6.5 The On-the-Job Training Investment Decision: Firm-Specific Training

his investment would be wiped out. (The earnings profile available to him at another firm is *UU'*.) If Don paid for all his training, he would have a strong incentive to remain with his employer, but his employer would have no particular reason to accord him any special protection from layoffs.

Similarly, the employer is unwilling to shoulder all the costs of firm-specific training because if Don were to quit, the firm would lose its investment. If the employer were to pay all the costs and receive all the returns, Don's profile would be *UU'*. He would have no special incentive to remain with the firm because he would be earning no more than he could get elsewhere. A temporary shift in demand that resulted in higher wages in another industry or even just more favorable working conditions at another firm might be sufficient to lure him away.

The solution is for the worker and the employer to share the costs of, and returns to, firm-specific training. In this case the specifically trained worker's profile is *SS'*. The worker (Don) has an incentive to remain with the firm after completing training because he earns more there than he can get elsewhere (given by profile *UU'*). The firm also has an incentive to retain a worker who has completed specific training, even in the face of, say, a dip in the demand for the firm's product. This is true because the specifically trained worker (again, Don in this case) is actually being paid less than his productivity—after point *M*, *SS'* lies below *GG'*.

There are two important implications of this analysis of firm-specific training. First, a relatively permanent attachment is likely to develop between the firm and the specifically trained worker. Such workers are less likely either to quit or to be laid off their jobs than untrained or generally trained workers. Second, because employers pay part of the costs of firm-specific training, they will be concerned about the expected employment stability of workers hired into jobs where such training is important. (We develop this point in greater detail later.)

As Figures 6.4 and 6.5 suggest, earnings will increase with experience for workers who have invested in training. Considerable empirical evidence does indeed show a positive relationship between labor market experience and earnings for workers of both sexes, although the return to experience has been found to be less for women than for men.[51] However, the return to experience for women increased relative to men's over the late 1970s and the 1980s.

EXPERIENCE AND PRODUCTIVITY

Human capital theory suggests that the reason why earnings tend to increase with experience in the labor market is that a worker's productivity is augmented by on-the-job training. However, critics of the human capital explanation have argued that it has not been proven that the productivity-enhancing effects of on-the-job training actually *cause* these higher earnings.[52]

For example, the rise in earnings with experience may simply reflect the widespread use of seniority arrangements, which appear to govern wage setting to some extent in the nonunion as well as the union sector. Of course, this does not explain why firms would adhere to this practice, if more senior workers were not also generally more able.

One interesting suggestion is that upward sloping earnings profiles, which reward experience with the firm (tenure), raise workers' productivity because employees are motivated to work hard so as to remain with the firm until retirement and, thus, reap the higher earnings that come with longer tenure.[53] This is in the interest of both workers and firms because the resulting increased productivity makes possible both higher earnings and higher profits. Note that, in this model, although workers are induced to put forth extra effort and be more productive, higher productivity is *not* due to training and productivity does *not* rise with experience. It should also be noted that such alternative explanations focus on the return to tenure (experience with a particular employer) and, thus, do not necessarily challenge the human capital explanation for the return associated with *general* labor market experience.

---

[51]   See, for example, Mincer and Polachek, "Family Investments in Human Capital."

[52]   See, for example, James L. Medoff and Katherine G. Abraham, "Are Those Paid More Really More Productive? The Case of Experience," *Journal of Human Resources* 16, no. 2 (spring 1981): 186–216.

[53]   Edward P. Lazear, "Why Is There Mandatory Retirement?" *Journal of Political Economy* 87 (December 1979): 1261–84. Another suggestion that has been made is that the observed return to tenure is just a statistical artifact: "Good matches" between workers and firms tend to last longer. So, at any point in time, workers with longer tenure will be higher paid, not because their earnings have risen with seniority but rather because workers with good, high-paying jobs are likely to keep them. See Katherine G. Abraham and Henry Farber, "Job Duration, Seniority, and Earnings," *American Economic Review* 77, no. 3 (June 1987): 278–97.

It is difficult to obtain empirical data to shed light on this controversy, since information on actual productivity of workers is seldom available. Available empirical evidence is mixed, with some studies supporting the human capital explanation and others refuting it.[54]

From the perspective of the individual, the factors influencing the investment decision are not affected by the reasons for the upward-sloping experience–earnings profile. It is the magnitude of costs *versus* benefits that is the individual's principal concern. When the upward-sloping experience–earnings profile reflects an incentive structure offered to the worker by a particular firm, the situation is similar to firm-specific training in that the higher earnings will only be available to the worker if he or she remains at that firm.

GENDER DIFFERENCES IN TRAINING INVESTMENT DECISIONS

EXPECTED WORK LIFE

Does our analysis of the training investment decision suggest that women will be less likely to invest in on-the-job training than men? Putting this somewhat differently, would they be less willing to spend time in relatively low-paid, entry-level positions in order to reap a return in terms of higher earnings later? Again, human capital theory suggests that adherence to traditional gender roles would lower women's incentives to invest.

The impact of women's shorter work lives is illustrated in Figure 6.6. Let us assume TT' represents the earnings profile of a worker with general training. Here we see that, just as in the case of formal education, the gross return to on-the-job training depends upon the number of years over which the return is earned. Jane, who plans to be in the labor market for a shorter period of time than Lisa, will find the investment in on-the-job training less profitable. For example, suppose she expects to work R' years, then return after an interruption of $R'' - R'$ years. Her benefits are reduced by the time spent out of the labor force when her earnings are zero. Further, it is expected that, due to depreciation of skills, the work force interruption will lower her earnings profile when she returns from TT' to II', resulting in a further loss of benefits. Although we have again shown the postinterruption profile (II') as approaching the profile of a continuous worker (TT'), a lifetime loss in earnings still occurs.

Jane's gross return to her investment in general training is equal to the sum of the two shaded areas, considerably less than Lisa's return shown in Figure 6.4. Given these reductions in benefits, women following traditional gender roles are likely to find it less profitable to make large investments in general training than will career-oriented men or women. Moreover, as we noted in our discussion of field of educational specialization, if occupations differ in the amount of depreciation associated with them, women who anticipate discontinuous work careers are likely to be attracted to fields in which such depreciation is relatively small.[55]

---

[54] Studies that do not support the training explanation include Medoff and Abraham, "Are Those Paid More?"; and Abraham and Farber, "Job Duration." Those providing support for the training hypothesis include Robert Topel, "Specific Capital, Mobility and Wages: Wages Rise with Job Seniority," *Journal of Political Economy* 99, no. 1 (February 1991): 145–76; and James Brown, "Why Do Wages Increase with Tenure?" *American Economic Review* 79, no. 5 (December 1989): 971–91.

[55] See, especially, Solomon W. Polachek, "Occupational Self-Selection."

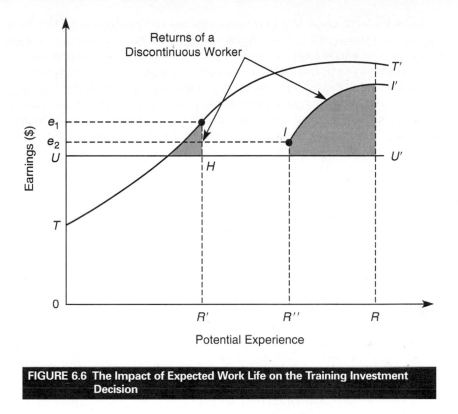

FIGURE 6.6 **The Impact of Expected Work Life on the Training Investment Decision**

Figure 6.6 may also be used to illustrate the consequences of the shorter and more discontinuous labor force participation of women following a traditional path for their incentives to invest in *firm-specific* training. Assume now that TT' is the earnings profile of a worker who has obtained firm-specific training. The impact of work interruptions is potentially even more serious in this case, depending crucially on whether or not a woman is able to return to her initial employer.

Suppose Jennifer has been out of the labor force for a substantial period of time and is unable to get her old job back. The firm-specific skills she has acquired are useless in other firms. Her earnings upon her return to the labor force will be only U dollars (the earnings of an individual without training), and her new earnings profile will be UU' (the profile of an individual without training). The returns to Jennifer's investment in firm-specific training have been completely wiped out by her withdrawal from the labor force! That is, the second shaded area shown in Figure 6.6 is eliminated, although she will still receive some returns for the brief period before she leaves the labor force. Of course, this conclusion depends on our assumption that she could not return to her original employer. But unless a woman is guaranteed reemployment, she must always face this risk. Thus, human capital theory suggests that women who anticipate work force interruptions of a long or uncertain duration will particularly avoid jobs where firm-specific training is important. Women who seek shorter, fixed-duration interruptions may, however, be covered by an employer's leave policy.

Considerable empirical evidence supports the prediction of the human capital model that women will receive less on-the-job training than men.[56] This is consistent with employer and worker decisions based on a lower expected probability of women remaining with the firm or in the work force. Interestingly, however, in one recent study that explicitly examined this issue, it was found that although women's higher probability of turnover can explain some of the gender training difference, a major portion remains unexplained even after this and other determinants of training are taken into account.[57] This suggests that differences in the amount of training men and women acquire may not be fully explained by factors emphasized in the human capital model, and that discrimination (discussed next) potentially plays a role.

As women's labor force attachment and career orientation increase, the profitability of on-the-job training investments for them, both general and firm specific, will increase; so too should their representation in jobs requiring such investments. Moreover, as more women are employed in jobs with training opportunities, the opportunity cost of work force interruptions is increased and their labor force attachment is further reinforced. The most important factor in the case of firm-specific training is attachment to a particular firm. This most likely requires that women keep any work force interruptions within the limits of their employers' leave policy and also raises the question of what such policies should be. We consider this issue in Chapter 10.

DISCRIMINATION

The explanation for gender differences in on-the-job training investment decisions suggested by human capital theory stresses differences between men and women in anticipated labor force participation over the life cycle. It is, however, important to point out that, just as in the case of men's and women's formal education decisions, societal discrimination may also be a factor increasing the (pecuniary and nonpecuniary) costs or decreasing the (pecuniary and nonpecuniary) returns to entry into traditionally male fields. Further, labor market discrimination, which is discussed in greater detail in Chapter 7, may also play a part in reducing women's representation in jobs where training is important. That is, overt or subtle discrimination on the part of employers, coworkers, or customers may prove an obstacle to women gaining access to jobs in such areas or reduce the pay of those who are able to obtain employment.

Consideration of firm-specific training introduces a particular rationale for employer discrimination that may be important. As illustrated in Figure 6.5, the employer is expected to share some of the costs of firm-specific training. The returns to the firm's (as well as to the worker's) investment depend on how long the individual remains with

---

[56]   Greg J. Duncan and Saul Hoffman, "On-the-Job Training and Earnings Differences by Race and Sex," *Review of Economics and Statistics* 61, no. 4 (November 1979); Joseph G. Altonji and James R. Spletzer, "Worker Characteristics, Job Characteristics, and the Receipt of On-the-Job Training," *Industrial and Labor Relations Review* 45, no. 1 (October 1991): 58–79; Lisa M. Lynch, "Private Sector Training and the Earnings of Young Workers," *American Economic Review* 82, no. 1 (March 1992): 299–312; Reed Neil Olsen and Edwin A. Sexton, "Gender Differences in the Returns to and the Acquisition of On-the-Job Training," *Industrial Relations* 35, no. 1 (January 1996): 59–77; and John Barron and Dan A. Black, "Gender Differences in Training, Capital and Wages," *Journal of Human Resources* 28, no. 2 (spring 1993): 342–64.

[57]   Anne Beeson Royalty, "The Effects of Job Turnover on the Training of Men and Women," *Industrial and Labor Relations Review* 49, no. 3 (April 1996): 506–21.

the firm. Thus, if an employer believes that women are less likely to stay at the firm than men, on average, he or she may prefer men for jobs that require considerable specific training. Employers' differential treatment of men and women on the basis of their perceptions of average gender differences in productivity or job stability has been termed **statistical discrimination.** Such behavior on the part of employers can restrict opportunities for career-oriented as well as noncareer-oriented women, if employers cannot easily distinguish between them.

Finally, labor market discrimination may indirectly lower women's incentives to invest in themselves by decreasing the rewards for doing so. The possibility of such "feedback effects" is considered in greater detail in the next chapter.

OCCUPATIONS AND EARNINGS

The analysis of gender differences in occupations and earnings based on the human capital model is quite straightforward. It is assumed that, given the traditional division of labor in the family, most women do indeed anticipate shorter and less continuous work careers than men. Thus, women are expected to select occupations requiring less investment in education and on-the-job training than those chosen by men. They will particularly avoid jobs in which firm-specific training is important, and employers will be reluctant to hire them for such jobs. Further, they will seek jobs where depreciation of earnings for time spent out of the labor force is minimal.

Hypothetical earnings profiles for predominantly male and predominantly female jobs are shown in Figure 6.7. For simplicity, we assume all workers have the same amount of formal schooling. Earnings profiles in predominantly male jobs are expected to slope steeply upward as does profile MM', since men are expected to undertake substantial investments in on-the-job training. Women, on the other hand, are expected to choose the flatter profile FF', representing smaller amounts of investment in on-the-job training. The existence of the crossover point, H, is crucial to this argument. Before H, profile FF' lies above profile MM'. It is argued that women choose higher earnings now in preference to higher earnings in the future because they do not expect to be in the labor market long enough for the larger human capital investment to pay off. Thus, we see that the human capital analysis of on-the-job training decisions, in conjunction with our previous discussion of formal education, can provide an explanation for the occupational segregation by gender detailed in Chapter 5.

The human capital analysis can also provide an explanation for gender differences in earnings. We have already seen why the human capital model implies that women are less likely to make large investments in formal schooling. To the extent that women in the labor force have been less likely than men to obtain a college or graduate education, their earnings would be reduced relative to men's. Of potentially more importance in explaining gender differences in earnings would be differences between men and women in fields of specialization, to the extent that men are likely to enter more lucrative areas.

For given levels of formal education, our consideration of on-the-job training investments also gives us reasons to expect women to earn less, on average, as illustrated in Figure 6.7: Mean female earnings are $\overline{E}_f$ dollars and are less than male mean earn-

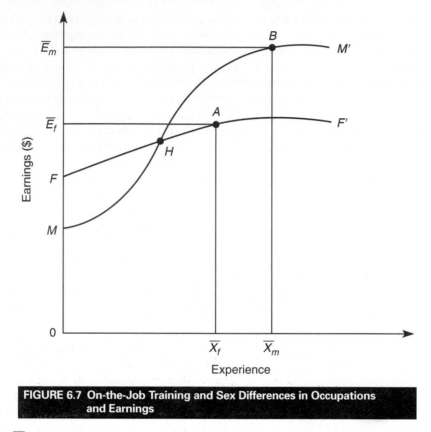

FIGURE 6.7 On-the-Job Training and Sex Differences in Occupations and Earnings

ings of $\overline{E}_m$ dollars. Why do women earn less? First, on average they have less labor market experience than men—$\overline{X}_f$ is less than $\overline{X}_m$. Because earnings tend to increase with experience, this decreases their earnings relative to men's. Second, for reasons given earlier, males have steeper profiles; this means that they experience larger increases in earnings for additional years of experience. After crossover point H, this produces a widening gap between male and female earnings with increasing labor market experience.

OTHER SUPPLY-SIDE FACTORS

Traditional gender roles, which result in women being viewed as the secondary earner in the family, may work to produce differences in economic outcomes in a variety of other ways. It has been found, for example, that wives in dual-earner couples who have the secondary career in their family tend to have lower wages than those who have the primary career, even controlling for any differences in levels of education or actual work experience, and the presence of children.[58] Below we briefly consider a number

[58] Anne E. Winkler and David C. Rose, "Career Hierarchy in Dual-Earner Families," *Research in Labor Economics,* ed. Solomon W. Polachek (Greenwich, CT: JAI Press, 2000), pp. 147–72.

of ways in which adherence to traditional gender roles in the family could reduce women's wages relative to men's. This issue receives considerably more attention in Chapters 9 and 10.

First, the longer hours that women tend to spend on housework may reduce the effort that they put into their market jobs and may thus decrease their hourly wage compared to men with similar qualifications.[59] And, indeed, it has been found that additional hours spent in housework by workers are associated with lower wages, all else equal.[60] Also consistent with women placing a greater priority on family responsibilities to the detriment of their labor market outcomes is the empirical evidence that women are more likely to quit their jobs for family related reasons, and that this negatively affects their subsequent earnings.[61] Interestingly, there is some evidence that this gender difference in the pattern of quits is concentrated among workers with a high school education or less, while little gender difference is found for those who have attended college.[62] This suggests that work force attachment of the latter group may be more nearly equal to their male counterparts.

Further evidence suggesting that women's nonmarket responsibilities may negatively affect their labor market outcomes is the widespread finding that the presence of children negatively affects the wages of women.[63] To some extent this reflects the labor force disruptions such women may experience. But there is also some evidence that even after adjusting for differences in experience, mothers earn less. One explanation for this finding is that, in the past, the birth or adoption of a child often resulted in women severing their tie to the firm. They would thus lose the returns to any firm-specific training they had acquired and forgo what might have been an exceptionally good job match. There is evidence that the availability of maternity leave significantly mitigates this negative effect, most likely because it enables women to take a short amount of time out but still maintain their attachment to the firm.

In contrast to the finding that children negatively affect the wages of women, married men tend to earn a wage premium compared to single men, whether or not children are present.[64] While this could reflect a selection of men with higher earnings potential into marriage, or even discrimination in favor of married men by employers, the

---

[59] See Gary S. Becker, "The Allocation of Effort, Specific Human Capital, and the Differences Between Men and Women in Earnings and Occupations," *Journal of Labor Economics* 3, no. 1, pt. 2 (January 1985): 33–58.

[60] See, for example, Joni Hersch and Leslie S. Stratton, "Housework, Fixed Effects and Wages of Married Workers," *Journal of Human Resources* 32, no. 2 (spring 1997): 285–307. On the other hand, using self-reports of effort levels, Denise D. Bielby and William T. Bielby do not find that women put in less effort; see "She Works Hard for the Money: Household Responsibilities and the Allocation of Work Effort," *American Journal of Sociology* 93, no. 5 (March 1988): 1031–59.

[61] Kristen Keith and Abagail McWilliams, "The Wage Effects of Cumulative Job Mobility," *Industrial and Labor Relations Review* 49, no. 1 (October 1995): 121–37.

[62] Anne Beeson Royalty, "Job-to-Job and Job-to-Nonemployment Turnover by Gender and Education Level," *Journal of Labor Economics* 16, no. 2 (April 1998): 392–443.

[63] See, for example, Victor R. Fuchs, *Women's Quest for Economic Equality* (Cambridge, MA: Harvard University Press, 1988); and Jane Waldfogel, "Understanding the 'Family Gap' in Pay for Women with Children," *Journal of Economic Perspectives* 12, no. 1 (winter 1998): 157–70.

[64] Sanders Korenman and David Neumark, "Does Marriage Really Make Men More Productive?" *Journal of Human Resources* 26, no. 2 (spring 1991): 282–307.

evidence suggests higher productivity is an important factor. This may in turn reflect the greater motivation or commitment of married men to their jobs, given some adherence to traditional gender roles in the family.

Second, to the extent that families place priority on the husband's, rather than the wife's, career in determining the location of the family, her earnings are likely to be decreased. She may be a "tied mover," relocating when it is not advantageous for her to leave a job where she has accumulated considerable seniority and firm-specific training. Alternatively, she may be a "tied stayer," unable to relocate despite good opportunities elsewhere.[65] Anticipation of a lesser ability to determine the geographic location of the family may also lead women to select occupations in which jobs are likely to be readily obtained in any labor market, thus constraining their occupational choices.

Third, if women tend to give greater priority than men to family concerns, they may restrict the amount of daily commuting they are willing to do,[66] their hours and work schedules, or their availability for work-related travel. Such constraints could also adversely influence women's occupational choices and reduce their earnings relative to men's.

Finally, if women anticipate a shorter work life than men, they may invest less time in searching out the best possible job and, as a consequence, receive lower earnings.[67]

As with the other supply-side influences we have discussed, it is important to bear in mind that women's decisions with regard to the priority they place on their own versus their husbands' careers, the adaptations they make in response to family responsibilities, and so on may reflect social pressures as well as voluntary choices. Further, to the extent that women face discrimination in the labor market that decreases their wages relative to their husbands', traditional gender roles in the family are reinforced. This is the case because the opportunity cost of wives sacrificing their career objectives to family demands is reduced relative to their husbands'.

THE HUMAN CAPITAL EXPLANATION: AN ASSESSMENT

The human capital model provides a clear, consistent theoretical explanation for gender differences in earnings and occupations in terms of the voluntary choices women and men make. In assessing the contribution of the model, however, it is important to

---

[65]   See, for example, Jacob Mincer, "Family Migration Decisions," *Journal of Political Economy* 86, no. 5 (October 1978): 749–73; and Joyce P. Jacobsen and Laurence M. Levin, "Marriage and Migration: Comparing Gains and Losses from Migration for Couples and Singles," *Social Science Quarterly* 78, no. 3 (September 1997): 688–709.

[66]   See Victor Fuchs, "Differences in Hourly Earnings Between Men and Women," *Monthly Labor Review* 94, no. 5 (May 1971). Janice Madden has suggested that the lesser willingness of women to commute increases the monopsony power of firms over their wages, thus decreasing their wages relative to men's; see "A Spatial Theory of Sex Discrimination," *Journal of Regional Science* 17, no. 3 (December 1977): 369–80. The monopsony model is discussed further in Chapter 7.

[67]   Some evidence consistent with this possibility is found in Steven H. Sandell, "Is the Unemployment Rate of Women Too Low? A Direct Test of the Economic Theory of Job Search," *Review of Economics and Statistics* 62, no. 4 (November 1980): 634–38.

consider the extent to which the data support it. Specifically, we want to know the answers to two questions: Do the factors emphasized by human capital theorists help to explain gender differences in labor market outcomes? If so, do they provide the *full* explanation? A voluminous literature in economics has grown up around investigating these questions. Actual estimates vary depending on the sources of the data used and the types of qualifications examined. Nonetheless, most studies find that human capital factors, particularly women's lesser labor market experience, are important in explaining the gender pay gap. In addition to gender differences in overall experience, other dimensions of work history that have been found to be important include tenure or length of time employed on a particular job, work interruptions, and the timing of past work experience.[68] However, most studies also find that a substantial portion of the pay gap cannot be explained by gender differences in qualifications. The portion of the pay gap that is not due to gender differences in qualifications is generally presumed to be due to labor market discrimination, although there are important measurement problems that need to be taken into account. We discuss this evidence at greater length in Chapter 7. Here we briefly sketch some of the reasoning and evidence underlying this conclusion.

One way to examine the explanatory power of the human capital explanation is to consider how well it explains gender differences in earnings at a point in time. We begin by returning to Figure 6.2, which presents the **age–earnings profiles** in real (1999) dollars for male and female high school and college graduates in 1974 and 1999. The age–earnings profiles shown in the figure indicate how earnings vary with age. As we saw in Figures 6.3 and 6.6, women's greater likelihood of work force interruptions means that, at any given age, they have, on average, less actual labor market experience than men. It is important to bear this in mind in comparing the profiles for males and females shown in Figure 6.2.

The figure suggests that gender differences in earnings are not fully explained by differences in educational attainment of men and women because, within each educational category, women tend to earn less than men. Of course, gender differences in labor market experience and investments in on-the-job training may also be a factor.

To consider this, let us compare Figure 6.2 to Figure 6.7. We see that, as predicted by the human capital model, women's age–earnings profiles tend to be flatter than men's. This is consistent with less investment in on-the-job training for women than for men. Note, however, that in the hypothetical diagram, Figure 6.7, there is a crossover point *H* between the male and female profiles. This implies that during their early years in the labor market, women should actually earn more than men with the same education, since men are investing in on-the-job training and women are not, or are doing so to a lesser extent. However, the actual data seen in Figure 6.2 do not show such a crossover point. On the contrary, within educational categories, men generally earn more than women at every age, even among the youngest workers who are recent entrants to the labor force. This suggests that gender differences in years

---

[68] See, for example, Mincer and Polachek, "Family Investments in Human Capital"; Blau and Kahn, "Swimming Upstream"; O'Neill and Polachek, "Why the Gender Gap"; Wellington, "Changes in the Male/Female Wage Gap"; and Audrey Light and Manuelita Ureta, "Early-Career Work Experience and Gender Wage Differentials," *Journal of Labor Economics* 13, no. 1 (January 1995): 121–54.

of formal education and on-the-job training do not fully explain gender differences in earnings.

Another piece of evidence that women's human capital investment decisions reflect the types of considerations emphasized by the human capital analysis is the finding that young women who expect to work at age 35 have experience–wage profiles that "begin at a lower point and have a steeper (initial) slope than those of their no-work-plans counterparts."[69] That is, the women who were more committed to the labor market were moving along an earnings profile like MM' in Figure 6.7, whereas the less committed women were moving along a profile like FF'. However, the data presented in Figure 6.2 (as well as other evidence reviewed in Chapter 7) suggest that *both* groups of women earn less than comparable men.

A comparison of the age–earnings profiles for 1974 and 1999 also discloses some interesting trends in gender differentials. First, as noted before, while in the mid-1970s female college graduates earned less than male high school graduates, by the late 1990s their earnings clearly exceeded those of male high school graduates. Interestingly, while a significant part of this change represents an increase in the real wages of women college graduates, a good bit of it also reflects falling real wages of male high school graduates; their real wages decreased across all age groups, with particularly sharp declines among younger men. Female high school graduates did better than male high school graduates in terms of real wage growth, experiencing only small real wage declines for younger workers and small real wage increases for older workers. This difference illustrates a general trend to be discussed in Chapter 8, that women tended to fare better than men in terms of real wage changes over this period. Second, the age-earnings profile of women, particularly of college graduates, became steeper over this period suggesting, that they were remaining in the labor force more consistently and investing more in on-the-job training.

As suggested by our discussion of Figure 6.7, the human capital model also provides an explanation for occupational segregation by gender in terms of women's optimizing behavior, given the traditional division of labor by gender within the family. Women are believed to choose occupations characterized by flatter experience–earnings profiles— illustrated by FF' in Figure 6.7. Men, on the other hand, are willing to undertake the larger human capital investments represented by profile MM'. This implies that women who do enter predominantly male occupations should be those who anticipate more continuous labor force participation and are willing to undertake the larger investments in on-the-job training required in male jobs. In return, they should reap higher returns to each year of their labor market experience. In other words, the human capital analysis suggests that women in predominantly male jobs should be moving along profile MM', whereas women in predominantly female jobs should be moving along profile FF'. Further, women who anticipate more work interruptions should enter predominantly female jobs where depreciation of earnings due to time spent out of the labor force is less than in predominantly male jobs.

---

[69]   Steven H. Sandell and David Shapiro, "Work Expectations, Human Capital Accumulation, and the Wages of Young Women," *Journal of Human Resources* 15, no. 3 (summer 1980): 335–43.

The research investigating the implications of the human capital theory as an explanation for gender differences in occupations has produced mixed results. On the one hand, women in predominantly male jobs have been found to earn more than women in predominantly female jobs at every age; that is, there is no evidence of the crossover point H in Figure 6.7 between the earnings profiles in predominantly male and predominantly female jobs, even when we look just among women. Further, women in predominantly male jobs are not found to earn greater returns to each year of experience than women in predominantly female occupations, as would be expected based on the hypothetical figure. Nor was it found in earlier research that the earnings of women in predominantly female jobs depreciate less during periods of time spent out of the labor force than do the earnings of women in predominantly male jobs. Finally, women who have discontinuous work histories have not been found to be more likely to be in a predominantly female occupation than women who have been employed more continuously.[70] These findings are surprising in light of the results reported previously that women who are more committed to the labor market *do* appear to have lower entry wages and steeper experience–wage profiles than women who are less committed. It appears that labor force commitment and participation in predominantly male and predominantly female jobs are not as closely associated as the human capital explanation for occupational segregation would lead us to expect.

On the other hand, some support for the human capital explanation is provided by empirical evidence that a substantial portion of the lower pay in female jobs is accounted for by differences in the skills required in male and female jobs.[71] Moreover, while, as noted above, there is no evidence that women in predominantly female jobs have lower earnings penalties for the total amount of time they have spent out of the labor force, a new study has found that married women have lower penalties for having *recently reentered* the labor force in female than in male occupations.[72] This latter finding is consistent with the predictions of the human capital model. Finally, the finding that women with more limited expected future labor force participation select occupations with lower job skills is also consistent with the human capital model of occupational choice.[73]

Given the mixed evidence on this question, it is difficult to reach firm conclusions regarding the importance of the factors identified by the human capital model in explaining occupational segregation by sex. While it is likely that the human capital ex-

[70] See, for example, Paula England, "The Failure of Human Capital Theory to Explain Occupational Sex Segregation," *Journal of Human Resources* 17, no. 3 (summer 1982): 358–70.

[71] Among the higher estimates for the effect of skills are those found in David A. Macpherson and Barry T. Hirsch, "Wages and Gender Composition: Why Do Women's Jobs Pay Less?" *Journal of Labor Economics* 13, no. 3 (July 1995): 426–71. For a review of the evidence, see also Elaine Sorensen, "The Crowding Hypothesis and Comparable Worth Issue," *Journal of Human Resources* 25, no. 1 (winter 1990): 55–89.

[72] John Robst and Jennifer VanGilder "Atrophy Rates in Male and Female Occupations," *Economic Letters* 69, no. 3 (2000): 407–13.

[73] Evelyn L. Lehrer and Houston Stokes, "Determinants of the Female Occupational Distribution: A Log Linear Analysis," *Review of Economics and Statistics* 67, no. 3 (August 1985): 395–404. See also Polachek, "Occupational Self-Selection."

planation accounts for a portion of the occupational differences between men and women, it appears unwarranted, based on the evidence, to conclude that it could fully account for these differences.

Another type of test of the explanatory power of the human capital explanation for gender differences in earnings is provided by an examination of the trends in the gender–pay differential. As we saw in Chapter 5, virtually no progress was made in closing the overall male–female pay gap during the 1960s and 1970s. Beginning in the late 1970s or early 1980s, the female-to-male earnings ratio began to increase. Gains were particularly marked over the 1980s. How do these trends correspond to shifts in women's qualifications, particularly their relative educational attainment and experience? In general, women's qualifications have been increasing as the pay gap has been declining. Though overall differences in educational attainment were never large, women's fields of study and propensity to pursue college and graduate education have become more similar to men's. Although women on average continue to have less labor market experience than men, the gender differential has declined here as well. As previously noted, while the average experience levels of women within age groups started to increase in the 1970s, the average level of experience of the female labor force as a whole did not start to rise relative to men's until the 1980s. This corresponds to the period of the fastest narrowing of the pay gap.

Thus, both the narrowing of the male–female pay gap and the time pattern of the trend is roughly consistent with the human capital model. This is also true of the trends in earnings ratios by age. Younger women have been most rapidly approaching males in terms of their college-going behavior and fields of study. They have also exhibited the largest increases in labor force attachment in recent years, as growing proportions of them have continued to work during the prime childbearing ages. And we did indeed find in Chapter 5 that younger women (those under 45) have experienced a substantial increase in their earnings relative to younger males.

This broad consistency of the human capital explanation with the observed trends in the female-to-male earnings ratio strongly suggests that human capital factors account for at least part of the male–female pay gap. This does not necessarily mean, however, that the human capital model provides the *sole* explanation of pay differences. Other factors, such as a decrease in discrimination against women, may well have contributed to the observed trends. We consider the sources of the declining gender pay gap more fully in Chapter 8. We generally conclude from our examination that decreasing human capital differences between men and women were an important part of the story, but do not appear to be the only reason for the fall in the pay gap.

CONCLUSION

In this chapter, we have examined supply-side explanations for gender differences in occupations and earnings, chiefly focusing upon the human capital model and its explanation for gender differences in investment in formal education and on-the-job training. Although the evidence suggests that such factors are important, they explain only part of the story. Discrimination against women in the labor market is also an important factor, to which we turn in the next chapter. In Chapter 10, we broadly consider the conflicts that female and increasingly male workers face in coping with dual demands of family and paid work and the policies that government or private employers have pursued, or might consider pursuing, to increase women's human capital and labor force attachment.

QUESTIONS FOR REVIEW AND DISCUSSION

* Indicates that the question can be answered using a diagram illustrating the individual's human capital investment decision as well as verbally. Consult with your instructor about the appropriate approach for your class.

1. What are the main economic factors that underlie the decision to go to college?
2. Carefully explain how the following hypothetical situations would affect the cost–benefit calculation of going to college:
   a. It is increasingly the case that full-time undergraduate students need 5 years to complete all of the requirements for a bachelor's degree.*
   b. The real earnings of college-trained workers increase while those for high school–trained workers decrease.*
3. As a future worker, explain the costs and benefits to you of obtaining highly specialized training from a particular firm.
4. What are the main reasons why women have frequently invested less in their human capital than men? Why has this been changing? Are there any government or employer policies that would be likely to accelerate this change?
5. To what extent and how did economic factors influence
   a. Your decision to attend college?
   b. Your choice of major?
   c. Your plans to go on or not to go on to graduate work?
   Would you expect any of these considerations to differ between men and women and if so why?
6. It is claimed that employers are reluctant to hire women for some jobs because of their higher expected quit rates. Assuming women are more likely to quit, use human capital theory to explain what kind of jobs an employer would be especially reluctant to hire women for. Explain the reasons for the employer's reluctance.* How valid do you think such employer assumptions about women are today?

Suggested Readings

American Association of University Women. *Gender Gaps: Where Schools Still Fail Our Children.* Washington, DC: American Association of University Women, 1998.

Becker, Gary S. *Human Capital: A Theoretical and Empirical Analysis, With Special Reference to Education,* 3rd ed. Chicago: University of Chicago Press, 1993.

Blau, Francine D., and Lawrence M. Kahn. "Gender Differences in Pay." *Journal of Economic Perspectives* 14, no. 4 (fall 2000): 75–99.

England, Paula. "The Failure of Human Capital Theory to Explain Occupational Sex Segregation." *Journal of Human Resources* 17, no. 3 (summer 1982): 358–70.

Mincer, Jacob, and Solomon W. Polachek. "Family Investments in Human Capital: Earnings of Women." *Journal of Political Economy* 82, no. 2, pt. 2 (March/April 1974): S76–S108.

O'Neill, June, and Solomon W. Polachek. "Why the Gender Gap in Wages Narrowed in the 1980s." *Journal of Labor Economics* 11, no. 1, pt. 1 (January 1993): 205–28.

Reskin, Barbara F., and Heidi I. Hartmann. *Women's Work, Men's Work: Sex Segregation on the Job.* Washington, DC: National Academy Press, 1986.

Tobias, Sheila. *Overcoming Math Anxiety.* New York: W. W. Norton, 1993.

Waldfogel, Jane. "Understanding the 'Family Gap' in Pay for Women with Children." *Journal of Economic Perspectives* 12, no. 1 (winter 1998): 157–70.

CHAPTER 7

DIFFERENCES IN OCCUPATIONS AND EARNINGS: THE ROLE OF LABOR MARKET DISCRIMINATION

Chapter Highlights

- Labor Market Discrimination: A Definition
- Empirical Evidence of Labor Market Discrimination
- Models of Labor Market Discrimination
- Policy Issue: The Government and Equal Employment Opportunity

In the preceding chapter, we examined the role of supply-side factors in producing the gender differences in earnings and occupational attainment that we observe in the labor market and that were described in Chapter 5. We now focus upon the demand side, specifically the role of labor market discrimination. As we explained at the end of Chapter 6, the available evidence suggests that both supply- and demand-side influences are responsible for gender differences in economic outcomes.

In this chapter, we begin by providing a definition of labor market discrimination. Next, we examine the empirical evidence on the extent of gender discrimination in the labor market with respect to earnings and occupations. We then turn to a detailed consideration of the various explanations that economists have offered for the existence and persistence of such discrimination. Although our focus is on gender discrimination, much of the analysis is equally applicable to discrimination based on other factors, such as race, ethnicity, age, or disability. In fact, most of the models of discrimination that we discuss were initially developed to explain racial discrimination.

Our primary concern here is to determine to what extent discrimination exists and its possible effects on women's status in the labor market. This is partly an issue of equity or fairness. However, there is also an issue of misallocation of resources when workers are not hired, promoted, or rewarded on the basis of their qualifications. Thus, efficiency, as well as considerations of equity, provides an important rationale for government intervention to combat labor market discrimination. We conclude by reviewing the government's antidiscrimination policies and examining their possible effects.

LABOR MARKET DISCRIMINATION: A DEFINITION

Labor market discrimination exists when *two equally qualified individuals are treated differently solely on the basis of their gender* (race, age, disability, etc.).[1] As we saw in Chapter 1, in the absence of discrimination, profit-maximizing employers in a competitive labor market will pay workers in accordance with their productivity. For similar reasons, they will also find it in their economic self-interest to make other personnel decisions, such as hiring, placement, or promotion, on the same objective basis. An individual's gender (or race, age, disability, etc.) would be an irrelevant consideration.

If labor market discrimination nonetheless exists, it is expected to adversely affect the economic status of women *directly* by producing differences in economic outcomes between men and women that are *not* accounted for by differences in productivity-related characteristics or qualifications. That is, men and women who, in the absence of discrimination, would be equally productive and would receive the same pay (or be in the same occupation) do not receive equal rewards. As we shall see, in some economic models of discrimination this inequality occurs because women are paid less than their marginal product due to discrimination. In other views of this process, labor market discrimination *directly* lowers women's productivity as well as their pay, as for instance, when a woman is denied access to an employer-sponsored training program or when customers are reluctant to patronize a female salesperson.

If such gender differences in *treatment* of equally qualified men and women are widespread and persistent, the behavior of women themselves may be adversely affected. As we saw in the preceding chapter, productivity differences among workers reflect, in part, the decisions they make as to whether or not to continue their schooling, participate in a training program, remain continuously in the labor market, and so on. Faced with discrimination in the labor market that lowers the returns to such human capital investments, women are likely to have less incentive to undertake them. To the extent that such indirect or **feedback effects** of labor market discrimination exist, they are also expected to adversely affect the economic outcomes of women compared to men.

Much of the theoretical and virtually all of the empirical work on labor market discrimination has focused on its more readily measured *direct* effects, that is, on pay or occupational differences between equally well-qualified (potentially equally productive) men and women. We shall follow that emphasis in this chapter. However, it is important to recognize that the *full* impact of discrimination also includes any feedback effects on women's behavior that result in their being less well qualified than men.[2] Thus, we also discuss such feedback effects.

---

[1] This definition is derived from the work of Gary S. Becker, *The Economics of Discrimination*, 2nd ed. (Chicago: University of Chicago Press, 1971).

[2] Note that the argument is *not* that *all* differences in qualifications between men and women are due to the indirect effects of discrimination, but, rather, that *some* of these differences may be a response to such discrimination.

The Subtle Barriers: Different Perceptions of Men and Women

One of the major difficulties in determining the existence of discrimination is that it may take very subtle forms. One of these is that men and women behaving in similar ways may, nonetheless, be perceived quite differently. Such attitudes are almost impossible to document, let alone measure, but that does not mean they do not exist. Here are some examples of typical reactions.*

The family picture is on HIS desk:
Ah, a solid, responsible family man.

The family picture is on HER desk:
Hmm, her family will come before her career.

HIS desk is cluttered:
He's obviously a hard worker and a busy man.

HER desk is cluttered:
She's obviously a disorganized scatterbrain.

HE's talking with co-workers:
He must be discussing the latest deal.

SHE's talking with co-workers:
She must be gossiping.

HE's not at his desk:
He must be at a meeting.

SHE's not at her desk:
She must be in the ladies' room.

HE's not in the office:
He's meeting customers.

SHE's not in the office:
She must be out shopping.

HE's having lunch with the boss:
He's on his way up.

SHE's having lunch with the boss:
They must be having an affair.

The boss criticized HIM:
He'll improve his performance.

The boss criticized HER:
She'll be very upset.

HE got an unfair deal:
Did he get angry?

SHE got an unfair deal:
Did she cry?

HE's getting married:
He'll get more settled.

SHE's getting married:
She'll get pregnant and leave.

HE's having a baby:
He'll need a raise.

SHE's having a baby:
She'll cost the company money in maternity benefits.

HE's going on a business trip:
It's good for his career.

SHE's going on a business trip:
What does her husband say?

HE'S leaving for a better job:
He recognizes a good opportunity.

SHE's leaving for a better job:
Women are undependable.

* From Natasha Josefowitz, *Paths to Power* (Reading, MA: Addison-Wesley Publishing Company, 1990). Copyright by Natasha Josefowitz. Reprinted by permission.

EMPIRICAL EVIDENCE

Having defined labor market discrimination, we now consider the empirical evidence as to the existence and extent of such discrimination. We restrict ourselves entirely to the direct effects of such discrimination and, thus, take as given any gender differences in qualifications. We seek to address more fully the types of questions raised at the end of Chapter 6. Are gender differences in labor market outcomes *fully* explained by gender differences in qualifications or (potential) productivity? If not, how large is the unexplained portion of the gender differential? It is this differential that is commonly used as an estimate of the impact of labor market discrimination. Unfortunately, as we shall see, though the questions are relatively straightforward, the answers are not so easily obtained. We turn first to a consideration of gender differences in earnings and then to an examination of gender differences in occupations.

Earnings Differences

Economists and other social scientists have studied the earnings gap between men and women workers extensively. Actual estimates vary depending on the source of the data used and the types of qualifications examined. However, virtually all studies find that a substantial portion of the pay gap cannot be explained by gender differences in qualifications.[3]

Representative findings from analyses of this type may be illustrated by results from a recent study using data from the Panel Study of Income Dynamics (PSID), which contains information on actual labor market experience for a large, nationally representative sample.[4] The data are for full-time workers aged 18 to 65 in 1989. (Information on wages relates to the preceding calendar year, 1988.) It would be desirable to have such findings for a more recent year. However, data on actual labor market experience are crucial for analyzing the gender pay gap and, unfortunately, this information is available only with a considerable lag.

Table 7.1 presents the average values of the various characteristics examined in this study for men and women separately. The gender differences in work-related characteristics shown in Table 7.1 are those we might expect based on information presented in previous chapters. There is virtually no gender difference in years of education, but women are a bit less likely to be college graduates or to have obtained an advanced degree.[5] The most important difference in qualifications between men and women is that,

---

[3] For summaries of this literature, see, for example, Joseph G. Altonji and Rebecca M. Blank, "Race and Gender in the Labor Market," in *Handbook of Labor Economics,* ed. Orley C. Ashenfelter and David Card, eds. (Amsterdam: North-Holland, 1999), pp. 3C: 3143–259; Francine D. Blau and Lawrence M. Kahn, "Gender Differences in Pay," *Journal of Economic Perspectives* 14, no. 4 (fall 2000): 75–99; Francine D. Blau and Marianne A. Ferber, "Discrimination: Empirical Evidence from the United States," *American Economic Review* 77, no. 2 (May 1987): 316–20; and Francine D. Blau, "Discrimination Against Women: Theory and Evidence," in *Labor Economics: Modern Views,* ed. William A. Darity Jr. (Boston: Kluwer-Nijhoff, 1984), pp. 53–89.

[4] Francine D. Blau and Lawrence M. Kahn, "Swimming Upstream: Trends in the Gender Wage Differential in the 1980s," *Journal of Labor Economics* 15, no. 1, pt. 1 (January 1997): 1–42.

[5] Note that the gender differences in the proportion with four or more years of college are somewhat smaller here than in Table 6.1. This reflects the focus on employed individuals and on full-time workers, in contrast to Table 6.1, which was for the full population. As we saw in Chapter 4, female participation is positively correlated with education. This is also true of male participation but the relationship is stronger for women. Thus, women in the labor force tend to be more highly educated relative to men than is the total female population.

TABLE 7.1   Average Characteristics of Full-Time Workers, 1989, Ages 18–65

	Men	*Women*
Years of education	13.37	13.38
Proportion with college degree	0.20	0.19
Proportion with advanced degree	0.08	0.07
Years of full-time experience	17.41	12.79
Years of part-time experience	1.61	2.46
Proportion white	0.92	0.89
Proportion in following occupations:		
Managers	0.19	0.12
Professional and technical	0.20	0.30
Clerical	0.04	0.31
Sales	0.05	0.03
Craft	0.24	0.01
Operatives	0.19	0.10
Service or laborers	0.10	0.13
Proportion in following industries:		
Mining, construction, and durable manufacturing	0.30	0.11
Nondurable manufacturing	0.10	0.08
Transportation	0.12	0.04
Wholesale trade	0.06	0.02
Retail trade	0.10	0.12
Finance, insurance, and real estate	0.04	0.11
Services	0.19	0.45
Government	0.09	0.06
Proportion unionized	0.22	0.17

Source: Francine D. Blau and Lawrence M. Kahn, "Swimming Upstream: Trends in the Gender Wage Differential in the 1980s," *Journal of Labor Economics* 15, no. 1, pt. 1 (January 1997): 1–42; Table A1. © 1997 by the University of Chicago. Reprinted by permission.

on average, women have less full-time work experience than men, over 4.5 years less. Although women do have a bit more part-time experience, that has been found to have a very low payoff in terms of current wages. In addition, men and women tend to be concentrated in different occupations and industries. Men are more likely to be in blue-collar jobs and to work in mining, construction, or durable manufacturing. Women are more likely to be in clerical or professional jobs and to work in the service industry. Women are also less likely to be in unionized employment.

The consequences of these differences in characteristics for the male–female wage differential are shown in Table 7.2. The results in the table are based on a statistical analysis of the contribution of each variable to the gender wage differential of 28 percent. This procedure is explained in detail in the appendix. The first column shows the results when only "human capital variables," that is, those relating to education and experience, are taken into account. (Race is also included, but its effect is small since the proportion of whites in the labor force is about the same for men and women.) Differences in qualifications, particularly labor market experience, are found to be significant determinants of gender wage differentials; gender differences in ex-

TABLE 7.2 Percentages of the Wage Differential Between Men and Women Explained by Differences in Measured Characteristics, 1988

Characteristics	Human Capital Variables Only	All Variables
Educational attainment	0.3	0.3
Labor force experience	30.8	26.2
Race	1.8	1.2
Occupational category	—	7.8
Industry category	—	22.6
Union status	—	3.8
Unexplained	67.1	38.0
Total	100.0	100.0
Wage differential (%)	27.6	27.6

Source: Calculated from results presented in Francine D. Blau and Lawrence M. Kahn, "Swimming Upstream: Trends in the Gender Wage Differential in the 1980s," *Journal of Labor Economics* 15, no. 1, part 1 (January 1997): 1–42.

perience explain 31 percent of the gender gap in wages. Although these findings suggest that gender differences in work-related characteristics are important, they also indicate that qualifications are only part of the story. The proportion of the wage differential that is *not* explained by these types of productivity-related characteristics serves as an estimate of the impact of labor market discrimination. In this case, 67 percent of the gender gap cannot be explained by differences in the education or experience of men and women.

The second column shows the results when gender differences in occupation, industry, and union status are taken into account, in addition to education and experience ("all variables"). The unexplained difference shrinks to 38 percent of the gender wage differential, suggesting that a considerable portion of the wage gap is due to wage differences between men and women with similar human capital who work in different industries or occupations or in union versus nonunion jobs. However, even taking such sectoral factors into account, which, as we shall see later, is a bit questionable, a substantial portion of the pay gap remains unexplained and potentially due to discrimination.

The results of this study are shown somewhat differently in Figure 7.1. The actual ("unadjusted") gender wage ratio is 72 percent; that is, women's wages are, on average, 72 percent of men's wages. If women had the same human capital characteristics as men (the first "adjusted" ratio), their wages would be 81 percent of men's wages. Finally, if, in addition, women had the same industry and occupational distribution and union coverage as men (the second "adjusted" ratio), their wages would rise to 88 percent of men's wages. Thus, while measured characteristics are important, women still earn considerably less than similar men even when all measured characteristics are taken into account.

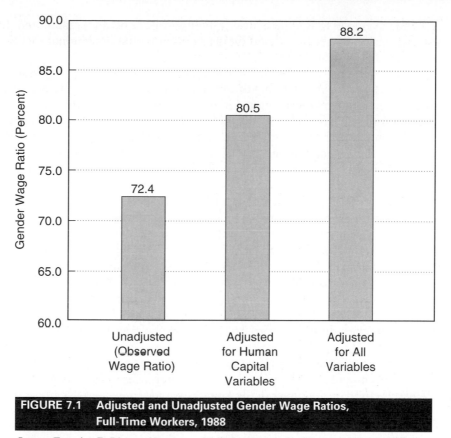

FIGURE 7.1   Adjusted and Unadjusted Gender Wage Ratios, Full-Time Workers, 1988

Source: Francine D. Blau and Lawrence M. Kahn, "Swimming Upstream: Trends in the Gender Wage Differential in the 1980s," *Journal of Labor Economics* 15, no. 1, part 1 (January 1997): 1–42.

How conclusive are such estimates? Certainly not entirely so; there are a number of problems with these types of analyses that may result in either upward or downward biases in the estimate of discrimination. One difficulty is that we do not have information on all the qualifications of individuals that are associated with their (potential) productivity. Some of the factors that affect earnings, such as motivation or work effort, cannot easily be quantified. Others (for example, college major) are frequently unavailable in a particular data set. Hence, in general, it is not possible to include all relevant job qualifications in a study of gender differences in wages.

For instance, although the study reported in Tables 7.1 and 7.2 accounts for differences between men and women in many important work-related factors, it lacks data on others that are potentially relevant. If men are more highly qualified with respect to the factors that are omitted from the analysis, the extent of labor market discrimination is likely to be *overestimated*. Some portion of the "unexplained" gender differential in Table 7.2 may, in fact, be due to men being more highly motivated or to gender differences in college major. However, it is also possible that women are more highly qualified in some respects not taken into account. They may have greater interpersonal skills, for example. In that case, discrimination would be underestimated. In general, more attention has been focused on the possibility that discrimination may be overestimated due to omitted factors.[6]

At the same time, some of the lower qualifications of women may be a direct result of labor market discrimination. For example, qualified women may be excluded from particular jobs due to discrimination in hiring or promotion. In Table 7.2, the results reported in the second column of the table include controls for variables like major occupation and industry category, which could themselves be impacted by such discrimination. To the extent that studies of discrimination control for qualifications that themselves reflect the direct effects of discrimination, the impact of discrimination on the pay gap will be *underestimated*.[7]

Analyses of the type presented in Table 7.2 also neglect the feedback effects of labor market discrimination on the behavior and choices of women themselves. For example, women have traditionally received lower returns to labor market experience than men. The lesser amount of work experience that they have accumulated may be due in part to their response to these lower returns. As another example, women may have been less likely to pursue college study in traditionally male fields in the past because of their perception that they would encounter job discrimination in these areas.

Some particularly persuasive evidence of discrimination comes from some recent studies that take a different approach to the question than most previous research. First, two studies have applied the same statistical techniques as those discussed above to especially homogeneous groups and employed particularly extensive controls for qualifications, thus minimizing the effect of gender differences in unmeasured characteristics. The first focused on graduates of the University of Michigan Law School classes of 1972 to 1975, 15 years after graduation.[8] The gap in pay between women and men was found to be relatively small at the outset of their careers, but 15 years later, women graduates earned only 60 percent as much as men. Some of this difference reflected choices that workers themselves had made, including the propensity of women lawyers to work shorter hours. However, even after accounting for differences in current hours worked, as well as an extensive list of worker qualifications and other factors, including family status, race, location, grades while in law school, and detailed work history data, such as years practiced law, months of part-time work, and type and size of employer, men still

---

[6] This problem is a bit less serious than it appears at first glance in that the included factors likely capture some of the effects of those that cannot be controlled for because of lack of information. For example, it is likely that more highly educated individuals are also more intelligent and more able, on average, than the less educated. For an interesting explication of the statistical issues raised by imperfect measures of productivity in empirical analyses, see Arthur Goldberger, "Reverse Regression and Salary Discrimination," *Journal of Human Resources* 19, no. 3 (summer 1984): 293–318.

[7] For a consideration of such issues, see Alan Blinder, "Wage Discrimination: Reduced Form and Structural Estimates," *Journal of Human Resources* 8, no. 4 (fall 1973): 436–55; and Ronald Oaxaca, "Male–Female Wage Differences in Urban Labor Markets," *International Economic Review* 14, no. 3 (October 1973): 693–709. For evidence on the issue of discrimination against women in access to on-the-job training, see Greg J. Duncan and Saul Hoffman, "On-the-Job Training and Earnings Differences by Race and Sex," *Review of Economics and Statistics* 61, no. 4 (November 1979): 594–603; John M. Barron, Dan A. Black, and Mark A. Lowenstein, "Gender Differences in Training, Capital and Wages," *Journal of Human Resources* 28, no. 2 (1993): 342–64; and Anne Beeson Royalty, "The Effects of Job Turnover on the Training of Men and Women," *Industrial and Labor Relations Review* 49, no. 3 (April 1996): 506–21.

[8] Robert G. Wood, Mary E. Corcoran, and Paul Courant, "Pay Differences Among the Highly Paid: The Male-Female Earnings Gap in Lawyers' Salaries," *Journal of Labor Economics* 11, no. 3 (July 1993): 417–41.

earned 13 percent more. In a similar vein, another study examined gender wage differences in 1985 among recent college graduates (who had graduated between one and two years earlier).[9] After controlling for narrowly defined college major, college grade point average, and specific educational institution attended, this study still found an unexplained pay gap of 10 to 15 percent between men and women.

In addition to providing evidence of unexplained pay differentials between men and women, the results of the study of lawyers suggest the danger in placing too much weight on how younger women fare relative to their male counterparts in assessing whether or not discrimination against women in the labor market exists. While the exceptionally large decreases in the gender pay gap among young workers that we reviewed in Chapter 5 are a welcome sign, it is important to realize that gender pay differences have tended in the past to increase over the work career.

A second set of studies used an experimental approach. One analyzed the results of a hiring "audit" in which male and female pseudo–job seekers were given similar résumés and sent to apply for jobs waiting on tables at the same set of 65 Philadelphia restaurants.[10] The results provided statistically significant evidence of discrimination against women in high-priced restaurants where earnings of workers are generally higher. In these restaurants, a female applicant's probability of getting an interview was 40 percentage points lower than a male's and her probability of getting an offer was 50 percentage points lower. A second study examined the impact of the adoption of "blind" auditions for musicians by symphony orchestras in which a screen is used to conceal the identity of the candidate.[11] The screen substantially increased the probability that a woman would advance out of preliminary rounds and be the winner in the final round. The switch to blind auditions was found to explain one quarter of the increase in the percentage female in the top five symphony orchestras in the United States, from less than 5 percent of all musicians in 1970 to 25 percent today.

Third, a recent study attempted to more directly estimate the productivity of women relative to men and then compare the magnitude of the productivity gap to the magnitude of the gender wage gap. It was found that women's estimated marginal product was somewhat lower than men's. However, women's wages fell short of men's by considerably more than can be explained by their lower marginal productivity. This finding is consistent with discrimination against women in the labor market.[12]

---

[9] Catherine J. Weinberger, "Race and Gender Wage Gaps in the Market for Recent College Graduates," *Industrial Relations* 37, no. 1 (January 1998): 67–84.

[10] David Neumark, with the assistance of Roy J. Blank and Kyle D. Van Nort, *Quarterly Journal of Economics* 111, no. 3 (August, 1996): 915–42. Such hiring audits have also found evidence of discrimination against minorities; for a summary see, U.S. Department of Labor, *Affirmative Action Review: Report to the President*, 1995.

[11] Claudia Goldin and Cecilia Rouse, "Orchestrating Impartiality: the Impact of 'Blind' Auditions on Female Musicians," *American Economic Review* 90, no. 4 (September 2000): 715–41.

[12] See Judith K. Hellerstein, David Neumark, and Kenneth R. Troske, "Wages, Productivity, and Worker Characteristics: Evidence from Plant-Level Production Functions and Wage Equations," *Journal of Labor Economics* 17, no. 3 (July 1999): 409–46. Their study, which focused on the manufacturing sector, estimated productivity by a statistical model that relates an establishment's output to the size and demographic composition of its work force, controlling for its input of capital and materials as well as industry and establishment size. See also Jonathan S. Leonard, "Antidiscrimination or Reverse Discrimination: The Impact of Title VII, Affirmative Action, and Changing Demographics on Productivity," *Journal of Human Resources* 19 no. 2 (spring 1984): 145–84.

Further evidence that labor market discrimination exists is provided by the many employment discrimination cases in which employers have been found guilty of discrimination in pay or have reached out-of-court settlements with the plaintiffs. A number of employment practices that explicitly discriminated against women used to be quite prevalent, including marriage bars restricting the employment of married women[13] and the intentional segregation of men and women into separate job categories with associated separate and lower pay scales for women.[14] While many such overt practices have receded, recent court cases still provide evidence of employment practices that produce discriminatory outcomes for women.

For example, in 1994, Lucky Stores, a major grocery chain, agreed to a settlement of $107 million after Judge Marilyn Hall Patel found that "sex discrimination was the standard operating procedure at Lucky with respect to placement, promotion, movement to full-time positions, and the allocation of additional hours." Similar lawsuits against several grocery chains have ended in settlements, including Publix Super Markets Inc. of Florida, which, in 1997, agreed to pay $81.5 million to settle a sex-discrimination lawsuit that accused the chain of keeping women in dead-end, low-wage jobs. Although women comprised half the company's work force, less than 5 percent of its 535 store managers were women.[15] In 2000, the U.S. Information Agency agreed to pay $508 million to settle a case in which the Voice of America rejected women who applied for high-paying positions in the communications field. A lawyer representing the plaintiffs said that the women were told things like, "These jobs are only for men," or "We're looking for a male voice." Similar issues were raised in another high profile case involving State Farm Insurance, which agreed in 1997 to pay $250 million to a group of women whose lawsuit claimed they were denied or deterred from positions as insurance agents.[16] A final example is the 1990 case against Price Waterhouse, a major accounting firm, in which the only woman considered for a partnership was denied the position, even though, of the 88 candidates for partner, she had brought in the most business. Her colleagues criticized her for being "overbearing, 'macho' and abrasive and said she would have a better chance of making partner if she would wear makeup and jewelry, and walk, talk and dress 'more femininely'." The court found that Price Waterhouse maintained a partnership evaluation system that "permitted negative sexually stereotyped comments to influence partnership selection."[17] We provide a review of the provisions of the employment discrimination laws and regulations later in this chapter.

Finally, it is suggestive that the perceptions of Americans, women and men, are consistent with the existence of such discrimination. A CBS News poll conducted in 1999 found that 67 percent of women and 58 percent of men thought that it was easier for men than women to get top executive jobs in business or government, while 70 percent

---

[13] Claudia Goldin, *Understanding the Gender Gap: An Economic History of American Women* (New York: Oxford University Press, 1990).

[14] See, for example, *Bowe v. Colgate-Palmolive Co.*, 416 F.2d 711 {7th Cir. 1969}; and *IUE* v. *Westinghouse Electric Co.*, 631 F.2d 1094 {3rd Cir. 1980}.

[15] *Stender* v. *Lucky Stores, Inc.* 803 F. Supp. 259; {N.D. Cal. 1992}; and Ronette King, "Women Taking Action Against Many Companies," *Times-Picayune*, 27 April 1997.

[16] *Federal Human Resources Week* 6, no. 47 (5 April 2000); King, "Women Taking Action."

[17] Bureau of National Affairs, *Daily Labor Report*, no. 235 (6 December 1990), pp. A11-A13 and F1-F10; and Tamar Lewin, "Partnership Awarded to Woman in Sex Bias Case," *New York Times*, 16 May 1990, pp. A1, A12.

of women and 59 percent of men believed that if a man and a woman are doing the same work, the man generally earns more than the woman.[18] Further evidence is provided by a 1995 poll of randomly selected top- and middle-management *Fortune* subscribers in which 77 percent of women and 43 percent of men believed that women need more experience or a higher degree level than men to qualify for the same job,[19] and a 1995 survey of female executives from *Fortune* 1000 companies by Catalyst, a women's professional support organization, which found that more than half of respondents said that "male stereotyping and preconceptions of women" had held back their careers.[20] Other perceived barriers are noted later in the section on the "glass ceiling."

Where does this leave us? It suggests that pinpointing the exact portion of the pay gap that is due to labor market discrimination is difficult. Nonetheless, the findings of most studies provide strong evidence of pay differences between men and women that are *not* accounted for by gender differences in measured qualifications, even when the list of qualifications is quite extensive. We conclude that discrimination does indeed exist. Although precisely estimating its magnitude is difficult, the evidence suggests that the *direct* effects of labor market discrimination may explain as much as half or more of the pay differential between men and women.

OCCUPATIONAL DIFFERENCES

As we saw in Chapter 5, not only do women earn less than men, they also tend to be concentrated in different occupations. In this section, we address two questions.

- What are the *consequences* for women of such occupational segregation? In particular, what is its relationship to the pay gap between men and women?
- What are the *causes* of these gender differences in occupational distributions? Specifically, what role does labor market discrimination play? Is there evidence of a "glass ceiling" limiting the upward mobility of women?

From a policy perspective, an understanding of the consequences of segregation is crucial for assessing how important a problem it is, and an analysis of its causes helps us to determine the most effective tools for attacking it.

Consequences of Occupational Segregation   In Chapter 5, we saw that women are more likely than men to be concentrated in clerical and service jobs, whereas men are more likely than women to work in higher-paying jobs such as skilled craft occupations. Similarly, although the representation of women in the professional category actually exceeds men's, men are more likely to work in lucrative professions such as law, medicine, and engineering, whereas women are more often employed in lower-paying ones such as elementary and secondary school teaching and nursing. Such observations suggest that women are concentrated in relatively low-paying occupations and that this helps to explain the male–female pay gap.

---

[18]   www.pollingreport.com.

[19]   "At Work: A Special Report on the Status and Satisfaction of Working Women and Initiatives for Their Advancement Conducted by FORTUNE Marketing Research for Deloitte & Touche LLP," *Fortune,* 4 March 1996.

[20]   "Women's Success Linked to Their Ability to Adapt," *St. Louis Post-Dispatch,* 28 February 1996.

On the other hand, there are factors other than gender composition that may help to account for pay differences between male and female jobs. For example, male jobs may tend to require more education and training than female jobs or call for the exercise of skills, like supervisory responsibility, that are more valuable to the employer. Also, some require more physical strength, inconvenient hours, and so on.

Such characteristics are important, but occupational differences do appear to be a significant factor in explaining the earnings gap, even when productivity-related characteristics of workers are held constant. The findings of the study reported in Table 7.2, for example, suggest that differences between men and women in major occupational categories account for about 8 percent of the pay difference between men and women. Other research that takes account of detailed occupational categories suggests that the lower pay in predominantly female jobs accounts for 14 to 23 percent of the gender wage gap, even when a variety of occupational-level and industrial-level characteristics are also controlled for.[21]

These findings are based on detailed census occupations. Although the number of occupational categories distinguished by the census—in excess of 400—is impressive, employers use considerably finer breakdowns. It is very likely that, were such extremely detailed categories available for the economy as a whole, an even higher proportion of the pay gap would be attributed to occupational segregation.[22] Moreover, within the same occupational category, women tend to be employed in low-wage firms and industries, whereas men tend to be employed in high-wage firms and industries. In the study reported in Table 7.2, for example, gender differences in major industry and union status together account for an additional 27 percent of the gender gap. Other research suggests that, even when controls for detailed occupational category are included, industry differences accounted for 12 to 17 percent of the pay gap among equally qualified male and female workers.[23]

In evaluating the negative consequences of occupational segregation for women, it is important to bear in mind that the focus upon earnings does not take into account any adverse nonpecuniary consequences of such segregation. For one, it is likely that occupational segregation reinforces cultural notions of exaggerated differences between men and women in capabilities, preferences, and social and economic roles. Such beliefs may adversely affect the opportunities and outcomes even of women in predominantly male jobs.

---

[21]   The 23 percent figure is from Elaine Sorensen, "The Crowding Hypothesis and Comparable Worth Issue," *Journal of Human Resources* 25, no. 1 (winter 1990): 55–89. The 14 percent figure is from George Johnson and Gary Solon, "Estimates of the Direct Effects of Comparable Worth Policy," *American Economic Review* 76, no. 5 (December 1986): 1117–25. The Sorensen article provides an extremely useful summary of the empirical findings in this area; see also David A. Macpherson and Barry T. Hirsch, "Wages and Gender Composition, Why Do Women's Jobs Pay Less?" *Journal of Labor Economics* 13, no. 3 (July 1995): 426–71.

[22]   For example, in one large fiduciary institution it was found that 76 percent of the pay gap between equally qualified men and women was due to gender differences in occupational distribution; see Francine D. Blau, "Occupational Segregation and Labor Market Discrimination," in *Sex Segregation in the Workplace: Trends, Explanations, Remedies,* ed. Barbara Reskin (Washington, DC: National Academy Press, 1984), pp. 117–43.

[23]   Sorensen, "The Crowding Hypothesis." For evidence of the importance of gender differences in employment by firm, see Francine D. Blau, *Equal Pay in the Office* (Lexington, MA: Lexington Books, 1977); Erica L. Groshen, "The Structure of the Female/Male Wage Differential: Is It Who You Are, What You Do, or Where You Work?" *Journal of Human Resources* 26, no. 3 (summer 1991): 457–72; and Kimberly Bayard, Judith Hellerstein, David Newmark, and Kenneth Troske, "New Evidence on Sex Segregation and Sex Difference in Wages from Matched Employee–Employer Data," NBER Working Paper No. 7003 (March 1999).

Causes of Occupational Segregation   As with earnings differences, the causes of occupational segregation may be classified into supply-side versus demand-side factors. It is only the latter—differences in treatment—that represent *direct* labor market discrimination. Of course, here again, the anticipation of, or experience with, labor market discrimination may indirectly influence women's choices via feedback effects.

In the preceding chapter, we considered human capital theory, which suggests that, because women generally anticipate shorter and less continuous work lives than men, it will be in their economic self-interest to choose female occupations, which presumably require smaller human capital investments and have lower wage penalties for time spent out of the labor market. We also discussed a variety of other supply-side factors that could influence women's occupational choices, including the socialization process and various subtle barriers to their obtaining training in traditionally male fields. On the demand side, employers may contribute to occupational segregation by discriminating against equally qualified women in hiring, placement, access to training programs, and promotion for traditionally male jobs.

There is considerable evidence to support the belief that gender differences in preferences play some role in gender differences in occupations.[24] The claim that discrimination is also important is more controversial, but here too there is quite a bit of evidence suggesting that discrimination plays a role as well. Of course, it is not an easy matter to distinguish between preferences and discrimination empirically especially when, as is likely, both contribute to observed differences.

Some persuasive evidence of the importance of discrimination comes from descriptions of institutional barriers that have historically excluded women from particular pursuits or impeded their upward progression.[25] In addition, many studies, although not all, have found that women are less likely to be promoted, all else equal.[26] It has also been found that a major portion of the gender difference in on-the-job training remains unexplained, even after gender differences in the probability of worker turnover and other variables are taken into account.[27] This suggests that women may encounter discrimination in access to on-the-job training; such training may be valuable in providing access to higher-paying jobs.

While such findings regarding promotion and training are certainly consistent with discrimination, it is important to note that they suffer from the same problems raised earlier in our analysis of the determinants of the gender pay gap. They may overstate discrimination if there are important nondiscriminatory factors that are omitted from the

[24]   Morley Gunderson, "Male–Female Wage Differentials and Policy Responses," *Journal of Economic Literature* 27, no. 1 (March 1989): 46–72.

[25]   Barbara F. Reskin and Heidi I. Hartmann, eds., *Women's Work, Men's Work: Sex Segregation on the Job.* (Washington DC: National Academy Press, 1986).

[26]   For examples of studies that find evidence of lower promotion rates, see Deborah A. Cobb-Clark and Yvonne Dunlop, "The Role of Gender in Job Promotions," *Monthly Labor Review* 122, no. 12 (December 1999): 32–38; Kristin McCue, "Promotions and Wage Growth," *Journal of Labor Economics* 14, no. 2 (1996): 175–209; and Robert Cabral, Marianne A. Ferber, and Carole A. Green, "Men and Women in Fiduciary Institutions: A Study of Sex Differences in Career Development," *Review of Economics and Statistics* 63, no. 4 (November 1981): 573–80. For an example of a study that does not find evidence of discrimination, see Joni Hersch and W. K. Viscusi, "Gender Differences in Promotions and Wages," *Industrial Relations* 35, no. 4 (October 1996): 461–72.

[27]   Royalty, "The Effects of Job Turnover"; see also Barron, Black, and Lowenstein, "Gender Differences"; and Duncan and Hoffman, "On-the-Job Training."

analysis, such as tastes for particular types of work, availability for travel, and so forth, which could help to account for the observed gender differences. On the other hand, discrimination would be understated to the extent some of the variables that are controlled for, such as initial job category in a promotion study, themselves reflect the impact of labor market discrimination.

Given these types of concerns, it is not possible to use these findings to ascribe a specific portion of gender differences in occupations to the choices individual men and women make versus labor market discrimination (that is, to supply-side versus demand-side factors).[28] However, as in the case of our review of evidence on the pay gap, the evidence suggests that both are important. And, as in the case of pay differences, evidence of discrimination may be found not only in statistical analyses but also in the audit studies discussed earlier and discrimination cases, like those reviewed above, in which employers have been found guilty of gender discrimination or have settled the cases out of court.

Two recent studies are especially suggestive of the importance of discrimination, including the types of subtle barriers that we consider below in our discussion of the glass ceiling. One, a study of small firms, found that male employers paid higher wages and employed fewer women.[29] The second, a study of managers in the California savings and loan industry, found that having more women at specific levels of the firm hierarchy creates more opportunities for women. Specifically, women's chances of being hired and promoted were greater when there was a higher proportion of women at the level of the job being filled.[30]

Is There a Glass Ceiling?   The *glass ceiling* is the name that has been given to the set of subtle barriers that are believed by many to inhibit women and minorities from reaching the upper echelons of corporate America, government, and academia. To the extent such barriers exist, they constitute a form of labor market discrimination. Is there a glass ceiling impeding women's occupational advancement? Disparities in the representation of women at the upper levels of many professions are easy to document. As our discussion above suggests, however, the reasons behind them may be harder to pin down. In this section, we consider the extent of the gender differences in representation at the higher levels of the job hierarchy, focusing first on management jobs and then academia, and summarize what is known about the reasons for women's underrepresentation at the upper levels, as well as steps that have been recommended to promote women's advancement.

---

[28] For additional evidence on the sources of gender differences in occupations, see Rosabeth Kanter, *Men and Women of the Corporation* (New York: Basic Books, 1977); Barbara F. Reskin and Patricia A. Roos, *Job Queues, Gender Queues: Explaining Women's Inroads into Male Occupations* (Philadelphia: Temple University Press, 1990); Virginia Valian, *Why So Slow? The Advancement of Women* (Cambridge MA: MIT Press, 1998); Paula England, "Socioeconomic Explanations of Job Segregation," in *Comparable Worth and Wage Discrimination: Technical Possibilities and Political Realities,* ed. Helen Remick (Philadelphia: Temple University Press, 1984), pp. 28–46; Patricia A. Roos and Barbara F. Reskin, "Institutional Factors Contributing to Occupational Sex Segregation," in *Sex Segregation in the Workplace: Trends, Explanations, Remedies,* ed. Barbara Reskin (Washington, DC: National Academy Press, 1984), pp. 235–60; and Reskin and Hartmann, *Women's Work, Men's Work.*

[29] William J. Carrington and Kenneth R. Troske, "Gender Segregation in Small Firms," *Journal of Human Resources* 30, no. 3 (summer 1995): 503–33.

[30] Lisa E. Cohen, Joseph P. Broschak, and Heather Haveman, "And Then There Were More? The Effect of Organizational Sex Composition on the Hiring and Promotion," *American Sociological Review* 63, no. 5 (October 1998): 711–27.

Looking first at the senior ranks of management, we have already noted in Chapter 5 the extremely low representation of women in these jobs. According to a report by Catalyst on Fortune 500 companies, only 11.9 percent of all corporate officers and 5.1 percent of top-level executives were women in 1999. Further, women held just 3.3 percent of the top five most highly paid executive positions in the company. This did, however, represent a substantial increase from 8.7 percent of officers, 2.4 percent of top-level executives, and 1.2 percent of top earners in 1995.[31] Women were also very sparsely represented on corporate boards of directors in these firms, holding 11.2 percent of board seats, up from 8.3 percent in 1993.[32] Finally, a recent survey found that women represent only 13 percent of American managers sent abroad, jobs that may represent considerable responsibility and contribute to upward progression in the firm.[33]

It is difficult in general to determine whether disparities like these are simply due to the fact that women are relative newcomers and it takes time to move up through the ranks or whether they represent particular barriers to women's advancement. This is particularly true in areas like management, where data on the available candidates for these positions do not exist and where norms regarding the speed of upward movement are not well defined. However, a recent study of executives does highlight the substantial impact on pay of gender differences in level of the job hierarchy and firm, although it does not shed light on the causes of such differences.[34] In a sample of the five highest-paid executives among a large group of firms, it was found that the 2.5 percent of the executives who were women earned 45 percent less than their male counterparts. Female executives were younger and thus had less seniority. Nonetheless, three-quarters of the gender pay gap was due to the fact that women managed smaller companies and were less likely to be the CEO, chair, or president of their company. Consistent with the Catalyst data presented above, this study found that over the 1992 to 1997 sample period, the representation of women in these top-earner executive jobs rose somewhat and women's representation at larger corporations increased as well.

While the evidence is not sufficient to fully resolve the issue of how disparities of the type we have outlined here arise, it is important to understand that, to the extent discrimination plays a role, it certainly need not manifest itself through overt and conscious acts of discrimination against women. The barriers women face are often subtle and difficult to document, let alone remove. One example is recruiting practices in which the use of personal contacts from the "old boys network" can leave women "out of the loop." In addition, women often remain outsiders to a "male" workplace culture. A study of female executives from *Fortune* 1000 companies by Catalyst found that women who do break through the glass ceiling are successful because "they've developed styles that make men comfortable." A prime example is that, because sports have traditionally been a male domain, successful women have often had to learn to play golf and talk sports.[35]

---

[31]   Top-level or "clout" positions include CEO, chair, vice chair, president, COO, senior VP, and executive VP; see Catalyst, *Fact Sheet: 1999 Catalyst Census of Women Corporate Officers and Top Earners.*

[32]   Catalyst, *Catalyst Census of Women Board Directors of the Fortune 1000,* 1999 and previous issues.

[33]   Catalyst, *Passport to Opportunity: U.S. Women in Global Business,* News Release, 18 October 2000.

[34]   Marianne Bertrand and Kevin F. Hallock, "The Gender Gap in Top Corporate Jobs," National Bureau of Economic Research Working Paper No. 7931 (October 2000).

[35]   "Women's Success Linked to Their Ability to Adapt," *St. Louis Post-Dispatch,* 28 February 1996.

There may also be stereotyped views about women's qualifications that result in able women receiving fewer opportunities. For example, it may be believed that women are not aggressive enough, are unwilling to relocate for higher positions, and that, when they have families, are less committed to their jobs than their male counterparts. In the increasingly important arena of international business, there are a number of preconceptions that limit women's access to these jobs, including that women are not as internationally mobile as men, that clients outside the United States are not as comfortable doing business with women as with men, and that women would find it more difficult than men to balance the dual demands of job-related international travel with nonjob activities and responsibilities.[36] Another subtle barrier that may limit women's advancement is the perception that men make better bosses. In a 1996 Gallup poll, 37 percent of men and 54 percent of women responded that they preferred male bosses. Since men have traditionally staffed upper-level positions in most firms, many men and women make this assessment without having had an opportunity to compare. One study found that when workers are exposed to women bosses, preexisting stereotypes tend to break down; both men and women who had ever had a female boss were considerably less likely to prefer a male boss.[37]

When *Fortune* magazine surveyed male and female middle and top managers among its subscribers in September 1995, both men and women agreed that women working in corporate America face considerable obstacles.[38] An overwhelming 91 percent of women and 75 percent of men believed that the "existence of a male-dominated corporate culture" is the single most important barrier for women. Among the other major barriers cited by women were the existence of a glass ceiling, women's exclusion from informal networking, management's belief that women are less career oriented, and the lack of female mentors. Men cited as the top reasons the difficulties women have balancing paid work and family, the lack of female mentors, few female bosses as role models, and the exclusion of women from informal networks.

The status of women in academia, discussed briefly in Chapter 5, is a subject that has attracted a great deal of attention among researchers. This may in part be due to the role faculty members can play as potential mentors and role models for students. Another reason is that there is a clear hierarchy for faculty, along with relatively well-defined criteria for progressing within this hierarchy. This makes the status of women in academia a particularly instructive case.

Table 7.3 provides data on the distribution of men and women in academia by rank in the 1970s, 1980s, and 1990s. In its broad outlines, the situation is quite clear. In each year, women were overrepresented at the lower end of the occupational hierarchy as assistant professors, whereas men were more highly represented at the upper ranks, as professors and associate professors—the categories that tend to have job security in the form of tenure. Women were also heavily overrepresented as instructors and lecturers,

---

[36]   Catalyst, *Passport to Opportunity.*

[37]   See "Bias Alive In Workplace," *St. Louis Post-Dispatch,* 27 March 1996; and Marianne Ferber, Joan Huber, and Glenna Spitze, "Preference for Men as Bosses and Professionals," *Social Forces* 58, no. 2 (1979): 466–76.

[38]   "At Work: A Special Report on the Status and Satisfaction of Working Women and Initiatives for Their Advancement Conducted by FORTUNE Marketing Research for Deloitte & Touche LLP," *Fortune,* 4 March 1996.

TABLE 7.3   Percent Female of Faculty in Institutions of Higher Education by Academic Rank, 1976–1977, 1987–1988, 1998–1999

Academic Rank	1976–1977	1987–1988	1998–1999
Professors	8.4	11.4	19.6
Associate professors	16.7	24.2	35.1
Assistant professors	29.7	36.6	46.6
Instructors	49.0	53.3	57.6
Lecturers	41.9	50.0	55.2
All Ranks	22.4	25.1	34.4

Source: *Academe*, August 1981 and March–April 1993: 1998–1999 figures calculated from *Academe* (March–April 1999), Table 12, p. 32.

job categories that tend to be considerably less desirable in terms of pay, promotion prospects, and job continuity. Other data indicate that there are also substantial differences by level of institution, with women tending to be underrepresented at the most highly ranked research universities and much more heavily represented at smaller, liberal arts institutions and two-year colleges.[39] Women also tend to be concentrated in less lucrative fields in the humanities, while men tend to dominate in the higher paying scientific and technical fields.

Disparities in the representation of women and men by level of the academic hierarchy may be due in whole or part to the more recent entry of women into academia and the time it takes to move up the ladder. And the data in Table 7.3 do suggest some female gains over time, consistent with the "pipeline" argument. For example, by 1998, women's share of associate professors (35.1 percent) nearly equaled their share of assistant professors 11 years earlier (36.6 percent), although the disparities are larger when we compare women's representation as associate professors in 1987 (24.2 percent) to their representation as assistant professors in 1976 (29.7 percent). Movement of women into the highest level has also occurred, though women remained sparsely represented at the top. The proportion of professors who were women increased from 8.4 percent in 1976 to 11.4 percent in 1987 and 19.6 percent in 1998, but women's share of professors in 1987 and 1998 remained below their share of associate professors 11 years earlier.

Detailed studies suggest that despite recent changes, discrimination does play a role in academia. For example, a recent study of faculty promotion in the economics profession found that, controlling for quality of Ph.D. training, publishing productivity, major field of specialization, current placement in a distinguished department, age and post-Ph.D. experience, female economists were still significantly less likely to be promoted from assistant to associate and from associate to full professor—although there was also some evidence that women's promotion opportunities from associate to full

---

[39]   For example, in 1998–1999, women constituted 46.6 percent of faculty at two-year colleges but were only 28.8 percent of the faculty at research universities that grant doctorates (*Academe*, March-April 1999, table 12, p. 32). See also Marianne A. Ferber and Jane W. Loeb, "Introduction," in *Academic Couples, Problems and Promise*, ed. Marianne A. Ferber and Jane W. Loeb (Champaign, IL: University of Illinois Press, 1997).

professor improved in the 1980s.[40] Moreover, women appear to face obstacles to their efforts to accumulate the publications and other credentials necessary to move up in the ranks. For example, it has been found that women in predominantly male fields are likely to have greater difficulty than men finding collaborators and in getting their papers accepted for publication. And, once published, their publications are less likely to be cited.[41] Other types of disparities in treatment may adversely affect the success of women in academia. For example, a recent report on faculty at MIT finds evidence of differential treatment of senior women that may encompass not simply differences in salary but also in space, awards, and resources, "with women receiving less despite professional accomplishments equal to those of their male colleagues."[42]

A bipartisan Federal Glass Ceiling Commission was established in 1991 to study this problem and make recommendations. In November 1995, the commission issued its final report.[43] The report recommended that government lead by example and strengthen enforcement of antidiscrimination laws. Later in this chapter, we will summarize these laws and consider what is known about their effectiveness. The report also stressed a variety of actions employers can take voluntarily to promote the advancement of women and minorities in the organization. It particularly highlighted the importance of strong leadership at the top. Among the recommendations were that CEOs (1) demonstrate a genuine commitment to diversity by ensuring that all written and oral information disseminated emphasize it as a "core value"; (2) link pay, promotions, and bonuses of managers to meeting goals of diversity; (3) ensure that all qualified individuals have equal access and opportunity to compete for positions; (4) expand searches for new employees to include individuals from "noncustomary" sources with varied backgrounds and experiences; (5) establish mentoring programs to prepare minorities and women for senior positions; (6) provide training to familiarize employees with the strengths and challenges of gender, racial, ethnic, and cultural differences; (7) initiate policies that help employees to balance the dual demands of career and family; and (8) encourage workers to participate in decision making and share information.

To better monitor progress in combating the glass ceiling, the report requested that both government and private corporations increase disclosure of data on workplace diversity. Finally, the report noted that society at large helps to perpetuate the glass ceiling. The commission recommended that the media carefully examine how they portray minorities and women, and that educators teach children about other cultures as well as encourage minorities and women to pursue careers in business. In addition, the report

---

[40] John M. McDowell, Larry D. Singell Jr., and James P. Ziliak, "Cracks in the Glass Ceiling: Gender and Promotion in the Economics Profession," *American Economic Review* 89, no. 2 (May 1999): 392–96. See also Massachusetts Institute of Technology, "A Study on the Status of Women Faculty in Science at MIT," unpublished report, Massachusetts Institute of Technology (1999); Donna K. Ginther and Kathy J. Hayes, "Gender Differences in Salary and Promotion in the Humanities," *American Economic Review* 89, no. 2 (May 1999): 397–402; and Sharon G. Levin and Paula E. Stephan, "Gender Differences in the Rewards to Publishing in Academe: Science in the 1970s," *Sex Roles* 38, no. 11–12 (June 1998): 1049–64.

[41] Marianne A. Ferber and Michelle L. Teiman, "Are Women Economists at a Disadvantage in Publishing Journal Articles?" *Eastern Economic Journal* 6, nos. 3–4 (August–October 1980): 189–94; and Marianne A. Ferber, "Citations and Networking," *Gender and Society* 2, no. 1 (March 1988): 82–89.

[42] Massachusetts Institute of Technology, "A Study on the Status of Women Faculty", p. 4.

[43] See "The Glass Ceiling," *CQ Researcher,* Congressional Quarterly Inc. 3, no. 40, 29 October 1993, pp. 937–59; and "A Solid Investment: Making Full Use of the Nation's Human Capital," Recommendations of the Glass Ceiling Commission, Washington, DC (November 1995).

urged educators to look beyond traditional measures such as standardized test scores in evaluating students' potential and to consider other factors that make for success such as leadership, teamwork, and analytical, communication, and interpersonal skills.

MODELS OF LABOR MARKET DISCRIMINATION

The empirical evidence suggests that there are indeed pay and occupational differences between men and women that are not accounted for by (potential) productivity differences. We now turn to an examination of how discrimination can produce such gender differences in economic outcomes and why this inequality has persisted over time. Economists have developed a variety of models that may be used to analyze these issues. Empirical research in this area has not, however, established which of these approaches most accurately describes the labor market. Indeed, for the most part, these explanations are *not* mutually exclusive and each may shed some light on how labor market discrimination affects women's economic outcomes.

Unless otherwise indicated, the analyses presented here assume that male and female labor are perfect substitutes in production. That is, it is assumed that male and female workers are equally well qualified and, in the absence of discrimination, would be equally productive and receive the same pay. Of course, we know that this assumption is not an accurate description of reality—there are gender differences in qualifications that explain some of the pay gap. However, this assumption is appropriate in that models of discrimination are efforts to explain the portion of the pay gap that is *not* due to differences in qualifications; that is, they are intended to explain pay differences between men and women who are (potentially) equally productive.

TASTES FOR DISCRIMINATION

The foundation for the modern neoclassical analysis of labor market discrimination was laid by Gary Becker.[44] Becker conceptualized discrimination as a personal prejudice, or what he termed a *taste*, against associating with a particular group. In his model, employers, coworkers, and customers may all potentially have such discriminatory tastes. In contrast to the case of racial discrimination that Becker initially analyzed, it may at first seem odd to hypothesize that men would not like to associate with women when, in fact, they generally live together in families. The issue here may be more one of socially appropriate roles than of the desire to maintain social distance, as Becker postulated was the case with race.[45]

Employers who have no reservations about hiring women as secretaries may be reluctant to employ them as pipefitters. Men who are willing to work with women in complementary or subordinate positions may dislike interacting with them as equals or superiors. Customers who are delighted to purchase stockings from female clerks may avoid

---

[44] Becker, *The Economics of Discrimination*. In our presentation of the tastes for discrimination model, we incorporate some of the insights of Kenneth Arrow; see "The Theory of Discrimination," in *Discrimination in Labor Markets,* ed. Orley Ashenfelter and Albert Rees (Princeton, NJ: Princeton University Press, 1973), pp. 3–33.

[45] The notion of socially appropriate roles may also be a factor in racial discrimination, as when blacks have little difficulty in gaining access to menial jobs but encounter discrimination in obtaining higher-level positions.

women who sell cars or are attorneys. If such discriminatory tastes reflect a dislike for interacting with women in these positions, rather than beliefs that women are less qualified than men for traditionally male pursuits, they are appropriately analyzed here.[46] The latter possibility is considered later under notions of statistical discrimination.

In order for such discriminatory tastes to have important consequences for women's earnings and employment, they must actually influence people's behavior. According to Becker, individuals with tastes for discrimination against women act as if there were nonpecuniary costs of associating with women—say, in what is viewed as a socially inappropriate role.[47] The strength of the individual's discriminatory taste is measured by his or her **discrimination coefficient** (that is, the size of these costs in money terms). We now examine the consequences of discrimination based on employer, employee, and customer preferences, respectively.

Employer Discrimination   If an employer has tastes for discrimination against women, he or she will act as if there were a nonpecuniary cost of employing women equal in dollar terms to d_r (the discrimination coefficient). To this employer, the costs of employing a man will be his wage, w_m, but the *full* costs of employing a woman will be her wage *plus* the discrimination coefficient ($w_f + d_r$). A discriminating employer will hire a woman only if the full cost of employing her ($w_f + d_r$) is no greater than the cost of employing a man (w_m) and will be indifferent between hiring a man or a woman if the full cost of a woman exactly equals the cost for a man. This implies that the discriminating employer will hire a women only at a lower wage than a man ($w_f = w_m - d_r$). Further, if we assume that men and women are equally productive, that is, their marginal products *(MP)* are the same, and that men are paid in accordance with their productivity, women will be hired only if they are paid less than their productivity.[48]

Becker's analysis showed that the consequences of this situation for female workers depend on the prevalence and size of discriminatory tastes among employers, as well as on the number of women seeking employment. Nondiscriminatory employers are willing to hire men and women at the same wage rate (that is, their discrimination coefficient equals 0). If there is a relatively large number of such nondiscriminatory employers or there are relatively few women seeking employment, they may all be absorbed by the nondiscriminatory firms. In this case, there will be no discriminatory pay differential based on gender, even though some employers have tastes for discrimination against women.

---

[46]   However, as we shall see, such discriminatory preferences on the part of workers or customers for men will cause women to be less productive from the point of view of the employer. For further consideration of the origin and persistence of occupational segregation, see Reskin and Roos, *Job Queues, Gender Queues;* and Myra H. Strober, "Toward a General Theory of Occupational Sex Segregation: The Case of Public School Teaching," in *Sex Segregation in the Workplace: Trends, Explanations, Remedies,* ed. Barbara F. Reskin (Washington, DC: National Academy Press, 1984), pp. 144–56.

[47]   Throughout, we assume that employers, coworkers, or customers have tastes for discrimination against women. It is also possible that they have positive preferences for employing, working with, or buying from men. This may be termed a kind of *nepotism.* See Matthew Goldberg, "Discrimination, Nepotism, and Long-Run Wage Differentials," *Quarterly Journal of Economics* 97, no. 2 (May 1982): 307–19 for an interesting analysis of the consequences of nepotism for the persistence of discrimination in the long run. See also David Neumark, "Employers' Discriminatory Behavior and the Estimation of Wage Discrimination," *Journal of Human Resources* 23, no. 3 (summer 1988): 279–95.

[48]   That is, if $w_m = MP$, where *MP* is equal to the marginal productivity of men (or women), then women will be paid $w_m - d_r$ which is less than their productivity.

However, if discriminatory tastes are widespread, or there are relatively many women seeking employment, some women will have to find jobs at discriminatory firms. As we have seen, the women obtain such employment only if w_f is less than w_m. If we assume that the labor market is competitive, all employers will pay the (same) going rate established in the market for workers of a particular sex. This is the case because no employer would be willing to pay more than the going rate, since additional workers are always available at that wage. No worker will accept less than the going rate, since jobs at other firms are always available to him or her at that wage. This means that, in equilibrium, the market wage differential between men and women must be large enough so that all the women who are looking for employment obtain it—including those who must find work at discriminatory firms. Thus, the more prevalent and the stronger employers' discriminatory tastes against women and the larger the number of women seeking employment, the larger will be the marketwide wage gap $(w_m - w_f)$ between men and women.

This model of employer tastes for discrimination is consistent with the inequalities between men and women that we observe in the labor market. Under this model, there may be a wage differential between equally qualified male and female workers because discriminatory employers will hire women workers only at a wage discount.[49] Further, since less discriminatory employers will hire more women workers than more discriminatory employers, male and female workers may be segregated by firm—as also appears to be the case. Finally, if, as seems likely, employer tastes for discrimination vary across occupations, occupational segregation by sex can also occur.

However, one problem that economists have identified with this model is that discrimination is not costless to the employer who forgoes the opportunity to hire more of the lower-priced female labor and less of the higher-priced male labor. Therefore, less discriminatory firms should have lower costs of production. Such a competitive advantage would enable them to expand and drive the more discriminatory firms out of business in the long run. As the less discriminatory firms expand, the demand for female labor would be increased and the male–female pay gap would be reduced. If there were enough *entirely* nondiscriminatory firms to absorb all the women workers, the pay gap would be eliminated. Hence, the question is how discrimination, which represents a departure from profit-maximizing behavior, can withstand the impact of competitive pressures.

One answer to this question is that discrimination may simply result from a lack of such competitive pressures in the economy. Becker hypothesized that, on average, employer discrimination would be less severe in competitive than in monopolistic industries, and some support has been obtained for this prediction. For example, it has been found that, with the deregulation of the banking industry beginning in the mid-1970s, the

---

[49] Some have proposed testing the employer discrimination model by comparing the gender pay gap among self-employed workers and employees. The claim is that if *employer* discrimination is responsible for the pay differential, female self-employed workers should fare relatively better than female employees, all else being equal. See Victor R. Fuchs, "Differences in Hourly Earnings Between Men and Women," *Monthly Labor Review* 94, no. 5 (May 1971): 9–15; and Robert L. Moore, "Employer Discrimination: Evidence from Self-Employed Workers," *Review of Economics and Statistics* 65, no. 3 (August 1983): 496–501. Although such studies have not supported the employer discrimination model, they do not provide an ideal test. There may be discrimination against women by lenders, suppliers, customers, and so on. In addition, in the presence of important economies of scale, women's lesser endowment of capital relative to men could lower their returns.

gender pay gap in banking declined.[50] This suggests that employers in banking were able to discriminate in part due to the monopolistic nature of the industry, but that their ability to do so was reduced when competition was increased.

Also consistent with Becker's reasoning is another recent study that found that, among plants with high levels of product market power (and hence an ability to exercise their tastes for discrimination in the Becker model), those employing relatively more women were more profitable.[51] This suggests that, among these firms, there is some discrimination against women and that less discriminatory firms benefit from the lower costs of production resulting from hiring more women.

Finally, unions may also, to some extent, be considered a barrier to competition in that wages may be set above the competitive level in the union sector. Unions are also more likely to arise in less competitive industries, and it is indeed the case that women are less highly represented in unionized employment. Thus, women do not benefit from the wage advantage of unionism to the same extent as men.[52] However, as we shall see in greater detail in Chapter 8, the gender difference in union representation has been narrowing.

It has also been suggested that *monopsony* power by employers in the labor market plays a role in producing and perpetuating the gender pay differential. One way in which a firm gains monopsony power is when it is a large buyer of labor relative to the size of a particular market.

To see how this can adversely affect women, consider the not uncommon case of a one-university town. In the past, when the husband's job prospects usually determined the location of the family, the faculty wife with a Ph.D. had little choice but to take whatever the university offered her—most considered themselves fortunate if they were able to obtain employment at all. Even the growing numbers of egalitarian Ph.D. couples cannot entirely avoid this problem. Although an increasing number of two-career couples, in academia and elsewhere, work in different locations and see each other, say, on weekends, most seek jobs in the same location. In order to change jobs, such couples must find *two* acceptable alternatives in a single location. This will obviously be harder to do than to find *one* desirable alternative. Thus, the Ph.D. couple will have fewer options than those with only one Ph.D. in the family. (Similar problems can arise for two-career couples in other fields.)

This situation gives the employer a degree of monopsony power and is likely to lower the pay of both members of the couple relative to Ph.D.'s who can relocate more

---

[50] Sandra E. Black and Philip E. Strahan, "Rent-Sharing and Discrimination: The Effects of Deregulation on the Labor Market," Working Paper, Federal Reserve Bank (May 1999). See also Sandra E. Black, "Investigating the Link Between Competition and Discrimination," *Monthly Labor Review* 122, no. 12 (December 1999): 39–43; Orley Ashenfelter and Timothy Hannan, "Sex Discrimination and Product Market Competition: The Case of the Banking Industry," *Quarterly Journal of Economics* 101, no. 1 (February 1986): 149–73; and William A. Luksetich, "Market Power and Sex Discrimination in White-Collar Employment," *Review of Social Economy* 37, no. 2 (October 1979): 211–24. Another possible reason for the persistence of employer discrimination in the long run is that it is based on a positive preference by employers for male workers (or "nepotism") rather than a disutility for employing female workers; see Goldberg, "Discrimination, Nepotism."

[51] Judith K. Hellerstein, David Neumark, and Kenneth Troske, "Market Forces and Sex Discrimination," National Bureau of Economic Research Working Paper No. 6321 (December 1997).

[52] For an analysis of the impact of unions on gender pay differences, see William E. Even and David A. MacPherson, "The Decline of Private-Sector Unionism and the Gender Wage Gap," *Journal of Human Resources* 28, no. 2 (spring 1993): 279–96.

easily. Note that among Ph.D. couples, both the husband's *and* the wife's salary may be adversely affected. However, because women with Ph.D.'s are more likely than male Ph.D.'s to have a Ph.D. spouse (there are still considerably fewer women than men who have Ph.D.'s), this factor is likely to have a larger adverse effect on academic women as a group than on academic men.[53]

The monopsony model has been offered as a general explanation for the gender pay gap. It is argued that employers have greater monopsony power over women than men due to such factors as occupational segregation and the power of male unions that may limit women's options. Further, as we saw in Chapter 6, women who adopt more traditional gender roles will tend to engage in less job search than men and to seek jobs that are closer to home.[54]

Consideration of job search suggests that another way in which firms may gain monopsony power is if workers lack perfect information about employment opportunities.[55] In a competitive model with perfect information, even a slightly higher wage at another firm will induce workers to move to that better opportunity. However, when information is imperfect, workers must search among employers for a good job match, thus incurring "search costs." These include the opportunity cost of the time spent looking for a job, as well as out-of-pocket costs for printing up a resume, transportation expenses to employment interviews, etc. Since search is costly, workers will be less mobile across firms than they would be if information was perfectly and costlessly available and it will take larger wage premiums at other firms to bid them away. The presence of search costs gives employers a degree of monopsony power over workers. If we further assume that some employers discriminate against women and are not willing to hire them, we see that women will have higher search costs than men. As a consequence employers will exploit this greater monopsony power over women and offer them lower wages than men. Thus, when information is imperfect and there are search costs, it is more credible that employer discrimination can persist in the long run.[56]

Another possible reason (not originally considered by Becker) for the persistence of discrimination in the labor market is that the employers' motivation for discriminating against women is not simply personal prejudice but is related to actual or perceived differences between male and female workers in productivity or behavior. We consider such models of **statistical discrimination** later in this chapter. A major contribution of

---

[53] There is evidence, at least for one institution, that both men and women in academic couples were paid less; see Marianne A. Ferber and Jane W. Loeb, "Professors, Performance and Rewards," *Industrial Relations,* 13, no. 1 (February 1974): 67–77.

[54] Janice F. Madden, *The Economics of Sex Discrimination* (Lexington, MA: Lexington Books, 1973). See also Alan Manning, "The Equal Pay Act as an Experiment to Test Theories of the Labour Market," *Economica* 63, no. 250 (May 1996): 191–212.

[55] We draw heavily here on Dan A. Black, "Discrimination in an Equilibrium Search Model," *Journal of Labor Economics* 13, no. 2 (April 1995): 309–34.

[56] A problem with the monopsony explanations, however, is that they require that women's labor supply to the *firm* be less sensitive to wages than men's. Yet, as we know from Chapter 4, women's labor supply to the *market* tends to more sensitive to wages than men's. While proponents of the monopsony view do suggest plausible reasons why women's mobility at the firm level may be reduced, these may or may not be sufficient to outweigh women's greater overall wage elasticity of labor supply to the market. In fact, after reviewing results from three studies of the quit behavior of men and women, Francine D. Blau and Lawrence M. Kahn find no evidence that men's labor supply is more sensitive to wages than women's at the firm level; see "Institutions and Laws in the Labor Market," in *Handbook of Labor Economics,* ed. Orley Ashenfelter and David Card (The Netherlands: Elsevier Science, B.V., 1999), chap. 25, pp. 3A:1399–461.

Becker's, however, is the realization that, even if employers themselves have no tastes for discrimination against women, their profit-maximizing behavior may result in gender discrimination in the labor market if employees or customers have such tastes. There is no conflict here with profit maximization by employers. Hence, there is no economic reason why this type of discrimination cannot continue.[57] We now consider the possibility of discriminating employees and customers.

Employee Discrimination   If a male employee has tastes for discrimination against women, he will act as if there were nonpecuniary costs of working with women equal to his discrimination coefficient, d_e. This is the premium he must be paid to induce him to work with women. Thus, if a discriminating male worker would receive w_m if he did not work with a woman, he would only be willing to work with a woman at a higher wage $(w_m + d_e)$. This is analogous to the compensating wage differential that economists expect workers to be offered for unpleasant or unsafe working conditions.

What will be the profit-maximizing employer's response to this situation? One solution would be for the employer to hire a sex-segregated work force. This would eliminate the necessity of paying a premium to male workers for associating with female workers. If all employers responded in this way (but had no taste for discrimination themselves), male and female workers would be paid the same wage rate, although they would work in segregated settings.

However, complete segregation may not be profitable where there are substantial costs of adjustment from the previous situation.[58] For example, the hiring of new workers entails recruitment and screening costs for the firm. Further, for jobs in which firm-specific training is important, the firm must incur the costs of these investments as well. Where there are such costs to changing from the current situation, history matters. Given rising female participation rates over time, women, as relatively new entrants, will find men already in place in many sectors. Further, as we saw in Chapter 2, women were heavily concentrated in a few female-dominated activities even when they constituted a small proportion of the labor force. Regardless of the various factors initially causing this segregation, adjustment costs in conjunction with employee tastes for discrimination could help to perpetuate it.

Given employee tastes for discrimination and adjustment costs, marketwide wage differences between male and female workers may result. Again, the size of the wage differential depends on the distribution and intensity of, in this case, *employees'* discriminatory tastes, as well as the relative number of women seeking employment. If there is a large proportion of employees with no taste for discrimination against women or relatively few women seeking jobs, then it may be possible for all the women to work with nondiscriminatory men; and no pay differential would occur.

However, if discriminatory tastes are widespread or there is a relatively large number of women seeking jobs, some of the women will have to work with discriminating male workers. Those males will require higher compensation to induce them to work with women. The result will be a wage differential between male and female workers,

---

[57]   Lawrence M. Kahn presents a model that shows that customer discrimination can produce persistent discriminatory wage differentials in "Customer Discrimination and Affirmative Action," *Economic Inquiry* 29, no. 3 (July 1991): 555–71.

[58]   Arrow, "The Theory of Discrimination."

on average, since some males will receive this higher pay, and women may be paid less to compensate for this. There also will be more variation in male workers' wage rates than would otherwise be the case. Discriminating male workers who do not work with women do not need to be paid a wage premium, nor do nondiscriminating males, regardless of whether or not they are employed with women.

In an empirical test of this prediction, one study compared the wages of men and women (within the same narrowly defined white-collar occupations) in sex-integrated and sex-segregated firms.[59] It was found that, contrary to what was expected on the basis of the employee discrimination model, men earned *more* in sex-segregated than in integrated firms, and women earned *more* when they worked with men than when they worked only with other women. These findings are more consistent with a situation in which high-wage (for example, monopolistic or unionized) employers are better able to indulge their preferences for hiring men than one in which the pay differential is due to employee discrimination. There may, however, be other cases in which employee discrimination has played an important role.

If such employee tastes for discrimination do in fact exist, and if they vary by occupation, employee discrimination may be a factor causing occupational segregation as well as pay differentials. For example, one reason why women may not be not hired for supervisory and managerial positions may be that even male employees who do not mind working with women do not like being supervised by them. As we have seen, there is evidence that some female as well as some male employees say that they would not like having women supervisors. This could create a barrier to the employment of women in such jobs.[60]

As Barbara Bergmann and William Darity have pointed out, employee discrimination may also adversely affect the morale and productivity of discriminating male workers who are forced to work with women, a possibility not initially considered by Becker.[61] This would make employers reluctant to hire women, especially when their male employees have considerable firm-specific training and are hard to replace. Further, if employers did hire women under such circumstances, they would pay them less to compensate for the reduction in the productivity of the discriminating male employees. In a sense, a woman's marginal productivity is lower than a man's because adding her to the work force causes a decline in the productivity of previously employed male workers. Adding an additional male worker causes no such decline in output.

Another way in which employee discrimination could affect worker productivity, also not initially considered by Becker, is that it can directly reduce the productivity of women in comparison to men. This is most likely to be a problem in traditionally male fields where the majority of workers are male. For example, on-the-job training frequently occurs informally as supervisors or coworkers demonstrate how things are done

---

[59] Blau, *Equal Pay in the Office.*

[60] However, one study found that both male and female employees earned *less* when they worked under a female supervisor. This is inconsistent with employee discrimination against female supervisors and suggests that the presence of a female supervisor is associated with less favorable characteristics of the job. See Donna S. Rothstein, "Supervisor Gender and the Early Labor Market Outcomes of Young Workers," in *Gender and Family Issues in the Workplace,* ed. Francine D. Blau and Ronald G. Ehrenberg (New York: Russell Sage, 1997): 210–55.

[61] Barbara R. Bergmann and William A. Darity Jr., "Social Relations in the Workplace and Employer Discrimination," *Proceedings of the Thirty-Third Annual Meetings of the Industrial Relations Research Association* (Madison: University of Wisconsin, 1981), pp. 155–62.

and give advice and assistance. When male employees have tastes for discrimination against women, they may be reluctant to teach them these important skills, and, as a result, women may learn less and be less productive.

Customer Discrimination   Customers or clients who have tastes for discrimination against women will act as if there were a nonpecuniary cost associated with purchasing a good or a service from a woman, equal to their discrimination coefficient, d_c. That is they behave as if the full price of the good or service is $p + d_c$ if it is provided by a women, but only p if it is sold by a man. Then, at the going market price, women will sell less. Alternatively, in order to sell as much as a comparable male, a woman would have to charge a lower price $(p - d_c)$. Again, discrimination, this time on the part of possible customers or clients, can result in potentially equally productive women being less productive (in terms of revenue brought in) than comparable males. They are, thus, less desirable employees and receive lower pay. If, as we speculated earlier, such customer discrimination exists in some areas but not in others, occupational segregation may also result.

Subtle Barriers   It is important to recognize that discrimination against women by employers, fellow employees, customers, or clients is not always or even usually conscious and overt. The subtle barriers of the sort we outlined in Chapter 6 with respect to women's acquisition of formal schooling also operate in the labor market. The barriers discussed above in connection with the glass ceiling are also relevant here. Women may participate less in the beneficial *mentor–protégé* relationships that often develop between senior and junior workers and may be excluded from the *informal networks* that tend to arise among peers at the workplace. As a result, they will be denied access to important job-related information, skills, and contacts, as well as the informal support systems that male workers generally enjoy. In these cases, although women are *potentially* equally productive, discrimination has the effect of reducing both their productivity and their pay.

Discrimination may also result from the perception that a woman would not "fit in" with the group as well as a man would and evaluations of a female employee's competence may be tainted by gender stereotypes of appropriate female behavior. A prime example of this is the Price Waterhouse case cited in our glass ceiling discussion above, in which a woman was denied a partnership at this prestigious accounting firm even though she had brought in the most business of all the partner candidates.

Discrimination by employers, employees, and customers may also be reinforced by habitual behavior that has the effect of disadvantaging women, even though its link to discriminatory outcomes may not be apparent at first. A good example of this is the role that all-male clubs traditionally played for business executives, high-level professionals, and civic leaders.[62] Some mistakenly perceived such clubs as "social" in their orientation. However, the significant business and professional relevance of such places has been increasingly recognized and many, under legal pressure or voluntarily, have opened their

---

[62] For further discussion of this issue, see Robin L. Bartlett, "Clubs that Exclude Women: 'Who You Know' vs. 'What You Know'," *Committee on the Status of Women in the Economics Profession (CSWEP) Newsletter* (spring 1984), pp. 11–14; and Robin L. Bartlett and Timothy I. Miller, "Executive Earnings by Gender: A Case Study," *Social Science Quarterly* 69, no. 4 (December 1988): 892–909.

doors to women. While there is no federal law prohibiting gender discrimination by private clubs, a number of major cities and several states, including New York, Florida, Michigan, and Minnesota, have banned the exclusion of women by business-oriented private clubs.[63]

STATISTICAL DISCRIMINATION

As noted earlier, models of statistical discrimination developed by Edmund Phelps and others[64] attribute a different motivation to employers for discrimination, one that is potentially more consistent with profit maximization and, thus, with the persistence of discrimination in the long run. In this view, employers are constantly faced with the need for decision making under conditions of incomplete information and uncertainty. Even if they carefully study the qualifications of applicants, they never know for certain how individuals will perform on the job or how long they will stay with the firm after being hired. Mistakes can be costly, especially where there are substantial hiring and training costs. Promotion decisions entail similar risks, although in this case employers have additional firsthand information on past job performance with the firm.

Perceptions of Average Gender Differences Can Result in a Pay Gap   In light of these uncertainties, it is not surprising that employers often use any readily accessible information that may be correlated with productivity or job stability in making difficult personnel decisions. If they believe that, *on average,* women are less productive or less stable employees, *statistical discrimination* against *individual* women may result. That is, employers may judge the individual woman on the basis of their beliefs about group averages. The result may be discrimination against women in pay or in hiring and promotion.

For example, suppose an employer is screening applicants for an entry-level managerial position and that the two major qualifications considered are level of education and grades. Assume further that the employer believes that at the same level of qualifications (say, an MBA with an A– average), women as a group will be less likely to remain with the firm than men. Then, for a given level of qualifications, the employer would hire a woman only at a lower wage or, perhaps, simply hire a man rather than a woman for the job. More careful screening of applicants might enable the employer to distinguish more from less career-oriented women (for example, a consideration of the candidate's employment record while a student or of extracurricular activities while in school), but it may not be cost-effective for the employer to invest the additional resources necessary to do this.

Judged on the basis of statements employers themselves make, such beliefs regarding differences in average ability or behavior by sex are quite common. For example, employers are often concerned that women do not take their careers as seriously as men and fear that they will quit their jobs when they have children. Other perceptions of average differences in behavior or performance of men and women were noted above

---

[63] Tom McNichol, "Is There a 'Glass Ceiling'?" *USA Weekend,* 16 November 1997, p. 8; and Cailin Brown, "Private Clubs Less Restrictive," *Times Union,* 14 May 1995, p. B1.

[64] See, for example, Edmund S. Phelps, "The Statistical Theory of Racism and Sexism," *American Economic Review* 62, no. 4 (September 1972): 659–61; and Dennis J. Aigner and Glen G. Cain, "Statistical Theories of Discrimination in Labor Markets," *Industrial and Labor Relations Review* 30, no. 2 (January 1977): 175–87.

in our consideration of issues related to the glass ceiling. If such employer beliefs are simply incorrect or exaggerated or reflect time lags in adjusting to a new reality, actions based on them are clearly unfair and constitute labor market discrimination as we have defined it. That is, they generate wage and occupation differences between men and women that are not accounted for by (potential) productivity differences. If such views are not simply rationalizations for personal prejudice, it might be expected that, over time, they will yield to new information. However, this process may be more sluggish than one would like and, in the meantime, employers make less than optimal choices.

The situation is different, and a bit more complicated, if the employer views *are* indeed correct *on average*. Employers make the best choices possible with imperfect knowledge, and, in a sense, labor market discrimination does not exist in this case: Any resulting wage and employment differences between men and women, on average, would be accounted for by *average* productivity differences.

Yet the consequences for *individual* women are far from satisfactory. A particular woman who would be as productive and as stable an employee as her male counterpart is denied employment or paid a lower wage. It seems fairly clear from a *normative* perspective that basing employment decisions on a characteristic like sex—a characteristic that the individual cannot change—is unfair. Indeed, the practice of judging an *individual* on the basis of *group* characteristics rather than upon his or her own merits seems the very essence of stereotyping and discrimination. Such behavior is certainly not legal under the antidiscrimination laws and regulations that we discuss later in this chapter. Yet it most likely still plays a role in employer thinking. Moreover, statistical discrimination, which is based on employers' *correct* assessment of average gender differences, is not likely to be eroded by the forces of competition.

Statistical Discrimination and Feedback Effects   As Kenneth Arrow has pointed out, the consequences of statistical discrimination are particularly pernicious where there are *feedback effects*.[65] For example, if employers' views of female job instability lead them to give women less firm-specific training and to assign them to jobs where the costs of turnover are minimized, women have little incentive to stay and may respond by exhibiting exactly the unstable behavior that employers expect. Employers' perceptions are confirmed, and they see no reason to change their discriminatory behavior. Yet if employers had believed women to be stable workers and had hired them into positions that rewarded such stability, they might well have been stable workers!

Hence, where statistical discrimination is accompanied by feedback effects, even employer behavior that is based on *initially* incorrect assessments of average gender differences may persist in the long run and be fairly impervious to competitive pressures.

Empirical Evidence on Gender Differences in Quitting   Some indication that such feedback effects are important is provided by studies of male and female quitting. This is an especially important area because employer views that women are more likely to quit their jobs than men tend to be fairly widespread. A number of studies have found that although women are on average more likely to quit their jobs than men, *most of this difference is explained by the types of jobs women are in and other individual char-*

---

[65] Arrow, "The Theory of Discrimination."

acteristics.[66] These findings suggest that, when a woman worker is confronted with the same incentives to remain on the job in terms of wages, advancement opportunities, and so on, a woman is no more likely to quit than a comparable male worker. Moreover, while some research suggests that the quit behavior of women was more difficult to predict than the quit behavior of men for earlier cohorts, this was not found to be the case for women born after 1950. Indeed, for a recent cohort of young, college-educated workers, little difference was found between men and women even in overall turnover rates.[67]

While these studies of gender differences in turnover imply that there may be little justification for employers to practice statistical discrimination against women based on presumed differences in quit rates, this does not necessarily mean that gender differences in quit behavior are unrelated to the pay gap. Women are more likely than men to quit their jobs for family related reasons or to exit the labor force entirely and less likely than men to quit in order to move to another job. Such behavioral differences and the resulting work force interruptions will contribute to the gender pay gap, although, interestingly, even in this aspect of quitting, college women's behavior now appears more similar to their male counterparts.[68]

THE OVERCROWDING MODEL

In the models we have discussed up to this point, gender segregation in employment (by firm or occupation) is a possible consequence of discrimination against women in hiring and job assignments, as are pay differentials. Both wage and employment differences are believed to result either from tastes for discrimination against women (among employers, employees, or customers) or from (real or perceived) gender differences in average productivity or job stability. Barbara Bergmann has developed an analysis of the pay gap that gives a more central role to employment segregation.[69]

Bergmann's overcrowding model demonstrates that, regardless of the reason for segregation (for example, socialization, personal preferences, or labor market discrimination), the *consequence* may be a male–female pay differential. This will occur if demand (job opportunities) in the female sector is small relative to the supply of women available for such work. The overcrowding model is consistent with the evidence presented earlier that, all else being equal, earnings tend to be lower in predominantly female than in predominantly male jobs. The fact that men in predominantly female occupations also receive low wages is not necessarily inconsistent with the overcrowding

---

[66] See, for example, Francine D. Blau and Lawrence M. Kahn, "Race and Sex Differences in Quits by Young Workers," *Industrial and Labor Relations Review* 34, no. 4 (July 1981): 563–77; W. Kip Viscusi, "Sex Differences in Worker Quitting," *Review of Economics and Statistics* 62, no. 3 (August 1980): 388–98; Nachum Sicherman, "Gender Differences in Departures from a Large Firm," *Industrial and Labor Relations Review* 49, no. 3 (April 1996): 484–505; and Anne Beeson Royalty, "Job-to-Job and Job-to-Nonemployment Turnover by Gender and Education Level," *Journal of Labor Economics* 16, no. 2 (April 1998): 392–443.

[67] Audrey Light and Manuelita Ureta, "Panel Estimates of Male and Female Job Turnover Behavior: Can Female Nonquitters Be Identified?" *Journal of Labor Economics* 10, no. 2 (April 1992): 156–81; and Royalty, "Job-to-Job."

[68] Sicherman, "Gender Differences in Departures from a Large Firm"; Royalty, "Job-to-Job"; and Kristin Keith and Abagail McWilliams, "The Wage Effects of Cumulative Job Mobility," *Industrial and Labor Relations Review* 49, no. 1 (October 1995), 121–37.

[69] Barbara R. Bergmann, "Occupational Segregation, Wages and Profits When Employers Discriminate by Race or Sex," *Eastern Economic Journal* 1, nos. 1–2 (April–July 1974): 103–10.

hypothesis. Although men as a group are obviously not excluded from the male sector, some of them may, nonetheless, enter female occupations because they have a strong preference or particular skills for this type of work. Or they may be simply unlucky or poorly informed about alternative opportunities. They will accept the lower wages paid in female jobs. However, this lower pay is primarily caused by the many women who "crowd" into these jobs due to their preferences for the work or a lack of alternative opportunities.

This model is illustrated in Figure 7.2. F jobs and M jobs are considered. As in the previous models of discrimination, it is assumed that male and female workers are perfect substitutes for each other (that is, they are potentially equally productive). The hypothetical situation in which there is no discrimination is represented by demand curves D_f and D_m and supply curves S_{f0} and S_{m0}. The nondiscriminatory equilibrium points in the two markets (E_{f0} and E_{m0}) are determined so that the wage rate (w_0) is the same for both types of jobs.

To see why this is the case, recall that we have assumed that all workers are equally well qualified for F and M jobs and that employers are indifferent between hiring male and female workers. Suppose that, by chance, the equilibrium wage in F jobs is higher than the equilibrium wage in M jobs. Then workers attracted by the higher wage rates would transfer from M jobs to F jobs. This process would continue until wages in F jobs were bid down to the level of wages in M jobs. Similarly, if by chance wages in M jobs were set above those in F jobs, workers would move from F jobs to M jobs until the differential was eliminated. Thus, in the absence of discrimination, worker mobility ensures that the wages paid for both types of work are the same, at least after there has been

FIGURE 7.2 An Illustration of the Overcrowding Model

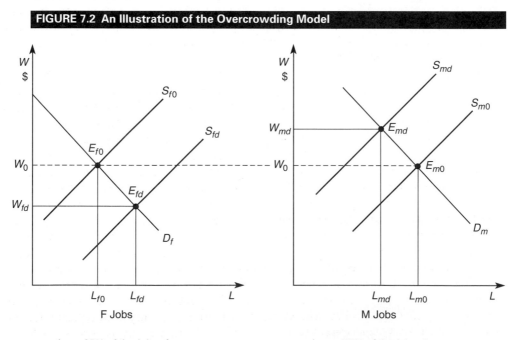

L_{f0} = 25% of the labor force
L_{fd} = 40% of the labor force

L_{m0} = 75% of the labor force
L_{md} = 60% of the labor force

time to make adjustments. This, of course, assumes that there are no *nonpecuniary* differences in the relative attractiveness of the two jobs that would result in a compensating wage differential.

In the hypothetical example given in Figure 7.2, demand conditions are such that, in the nondiscriminatory equilibrium, L_{f0} workers (25 percent of the labor force) are employed in F jobs and L_{m0} workers (75 percent of the labor force) work in M jobs. F and M jobs have no sex labels associated with them and both women and men are randomly divided between the two sectors.

How does the situation differ when there is discrimination against women in "male" occupations or when, for a variety of reasons, women choose to concentrate in typically female jobs? The consequences of such segregation may be ascertained by comparing this situation to the hypothetical situation in which there is no segregation. In our example, the restriction of M jobs to men results in an inward shift of the supply curve to M jobs from S_{m0} to S_{md}, causing wages to be bid up to W_{md}. At this higher wage, only L_{md} workers (60 percent of the labor force) are employed in M jobs. The exclusion of women from M jobs means that all the women must (or choose to) "crowd" into the F jobs. The expanded supply of labor in F jobs, represented by an outward shift of the supply curve from S_{f0} to S_{fd}, depresses wages there to W_{fd}. Now L_{fd} workers (40 percent of the labor force) are employed in F occupations.

The overcrowding model shows how gender segregation in employment may cause a wage differential between otherwise equally productive male and female workers. This will occur if the supply of women seeking employment is large relative to the demand for labor in the F jobs. This may well be what actually takes place in the labor market. Nevertheless, the analysis also shows that gender segregation in employment need not always result in a wage differential between men and women. If it so happens that the wage rate that equates supply and demand in the F sector is the same as the wage that equates supply and demand in the M sector, no wage differential will result (that is, if the female sector is not overcrowded). However, this will happen only by chance. Labor market discrimination (or some other barrier) has eliminated the free mobility of labor between the two sectors that would otherwise ensure wage equality between M and F jobs.

Returning to the more likely situation illustrated in Figure 7.2, in which segregation does lower women's pay, we may examine its impact on the *productivity* of women relative to men. Employers of women in F jobs accommodate a larger number of workers (L_{fd} rather than L_{f0}) by substituting labor for capital. The relatively low wages of the women, W_{fd}, make it profitable to use such labor-intensive production methods. On the other hand, the higher wage in the male sector, W_{md}, encourages employers to substitute capital for labor to economize on relatively high-priced labor. In the overcrowding model, women earn less than men, but both are paid in accordance with their productivity. Discrimination causes differences in both wages and productivity between *potentially* equally productive male and female labor—women are less productive than men because, due to segregation and crowding, they have less capital to work with.

The claim that the supply of labor to a particular occupation (or industry) helps to determine the wage rate is relatively noncontroversial. But the crowding hypothesis, in and of itself, does not explain why so many women are employed in typically female sectors. Controversy has centered on the question of whether this is because men and women have inherently different talents or preferences for different types of work; because, due to differences in socialization or in household responsibilities, women are willing to trade higher wages and steeper lifetime earnings profiles for more favorable working conditions and lower penalties for discontinuous labor force participation; or because employers, coworkers, or customers discriminate against women in some occupations but not in others.

INSTITUTIONAL MODELS

The idea that the male–female pay gap is closely related to employment segregation is echoed in institutional models of discrimination.[70] Such explanations emphasize that labor markets may not be as flexible as the simple competitive model assumes. Rigidities are introduced both by the institutional arrangements found in many firms and by various barriers to competition introduced by the monopoly power of firms in the product market or of unions in the labor market.

The Internal Labor Market   Institutionalists point out that the job structure of many large firms looks like the illustration in Figure 7.3a. Firms hire workers from the outside labor market for so-called entry jobs. The remainder of the jobs are internally allocated by the firm as workers progress along well-defined promotion ladders by acquiring job-related skills, many of which are firm specific in nature. When firm-specific skills are emphasized and a high proportion of jobs are filled from internal sources, the firm has an *internal labor market.* That is, it determines wages for each job category and the allocation of workers among categories and is insulated to some extent (although not entirely) from the impact of market forces.

To administer their personnel systems, larger firms often take the occupational category as the decision unit, establishing pay rates for each category (with some allowance for seniority and merit considerations), and linking jobs together into promotion ladders. Thus, group treatment of individuals is the norm, and it will be to the employer's advantage to make sure that workers within each job category are as similar as possible. If it is believed that men and women (as well as, say, whites and nonwhites) differ in their productivity-related characteristics (like quit and absenteeism rates), statistical discrimination is likely to result in their being channeled into different jobs.

Primary and Secondary Jobs   The dual labor market model developed by Peter Doeringer and Michael Piore takes this analysis a step further and emphasizes the distinction between primary and secondary jobs.[71] Primary jobs emphasize high levels of firm-specific skills and, thus, pay high wages, have good promotion opportunities, and emphasize long-term attachment between workers and firms. In secondary jobs, firm-specific skills are not

---

[70]   See, for example, Peter B. Doeringer and Michael J. Piore, *Internal Labor Markets and Manpower Analysis* (Lexington, MA: D. C. Heath and Co., 1971); Michael J. Piore, "The Dual Labor Market: Theory and Implications," in *Problems in Political Economy: An Urban Perspective,* ed. David M. Gordon (Lexington, MA: D. C. Heath and Co., 1971), pp. 90–94; Blau and Jusenius, "Economists' Approaches to Sex Segregation in the Labor Market"; Glen G. Cain, "The Challenge of Segmented Labor Market Theories to Orthodox Theory: A Survey," *Journal of Economic Literature* 14, no. 4 (December 1976): 1215–57; David M. Gordon, Richard Edwards, and Michael Reich, *Segmented Work, Divided Workers: The Historical Transformation of Labor in the United States* (Cambridge: Cambridge University Press, 1982); and Michael Wachter, "Primary and Secondary Labor Markets: A Critique of the Dual Approach," *Brookings Papers on Economic Activity,* vol. 3 (1974): 637–94.

[71]   Doeringer and Piore, *Internal Labor Markets;* and Piore, "The Dual Labor Market."

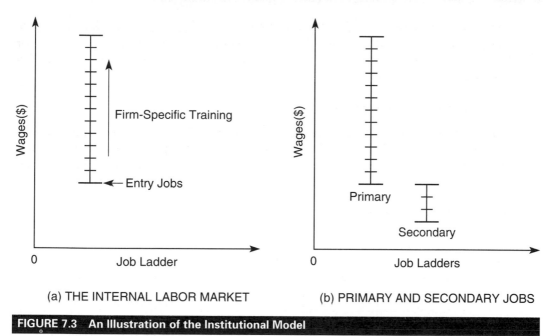

(a) THE INTERNAL LABOR MARKET   (b) PRIMARY AND SECONDARY JOBS

FIGURE 7.3   An Illustration of the Institutional Model

as important. Such jobs will pay less, offer relatively fewer promotion opportunities, and have fairly high rates of labor turnover. This situation is depicted in Figure 7.3b. Applying the dual labor market model to gender discrimination leads us to expect that men would be more likely to be in primary jobs and women in secondary jobs.

The distinction between primary and secondary jobs may occur within the same firm—say, between the managerial and clerical categories. In addition, it is believed that primary jobs are more likely to be located in monopolistic, unionized industries that are generally higher paying and have traditionally offered more stable employment and that secondary jobs are more likely to be found in lower-paying, competitive industries where there is more labor turnover. This is an additional reason for expecting women to be more concentrated in the competitive sector.

Radical economists further argue that employers as a group benefit from such segmentation of the labor force by gender and race because it prevents workers from seeing their common interests across gender and race lines. That is, capitalists (employers) practice "divide and rule" tactics to thwart unionization and other attempts by workers to share power. As we noted in Chapter 3, radical feminists add another element to this analysis. In their view, one must take into account the effects not only of capitalism, but also of patriarchy, which is defined as a system of male oppression of women. Thus, they point to the role of male workers and of their unions, as well as of employers, in maintaining occupational segregation.[72]

Segmentation of male and female workers into primary and secondary jobs is likely to produce both pay and productivity differences between them due to unequal access to on-the-job training. Institutionalists also point out that feedback effects are likely to

---

[72]   See Gordon, Edwards, and Reich, *Segmented Work, Divided Workers* for the radical view, and, for the radical feminist analysis, Heidi I. Hartmann, "Capitalism, Patriarchy and Job Segregation by Sex," *Signs: Journal of Women in Culture and Society* 1, no. 3, pt. 2 (spring 1976): 137–69.

magnify any initial productivity differences, as women respond to the lower incentives for employment stability in the secondary sector.

The institutional analysis also reinforces the point made earlier that labor market discrimination against women is not necessarily the outcome of conscious, overt acts by employers. Once men and women are channeled into different types of entry jobs, the normal, everyday operation of the firm—"business as usual"—will virtually ensure gender differences in productivity, promotion opportunities, and pay. This is termed *institutional discrimination.*[73] Even gender differences in initial occupational assignment may be in part due to adherence to traditional policies that tend to work against women; for example, referrals from current male employees or an informal network of male colleagues at other firms, sexist recruitment materials picturing women in traditionally female jobs and men in traditionally male jobs, and lack of encouragement of female applicants to broaden their sights from traditional areas.

FEEDBACK EFFECTS

As we have noted several times, labor market discrimination or unequal treatment of women in the labor market may adversely affect women's own decisions and behavior.[74] This is illustrated in Figure 7.4. Human capital theory and other supply-side explanations for gender differences in economic outcomes tend to emphasize the role of the gender division of labor in the family in causing differences between men and women in labor market outcomes. This is indicated by the arrow pointing to the right in the figure.

This relationship undoubtedly exists; however, such explanations tend to neglect the impact of labor market discrimination in reinforcing the traditional division of labor (shown by the arrow pointing to the left). Even a relatively small amount of initial labor market discrimination can have greatly magnified effects if it discourages women from making human capital investments, weakens their attachment to the labor force, and provides economic incentives for the family to place priority on the husband's career. Although it is unlikely that labor market discrimination is responsible for initially causing the traditional division of labor in the family, which clearly predates modern labor markets, it may well help to perpetuate it by inhibiting more rapid movement toward egalitarian sharing of household responsibilities today.

The net result is what might be viewed as a vicious circle. Discrimination against women in the labor market reinforces traditional gender roles in the family, while adherence to traditional roles by women provides a rationale for labor market discrimination. However, this also means that effective policies to end labor market discrimination can have far-reaching effects, particularly when combined with simultaneous changes in social attitudes toward women's roles. A decrease in labor market discrimination will have feedback effects as the equalization of market incentives between men and women induces further changes in women's supply-side behavior. This would in turn further en-

---

[73]   See Roos and Reskin, "Institutional Factors," for a description of business practices that tend to adversely affect women.

[74]   A number of authors have emphasized the importance of feedback effects in analyzing discrimination in pay and employment. See, for example, Arrow, "The Theory of Discrimination"; Shelly J. Lundberg and Richard Startz, "Private Discrimination and Social Intervention in Competitive Labor Markets," *American Economic Review* 73, no. 3 (June 1983): 340–47; and Yoram Weiss and Reuben Gronau, "Expected Interruptions in Labour Force Participation and Sex-Related Differences in Earnings Growth," *Review of Economic Studies* 48, no. 4 (October 1981): 607–19.

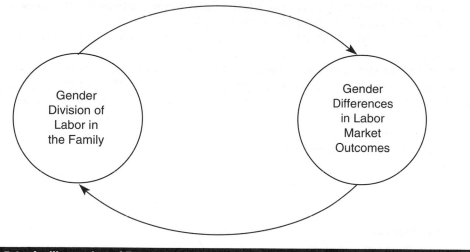

FIGURE 7.4   An Illustration of Feedback Effects

courage employers to reduce statistical discrimination against women. In addition, as more women enter previously male-dominated fields, the larger number of female role models for younger women is likely to induce still further increases in the availability of women for such jobs. Thus, demand-side policies can be expected to play an important role in sustaining a process of cumulative change in women's economic status.

POLICY ISSUE: THE GOVERNMENT AND EQUAL EMPLOYMENT OPPORTUNITY

Government policies to combat labor market discrimination against women can potentially be justified on at least two grounds. One is equity or fairness—"a matter of simple justice."[75] Thus, government intervention may be rationalized to assure equal treatment for all participants in the labor market, regardless of gender (or race, ethnic origin, etc.).

As well as being unfair, unequal treatment on the basis of gender may result in an inefficient allocation of resources. This provides a second rationale for government intervention. To see this, consider the case where equally productive men and women are hired for different jobs and women's jobs are lower paid (as in the overcrowding model). Under these circumstances, prices do not serve as accurate indicators of social costs. In comparison to the nondiscriminatory situation, society produces "too little" of the outputs that use "overpriced" male labor, given that equally productive female labor is available at a lower price to expand production. Society produces "too much" of the outputs that use "underpriced" female labor, given that the contribution of equally productive labor is valued more highly in the male sector (as measured by its price).

The inefficiency caused by discrimination is even greater when we take into account feedback effects. If women are deterred from investing in their human capital because of discrimination, society loses a valuable resource. Thus, opening doors to women that were previously closed (or only slightly ajar) potentially benefits society as well as in-

---

[75] This was the title of the Report of the President's Task Force on Women's Rights and Responsibilities (Washington, DC: U.S. Government Printing Office, April 1970).

dividual women by bringing their talents and abilities to bear in new areas. As Nobel laureate Paul A. Samuelson commented, "To the degree that women are getting an opportunity they didn't have in the past, the economy is tapping an important and previously wasted resource."[76]

Weighed against these potential gains are the costs of the increased government intervention in society that may be necessary to produce this result. These costs loom large indeed to those who are skeptical of the evidence of labor market discrimination against women presented earlier. Some may also fear what they regard as the possible excesses of such policies in the form of reverse discrimination or preferential treatment for women and minorities. However, research to date provides no evidence that the increased employment of women and minorities encouraged by legislation has entailed such efficiency costs.[77] We examine the record of government intervention in this area next.[78]

EQUAL EMPLOYMENT OPPORTUNITY LAWS AND REGULATIONS

Government has long been involved in shaping conditions encountered by women in the labor market. During the period following the Civil War, in response to concern and agitation by workers and their sympathizers, a number of states passed protective labor laws limiting hours and regulating other terms of employment for all workers. At first, the Supreme Court struck down these laws as unconstitutional on the basis that they interfered with the freedom of workers to enter contracts. Subsequently, in its 1908 decision in *Muller* v. *Oregon,*[79] the Court upheld such laws when they were confined to women alone, arguing that individual rights may be abridged because the state has a legitimate interest in the possible social effects of women's work. Louis Brandeis, later to become a Supreme Court Justice known for his support of individual human rights, wrote the following about the case:

> The two sexes differ in structure of body, in the functions performed by each, in the amount of physical strength, in the capacity for long-continued labor, particularly when done standing, the influence of vigorous health upon the future well-being of the race, the self-reliance which enables one to assert full rights, and in the capacity to maintain the struggle for subsistence. The difference justifies a difference in legislation, and upholds that which is designed to compensate for some of the burdens which rest upon her.

---

[76] *Business Week,* 28 January 1985, p. 80.

[77] Leonard, "Antidiscrimination or Reverse Discrimination"; Harry Holzer and David Neumark, "Are Affirmative Action Hires Less Qualified? Evidence from Employer–Employee Data on New Hires," *Journal of Labor Economics* 17, no. 3 (July 1999); and Marianne A. Ferber and Carole A. Green, "Traditional or Reverse Sex Discrimination? A Case Study of a Large Public University," *Industrial and Labor Relations Review* 35, no. 4 (July 1982): 550–64.

[78] For excellent summaries of the legal situation, see Susan Deller Ross, Isabelle Katz Pinzler, Deborah A. Ellis, and Kary L. Moss, *The Rights of Women: The Basic ACLU Guide to a Woman's Rights,* 3rd ed. (Carbondale: Southern Illinois University Press, 1993); and Claire Sherman Thomas, *Sex Discrimination,* 2nd ed. (St. Paul: West Publishing Co., 1991).

[79] *Muller* v. *Oregon,* 208 U.S. 412 (1908).

In time, however, the concern shifted from protection to equal opportunity. Indeed, protective laws came eventually to be viewed as undesirable impediments to the advancement of women. Supreme Court Justice Brennan expressed this view very well in a 1973 case: "Traditionally, discrimination was rationalized by an attitude of romantic paternalism which in practical effect put women not on a pedestal but in a cage."[80]

As early as 1961, President Kennedy issued an Executive Order calling for a Presidential Commission on the Status of Women. Two years later, the **Equal Pay Act** of 1963 was passed, which requires employers to pay the same wages to men and women who do substantially equal work, involving equal skill, effort, and responsibility, and performed under similar conditions in the same establishment. In 1964, **Title VII** of the Civil Rights Act was enacted. The legislation was originally written to prohibit discrimination in employment on the basis of race, religion, and national origin, but was changed at the last minute to include the word *sex*.[81] Title VII prohibits sex discrimination in virtually all aspects of employment, including hiring and firing, training, promotions, wages, fringe benefits, or other terms and conditions of employment. As amended, it covers all businesses employing 15 or more workers, including federal, state, and local governments and educational institutions. It also prohibits discrimination by employment agencies and labor organizations. The **Equal Employment Opportunity Commission** (EEOC) is the federal agency charged with enforcing the Equal Pay Act and Title VII.

Executive Order 11246 issued in 1965, and amended in 1967 to include sex, bars discrimination in employment by all employers with federal contracts and subcontracts. It also requires affirmative action for classes of workers disadvantaged by past discrimination. Contractors are required to analyze their own employment patterns to determine where women and minorities are underrepresented. Whenever such deficiencies are found, they are to set up "goals and timetables" for the hiring of women and minorities and to make good faith efforts to reach their goals in the specified period.[82] The Executive Order is enforced by the Office of Federal Contract Compliance. Violators face possible loss of their government contracts, although this sanction has been very seldom invoked.

In the years since their passage and implementation, the federal antidiscrimination laws and regulations have been interpreted and clarified by the courts, with the final arbiter being the United States Supreme Court. This process has been especially important for Title VII of the Civil Rights Act, the broadest law and the centerpiece of the federal government's antidiscrimination enforcement effort. In some cases, the Court's interpretations of the law have changed as the membership on the Court has shifted, and this is likely to continue to be the case in the future. Bearing this is mind, in order to better understand what activities are currently prohibited under Title VII, we turn to a brief summary of some of the more important Court decisions.

---

[80] *Frontiero* v. *Richardson,* 411 U.S. 677 (1973).

[81] Since it was Howard Smith, a conservative congressman from Virginia, who proposed this amendment, it is widely believed that his purpose in doing so was to increase opposition to the bill, and reduce the chances of its passage.

[82] In *Adarand Constructors Inc.* v. *Pena* (Sup. Ct., No. 93–1841, 6/12/95), the Supreme Court placed significant limits on federal government programs that favor racial minorities (or presumably women), stating that such programs must be subject to "strict scrutiny." That is, they must serve a compelling governmental interest and be narrowly tailored; see Bureau of National Affairs, *Daily Labor Report,* no. 113 (13 June 1995), AA-1–AA-2. Since this case dealt with preferences for minority-owned firms in awarding contracts, it is unclear whether it will affect employment programs under the Executive Order that do not confer similar types of tangible benefits.

Title VII permits exceptions to its ban on gender discrimination when sex is found to be a bona fide occupational qualification (BFOQ). When the law was passed in the mid-1960s, it was not entirely clear what this exemption would mean as a practical matter. At that time, social views widely accepted the notion that a considerable number of jobs were particularly suitable for women and a goodly number of others especially appropriate for men. Indeed, newspapers routinely divided portions of their help wanted sections into "help wanted male" and "help wanted female." The former might include openings for such jobs as manager or construction worker, while the latter might include "girl friday" (that is, administrative assistant) or receptionist. Thus, the interpretation of the bona fide occupational qualification exemption by the courts is extremely important. Had it been interpreted broadly, to match the social views of the day, considerable gender discrimination would have been permissible under Title VII in that sex might have been viewed as a valid qualification for a host of traditionally male and traditionally female jobs. However, both the EEOC and the courts have taken the position that this exception should be interpreted narrowly. That is, men and women are entitled to consideration on the basis of their individual capabilities, rather than on the basis of characteristics generally attributed to the group. The court has, for example, rejected the BFOQ exemption for predominately male jobs in which heavy lifting is required as well as for the predominately female position of flight attendant where it was argued by the employer that airline passengers preferred women in the job. Also, as discussed in the inset on "fetal protection," the court has ruled that it is discriminatory to bar all women of childbearing age from jobs where they would work with substances that might be hazardous to unborn children. In the only major case to date in which gender was found to be a bona fide occupational qualification, the 1977 *Dothard* v. *Rawlinson* case, the Supreme Court allowed the hiring of males only for the position of guard in Alabama's maximum security male prisons. The Court reasoned that due to the nature of the prison population, as well as the atmosphere of the prison, women would be particularly subject to sexual assault, which would interfere with their job performance. Regardless of whether or not one agrees with this reasoning, this case has not resulted and is not likely to result in substantially greater acceptance by the courts of the BFOQ exception for other jobs, given its unusual circumstances.[83]

The Court has also found that sex cannot be used in combination with some other factor as a legal basis for discrimination under Title VII. The Court has held, for example, that an employer cannot refuse to hire women with preschool-age children while men with preschool-age children are hired.[84] Furthermore, it is illegal to pay women lower monthly pension benefits than men.[85] In the past, this practice had been justified on the basis that, on average, women live longer and, thus, it would be more costly to provide them with the same monthly benefit. The courts have ruled that each woman is entitled to be treated as an individual, rather than as a group member.

Disparate treatment of women and minorities, that is, differential treatment of these groups with the intention to discriminate, is a clear violation of Title VII. A more complex

---

[83] *Dothard* v. *Rawlinson,* 433 U.S. 321 (1977); see Ross et al., *The Rights of Women* for a consideration of this and other cases. Major cases in which the court has rejected a BFOQ exemption include *Weeks* v. *Southern Bell Telephone and Telegraph,* 408 F.2d 228 (5th Cir. 1969); *Rosenfeld* v. *Southern Pacific Company,* 444 F.2d 1219 (9th Cir. 1971); and *Diaz* v. *Pan American World Airways, Inc.,* 442 F.2d 385 (5th Cir. 1971).

[84] *Philips* v. *Martin Marietta Corp.,* 400 U.S. 542 (1971).

[85] *City of Los Angeles, Dept. of Water* v. *Manhart,* 435 U.S. 702 (1978).

issue addressed by the courts in interpreting Title VII concerns unintentional discrimination. This arises when a firm's apparently neutral hiring or promotion practices have a **disparate impact** on women or minorities. *Disparate impact* means that the practice or practices have a disproportionately adverse effect on women or minorities. An example of this potentially affecting women might be a minimum height and weight requirement for the position of police officer that screens out a higher proportion of women than men. Based on a 1971 Supreme Court decision in *Griggs,* apparently neutral practices having a disparate impact on women and minorities may be illegal even if the discrimination is not intentional. Once the plaintiffs have shown that the practice has a disparate impact, the burden of proof is shifted to the employer to show that the practice is a matter of "business necessity" or that the requirement is job related; otherwise there would be a finding of discrimination.[86]

A later 1989 Supreme Court decision[87] held that even after a disparate impact had been demonstrated, the burden of proof remained with the plaintiffs to show that the employer had no business necessity justification for the practice. This decision was widely criticized by civil rights advocates. The original interpretation of the law that places the burden of proof on the *employer* was reestablished in November 1991, when a new civil rights law was enacted. In addition to this provision, the new law permits women to obtain compensatory and punitive damages for intentional discrimination, although the amounts are limited. (Racial minorities had such rights under existing law.)

Finally, an issue that has been the focus of considerable attention in recent years is sexual harassment.[88] Sexual harassment potentially encompasses a broad range of objectionable behaviors ranging from the making of sexual demands where a refusal results in an adverse action (such as dismissal, the loss of a promotion, reduced benefits, etc.), generally called "quid pro quo" harassment, to various actions that are sufficiently offensive to result in a hostile work environment. Deciding whether sexual harassment was indeed covered under Title VII and demarcating the conditions under which the behavior was egregious enough to be illegal has proved challenging for the courts. A major step forward was the Supreme Court's 1986 decision in *Meritor,* which held that sexual harassment is illegal under Title VII if it is unwelcome and "sufficiently severe or pervasive to alter the conditions of the victim's employment and create an abusive working environment."[89] Following the Court's ruling, there was some controversy over what constituted evidence of a hostile environment with some lower courts requiring evidence of severe psychological injury or diminished job performance. In its 1993 *Harris*[90] case, the Supreme Court clarified this issue, overturning a

---

[86]   *Griggs* v. *Duke Power Co.,* 401 U.S. 424 (1971).

[87]   *Wards Cove Packing Co.* v. *Atonio,* 109 Sup. Ct. 2115 (1989). For a discussion of this case and its implications, see the articles in "Special Report: Setback for Civil Rights? The Supreme Court's 1989 Discrimination Rulings," *ILR Report* 27, no. 2 (spring 1990).

[88]   This issue attracted particular attention during the 1991 confirmation hearings of Supreme Court Justice Clarence Thomas, when charges of sexual harassment were made against the nominee by Anita Hill, a law professor who had formerly worked as his assistant. Although Justice Thomas was confirmed, the airing of this issue in a national forum greatly heightened public awareness of this problem.

[89]   *Meritor Savings Bank* v. *Vinson,* 106 Sup. Ct. 2399 (1986); the quotation was cited in "Ending Sexual Harassment: Business Is Getting the Message," *Business Week,* 18 March 1991, p. 99.

[90]   *Harris* v. *Forklift Systems Inc.,* Sup.Ct., No. 92–1168, 11/9/93. The summary of the case and quotation from the opinion are from Linda Greenhouse, "Court, 9–0, Makes Sex Harassment Easier to Prove," *New York Times,* 10 November 1993, pp. A1–A14; see also "Psychological Injury Not Needed to Prove Sex Harassment, Unanimous Supreme Court Rules," Bureau of National Affairs, *Daily Labor Report,* no. 216, 10 November 1993, pp. AA-1–AA2.

lower court ruling that an employee who was subjected to the company president's repeated offensive and demeaning comments of a sexual nature was not entitled to redress under the law because she had not suffered sufficient psychological damage. The standard put forth by the Court in its decision is essentially that a hostile environment is one that a *reasonable person* would perceive to be "hostile or abusive." Writing for the majority, Justice Sandra Day O'Connor said that the protection of federal law "comes into play before the harassing conduct leads to a nervous breakdown." The Court has since ruled that Title VII prohibits sexual harassment between members of the same sex under the same legal standards as those used to evaluate claims of sexual harassment by a member of the opposite sex.[91]

Since sexual harassment generally results from interactions between employees, the question arises as to when employers are held liable for the actions of their employees. This is an important issue because it is employers that have the "deep pockets"; that is, who can potentially pay financial compensation to individuals who are the victims of harassment. The stakes involved may be considerable. In 1998, in the largest sexual harassment settlement negotiated up to that point, Mitsubishi Motor Corporation agreed to pay $34 million to end a government lawsuit charging that hundreds of female employees at its automobile assembly plant in Normal, Illinois, had been sexually harassed.[92] Prior to two 1998 Supreme Court decisions,[93] it was believed based on a lower court ruling that employers could only be held liable for sexual harassment if they knew or should have known that the harassment had taken place. In its recent decisions, the Supreme Court extended the employer's liability well beyond this situation, making it clear that employers bear the fundamental responsibility for preventing and eliminating sexual harassment from the workplace. The Court ruled that when sexual harassment results in "a tangible employment action, such as discharge, demotion or undesirable assignment" (this is the quid pro quo type of case described above), the employer's liability is absolute. Where there is no tangible action (this would include hostile environment cases), an employer could still be liable but can defend itself by establishing that "reasonable care to prevent and correct promptly any sexually harassing behavior" has been taken and that the employee "unreasonably failed to take advantage of any preventive or corrective opportunities" provided. It is widely believed that a strong, well-publicized employer policy against harassment coupled with an effective grievance (complaint) procedure are the best tools currently available to employers to combat sexual harassment at the workplace and to safeguard themselves from liability. Such a policy cannot simply be "on the books." The employer must make sure that the policy is effectively communicated to employees, complaints are promptly investigated, and corrective action, where merited, is promptly taken.

---

[91]   This was in the 1998 case of *Oncale* v. *Sundowner Offshore Services, Inc.*; see Charles J. Muhl, "The Law at Work: Sexual Harassment," *Monthly Labor Review* 121, no. 7 (July 1998): 61–62.

[92]   Barnaby J. Feder, "$34 Million Settles Suit for Women at Auto Plant," *New York Times,* 12 June 1998 (www.nytimes.com).

[93]   The two cases, both decided in 1998, are *Faragher* v. *City of Boca Raton* and *Burlington Industries, Inc.* v. *Ellerth.* The quotations are from Linda Greenhouse, "The Supreme Court: The Workplace; Court Spells Out Rules for Finding Sex Harassment," *New York Times,* 27 June 1998 (www.nytimes.com). See also Muhl, "The Law at Work"; and Steven Greenhouse, "Companies Set to Get Tougher on Harassment," *New York Times,* 28 June 1998 (www.nytimes.com).

Women's Job Rights Versus "Fetal Protection"

One controversial issue raised by the antidiscrimination statutes relates to the employment of women in jobs where they would work with substances like lead that might be hazardous to unborn children. During the 1970s and the 1980s, a number of employers adopted policies excluding fertile women from such employment: they claimed to fear liability in future lawsuits on behalf of children who were born with birth defects caused by their mothers' work environment. Such policies generally barred all women of childbearing age who had not been sterilized, arguing that temporary birth control measures might fail, and that fetal damage could occur during the early months of pregnancy when many women are unaware that they are pregnant and thus would not request a transfer to a safer job.

Opponents of fetal protection policies, including many women's groups and labor unions, argued that such policies constituted sex discrimination and were illegal under Title VII. Like protective labor laws, fetal protection policies resulted in women being denied access to high-paying jobs. Critics also noted that toxic substances had been found to harm the male as well as the female reproductive system and held that women, like men, should be able to choose whether or not to incur the higher risks in exchange for the higher pay in these jobs. They advocated addressing the safety issue by further efforts to reduce the level of exposure of all workers to toxic substances, rather than by excluding particular groups claimed to be at special risk. Finally, they feared that if fetal protection policies were found to be legal, they would be adopted by many additional employers, eventually affecting millions of women in various industries.

In 1991, the Supreme Court addressed these issues in the Johnson Controls* case. Johnson Controls, an automobile battery manufacturer, "banned women who could not prove they were infertile from working in areas of the plant where they were exposed to lead, the principal material used in making batteries."† The plaintiffs consisted of all employees who were potentially affected by the policy. Among the individual plaintiffs in the case were a woman who was sterilized to avoid losing her job, a 50-year-old divorced woman who suffered a substantial loss in earnings when she was transferred out of a job where she was exposed to lead, and a man who was denied a leave of absence that he had requested in order to lower his lead level because he intended to become a father. The Court found for the plaintiffs. It held the fetal protection policy to be discriminatory because "fertile men, but not fertile women, are given a choice as to whether they wish to risk their reproductive health for a particular job." It also clarified that the bona fide occupational qualification exemption of Title VII "must relate to ability to perform the duties of the job" rather than to any danger or risk to the woman herself. This is in line with the narrow interpretation of this exemption in prior Court decisions. Finally, the Court concluded that the risk of employer liability was slight given that "Title VII bans sex-specific fetal-protection policies, the employer fully informs the woman of the risk, and the employer has not acted negligently. . . ."

* United Auto Workers v. Johnson Controls, Inc., U.S. Sup. Ct., No. 89-1215 (1991). In this discussion, we draw on the summary of the Johnson Controls case and the printed text of the decision in Bureau of National Affairs, *Daily Labor Report*, no. 55 (21 March 1991), pp. A1–A3 and D1–D11. For the response to the case on the part of business, see also the following issues of the *Daily Labor Report*, no. 55 (22 March 1991), pp. A11–A13; and no. 62 (1 April 1991), pp. A2–A4.
† The quotations from the Court's decision presented here are from Bureau of National Affairs, *Daily Labor Report*, no. 55 (21 March 1991), p. A1.

EFFECTIVENESS OF THE GOVERNMENT'S ANTIDISCRIMINATION EFFORT

Much remains to be learned about the functioning of these laws and regulations. Questions have been raised both about their effectiveness in improving opportunities for the protected categories and about the possibility that they might result in reverse discrimination against groups that are not covered.

It is highly likely that the Equal Pay Act has had relatively little impact. The major reason is that men and women rarely do exactly the same kind of work in the same firm. However, the protection offered by this law may be growing more important as occupational segregation continues to decline.

Considerably less agreement exists on the effects of Title VII and the Executive Order. Although some empirical work has been done examining their effectiveness, the results have not been entirely conclusive, in large part because it is difficult to isolate the effect of legislation from other changes that have been occurring.

A review of the trends in the male–female pay gap was presented in Chapter 5. It gave no indication of a notable improvement in women's economic status in the post-1964 period that might be attributable to the effects of the government's antidiscrimination effort, at least through the late 1970s or early 1980s. During this time period, blacks experienced considerable increases in their earnings relative to whites that many have ascribed, at least in part, to the impact of the antidiscrimination laws.

On the other hand, some detailed studies do find positive effects of the government's policies on women's earnings and occupations.[94] Studies focusing specifically on the impact of affirmative action also suggest modest employment gains for women attributable to this program. Such programs also appear to boost the relative wages of women, both because establishments using affirmative action are higher paying, controlling for the characteristics of workers employed in them, and because sex differences in wages are smaller in such establishments.[95] It might also be argued that the improvement in women's economic position that began around 1980 could be due at least in part to the opportunities created by the government's antidiscrimination laws and regulations. This would potentially include both the direct effect of improving the treatment of women in the labor market and, in response to that, the indirect effect of increasing the incentives for women to train for nontraditional jobs.

---

[94] For example, one study suggests that a trend toward *larger* male–female earnings differentials was reversed in the mid-1960s, about the time the effect of the government legislation would be expected to become apparent. See Ronald Oaxaca, "The Persistence of Male–Female Earnings Differentials" in *The Distribution of Economic Well-Being,* ed. Thomas F. Juster (Cambridge, MA: Ballinger Publishing Company, 1977), pp. 303–44. Two other studies that also obtained positive findings attempted to measure the impact of Title VII through regional differences in its enforcement. They find that, between 1967 and 1974, enforcement of Title VII narrowed the sex differential in earnings by about 7 percentage points and sex differences in the probability of being employed in a male occupation by about 6 percentage points, all else equal. See Andrea H. Beller, "The Impact of Equal Employment Opportunity Laws on the Male/Female Earnings Differential," in *Women in the Labor Market,* ed. Cynthia B. Lloyd, Emily Andrews, and Curtis L. Gilroy (New York: Columbia University Press, 1979), pp. 304–30; and Andrea H. Beller, "Occupational Segregation by Sex: Determinants and Changes," *Journal of Human Resources* 17, no. 3 (summer 1982): 317–92.

[95] Harry Holtzer and David Neumark, "Assessing Affirmative Action," *Journal of Economic Literature* 38 no. 3 (September 2000): 483–568; see also Holtzer and Neumark, "What Does Affirmative Action Do?"; and Jonathan S. Leonard, "Women and Affirmative Action," *Journal of Economic Perspectives* 3, no. 1 (winter 1989): 61–75.

In recent years it appears that the government has scaled back its antidiscrimination enforcement efforts. It has been reported that the government's efforts to enforce affirmative action in the contract sector were reduced in the 1980s.[96] Also notable is the decline in cases in which the EEOC has brought class actions under Title VII, alleging a pattern and practice of discrimination against women or minorities on the part of an employer. The resolution of such suits on behalf of the plaintiffs potentially has a much larger labor market impact than the resolution of individual complaints. Interestingly, however, the number of class action and other employment discrimination suits is again on the increase, due to a rising number that are brought by employees themselves either individually or banding together and being represented by private law firms. There were 68 class action suits in 1996, up from 30 in 1992, with such suits estimated to cover at least 100,000 workers in 1996. While more recent data on class action suits are not available, there is evidence that job bias lawsuits overall grew rapidly over the 1990s, from 6,936 in 1990 to 21,540 in 1998, largely due to an increase in private cases. This development may be related to the incentives established by the 1991 federal law, discussed above, which makes it more lucrative for private law firms to represent employees alleging discrimination. Under the original antidiscrimination legislation, monetary redress was generally limited to back pay. Now, in cases of intentional discrimination, it is possible to sue for distress, humiliation, and punitive damages. In addition, the new law allows discrimination cases to be argued before juries as well as judges, rather than only before judges as had previously been the case. In 1994, workers won 43.3 percent of all employment discrimination cases heard by juries compared to 22.1 percent of those heard by judges.[97]

AFFIRMATIVE ACTION

Just as there is disagreement on the effectiveness of the government's antidiscrimination effort, so there is controversy about the form it should take. Debate has particularly centered on the desirability of affirmative action to remedy past underrepresentation of women and minorities. Affirmative action may be defined as ". . . pro-active steps . . . to erase differences between women and men, minorities and nonminorities, etc." in the labor market, and contrasts with laws and regulations that simply require employers not to discriminate against these groups.[98] Thus, affirmative action refers to a broad array of possible activities ranging from efforts to more vigorously recruit women and minorities for job openings to some sort of preferences for women and minorities.

---

[96]   Leonard, "Women and Affirmative Action."

[97]   Allen Myerson, "As U.S. Bias Cases Drop, Employees Take Up Fight," *New York Times,* 12 January 1997 (www.nytimes.com); and Michael J. Sniffen, "Work-Related Bias Lawsuits Soared During '90s," *Chicago Sun-Times,* 17 January 2000, p. 21. A 1999 Supreme Court ruling may, however, make it less likely that employees who bring successful discrimination suits against their employers will be able to collect punitive damages. In *Kolstad* v. *American Dental Association,* the Court ruled that when a company has made "good faith efforts" to comply with the civil rights law, it cannot be required to pay punitive damages for the discriminatory actions of managers who violate company policy; see Linda Greenhouse, "Ruling Raises Hurdle in Bias-Award Cases," *New York Times,* 23 June 1999 (www.nytimes.com).

[98]   Holtzer and Neumark, "Assessing Affirmative Action," p. 484. The Holtzer and Neumark article, as well as Barbara R. Bergmann, *In Defense of Affirmative Action* (New York: Basic Books, 1996) provide extremely useful treatments of the issues surrounding affirmative action and assessments of the empirical evidence.

Affirmative action plans are legally mandated in only two cases. First, the Executive Order requires affirmative action by government contractors who are found to under-utilize women or minorities. Such employers are required to set goals based on estimates of the availability of protected groups for similar types of positions and to set reasonable timetables for meeting those goals. Thus, contrary to popular belief, the government contract compliance program does not impose hiring quotas on employers. Second, affirmative action may be imposed by the courts in cases where employers have been found guilty of discrimination or settlements have been reached in discrimination suits. While quotas may sometimes be ordered in such instances, quotas remain extremely rare in the labor market. In addition to these legal requirements, some employers have voluntarily adopted affirmative action programs. They may be motivated by a sincere desire to expand their utilization of protected groups, the hope of heading off potential lawsuits by women and minorities, the potential public relations benefits of such efforts, or some combination of all of these.

A variety of different views is held about affirmative action. First, there are those who argue that there is no conclusive evidence that there has been serious discrimination in the past and that, even if there had been, removing it would be sufficient and affirmative action is not needed. Second, there are others who accept the need for some form of affirmative action but oppose the use of goals and timetables for fear that they will be too rigidly enforced and become de facto quotas. There is a difference of opinion, even among strong proponents of affirmative action, whether it should take the form of sincere efforts to find and encourage fully qualified candidates from the protected groups or go so far as to hire them preferentially. Some believe that preferential treatment may at times be needed to overcome the effects of past discrimination, while others do not believe such steps are warranted.

Although affirmative action programs that include preferences for women or minorities in employment are controversial in the public debate, such programs have generally been found by the courts to be legitimate approaches to remedying past discrimination in the labor market. The legal status of court-mandated affirmative action plans that include employment preferences is not in question. Similarly, those required by the Executive Order have generally not been challenged. This may change given the Supreme Court's ruling in the 1995 *Adarand* case, which placed significant limits on federal government programs that favor racial minorities (and presumably women). That case dealt with preferences for minority-owned firms in awarding contracts rather than with employment, however.

The Supreme Court has also found that voluntary programs incorporating employment preferences are legal under certain circumstances. Specifically, employers can give employment preferences to women and minorities as a temporary measure to remedy manifest imbalances in traditionally segregated job categories.[99] At the same time, the Court has stressed the need for affirmative action plans to be flexible, gradual, and limited in their adverse effect on men and whites; it has also tended to disapprove of strict numerical quotas except where necessary to remedy demonstrated cases of severe past discrimination. Furthermore, although the Court has ruled that employers may give preference to women and minorities in hiring and promotion under certain circum-

---

[99] *Steelworkers* v. *Weber,* 443 U.S. 193 (1979) and *Johnson* v. *Santa Clara County Transportation Agency,* 480 U.S. 616 (1987).

stances, it has rejected the use of such preferences to protect women and minorities from layoffs.[100] This may be due to a concern over the rights of third parties, that is, members of nonprotected groups who are adversely affected by the affirmative action program. Being denied a potential benefit like getting hired for a particular job, gaining admittance to a training program, or securing a promotion may be viewed as a less serious cost than being laid off from a job, especially after accumulating considerable seniority.

It is important to recognize, however, that most affirmative action programs do not require employment preferences. Indeed, affirmative action programs may improve personnel management systems because, in the face of affirmative action pressures, many companies have implemented wider and more systematic search procedures and developed more objective criteria and procedures for hiring and promotion. In recent studies comparing workers in firms using affirmative action and firms that did not, little evidence was found that women or minorities hired under affirmative action performed worse. In fact, where affirmative action was used in *recruitment only* (as compared to hiring), the results indicated that women and minorities, if anything, performed better than white males.[101] These findings are consistent with empirical research which strongly suggests that rigid employment quotas and reverse discrimination are not the norm in the labor market. One study found that the employment goals of government contractors covered under the Executive Order were not filled with the rigidity one would expect if they were really quotas. That is, firms tended to fall short of their employment goals for women and minorities. Nonetheless, the setting of goals did appear to have a positive effect on the employment of these groups in that establishments that promised to employ more women and minorities in the future tended to do so in subsequent years.[102]

As in the case of affirmative action, it has been found, with respect to the broader issue of antidiscrimination policy as a whole, that the increased employment of women has been achieved without substantial reverse discrimination. Specifically, there is no evidence at the industry level that the productivity of women fell relative to men as their employment increased—as would have been the case if there had been substantial reverse discrimination. Direct tests at the company level of the effect of affirmative action pressure, Title VII litigation, and changing proportions of women and minorities on profits also failed to show any adverse effect.[103] Indeed, rather than having produced an epidemic of reverse discrimination, research suggests that the government's enforcement of the Executive Order was in fact scaled back in the 1980s.[104]

Given that the government's efforts to enforce affirmative action in the contract sector appear to have declined considerably and there is little evidence that affirmative action has produced ill effects in any event, one may wonder why it has excited so much public opposition. One reason may be that it is unclear who the "victims" of affirmative

---

[100] Stuart Taylor, "Court's Change of Course," *New York Times,* 27 March 1987, p. 1; and Steven A. Holmes, "Quotas: Despised by Many, but Just What Are They?" *New York Times,* 2 June 1991, p. 20.

[101] Holtzer and Neumark, "Are Affirmative Action Hires Less Qualified?"; and Holtzer and Neumark, "What Does Affirmative Action Do?"

[102] Jonathan S. Leonard, "What Promises Are Worth: The Impact of Affirmative Action Goals," *Journal of Human Resources* 20, no. 1 (winter 1985): 3–20.

[103] Leonard, "Antidiscrimination or Reverse Discrimination"; see also Holzer and Neumark, "Are Affirmative Action Hires Less Qualified?"

[104] Leonard, "Women and Affirmative Action."

action efforts are and, hence, it is easy to form exaggerated views of their numbers. So, for example, when a woman or minority gets a position, observers may leap to the conclusion that the individual is an "affirmative action hire," which may or may not be true in the first place. Then, since it is generally not known who would have otherwise been hired, all those who did not get the job may feel that it was "because" of affirmative action. Of course, in reality, no more than one of the rejected applicants would have been hired. A second reason for the upsurge of public opinion against affirmative action is that, as we shall see in greater detail in Chapter 8, despite vigorous employment growth, these have been in some respects difficult and uncertain times in the labor market, especially for the less skilled. Affirmative action becomes a ready scapegoat for those who feel adversely affected by what are in truth broader economic trends that are unrelated to the government's antidiscrimination effort.

Exaggerated public perceptions of the negative effects of affirmative action and other government antidiscrimination programs constitute a serious concern, since they may adversely affect attitudes toward women and minorities in the workplace. A related problem is that women and minorities may, as noted earlier, be branded as affirmative action hires and stigmatized as less competent. Such perceptions could sap their confidence and make it difficult for them to function effectively in their jobs. On the other hand, if the alternative to affirmative action is greater discrimination against women and minorities, the absence of good advancement opportunities could, through feedback effects, discourage these groups from investing in job skills.

COMPARABLE WORTH

In the latter half of the 1970s, impatience with the slow progress in closing the male–female earnings gap, as well as some reluctance to accept the movement of women into different occupations as a necessary component of the solution, led to great interest in a possible alternative approach to increasing women's wages. The new idea, in simple terms, amounts to extending the notion of equal pay for equal work to the broader concept of equal pay for work of comparable worth within the firm.[105] Proponents argue this is a reasonable interpretation of Title VII and a feasible way of achieving a more rapid reduction in the male–female pay gap. Opponents point to the difficulties involved in determining exactly what comparable worth means in practical terms. They are also concerned about interfering with the working of the market and the possibility of bringing about a substantial imbalance in the supply of and demand for female workers.

Comparing the value to the firm of workers employed in different jobs is a difficult task involving the establishment of equivalences for various fields of education, different types of skill, and varying work environments. Nonetheless, job evaluation is widely used to determine pay scales, not only by governments, but also by many larger firms.

---

[105] For an early article articulating the legal basis for this approach, see Ruth G. Blumrosen, "Wage Discrimination, Job Segregation, and Title VII of the Civil Rights Act of 1964," *University of Michigan Journal of Law Reform* 12, no. 3 (spring 1979): 399–502. For examinations of the economic and social issues involved, see, for example, Barbara R. Bergmann, *The Economic Emergence of Women* (New York: Basic Books, 1986), chap. 8; Mark R. Killingsworth, *The Economics of Comparable Worth* (Kalamazoo, MI: W. E. Upjohn Institute for Employment Research, 1990); Paula England, *Comparable Worth: Theories and Evidence* (New York: Aldine De Gruyter, 1992); Robert T. Michael, Heidi Hartmann, and Brigid O'Farrell, eds., *Pay Equity: Empirical Inquiries* (Washington, DC: National Academy Press, 1989); and Heidi I. Hartmann and Stephanie Aaronson, "Pay Equity and Women's Wage Increases: Success in the States, A Model for the Nation," *Duke Journal of Gender Law & Policy* 1 (1994): 69–88.

This certainly shows that the approach is feasible. However, it should be noted that such a procedure is generally used in conjunction with information about market wage rates, rather than as a completely separate alternative to the market. Moreover, existing job evaluation schemes have themselves been criticized for undervaluing the skills and abilities that are emphasized in female jobs. Finally, when unions are involved in determining and implementing comparable worth or pay equity adjustments, alterations in pay rates across jobs may in part be determined through the negotiation process rather than solely through job evaluation.

Turning to the issue of setting wages at a level other than that determined by the market, the strongest opposition to such a policy comes primarily from those who believe that the existing labor market substantially resembles the neoclassical competitive model. In such a market, only the person's qualifications and tastes limit access to jobs, and all workers are rewarded according to their productivity. In this view, raising women's wages is not only unnecessary but would lead to excess supply, hence, unemployment and a misallocation of resources.

On the other hand, many of those in favor of the comparable worth approach begin with a view of a segmented labor market, where workers' access to highly paid positions is often limited by discriminating employers, restrictive labor organizations, entrenched internal labor markets, and differences in the prelabor market socialization of men and women. Under such circumstances, the crowding of women into traditional occupations is believed to represent a misallocation of resources, which is permitted to continue by societal and labor market discrimination against women. Mandating higher wages would bring the earnings of those who remain in women's jobs closer to the level of comparably qualified men.

However, raising women's wages without changing the underlying conditions that produced them could still result in job loss. This is illustrated in Figure 7.2. Suppose we begin with the discriminatory situation. The relevant supply curves are S_{fd} and S_{md}, and wages are W_{fd} and W_{md}, in the female and male sectors, respectively. Suppose further that a comparable worth system set wages in female jobs at W_0, the rate that would prevail in the absence of discrimination. At that wage, only L_{f0}, rather than L_{fd} workers, would be demanded by employers. The remainder, $L_{fd} - L_{f0}$, would be displaced from their jobs.

If such shifts were major and abrupt (which, of course, need not be the case), the transition period might be quite protracted. To the extent that not only new entrants but experienced workers were involved, it would be disruptive and painful. Female unemployment rates might well be increased. The costs associated with this policy depend crucially on how many workers are displaced, how quickly, and what happens to them.

It is also worth noting that the approach of raising women's pay through the principles of equal pay for equal work and equal employment opportunity also has the potential for increasing the wages even of women who remain in female jobs. This may also be illustrated in Figure 7.2. Suppose that we again begin with the discriminatory situation. If the barriers to entry into male jobs are reduced, women will transfer from F jobs to M jobs. The supply curve in F jobs will shift inward toward S_{f0} while the supply curve in M jobs shifts outward toward S_{m0}. Wages in the female sector are increased by the reduction of overcrowding there. A completely successful antidiscrimination policy would result in a wage of W_0 being established for both types of jobs. Proponents of comparable worth contend, however, that existing policies have not achieved notable success as yet and that a new strategy is called for.

Thus far, we have emphasized the economic issues relevant to the subject of comparable worth—issues that are paramount in concluding whether or not, and for whom, such a policy would be beneficial. However, the courts are making decisions concerning the issue on purely legal grounds. Currently, the status of comparable worth as a legal doctrine under Title VII is unclear because the matter has not been definitively addressed by the Supreme Court.[106] Nor is there much evidence of the adoption of comparable worth in the private sector, although many state and local governments have implemented or begun to implement some version of comparable worth.[107] In addition, some unions, particularly those in the public sector, have pressed for pay equity as a collective bargaining demand.

Empirical evidence on the potential impact of comparable worth in the United States is based on analyses of its implementation for state and municipal government employees, since there has been little experience with comparable worth in the private sector. Such studies have tended to find positive effects on women's relative wages. When employment effects were also examined, adverse effects on the growth of women's relative employment were usually found, although such effects were generally small.[108] Some additional light can be shed on these issues by examining what happened in Australia when wages in female occupations were abruptly raised by introducing a comparable worth policy. The experience of that country will be described in Chapter 11, but overall it tends to be relatively positive in that a considerable narrowing of the pay gap was achieved with relatively modest negative employment effects.

However, it may be difficult to extrapolate the results of studies that focus on government employees to the impact of the adoption of a nationwide comparable worth policy that includes the private sector. Even studies of comparable worth as imple-

---

[106] In *County of Washington* v. *Gunther,* 452 U.S. 161 (1981), the Supreme Court removed a major legal stumbling block to the comparable worth doctrine by ruling that it is not required that a man and woman do "equal work" in order to establish pay discrimination under Title VII. However, many other issues remain unresolved, and the Court stopped short of endorsing the comparable worth approach. See Ross et al., *The Rights of Women,* pp. 26–29. A major legal victory for proponents of comparable worth was attained in September 1983 when a federal court ruled in favor of the American Federation of State, County, and Municipal Employees (AFSCME) and found that the State of Washington had violated Title VII by paying employees in traditionally female job classifications less than employees in traditionally male occupations. A 1974 comparable worth study, commissioned by the state, found that women received 20 percent lower pay than men for jobs requiring equal skill and responsibility. When Washington state failed to eliminate the disparity, AFSCME filed suit. The ruling in favor of the plaintiffs was later overturned on appeal (see *American Federation of State, County and Municipal Employees* v. *State of Washington,* 770 F.2d 1401 [1985]). In 1986, the parties settled out of court. Thus, the Supreme Court has not issued a definitive ruling on the comparable worth issue. See Bureau of National Affairs, *Daily Labor Report,* no. 181 (16 September 1983); and "Washington State Settles Dispute Over Pay Equity," *New York Times,* 2 January 1986, p. A15.

[107] It has been reported that all but five states have initiated some degree of pay equity activity (for example, salary increases for female-dominated or minority-dominated job categories), and eight states have fully implemented a pay equity plan; see Susan E. Gardner and Christopher Daniel, "Implementing Comparable Worth/Pay Equity: Experiences of Cutting-Edge States," *Public Personnel Management* 27, no. 4 (winter 1998): 475–489, as cited in Michael Baker and Nicole M. Fortin, "Does Comparable Worth Work in a Decentralized Labor Market," National Bureau of Economic Research Working Paper No. 7937 (October 2000).

[108] See, for example, Killingsworth, *The Economics of Comparable Worth;* Peter F. Orazem and J. Peter Mattila, "The Implementation Process of Comparable Worth: Winners and Losers," *Journal of Political Economy* 98, no. 1 (February 1990): 134–52; and June O'Neill, Michael Brien, and James Cunningham, "Effects of Comparable Worth Policy: Evidence from Washington State," *American Economic Review* 79, no. 2 (May 1989): 305–9. In addition, the potential effect of a national comparable worth policy on the gender pay gap has been simulated by economic analyses that employ estimates of the effect of the occupational segregation on the pay gap. Such studies were reviewed above.

mented in Australia may be less than fully instructive because the labor market in that country tends to be highly centralized with a large role for government tribunals and unions in setting wage rates. This contrasts strongly with the highly decentralized U.S. labor market, which relies much more heavily on the market and generally gives firms considerable autonomy in setting wages. In this respect a recent study, which focused on the consequences of a pay equity initiative in one Canadian province, Ontario, beginning in the early 1990s, may be more relevant, since the Canadian labor market is more similar to the United States in being relatively decentralized. The results of this study suggest some caution in implementing comparable worth in such circumstances. Substantial lapses in compliance and implementation of the law were found. These tended to center on small firms that lacked the resources to undertake the necessary job evaluation programs and often did not have a sufficient sample of male and female jobs to make meaningful comparisons. Since such small firms employed the majority of both male and female workers in Ontario, little evidence was found of a positive impact of the policy on women's relative pay overall. Even among large firms, where compliance was fairly complete, estimated positive effects on women's pay in female jobs were modest and typically statistically insignificant.[109] It is also possible that the ineffectiveness of pay equity legislation, in this case, reflects additional factors specific to the situation in Ontario, such as the particular law implemented there or a change in the governing party that occurred a few years after the passage of the law.

Job Evaluation

The implementation of comparable worth requires an evaluation of the contribution of the many different jobs within an enterprise.* At present, formal job evaluation procedures are already used by the federal government, a number of state governments, and many large private firms as an aid in determining pay rates. Employers rely on such evaluations because many positions are filled entirely from within the firm itself through promotion and upgrading of the existing work force. Job evaluation may be useful in setting pay ratios in such jobs, especially since some of them are unique to a particular enterprise. This means that "going rates" for all jobs are not always available in local labor markets. Thus, employers may find it necessary to establish wages for such jobs, rather than simply to accept those determined by the market. It is important to bear in mind that this does not mean that market forces are ignored. In setting wages, most firms and governmental units try to take into account whatever information is available on prevailing wages for different types of labor. At the same time, the existence of job evaluation and other procedures for setting wages tends to make wages less responsive to short-term shifts in market conditions than they would otherwise be.

The actual methods used differ in detail but share the same basic rationale and approach. The first step is always a description of all the jobs within the given organization. The next step is to rate each according to all the various features that it is believed deter-

* Job evaluation is discussed in Donald J. Treiman and Heidi I. Hartmann, eds., *Women, Work and Wages: Equal Pay for Jobs of Equal Value* (Washington, DC: National Academy Press, 1981), pp. 71–74. Institutional models, discussed earlier, emphasize the importance of job evaluation and other administrative procedures for determining wages. See Peter B. Doeringer and Michael J. Piore, *Internal Labor Markets and Manpower Analysis* (Lexington, MA: D. C. Heath and Co., 1971).

[109] Baker and Fortin, "Does Comparable Worth Work?"

mine pay differences across jobs. Last, these ratings are combined to create a score for each job, which may then be used to help determine wages.

Among the factors used to construct job scores are such characteristics as level of education, skills, and responsibility, as well as the environment in which the work is performed. Commonly, multiple regression is used to link these to the existing pay structure. At other times, weights are assigned according to the judgment of the experts constructing the scale. In theory, various jobs can be assigned values objectively, presumably not influenced by irrelevant factors such as the gender and race of the incumbent, and quite different jobs may be assigned equal values, if warranted.

It would be a mistake, however, to take the objectivity of such procedures for granted. Both prevailing wage structures and the judgments of individuals may be tainted by existing inequalities in the economy and in society. An additional problem with the job evaluation approach is that it is most readily implemented in large firms. All one can conclude at this point is that the use of job evaluation to determine pay rates is neither an impractical pipe dream nor a surefire cure for discrimination.

CONCLUSION

Economists define labor market discrimination as a situation where two equally qualified individuals are treated differently on the basis of gender (race, age, etc.). Such discrimination against a particular group is likely to be detrimental, both directly and indirectly through feedback effects on their accumulation of human capital. Empirical studies have used available evidence on differences in the characteristics of male and female workers to explain the pay gap and the differences in occupational distributions between the two groups. Productivity-related factors have not been able to account for all of the gender differences in economic outcomes, suggesting that discrimination does play a part, accounting for perhaps half of the male–female earnings differential.

As much attention as has been focused on the issue of whether or not discrimination exists, there has been almost equal interest in the question of who discriminates, why, and how. We reviewed theories suggesting that

- employers, coworkers, or customers have tastes for discrimination against women;
- employers judge individual women in terms of the average characteristics of the group (statistical discrimination);
- women's wages are depressed because they are crowded into a few sectors;
- women are concentrated in dead-end jobs with few opportunities for on-the-job training and promotion.

Last, we examined the government's equal employment opportunity policies and considered the pros and cons of comparable worth.

There is good reason to believe that each of the models of discrimination that we have considered contributes to our understanding of a complex reality, where factors keeping women in segregated and poorly paid jobs, rather than being mutually exclusive, are far more likely to reinforce each other. By the same token, however, we pointed out that any improvement in women's labor market outcomes is likely to have feedback effects. By rewarding women more highly for their human capital, they are encouraged to accumulate more human capital on which they can gather rewards.

A P P E N D I X

Regression Analysis and Empirical Estimates of Labor Market Discrimination

In Table 7.2, we presented empirical estimates of labor market discrimination. In this appendix,[110] we explain in more detail how economists arrive at such estimates. The goal is to be able to "decompose" the gender wage gap into a portion due to measured productivity-related characteristics and a portion that cannot be explained by differences in characteristics and is, therefore, potentially due to labor market discrimination.

The starting point of such analyses is the estimation of a wage regression, which expresses wages as a function of such factors as experience and education. For simplicity, let's begin with the case in which there is only one explanatory variable, experience. Figure 7.5 shows a hypothetical scatter of points, "observations," for individual women with each point representing one woman's wage rate and experience.

FIGURE 7.5   Scatter Plot and Regression Line for Women's Wages

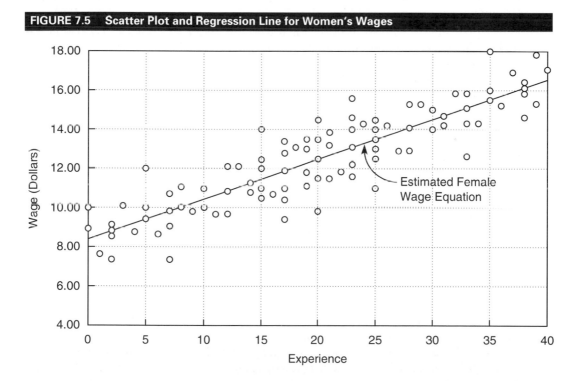

---

[110] In formulating this section we have benefited from reviewing Ronald G. Ehrenberg and Robert S. Smith, *Modern Labor Economics,* 6th ed. (Reading, MA: Addison Wesley, 1996), Appendix 1A, pp. 17–24; and Mark Killingsworth, "Where Does the Pay Gap Come From?" Class Handout for Economics 375, Women in the Economy, Rutgers University. For a more detailed treatment of regression analysis, see a statistics or econometrics text.

To better understand how wages are determined, we would like to use this information to estimate the effect of an additional year of work experience on wages. As can be seen, if we were to fit a straight line to the points in Figure 7.5, it would be an upward sloping line, suggesting that wages increase with additional years of labor market experience.

Before considering the technique that we would use to estimate the line shown in the figure, let's begin with the following equation that models the general relationship between wages and experience.

$$WAGE_i = a_0 + a_1 X_i + e_i$$

In this equation WAGE represents the wage rate of individual i and is called the **dependent variable.** The **independent** or **explanatory variable** is X, which represents the individual's level of experience. The regression coefficients, a_0 and a_1, specify the relationship between the dependent and independent variable: a_0 is the intercept of the line on the y-axis and a_1 is the slope of the line. The intercept gives the wage rate corresponding to zero years of work experience, that is, for a new entrant into the labor market. The slope of the line tells us by how much wages increase for each additional year of experience. The last term, e, is a random error term. It is included because we do not expect each observation to lie along the straight line. This is due to the fact that there are likely to be random factors which are unrelated to experience that also influence wages. (We shall see below that systematic factors like education, which also affect wages, can be incorporated in multiple regression analysis.)

How do we find the straight line that best fits the points in the figure? This amounts to estimating a_0 and a_1. The statistical technique that is generally used to do this is called **least squares regression analysis.** It is estimated by finding the line that minimizes the sum of the squared deviations (vertical differences) of each point from the line.

If we estimate a least squares regression using the points in Figure 7.5, we obtain the following estimated line:

$$WAGE_i = 8.5 + .2X_i$$

The estimate of $a_0 = 8.5$ and the estimate of $a_1 = 0.2$ mean that a new entrant into the labor market is expected to earn \$8.50 per hour and an individual's wages are expected to increase by \$0.20 with each additional year of experience.

There are at least two potential problems with this estimate. First, the hypothetical and the actual earnings profiles we showed in Chapter 6 were not straight lines but rather curved lines, which suggests that while earnings rise with experience, the rate of increase tends to fall over time. Such a relationship can readily be estimated using regression analysis and in fact most studies by economists allow for this.[111] We, however, will stick to a straight line as in Figure 7.5 to simplify our exposition.

Second, economic theory tells us that there are a number of other explanatory variables that are potentially important determinants of wages. These additional explanatory variables can be incorporated by using **multiple regression analysis.** We illustrate this by adding education as an additional explanatory variable. Our wage equation now becomes:

---

[111] To do this we include experience squared (X^2), in addition to X, as an explanatory variable in the regression.

$$\text{WAGE}_i = a_0' + a_1'X_i + a_2'ED_i + e_i'$$

ED is a variable measuring years of schooling completed. Each regression coefficient now tells us the impact of a unit change in each explanatory variable on the dependent variable, *holding the other independent variables constant.* So, for example, a_1' gives the effect of an additional year of experience on wages, holding education constant. Thus, the regression coefficients a_0' and a_1' are not necessarily equal to a_0 and a_1, since their interpretation has changed. This new relationship estimated by multiple regression analysis is found to be:

$$\text{WAGE}_i = 2 + .3X_i + .5ED_i$$

That is, we find that, holding education constant, each additional year of experience raises wages by $0.30; and, holding experience constant, each additional year of education raises wages by $0.50.

Note that including education changed our estimate of the effect of experience. This is because education is *correlated* with experience: Given the trend toward rising educational attainment, younger women have higher levels of education, on average, but less experience than older women. The estimated experience coefficient in the simple regression (the one that includes only experience) is *smaller* than in the multiple regression because the positive effect of experience on earnings is offset somewhat by the tendency of older people (who have higher levels of experience) to be less well educated. Thus, education is an important *omitted variable* and not taking it into account results in a *biased* estimate of the effect of experience; specifically, the estimated effect of experience is *biased downward* when education is omitted from the regression.

The results obtained with multiple regression analysis for the relationship between wages and experience can still be summarized in a simple diagram if we evaluate them at a specific level or specific levels of education. This is shown in Figure 7.6 for $ED = 12$ (high school graduates) and $ED = 16$ (college graduates).

Now that the basics of regression analysis are clear, we can consider how it may be used to obtain statistical estimates of the extent of labor market discrimination. We do this first in terms of a diagram and then present a general formula.

Figure 7.7 shows hypothetical male and female wage regression lines for college graduates. By focusing on one education group, we can proceed in terms of simple regression with one explanatory variable, experience. As may be seen in the figure, women's average wages, $\overline{w}_f$, are lower than men's, $\overline{w}_m$. At the same time, women have less experience on average, $\overline{x}_f$, than men do, $\overline{x}_m$. How much of the difference in average wages between men and women, $\overline{w}_m - \overline{w}_f$, is due to the gender difference in average levels of experience, $\overline{x}_m - \overline{x}_f$, and how much cannot be explained by this difference in qualifications? This "unexplained" portion is our estimate of discrimination.

We begin by observing that the female regression line lies below the male line and that it is also flatter. This shows that women earn less than men with the same experience both because they earn less at the outset of their careers than men do (the intercept of the female line is below the intercept of the male line) and because they receive a smaller return than men for each additional year of experience (the female line is flatter than the male line). We would like our estimate of discrimination to capture these differences.

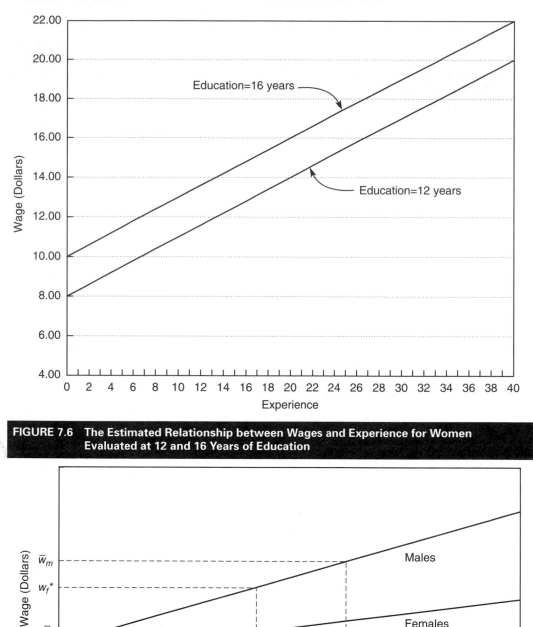

FIGURE 7.6 The Estimated Relationship between Wages and Experience for Women Evaluated at 12 and 16 Years of Education

FIGURE 7.7 Hypothetical Regression Lines for Male and Female College Graduates

To estimate how much of the gender wage gap is due to gender differences in experience, we ask what women's wages would be if they were rewarded the same way men were for their experience. Reading off of the male regression line, we see that a man with $\overline{x}_f$ years of experience would receive a wage of w_f^*. Thus, the portion of the gender wage gap attributable to women's lower average level of experience is $\overline{w}_m - w_f^*$. The remainder, $w_f^* - \overline{w}_f$ is unexplained and potentially due to discrimination. The unexplained portion of the gender gap is due to gender differences in the estimated coefficients of the wage regression (a_0 and a_1).

We can express this mathematically as follows:

Gender wage difference = Difference due to qualifications + Unexplained difference

$$= \overline{w}_m - \overline{w}_f = (\overline{w}_m - w_f^*) + (w_f^* - \overline{w}_f)$$

where:

$$\overline{w}_m = a_{0m} + a_{1m} \times \overline{x}_m$$
$$\overline{w}_f = a_{0f} + a_{1f} \times \overline{x}_f$$
$$w_f^* = a_{0m} + a_{1m} \times \overline{x}_f.$$

In the preceding equations, a_{0m} and a_{1m} are the intercept and slope of the male regression and a_{0f} and a_{1f} are the intercept and slope of the female regression.

The portion of the wage difference that is due to differences in qualifications, in this case experience, $(\overline{w}_m - w_f^*)$, is obtained by evaluating both men's and women's average levels of experience using the male regression coefficients. The unexplained portion of the gender difference is estimated by the difference between what women's wages are when their average experience is evaluated using the male regression versus when they are evaluated using the female regression. This approach can readily be applied in the multiple regression context and underlies estimates like those presented in Table 7.2.[112]

QUESTIONS FOR REVIEW AND DISCUSSION

1. How do economists generally measure the extent of labor market discrimination against women statistically? Are there important qualifications that need to be noted about such estimates? Do such studies indicate that discrimination against women in the labor market continues to exist? Is there any evidence that there is now reverse discrimination as a general pattern in the labor market?
2. What factors explain why some researchers conclude that labor market discrimination against women is very small while others come to a very different conclusion? [Hint: you may also want to consult the inset on the gender pay gap in Chapter 5.]
3. Suppose you are given data on a firm that indicate that the average wage of male employees is $15.00/hour and the average wage of female employees is $10.50/hour. Define "labor market discrimination" against women. Does the data

---

[112] Our ability to perform this decomposition is aided by the property of least squares regression that the regression line passes through the means of the dependent and explanatory variables. Thus, the point $(\overline{w}_f \, \overline{x}_f)$ will lie on the female regression line and the point $(\overline{w}_m \overline{x}_m)$ will lie on the male regression line. This analysis is sometimes known as a "Oaxaca Decomposition," after the economist who was one of the first to use it; he provides a detailed description in Ronald Oaxaca, "Male–Female Wage Differentials in Urban Labor Markets," *International Economic Review* 14 (October 1973): 693–709.

above prove that the firm discriminates against women? What kind of additional information would you need to have to determine whether or not such discrimination exists?

4. Prohibition of discrimination, affirmative action, and comparable worth are all possible means of reducing the wage gap. Which, if any, are likely to be effective? Why or why not? Do you see them as substitutes or as complements and why?

5. To the extent that it is true that women earn less because they spend less time in the labor market and that they spend less time in the labor market because they are paid less, how can this vicious circle be broken?

6. Given the discussions in Chapters 6 and 7, why do you think the income ratio for black females to black males is so much higher than for all women relative to all men, as shown by data presented in Chapter 5?

7. "Excluding women from occupations that require physical strength is justified because men tend to be stronger than women." Evaluate the validity of this argument.

Suggested Readings

Altonji, Joseph G., and Rebecca M. Blank. "Race and Gender in the Labor Market." In *Handbook of Labor Economics,* edited by Orley C. Ashenfelter and David Card, pp. 3C: 3143–259. Amsterdam: North-Holland, 1999, pp. 3143–3259.

Becker, Gary S. *The Economics of Discrimination,* 2nd ed. Chicago: University of Chicago Press, 1971.

Bergmann, Barbara R. *In Defense of Affirmative Action.* New York: Basic Books, 1996.

Blau, Francine D. "Discrimination Against Women: Theory and Evidence." In *Labor Economics: Modern Views,* edited by William A. Darity Jr., pp. 53–89. Boston: Kluwer-Nijhoff, 1984.

Blau, Francine D., and Lawrence M. Kahn. "Gender Differences in Pay." *Journal of Economic Perspectives* 14, no. 4 (fall 2000): 75–99.

Darity, William A. Jr., and Patrick L. Mason. "Evidence on Discrimination in Employment: Codes of Color, Codes of Gender." *Journal of Economic Perspectives* 12 no. 2 (spring 1998): 63–90.

Gunderson, Morley. "Male–Female Wage Differentials and Policy Responses." *Journal of Economic Literature* 27, no. 1 (March 1989): 46–72.

Holzer, Harry, and David Neumark. "Assessing Affirmative Action." *Journal of Economic Literature* 38, no. 3 (September 2000): 483–568.

Madden, Janice F. *The Economics of Sex Discrimination.* Lexington, MA: Lexington Books, 1973.

Reskin, Barbara F., and Heidi I. Hartmann, eds. *Women's Work, Men's Work: Sex Segregation on the Job.* Washington, DC: National Academy Press, 1986.

Reskin, Barbara F., and Patricia A. Roos. *Job Queues, Gender Queues: Explaining Women's Inroads into Male Occupations.* Philadelphia: Temple University Press, 1990.

Strober, Myra H. "Toward a General Theory of Occupational Sex Segregation: The Case of Public School Teaching." In *Sex Segregation in the Workplace: Trends, Explanations, Remedies,* edited by Barbara F. Reskin, pp. 144–56. Washington, DC: National Academy Press, 1984.

Valian, Virginia. *Why So Slow? The Advancement of Women.* Cambridge MA: MIT Press, 1998.

CHAPTER 8

RECENT DEVELOPMENTS IN THE LABOR MARKET: THEIR IMPACT ON WOMEN AND MEN

Chapter Highlights

- Trends in Female and Male Wages
- The Declining Gender Pay Gap
- The Rising Payoff to Education
- Changing Labor Market Dynamics: Restructuring and Job Loss
- The Rise of the Nonstandard Work Force
- The Growth in Self-Employment
- The Changing Face of Labor Unions

In previous chapters we examined historic developments and long-term trends in the status of women and discussed various explanations for them. We have chronicled dramatic changes in women's participation in the labor force and their roles within the family. We have also documented some substantial improvements in women's labor market outcomes, notably the significant decrease in the gender pay gap that occurred beginning in the 1980s. This is only one of a number of dramatic labor market shifts that have taken place in recent years. Other changes include a flattening of the growth in real wages that American workers had long taken for granted, and a widening wage gap between high- and low-skilled workers that has been associated with a rising payoff to education. In addition there have been increased concerns about job security in the face of corporate restructuring and downsizing, growth in nonstandard employment arrangements and self-employment among workers, and a continued decline in the share of the work force that is unionized. In this chapter we focus on these important developments and examine their impact on women and men.

TRENDS IN FEMALE AND MALE WAGES

One of the most notable labor market trends in recent years has been the dramatic increase in **wage inequality** among both male and female workers, which began in the 1970s, intensified in the 1980s, and continued at a slower pace in the 1990s. By increasing wage inequality, we mean a widening dispersion in the distribution of earnings within each group (that is, men and women), so that the wage gap between those at the bottom and those at the top has widened considerably. This has also been a time of stagnating overall **real wages** of male workers. Real wages are wages that have been adjusted for changes in the cost of living or price inflation. In the presence of constant or falling real wages for males overall, rising wage inequality has meant substantial declines in the real wages of less-educated men who are at the lower end of the wage distribution.[1]

The declining relative labor market position of the less skilled is believed to reflect an increase in demand for skilled workers relative to the demand for unskilled workers. This has raised the **returns to skill** or the rewards that the labor market gives for various worker skills or qualifications. The reasons for this increase in demand are not fully understood, but most studies point to the importance of technological change and increasing international competition, both of which are believed to have had a negative effect on the relative demand for less skilled workers. In addition, institutional factors including the decline in unionism, which we discuss at the end of this chapter, and the decreasing real value of the minimum wage have also played a role.[2]

The trends in real earnings for men and women since 1960 are summarized in Table 8.1, which shows changes in the median annual earnings of year-round, full-time workers after adjustment for inflation. While male real earnings rose substantially during the 1960s and moderately during the 1970s, they declined over the 1980s and increased only slightly in the 1990s. Indeed, Figure 8.1 indicates that male real earnings actually peaked in 1973 and have fallen 7.6 percent since then. The real earnings trends for women are fairly similar to men's, decade by decade, with the important exception of the 1980s. During the 1980s, the period of major convergence in the gender wage gap, women's real earnings increased by 11.3 percent while men's real earnings fell by 2.5 percent. Overall, in stark contrast to the experience of men, women's real earnings have increased by nearly 18 percent since 1973. Thus, the decline in the

---

[1] For summaries of these trends, see, for example, Frank Levy, *The New Dollars and Dreams: American Incomes and Economic Change* (New York: Russell Sage Foundation, 1998); Frank Levy and Richard J. Murnane, "U.S. Earnings Levels and Earnings Inequality: A Review of Recent Trends and Proposed Explanations," *Journal of Economic Literature* 30, no. 3 (September 1991): 1222–381; and Francine D. Blau, "Trends in the Well-Being of American Women: 1970–95," *Journal of Economic Literature* 36, no. 1 (March 1998): 112–65.

[2] For an excellent summary of the evidence, see Lawrence F. Katz and David H. Autor, "Changes in the Wage Structure and Earnings Inequality," in *Handbook of Labor Economics,* ed. Orley C. Ashenfelter and David Card (Amsterdam: Elsevier, 1999), pp. 3A:1463–555. Some of the better known studies include Chinhui Juhn, Kevin M. Murphy, and Brooks Pierce, "Wage Inequality and the Rise in Returns to Skill," *Journal of Political Economy* 101, no. 3 (June 1993): 410–42; Lawrence F. Katz and Kevin M. Murphy, "Changes in Relative Wages, 1963–87: Supply and Demand Factors," *Quarterly Journal of Economics* 107, no. 1 (February 1992): 35–78; and John DiNardo, Nicole M. Fortin, and Thomas Lemieux, "Labor Market Institutions and the Distribution of Wages, 1973–1992: A Semiparametric Approach," *Econometrica* 64, no. 5 (September 1996): 1001–44.

TABLE 8.1   Change in Real Median Earnings of Men and Women, Year-Round, Full-Time Workers, Selected Periods, 1960–1999

Period	Men (%)	Women (%)
1960–1969	28.7	24.9
1970–1979	5.9	6.4
1980–1989	–2.5	11.3
1990–1999	3.4	4.2
1973–1999	–7.6	17.7
1960–1999	31.3	56.2

Notes: Persons 15 years old and over beginning in 1980, and persons 14 years old and over for previous years. Adjusted for inflation using the Consumer Price Index.

Source. U.S. Census Bureau, *Current Population Reports,* Historical Tables, and Series P-60.

FIGURE 8.1   Median Earnings of Year-Round, Full-Time Workers by Sex, 1960–1999 (1999 dollars)

gender gap was due in part to real earnings gains for women, but also reflects the worsening economic position of men.[3]

THE DECLINING GENDER PAY GAP

As we saw in Chapter 5, starting in the late 1970s or early 1980s, the gender pay gap began a steady decline. Between 1978 and 1999, for example, the weekly earnings of women full-time workers increased from 61 to 77 percent of men's weekly earnings. The pace of change was most rapid over the 1980s and appears to have slowed considerably over the 1990s. In order to fully understand both the reasons for the progress in narrowing the gender gap as well as the consequences of this development for women's economic well-being, it is important to consider the labor market context in which this change has taken place, most importantly the fact that overall wage inequality has increased. This raises the question of how women have succeeded in narrowing the gender gap in pay in the face of overall labor market trends that have become increasingly unfavorable for low-wage workers in general, since women are disproportionately represented at the bottom of the wage distribution.

We begin our analysis of the trends in the gender pay gap with a consideration of the determinants of the pay gap from a theoretical perspective. We then apply these concepts to understanding the trends in the pay gap and review empirical results for the 1980s and 1990s. We also briefly consider what is known about trends in the race pay gap during this same period.

DETERMINANTS OF TRENDS IN THE GENDER PAY GAP

In analyzing the theoretical reasons for the decline in the gender pay gap, it makes sense to start with the two major explanations economists have developed for the pay gap that we reviewed in previous chapters:

- **differences in human capital investments** or other gender differences in qualifications, which we considered in Chapter 6
- **labor market discrimination** or differences in the treatment of equally qualified men and women, which we considered in Chapter 7

As we have seen, these two explanations do not necessarily constitute mutually exclusive sources of gender wage differentials. Both may play a role in explaining the gender pay gap and there may also be important feedback effects if discrimination in the labor market lowers women's incentives to invest in their qualifications and women's lower qualifications reinforce statistical discrimination against them. The empirical research re-

---

[3] Estimated trends in real earnings vary to some extent depending on the earnings measure and price deflator used, the data set employed, and the starting and ending years selected. While the trends reported here, based on government data, are broadly consistent with the findings in the literature, we note that, in recent years, there has been considerable controversy about the measurement of price changes. See, for example, Michael J. Boskin, "The CPI Commission: Findings and Recommendations," *American Economic Review* 87, no. 2 (May 1997): 78–83; and Katharine Abraham, John S. Greenlees, and Brent R. Moulton, "Working to Improve the Consumer Price Index," *Journal of Economic Perspectives* 12, no. 1 (winter 1998): 27–36.

viewed in previous chapters provides considerable support for each set of factors in explaining the gender pay gap.

Following this reasoning, we would expect the pay gap to decline if (1) women increased their qualifications relative to men's or (2) labor market discrimination against women decreased. There is some reason to believe that both these developments have occurred. As we saw in Chapter 6, women have narrowed the experience gap with men and increased their representation in professional schools and in traditionally male fields of study. At the same time, women's increasing commitment to market work may have induced employers to reduce the extent of statistical discrimination against them. That is, employers may judge individual women less negatively for being members of a group they view as less committed to the labor market, on average.

However, recent research suggests that explaining trends over time in the gender pay differential requires that we also consider a third factor, one we have not mentioned in earlier chapters—overall trends in wage structure:[4]

- **wage structure** refers to the returns that the labor market offers for various skills and for employment in higher-paying industries or occupations

Both the human capital and discrimination explanations of the pay gap suggest an important role for trends in wage structure in determining how women fare over time. For example, despite important recent gains, women still have less experience than men, on average. This means that if the market return to experience (that is, the increase in wages associated with each additional year of experience) rises over time, women will be increasingly disadvantaged by their lesser amount of experience. In addition, both the human capital and discrimination models suggest reasons why women are likely to be employed in different occupations and perhaps in different industries than men. This implies that an increase in the rewards for employment in "male" occupations or industries will also place women at an increasing disadvantage. In fact, the patterns of rising overall wage inequality that have been found for both men and women in the labor market resulted from precisely such increases in the market rewards to skill and to employment in high-paying male sectors. This means that women as a group have essentially been "swimming upstream" in a labor market growing increasingly unfavorable for workers with below-average skills—in this case experience—and for workers employed in disproportionately female occupations and industries.

EMPIRICAL RESULTS FOR THE 1980s

How can we explain the decrease in the gender pay gap in the 1980s in the face of overall shifts in labor market returns that have worked against women as a group? We focus here on the 1980s, both because this was the period of the greatest narrowing of the gender gap and because the data are available for this time period to undertake a detailed analysis. In the next subsection we examine the considerably sketchier information that

---

[4] Francine D. Blau and Lawrence M. Kahn, "Rising Wage Inequality and the U.S. Gender Gap," *American Economic Review Papers and Proceedings* 84, no. 2 (May 1994): 23–28; and Francine D. Blau and Lawrence M. Kahn, "Swimming Upstream: Trends in the Gender Wage Differential in the 1980s," *Journal of Labor Economics* 15, no. 1, pt. 1 (January 1997): 1–42.

is available for the 1990s. According to a study by Francine Blau and Lawrence Kahn,[5] it appears that women were able to overcome the effect of adverse shifts in overall wage structure (that is, rising labor market returns to skills and to employment in high-paying male sectors) on their relative wages in the 1980s, in part, by improving their qualifications relative to men. So, although women continue to have lower skills than men, on average, particularly less labor market experience, they have *narrowed the gender difference in skills*. Women have also benefited from a decrease in the "unexplained" pay gap, which may reflect (1) a decrease in discrimination against women, (2) an improvement in women's unmeasured factors that it is not possible to include in the analysis, like motivation or commitment, or (3) favorable shifts in the demand for female versus male workers.

The results from the Blau-Kahn study, which focuses on full-time workers, are shown in greater detail in Table 8.2. This table looks a great deal like Table 7.2 in Chapter 7, which is derived from the same study. However, while our goal there was to understand the reasons for the gender wage gap in a particular year, 1988, our goal here is to understand the reasons for the *increase* in the gender wage ratio between 1979 and 1988. Note that the gender wage *gap* is equal to the difference between 100 percent and the gender wage *ratio* (gap = 100% – ratio). So that a gender wage ratio of 62 percent, for example, corresponds to a gender wage gap of 38 percent. In the Blau-Kahn study, the ratio of women's to men's wages was 62 percent in the first year and rose to 72 percent by 1988, an increase of 16 percent.[6] Each entry in the table gives the contribution of the indicated factor to the total change in the gender wage ratio (16 percent). A positive sign means that the factor worked to *increase* the ratio; a negative sign means that the factor worked in the opposite direction, that is, to *reduce* the wage ratio.

The table indicates that improvements in women's characteristics had a large positive effect on the gender wage ratio. Of particular importance was the decline in the experience difference between men and women: the gender gap in full-time experience fell from 7.5 to 4.6 years over this period. Shifts in major occupations played a significant role too, as the employment of women as professionals and managers rose relative to men's, while their relative employment in clerical and service jobs fell. Women's wages also increased relative to men's because of deunionization, or the decline of unions, which had a larger negative impact on male than female workers: Men, who have traditionally been more likely than women to be unionized, experienced a larger decline in unionization than women. The combined effect of these changes in characteristics would have led to a 13 percent increase in the gender wage ratio. Another factor that worked to increase the gender pay ratio substantially was a decrease in the unexplained portion of the gender differential. The contribution of this factor was to increase the ratio by 14 percent.

---

[5] Blau and Kahn, "Swimming Upstream." We draw heavily on the results of this study in this section. Other research on the convergence of the gender gap that emphasizes the importance of women's increasing skills includes June O'Neill and Solomon W. Polachek, "Why the Gender Gap in Wages Narrowed in the 1980s," *Journal of Labor Economics* 11, no. 1, pt. 1 (January 1993): 205–28; Elaine Sorensen, *Exploring the Reasons Behind the Narrowing Gender Gap in Earnings* (Washington, DC: Urban Institute Press, 1991); and Alison J. Wellington, "Changes in the Male/Female Wage Gap, 1976–85," *Journal of Human Resources* 28, no. 2 (spring 1993): 383–411.

[6] That is, $(72.4 - 62.2)/62.2 = 0.164$.

TABLE 8.2   Explaining the Percentage Increase in the Female–Male Wage Ratio, 1979–1988

Explanatory Factors	Contribution to the Change in the Ratio (%)
Change in Gender Differences in Characteristics	13.4
Educational attainment	0.9
Labor force experience	5.7
Race	0.1
Occupational category	4.9
Industry category	–0.1
Union status	1.9
Change in Prices of Characteristics	–10.8
Change in the Unexplained Gap	13.8
Total	16.4

Notes: The figures presented in this table differ slightly from those in the study by Blau and Kahn from which they are derived. The Blau-Kahn study decomposes the 1979–1988 change in the gender log wage gap (= –.152). This is approximately equal to the more intuitive concept that we focus upon, the percentage change in the gender wage ratio presented in the table of 16.4% (multiplied by –1). The contribution of each of the explanatory factors given in the table to the percentage change in the gender wage ratio was estimated by applying the proportion of the change in the gender log wage gap that was due to the indicated factor, to the 16.4% change in the ratio.

Source: Calculated from results presented in Francine D. Blau and Lawrence M. Kahn, "Swimming Upstream: Trends in the Gender Wage Differential in the 1980s," *Journal of Labor Economics* 15, no. 1, pt. 1 (January 1997): 1–42.

Taken together, changes in qualifications and in the unexplained gap would have increased the gender wage ratio by 27 percent. The reason that the actual ratio rose by only 16 percent is that changes in wage structure (or returns to characteristics) over this period favored men over women. Of particular importance were a rise in the return to experience (since women have less of it) and increases in returns to employment in major occupations and industries where men are more highly represented. These adverse shifts in labor market returns by themselves would have reduced the gender ratio substantially, by 11 percent. Thus, in order for the wage gap to decline, the factors favorably affecting women's wages had to be large enough to more than offset the impact of unfavorable shifts in returns. Another way to look at this is that the convergence in male and female wages would have been considerably greater had these unfavorable shifts in wage structure not occurred.

Can we say anything about the reasons for the decline in the unexplained gender wage gap that occurred over the 1980s? As noted above, such a shift may reflect an upgrading of women's unmeasured labor market skills, a shift in labor market demand favoring women over men, or a decline in labor market discrimination against women. Indeed all of these factors may well have played a role, and all appear credible during this period.

Since women improved their relative level of measured skills, as shown by the narrowing of the gap in full-time job experience, it is plausible that they also enhanced their relative level of unmeasured skills. For example, women's increasing labor force attachment may have encouraged them to acquire more on-the-job training. And, as we saw in Chapter 6, gender differences in college major, which have been found to be strongly related to the gender wage gap among college graduates, decreased over the 1970s and 1980s. Thus, the marketability of women's education has probably improved. As we also saw in Chapter 6, the male–female difference in SAT math scores has also declined. This could be a sign of improved quality of women's education.

The argument that discrimination against women declined in the 1980s may seem less credible than that their unmeasured human capital characteristics improved, since the federal government scaled back its antidiscrimination enforcement effort during the 1980s.[7] However, as women increased their commitment to the labor force and improved their job skills, the rationale for statistical discrimination against them diminished; thus it is plausible that this type of discrimination decreased. Further, in the presence of feedback effects, employers' revised views can generate additional increases in women's wages by raising women's returns to investments in job qualifications and skills. To the extent that such qualifications are not fully controlled for in the statistical analysis used to explain the change in the gender wage gap, this may also help to account for the decline in the "unexplained" gap. Another possible reason for a decline in discrimination against women is that changes in social attitudes have made such discriminatory tastes increasingly less acceptable.

Finally, the underlying labor market demand shifts that widened wage inequality over the 1980s may have favored women relative to men in certain ways, and thus may have also contributed to a decrease in the unexplained gender gap. Overall, manufacturing employment declined. In addition, there is some evidence that technological change has produced within-industry demand shifts that have favored white-collar workers in general. Given the traditional male predominance in blue-collar jobs (that is, as craftsworkers, operatives, and laborers), this shift might be expected to benefit women relative to men, and would tend to offset the large increase in female labor supply that also occurred during this time.[8] Moreover, one aspect of technological change, increased computer use, favors women both because they have been found to be more likely than men to use computers at work and because computers restructure work in ways that de-emphasize physical strength.[9]

In light of these trends, it may be surprising that Table 8.1 indicates that shifts in employment by industry had little impact on changes in the gender wage ratio during this period. However, as we have seen, some of the changes occurred within industries and likely resulted in economy-wide effects impacting men and women regardless of where they were employed. In addition, detailed analyses reported in the Blau-Kahn study suggest that the impact of changes in employment by industry differed across skill groups. Among low-skilled workers, shifts in employment across major industries were

---

[7] Jonathan S. Leonard, "Women and Affirmative Action," *Journal of Economic Perspectives* 3, no. 1 (winter 1989): 61–75.

[8] Eli Berman, John Bound, and Zvi Griliches, "Changes in the Demand of Skilled Labor Within U.S. Manufacturing Industries: Evidence from the Annual Survey of Manufacturing," *Quarterly Journal of Economics* 109, no. 2 (May 1994): 367–97; and Blau and Kahn, "Swimming Upstream."

[9] Alan B. Krueger, "How Computers Have Changed the Wage Structure: Evidence from Microdata, 1984–1989," *Quarterly Journal of Economics* 108, no. 1 (February 1993): 33–60; and Bruce Weinberg, "Computer Use and the Demand for Female Workers," *Industrial and Labor Relations Review* 53, no. 2 (January 2000): 290–308. The growing importance of "brains" relative to "brawn" as a factor narrowing the gender pay gap is particularly emphasized by Finis Welch in "Growth in Women's Relative Wages and in Inequality Among Men: One Phenomenon or Two?" *American Economic Review* 90, no. 2 (May 2000): 444–49.

indeed an important factor working to lower the gender wage gap, as low-skilled men lost jobs in high-paying industries.[10] On the other hand, among middle-skilled workers, industry shifts had little effect on the gender wage gap, while among high-skilled workers, industry shifts actually worked to raise men's wages relative to women's. Thus, for men and women as a whole, changes in employment by industry had relatively little effect on relative wages, although this was indeed an important factor benefiting low-skilled women relative to low-skilled men.

The framework employed in obtaining the results reported in Table 8.1 assumes that labor market returns to skills and to employment in particular sectors, as estimated from a sample of male workers, are determined by forces outside the gender pay gap and are a useful indicator of the market rewards facing both men and women.[11] Consistent with this assumption is evidence that widening wage inequality in the 1980s and 1990s was importantly affected by the economy-wide forces discussed above, including technological change, international trade, the decline in unionism, and the falling real value of the minimum wage.[12] Moreover, increases in wage inequality during this period were similar for men and women, suggesting that both groups may have been similarly affected by these trends. This suggests that the assumptions underlying Table 8.1 are reasonable. However, under some circumstances, the gender pay gap could influence male inequality. For example, suppose there is a fixed overall hierarchy of jobs and that jobs determine wages. In this case, as women succeed in narrowing the gender pay gap by moving up in the overall distribution of jobs (and wages), men who are displaced move down resulting in widening male inequality. It has been argued that recent trends in the gender pay gap and male wage inequality are consistent with such a model.[13] In this view, women's gains have to some extent come at the expense of men's losses.

The experience of blacks in the 1980s stands in sharp contrast to that of women. As we saw in Chapter 5, while the gender pay gap narrowed considerably, there was little evidence of further reductions in the race gap during the 1980s and there have been only moderate signs of further wage convergence since then. Some research suggests that recent changes in wage structure may provide at least a partial explanation for the lack of progress of blacks over the 1980s. Blacks, on average, have lower educational attainment than whites and, as a consequence, have been more adversely affected than whites by declining relative wages for less-educated workers. In addition, although blacks continued to reduce the race gap in education over the 1980s, their rate of progress was slower during that period than in previous decades. Some evidence has also been found that the decline in blue-collar jobs in manufacturing particularly negatively affected black males. Further, while the exit of black women from extremely low-paying, private household employment was an important factor in their narrowing the

---

[10]   See also Jane Waldfogel and Susan E. Mayer, "Gender Differences in the Low-Wage Labor Market," in *Finding Jobs: Work and Welfare Reform,* ed. David Card and Rebecca M. Blank (New York: Russell Sage Foundation, 2000), pp. 193–232.

[11]   Male wage regressions are used to estimate the returns to the various characteristics listed in Table 8.1. See the appendix to Chapter 7 for a brief description of the application of regression analysis to analyzing wages.

[12]   See, for example, Katz and Autor, "Changes in the Wage Structure."

[13]   Nicole M. Fortin and Thomas Lemieux, "Are Women's Wage Gains Men's Losses? A Distributional Test," *American Economic Review* 90, no. 2 (May 2000): 456–60.

race gap in earlier years, this process had pretty much played itself out by the 1980s as black women's representation in these jobs approached levels for whites. Despite these interesting insights, the full explanation for the unfortunate stalling of progress in narrowing the race gap in the 1980s and beyond remains elusive.[14]

The data presented in Chapter 5 also indicated that the wages of Hispanic women and men have been falling relative to those of whites. Education gaps between Hispanics and whites are considerably larger than those between blacks and whites, so it is likely that they have been particularly negatively affected by the declining relative wages of less-educated workers and the decrease in blue-collar and manufacturing employment. In addition, as noted in Chapter 5, a large and growing proportion of Hispanics are recent immigrants to the United States, hence their earnings are reduced because they tend to be relatively young, may not speak English well, and are likely to face other difficulties in adjusting to their new environment. There is also some evidence that the economic status of immigrants has deteriorated relative to natives in recent years.[15]

EMPIRICAL RESULTS FOR THE 1990S

As noted above, unfortunately the data are not yet available to undertake for the 1990s the type of detailed study of changes in the gender wage ratio that we summarized for the 1980s. Most importantly, data sets that contain information on actual labor market experience, a crucial variable for analyzing the male–female pay gap, have not yet been released for a period that covers most of the decade. However, one recent study has endeavored to summarize what could be learned from preliminary analyses of available data.[16] This study concluded that changes in the composition of male and female workers by age and education could *not* account for the slowing of convergence in the gender pay gap in the 1990s, nor did it appear that there was a more adverse effect of

---

[14] For studies of black–white trends, see Francine D. Blau and Andrea H. Beller, "Black–White Earnings over the 1970s and 1980s, Gender Differences in Trends," *Review of Economics and Statistics* 74, no. 2 (May 1992): 276–86; John Bound and Richard B. Freeman, "What Went Wrong? The Erosion of Relative Earnings and Employment Among Young Black Men in the 1980s," *Quarterly Journal of Economics* 107, no. 1 (February 1992): 201–32; Chinhui Juhn, Kevin M. Murphy, and Brooks Pierce, "Accounting for the Slowdown in Black–White Wage Convergence," in *Workers and Their Wages,* ed. Marvin Kosters (Washington, DC: AEI Press, 1991), pp. 107–43. As noted in Chapter 5, the issue of selection bias has received considerable attention in analyzing the male trends. For studies that include the 1980s see Chinhui Juhn, "Labor Market Dropout, Selection Bias, and Trends in Black and White Wages," Working Paper, University of Houston (1997); James J. Heckman, Thomas M. Lyons, and Petra E. Todd, "Understanding Black–White Wage Differentials, 1960–1990," *American Economic Review* 90, no. 2 (May 2000): 344–49; and Amitabh Chandra, "Labor-Market Dropouts and the Racial Wage Gap: 1940–90," *American Economic Review* 90, no. 2 (May 2000): 333–38.

[15] For analyses of Hispanic and immigrant earnings, see Maury B. Gittleman and David R. Howell, "Changes in the Structure and Quality of Jobs in the United States: Effects by Race and Gender, 1973–1990," *Industrial and Labor Relations Review* 48, no. 3 (April 1995): 420–40; Gregory DeFreitas, *Inequality at Work: Hispanics in the U.S. Labor Force* (Oxford: Oxford University Press, 1991); George J. Borjas, "Assimilation and Changes in Cohort Quality Revisited: What Happened to Immigrant Earnings in the 1980s?" *Journal of Labor Economics* 13, no. 2 (April 1995): 201–45; and Barry R. Chiswick, "Speaking, Reading, and Earnings Among Low-Skilled Immigrants," *Journal of Labor Economics* 9, no. 2 (April 1995): 149–70.

[16] Francine D. Blau and Lawrence M. Kahn, "Gender Differences in Pay," *Journal of Economic Perspectives* 14, no. 4 (fall 2000): 75–99. Specifically, the authors analyzed data from the *Current Population Surveys,* in contrast to the Panel Study of Income Dynamics, which was employed for the analysis underlying Table 8.1.

changes in wage structure in the 1990s than in the previous decade. These findings suggest that the slower progress of women during the 1990s as compared to the 1980s was probably due to one or more of the following factors: less improvement in women's qualifications (such as experience) relative to men's in the 1990s than in the 1980s; a smaller decline in discrimination against women in the 1990s than in the 1980s; or less favorable demand shifts for women in the 1990s than in the 1980s. Future research is needed to sort out these explanations.

THE RISING PAYOFF TO EDUCATION

The more favorable real earnings experience of women and the declining gender pay gap over the past 25 years have resulted in significant gender differences in earnings trends. However, when we compare how the less educated have fared relative to the more highly educated, the experiences of men and women are more similar. Among both women and men, the less educated are increasingly falling behind others, as earnings disparities by education have grown. Among men, these have been associated with declining real wages for the less educated, while among women, though their real wages have not declined, real wage growth has been considerably slower for the less educated.

These trends are seen in Tables 8.3 and 8.4. Table 8.3 gives the median earnings of year-round, full-time workers in each educational category relative to those of high school graduates for 1967 and 1999. It is clear that, relative to high school graduates, the earnings of those who have not completed high school have fallen, while the relative earnings of college graduates have increased considerably. For instance, in 1999, women and men with a college degree earned 80 percent more than a high school graduate, compared to 50 percent more in 1967.[17] Those with some college also increased their earnings relative to high school graduates, but to a lesser extent than

TABLE 8.3	Ratios to Median Incomes of High School Graduates for Men and Women Year-Round, Full-Time Workers, 1967 and 1999 (%)			
	1967		*1999*	
Education	*Men*	*Women*	*Men*	*Women*
High school				
1–3 years	89.1	82.3	75.4	73.8
4 years	100.0	100.0	100.0	100.0
College				
1–3 years	114.0	116.8	120.5	125.0
4 or more years	149.7	151.1	181.4	181.0

Notes: Data refer to workers 25 years of age and older. Definitions of educational categories are not exactly comparable for the two years. In 1999, median income for 1–3 years of college is computed as a weighted average of the medians for "some college, no degree" and "associate degree."

Source: U.S. Census Bureau, *Current Population Reports,* Consumer Income Series P-60, various issues.

---

[17]   Of course, the costs of going to college have risen as well, but even taking this into account, the figures suggest an increase in the return to a college education.

TABLE 8.4 Change in Real Median Income of Men and Women by Education for Year-Round, Full-Time Workers, 1967–1999

Education	Men (%)	Women (%)
High School		
1–3 years	–20.8	0.1
4 years	–6.5	11.7
College		
1–3 years	–1.2	19.6
4 or more years	13.4	33.8

Notes: Data refer to workers 25 years of age and older. Definitions of educational categories are not exactly comparable for the two years. In 1999, median income for 1 to 3 years of college is computed as a weighted average of the medians for "some college, no degree" and "associate degree."

Source: U.S. Census Bureau, *Current Population Reports,* Consumer Income Series P-60, various issues.

college graduates did. Interestingly, the ratios of each educational category's earnings relative to high school graduates are quite similar for men and women in both years, indicating that the extent of earnings differentials by education is about the same for both. This means that the increase in earnings inequality over this period, as measured by the widening disparities across educational groups, was similar for men and women.

Table 8.4 shows the consequences of widening inequality in earnings by education for trends in real earnings. For both men and women, more highly educated workers did considerably better in terms of real earnings changes. Among men, only college graduates experienced an increase in real earnings; for others real earnings decreased. The largest decline was for high school dropouts: Their real earnings fell by 21 percent over the period, while the real earnings of men with some college decreased by only 1 percent. In contrast, male college graduates experienced an *increase* in their real earnings of 13 percent. Women fared better than their male counterparts within each educational category. However, here too we observe that the more highly educated did a great deal better: Real earnings remained roughly constant among female dropouts but rose by 34 percent among female college graduates. Note that real wage changes for men and women overall are determined not just by the wage trends for each education group but also by changes in the relative importance of each education group in the total. In this respect, rising educational attainment has helped to boost the real earnings of both men and women, although, as we have seen, male real earnings have nonetheless been stagnating since the early 1970s.

These trends indicate a rising payoff to a college education for both men and women. This also means that, among both men and women, the earnings of the less educated fell compared to others. The deteriorating earnings situation of less educated women and men tell only part of the story of the falling economic status of the less educated. To be included in these tabulations, an individual must not only be employed, but work year-round and full-time. Another piece of the story is that, as we saw in Chapter

4, among both men and women, over the past 25 years, the less educated have become increasingly less likely to be in the labor force than the more highly educated. Among women, this reflects considerably smaller increases in participation rates for those with less than four years of high school in comparison to substantial increases for those with higher levels of education. Among men, there have been decreases in participation rates among all education groups, but the declines have been especially precipitous among those who have not completed high school. A final piece of the story is the rising incidence of mother-only families that we will examine in the next chapter; it has been particularly pronounced among the less educated, placing them and their families at even greater economic disadvantage.[18]

CHANGING LABOR MARKET DYNAMICS: RESTRUCTURING AND JOB LOSS

THE HIGH-CHURNING U.S. LABOR MARKET

The economic expansion in the United States, which began in the early 1990s, was the longest ever experienced, with high rates of growth in output and very low unemployment rates combined with low levels of inflation. By spring 2000, the overall national unemployment rate was at its lowest level in 30 years, just under 4 percent, producing an exceptionally "tight" labor market. Employers responded by offering a variety of enticements to attract workers ranging from higher pay, additional benefits, signing bonuses, and, in some cases even stock options. High wage and even some "minimum wage" workers job-hopped in an effort to obtain the best opportunity.[19] At the same time, however, other workers suffered involuntary job loss as a result of corporate restructuring. Corporations that announced significant layoffs or plans for sizable reductions in their workforces during the mid-to late 1990s included AT&T, IBM, General Motors, Boeing, and Xerox, among others.[20] While such downsizing may reflect decreases in demand in particular sectors, more often than in the past it represents an effort by firms to streamline their operations and increase efficiency.[21] Thus, a significant amount of such job loss may occur at any point in the business cycle, including the buoyant economy of this period. As the economy weakens, job loss is expected to increase further. Less-educated workers with fewer skills, who cannot take advantage of the new opportunities available, as well as older workers, who find it is difficult to "retool" or who may face age discrimination, are at a particular disadvantage when such downsiz-

---

[18]   This development is particularly emphasized in Blau, "Trends in the Well-Being of American Women."

[19]   See Ron Scherer and Daphne Eviatar, "High-Churn American Workforce," *Christian Science Monitor,* 1 February 2000.

[20]   "The Hit Men," *Newsweek,* 26 February 1996, pp. 44–48; Laurence Zuckerman, "Boeing to Eliminate as Many as 7,000 Jobs," *New York Times,* 14 May 1999, p. C5; and Claudia H. Deutsch, "Xerox to Take $625 Million Write-Off and Eliminate 5,000 Jobs," *New York Times,* 1 April 2000 (http://www.nytimes.com).

[21]   Peter Cappelli, "Examining the Incidence of Downsizing and Its Effect on Establishment Performance," National Bureau of Economic Research Working Paper No. 7742 (June 2000); and Henry S. Farber and Kevin F. Hallock, "Have Employment Reductions Become Good News for Shareholders? The Effect of Job Loss Announcements on Stock Prices, 1970–97," National Bureau of Economic Research Working Paper No. 7295 (August 1999).

ing occurs.[22] This section investigates the dynamics of the labor market, with particular focus on the nature of the corporate restructuring that has taken place, as well as its economic consequences for employment probabilities, earnings, and job stability of women and men.

CORPORATE RESTRUCTURING IN THE 1980S AND 1990S

The structure of the U.S. economy has been rapidly changing from one with primarily an industrial base to a high-technology, service-oriented economy. For instance, between 1980 and 1999, the share of employment in manufacturing fell from 22 to 15 percent, while the share of service jobs expanded from 29 to 36 percent. These developments dramatically decreased the ranks of blue-collar workers.[23] Technological change has been an important force within all sectors of the economy and there have also been increasing pressures on firms to compete in the global market. An additional change is the increased practice of outsourcing, where companies contract out work within the United States or elsewhere rather than doing the work in-house, in part to avoid overhead costs associated with pensions and rising health insurance premiums, as well as the demands of unions. These factors have all served to increase involuntary terminations.

While highly publicized and dramatic layoffs as those noted above appear to have given the public an exaggerated view of the rising prevalence of job loss, economists are accumulating some economy-wide evidence of a moderate worsening of the displacement problem in the 1990s.[24] Table 8.5 provides data on the **job loss rate**—that is, the number of workers who suffered involuntary job loss during the past three years as a percentage of those employed. Reasons for such involuntary job losses include a shift or position being abolished, slack work conditions, or a plant closing. Table 8.5 and Figure 8.2 show that the job loss rates for the recessions of the early 1980s and early 1990s were virtually the same; about 13 percent of all workers lost their jobs during the three-year period 1981 to 1983 and again during the period 1991 to 1993. However, the recession of the early 1980s was considerably more severe than that of the early 1990s. From that perspective, we would have expected the job loss rate to be substantially lower in the early 1990s than in the early 1980s. The suggestion of a worsening problem is reinforced by the most recent data for the mid-1990s, which shows that the job loss rate increased even further, to 15 percent, despite the ensuing economic expansion.

Women have traditionally had lower rates of job loss than men, particularly in downturns. As discussed in greater detail in the section on gender differences in unemployment,

---

[22] See, for instance, Robert Tomsho, "Joblessness Is Low, So It's All the Harder Being Without a Job," *Wall Street Journal,* 25 July 2000, pp. A1, A12.

[23] U.S. Department of Labor, *Employment and Earnings* (January 1981 and January 2000). For further discussion see Susan N. Houseman, "Job Growth and the Quality of Jobs in the U.S. Economy," Special issue of *Labour* (1995): S93–S124.

[24] See Henry S. Farber, "The Changing Face of Job Loss in the United States, 1981–1995," *Brookings Papers on Economic Activity* (Microeconomics 1997): 55–128. While some other researchers did not find an *increase* in the risk of job loss in the 1990s, the fact that the rate of job loss was no *lower* in the 1990s than in the 1980s suggests a worsening displacement problem: Since economic conditions were better in the 1990s, a *reduction* in layoff rates would have been expected. See, for instance, Lori G. Kletzer and Robert W. Fairlie, "The Long-Term Costs of Job Displacement Among Young Workers," unpublished working paper, University of California, Santa Cruz (January 1999); and Steven Hipple, "Worker Displacement in an Expanding Economy," *Monthly Labor Review* 120, no. 12 (December 1997): 26–39. For a good review of the literature, see Lori G. Kletzer, "Job Displacement," *Journal of Economic Perspectives* 12, no. 1 (winter 1998): 115–36.

TABLE 8.5   Rate of Job Loss by Reason, 1981–1983, 1991–1993, 1993–1995[a]

	1981–1983		*1991–1993*		*1993–1995*	
	Total Job Loss	*Due to Position or Shift Abolished*	*Total Job Loss*	*Due to Position or Shift Abolished*	*Total Job Loss*	*Due to Position or Shift Abolished*
Overall, age 20–64	13.3	1.4	12.8	2.2	15.1	2.4
Men, age 20–64	15.2	1.4	14.4	2.3	15.8	2.3
Women, age 20–64	11.0	1.3	11.0	2.2	14.3	2.5
Age						
20–24	16.5	1.4	13.5	1.4	20.2	1.6
25–34	15.5	1.5	13.8	2.1	16.8	2.2
55–64	10.9	1.2	13.0	2.5	13.0	2.6
Education						
Less than high school	19.3	1.2	16.6	0.9	20.3	1.2
High school	14.8	1.3	13.5	1.8	16.1	2.0
4 years of college or more	7.4	1.5	9.5	2.7	11.3	3.2
Occupation						
Managers	8.2	1.4	9.7	3.0	7.8	2.4
Craftsworkers, operatives, and laborers	21.2	1.5	13.7	1.5	13.5	1.7

[a] Rate is the number of workers who involuntarily left a firm due to a shift or position being abolished, slack work conditions, a plant closing, or some other reason during the past three years as a percentage of those employed at the survey date.

Source: Figures are from Henry S. Farber, "The Changing Face of Job Loss in the United States, 1981–1995," *Brookings Papers on Economic Activity,* Special Issue, 1997: 55–128. Copyright ©1997. Used by permission of Brookings Institution.

this may be related to gender differences in occupations. Men have been more likely to hold cyclically sensitive blue-collar, manufacturing jobs, while women are more highly concentrated in white-collar and service jobs and in nonmanufacturing industries, making them less subject to job loss. However, as Table 8.5 and Figure 8.2 show, while job loss rates have risen for both men and women since the early 1990s, the increases were larger for women than for men. Thus, the gender gap in job loss rates has been cut in half, from 3.4 percentage points in 1991 to 1993 to 1.5 points in 1993 to 1995. At the same time, as indicated in Table 8.5, the job loss rate of blue-collar workers (craftsworkers, operatives, and laborers) was considerably lower relative to the overall rate in the early 1990s than it had been in the early 1980s. Further, while a blue-collar worker had a greater risk of job loss than workers overall during 1991 to 1993, such a worker had a lower risk during 1993 to 1995. Since economic conditions differed substantially over these periods, it is difficult to evaluate these changes, but they suggest that employment in white-collar jobs no longer shields workers from layoffs to the extent that it did in the past.

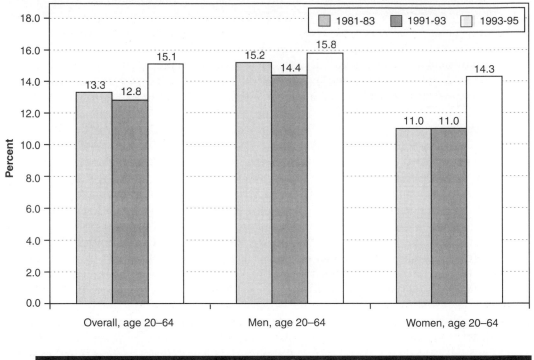

FIGURE 8.2 Total Job Loss Rates Computed Over Three Years

Source: See Table 8.5.

Recent layoffs are also significantly different from those in the past in several other ways. First, for both men and women, job loss due to a job or shift being abolished has become more prevalent since the 1980s, indicative of the process of downsizing and restructuring that has taken place in recent years.[25] Second, in addition to women becoming more prone to job loss compared to men, there have been other changes in the risk of job loss for particular groups. As may be seen in Table 8.5, more highly educated and older workers became increasingly vulnerable to layoffs between the early 1980s and the early 1990s, while job loss rates for younger and less-educated workers fell. Since then, job loss rates have risen for workers in all age and educational categories. Looking at the entire period, from the early 1980s through mid 1990s, the highly educated were the group that experienced the largest percentage increase in their rate of job loss, an increase of over 50 percent. This is consistent with a growing impact of corporate restructuring. In addition, the rate of job loss for managers increased initially in the early 1990s, though it declined thereafter. It has been suggested that this increase in their displacement rate may reflect a one-time adjustment, as firms modified their organizational structure and cut back on management in response to changes in information technology.[26]

---

[25] In addition, the catchall category "other reason for job loss" has increased substantially, though the reasons for this are not well understood; see Farber, "The Changing Face of Job Loss."

[26] Farber, "The Changing Face of Job Loss."

Job loss imposes real costs on workers, which cannot be masked by recent "layoff-speak" reminiscent of George Orwell's *1984* such as "downsizing," "separation," "being unassigned," or notification that a job "is not moving forward." Displaced workers may suffer subsequent unemployment, lower income, movement into part-time jobs, or underemployment in full-time jobs.[27] Even workers who retain their positions may be assailed by a sense of insecurity and the thought that "next time it could be me." The loss of coworkers can also lead to increased workloads and greater work-related pressures for those who remain. One recent study finds that men's and women's perceptions of job insecurity are fairly similar, but perceptions do vary substantially by race; blacks are twice as likely to expect that they will lose their jobs as whites.[28] Not surprisingly, those with higher levels of schooling tend to be less concerned about job security, on average, than those who have less education.

Still, it is important to place job loss in context. The U.S. economy generated a tremendous number of new jobs in the 1990s, much to the envy of many other economically advanced nations. Also, despite considerable concern, there is some evidence that the quality of the new jobs that are being created is not very different from existing jobs.[29] Nonetheless, the fact that these jobs are not very different does not necessarily bode well for workers with fewer skills, given evidence of a widening pay gap based on skill in existing jobs. In addition, newly hired workers are less likely to be eligible for employer-provided health insurance than in the past.[30] Before going on to consider the consequences of corporate restructuring and, more broadly, the implications of the changing labor market for women and men in greater detail, we first define the concepts of unemployment, underemployment, and discouraged workers and examine their prevalence in the labor market.

UNEMPLOYMENT

As we saw in Chapter 4, the official definition of **unemployment** includes all individuals not currently working for pay but actively looking for work or persons temporarily laid off from a job to which they expect to return.[31] The overall unemployment rate includes four types of unemployment: frictional, seasonal, structural, and cyclical. **Frictional unemployment** occurs when new entrants and reentrants enter the labor force, as well as when workers are between jobs, either having just quit or lost their last job. Given imperfect information, it will often take such individuals some time to find a job, even when

---

[27]   For a discussion of the personal consequences of corporate layoffs, see Alan Downs, *Corporate Executions* (New York: American Management Association, 1995).

[28]   Charles F. Manski and John D. Straub: Worker Perceptions of Job Insecurity in the Mid-1990s," *Journal of Human Resources* 35, no. 3 (summer 2000): 447–79.

[29]   Susan N. Houseman reports that the common view that new jobs are of poorer quality does not hold in many instances, though again opportunities for less-educated workers do appear to have deteriorated, in "Job Growth." For example, the general changes in the wage distribution, including the widening gap in pay between lesser and higher-skilled workers, is evident in both newly created and existing jobs.

[30]   Henry S. Farber and Helen Levy, "Recent Trends in Employer-Sponsored Health Insurance Coverage: Are Bad Jobs Getting Worse?" *Journal of Health Economics* 19, no. 1 (January 2000): 93–119.

[31]   For a formal definition, see U.S. Department of Labor, "How the Government Measures Unemployment," Report 864 (February 1994).

enough appropriate job openings are available.[32] **Seasonal unemployment** occurs due to seasonal variations in employment, such as a lack of jobs for construction workers in the snowbelt during the winter and for ski instructors during the summer. A more serious type of unemployment is **structural unemployment,** when those looking for work do not have the right skills or are not in the right location to fill the vacancies that exist. It is likely to be more persistent because these difficulties are not easily or quickly remedied. **Cyclical unemployment,** associated with an overall deficiency in demand, occurs when there is an excess of workers in relation to unfilled positions. Because the first three types of unemployment will exist to a greater or lesser degree even when there is no deficiency in overall demand, there is still some amount of unemployment even in an economy that has achieved full employment. The acceptable level of unemployment is typically called the **full-employment unemployment rate** or the **natural rate of unemployment.** It had for a long time been estimated to be around 5.5 percent, though the very low unemployment rates of the late 1990s and early 2000s, which were not accompanied by a surge of inflation, suggest it is now considerably lower.[33]

The ranks of the unemployed include new entrants into the labor market, reentrants, job losers (including displaced workers), and job leavers. New entrants are likely to be those who have recently left school or women entering the labor force after caring for their children full-time. Reentrants might be persons who left the labor market to get additional education, or women who did so in order to take care of their children. Job losers are workers who were involuntarily separated from their jobs for whatever reason. Finally, job leavers are those who voluntarily terminate employment and immediately begin (or perhaps continue) looking for another job.

Table 8.6 shows unemployment rates by gender, age, race, and Hispanic origin at various points in the business cycle for several years since 1979. These data indicate that unemployment rates are particularly high among blacks of all ages, around double those of whites, for both men and women.[34] Possible explanations include lower levels of education and fewer skills, a lack of jobs located near communities where blacks live, regional shifts in the demand for workers that have been unfavorable to blacks, and racial discrimination.[35] Black unemployment has also been found to be especially responsive to local labor market conditions, with black men and women ben-

---

[32] The majority of those who change jobs do not, however, experience unemployment because most workers search while holding on to the old job until they have found a new one. See J. Peter Mattila, "Job Quitting and Frictional Unemployment," *American Economic Review* 64, no.1 (March 1974): 235–39. Similarly, many labor market entrants never experience a period of unemployment; see Ronald G. Ehrenberg, "The Demographic Structure of Unemployment Rates and Labor Market Transition Probabilities," in *Research in Labor Economics,* vol. 3, ed. Ronald G. Ehrenberg (Greenwich, CT: JAI Press, Inc., 1980), p. 253.

[33] Ronald G. Ehrenberg and Robert S. Smith, *Modern Labor Economics: Theory and Public Policy,* 7th ed. (Reading, MA: Addison-Wesley, 2000), p. 595. For an analysis of the factors contributing to the decline in the U.S. unemployment rate from the 1980s to the late 1990s, see Lawrence F. Katz and Alan B. Krueger, "The High-Pressure U.S. Labor Market of the 1990s," *Brookings Papers on Economic Activity,* no. 1 (1999): 1–65.

[34] Also of concern, as we saw in Chapter 4, a much higher fraction of black as compared to white men are not included in the labor force at all, or are incarcerated and hence not included in workforce statistics. For figures based on the 1990 census, see Chandra, "Labor-Market Dropouts."

[35] See Harry Holzer, for example, "Black Employment Problems: New Evidence, Old Questions," *Journal of Policy Analysis and Management* 13, no. 4 (fall 1994): 699–722; and Robert W. Fairlie and William A. Sundstrom, "The Emergence, Persistence, and Recent Widening of the Racial Unemployment Gap," *Industrial and Labor Relations Review* 52, no. 2 (January 1999): 252–70.

TABLE 8.6 Unemployment Rates by Sex, Age, Race, and Hispanic Origin, Selected Years[a]						
	1979	*1983*	*1990*	*1992*	*1995*	*1999*
All, age 16–19						
Men	15.9	23.3	16.3	21.5	18.4	14.7
Women	16.4	21.3	14.7	18.5	16.1	13.2
All, age 20 and over						
Men	4.2	8.9	4.9	7.0	4.8	3.5
Women	5.7	8.1	4.9	6.3	4.9	3.8
Whites, age 16 and over						
Men	4.5	8.8	4.8	6.9	4.9	3.6
Women	5.9	7.9	4.6	6.0	4.8	3.8
Blacks, age 16 and over						
Men	11.4	20.3	11.8	15.2	10.6	8.2
Women	13.8	18.6	10.8	13.0	10.2	7.8
Hispanics, age 16 and over						
Men	7.0	13.5	7.8	11.5	8.8	5.6
Women	10.3	13.8	8.3	11.3	10.0	7.6

[a] Civilian labor force

Source: Employment and Training Report of the President (1982); *Employment and Earnings* (January), various issues.

efiting much more from tighter labor markets than do whites.[36] Hispanics of all ages also tend to have higher unemployment rates than whites, although among males the difference is less than between blacks and whites. The unemployment rate of Hispanic men and women has been found to be more responsive to local labor market conditions than that of whites, but less so than that of blacks.[37] Table 8.6 also shows that teens have substantially higher unemployment rates than adults. Differences in teen unemployment by sex and race for 1999 are highlighted in Figure 8.3. All groups of teens had unemployment rates that were considerably above the overall national rate of about 4 percent. Black teens had the highest rates, with nearly one-third of young black men and about one-quarter of young black women unemployed. While young black women had considerably lower unemployment rates than young black men, gender differences in unemployment rates were small for Hispanic and white teens. These figures clearly show that it is young black men who are at the greatest disadvantage in the labor market, even a buoyant one, as compared to all other groups.

For the population as a whole, gender differences in the unemployment rate tended to be fairly small compared to differences between whites and minorities or teens and adults. For instance, Table 8.6 shows that in 1979 the unemployment rate of women was 1.5 points higher than men's. As we shall see in greater detail later, this illustrates a gen-

---

[36] Cordelia W. Reimers, "The Effect of Tighter Labor Markets on Unemployment of Hispanics and African Americans: The 1990s Experience" and Richard B. Freeman and William M. Rodgers III, "Area Economic Conditions and the Labor-Market Outcomes of Young Men in the 1990s Expansion," in *Prosperity for All? The Economic Boom and African Americans,* ed. Robert Cherry and William M. Rodgers III (New York: Russell Sage Foundation, 2000), pp. 3–49 and 50–87.

[37] Reimers, "The Effect of Tighter Labor Markets"; however, Reimers finds that while blacks benefit more from labor market tightness than whites, even controlling for industry, occupation, education, and age, Hispanic unemployment, especially of men, tends to be less sensitive to local unemployment rates than that of whites once these controls are added.

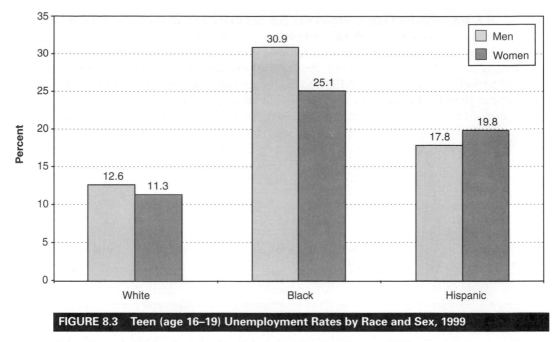

FIGURE 8.3 Teen (age 16–19) Unemployment Rates by Race and Sex, 1999

Source: Bureau of Labor Statistics, *Employment and Earnings* (January 2000).

eral pattern prevailing prior to the early 1980s when the female unemployment rate tended to be higher than the male rate, especially in relatively prosperous times. Interestingly, that pattern still prevails to some extent among Hispanics, though not among whites or blacks. For the other years shown in the table, the unemployment rates of men and women overall tend to be about the same in prosperous years, while in recession years, the male rate tends to exceed the female rate.

OTHER INDICATORS OF EMPLOYMENT PROBLEMS

While the unemployment rate is a useful indicator of the health of the economy, it is an incomplete tool for fully assessing either economic hardship for workers or loss of output for the economy. For one thing, unemployment rates fail to provide information about underemployed workers. **Underemployment** occurs when workers have to take jobs for which they are clearly overqualified, or when they work fewer hours than they would prefer. Examples of the former would be an MBA taking a housecleaning job or a skilled automobile worker harvesting fruit. Examples of the latter are persons who would prefer to work full-time but are unable to find such employment and so work part-time. They are classified as **part-time for economic reasons** or sometimes called **involuntary part-time workers.**[38] These problems tend to arise more often in a slack labor market, when the recorded unemployment rate is also high.

---

[38] Specifically, this measure only counts those who worked part-time in the survey week *and* who usually work part-time for economic reasons, as discussed in Leslie S. Stratton, "Reexamining Involuntary Part-Time Employment," *Journal of Economic and Social Measurement* 20 (1994): 95–115; and Thomas J. Nardone, "Part-Time Workers: Who Are They?" *Monthly Labor Review* 109, no. 2 (1986): 13–19.

Second, measured unemployment rates fail to include **discouraged workers.** These are individuals who would like a job, but have not looked for work within the prior four weeks because they believe their search would be futile. Thus, since they are not classified as currently looking for work, they are not included among the unemployed nor in the labor force. Since January 1994, to be counted as a discouraged worker, individuals must explicitly state that they are available to take a job and must have looked for work within the past year; this was not the case in the past. Primarily as a result of these changes in definition, estimates of the number of discouraged workers were substantially reduced. Moreover, women were affected to a greater extent than men: The number of women classified as discouraged fell by two-thirds, while the number of men declined by 50 percent.[39] Women who, as a group, are likely to have weaker attachment to the labor market than men traditionally had higher rates of discouragement than men, although, under the new, more stringent definition, female and male rates are about the same.

TRENDS IN THE GENDER DIFFERENCE IN UNEMPLOYMENT AND RELATED MEASURES

The gender difference in the overall unemployment rate for men and women, shown in greater detail in Figure 8.4, has fluctuated over time. While women traditionally had higher unemployment rates than men, in recent years, this differential has virtually disappeared. The small and changing gender gap in unemployment rates shown in the figure has been the net result of various factors working in opposing directions. It appears that, over time, the balance of these forces has shifted.

The first major factor affecting unemployment is *labor force attachment.* On average, women are less firmly attached both to the labor force as a whole and to particular jobs than men, although, as discussed in Chapter 4, the difference has been declining. The higher labor force turnover of women in comparison to men has an ambiguous effect on their relative unemployment rates.

On the one hand, the larger proportion of entrants or reentrants among women in the labor force tends to increase female relative to male unemployment rates. This is the case because many will undergo a period of frictional unemployment as they search for jobs. As a consequence, a higher proportion of unemployed women than unemployed men is comprised of labor market entrants or reentrants; in 1999, for example, this was true of 42 percent of unemployed women, but only 26 percent of unemployed men.[40] On the other hand, unemployed women are considerably more likely than unemployed men to exit the labor force. This results in their being counted as "out of the labor force" rather than unemployed. This factor is particularly important during recessions and helps to explain why the female rate of measured unemployment tends to rise less than the male unemployment rate during economic downturns. Indeed, in both

---

[39] See U.S. Department of Labor, Bureau of Labor Statistics, "Revisions in the Current Population Survey Effective January 1994," *Employment and Earnings* (February 1994), table 9. There is some question about whether categories that are used by the Bureau of Labor Statistics such as "unemployed," "marginally attached," and "discouraged" provide meaningful distinctions. For a discussion, see, Stephen R. G. Jones and W. Craig Riddell, "The Measurement of Unemployment: An Empirical Approach," *Econometrica* 67, no. 1 (January 1999):147–62.

[40] The 1999 figures on the reasons for unemployment cited here and later are from U.S. Department of Labor, *Employment and Earnings* (January 1999), p. 203.

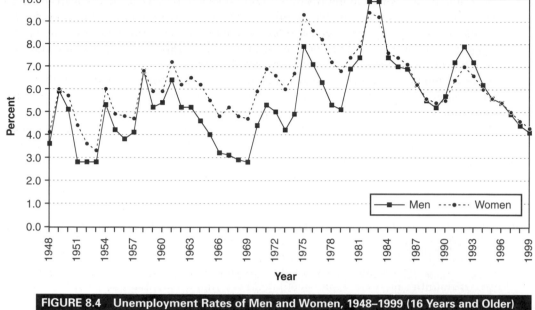

FIGURE 8.4 Unemployment Rates of Men and Women, 1948–1999 (16 Years and Older)

the 1982–1983 and 1990–1991 recessions, the male unemployment rate exceeded the female unemployment rate.

The second major factor that contributes to differences in male and female unemployment rates is that men and women tend to be employed in different occupations and industries. Like labor force attachment, gender differences in *employment by occupation and industry* have an ambiguous effect on the gender gap in unemployment rates. On the one hand, men are more heavily represented in blue-collar jobs and in durable manufacturing, sectors that have above-average layoff and unemployment rates. Women are more likely to be employed in white-collar jobs, which have lower layoff and unemployment rates. On the other hand, women are also disproportionately represented in service occupations, which have above-average unemployment rates. On balance, occupational distribution appears to lower the female unemployment rate relative to the male rate as suggested by the higher proportion of men than women who tend to be unemployed because they lost their last job. For example, in 1999, 60 percent of unemployed men compared to 43 percent of unemployed women were job losers.[41] The fact that blue-collar jobs and durable-goods manufacturing industries, which have a larger proportion of male workers, are subject to greater cyclical variations in employment also helps to explain why the difference in male and female unemployment rates changes over the business cycle. Men's unemployment rate tends to rise more in downturns than women's, but also declines more during upswings.

---

[41] See also Francine D. Blau and Lawrence M. Kahn, "Causes and Consequences of Layoffs," *Economic Inquiry* 19, no. 2 (April 1981): 270–96.

Prior to the 1980s, the net result of these opposing forces was that women's unemployment rates were higher than men's. An added factor may have been that, during this earlier period, women faced considerable competition for entry jobs from the growing number of young workers, both male and female, who were also seeking employment, as the large baby boom cohort entered the job market.

Beginning in the 1980s, women's unemployment rates have tended to be about the same as men's, or, during recessions, even lower. One reason for this may be the increase in women's labor force attachment, which, as we saw in Chapter 4, has reduced their labor force turnover relative to men's. In addition, demand shifts have benefited women relative to men, as the service industries, which have traditionally had a high concentration of women, have expanded relative to the manufacturing industries, which disproportionately employ men. In addition, as the baby bust cohort has entered the job market, there has been a declining number of young people competing with women for entry-level jobs.

Figures on discouraged workers and involuntary part-time employment also indicate some differences by gender and changes over time, as shown in Table 8.7. Each category is shown as a percentage of the total labor force. As previously noted, the discouraged worker rate, which has historically been higher for women than men, is now about the same for each group as a result of the change in the definition of this measure. The impact of this change may be seen by comparing the discouraged worker rates for 1995 with those for 1979 and 1990, before the change in the definition. Although the unemployment rate was about the same in each of the three years, the measured discouragement rate was higher for both men and women in 1979 and 1990 than afterwards. Moreover, in the earlier years, the female rate exceeded the male rate whereas, under the new measure of discouragement, the female and male rates are the same.

Table 8.7 also shows that, in each year, a larger proportion of women than men in the labor force are employed part-time for economic reasons. One explanation on the supply side is that women may perceive themselves to be less stigmatized than men when they work part time and, therefore, be more willing to take such jobs when they have problems finding full-time work. On the demand side, higher female rates of involuntary part-time employment may reflect employer behavior. For instance, some employers may prefer to hire women on a part-time basis, despite the women's own preferences for full-time work, in order to evade government mandates that they perceive as costly, such as the Family and Medical Leave Act.[42] While this is a potential concern, the data for 1995 and 1999 do not provide any evidence that rates of involuntary part-time employment have increased for women since the passage of this legislation, either absolutely or relative to men.

ECONOMIC CONSEQUENCES OF RESTRUCTURING AND LAYOFFS

The economic and emotional toll of job loss depends, in large part, on workers' ability to find new jobs and the wages associated with these jobs. Table 8.8 shows the employment outcomes of workers with three or more years of job tenure who were displaced between January 1997 and December 1999. It indicates that nearly three-fourths had

---

[42]   See Leslie Stratton, "Are Involuntary Part-Time Workers Indeed 'Involuntary?' " *Industrial and Labor Relations Review* 49, no. 3 (April 1996): 522–36.

TABLE 8.7   Alternative Measures of Employment Problems of Men and Women, Selected Years

Year and Group	Official Unemployment Rate (%)	Discouraged Worker Rate (%)	Involuntary Part-Time Rate (%)
1979			
Total	5.8	0.7	1.9
Men	5.1	0.5	1.2
Women	6.8	1.1	2.9
1990			
Total	5.5	0.7	2.6
Men	5.6	0.5	2.0
Women	5.4	0.9	3.3
1995			
Total	5.6	0.3	2.4
Men	5.6	0.3	2.0
Women	5.6	0.3	3.0
1999			
Total	4.2	0.2	1.6
Men	4.1	0.2	1.3
Women	4.3	0.2	2.0

Notes: Data refer to civilians 16 years of age and over. The unemployment, discouraged worker, and involuntary unemployment rates are computed as percentage of the labor force. Part-time rates were based on nonagricultural workers for 1979 and all workers for the remaining years. As explained in the text, data on discouragement for 1995 and 1999 are not comparable to earlier years.

Sources: U.S. Department of Labor, *Employment and Earnings* (January issues); U.S. Department of Labor, *Handbook of Labor Statistics,* 1989.

found new jobs as of February 2000. While most, though not all, displaced workers find employment, many of these workers initially end up in nonstandard employment arrangements—temporary work, performing work they used to do on a contract basis, starting a consulting business selling their services, or working part-time involuntary—outcomes generally associated with lower pay. For instance, one recent study finds that while only 12 percent of displaced workers were displaced from part-time jobs in the mid-1990s, 17 percent of displaced workers found reemployment in part-time jobs. However, there is evidence that such arrangements tend to be only temporary in nature, part of a transitional process back to full-time, regular employment.[43]

Not surprisingly, it has been found that reemployment rates are higher when jobs are relatively plentiful, as was the case in the 1990s after the 1990–1991 recession. Reemployment rates also tend to be higher for workers in service-producing industries and

---

[43] Farber, "The Changing Face of Job Loss"; and Henry S. Farber, "Alternative and Part-Time Employment Arrangements as a Response to Job Loss," *Journal of Labor Economics* 17, no. 4, pt. 2 (October 1999): 142–69.

TABLE 8.8   Employment Outcomes of Workers Displaced from Their Jobs Between January 1997 and December 1999

	Total Number Displaced (in millions)	Employment Status as of February 2000 (%)		
		Re-employed	Unemployed	Not in Labor Force
Total				
Age 20 and older	3.28	73.5	10.4	16.1
Age 55–64	0.52	56.0	13.6	30.4
Men				
Age 20 and older	1.77	78.9	9.6	11.5
Age 55–64	0.28	62.9	13.3	23.8
Women				
Age 20 and older	1.51	67.3	11.3	21.4
Age 55–64	0.24	47.9	14.0	38.1

Notes: Figures are for workers who had three or more years of tenure on their last job and were displaced between January 1997 and December 1999 because of plant or company closings or moves, insufficient work, or the abolishment of their positions or shifts.

Source: Bureau of Labor Statistics, "Worker Displacement During the Late 1990s," USDL 00-223 (9 August 2000).

for those in white-collar versus blue-collar occupations. Nonetheless, women, who are more likely than men to be in service industries and white-collar occupations, typically have lower rates of reemployment overall and are much more likely to drop out of the labor force altogether following a job loss. This pattern, which is reflected in Table 8.8, is consistent with historically higher rates of discouragement among women than men. It may reflect traditional gender roles that make it easier for women to fall back on the homemaker role, as well as difficulties they face in the labor market that lower the probability of reemployment and the rewards to extended search. Table 8.8 further shows that older workers, especially older women, are less likely to be reemployed, either because of the difficulty of retooling, the decision to take early retirement, or because of age discrimination. It has also been found that reemployment rates depend on the displaced worker's educational attainment: More highly educated workers tend to have higher rates of reemployment because they can better take advantage of new labor market opportunities.[44]

Workers who find new jobs frequently receive lower wages than in their prior positions. It has been estimated that five or more years after displacement, displaced workers earn 10 to 18 percent below what their counterparts who were not displaced earned.[45] The wage penalty due to displacement can arise for two reasons, either be-

---

[44] For evidence on the various factors mentioned, see Farber, "The Changing Face of Job Loss." See also Robert W. Fairlie and Lori G. Kletzer, "Jobs Lost, Jobs Regained: An Analysis of Black/White Differences in Job Displacement in the 1980s," *Industrial Relations* 37, no. 4 (October 1998): 460–77.

[45] This estimate, based on a review of the literature, is from Kletzer and Fairlie, "The Long-Term Costs." See also Kletzer, "Job Displacement."

cause the worker is not able to reap the rapid early career wage growth he or she would have experienced in the initial position, or because of the decline in wages due to the loss of firm-specific human capital that results from changing jobs. One study finds that for young workers it is the former effect that is quite large, while for older workers it is the latter effect that is more important.[46] In considering the full economic costs of displacement, it is important to also take account of the fact that some workers end up in part-time work although they would have preferred full-time employment, others end up in full-time jobs but are underemployed, while still others may fail to find a new job altogether.

For families, the economic consequences of job loss may also depend on whether there is more than one wage earner. Dual-earner families, as compared with traditional families with a single (male) wage earner, are more likely to be buffered from the full consequences of unemployment, especially if the husband and wife work in different industries or at least for different firms. Consequently, one might speculate that the risk of marital dissolution as a result of layoffs is likely to be particularly high for single-earner families. For them, layoffs not only mean financial hardship but may also increase the risk of marital dissolution because of the related stress associated with the job loss of the sole breadwinner.

A final issue concerns the question of whether or not and to what extent the patterns of job loss, reemployment, earnings, and job stability have changed over time. We have already seen that rates of job loss are up somewhat, compared to earlier periods. Further, rates have particularly increased among older and more highly educated workers, though these groups continue to have lower rates than younger, less-educated workers. In contrast, the evidence suggests that the consequences of job loss in terms of re-employment and earnings do not appear to have changed much from the early 1980s to the mid-1990s.[47]

Moreover, while it does appear that employment relationships between workers and firms weakened somewhat in the 1990s, there is not yet evidence of a long-term decline in job tenure for workers overall.[48] However, there does appear to have been a compositional shift in who holds these jobs. Women, especially those with a high school education or more, are now considerably more likely to have jobs that have lasted 20 years or more, while less-educated men are much less likely than previously to hold such jobs.[49] This signals progress for women, but also points to yet another negative effect of low education on economic outcomes. That is, low education is not only associated with low real earnings increases and falling employment rates, but also with a lower probability of reemployment following job loss and a lower probability of "lifetime" employment.

---

[46]   Kletzer and Fairlie, "The Long-Term Costs."

[47]   Farber, "The Changing Face of Job Loss."

[48]   For two recent comprehensive reviews of the evidence, see David Neumark, "Changes in Job Stability and Job Security: A Collective Effort to Untangle, Reconcile, and Interpret Evidence," National Bureau of Economic Research Working Paper No. 7472 (January 2000); and David A. Jaeger and Ann Huff Stevens, "Is Job Stability in the United States Falling? Reconciling Trends in the Current Population Survey and Panel Study of Income Dynamics," *Journal of Labor Economics* 17, no. 4, pt. 2 (October 1999): 1–28.

[49]   Henry S. Farber, "Are Lifetime Jobs Disappearing? Job Duration in the U.S.: 1973–1993," in *Labor Statistics Measurement Issues,* ed. John Haltiwanger, Marilyn Manser, and Robert Topel (Chicago: University of Chicago Press, 1996): pp. 157–206.

Summary on Restructuring and Job Loss

This section examined the impact of corporate restructuring on reemployment, earnings, and job stability. When evaluating gender differences in the effects of corporate restructuring and the overall incidence of employment problems, the picture is mixed. On the one hand, the displacement rate has tended to be lower for women than men and unemployment rates of men and women are now about the same. On the other hand, women are less likely than men to be reemployed after a job loss and are considerably more likely to leave the labor force, which may have a particularly negative effect on their long-term wage and employment prospects. Nonetheless, women who retain their jobs appear to be staying in them longer. This section also provides evidence that the consequences of displacement are more serious for older workers and that less-educated workers confront a declining probability of obtaining long-term, stable employment.

Looking toward the future, it is very likely that workers of both sexes will continue to face the prospect of job loss and downsizing as the economy continues to adapt to changing technology, globalization, and other developments. Policies can be designed to reduce the cost of job loss to the individual somewhat. Among the improvements suggested by policy makers are programs aimed at enhancing workers' education and job skills to keep pace with advances in technology and computerization.[50] In addition, legislation was enacted in 1996 to allow workers who had health insurance through their employer to remain covered when they suffer a job loss or change jobs. This law should be helpful in assisting workers, especially those with preexisting conditions, in coping with job loss, as well as facilitating voluntary job moves. It does not, however, ensure that coverage will be affordable or provide assistance for those workers who are currently uninsured to become insured.

THE RISE OF THE NONSTANDARD WORK FORCE

There is some evidence that the proportion of people in the labor force who do not have "regular" full-time jobs has been increasing, with estimates for the 1990s ranging between 25 to 30 percent of the work force when part-time workers, as well as workers in various alternative employment arrangements, are included.[51] This section defines the nonstandard work force, explains recent trends, and then looks at the consequences of these trends for American workers and their families.

Definition of the Nonstandard Work Force

Nonstandard workers are those who do not hold "regular," full-time jobs. They include workers defined by the Bureau of Labor Statistics (BLS) as having "alternative" or nontraditional employment arrangements; that is, "individuals whose employment is

---

[50]   Robert B. Reich, "Rescuing Castoff Workers," *St. Louis Post-Dispatch,* 8 March 1996, page 7B.

[51]   See, for instance, Richard S. Belous, *The Contingent Economy: The Growth of the Temporary, Part-Time, and Subcontracted Workforce* (McLean, VA: National Planning Association, 1989); and Marianne A. Ferber and Jane Waldfogel, " 'Contingent' Work: Blessing or Curse," Radcliffe Public Policy Institute paper, February 1996. For a comprehensive examination of this type of employment, see the contributions by Francoise Carré, Marianne A. Ferber, Lonnie Golden, and Steve Herzenberg, eds., *Nonstandard Work Arrangements and the Changing Labor Market: Dimensions, Causes, and Institutional Responses,* Industrial Relations Research Association Research Volume (2000).

arranged through an employment intermediary such as a temporary help firm, or individuals whose place, time, and quantity of work are potentially unpredictable."[52] Four major categories of workers in alternative arrangements have been identified by the BLS: **temporary help agency workers ("temps"), on-call workers, contract workers,** and **independent contractors.** Many of these workers, particularly among those employed as temps and on-call workers, would be classified as in "contingent" jobs, that is, jobs in which an individual "does not have an explicit or implicit contract for long-term employment."[53] Our definition of the nonstandard work force also includes **part-time workers,** those who work less than 35 hours per week.

Temporary help agency workers are employed by agencies and sent out to other businesses as they are needed. **On-call workers** or limited duration hires are only employed as needed, generally for a short time; they include, for instance, substitute teachers and construction workers supplied by a union hiring hall. **Contract workers** are employed by a firm that contracts out employees or services to other companies; they supply such services as cleaning, security, landscaping, or computer programming.[54] **Independent contractors** or freelance workers are individuals who obtain customers on their own to whom they provide a product or service. Management consultants, freelance writers, and textbook editors are all examples of occupations in which some individuals work on a freelance basis. Individuals who are self-employed business operators, such as shop owners or restaurateurs, are not included in this category.

The status of **part-time workers** is less clear since many are employed by a single employer for an extended period of time, and so, perhaps from this perspective, should not be included. They are, however, included in our estimates of the nonstandard work force on the basis that they share a number of the same problems as others in this category, such as often having limited training and promotion opportunities and receiving few if any benefits.

Table 8.9 gives a breakdown of the employment arrangements included in our definition of nonstandard work. In all, about 9 percent of employed workers were in alternative employment arrangements as temps, on-call workers, independent contractors, and contract workers.[55] Including part-timers in otherwise traditional employment arrangements brings the total to 25 percent. Women are overrepresented among nonstandard workers; it is estimated that 57 percent of such workers were women, as compared to 46 percent of all employed workers. However, the representation of women varies consid-

---

[52] Anne E. Polivka, "Contingent and Alternative Work Arrangements, Defined," *Monthly Labor Review* 119, no. 10 (October 1996): 3–9, p. 7.

[53] Polivka, "Contingent and Alternative Work Arrangements, Defined," p. 4. A recent government report estimated that 56 percent of temps, 28 percent of on-call workers, and 20 percent of contract workers were contingent, but this was true of only 3 percent of independent contractors. In contrast, 3 percent of workers in traditional employment arrangements were classified as contingent. See U.S. Department of Labor, Bureau of Labor Statistics, "Contingent and Alternative Employment Arrangements, February 1999," *News,* USDL 99–362, 21 December 1999.

[54] To be included under alternative employment arrangements, contract workers had to report that they usually had only one customer and worked at the customer's worksite. These requirements distinguish contract workers from those employed by companies that obtain contracts to carry out work assignments, such as advertising agencies, equipment manufacturers, lawyers, or employees of economic "think tanks." See Polivka, "Contingent and Alternative Work Arrangements, Defined," p. 8.

[55] Focusing on contingent workers, that is, workers without an implicit or explicit contract for long-term employment, the Bureau of Labor Statistics estimates that 1.9 to 4.3 percent of workers are contingent; see U.S. Department of Labor, Bureau of Labor Statistics, "Contingent and Alternative Employment

TABLE 8.9　Nonstandard Workers in the Labor Force, 1999

	Percent Female	*Percent of All Employed*
I.　Alternative Employment Arrangements		
On-call workers	51.2	1.5
Temporary help agency workers	57.8	0.9
Independent contractors	33.8	6.3
Workers provided by contract firm	29.5	0.6
Subtotal	38.8	9.3
II.　Part-Time Workers (not included above)	67.6[a]	15.5
III.　Total Nonstandard Workers (sum of I and II)	56.8[a]	24.8

[a] Percentage female for "Part-Time Workers (not included above)" is based on all part-time workers.

Sources: U.S. Department of Labor, Bureau of Labor Statistics, "Contingent and Alternative Employment Arrangements, February 1999," Report 99-362 (December 1999); and U.S. Department of Labor, Bureau of Labor Statistics, *Employment and Earnings* (January 2000).

erably by employment arrangement. Women comprise the vast majority of part-time workers, and are overrepresented among temps and on-call workers. They are, however, underrepresented among independent contractors and contract workers. As we shall see, the latter two categories include the largest proportions of highly educated workers and those in managerial and professional jobs, and are also relatively well-paid compared to the others.

The largest fraction of nonstandard workers are part-timers, a group that has long been a feature of the labor market. In the 1950s, they comprised 12 percent of employed workers. That number had risen to 17 percent by 1999, 68 percent of whom were women. The proportion of involuntary part-time workers (those who could not find full-time jobs) has ranged from a low of 17 percent of all part-time workers during relatively prosperous periods, to a high of 32 percent during recessions.[56] Even so, the proportion of voluntary part-time workers remains large, especially among women, often homemakers; young people, often students; and older people, often retired or in transition to retirement.

DIFFERENCES AMONG NONSTANDARD WORKERS

Additional information about workers in alternative employment arrangements is shown in Table 8.10, with the last column of the table giving the characteristics of workers in traditional arrangements for purposes of comparison. Taken together, Tables 8.9 and 8.10 show that nonstandard workers are quite heterogeneous, differing substantially by sex, race, age, and level of education. As noted earlier, women, young people, and the elderly

Arrangements." An additional category of workers who might be considered in alternative employment arrangements is **direct-hire temporaries** who were hired into a temporary job directly by a company rather than through a temporary agency. The BLS does not explicitly collect information on this category, but it was estimated to be 2.6 percent of employed workers in 1997; see Anne Polivka, Sharon R. Cohany, and Steven Hipple, "Definition, Size, Types and Demographic Composition of the Nonstandard Work Force," in Carré et al., *Nonstandard Work Arrangements,* pp. 41–94.

[56]　Chris Tilly, "Reasons for the Continuing Growth of Part-Time Employment," *Monthly Labor Review* 114, no. 3 (March 1991): 10–18; and U.S. Department of Labor, *Employment and Earnings.*

TABLE 8.10 Characteristics of Workers in Selected Alternative Employment Arrangements,1999

	Independent Contractors (%)	*On-Call Workers (%)*	*Temporary Help Agency Workers (%)*	*Contract Firms (%)*	*Workers in Traditional Arrangements (%)*
Sex					
Female	33.8	51.2	57.8	29.5	47.6
Male	66.2	48.8	42.2	70.5	52.4
Race and Hispanic Origin					
White	90.6	84.2	74.3	79.2	84.0
Black	5.8	12.7	21.2	12.6	11.4
Hispanic origin	6.1	11.6	13.6	6.0	10.4
Education					
Bachelor's degree or more	34.3	27.9	21.2	38.9	31.1
Occupation					
Executive, administrative, and managerial	20.5	5.3	4.3	12.0	14.6
Professional specialty	18.5	24.3	6.8	28.8	15.5
Technicians and related support	1.1	4.1	4.1	6.7	3.3
Sales occupations	17.3	5.7	1.8	1.5	12.0
Administrative support	3.4	8.2	36.1	3.4	15.0
Service occupations	8.8	23.5	8.1	18.8	13.7
Precision production, craft, and repair	18.9	10.1	8.7	16.0	10.5
Operators, fabricators, and laborers	7.0	16.0	29.2	10.7	13.6
Farming, forestry, and fishing	4.4	2.9	0.9	2.2	2.0
Employment Status					
Part-time	24.9	50.7	21.5	13.2	17.1

Note: Persons of Hispanic origin may be of any race.

Source: U.S. Department of Labor, Bureau of Labor Statistics, "Contingent and Alternative Employment Arrangements, February 1999," USDL 99-362 (December 1999).

are considerably more likely to work part-time than prime-age men. Similarly, women are overrepresented among on-call and temporary help workers, but underrepresented among independent contractors and workers provided by contract firms. Table 8.10 shows that minorities were also heavily represented among temporary workers and underrepresented among independent contractors and Hispanics, but not blacks, are underrepresented among contract workers. In addition, the representation of both blacks and Hispanics among on-call workers is similar to their representation in traditional arrangements.

There are also large differences in the occupational distribution of different types of nonstandard workers. Temps are frequently employed in administrative support positions. Most of the smaller but growing proportion of men in this category are nonwhite, and tend to be mainly in industrial jobs. On-call workers increasingly include skilled as well as unskilled, and white-collar as well as blue-collar workers. Some firms have also been forming pools of retirees who agree to be on call. Unlike most other nonstandard workers, a large number of independent contractors are employed in executive and managerial positions, as well as professional and sales jobs. In fact, these workers are found in a broad array of occupations, from textbook editors and real estate agents, to building cleaners. Workers provided by contract firms to other companies are most likely to be in service occupations, such as landscaping or janitorial work, and professional specialties, including computer programmers, as well as blue-collar categories, including skilled precision production and craft jobs. Not surprisingly, given these occupational breakdowns, independent contractors and workers in contract firms are more likely than workers in traditional arrangements to have completed a bachelor's degree or more, with some 34 to 39 percent in this category, compared to 31 percent of workers in traditional arrangements. On-call workers are somewhat less likely to have college degrees than traditional workers and temps are considerably less likely.

Overall, contract workers and independent contractors tend to outearn similar workers in traditional arrangements, while on-call and temporary workers earn less. Similarly, while workers in all alternative arrangements were less likely than those in traditional arrangements to be covered by health insurance and pensions, among them, contract workers and independent contractors were most likely to be covered while on-call and temporary workers were least likely to be covered.[57]

EXPLANATIONS BEHIND THE RISE
OF NONSTANDARD WORKERS

There is little agreement about the extent to which such growth as there has been in nonstandard jobs has been caused by increased demand on the part of employers or an increase in the supply of workers who prefer such arrangements.

On the demand side, small and medium-size firms, especially, may benefit from the use of contracted services in specialized areas like computer support, since it may not be cost effective for them to hire a full computer support staff if skills, such as programming, are needed only occasionally. It has also been argued that if production is characterized by peak and off-peak periods, firms may find it cost effective to contract out during peak periods in order to dispense with the need to carry surplus workers in slow times or avoid the costs of repeated hiring and firing of workers. One study finds evidence in favor of both of these explanations in influencing a firm's decision to "contract out."[58] In addition, there is also evidence that the use of nonstandard workers provides a way to screen future employees.[59] Losses of regular jobs have also been caused

---

[57] Steven Hipple and Jay Stewart, "Earnings and Benefits of Workers in Alternative Work Arrangements," *Monthly Labor Review* 119, no. 10 (October 1996): 46–54.

[58] Katherine G. Abraham and Susan K. Taylor, "Firms' Use of Outside Contractors: Theory and Evidence," *Journal of Labor Economics* 14, no. 3 (July 1996): 394–424. Looking more broadly at market-mediated work arrangements, another study reports that an important reason for the employment of temporary workers is to buffer the firm from fluctuations in demand, while employment of contract workers is often explained by the desire for specialized services that cannot be economically provided in-house; see Katherine G. Abraham, "Restructuring the Employment Relationship: The Growth of Market-Mediated Work Arrangements," in *New Developments in the Labor Market,* ed. Katherine G. Abraham and Robert B. McKersie (Cambridge, MA: MIT Press, 1990), pp. 85–118.

[59] See Dale Belman and Lonnie Golden, "Contingent and Nonstandard Work Arrangements in the United States: Dispersion and Contrasts by Industry, Occupation and Job Type," in Carré et al., eds., *Nonstandard Work Arrangements,* pp. 167–212; and David H. Autor, "Why Do Temporary Help Firms Provide Free General Skills Training?" National Bureau of Economic Research Working Paper No. 7637 (April 2000).

in part by businesses abolishing them or shifting them to nonstandard positions in an attempt to cut costs. Indeed, a recent trend has been for firms that have downsized to hire back some workers on a contingent basis.[60] Further, some high-wage companies contract out for services rather than use their regular work force because they want to pay relatively lower wages or reduced benefits, but do not want to create inequities within the ranks of their own workers.

From the supply-side perspective, there is no doubt that various types of nonstandard work have attracted men and women, whether they are students, young people exploring career options, adults reentering the labor market, homemakers in need of flexibility because of family responsibilities, or older people in transition to retirement. Also, some nonstandard jobs can be very attractive, and on occasion pay higher wages to compensate for the uncertainty and lower benefits.[61]

While the reasons just offered explain why firms and workers might choose to make use of nonstandard arrangements, they do not explain why such employment appears to have increased. Among the possible explanations may be that job growth has been more rapid in industries where nonstandard work arrangements are more common, although, for temporary help, it has been found that practically all of the growth in such jobs between 1977 and 1997 was due to a change in the hiring behavior of firms, rather than to a disproportionate increase in the size of industries that use temporary help more intensively.[62] Another factor may be that the cost of benefits, health insurance especially, has risen substantially, increasing the incentive for firms to hire nonstandard workers in order to avoid these expenses. In addition, over the period of expansion in the temporary help services industry, there have been growing restrictions on firms' ability to hire and fire workers due to state judicial decisions limiting the common law doctrine of "employment at will."[63] Finally, there are greater numbers of small firms, and, as noted earlier, these firms are most likely to benefit from the purchase of specialized skills from outside sources.

---

[60] The Bureau of Labor Statistics estimates that, in 1995, 19 percent of on-call workers, 9 percent of temps, 12 percent of contract workers, and 22 percent of independent contractors had previously worked for their current employer under another arrangement. (Note that these figures may include retirees and others who have voluntarily left their regular jobs, as well as workers who have been involuntarily terminated.) Similarly, a survey by the American Management Association of 720 firms that had recently downsized found that 30 percent had brought back terminated employees on contract or as rehired employees. See Louis Uchitelle, "More Downsized Workers Are Returning as Rentals," *New York Times,* 8 December 1996, pp. 1 and 34.

[61] As we have seen, among workers in alternative employment arrangements, contract workers and independent contractors have especially high wages. It has been pointed out there are "good" and "bad" part-time jobs as well; see Rebecca M. Blank, "Are Part-Time Jobs Bad Jobs?" in *A Future of Lousy Jobs?* ed. Gary Burtless (Washington, DC: Brookings Institution, 1990), pp. 123–55; and Chris Tilly, "Two Faces of Part-Time Work: Good and Bad Part-Time Jobs," in *Working Part-Time: Risks and Opportunities,* ed. Barbara D. Warme, Katherina L. P. Lundy, and Larry A. Lundy (New York: Praeger, 1992).

[62] Marcello Estavao and Saul Lach, "The Evolution of the Demand for Temporary Help Supply Employment in the United States," in Carré et al., eds., *Nonstandard Work Arrangements,* pp. 123–44.

[63] David H. Autor estimates that firms' response to these decisions accounts for 20 percent of the growth of the temporary help services industry between 1973 and 1995, in "Outsourcing at Will: Unjust Dismissal Doctrine and the Growth of Temporary Help Employment," National Bureau of Economic Research Working Paper No. 7557 (February 2000).

CONSEQUENCES FOR WORKERS AND THEIR FAMILIES

Nonstandard work is likely to have consequences for workers and their families. Most obviously, such workers will tend to have less job security because the average duration of their jobs is relatively short as compared with regular full-time jobs.[64] Part-time workers may be more attached to their employers than others in nonstandard jobs, but even they have shorter tenure on average than those who work full-time, are more likely to be assigned to routine jobs, and often receive less training as well as fewer promotions. In addition, nonstandard workers generally lack the protection provided by labor unions, in part because they are especially difficult to organize, in part because unions for a long time opposed part-time employment. Perhaps most importantly, while it is not clear whether or not nonstandard workers earn lower wages than regular workers with comparable qualifications, they usually receive substantially fewer benefits, including sick pay, holidays, health insurance, and unemployment coverage; nor do most of them accumulate pension rights, and they generally accumulate fewer Social Security benefits.[65]

To the extent that many of these problems tend to have more serious effects in the long run than in the short run, and to the extent that individuals are unaware of this or have a short planning horizon, it may be that even many people who choose nonstandard employment voluntarily will eventually suffer serious negative consequences as a result of their choice. This is not likely to be true for young people who take these kinds of jobs while they are students and are building up their human capital in preparation for entering the labor market full-time, or for women who work part-time or in an alternative employment arrangement for a few years while their children are small, instead of dropping out of the labor force entirely.[66] It is, however, a more serious concern for those who use nonstandard employment as a long-term substitute for, rather than as a prelude to, a regular job.

For instance, young people who have earnings more or less comparable to their peers in standard jobs may not be unduly concerned about the fact that their wages are likely to rise less over the years or that they often have no health insurance or pension rights. They may not look ahead to the time when they have greater problems finding a new job if the need arises because their discontinuous employment history is likely to be held against them by potential employers. Others may be less concerned about benefits because they are married and covered under their spouse's policy. Should the re-

---

[64] Susan N. Houseman and Anne E. Polivka, "The Implications of Flexible Staffing Arrangements for Job Security," (New York: Russell Sage Foundation, forthcoming).

[65] For example, while 58 percent of workers with traditional employment arrangements were covered by employer-provided health insurance, this was true of only 21 percent of on-call workers and 9 percent of temps. Health benefit coverage of workers employed by contract firms was, however, fairly similar to that of traditional workers. (No information was available for independent contractors.) Employer-provided pension coverage was also considerably lower for independent contractors, on-call workers, and temps than for those in traditional arrangements, but, again, coverage was similar for workers employed by contract firms. See U.S. Department of Labor, Bureau of Labor Statistics, "Contingent and Alternative Employment Arrangements."

[66] Among employed women in their thirties, those who had given birth during the preceding two years were much less likely to be in a regular full-time work arrangement than were women who did not have a birth; see Donna S. Rothstein, "Entry into and Consequences of Nonstandard Work Arrangements," *Monthly Labor Review* 119, no. 10 (October 1996): 75–82.

lationship end, however, their lack of benefits could become a serious difficulty. Single heads of families with young children may take nonstandard jobs, even though they find it very difficult to manage with the low earnings and scanty benefits, because they value the flexibility. Their situation may deteriorate further when, in time, they are faced with education expenses for their children, occasional medical emergencies, and, eventually, retirement, without adequate provisions for any of these eventualities.

SUMMARY ON NONSTANDARD WORKERS

The proportion of the labor force that holds nonstandard jobs has risen in part because employers often find alternative arrangements more advantageous, but also in part because there are men, and even more women, who find some of these alternative arrangements attractive.[67] Nonetheless, lack of benefits, job security, and opportunities for training and promotion are undesirable features of many of these jobs. In this respect, it is of concern that women are overrepresented among these workers. Because it is likely that some workers desire these employment arrangements and others would be unsuccessful in obtaining regular jobs, it would be counterproductive to advocate restrictions on such jobs. However, as such arrangements continue to expand, policy makers need to consider how important benefits like health care and pensions may be provided to growing numbers of workers who do not receive them from their employers.

THE GROWTH IN SELF-EMPLOYMENT

Another labor market trend in recent years has been the increase since the 1970s in the share of the nonagricultural labor force that is self-employed, although this trend appears to have flattened out since the mid-1990s.[68] As may be seen in Table 8.11, between 1975 and 1996, the self-employment rate (percentage of workers who are self-employed) increased from 7.4 to 9.6 percent. Of particular note is the sharp rise in the self-employment rate for women from 4.1 percent in 1975 to 7.1 percent in 1996. The increase has been slower for men, thus, the gender "self-employment gap" has been narrowing. Nonetheless, nearly 12 percent of men were self-employed in 1996 as compared with just over 7 percent of women. The patterns identified in Table 8.11—men's higher rates of self-employment along with larger increases in women's rate of self-employment—have also been found for an extensive set of race and ethnic groups. However, rates for women in the United States vary considerably by group; for instance, the self-employment rate for Korean women was 9 times higher than the rate for African American women.

---

[67] In 1999, only 9 percent of independent contractors reported that they preferred a traditional employment arrangement; this was, however, true of higher fractions of on-call workers and temps, 47 percent and 57 percent, respectively; see U.S. Department of Labor, Bureau of Labor Statistics, "Contingent and Alternative Employment Arrangements."

[68] Self-employment is defined here to include both those individuals who identify themselves as mainly self-employed in their own unincorporated businesses, typically sole proprietorships with no employees, as well as those running their own, typically larger, incorporated businesses. In contrast, the U.S. Bureau of Labor Statistics includes only individuals in an unincorporated business as self-employed and counts those running an incorporated business as wage and salary workers. Based on the BLS definition, the number and share of Americans outside of agriculture who were self-employed decreased between 1994 and 2000; see David Leonhardt, "Self-Employment on the Decline," *New York Times,* 1 December 2000 (www.nytimes.com).

TABLE 8.11   Self-Employment Rates of Women and Men in the Nonagricultural Sector, 1975–1996 (percent)

Year	*Self-Employment Rate*		
	Total	*Women*	*Men*
1975	7.4	4.1	10.0
1979	8.6	5.3	11.3
1989	9.4	6.6	11.9
1996	9.6	7.1	11.9

Notes: Includes individuals 16 years of age and older. The self-employed include workers in both unincorporated and incorporated businesses.

Sources: 1975 data: Theresa J. Devine, "Characteristics of Self-Employed Women in the United States," *Monthly Labor Review* 117, no. 3 (March 1994): 20–34. Remaining years from Marilyn E. Manser and Garnett Picot, "The Role of Self-Employment in U.S. and Canadian Job Growth," *Monthly Labor Review* 122 no. 4 (April 1999): 10–25.

More generally, rates of self-employment among African Americans, both men and women, are among the lowest of any group, in part due to the fact that they tend to have fewer assets and less access to credit than other groups.[69]

These recent trends raise at least two interrelated questions. First, what are the reasons for the increase in female self-employment? Second, what are its implications for women's economic status? With respect to the second question, it is highly likely that, on balance, the breakthrough of women into a new area represents an expansion of opportunities and choices and is thus a positive development. However, as we have seen, workers sometimes turn to self-employment when they are displaced from their jobs and, in addition, some of the growth in self-employment likely reflects the increase in independent contractors who comprise one component of the nonstandard work force. Moreover, while there are a number of complex measurement issues, the average hourly earnings of female self-employed workers are lower than those of female wage and salary workers, even among those who work full-time and full-year, while the opposite is the case for men.[70] The earnings difference between female self-employed and wage and salary workers might reflect productivity differences between the two groups. Although self-employed women are typically older and better educated than wage and salary women,[71] there is some evidence that earnings differences in part reflect less favorable unmeasured characteristics of self-employed women.[72] Women may also be

---

[69]   Robert W. Fairlie and Bruce D. Meyer, "Ethnic and Racial Self-Employment Differences and Possible Explanations," *Journal of Human Resources* 31, no. 4 (fall 1996): 757–93; Robert W. Fairlie, "The Absence of the African-American Owned Business: An Analysis of the Dynamics of Self-Employment," *Journal of Labor Economics* 17, no. 1 (January 1999): 80–108; Jan E. Christopher, "Minority Business Formation and Survival: Evidence on Business Performance and Viability," *Review of Black Political Economy* 26, no. 1 (summer 1998): 37–72; and Timothy Bates, *Race, Self-Employment and Upward Mobility* (Baltimore, MD: Johns Hopkins Press, 1997), pp. 261–68.

[70]   Theresa J. Devine, "Characteristics of Self-Employed Women in the United States," *Monthly Labor Review* 117, no. 3 (March 1994): 20–34.

[71]   Devine, "Characteristics of Self-Employed Women"; and Karen V. Lombard, "Female Occupational Choice: Working for Oneself or Someone Else" (Ph.D. diss., University of Chicago, June 1993).

[72]   This view receives some support from an examination of the effects of changes in type of employment on wage growth by Marianne A. Ferber and Jane Waldfogel, "The Long-Term Consequences of Nontraditional Employment," *Monthly Labor Review* 121, no. 5 (May 1998): 3–12.

willing to forgo some income for the ability to determine their own hours and other work arrangements as self-employed workers. Earnings differences of this type would fall under the category of a compensating differential. However, it is also true that self-employed workers are less likely to have health care coverage, and, when they are covered, particularly among women, they are less likely to receive coverage through their own jobs.[73] Moreover, it has been found that women returning to the wage and salary sector after a spell of self-employment experience lower earnings growth upon return, perhaps due to the depreciation of firm or sector-specific capital. In contrast, little or no effect on earnings has been found for men who return to the wage and salary sector from self-employment.[74]

A variety of explanations have been offered for the growth in women's self-employment. Perhaps a reasonable starting place is to inquire what motivates women and men to enter self-employment in the first place. For both groups, the greater their earnings potential in self-employment, the more likely they are to choose it. Moreover, the ability to set one's own hours is likely to be attractive to both men and women, but particularly to women seeking to combine family and work responsibilities. In addition, the presence of a spouse who already has health insurance coverage would make the choice of self-employment more attractive.[75] Finally, it has been suggested that women seek to enter self-employment to escape from a glass ceiling that limits their advancement in the wage and salary sector.[76] While all these factors may contribute to individual decisions about whether or not to become self-employed, some evidence suggests that the rising relative earnings potential of women in self-employment explains most of the *upward trend* in the self-employment of married women between 1970 and 1990.[77] This also reinforces the notion that the growing move into self-employment of women does represent a desirable expansion in their opportunities.

---

[73] Devine, "Characteristics of Self-Employed Women"; and Ferber and Waldfogel, "The Long-Term Consequences of Nontraditional Employment."

[74] Donald R. Williams, "Consequences of Self-Employment for Women and Men in the United States," *Labour Economics* 7, no. 5 (September 2000): 665–87; see also Ferber and Waldfogel, "The Long-Term Consequences of Nontraditional Employment."

[75] Karen V. Lombard finds evidence for each of these explanations for married women's self-employment decision; see "Female Self-Employment and the Demand for Flexible, Non-Standard Work Schedules," unpublished working paper, University of Miami, January 1996. For evidence on the attractiveness to women of the greater flexibility offered by self-employment, see also Richard J. Boden Jr., "Flexible Working Hours, Family Responsibilities, and Female Self-Employment: Gender Differences in Self-Employment Selection," *Journal of Economics and Sociology* 58, no. 1 (January 1999): 71–83; and Greg Hundley, "Male/Female Earnings Differences in Self-Employment: The Effects of Marriage, Children, and the Household Division of Labor," *Industrial and Labor Relations Review* 54, no. 1 (October 2000): 95–114.

[76] See, for example, Dorothy P. Moore and E. Holly Buttner, *Women Entrepreneurs Moving Beyond the Glass Ceiling* (Thousand Oaks, CA: Sage Publications, 1997).

[77] Lombard, "Female Occupational Choice: Working for Oneself or Someone Else." Consistent with this, Devine, "Characteristics of Self-Employed Women in the United States," reports that earnings of female self-employed workers rose relative to those of wage and salary workers between 1975 and 1990. In addition, Theresa J. Devine obtains findings that are not consistent with the rise in female self-employment being primarily a response to a glass ceiling on women wage and salary workers in "Changes in Wage-and-Salary Returns to Skill and the Recent Rise in Female Self-Employment," *American Economic Review* 84, no. 2 (May 1994): 108–13.

THE CHANGING FACE OF LABOR UNIONS

One of the reasons for the lower wages of women has been their low representation in unions compared to men. However, over the past 30 years, union membership has undergone a major transition and is becoming increasingly female. In this section we take a closer look at these trends.

REPRESENTATION OF WOMEN IN LABOR UNIONS

Overall union membership, which reached a high of about one-quarter of the U.S. labor force in the mid-1950s, has been declining steadily since then. As may be seen in Table 8.12, by 1999 only 13.9 percent of workers were in unions. One reason for this decline was the shift in industrial structure away from heavily unionized sectors like manufacturing. Because these have largely been the bastions of men, this has also resulted in a decline in the gender difference in unionization. At the same time, there has been an increase in unionization in sectors in which women are heavily represented, such as the public sector, and among white-collar and service workers, including clerical, grocery, and health care workers.[78] Thus, while women continue to be underrepresented in labor unions in comparison to their share of the labor force, as of 1999 they comprised nearly 40 percent of union members, up from less than 20 percent in the mid-1950s.

BENEFITS OF UNION MEMBERSHIP FOR WORKERS

The historic underrepresentation of women in unions is a cause for concern to some because unions confer benefits on their members that women thus enjoy to a lesser extent than men. Unions have been found to increase the wages of their members, although the union wage premium tends to vary by occupation and industry. Overall, the union relative wage advantage appears to have remained fairly constant from the mid-1950s to the early 1990s, at around 15 percent.[79] Most research suggests that the union wage gain is at least as large for women as it is for men, and there is some evidence that unions may raise women's wages more than men's.[80] As women become more attached to the labor force and gain seniority, the economic advantages of unionization to them may increase because unions tend to provide generous benefits to workers with more

---

[78]   See Richard B. Freeman and Jonathan S. Leonard, "Union Maids: Unions and the Female Work Force," in *Gender in the Workplace,* ed. Clair Brown and Joseph A. Pechman (Washington, DC: The Brookings Institution, 1987), pp. 189–216; and Julie Kosterlitz, "Luring Women to Labor's Ranks," *National Journal* 29, no. 11 (March 15, 1997): 541.

[79]   See H. Gregg Lewis, *Union Relative Wage Effects: A Survey* (Chicago: University of Chicago Press, 1986), cited in Robert J. Flanagan, Lawrence M. Kahn, Robert S. Smith, and Ronald G. Ehrenberg, *The Economics of the Employment Relationship* (Glenview, IL: Scott, Foresman, and Co., 1989), pp. 552–53; and David G. Blanchflower, "Changes Over Time in Union Relative Wage Effects in Great Britain and the U.S." National Bureau of Economic Research Working Paper No. 6100 (July 1997). For international evidence, see Lawrence M. Kahn, "Collective Bargaining and the Interindustry Wage Structure: International Evidence," *Economica* 65, no. 260 (November 1998): 507–34.

[80]   Blanchflower finds no differences by race or gender in the union wage advantage for the United States in "Changes Over Time"; but Freeman and Leonard, "Union Maids," do find some evidence that union wage gains in the public sector are higher for women than men. See also Heidi Hartmann, Roberta Spalter-Roth, and Nancy Collins, "What Do Unions Do for Women?" *Challenge* 37, no. 4 (July/August 1994): 11–18.

TABLE 8.12   Representation of Women in Labor Organizations, Selected Years, 1956–1999

| Year | Women's Share of | | Union Membership as a Percent of Employed Workers | | |
	All Employed Workers	Membership in Labor Organizations	Men	Women	Total
Unions only:					
1956	32.0	18.5	32.2	15.7	27.0
1966	35.6	19.3	30.7	13.1	24.4
Unions and associations:					
1970	37.7	23.9	32.9	16.9	26.8
1980					
All	42.4	30.1	25.1	14.7	20.7
Whites	41.7	28.3	24.4	13.4	19.8
Blacks[a]	48.1	40.7	31.5	23.2	27.5
1990					
All	47.2	36.9	19.3	12.6	16.1
Whites	46.7	35.4	18.8	11.7	15.5
Blacks	51.5	44.0	24.4	18.0	21.1
Hispanics[b]	40.5	34.3	16.3	12.5	14.8
1999					
All	48.0	39.6	16.1	11.4	13.9
Whites	47.1	38.2	15.7	10.9	13.5
Blacks	54.1	45.3	20.5	14.4	17.2
Hispanics[b]	41.8	36.7	13.0	10.4	11.9

[a] Includes other nonwhites.

[b] Hispanics may be of any race.

Sources: U.S. Department of Labor, Bureau of Labor Statistics, "Earnings and Other Characteristics of Organized Workers," Bulletin 2105 (May 1980), Table 2, p. 2; Linda H. LeGrande, "Women in Labor Organizations: Their Ranks Are Increasing," *Monthly Labor Review* 101, no. 8 (August 1978), Table 1, p. 9; *Employment and Training Report of the President* (1981), Table A-16, pp. 144–46; *Employment and Earnings* 38, no. 1 (January 1991), p. 228; and U.S. Department of Labor, Bureau of Labor Statistics, *News,* February 9, 1996; and U.S. Department of Labor, Bureau of Labor Statistics, "Union Members in 1999" (January 2000).

seniority.[81] Nonetheless, as long as women continue to be underrepresented in unions (as compared with their representation in the labor force as a whole), the impact of unions is to widen the male–female pay gap since men benefit from the union wage premium to a greater extent than women. Indeed, as we have seen, the *decrease* in unionism has contributed to a reduction in the male–female wage gap because it has been associated with a *decrease* in the male advantage in unionization. The mechanism for this narrowing has been a greater loss of high-paying union jobs for men, as unionism fell more for them than for women.[82]

---

[81]   William E. Even and David A. Macpherson, "The Decline of Private Sector Unionism and the Gender Wage Gap," *Journal of Human Resources* 28, no. 2 (1993): 279–96.

[82]   Even and Macpherson, "The Decline of Private Sector Unionism"; Francine Blau and Lawrence Kahn, "Rising Wage Inequality and the U.S. Gender Gap," *American Economic Review* 84, no. 2 (May 1994): 23–28; and Blau, "Trends in the Well-Being of American Women." In the latter paper, Blau reports that the decline in unionism lowered the real wages of men by 2.8 percent and of women by 1.6 percent, thereby narrowing the gender gap.

Unions have also been found to increase the fringe benefits of their members relative to their nonunion counterparts. Indeed, their effect on benefits has been found to be greater (in percentage terms) than on wages. Finally, some argue that unions provide important nonpecuniary benefits to their members, chiefly by giving them a greater opportunity to shape their work environment by communicating their preferences to employers through the collective bargaining process and by providing for grievance procedures.[83] From a broader social perspective, unions, on balance, reduce wage inequality among all workers by providing relatively high-paying job opportunities for many less-skilled workers. This means that deunionization has contributed to rising wage inequality in the United States.[84] There have also been reports of unions working to eliminate gender-based tracking in a variety of industries, so that entry-level workers, whether in a female-dominated or male-dominated job, could have the same opportunities for promotion.[85] Unions also have the potential to help reduce tension between work and family by negotiating for family leave, on-site day care, and flexible schedules. Such benefits are not only particularly important for women workers, but also increasingly for men, as they share more household responsibilities.

While unions offer many potential advantages to workers, including higher wages and greater fringe benefits, to the extent that the demand for labor is responsive to cost, unionization is also associated with lower employment. Hence, the gains of those who get greater rewards are in part at the expense of those who are not hired, or are displaced, due to unionization.

REASONS FOR THE UNDERREPRESENTATION OF WOMEN IN UNIONS

In light of the advantages of union membership, how do we explain the underrepresentation of women in unions?

On the one hand, there is no evidence that women have a lesser "taste" or preference for unionism. In fact, survey evidence indicates that women tend to be more supportive of collective action to achieve goals than men and are more likely to vote for a union.[86] On the other hand, women tend to be concentrated in industries and occupations where, for whatever reason, unionization is below average. Traditionally, unionization has been highest among blue-collar workers in manufacturing, whereas women have been concentrated in clerical and service occupations and in service industries, which have much lower rates of unionization. Moreover, within the manufacturing sector, women are concentrated in the more competitive industries, while unionization has been higher in monopolistic industries. It has been found that three-fourths of the difference in unionization between men and women is explained by the underrepresenta-

---

[83]   Richard B. Freeman has termed this the "voice effect" of unions; see "Individual Mobility and Union Voice in the Labor Market," *American Economic Review* 66, no. 2 (May 1976): 361–68. The evidence on fringes is from Richard B. Freeman and James L. Medoff, *What Do Unions Do?* (New York: Basic Books, 1984).

[84]   Richard B. Freeman, "How Much Has De-Unionization Contributed to the Rise in Male Earnings Inequality?" in *Uneven Tides: Rising Inequality in America,* ed. Sheldon Danziger and Peter Gottschalk (New York: Russell Sage Foundation, 1993), pp. 133–64.

[85]   Amy Waldman, "Labor's New Face," *Nation* 265, no. 8 (22 September 1997): 11–16.

[86]   Freeman and Medoff, *What Do Unions Do?* Other evidence is provided by a 1996 survey as cited in Waldman, "Labor's New Face."

tion of women in highly organized occupations and sectors. But this also means that the economy-wide shift away from blue-collar and manufacturing jobs has worked to decrease the gender gap in unionization in recent years.[87]

Historically, the policies of unions themselves have no doubt also contributed to women's underrepresentation among their ranks. Male craft unions did not begin to admit women until the late 1800s[88] and failed to be hospitable to women (or blacks) long after they no longer formally excluded them. Also, unions have been criticized for their less than vigorous efforts to organize women workers and lack of support for women's own efforts to unionize. Moreover, unions have tended to emphasize issues of concern to male workers and to neglect female concerns, thus lowering the appeal of unions for women. For example, the emphasis of unions on fringe benefits like health insurance would be of less value to women workers because many of them are members of two-earner families and are frequently already covered under their husbands' plans. On the other hand, the growing emphasis in recent years on provision of such benefits as parental leave and day care is likely to be of greater interest to women than to men.

THE GLASS CEILING IN UNION LEADERSHIP

As in corporate America, women appear to face a glass ceiling when it comes to union leadership positions, especially top posts at both the national and local levels. Although comprehensive data on the number of women in leadership positions in unions are not collected on a regular basis, there is considerable evidence to support this contention. Among the nearly 70 national unions affiliated with the American Federation of Labor-Congress of Industrial Organization (AFL-CIO) in 1997, just three had a female president (the Retail, Wholesale, and Department Store Union, the Association of Flight Attendants, and the American Federation of Teachers), although this represented a slight improvement over 1975 when there were none.[89] In addition, in 2000 only 12 percent of AFL-CIO executive council members were women.[90] The Coalition of Labor Union Women (CLUW), an advocacy group, was formed in 1974 with the express goal of moving women into such positions, but its impact at that level appears to have been fairly modest to date.

Women have been somewhat more successful in attaining middle-level positions at the local level such as union steward or member of the local executive board, and have even reached some top-level positions. In the early 1990s, more than 35 percent of local officers in the American Federation of State, County and Municipal Employees (AFSCME), the American Federation of Teachers (AFT), the National Education Association (NEA), the Communications Workers Association (CWA), and the Service Employees' International Union (SEIU) were women. Even in local unions with largely

---

[87] Even and Macpherson, "The Decline of Private Sector Unionism."

[88] Barbara M. Wertheimer and Anne H. Nelson, " 'Union Is Power': Sketches from Women's Labor History," in *Women: A Feminist Perspective,* 4th ed., ed. Jo Freeman (Palo Alto, CA: Mayfield, 1989), pp. 312–28. See also Margaret S. Coleman, "Undercounted and Underpaid Heroines: The Path to Equal Opportunity Employment During the Twentieth Century," *Working USA* 3, no. 5 (January/February 2000): 37–65.

[89] Figure for 1975 cited in Dale Melcher, Jennifer L. Eichstedt, Shelley Eriksen, and Dan Clawson, "Women's Participation in Local Union Leadership: The Massachusetts Experience," *Industrial and Labor Relations Review* 45, no. 2 (1992): 267–80; figure for 1997 cited in Waldman, "Labor's New Face."

[90] "About AFL-CIO," AFL-CIO web site (May 2000), www.aflcio.org.

male memberships such as the United Auto Workers (UAW), there are now some women in key positions. Nonetheless, among the four major elected posts, president, vice-president, treasurer, and secretary, women tend to be most heavily represented in the secretary position, which is the lowest rung.[91] In fact, one study of unions affiliated with the local AFL-CIO in Massachusetts found that over one-half of women in the top four positions held that job. Moreover, every female president and vice-president was in a local with at least 40 percent female members. Women were also significantly under-represented in other key officer positions including steward, which is often a stepping-stone to higher office, and as chair of negotiations and grievance committees.[92]

The reasons for the lack of women in key leadership roles are complex, but most likely reflect the same types of barriers encountered by women in other organizations, from corporations and foundations to government elective office. Studies point to a variety of obstacles that inhibit women's participation at high levels. First, since women generally have primary responsibility in the home, employed women must juggle home and job responsibilities, leaving little time available for union activities. Such participation can require as much as 20 to 40 hours of work per week and, at the local level, is often unpaid. A second and related factor is that election to leadership positions often takes years of working with the rank and file members in order to reach top posts. Many men begin these activities in their twenties, while many women find it particularly difficult to participate at that age, which coincides with their childbearing years.[93] Third, it has been found that women tend to underestimate their abilities and are thus less likely to place themselves on a leadership "career track."

As is true in other organizations, the underrepresentation of women in union leadership positions itself also hinders women's advancement because it reduces the opportunities for women to receive informal mentoring and to find role models. It also makes it more likely that women will be perceived as outsiders. In addition, women must often contend with overt sexual harassment as well as the perception that women are not "tough" enough to negotiate contracts or participate in bargaining. Finally, women frequently lack the crucial education and experience required for leadership positions, such as negotiating skills and institutional knowledge about union offices.[94]

IMPROVED PROSPECTS FOR WOMEN IN UNIONS

In the face of all these problems, there have been important recent efforts at the national level in the AFL-CIO and among international unions to open up leadership positions to women. Under the auspices of its president, John Sweeney, the AFL-CIO has created the position of executive vice-president to be filled by a woman trade union activist. In addition, the executive council was expanded to allow for greater female representation, and one position was designated for a representative from the Coalition of

---

[91]   Lois S. Gray, "The Route to the Top: Female Union Leaders and Union Policy," in *Women and Unions: Forging a Partnership,* ed. Dorothy Sue Cobble (Ithaca, NY: ILR Press, 1987). See also Helen Elkiss, "Training Women for Union Office: Breaking the Glass Ceiling," *Labor Studies Journal* 19, no. 2 (summer 1994): 25–41.

[92]   Melcher et al., "Women's Participation."

[93]   Helen Elkiss finds that most women in union administration are white, middle-aged single women who either have grown children or no children; see "Training Women for Union Office."

[94]   See Gray, "The Route to the Top."

Labor Union Women, signaling the importance of this group. Another step was to create a Working Women's Department in an effort to reach out to current and potential women union members. To promote grass roots change, the national AFL-CIO is helping local unions with outreach and training for women. Still, change is likely to come slowly, even at the local level, because women's representation in leadership roles is starting from such a low level.

Individual unions have also taken steps to expand opportunities for women.[95] Many have formed women's committees to take greater account of women workers' needs. Although taking this approach runs the risk of marginalizing women's issues, such committees provide women with the opportunity to actively participate in the union and gain leadership experience. Further, an increasing number of unions have begun to reserve seats on executive committees for women, and some have guaranteed women proportional representation on executive boards. Again, there is a risk. It is possible that women will be viewed as mere tokens, especially if they are appointed to such posts rather than elected. But these positions do provide them with an up close view of the decision-making process. Finally, international unions have directed specific efforts toward education, including emphasis on public speaking, negotiating, and building self-confidence, in an effort to develop women's leadership skills.

Some routes to leadership positions for women do not require special efforts by unions. Founders of new unions typically end up as leaders. This was true, for example, of Karen Nussbaum, who was a founder of 9 to 5, which was subsequently affiliated with the SEIU. A more likely route that may help women reach the top is working for a union in an area of technical expertise, such as in human resources, pensions, occupational safety and health, education, or the legal department.[96]

SUMMARY ON UNIONS

Women have long been underrepresented in unions and thus have been less likely than men to receive the benefits that unions can confer on their members, including higher wages and fringe benefits and a greater say in workplace decisions. Nonetheless, changes are occurring. Ironically, since the decline in unionism has proceeded more rapidly among men than women, women's share of union membership has increased considerably. In addition, perhaps because unions increasingly perceive the importance of organizing women to halt further declines in their membership, they are making greater efforts to bring women into leadership positions.

CONCLUSION

In this chapter we began by emphasizing that the gender wage gap has narrowed considerably since the late 1970s. During these years women's real wages continued to rise while those of men stagnated, and real wages of low-skilled men even declined as earnings inequality rose rapidly. In the face of rising returns to skill, women, who on aver-

[95] Anne Trebilcock, "Strategies for Strengthening Women's Participation in Trade Union Leadership," *International Labour Review* 130, no. 4 (1991): 407–26.

[96] Gray, "The Route to the Top"; and Michelle Hoyman, "Working Women: The Potential of Unionization and Collective Action in the United States," *Women's Studies International Forum* 12, no. 1 (1989): 51–58.

age still have lower qualifications than men, managed to overcome this disadvantage by substantially upgrading their qualifications, especially their experience and occupations. They also benefited from a decrease in the unexplained gender gap, which may represent a decline in discrimination, an improvement in women's qualifications that we are not able to measure using conventional data sources, or more favorable demand shifts for women than for men.

Next we examined a number of other developments in the labor market, from restructuring and the growth of nonstandard work and self-employment, to the decline and changing role of labor unions, and considered the impact of each on the position of women in the labor force. Some have enhanced women's advancement, while others have tended to inhibit it, but it is clear that, overall, women as a group have managed to make steady progress. On the other hand, this is far less true of women who have few educational credentials. Moreover, a growing proportion of them head single-parent families. The difficulties faced by single-parent families is one of the subjects discussed in Chapter 9. Chapter 10, in turn, discusses recent changes in welfare policy and their impact on these families.

QUESTIONS FOR REVIEW AND DISCUSSION

1. Discuss the advantages and disadvantages of our "high-churning" economy. How does your answer differ for women? less-skilled workers? older women? older men? minority workers?

2. Explain why economists, especially in times of recession, try to keep track of discouraged workers, as well as those who are unemployed. How do these groups differ?

3. It is said that there are factors that "push" and "pull" individuals into self-employment. Provide an example or two of each.

4. Explain why teen unemployment rates are so much higher than for workers who are age 20 and over.

5. What factors caused the gender earnings ratio in the United States to increase from 61 percent in 1979 to 75 percent by 1988, according to the study by Blau and Kahn cited in the text? Based on these results, can you conclude discrimination against women in the labor market has declined? Why or why not?

6. What are the pros and cons of being employed in nonstandard employment?

7. For many individuals in the United States, health insurance depends on their employment. Consider this situation in light of the recent employment trends discussed in the text.

Suggested Readings

Blau, Francine D., and Lawrence M. Kahn. "Swimming Upstream: Trends in the Gender Wage Differential in the 1980s." *Journal of Labor Economics* 15, no. 1, pt. 1 (January 1997): 1–42.

Carré, Francoise, Marianne A. Ferber, Lonnie Golden, and Steve Herzenberg, eds. *Nonstandard Work Arrangements and the Changing Labor Market: Dimensions, Causes, and Institutional Responses.* Industrial Relations Research Association Research Volume, 2000.

Cobble, Dorothy Sue, ed. *Women and Unions: Forging a Partnership.* Ithaca, NY: ILR Press, 1987.

Devine, Theresa J. "Characteristics of Self-Employed Women in the United States," *Monthly Labor Review* 117, no. 3 (March 1994): 20–34.

Freeman, Richard B., and Peter Gottschalk. *Generating Jobs: How to Increase Demand for Less-Skilled Workers.* New York: Russell Sage Foundation, 1998.

Freeman, Richard B., and James L. Medoff. *What Do Unions Do?* New York: Basic Books, 1984.

Hartmann, Heidi, Roberta Spalter-Roth, and Nancy Collins. "What Do Unions Do for Women?" *Challenge* 37, no. 4 (July/August 1994): 11–18.

Holzer, Harry. "Black Employment Problems: New Evidence, Old Questions," *Journal of Policy Analysis and Management* 13, no. 4 (fall 1994): 699–722.

Juhn, Chinhui, Kevin M. Murphy, and Brooks Pierce. "Wage Inequality and the Rise in Returns to Skill." *Journal of Political Economy* 101, no. 3 (June 1993): 410–42.

Katz, Lawrence F., and Kevin M. Murphy. "Changes in Relative Wages, 1963–87: Supply and Demand Factors." *Quarterly Journal of Economics* 107, no. 1 (February 1992): 35–78.

Kruse, Douglas, and Joseph Blasi. "The New Employee-Employer Relationship." In *A Working Nation: Workers, Work, and Government in the New Economy,* by David T. Ellwood, Rebecca M. Blank, Joseph Blasi, Douglas Kruse, William A. Niskanen, and Karen Lynn-Dyson, chap. 2, pp. 42–91. New York: Russell Sage Foundation, 2000.

Levy, Frank. *The New Dollars and Dreams: American Incomes and Economic Change.* New York: Russell Sage Foundation, 1998.

Levy, Frank, and Richard J. Murnane. "U.S. Earnings Levels and Earnings Inequality: A Review of Recent Trends and Proposed Explanations." *Journal of Economic Literature* 30, no. 3 (September 1991): 1222–381.

U.S. Department of Labor, Bureau of Labor Statistics. "Contingent Workers and Alternate Work Arrangements." *Monthly Labor Review* 119, no. 10 (October 1996): 3–83.

CHAPTER 9

CHANGING WORK ROLES AND THE FAMILY

Chapter Highlights

- Economic Explanations for Family Formation
- Marriage
- Divorce
- Fertility
- Cohabitation: Opposite Sex and Gay and Lesbian Couples
- Changing Family Structure and Economic Well-Being

In earlier chapters, we discussed the family as an economic institution and the allocation of time of husband and wife between the household and the labor market. We now turn our attention to the impact a woman's employment has on her family and also consider a number of issues associated with changing family structure. One important difference between our approach here and in Chapter 4 is that there we accepted marital status and fertility as given, exogenous to our models, and focused on the effects of these factors on women's labor force participation. In this chapter, we turn the tables and examine the impact of economic factors, including women's labor force participation, on demographic outcomes.

The first sections of this chapter deal with the effect of economic factors on the incidence of marriage, divorce, opposite-sex cohabitation, gay and lesbian couples, and fertility. Next, we look at the effect of changing family structure on economic well-being, focusing on dual-earner families and single-parent families. One of the most important issues associated with changing family structure and labor market activity that we consider is their consequences for the well-being of children. Thus, we review the literature on the effect of maternal employment on children's development and well-being, and then examine the effect of family structure on children's future success as measured by high school dropout rates and teen pregnancy.

ECONOMIC EXPLANATIONS FOR FAMILY FORMATION

What is the expected effect of economic factors, including women's increased labor force participation, on family formation? From the viewpoint of neoclassical economics, the determining factor in decisions concerning family issues such as marriage, divorce, and fertility is whether or not the benefits exceed the costs.[1] Thus, the question arises as to the effect women's rising labor force participation and other economic factors have had on the costs and benefits associated with these decisions—do more or fewer couples choose to marry, divorce, or bear children? The answer to this question is not obvious from a theoretical point of view. That is, there are forces operating both to reduce and to increase the benefits and costs of these decisions.

MARRIAGE

Marriage is encouraged by a number of factors, though perhaps the one most emphasized by neoclassical economists is that it makes possible the specialization and exchange that potentially increase the couple's productivity and economic well-being. In general, the more the comparative advantage in producing home and market goods *differs* between the two partners, the larger the potential gain, for each may then specialize mainly or entirely in his or her area of higher relative productivity. As women have been acquiring more job-oriented education and training, and perhaps encountering less discrimination in the labor market, their market productivity has increased relative to their home productivity. This leads to smaller gains from specialization and exchange than in the days when women prepared for the traditional role of homemaker in a family with only a male breadwinner. From this perspective, rising female labor force participation is expected to result in lower marriage rates. Working hand in hand with this, women's improved opportunities for earning their own living are expected to reduce their incentives to marry because they present women with a viable alternative to marriage, making it economically feasible to postpone or altogether forgo such a commitment. Thus, it would appear that women's increasing labor force participation tends to lower marriage rates, but the matter is not quite that simple.

The much greater acceptability of market work for married women today may encourage marriage by reducing its opportunity cost. That is, women are no longer pressured to choose between employment on the one hand and marriage on the other. Although many women continue to accommodate their paid work to what are still perceived to be their household responsibilities, they are far less likely than in the past to cut short their education or leave the labor market entirely at the time they get married. Working in the same direction, some sociologists have argued that men may prefer women who can make a larger contribution to family income.[2]

---

[1] Seminal work by neoclassical economists on the economics of the family was first done by Gary S. Becker and has been summarized by him in *A Treatise on the Family* (Cambridge, MA: Harvard University Press, 1991). See also Robert Willis, "What Have We Learned from the Economics of the Family?" *American Economic Review* 77, no. 2 (May 1987): 68–81; Shoshana Grossbard-Shechtman, *On the Economics of Marriage* (Boulder, CO: Westview Press, 1993); and Mark R. Rosenzweig and Oded Stark, eds., *Handbook of Population and Family Economics,* vol. 1A and 1B (Amsterdam: Elsevier, 1997).

[2] See, for instance, Valerie Kincade Oppenheimer, "Women's Rising Employment and the Future of the Family in Industrial Societies," *Population and Development Review* 20, no. 2 (June 1994): 293–342.

In sum, it is not entirely clear that women's rising labor force participation would negatively affect marriage rates. There are possible effects in both directions. However, most of the theoretical considerations tend to suggest a negative effect of women's rising labor force participation on marriage.

As we saw in Chapter 3, several other economic factors, unrelated to changes in women's labor force participation, may work to encourage marriage. Marriage provides a benefit in the form of economies of scale. That is, the cost of housing and food is much less on a per person basis if shared. In addition, marriage makes possible the consumption of public goods such as a well-tended garden or a newly mowed lawn. While many of these advantages can also be reaped by unmarried couples, roommates, or those living with extended families, given prevailing tastes and norms, these other alternatives are often less desirable or less socially acceptable. Also, the contractual relationship of marriage encourages marriage-specific investments. Thus, even as the rewards to specialization based on the traditional division of labor diminish, marriage may remain quite prevalent, especially when we additionally take into account noneconomic considerations like affection and companionship.[3] In fact, two-earner couples are particularly likely to benefit from marriage to the extent that they have more similar tastes than traditional couples and are more likely to participate in the same activities, thus enhancing each other's enjoyment. Also, more similar tastes tend to reduce disagreements over the combination of commodities to consume. In addition, having two wage earners reduces the economic risks for such families because they are not entirely dependent on one income.

Another factor that has received tremendous attention as possibly affecting trends in marriage rates is the role of income support available outside of marriage, such as welfare. A concern that influenced the policy debate to redesign welfare in the mid-1990s was that since welfare largely provided government support for single mothers, it may have discouraged women from getting married. While such effects are possible, it is important to note that welfare could not have affected most women's marriage decisions because it was only available to those with very low incomes. Further, as will be discussed in Chapter 10, a large body of research supports the view that, contrary to popular perception, welfare cannot explain the large shift in family structure away from marriage toward single-parent families that has occurred since the 1970s, even among low-income women.[4]

A shortage of "marriageable" men is another explanation offered for declining marriage rates. Insufficient supply may be a result of men's lack of economic opportunities, either as reflected by declining real wages, lack of stability in employment, or joblessness,[5] as

---

[3] It is also the case that government and employer policies often favor married couples. This point is considered further in Chapter 10.

[4] Robert A. Moffitt, "Welfare Benefits and Female Headship in U.S. Time Series," *American Economic Review* 90, no. 2 (May 2000): 373–77; and for a review, Robert A. Moffitt, "The Effect of Welfare on Marriage and Fertility" in *Welfare, the Family, and Reproductive Behavior: Research Perspectives,* ed. Robert A. Moffitt (Washington, DC: National Research Council, 1998), pp. 50–97.

[5] This theory was put forward by William J. Wilson and Kathryn Neckerman, "Poverty and Family Structure: The Widening Gap Between Evidence and Public Policy Issues," in *Fighting Poverty: What Works and What Doesn't,* ed. Sheldon Danziger and Daniel Weinberg (Cambridge, MA: Harvard University Press, 1986), pp. 232–59. For the perspective of single mothers themselves, see Kathryn Edin, "What Do Low-Income Single Mothers Say About Marriage?" Joint Center for Poverty Research Working Paper No. 100 (July 1999).

well as of a lower ratio of men to women in the population.[6] Concern about men's economic opportunities is particularly relevant for less educated men, whose labor market status has been declining in recent years. Minorities have, on average, less education than whites, and may also face discrimination; thus they would be expected to be disproportionately affected by these trends. Related to this, as seen in Chapter 5, the gender differential in wages among minorities is much smaller as compared to whites, which means that the gains to marriage from specialization and exchange are also smaller, all else equal.

Economic considerations are not, however, the only ones that play a role in demographic changes, including marriage. One factor that has undoubtedly contributed to the growing number of unmarried young people is the dramatic liberalization in attitudes toward divorce, cohabitation, and sex outside of marriage in the 1960s and 1970s.[7] As a result, marriage and sex are no longer as closely linked together as they once were.

Taken together, the factors summarized above, including rising labor force participation as well as the other considerations, have an ambiguous effect, some serving to increase marriage rates and others to reduce them. However, the empirical evidence suggests that the latter have been dominant, most likely because of the rapid entry of women into the labor market, which has largely operated to reduce incentives to marry, along with the liberalization of social attitudes. Indeed, as Table 9.1 shows, the marriage rate fell from 10.6 marriages per 1,000 population in 1970 to 8.3 by 1998. The decline has been particularly precipitous among young women. In 1970, 36 percent of women age 20 to 24 had never been married as compared with 70 percent in 1998. This trend, related to the rising median age of first marriage, is consistent with increased economic opportunities for women, which have encouraged them to stay in school longer and made them less likely to marry at an early age.[8] In conjunction with these developments, the declining labor market opportunities of less educated men have also played a role in discouraging marriage. Even so, most individuals eventually marry; the proportion of people who never marry in their lifetime, in recent years about 5 percent, is not expected to increase to more than 10 percent in the foreseeable future.[9] However one important difference from past patterns is that more children are now being born to unmarried mothers.

---

[6] Grossbard-Schectman provides a theoretical model that integrates marriage and labor markets in *On the Economics of Marriage,* chap. 4 and 5; and in "Women's Hours of Work and Marriage Market Imbalances," in *Economics of the Family and Family Policies,* ed. Inga Persson and Christina Jonung (London: Routledge, 1998), pp. 100–118. See also Scott J. South and Kim M. Lloyd, "Marriage Opportunities and Family Formation: Further Implications of Imbalanced Sex Ratios," *Journal of Marriage and the Family* 54, no. 2 (May 1992): 440–51.

[7] Arland Thornton, "Changing Attitudes Toward Family Issues in the United States," *Journal of Marriage and the Family* 51, no. 4 (November 1989): 873–93; and Tom W. Smith, "The Emerging 21st Century American Family," GSS Social Change Report No. 42 (University of Chicago: National Opinion Research Center, 1999). See also Claudia Goldin and Lawrence F. Katz, "Career and Marriage in the Age of the Pill," *American Economic Review* 90, no. 2 (May 2000): 461–65.

[8] Evidence that women's improved labor market opportunities have lead to a decline in marriage is provided by T. Paul Schultz, "Marital Status and Fertility in the United States," *Journal of Human Resources* 29, no. 2 (spring 1994): 637–69; and Francine D. Blau, Lawrence M. Kahn, and Jane Waldfogel, "Understanding Young Women's Marriage Decisions: The Role of Labor Market and Marriage Market Conditions," *Industrial and Labor Relations Review* 53, no. 4 (July 2000): 624–47. However, Valerie Kincade Oppenheimer and Vivian Lew question the emphasis placed on this factor in explaining trends; see "American Marriage Formation in the 1980s: How Important Was Women's Economic Independence?" in *Gender and Family Change in Industrialized Countries,* ed. Karen Oppenheim Mason and An-Magitt Jensen (Oxford: Clarendon Press, 1995).

[9] This projection was made by Steve W. Rawlings of the Census Bureau and cited in Margot Slade, "Siblings: Now You Can't Live with Them or Without Them," *New York Times,* 25 July 1991, p. B1.

TABLE 9.1   Trends in Family Structure, 1970–1998

	1970	*1980*	*1990*	*1998*
Marriage				
Marriage rate per 1,000 population	10.6	10.6	9.8	8.3
Median age at first marriage				
Men	23.2	24.7	26.1	26.7
Women	20.8	22.0	23.9	25.0
% Never-married men				
Age 20–24	54.7	68.8	79.3	83.4
Age 30–34	9.4	15.9	27.0	29.2
Age 40–44	6.3	7.1	10.5	15.6
% Never-married women				
Age 20–24	35.8	50.2	62.8	70.3
Age 30–34	6.2	9.5	16.4	21.6
Age 40–44	4.9	4.8	8.0	9.9
% Married adults	71.7	65.5	61.9	59.7
Whites	72.6	67.2	64.0	62.1
Blacks	64.1	51.4	45.8	41.8
Hispanic origin	71.8	65.6	61.7	58.9
Divorce				
Divorce rate per 1,000 married women, age 15+	14.9	22.6	20.9	19.8[a]
Cohabitation				
Cohabitors (unmarried, opposite-sex couples) per 100 married couples	1	3	5	8

[a] Figure is from 1997.

Sources: U.S. Department of Health and Human Services, *National Vital Statistics Reports* 47, no. 1 (6 July 1999); U.S. Department of Health and Human Services, *Monthly Vital Statistics Report* (various issues); U.S. Census Bureau, *Statistical Abstract of the United States: 1999* (marriage and divorce rates); U.S. Census Bureau, "Marital Status and Living Arrangements: March 1998," *Current Population Reports* P20-514; Table 1, Table 7, Table C, Table AD-2 (cohabitation, other marriage statistics).

As may be seen in Table 9.1, the largest decline in marriage has been among blacks. This appears to reflect black women's rising economic opportunities combined with black men's often very poor job prospects.[10] In inner cities, especially, high rates of homicide and incarceration have further reduced the supply of "marriageable" men.

---

[10]   T. Paul Schultz finds that black women's marriage rates are more greatly affected by their husband's economic prospects than by their own in "Eroding the Economic Foundations of Marriage and Fertility in the United States," *Structural Change and Economic Dynamics* 9, no. 4 (December 1998): 391–413. See also William J. Wilson and Kathryn Neckerman, "Poverty and Family Structure," *Structural Change and Economic Dynamics* 9, no. 4 (December 1998): 391–414; and William A. Darity Jr. and Samuel L. Myers Jr., "Family Structure and the Marginalization of Black Men: Policy Implications," in *The Decline in Marriage Among African Americans,* ed. M. Belinda Tucker and Claudia Mitchell-Kernan (New York: Russell Sage Foundation, 1995), pp. 263–308. On the other hand, Robert G. Wood finds weaker evidence regarding this factor in "Marriage Rates and Marriageable Men," *Journal of Human Resources* 30, no. 1 (winter 1995): 163–93.

As already noted, economic considerations are not the only ones that play a role in demographic changes, including marriage. Another factor behind the decline in marriage in recent decades is the changing attitude toward cohabitation. Table 9.1 shows that the ratio of unmarried to married couples increased from 1:100 in 1970 to 8:100 in 1998. Obviously, many more individuals have cohabited at some point, if only briefly. Yet as will be seen in Chapter 11, despite the fact that the marriage rate in the United States has fallen since the 1970s, it remains among the highest of the economically advanced nations. Furthermore, most people who get divorced do eventually remarry, though the remarriage rate has declined, no doubt for the same reasons that have caused marriage rates to fall.[11] The fact that marriage and remarriage rates continue to be so high suggests that, in spite of all the changes, marriage remains central to the lives of many Americans.

DIVORCE

A related set of economic and social factors affects marital dissolution—that is, separation or divorce.[12] Among traditional married couples, the interdependence of husband and wife due to specialization and exchange is probably the single most important economic deterrent to divorce. In the case of the breadwinner husband and homemaker wife, the wife generally has relatively few market skills that would enable her to earn enough money on her own to buy whatever she requires of market goods and services, while the husband has little training for household tasks and needs someone to look after home and children. Investments in marriage-specific human capital by the couple further cement this relationship.

As the traditional division of labor breaks down, the economic incentives for remaining married are reduced. This suggests that women's increased economic opportunities are expected to increase the propensity to divorce. This does not mean, however, that divorce is no longer costly, or that there are no longer any economic advantages to marriage. As to the costs of divorce, while the higher income of two-earner couples gives them the opportunity to acquire more assets, dividing them, especially such illiquid assets as a house or a car, often creates problems. As to other economic advantages of marriage, benefits such as joint consumption will remain or may even be enhanced for two-earner couples. Moreover, though such couples have less time, they have more money than those with only one paycheck. Not only does their higher income permit them to consume more of the market goods and services they desire, it also presumably reduces at least one common area of potential stress and disagreement—conflicts over the use of scarce dollars. Finally, sharing both market work and housework might be expected to create greater understanding and empathy between husband and wife. One may well conclude that the dominant effect of women's increased labor force participation is not that it makes married people less happy, but rather that it provides those who are unhappy with more attractive alternatives than were previously available.

Other factors also influence the probability of divorce. One of these is that unexpected events, such as a sudden increase or decrease in the earnings ability of one or

---

[11] Pamela J. Smock, "Remarriage Patterns of Black and White Women: Reassessing the Role of Educational Attainment," *Demography* 27, no. 3 (August 1990): 467–73.

[12] Gary S. Becker, Elisabeth M. Landes, and Robert T. Michael, "An Economic Analysis of Marital Instability," *Journal of Political Economy* 85, no. 6 (December 1977): 1141–87.

both partners may create frictions in the marriage.[13] Another is that individuals' preferences and needs may change as time passes, especially during times of rapid shifts in long-accepted standards and norms, such as those that have been taking place in recent years. Similarly, changes in the rules governing legal termination of marriage, whether concerning alimony and child support or the introduction of no-fault divorce laws, might be expected to have some effect. Just what the effects of higher expected awards to a former spouse would be is not, however, clear a priori. The spouse who expects to get the payments would presumably be more willing to terminate a marriage because these payments provide a financial cushion; at the same time the partner who has to make them would be less likely to favor breaking up the marriage.[14] On the other hand, liberalization of the divorce laws, introduced in many states during the 1970s, might be expected to increase the likelihood of marital dissolution, although evidence on this is mixed.[15] Religious beliefs and other broad social attitudes also likely play a role.

For some time, the factors just cited that serve to increase divorce appeared to dominate the effect of those that encourage the continuation of marriage. Specifically, the figures in Table 9.1 show a sharp rise in the divorce rate from 14.9 divorces per 1,000 married women in 1970 to 22.6 in 1980. As noted earlier, women's rising economic opportunities likely help to account for the upward trend because they reduce interdependence. The research evidence on this, however, is mixed, perhaps because similar lifestyles of husbands and wives enhance the quality of some marriages.[16] Since 1980, the divorce rate has leveled off and has even declined somewhat to 19.8 in 1998, though it is estimated that at current rates about one-half of all marriages will end in divorce.[17] One possible explanation for this recent trend is that the decreasing economic and social pressures to marry, associated with women's rising labor force participation, have led

---

[13]   Yoram Weiss and Robert Willis, "Transfers Among Divorced Couples: Evidence and Interpretation," *Journal of Labor Economics* 11, no. 4 (October 1993): 629–79.

[14]   Lucia Nixon finds that the latter effect dominates, leading stronger child support enforcement to discourage divorce in "The Effect of Child Support Enforcement on Marital Dissolution," *Journal of Human Resources* 32, no. 1 (winter 1997): 159–81.

[15]   For evidence that no-fault divorce did not increase the divorce rate, see H. Elizabeth Peters," Marriage and Divorce: Informational Constraints and Private Contracting," *American Economic Review* 76, no. 3 (June 1986): 437–54; and Jeffrey S. Gray, "Divorce-Law Changes and Married Women's Labor Supply," *American Economic Review* 88, no. 3 (June 1998): 628–42. For evidence on the other side, see Leora Friedberg, "Did Unilateral Divorce Raise Divorce Rates?" *American Economic Review* 88, no. 3 (June 1998): 608–27.

[16]   For papers that support the hypothesis that women's increased employment or rising wages caused a higher divorce rate, see Steven Ruggles, "The Rise of Divorce and Separation in the United States, 1890–1990," *Demography* 34, no. 4 (November 1997): 455–566; Robert Michael, "Why Did the U.S. Divorce Rate Double Within a Decade?" *Research in Population Economics* 6 (1988): 367–99; and John H. Johnson IV, "Do Long Work Hours Contribute to Divorce?" University of Illinois at Urbana-Champaign Office of Research Working Paper No. 99–0130 (March 2000). For papers that come to a different conclusion, see Valerie Kincade Oppenheimer, "Comment on 'The Rise of Divorce and Separation in the United States, 1880–1990'," *Demography* 34, no. 4 (November 1997): 467–72; and Saul D. Hoffman and Greg J. Duncan, "The Effect of Incomes, Wages, and AFDC Benefits on Marital Disruption," *Journal of Human Resources* 30, no. 1 (winter 1995): 19–41.

[17]   Suzanne M. Bianchi, "The Changing Demographic and Socioeconomic Characteristics of Single Parent Families," *Marriage and Family Review* 20, nos. 1–2 (spring 1995): 71–97. Projections are, however, necessarily hazardous because they are based on assumptions about future rather than merely past and present behavior. See Robert Schoen, William L. Urton, Karen Woodrow, and John Bay, "Marriage and Divorce in 20th Century American Cohorts," *Demography* 22, no. 1 (February 1985): 101–14.

young people to postpone marriage. This has served to promote marital stability because couples who get married at older ages are less likely to break up.[18] It has also been suggested that increases in cohabitation might explain recent trends to the extent that breakups of these unions are not counted in the divorce statistics. However, research to date does not support these explanations, leaving the question open as to what has caused the leveling off and modest decline in divorce rates.[19] Looking ahead, while the divorce rate may continue to decline a bit, whatever the reason, it is not likely to fall to the levels that prevailed when traditional marriages were the norm and when social attitudes toward divorce were extremely negative.

Whatever the pros and cons of divorce, it leaves full-time homemakers and their children particularly vulnerable. The housewife is dependent on her husband not only for money income but also for her social status and even, at times, for much of her circle of friends. For children, family disruption has potential effects on their future development, including educational attainment, wages, and teen pregnancy, in part because family disruption leads to reduced incomes but very likely for other reasons as well. These issues will be discussed shortly.

Custody Battles: It Would Take a Solomon

In the "traditional family" the father was the wage earner; the mother was the homemaker who tended home and hearth and took care of their children.* Thus, life was simple in the "good old days." Or was it? In fact, poor women frequently worked for pay, with children often working alongside them or fending for themselves as best they could; and the well to do often hired others to care for their children, at times beginning with wet nurses, going on to nannies, and then sending the youngsters to boarding school at an early age. Nonetheless, matters have become more complicated, in substantial part because of the large proportion of children whose parents do not live together. The most heartbreaking cases are, no doubt, those where neither mother nor father wants the child, although we hear very little about these cases. We do, however, hear a great deal about legal battles when both parents want custody, or when the noncustodial parent does not want to permit their children to move out of their community. Such cases too raise very serious issues. They deserve all the more attention because the number of such disputes are expected to continue to rise as more and more women are increasingly committed to their work, and as fathers continue to become more involved with their children.

Traditionally, the mother was routinely awarded custody, barring overwhelming evidence that she was unfit and, in general, this continues to be the case. However, increas-

* This inset draws on Susan Chira, "Custody Fight in Capital: A Working Mother Loses," *New York Times,* 20 September 1994, sec. A, p. 1; Anna Quindlen, "Sometimes You Just Can't Win for Losing. Particularly If You're a Single Mother in America," *New York Times,* 10 July 1994, sec. 1, p. 19; Raymond Hernandez, "Court Ruling Gives Divorced Parents Right to Leave the State," *New York Times,* 27 March 1996, sec. A, p. 1; and *Jennifer Ireland, Plaintiff-Appellant, Cross Appellate* v. *Steve Smith a/k/a Steven J. Smith, Defendant-Appellee, Cross-Appellant,* Nos. 177431, 182369, Court of Appeals of Michigan, 214 Mich. App. 235; 1995 Mich. App. LEXIS 478, May 3, 1995, Submitted; November 7, 1995, Decided.

---

[18] Alan Booth and Lynn White, "Thinking About Divorce," *Journal of Marriage and Family* 42, no. 3 (August 1980): 605–16; and Julie DaVanzo and M. Omar Rahman, "American Families: Trends and Correlates," *Population Index* 59, no. 3 (fall 1993): 350–86.

[19] Joshua R. Goldstein, "The Leveling of Divorce in the United States," *Demography* 36, no. 3 (August 1999): 409–14.

ingly more fathers are aggressively seeking custody, and they are winning a majority of contested cases. The questions involved are complex. There is justified concern about the usual presumption that the mother should automatically be given preference, and that the father, especially when not married to the mother of the child, has few rights. There is equally justified concern that courts appear to look askance at mothers who have a career, or aspire to one, but have no such reservations about "career fathers." In addition to these problems, there are inevitable difficulties when charges and countercharges are raised by the contestants and their respective supporters that are difficult to verify with any degree of certainty. A brief summary of two high-profile cases, and a court ruling concerning permission for the custodial parent to move, well illustrate the problems involved.

The first case attained celebrity status in part because Sharon Prost, the mother of two boys, worked as counsel to conservative Senator Orrin G. Hatch of Utah. Kenneth Greene, the father, was assistant executive director of the American Federation of Television and Radio Artists. They were married in 1984 and separated eight years later. The judge awarded custody of the children to Mr. Greene in a sharply worded opinion that cited his friends and relatives who described the wife as a driven workaholic, while claiming that he was a playful and affectionate parent. Partisans of Prost, including Senator Hatch, on the other hand, claimed that this picture was distorted and ignored the maximum efforts she made to be a responsible parent, while her husband chose not to take care of the children full-time while he was unemployed. They objected that the judge gave the father credit for any time he participated in activities at the children's kindergarten, and for coming home first in the evening, but ignored the teacher's description of Ms. Prost as "surrogate room mom" as well as the fact that she regularly got up at 5:30 A.M. to play with the children before she left for work at 8 o'clock. In sum, they charged that the judgment involved sex bias. The judge, a mother herself, who had worked part-time while her children were young, explained that a woman was entitled to put her career ahead of other demands in her life but, having made that decision, she must live with the consequences. Whether one agrees with the judge's decision or not, it must be expected to make some professional women fearful that courts may use a double standard, because they are likely to compare them to other mothers, who often are employed only part-time, or not at all, while fathers will be compared to other men with children, who almost invariably are employed full time. Such comparisons would tend to make career mothers look bad as compared to similarly positioned fathers.

The second case involved very different circumstances but also raised issues with implications for the role of women as mothers, albeit somewhat more indirectly. The mother had given birth to a daughter in 1991, when both she and the defendant were 16 years old and unmarried. She first agreed to give the baby up for adoption, but three weeks later changed her mind and decided to raise the child herself. Both mother and father lived with their respective families, continued to go to high school, and eventually graduated. The father had no contact with the infant during the first year of her life, but after that visited her regularly. In the fall of 1993 the plaintiff and her child moved to Ann Arbor, where she attended the University of Michigan on a scholarship. They lived in university family housing and the child attended university-approved day care. Expenses were covered by the maternal grandmother, while the child received occasional gifts from the father and his family. At no time were there charges that the child was less than adequately cared for, or that the relationship between mother and child was anything less than warm and satisfactory. The child was found to have a strong emotional attachment to both parents.

There were no problems until the mother filed an action for child support. Only then did the father claim that he should obtain custody of his daughter because it would be better for her to be looked after by his mother (the child's paternal grandmother) rather than in a day care center. The court sided with the father, but the child was not removed from the mother's custody because she appealed the case. The decision was later reversed in a higher court. This reversal clearly stated that a party's arrangements for the child's care while a parent worked or went to school is not an appropriate consideration.

The implications of the issue at stake in this instance go well beyond custody cases. The initial decision, which was explicitly made on the grounds that it is preferable for a child to be cared for by a blood relative (her paternal grandmother) than by strangers (day care center workers), ignored the substantial amount of contact parents and children have, and the substantial amount of parental care children receive even when they spend eight hours a day, five days a week, at a center. Furthermore, this decision, which overruled the recommendations of two impartial child welfare groups, obviously implies that day care is always second best to having children taken care of by their own parents, or in this instance even grandparents. Realistically, that suggests that a woman who really cares about her children should stay home and give up, or at least interrupt, her career; it also means that if she does not, it might one day be held against her if anyone chooses to question her fitness as a mother. Wide acceptance of this view, even though it is contrary to the evidence of the great preponderance of research, could prove to be an obstacle in the path of women's further progress toward equality in the labor market.

A question related to custody that can be as difficult to resolve as the questions involved in custody cases themselves is whether or not and under what circumstances the custodial parent, most often the mother, should be permitted to move out of state. On the one hand, the father will find it more difficult to see his children regularly if they live further away; on the other hand, not being able to move may impose serious constraints on a woman who needs to find a job or is offered better opportunities elsewhere, or who wants to marry someone who lives in another state. In the past, it was not unusual to permit such a woman to move only under "exceptional" circumstances. In March 1996 the highest court of New York State, however, unanimously decided that the well-being of the children should take precedence over the desire to keep the family in close proximity, and in April of the same year the highest court of California handed down a similar ruling. It is widely thought that this is likely to be part of a more general trend toward greater permissiveness.

COHABITATION: OPPOSITE-SEX, UNMARRIED COUPLES

Opposite-sex cohabitation has emerged as an increasingly common living arrangement since the 1970s, in large part due to changing attitudes about premarital sex. As noted earlier, the ratio of unmarried to married couples increased considerably from 1970 to 1998. Economic explanations for the rise in cohabitation since the 1970s are, however, less well understood than those for trends in marriage and divorce.

Like marriage, cohabitation involves two individuals living together in a single household. There are the same possibilities for economies of scale, but there are also important differences. A number of factors, including the financial and economic resources of the two partners, are likely to influence whether a couple chooses to marry or cohabit, or if already cohabiting, whether or not they subsequently decide to marry. For instance, because current employment provides important information about long-term economic security, individuals may choose to cohabit until one or both partners have good job prospects.[20] Also, as discussed in Chapter 3, marriage establishes prop-

---

[20] Pamela J. Smock and Wendy D. Manning find that it is only men's economic resources that matter in making the transition from cohabitation to marriage in "Cohabiting Partners' Economic Circumstances and Marriage," *Demography* 34, no. 3 (August 1997): 331–41. See also Debra L. Blackwell and Daniel T. Lichter, "Mate Selection Among Married and Cohabiting Couples," *Journal of Family Issues* 21, no. 3 (April 2000): 275–302.

erty rights between the two individuals regarding any assets brought into or acquired after setting up a joint household. Thus, one would expect individuals who want to live together to be more likely to cohabit rather than marry if little or no legal protection of property is needed.[21] Other factors influencing the decision are likely to include the degree of commitment to the relationship, as well as the desire for and presence of children.[22] As noted earlier, the propensity to cohabit is strongly influenced by social attitudes, which except among the very religious have grown increasingly more liberal.

We expect cohabitors to be more prone to break up or to remain together for a shorter period of time than married couples. One reason for this is that cohabitation does not provide legal guarantees for a partner who specializes in homemaking and forgoes the opportunity to maintain and increase labor market skills to the same extent marriage does. Consequently, cohabitors are less likely to become economically interdependent. In addition, the fact that cohabitation creates few, if any, legal commitments, makes it more likely that any personal problems or economic setbacks that arise will lead to breakups.

Gradually we are learning more about cohabitation. Consistent with our expectations, it has been found that the median length of time couples spend cohabiting is as short as a year or so, with the cohabitation ending in the marriage or the breakup of the couple. Indeed, overall, more than 50 percent of cohabiting couples eventually get married, suggesting that cohabiting is often not so much an alternative to marriage as a prelude to it.[23] It might be expected that premarital cohabitation would stabilize marriage by providing the partners with more information about whether or not they could successfully cooperate and make household decisions as compared with couples who have never lived together. Surprisingly, however, there is little evidence that premarital cohabitation has this stabilizing effect on marriage.[24]

Rates of cohabitation have increased substantially among all cohorts but especially among the young. As of 1995, it was estimated that just over 40 percent of the population 15 to 44 years of age had cohabited at some time in their lives.[25] For many, cohabitation, albeit brief, serves as part of a larger "family building" process that often includes nonmarital childbearing as well as marriage.[26] One consequence of rising rates of cohabitation is that increasing numbers of children are living with cohabiting par-

---

[21] There have been a number of important court cases that have sought to increase cohabitors' rights, but married couples and cohabitors continue to be treated very differently after a union is dissolved.

[22] See Pamela J. Smock and Sanjiv Gupta, "Cohabitation in North America," unpublished working paper, University of Michigan (October 2000); and Deborah Roempke Graefe and Daniel T. Lichter, "Life Course Transitions of American Children: Parental Cohabitation, Marriage, and Single Motherhood," *Demography* 36, no. 2 (May 1999): 205–17.

[23] Larry L. Bumpass and James A. Sweet, "The Role of Cohabitation in Declining Rates of Marriage," *Journal of Marriage and the Family* 53, no. 4 (November 1991): 913–27; and Larry Bumpass and H.-H. Lu, "Trends in Cohabitation and Implications for Children's Family Context in the United States," *Population Studies* 54, no. 1 (March 2000): 29–41.

[24] Lee A. Lillard, Michael J. Brien, and Linda J. Waite have found the opposite to be the case and conclude that the reason for this is that cohabitors are poor marriage material. Still, even after they account for this "selectivity" problem, they do not find that cohabitation reduces marital dissolution in "Pre-Marital Cohabitation and Subsequent Marital Dissolution: Is It Self-Selection?" *Demography* 32, no. 3 (August 1995): 437–58.

[25] U.S. Census Bureau, *Statistical Abstract of the United States: 1999,* table 66.

[26] See Michael J. Brien, Lee A. Lillard, and Linda J. Waite, "Interrelated Family-Building Behaviors: Cohabitation, Marriage and Nonmarital Conception," *Demography* 36, no. 4 (November 1999): 535–51.

ents. For instance, in the mid-1990s, nearly 40 percent of children born to unmarried mothers were in fact born to opposite-sex cohabiting parents. Moreover, it is projected that 40 percent of *all* children will spend at least some time in a cohabiting family during their childhood.[27]

Looking toward the future, although it is not yet clear to what extent cohabitation will replace marriage rather than remain a prelude to it, it is expected that cohabitation rates will continue to rise. One reason for expecting this is that rates are even higher in a number of other economically advanced countries, particularly Sweden, where as many as one in five of all couples are unmarried. However, one important difference is that cohabitation tends to be of longer duration in Sweden and other Scandinavian countries, perhaps for historical or cultural reasons.[28]

COHABITATION: GAY AND LESBIAN COUPLES

Like traditional marriage and opposite-sex cohabitation,[29] same-sex relationships offer the partners not only companionship and affection, but economic benefits, including the ability to share economic resources and realize economies of scale. However, while partners in a same-sex couple may also differ in terms of their comparative advantage in the home and in the market to some degree,[30] neither partner is likely to specialize in home production to the same degree as the average married woman. First, as in the case of unmarried opposite-sex couples, same-sex couples have far fewer legal protections than married couples, which makes investment in homemaking particularly costly in the event that the couple breaks up.[31] Second, to the extent that young women know that they are not likely to enter an opposite-sex relationship, they will have little incentive to specialize in homemaking skills. Specifically, those expecting to have partnerships with other women are more likely, all else equal, to accumulate human capital useful for the labor market as compared with those expecting to be members of a more traditional household. At the same time, since men have traditionally had the role of breadwinner, young gay men are likely to acquire skills useful for the labor market rather than invest heavily in homemaking skills.[32]

[27] Bumpass and Lu, "Trends in Cohabitation."

[28] Constance Sorrentino, "The Changing Family in International Perspective," *Monthly Labor Review* 113, no. 3 (March 1990): 41–58.

[29] While the term "mixed-sex" or "different-sex" is used by some researchers to distinguish men–women couples from gay and lesbian couples, we use the term "opposite-sex" couple here because of its usage by the Census Bureau and the general public. For a historical perspective on gay and lesbian couples, see Julie Matthaei, "The Sexual Division of Labor, Sexuality, and Lesbian/Gay Liberation: Toward a Marxist–Feminist Analysis of Sexuality in U.S. Capitalism," in *Homo Economics: Capitalism, Community, and Lesbian and Gay Life,* ed. Amy Gluckman and Betsy Reed (New York: Routledge, 1997), pp. 135–64.

[30] See Lisa A. Giddings, "Political Economy and the Construction of Gender: The Example of Housework Within Same-Sex Households," *Feminist Economics* 4, no. 2 (summer 1998): 97–106; and M. V. Lee Badgett, "Gender, Sexuality, and Sexual Orientation," *Feminist Economics* 1, no. 1 (spring 1995): 121–39.

[31] Unlike opposite-sex couples, same-sex couples in the United States do not have the opportunity to get married except that since July 2000, they may obtain "civil union" licenses in Vermont, which provide many of the same protections as marriage.

[32] It is also the case that gay men will not reap the same benefits to specialization as most married men and so are expected to have lower wages, all else equal. For a discussion of the effects of sexual orientation on wages, see Dan A. Black, Hoda R. Makar, Seth G. Sanders, and Lowell Taylor, "The Effects of Sexual Orientation on Earnings," unpublished working paper, University of Kentucky (September 1998); and M. V. Lee Badgett, "The Wage Effects of Sexual Orientation Discrimination," *Industrial and Labor Relations Review* 48, no. 4 (July 1995): 726–39.

While even today little is known about the number of gay men and lesbians, let alone about partnerships with and without children, some estimates are available based on a number of extensive surveys. According to one recent study, the fraction of men who are gay is approximately 2.5 percent and the fraction of women who are lesbians is approximately 1.4 percent.[33] It is further estimated that around 29 percent of gay men and 44 percent of lesbians were living with a same-sex partner at the time they were surveyed. As would be expected, the percentage of gays and lesbians who have ever had a live-in partner is considerably higher, 68 percent and 94 percent, respectively.

Although a smaller fraction of same-sex couples than opposite-sex couples have children, it has nonetheless been estimated that around 5 percent of gay couples and nearly 22 percent of lesbian couples have children. Other estimates, which include currently unpartnered gay men and currently unpartnered lesbians, indicate that as many as 14 percent of gay men and 28 percent of lesbians have children, many of them from a prior marriage. These figures suggest that children's living arrangements are far more diverse than would appear based on standard Census Bureau categorizations. Moreover, "family" for these children tends to be more broadly defined than for many of those living in heterosexual families. In particular, lesbian and gay families often consist of networks of adults and children, who may live in the same or different households.[34]

As for future trends, it is expected that the fraction of same-sex couples, including those with children, will increase to the extent that societal attitudes toward them become more tolerant and other states follow Vermont's lead and solidify the legal rights of gay and lesbian couples, including rights regarding adoption. Further, to the extent that alternative reproductive technologies become less expensive and more acceptable, this will further increase the fraction of children raised in nontraditional living arrangements.

FERTILITY

Neoclassical economic theory sheds considerable light on people's decisions as to whether or not to have children, how many to have, and to what extent scarce resources should be allocated to them.[35] To make such decisions rationally, one must weigh expected costs against expected benefits. The costs of raising children include direct money expenditures for food, clothing, housing, and education. Such expenditures are substantial. The U.S. Department of Agriculture estimated that, in 1999, the expenditures required for an average married couple to raise a child until age 18 amounted to

---

[33]   The estimates are based on survey data pooled from 1989 through 1996. Gays and lesbians are defined as those who reported having had exclusively same-sex relationships during the prior year. These figures, as well as those that follow, are from Dan A. Black, Gary Gates, Seth G. Sanders, and Lowell Taylor, "Demographics of the Gay and Lesbian Population in the United States: Evidence from Available Systematic Data Sources," *Demography* 37, no. 2 (May 2000): 139–55. One difficulty in obtaining reliable estimates is that gay men and lesbians may be reluctant to identify themselves given prevailing attitudes.

[34]   Nancy E. Rose and Lynn Bravewomon, "Family Webs: A Study of Extended Families in the Lesbian/Gay/Bisexual Community," *Feminist Economics* 4, no. 2 (summer 1998): 107–9.

[35]   For an extended theoretical treatment, see V. Joseph Hotz, Jacob Alex Klerman, and Robert J. Willis, "The Economics of Fertility in Developed Countries," in *Handbook of Population and Family Economics*, vol. 1A, ed. Mark R. Rosenzweig and Oded Stark (Amsterdam: Elsevier, 1997), pp. 275–348.

$160,140.[36] Moreover, a very large part of total costs are not included in this figure, namely the time parents devote to childrearing. Even when a great deal of child care is purchased, parents, most often mothers, must still devote time to finding suitable caretakers and taking care of emergencies; in addition they tend to spend considerable time with their children providing education, recreation, and other enrichment. The time and energy they devote to these purposes could otherwise be used to get more education or training for themselves, to earn money, or to enjoy leisure.[37] Giving up some or all of these constitutes the opportunity cost of rearing children.

The economic opportunities of women and men are likely to have an important influence on the fertility decision. Women's growing potential for market earnings increases the opportunity cost of children and would, accordingly, be expected to have a negative substitution effect. This may well be one of the main determinants of fertility. The growing career orientation of highly educated women would reinforce this effect.[38] At the same time, however, greater earnings would also have a positive income effect, since the family can now better afford the money costs of having more children. Nonetheless, the substitution effect is expected to dominate for women. On the other hand, the income effect is likely to dominate when men's wages rise, as long as they do not generally give up much of their time for child care.[39] Thus, fertility is expected to be negatively associated with women's wages (and labor force participation), but positively associated with men's wages.

In addition to women's wages, a number of other factors may work to reduce fertility. For instance, the growing demand for "higher-quality" children, with better health and more education, is expected to have a negative effect.[40] In addition, the introduction of new and more effective methods of birth control, including the pill and IUD, have allowed couples to limit their fertility more easily and effectively.[41]

Table 9.2 and Figure 9.1 indicate that the total fertility rate has fluctuated considerably since the 1940s. From the end of World War II until the early 1960s was the period of the "baby boom." The fertility rate reached a peak of 3.7 children per woman (3,690 children per 1,000 women) between 1955 and 1959, far above the replacement rate of 2.1 children per woman. By 1976, however, during what has been termed the "baby bust" period, it had declined to as low as 1.7. It has fluctuated since then, but has recently been at or just below the replacement level. Apart from the fertility rate, the

---

[36] This figure is from the Department of Agriculture's annual report, "Expenditures on Children by Families," as cited in Tamar Lewin, "The Way We Live Now," *New York Times,* 14 May 2000, sec. 4, p. 3.

[37] It is worth noting that some of the time spent with children is often as enjoyable as any leisure.

[38] For instance, McKinley L. Blackburn, David E. Bloom, and David Neumark found that late childbearers tend to invest more heavily in human capital than early childbearers in "Fertility Timing, Wages and Human Capital," *Journal of Population Economics* 6, no. 1 (1993): 1–30. In addition, late childbearing would also be expected to reduce the number of children per woman, all else equal. See also Ronald R. Rindfuss, S. Philip Morgan, and Kate Offutt, "Education and the Changing Age Pattern of American Fertility: 1963–1989," *Demography* 33, no. 3 (August 1996): 277–90.

[39] The importance of both the substitution and income effects was initially identified by William P. Butz and Michael P. Ward, "The Emergence of Countercyclical U.S. Fertility," *American Economic Review* 69, no. 3 (June 1979): 318–28. These findings have been reexamined and, to some degree, contested by Diane Macunovich in "The Butz-Ward Model in Light of More Recent Data," *Journal of Human Resources* 30, no. 2 (spring 1995): 229–55.

[40] Becker, *A Treatise on the Family.*

[41] For consequent effects on career and marriage, see Goldin and Katz, "Career and Marriage in the Age of the Pill."

TABLE 9.2   Total Fertility Rates, 1940–1998

Years	Total Fertility Rate[a]
1940–1944	2,523
1945–1949	2,985
1950–1954	3,337
1955–1959	3,690
1960–1964	3,449
1965–1969	2,622
1970–1974	2,094
1975–1979	1,774
1980–1984	1,819
1985–1988	1,870
1989	2,014
1990	2,081
1991	2,073
1992	2,065
1993	2,046
1994	2,036
1995	2,019
1996	2,027
1997	2,033
1998	2,059

[a] The number of births that a cohort of 1,000 women would have if they experienced the age-specific birthrates occurring in the current year throughout their childbearing years. Dividing by 1,000 provides a measure of births per woman.

Source: U.S. Census Bureau, *Statistical Abstract of the United States,* 1984, 1999; U.S. Department of Health and Human Services, "Births: Final Data for 1998," *National Vital Statistics Reports* 48, no. 3 (28 March 2000).

total number of births is also related to the absolute number of women in their childbearing years. The baby boomers produced a large cohort of children starting in the early to mid-1980s referred to as the "echo of the baby boom" or the "baby boomlet."

The fluctuations in the fertility rate have occurred, in substantial part, as a result of variations in the strength of the opposing factors discussed earlier. The baby boom took place in a time of prosperity and rising real wages of men and women. Since relatively few married women in the childbearing ages worked at that time, the main effect was an increase in fertility due to the income effect of husbands' rising wages. Nonetheless, the magnitude of the baby boom probably cannot be fully explained without taking into account the postponement of births during the Great Depression of the 1930s and World War II, as well as social and cultural factors.

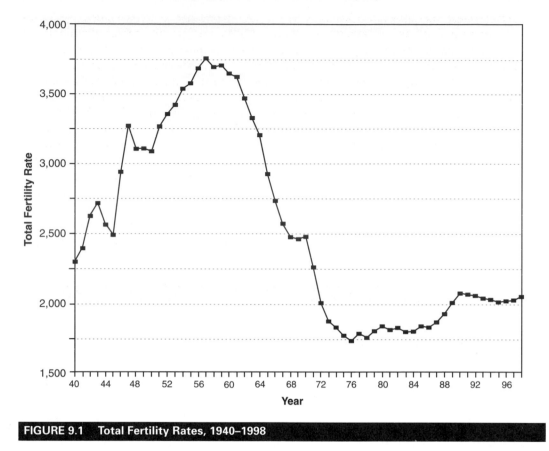

FIGURE 9.1 **Total Fertility Rates, 1940–1998**

The sharp drop in fertility beginning in the early 1960s, following the baby boom, coincided with rapid increases in the labor force participation rate of young women and advances in contraceptive techniques. The downward trend can also be explained in part by the higher cost of dropping out of the labor force to bear and raise children for women who have become increasingly committed to their careers. Such women are also more inclined to find their work absorbing and fulfilling. Turning to the most recent period, Figure 9.1 shows that, overall, there has been a modest rise in fertility from the mid-1980s to 1998. This may reflect the fact that some women who did not have children earlier chose to have them at a later time,[42] while younger couples may not have waited as long to start a family, perhaps because of publicity about the fertility problems of older couples.

We conclude that while the fertility rate may continue to increase very slightly for a time, it is unlikely to rise significantly. Women's growing commitment to market work is expected to keep fertility relatively low. As noted earlier, highly educated and career-oriented women tend to have the fewest children, and both level of education and career orientation of women are continuing to increase. At the same time, the negative ef-

---

[42] DaVanzo and Rahman, "American Families." Blackburn, Bloom, and Neumark, "Fertility Timing, Wages and Human Capital," suggest that this postponement was associated with women's greater investment in human capital.

fect of these factors on fertility may be mitigated, at least to some extent, by the increasing involvement of fathers with their children, and by the greater availability of good alternative child care, as well as any new tax provisions or subsidies reducing the financial burden of raising and educating children that are enacted in the future.

While there have been sizable fluctuations in the overall fertility rate, the share of births to unmarried mothers out of all births has increased markedly since the 1970s, though it appears to have leveled off in recent years. As shown in Table 9.3, births to unmarried mothers rose from just over one-tenth of all births in 1970 to around one-third in the late 1990s. Several factors contributed to the dramatic increase. First, there was a decline in births to married women. Hence, even if there had been no increase in births to unmarried women, this would have caused the proportion of such births to rise. Second, this figure depends on both the number of unmarried women as well as their probability of giving birth. As shown in Table 9.3, the birthrate among unmarried women actually declined among blacks between 1980 and 1998, and remains relatively low among whites, though it is on the increase. What has changed most significantly is the number of unmarried women, which increased substantially.[43]

TABLE 9.3 Births to Teens and Unmarried Women, 1970–1998				
	1970	*1980*	*1990*	*1998*
Birth Rates (Births per 1,000 Women in Specified Group)[a]				
Unmarried birth rate, ages 15–44	26.4	29.4	43.8	44.3
Whites	n.a.	18.1	32.9	37.5
Blacks	n.a.	81.1	90.5	73.3
Teen birth rate, ages 15–19	68.3	53.0	59.9	51.1
Unmarried teen birth rate, ages 15–19	22.4	27.6	42.5	41.5
Whites	n.a.	16.5	30.6	34.0
Blacks	n.a.	87.9	106.0	83.4
Older mother birth rate, ages 40–44	8.1	3.9	5.5	7.3
Unmarried older mother birth rate, ages 40–44	3.5	2.6	3.6	4.6
Types of Births (in Percent)				
Unmarried births as % of all births	10.7	18.4	28.0	32.8
Unmarried teen births as % of all teen births	31.9	48.3	67.6	78.5
Unmarried teen births as % of all unmarried births	50.1	40.8	31.0	29.4

n.a. Consistent series not available.

[a] For instance, unmarried birth rate is births to unmarried women per 1,000 unmarried women.

Sources: U.S. Department of Health and Human Services, "Births: Final Data for 1998," *National Vital Statistics Reports* 48, no. 3 (28 March 2000); U.S. Department of Health and Human Services, "Advance Report of Final Natality Statistics: 1994," *Monthly Vital Statistics Report* 44, no. 11, Tables 4 and 15; U.S. Department of Health and Human Services, *U.S. Vital Statistics,* Volume I, Natality; and U.S. Census Bureau, *Statistical Abstract of the United States: 1999.*

---

[43] Rebecca Blank, "Teen Pregnancy: Government Programs Are Not the Cause," *Feminist Economics* 1, no. 2 (summer 1995): 47–58. For trends by race, see Herbert L. Smith, S. Philip Morgan, and Tanya Korepeckyj-Cox, "Trends in Nonmarital Fertility," *Demography* 33, no. 2 (May 1995): 141–51.

Births to unmarried mothers are related to the same factors that have generally reduced incentives to marry. Women's increased labor market opportunities have provided them with greater financial means to support a family. In addition, men's ability to support a family has declined among the less educated, and welfare also appears to have played a role, albeit a small one.[44] Finally, premarital sex and unmarried childbearing are more widely accepted than in the past.

Interestingly, in many cases, unmarried mothers live with their child's father; as noted earlier, as many as 40 percent of all nonmarital births in the United States in the early 1990s were to cohabiting couples, rather than to women living alone.[45] Moreover, whether or not the child's parents are living together, a recent study finds that the fathers are often around at the time of the birth, want to help raise their children, and more often than not are romantically involved with the mother.[46] These couples have been termed "fragile families," because, quite often, the parents have low levels of educational attainment, unstable employment histories, and low earnings, and therefore are quite susceptible to breakup.

More serious than the high proportion of births to unmarried mothers is that the teen birthrate is considerably higher in the United States than in other economically advanced countries. Furthermore, Table 9.3 shows that over three-fourths of these births are to unmarried teens, as compared with only one-third in 1970. The rising percentage of unmarried teen births in the United States has largely been a result of declining marriage rates for teenagers, combined with increased birthrates among unmarried teens.[47] These trends, in turn, may be related to poor labor market prospects for less-educated young people, which lower the opportunity cost of pregnancy and reduce the availability of marriage partners with good economic prospects.[48] Other factors, including the availability of welfare, access to contraceptives, and the availability and affordability of abortion, may also affect trends in teen pregnancy and childbearing.[49]

It is encouraging that in the 1990s there has been a modest decline in the overall teen birthrate, from a recent high of 62 births per 1,000 teens in 1991 to 51 births per 1,000 in 1998. Birthrates have declined most for African American teens, though their rate remains substantially higher than that for white teens. These recent trends are a result of a decline in teen pregnancy due to reduced sexual activity and increased use of contraceptives, not the result of an increase in abortions.[50] As young women defer their

---

[44] For evidence on the poor job prospects of low-skilled workers, see Chinhui Juhn, "Decline of Male Labor Market Participation: The Role of Declining Market Opportunities," *Quarterly Journal of Economics* 107, no. 1 (February 1992): 79–122. Regarding the effect of welfare, see Moffitt, "The Effect of Welfare on Marriage and Fertility." Robert J. Willis also suggests that unmarried fertility may be a result of an imbalance in the sex ratio in "The Economics of Fatherhood," *American Economic Review* 90, no. 2 (May 2000): 378–82.

[45] Bumpass and Lu, "Trends in Cohabitation."

[46] Sara McLanahan and Irwin Garfinkel, "The Fragile Families and Child Well-Being Study: Questions, Design, and a Few Preliminary Results" (University of Wisconsin-Madison: Institute for Research on Poverty), Discussion Paper No. 1208–00 (May 2000).

[47] Blank, "Teen Pregnancy."

[48] For a discussion of these factors, see Ann Horvath and H. Elizabeth Peters, "Welfare Waivers and Non-Marital Childbearing," unpublished working paper, Cornell University (September 1999).

[49] See Shelly Lundberg and Robert D. Plotnick, "Adolescent Premarital Childbearing: Do Economic Incentives Matter?" *Journal of Labor Economics* 13, no. 2 (April 1995): 177–200; Daniel T. Lichter, Diane K. McLaughlin, and David C. Ribar, "State Abortion Policy, Geographic Access to Abortion Providers and Changing Family Formation," *Family Planning Perspectives* 30, no. 6 (December 1998): 281–87; and Moffitt, "The Effect of Welfare on Marriage and Fertility."

[50] National Center For Health Statistics, "Highlights of Trends in Pregnancies and Pregnancy Rates," *National Vital Statistics Reports* 47, no. 29 (December 15, 1999), p. 2.

first birth, this should lead to several positive developments, including improved health outcomes for children, since babies born to teens tend to have more health problems, beginning with premature birth and low birth weight. For young women themselves, deferring the birth of their first child enables them to spend more time acquiring education and job skills, which will ultimately place them and their future children in a much better economic position.[51]

Finally, Table 9.3 indicates an interesting trend in the birthrate among older mothers, those age 40 to 44. In 1970, their birthrate was relatively high, at 8.1 births per 1,000 women. At that time, family size was larger, so many of these births were to women who had started their childbearing in their 20s or 30s. As family size fell, so did births to older mothers. In recent years, births to older mothers have increased and are now close to their 1970 level, not because average family size has increased, but because more women are starting their families much later. Of particular note, births among "Murphy Brown" type mothers—those who are older and unmarried—have increased, though again their numbers are few. These trends likely reflect women's increased career orientation along with the delay in first marriage[52] and are expected to continue, especially as technological advances enable childbearing among larger fractions of women into their mid to late 40s.

Broadening the Economic Model of Fertility

A central feature of the application of the model of fertility initially formulated by Gary Becker to explain the trends in fertility is the expectation that, for women, the negative substitution effect of rising wages will outweigh the positive income effect, while the opposite will likely be true for men. There are, however, other scholars who believe that predictions drawn from the Becker model do not mesh well with actual trends. Diane Macunovich, for instance, argues that this model would have predicted much lower rates of fertility than we have had since the mid-1970s. She argues that this implies something else must have been going on, in addition to the rising opportunity cost of time for mothers. Following Richard A. Easterlin, she suggests that **relative income**—income relative to one's parents—is another important factor.

According to the Easterlin model, the driving force behind changes in fertility and female labor force participation is that people aspire to achieve at least the same income their parents had. If members of a particular birth cohort are worse off than their parents had been, female labor force participation will rise to compensate and, hence, fertility will decline. If, on the other hand, their income is higher than that of their parents, the effect on fertility will be positive.

Like the Becker model, the Easterlin theory, on its own, has not been completely successful at explaining fertility trends. However, Macunovich, among others, has worked to bring these theories together by incorporating elements of each in her model of fertility.[*] Focusing on young women age 20 to 24 for the period 1962 to 1994, Macunovich includes measures of wives' wages and husbands' relative income. Consistent with the two theories,

[*] Diane Macunovich, "Relative Income and Price of Time: Exploring Their Effects on U.S. Fertility and Female Labor Force Participation," in *Population and Development Review* 22, (supplement 1996): 223–57.

---

[51] For a discussion of policies that can be used to hasten this trend, see Isabel V. Sawhill, "Welfare Reform and Reducing Teen Pregnancy, *Public Interest 138* (winter 2000): 40–51.

[52] See, for instance, Steven P. Martin, "Diverging Fertility Among U.S. Women Who Delay Childbearing Past Age 30," *Demography* 37, no. 4 (November 2000): 523–33.

she finds that rising female wages negatively affect fertility, while increases in husbands' relative income serves to increase fertility. She also provides evidence that the net effect of rising female wages depends on the level of husbands' relative income. That is, when husbands have relatively low income compared to what their parents had, the income effect associated with their wives' wages is stronger and her earnings become more important in determining whether or not the family feels affluent enough to raise children. These findings suggest that a complex set of forces and interactions, rather than a single variable, is likely responsible for the dramatic fluctuations observed in fertility rates since the early 1960s.

Sources: Gary A. Becker, "An Economic Analysis of Fertility," in *Demographic and Economic Change in Developed Countries* (Princeton, NJ: Princeton University Press for the National Bureau of Economic Research, 1960); Richard A. Easterlin, "On the Relation of Economic Factors to Recent and Projected Fertility Changes," *Demography* 3 (August 1966): 131–53; Diane J. Macunovich, "A Review of Recent Developments in the Economics of Fertility" in *Household and Family Economics,* ed. Paul Menchik (Boston, MA: Kluwer Academic Press, 1996); and Macunovich, "Relative Income and Price of Time." For a discussion of other ways to broaden the model, see Robert Pollak and Susan Cotts Watkins, "Cultural and Economic Approaches to Fertility: Proper Marriage or Mesalliance?" *Population and Development Review* 19, no. 3 (September 1993): 467–96.

CHANGING FAMILY STRUCTURE AND ECONOMIC WELL-BEING

The U.S. labor force was once composed almost entirely of workers with few if any responsibilities for homemaking. The majority were married men with wives who were full-time homemakers, while most of the others were single. Today the labor force includes a growing proportion of workers from **dual-earner families,** in which both husbands and wives participate in the paid labor force, and from **single-parent families.** As we shall see, the structure of workers' families has substantial implications for the well-being of workers and their families. The policy issues raised by these changes will be discussed in Chapter 10.

DUAL-EARNER FAMILIES

As shown in Table 9.4, over the period 1976 to 1998 dual-earner families emerged as the predominant structure among married couples, rising from 50 to 60 percent of all such families.[53] Even more striking, in 1998, dual-earner families constituted 75 percent of all those that had an employed husband, and in just over 50 percent of dual-earner families, both spouses worked full-time, full-year. As would be expected, the explanations for the rise in dual-earner families are much the same as those offered for women's increased labor force participation discussed in Chapter 4. In large part, they indicate women's response to their own increased labor market opportunities. This view is consistent with the fact that increases in labor force participation have been most pronounced among women who earn high wages who are also married to high-wage men.[54]

---

[53] Despite anecdotal reports, families comprised of a breadwinner wife and stay-at-home husband remain quite rare as indicated by Smith, "The Emerging 21st Century American Family."

[54] For a detailed discussion of trends in earnings and employment among spouses, see Chinhui Juhn and Kevin M. Murphy, "Wage Inequality and Family Labor Supply," *Journal of Labor Economics* 15, no. 1, pt. 1 (January 1997): 72–97.

TABLE 9.4   Dual-Earner Families, 1976–1998ª

	1976	1980	1990	1998
Dual earners as % of all married couples	50.1	53.5	59.4	60.0
Dual earners as % of all married couples with employed husband	59.4	64.5	73.4	75.2
Dual earners, where both spouses employed full-time, full-year, as % of all dual earners	33.0	36.0	44.1	50.8
Median income of married-couple families ($1998) All married couples	n.a.	n.a.	$49,754	$54,180
Husband only employed	n.a.	n.a.	$44,301	$45,541
Dual earners	n.a.	n.a.	$59,032	$65,411
Both spouses employed full-time, full-year	n.a.	n.a.	$68,677	$68,075
Ratio of median income of dual earners to those with husband only employed	n.a.	n.a.	1.3	1.4

n.a. Not available.

ª Dual-earner couple defined as married couple with both spouses employed.

Source: U.S. Census Bureau, Historical Income Tables, "Work Experience of Husband and Wife—Married-Couple Families (All Races), by Median and Mean Income, 1976 to 1998," www.census.gov.

Also, as we saw in Chapter 3, there are considerable risks for women who completely specialize in homemaking in the event of divorce. It is expected that some married women work for pay to avoid these risks. Another explanation is that many families cannot achieve an acceptable standard of living unless both partners are employed.

In any case, married women's earnings are an important source of family income today. As shown in Table 9.4, dual-earner married couples, on average, have incomes that are 40 percent higher than those with just an employed husband. One consequence of women's improved qualifications and increasing labor market opportunities, in conjunction with declines in the real earnings of less-educated men, is that the percentage of wives who had higher annual earnings than their husbands increased, from 16 percent in 1981 to 23 percent by 1998.[55] As discussed in Chapter 3, wives' greater earnings may be expected to increase their bargaining power within marriage. Related to this, husbands' and wives' relative earnings also tend to affect decisions about whose career takes precedence. Generally, wives have had the secondary career in their families, while their husbands have had the primary one. This is likely to negatively affect the level and growth of their wages for a couple of reasons. First, those with secondary careers are less able to determine their place of residence so as to maximize their wages and opportunities for advancement. Further, this reduces their bargaining power vis-à-vis their current employer because they cannot make a credible threat to leave. Some research indicates that wages are lower for wives who

---

[55] U.S. Census Bureau, "Historical Income Tables," www.census.gov. See also Anne E. Winkler, "Earnings of Husbands and Wives in Dual-Earner Families," *Monthly Labor Review* 121, no. 4 (April 1998): 42–48.

have the secondary career in their family than for those who have the primary career.[56] As husbands' and wives' relative earnings change, one would expect more instances in which the careers of both spouses are regarded as equal and where wives even have the primary career. Equal careers may, however, lead to a wage penalty for both husbands and wives, particularly if they live in a small community with few alternative job opportunities. Residing in a big city is one potential solution.[57]

There is considerable evidence that women also suffer a wage penalty if they have children. For instance, in 1991, among young women (average age of 30), those without children earned 90 percent as much as young men, but mothers earned 73 percent as much. This difference cannot be fully accounted for by the lesser amounts of experience and education mothers tend to have. Further, there is evidence that this "family gap"—the difference in earnings between women with and without children—has been rising.[58] One possible explanation for the family gap is that mothers put less effort into their job, perhaps because they are overburdened by working a double shift at home and work.[59] Alternatively, perhaps employers discriminate against women with children, or mothers lack sufficient access to job-protected maternity leave, causing them to lose out on the benefits of accumulated human capital when they have children.[60] Another possibility is that women who are especially career-oriented, with a higher potential wage, may choose to remain childless. In this case, while the presence of children is associated with lower wages, children do not *cause* lower wages. Indeed, one recent study finds that even prior to the birth of their first child, women who eventually have children had lower wages than those who remained childless.[61]

Conversely, there is evidence that marriage increases men's wages and that fatherhood may do so as well, most likely due to the benefits of specialization in the family.[62] However, there may be a wage penalty for having a career-oriented wife as com-

---

[56] Anne E. Winkler and David C. Rose, "Career Hierarchy in Dual-Earner Families," *Research in Labor Economics* 19, ed. Solomon Polachek (Greenwich, Connecticut: JAI Press, 1999), pp. 147–72. For recent research on the effect of migration and job mobility on wages, see Joyce Jacobsen and Laurence M. Levin, "Marriage and Migration: Comparing Gains and Losses from Migration for Couples and Singles," *Social Science Quarterly* 78, no. 3 (September 1997): 688–709; and Kristin Keith and Abagail McWilliams, "Job Mobility and Gender-Based Wage Growth Differentials," *Economic Inquiry* 35, no. 2 (April 1997): 320–33.

[57] Dora L. Costa and Matthew E. Kahn, "Power Couples: Changes in the Locational Choice of the College Educated, 1940–1990," *Quarterly Journal of Economics* 115, no. 4 (November 2000): 1287–316.

[58] These figures are from Jane Waldfogel, "Understanding the 'Family Gap' in Pay for Women with Children," *Journal of Economic Perspectives* 12, no. 1 (winter 1998): 137–56. See also Sanders Korenman and David Neumark, "Marriage, Motherhood, and Wages," *Journal of Human Resources* 27, no. 2 (spring 1992): 233–55.

[59] For theory, see Gary Becker, "Human Capital, Effort, and the Sexual Division of Labor," *Journal of Labor Economics* 3, no. 1, pt. 2 (January 1985): 33–58; and for evidence see Joni Hersch and Leslie Stratton, "Housework, Fixed Effects, and Wages of Married Workers, *Journal of Human Resources* 32, no. 2 (spring 1997): 285–307.

[60] Waldfogel, "Understanding the 'Family Gap' in Pay."

[61] Shelly Lundberg and Elaina Rose, "Parenthood and the Earnings of Married Men and Women," *Labour Economics* (forthcoming).

[62] See, for instance, Sanders Korenman and David Neumark, "Does Marriage Really Make Men More Productive?" *Journal of Human Resources* 26, no. 2 (spring 1991): 282–307; and Shelly J. Lundberg and Elaina Rose, "The Effects of Sons and Daughters on Men's Labor Supply and Wages," unpublished working paper, University of Washington (October 1999).

pared to being the sole earner in the family.[63] Possible reasons why men with employed wives may not do as well are that employers might look askance at men who do not have a "traditional" family or might believe these men do not need as much income. As noted above, the wife's employment may also restrict the husband's mobility, or his productivity may be lower as a result of less spousal career support.[64] On the other hand, the husband's lower earnings could be the cause rather than the result of the wife's employment. At any rate, although a wife's employment may have a negative effect on her husband's earnings, it is clear that, on balance, her paycheck increases total family income and has helped to raise many families above the poverty line.

Apart from considering the effect of the rise in dual-earner families on wives' and husbands' incomes, separate and combined, it is also instructive to consider the effect of this trend on income inequality among married couples. Over the past several decades, income inequality among married couples has been rising. On the one hand, the larger proportion of women in the labor force has served to reduce income inequality among married couples because there are now fewer couples with wives who have zero earnings. On the other hand, the correlation between the earnings of husbands and wives has increased. While this positive relationship, which simply reflects the fact that men and women with higher earnings potential tend to be married to one another, has always existed, it has grown stronger.[65] To date, it is not clear if, on net, the rising employment and earnings of wives have increased inequality or caused inequality to rise less than might have otherwise been the case.[66] In any case, it is clear that the primary factor causing inequality to rise has been the large increase in earnings inequality among husbands.

MATERNAL EMPLOYMENT AND CHILDREN'S OUTCOMES

A particularly emotionally charged issue concerns the effect of maternal employment on children's development. In principle, the question should be asked about parental rather than maternal employment; however, it is still commonly accepted that the father will be working for pay and, as of now, that is a realistic assumption. Even so, while

---

[63] For evidence that having an employed wife leads to a wage penalty see Julie L. Hotchkiss and Robert E. Moore, "Testing for and Decomposing the Working Spouse Effect: Accounting for Endogeneity of the Wife's Decision to Work," *Industrial and Labor Relations Review* 52, no. 3 (April 1999): 410–23; and Jeffrey S. Gray, "The Fall in Men's Return to Marriage: Declining Productivity Effects or Changing Selection?" *Journal of Human Resources* 32, no. 3 (summer 1997): 481–504. On the other hand, Joyce P. Jacobsen and Wendy L. Rayack find no effect of wives' employment on husbands' wages in "Do Men Whose Wives Work Really Earn Less?" *American Economic Review* 86, no. 2 (May 1996): 268–73.

[64] These reasons are cited in Hotchkiss and Moore, "Testing for and Decomposing the Working Spouse Effect."

[65] John Pencavel, "Assortative Mating by Schooling and the Work Behavior of Wives and Husbands," *American Economic Review* 88, no. 2 (May 1998): 326–29.

[66] For evidence that rising wives' employment did not increase married-couple inequality, see Maria Cancian, Sheldon Danziger, and Peter Gottschalk, "Working Wives and Family Income Inequality Among Married Couples, in *Uneven Tides: Rising Inequality in America*, ed. Sheldon Danziger and Peter Gottschalk (New York: Russell Sage Foundation, 1993); and Maria Cancian and Deborah Reed, "The Impact of Wives' Earnings on Income Inequality: Issues and Estimates," *Demography* 36, no. 2 (May 1999): 173–84. Lynn Karoly and Gary Burtless reach the opposite conclusion in "Demographic Changes, Rising Earnings Inequality, and the Distribution of Personal Well-Being, 1959–1989," *Demography* 32, no. 3 (August 1995): 379–406.

in the past most research ignored the role of the father entirely, some limited attention is now being paid to the influence of fathers' employment on their children.[67]

Research has clearly shown that children's development is determined by a great many factors in addition to mother's employment. These include the innate characteristics of the children themselves, their sex, the number of children in the family, the family's level of resources, the role in their lives of their father, of other family members, and of close friends, the quality of their alternative care, and last but by no means least, the nature of the community where their family lives. In addition, there are many aspects of children's development to consider other than merely progress in cognition, educational attainment, and whether or not a girl becomes pregnant in her teens, the criteria most frequently employed by economists for child outcomes. Social and emotional development are obviously important as well, as are such long-term outcomes as the stability of their own marriages and their success in raising their own children. Again there is evidence that many different factors influence these various outcomes as well.[68]

Another factor to consider, as discussed in Chapter 3, is that nonemployed women often engage in other household activities when at home with their children, so that the difference between the amount of time that employed and nonemployed mothers spend in one-on-one activities with their children is smaller than might initially be suspected. Also, as indicated in Chapter 3, fathers' time with children has increased in many families, which should also serve to reduce any potential negative effects of mothers' employment on children's development.[69]

The general consensus among researchers is that children between ages two and four tend to do better in center day care both intellectually and socially than children cared for entirely at home. For infants and toddlers, the evidence has been more mixed, with some researchers finding negative effects on children's social and cognitive development during the first year, while most, but not all, find that these are offset by positive effects in subsequent years.[70] Early studies also raised some concern about the effect of nonmaternal care on children's attachment to their mother. However, a 1996

---

[67] Toby L. Parcel and Elizabeth G. Meaghan, *Parents' Jobs and Children's Lives* (New York: Aldine de Gruyter, 1994), for instance, investigates the impact of both mothers' and fathers' work on children's outcomes and find that fathers' failure to have a full-time job has negative consequences on children, perhaps because of the norm of father as breadwinner. In a related study, Christopher J. Ruhm finds some evidence that paternal and maternal employment have qualitatively similar negative effects on children's cognitive development in "Parental Employment and Child Cognitive Development," unpublished working paper, University of North Carolina at Greensboro (May 2000).

[68] For a review of the issues, see Cheryl D. Hayes, John L. Palmer, and Martha Zaslow, eds., *Who Cares for America's Children? Child Care Policy for the 1990s,* National Research Council (Washington, DC: National Academy Press, 1990).

[69] Suzanne M. Bianchi, "Maternal Employment and Time with Children: Dramatic Change or Surprising Continuity? *Demography* 37, no. 4 (November 2000): 401–14; and Joseph H. Pleck, "Balancing Work and Family," *Scientific American Presents* 10, no. 2 (summer 1999): 38–43.

[70] This general assessment of the literature is made by Ruhm, "Parental Employment and Child Cognitive Development," though his own analysis leads him to the conclusion that these earlier studies may have been "overly optimistic." For other evidence, both positive and negative, see Francine D. Blau and Adam J. Grossberg, "Maternal Labor Supply and Children's Cognitive Development," *Review of Economics and Statistics* 74, no. 3 (August 1992): 474–81; K. Alison Clarke-Stewart, "A Home Is Not a School: The Effects of Child Care on Children's Development," *Journal of Social Issues* 47, no. 2 (1991): 105–23, and "Infant Day Care: Maligned or Malignant," *American Psychologist* 44, no. 2 (1989): 266–73; and Jay Belsky, "The 'Effects' of Infant Day Care Reconsidered," *Early Childhood Research Quarterly* 3 (1988): 235–72.

study on the impact of day care on infants conducted by 25 researchers sponsored by the National Institute of Child Health and Human Development (NICHD) found that an infant's sense of trust in his or her mother was not affected by being in day care, the number of hours spent in day care, the age when the infant entered day care, or how many times the arrangement was changed. Instead, the key factor was the mother's sensitivity and responsiveness to her child.[71] Similarly, NICHD recently found virtually no relationship between hours spent in day care and young children's cognitive, linguistic, and social development. Again, it was the mother's sensitivity to her child that was most important as well as her level of education.[72] A particular challenge faced by researchers and those interpreting these findings is that the factors discussed earlier that affect children's outcomes are highly interrelated, making it extremely difficult to isolate the influence of a single factor.[73]

A further dimension of this issue is the extent to which the *quality* of nonmaternal child care affects children's development. Quality has been measured either in terms of institutional features of child care settings such as teacher training, group size, and child–teacher ratios, or in terms of children's experiences in child care, such as the amount of verbal interaction between children and teachers or whether "developmentally appropriate" activities are provided. As might be expected, settings that tend to be of high quality in one dimension tend to also be of high quality in the other. Findings vary but there is evidence that quality of care does matter.[74] For instance, recent research found that the amount of verbal interaction between child care providers and children positively influences cognitive outcomes, though factors related to the child's own family environment were stronger predictors of their cognitive development.[75] This conclusion is also supported by the success of Head Start, a preschool program targeted at low-income children funded by the federal government, as well as by positive results from other early intervention programs.[76]

The impact on school-aged and older children of mothers' employment appears to be favorable. Recent evidence indicates that it has positive effects on daughters' and sons' academic achievements. Further, maternal employment during a daughter's teen years does not appear to have any effect on her likelihood of becoming a teen mother,

---

[71] National Institute of Child Health and Human Development, "Infant Child Care and Attachment Security: Results of the NICHD Study of Early Child Care" (20 April 1996).

[72] National Institutes of Health, "Only Small Link Found Between Hours in Child Care and Mother–Child Interaction," *NIH News Alert* (7 November 1999).

[73] Moreover, causation between mothers' employment and children's outcomes may go either way. For instance, Karen Norberg finds that mothers of "high risk" infants, such as those born prematurely, as well as those with developmental delays, are slower to return to employment in "The Effects of Daycare Reconsidered," National Bureau of Economic Research Working Paper No. 6769 (October 1998).

[74] For evidence that quality matters, see Council of Economic Advisers, "The First Three Years: Investments that Pay," Executive Summary (17 April 1997); and Janet Currie, "Early Childhood Intervention Programs: What Do We Know?" Joint Center for Poverty Research Working Paper No. 169 (May 2000). On the other hand, David M. Blau finds that institutional features, alone, have no effect on children's cognitive development in "The Effect of Child Care Characteristics on Child Development," *Journal of Human Resources* 34, no. 4 (fall 1999): 786–822.

[75] National Institutes of Health, "Results of NICHD Study of Early Child Care Reported at Society for Research in Child Development Meeting," *NIH News Alert* (3 April 1997). See also Currie, "Early Childhood Intervention Programs."

[76] Janet Currie and Duncan Thomas, "Does Head Start Make a Difference?" *American Economic Review* 85, no. 3 (June 1995): 341–64; and Currie, "Early Childhood Intervention Programs."

nor on her chance of being a future welfare recipient. Finally, mother's employment appears to have positive effects on daughters' self-esteem.[77]

SINGLE-PARENT FAMILIES

As the demographic trends reviewed earlier suggest, single-parent families are increasingly common in the United States, especially families maintained by mothers. Table 9.5 indicates that, from 1970 to 1998, the percentage of families with one or more children under age 18 maintained by a mother increased from nearly 12 percent to 26 percent. In addition, just under 6 percent of families were father only, a figure that has quadrupled since 1970.[78] These figures on single-parent families include those who head their own household as well as those who live in someone else's household, whether a parent's or nonrelative's.

Differences in family types by race are substantial. Historically, mother-only families have been more common among African Americans, but as shown in Table 9.5 and

TABLE 9.5 Trends in Types of Families With Own Children Under Age 18, 1970–1998[a]				
	As a % of All Families			
	1970	*1980*	*1990*	*1998*
Mother-Only Families				
All races	11.5	19.4	24.2	26.1
White	8.9	15.1	18.8	20.9
Black	33.0	48.7	56.2	57.3
Hispanic origin[b]	n.a.	24.0	29.3	29.9
Father-Only Families				
All races	1.3	2.1	3.9	5.6
White	1.2	2.0	3.8	5.8
Black	2.6	3.2	4.3	5.0
Hispanic origin[b]	n.a.	1.9	4.0	5.8
Two-Parent Families				
All races	87.1	78.5	71.9	68.3
White	89.9	82.9	77.4	73.4
Black	64.3	48.1	39.4	37.7
Hispanic origin[b]	n.a.	74.1	66.8	64.4

n.a. Not available.

[a] Families include those heading their own households and those living in the households of others (subfamilies).

[b] Persons of Hispanic origin can be of any race.

Source: U.S. Census Bureau, "All Parent/Child Situations by Type, Race, and Hispanic Origin of Householder or Reference Person: 1970 to Present," www.census.gov.

---

[77]   Robert Haveman and Barbara Wolfe, "The Determinants of Children's Attainments: A Review of Methods and Findings," *Journal of Economic Literature* 33, no. 4 (December 1995): 1829–78; Robert Haveman and Barbara Wolfe, *Succeeding Generations: On the Effects of Investments in Children* (New York: Russell Sage Foundation, 1994), chap. 5 and 8; and Paul Amato and Alan Booth, *Generation at Risk: Growing Up in an Era of Family Upheaval* (Cambridge MA: Harvard University Press, 1997).

[78]   See Steven Garasky and Daniel R. Meyer, "Reconsidering the Increase in Father-Only Families," *Demography* 33, no. 3 (August 1996): 385–93.

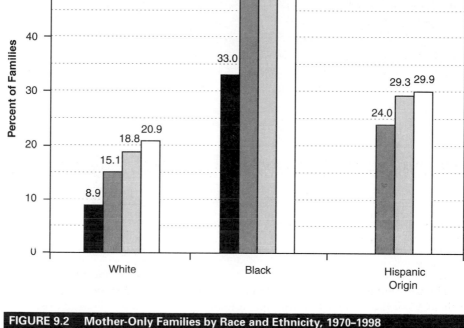

FIGURE 9.2   **Mother-Only Families by Race and Ethnicity, 1970–1998**

Figure 9.2, there has been a considerable increase in the proportion of these families among whites since 1970.[79] As of 1998, 57 percent of black families with children were maintained by mothers as compared with 21 percent of white families, while the figure for those of Hispanic origin was 30 percent.

There is considerable concern about single-parent families, particularly in relation to child well-being. First, such families, especially those maintained by women, have a high incidence of poverty. Second, it is believed that growing up in a family with only one adult may have long-term negative consequences for children, both economic and social.

Table 9.6 shows the income status of single-adult female and male-headed families as compared to married-couple families in 1999. These figures are available for household heads only (and do not include single-parent families living in someone else's household). Most strikingly, the median income of female-headed families was less than

---

[79]   Michael S. Rendall observes, however, that in contrast to black families, many white families still have two parents present, whether married or cohabiting, in "Entry or Exit? A Transition-Probability Approach to Explaining the High Prevalence of Single Motherhood Among Black Women," *Demography* 36, no. 3 (August 1999): 369–76.

TABLE 9.6 Incidence of Poverty by Type of Family, 1999[a]			
	Percent of Families	*Median Income ($)*	*Percent in Poverty*
All Families	100.0	48,950	9.3
White	83.7	51,224	7.3
Black	12.0	31,778	21.9
Hispanic origin[b]	10.5	31,663	20.2
Type of Family			
Married-couple families	76.8	56,676	4.8
Male householder, no wife present	5.6	37,396	11.7
Female householder, no husband present	17.6	23,732	27.8
White	13.9	26,529	22.5
Black	44.0	18,244	39.3
Hispanic origin[b]	23.4	18,701	38.8

[a] Figures are for household heads only. Children under age 18 may or may not be present.

[b] Persons of Hispanic origin may be of any race.

Sources: U.S. Census Bureau, "Money Income in the United States: 1999," *Current Population Reports* P60-209 (September 2000); and U.S. Census Bureau, "Poverty in the United States: 1999," *Current Population Reports* P60-210 (September 2000).

half that of married couples. Around 28 percent were poor, compared to less than 5 percent of married couples. Families headed by women are also more likely to have incomes below the poverty line for an extended period of time.[80] This gives some indication of why there is so much discussion about the "feminization" of poverty.

Poverty rates are particularly high for African American and Hispanic female-headed families, with nearly 40 percent of both living in poverty in 1999, although these figures are well below the recent highs of 50 percent in the early 1990s. Among whites the poverty rate for 1999 was 23 percent. Inevitably, the very high rates of poverty among single-parent families are a major factor behind the high rates of poverty for children, overall. In 1999, fully 17 percent of all children, 14 percent of white, 30 percent of Hispanic, and 33 percent of black children lived in poverty.[81]

In interpreting poverty statistics, it is important to understand the way in which the official poverty rate is currently determined. On the one hand, income used to determine poverty status does not include such items as food stamps, Medicaid, housing subsidies, and other in-kind transfers so that it understates real income. On the other hand, while the poverty threshold is updated for changes in inflation, it remains a fixed multiple of the income needed to provide food for the family, established as long ago as the 1960s, ignoring the fact that expenditures on food have increased substantially less than have those for other items such as housing, health insurance, and education. In view of these concerns, alternative measures of poverty are currently being calculated as well,

---

[80] U.S. Census Bureau, "Female-Householder Families Most Likely to Stay Poor, Census Bureau Says," Press Release, CB95–129, 20 July 1995.

[81] U.S. Census Bureau, "Poverty in the United States: 1998" *Current Population Reports,* P60–207 (September 1999).

but the official poverty rate continues to serve as a major indicator of economic well-being.[82]

It is not difficult to understand why single-parent families have incomes so much lower than families with two parents. First, they have a lower ratio of adults to children, thus fewer potential earners as well as fewer caregivers per dependent. This double burden makes it far more difficult to do justice both to job and family, not to mention the reduction in leisure time.[83] Second, there is a higher incidence of female-headed families among the less educated, which further accounts for their lower income.[84] Third, as we have seen, women tend to earn considerably less than men with comparable qualifications, and mothers tend to accumulate less labor force experience than other workers.

As noted earlier, single mothers may live independently or they may live in extended households, typically with their parents (their child's grandparents) or other relatives. In 1998, over one-fifth of single mothers were in the latter arrangement.[85] Such doubling up involves some loss of privacy, but also reduces costs, because of economies of scale. In addition, other household members can provide financial assistance and emotional support as well as in-house child care.

As discussed earlier, some single mothers cohabit with a male partner. A recent study estimated that 12 percent did so in 1995.[86] Since the U.S. Census Bureau does not count unmarried partners as part of the family, their income is not taken into consideration in determining the family's poverty status. The mother and her children may, nevertheless, benefit from some degree of income sharing with the partner, depending on factors such as the length of time the couple has been together and whether or not the partner is the children's biological father.[87] One study finds that the poverty rate for children would fall very slightly, but that many would remain poor even if cohabitors' incomes were included because many cohabitors have low or no incomes.[88]

---

[82]   The National Research Council has offered a number of recommendations to revise the poverty measure, and several experimental measures are now being tracked. See, for instance, U.S. Census Bureau, "Experimental Poverty Measures: 1970 to 1990," *Current Population Reports*, P60–205 (June 1999). For a detailed look at how poor single mothers keep their families afloat, see Kathryn Edin and Laura Levin, *Making Ends Meet: How Single Mothers Survive Welfare and Low-Wage Work* (New York: Russell Sage Foundation, 1997).

[83]   For a discussion, see Clair (Vickery) Brown, "The Time-Poor: A New Look at Poverty," *Journal of Human Resources* 12, no. 1 (winter 1977): 27–48. The issue is also discussed in Clair (Vickery) Brown, "Women's Economic Contribution to the Family," in *The Subtle Revolution,* ed. Ralph E. Smith (Washington, DC: The Urban Institute, 1979), pp. 159–200.

[84]   Francine D. Blau, "Trends in the Well-Being of American Women, 1970–1995," *Journal of Economic Literature* 36, no. 1 (March 1998): 112–65.

[85]   Figure computed from U.S. Census Bureau, "Families, by Presence of Own Children Under 18: 1950 to Present," and "All Parent/Child Situations by Type, Race, and Hispanic Origin of Householder or Reference Person: 1970 to Present," www.census.gov. For recent evidence on the rising number of families with grandparents present, see Lynne M. Casper and Kenneth R. Bryson, "Co-resident Grandparents and Their Grandchildren: Grandparent Maintained Families," Population Division Working Paper No. 26 (Washington, DC: U.S. Census Bureau, March 1998).

[86]   Rebecca A. London, "Trends in Single Mothers' Living Arrangements, 1970–1995," *Demography* 35, no. 1 (February 1998): 125–31.

[87]   Anne E. Winkler, "Economic Decisionmaking Among Cohabitors: Findings Regarding Income Pooling," *Applied Economics* 29, no. 8 (August 1997): 1079–90.

[88]   Marcia Carlson and Sheldon Danziger, "Cohabitation and the Measurement of Child Poverty," *Review of Income and Wealth* 45, no. 2 (June 1999): 179–91. See also Gregory Acs and Megan Gallagher, "Income Inequality Among America's Children," Assessing the New Federalism Series B, No. B-6 (Washington, DC: Urban Institute, January 2000).

The economic circumstances of families maintained by women also vary considerably depending on the woman's age and marital status. Never-married mothers tend to have particularly low incomes, not only because they are less likely than divorced mothers to receive child support from absent fathers, but also they are, on average, younger and have less education. Women who become parents as teenagers, most of whom are not married, tend to be at a particular economic and social disadvantage throughout their lives. They tend to have low levels of educational attainment, and if they work, they generally earn low wages, causing many to be poor. At first, researchers assumed that it was early childbearing that led to these negative outcomes. More recently, however, it has been suggested that many of these women would not have done well even if they had delayed childbearing until their 20s, because many are, themselves, from economically and socially disadvantaged backgrounds. While the research evidence is mixed, it appears that early childbearing, per se, does have some detrimental effect on young women and their children, though findings differ considerably regarding the magnitude of this effect.[89]

Divorced women tend to fare somewhat better than never-married women, in part because they are more likely to receive child support payments. Yet many struggle financially. It has been estimated that women's income falls by 20 to 30 percent after divorce, even after the smaller size of the family is taken into account.[90] For both never-married and divorced mothers, a significant reason for their low income is that if noncustodial parents provide any child support at all, they tend to contribute less than what would generally be considered their fair share. In 1997, only 56 percent of custodial parents had a child support award; of those who were supposed to receive payments the same year, nearly 41 percent received the full amount they were awarded, just under 27 percent received partial payment, and the remaining 33 percent received no payment at all.[91] Nonetheless, child support payments that are received do provide a considerable supplement to income, especially for poor parents.[92]

A number of factors contribute to low rates of child support collection.[93] Some parents fail to pay child support they could well afford because they believe that the custodial parent does not spend the entire amount on their children. Of course, the question arises as to what extent they take into account a share of overhead items such as the cost

[89] For evidence that early childbearing has little effect, see Arline T. Geronimus and Sanders Korenman, "The Socioeconomic Consequences of Teen Childbearing Reconsidered," *Quarterly Journal of Economics* 107, no. 4 (November 1992): 1187–214; and Joseph Hotz, Susan McElroy, and Seth Sanders, "The Impact of Teenage Childbearing on the Mothers and the Consequences of Those Impacts for Government," in *Kids Having Kids,* ed. Rebecca Maynard (Washington, DC: The Urban Institute, 1997), pp. 55–94. For evidence of negative consequences, see Saul Hoffman, E. Michael Foster, and Frank F. Furstenberg, "Reevaluating the Costs of Teenage Childbearing," *Demography* 30, no. 1 (February 1993): 1–13; and Daniel Klepinger, Shelly Lundberg, and Robert Plotnick, "How Does Adolescent Fertility Affect the Human Capital and Wages of Young Women?" *Journal of Human Resources* 34, no. 3 (summer 1999): 421–43.

[90] Karen C. Holden and Pamela J. Smock, "The Economic Costs of Marital Dissolution: Why Do Women Bear a Disproportionate Cost?" *Annual Review of Sociology* 17 (1991): 51–78. For evidence on the gender gap in economic well-being between spouses following separation, see Suzanne M. Bianchi, Lekha Subaiya, and Joan R. Kahn, "The Gender Gap in the Economic Well-Being of Nonresident Fathers and Custodial Mothers," *Demography* 36, no. 2 (May 1999): 195–203.

[91] Figures are from U.S. Census Bureau," Child Support 1997," www.census.gov.

[92] Judi Bartfeld, "Child Support and the Postdivorce Economic Well-Being of Mothers, Fathers, and Children," *Demography* 37, no. 2 (May 2000): 203–13; while Daniel R. Meyer and Mei-Chen Hu find more modest effects in "A Note on the Antipoverty Effectiveness of Child Support Among Mother-Only Families," *Journal of Human Resources* 34, no. 1 (winter 1999): 225–34.

[93] For a formal treatment and discussion, see Andrea Beller and John W. Graham, *Small Change: The Economics of Child Support* (New Haven, CT: Yale University Press, 1993), chap. 3.

of housing, maintenance, and so on. Others may also withhold payments in retaliation for limited visitation rights or simply because of resentment against the former spouse. Also, in a few cases the other parent may be deceased. Far more frequently, however, absent parents are themselves poor and it would be genuinely difficult for them to pay more.[94] Unfortunately, it is most often the mothers, who are the least able to stand on their own, with little education, little or no labor market experience, and few other resources, who are also the least likely to receive any support from their children's father(s).

This review makes clear that single-parent families are at a particular economic disadvantage. In Chapter 10 we review government policies intended to raise their incomes, pointing to both the successes and limitations of these policies.

FAMILY STRUCTURE AND CHILDREN'S OUTCOMES

As we have seen, the share of single-parent families has increased considerably. From the perspective of children, this means that an increasing fraction of them are being raised in these families. As shown earlier in Table 3.4, only 68 percent of children under age 18 lived in a married couple family in 1998.[95] Moreover, these figures refer to a single point in time and thus mask the disruption and change that an even larger fraction of children experience during their childhood. It is estimated that one-half of all children born in the early 1980s will spend some time without one of their biological or adoptive parents living in their home, before they themselves leave to set up their own household.[96] Transitions between living arrangements may create difficulties for children, both in terms of financial and emotional support.[97] Hence, it is important to focus not only on the influence of the current family structure, but also on the changes in family structure that the children have experienced. In terms of economic outcomes, it is particularly relevant to examine educational attainment, labor force participation, and teen pregnancy.

A study by Sara McLanahan and Gary Sandefur, which has received considerable attention, found that children raised in married-couple two-parent families do better in these respects than those from single-parent families.[98] For instance, they report that children raised in single-parent families have a greater high school dropout rate than those from two-parent families, even after taking account of parents' educational levels[99] and

---

[94] See, for instance, Maureen Waller and Robert Plotnick, *Child Support and Low-Income Families: Perceptions, Practices and Policies* (San Francisco, CA: Public Policy Institute of California, 1999).

[95] U.S. Census Bureau, "Living Arrangements of Children Under 18 Years Old: 1960 to Present," table CH-1, www.census.gov.

[96] Larry Bumpass and James Sweet, "Children's Experiences in Single-Parent Families: Implications of Cohabitation and Marital Transitions," *Family Planning Perspectives* 21, no. 6 (November/December 1989): 256–60; and Bumpass and Lu, "Trends in Cohabitation."

[97] Graefe and Lichter, "Life Course Transitions of American Children."

[98] Sara McLanahan and Gary Sandefur, *Growing Up With a Single Parent: What Hurts, What Helps?* (Cambridge, MA: Harvard University Press, 1994). Unfortunately, the data sets they examine do not permit them to analyze the effects of cohabitation on children's outcomes. For a review of studies that have started to look at this question, see Wendy D. Manning, "The Implications of Cohabitation for Children's Well-Being," unpublished working paper, Bowling Green University (October 2000).

[99] McLanahan and Sandefur observe that parents' education is a very important determinant of children's future educational attainment in *Growing Up With a Single Parent.* Similarly, David M. Blau finds that family background characteristics including parental education have a far greater effect on children's development than income in "The Effect of Income on Child Development," *Review of Economics and Statistics* 81, no. 2 (May 1999): 261–76. For other evidence on the role of parental education, see Haveman and Wolfe, "The Determinants of Children's Attainments."

race. Estimates of the remaining difference range from 7 to 16 percentage points, but much of this rather large difference is explained by factors other than single parenthood itself. Income explains as much as half of it. With less income, single parents have little money for after-school care, let alone enrichment programs. Children in such families are also thought to be at a disadvantage because there is one less adult to provide ties to the community. This disadvantage is often exacerbated by the more frequent moves of such families. Community ties are important because a community network can help with schooling decisions and getting a job, as well as with solving personal problems that may arise. Finally, children in single-parent families tend to receive less parental attention and supervision at home. This study also found that outcomes are not as favorable for children in stepparent families as for those living with both biological or adoptive parents.

In spite of this evidence, researchers continue to debate whether, and to what extent, growing up in a single-parent family is the real cause of children performing poorly in school. Some argue that there may be other factors present that lead to both children's poor school performance and parents' divorce, such as a parent's substance abuse problem or a high degree of family conflict. In these cases, the child might well have performed poorly in school even if the parents had not separated. As a result, researchers have made additional efforts to try to disentangle causation from association. Some of this research tends to confirm McLanahan and Sandefur's findings that living in single-parent families or living with one stepparent rather than both biological or adoptive parents has unfavorable effects on educational outcomes, but others have found more mixed evidence.[100] One researcher has even taken the extreme view that what parents do does not matter at all in terms of children's developmental outcomes.[101]

In interpreting these research findings it is important to keep in mind that even if growing up in a single-parent family tends to have negative effects, this only means that the risks of particular outcomes are increased, not that they are assured or that they are nonexistent for children in two-parent families. For one, there are not always two good, loving, attentive parents in every family where there are two biological parents, and there are many single parents and stepparents who love their children and devote considerable time and energy to them.

---

[100] For further evidence that family structure influences educational attainment see Gary D. Sandefur and Thomas Wells, "Does Family Structure Really Influence Educational Attainment?" *Social Science Research* 28 (December 1999): 331–57; Gary Painter and David I. Levine, "Family Structure and Youths' Outcomes: Which Correlations are Causal?" *Journal of Human Resources* 35, no. 3 (summer 2000): 524–49; and Anne Case, I-Fen Lin, and Sara McLanahan, "Household Resource Allocation in Stepfamilies: Darwin Reflects on the Plight of Cinderella," *American Economic Review* 89, no. 2 (May 1999): 234–38. For some evidence on the other side, along with a discussion of the methodological challenges, see Donna K. Ginther and Robert A. Pollak, "Does Family Structure Affect Children's Educational Outcomes?" unpublished working paper, Washington University (May 2000).

[101] Judith Rich Harris argues that only genetics and peer groups matter in *The Nurture Assumption: Why Children Turn Out the Way They Do* (New York: Free Press, 1998). For a useful synthesis of this and much of the aforementioned literature, see Andrew J. Cherlin, "Going to Extremes: Family Structure, Children's Well-Being, and Social Science," *Demography* 36, no. 4 (November 1999): 421–28.

CONCLUSION

This chapter has considered the effect of a woman's labor force participation and other factors on the formation, functioning, and possible breakup of families. The net result is that dual-earner families and female-headed families are becoming far more common, swiftly replacing the traditional married-couple family of the breadwinner husband and homemaker wife. The research provides little evidence that maternal employment has negative consequences for children, and some evidence of beneficial effects for preschoolers and older children. We have also seen that women who head families face severe economic problems as well as some evidence that children growing up in these families do not, on average, fare as well as those in two-parent families.

QUESTIONS FOR REVIEW AND DISCUSSION

1. Describe the main changes in the typical family in the United States over the last 30 to 40 years and explain their causes.
2. Women's rising labor force participation might either increase or reduce marriage rates. Explain why the effect could go either way.
3. There is a negative relationship between women's labor force participation and fertility. Is higher labor force participation the cause of the lower birthrate or vice versa? Discuss.
4. Increasing numbers of children are being raised in families in which mothers are cohabiting, either with the child's father or with a boyfriend. Consider the pros and cons for children of these arrangements versus living with a single parent.
5. In what ways are marriage and cohabitation similar and in what ways do they differ?
6. Explain why child support enforcement might encourage some married couples to stay together while it might encourage others to break up.
7. What are the advantages and disadvantages of the rising age of marriage?
8. Women who become mothers when they are teenagers are less likely to obtain a college degree than those who delay their childbearing until at least their mid 20s. Discuss why this is the case [Hint: refer back to the human capital model in Chapter 6] and what the consequences for these women and their families are likely to be.

Suggested Readings

Beller, Andrea H., and John W. Graham. *Small Change: The Economics of Child Support.* New Haven, CT: Yale University Press, 1993.

Bianchi, Suzanne. "The Changing Demographic and Socioeconomic Characteristics of Single Parent Families." *Marriage and Family Review* 20, nos. 1–2 (spring 1995): 71–97.

Blau, Francine D. "Trends in the Well-Being of American Women, 1970–1995." *Journal of Economic Literature* 36, no. 1 (March 1998): 112–65.

DaVanzo, Julie, and M. Omar Rahman. "American Families: Trends and Correlates." *Population Index* 59, no. 3 (1993): 350–86.

Edin, Kathryn, and Laura Lein. *Making Ends Meet: How Single Mothers Survive Welfare and Low-Wage Work.* New York: Russell Sage Foundation, 1997.

Gluckman, Amy, and Betsy Reed, eds. *Homo Economics: Capitalism, Community, and Lesbian and Gay Life.* New York: Routledge, 1997.

McLanahan, Sara, and Gary Sandefur. *Growing Up With a Single Parent: What Hurts, What Helps?* Cambridge, MA: Harvard University Press, 1994.

Moffitt, Robert A., ed. *Welfare, the Family, and Reproductive Behavior: Research Perspectives.* Washington, DC: National Research Council, 1998.

Rosenzweig, Mark R., and Oded Stark, eds. *Handbook of Population and Family Economics.* Vol. 1A and 1B. Amsterdam: Elsevier, 1997.

Smith, Tom W. "The Emerging 21st Century American Family." GSS Social Change Report No. 42. University of Chicago: National Opinion Research Center, 1999.

Tucker, M. Belinda, and Claudia Mitchell-Kernan. *The Decline in Marriage Among African-Americans.* New York: Russell Sage Foundation, 1995.

Waite, Linda, and Maggie Gallagher. *The Case for Marriage: Why Married People Are Happier, Healthier, and Better Off Financially.* New York: Doubleday & Company, 2000.

10

POLICIES AFFECTING PAID WORK AND FAMILY

Chapter Highlights

- Policies to Alleviate Poverty
- Taxes, Specialization, and Marriage
- The Competing Demands of Work and Family
- Who Is Responsible for Children?
- Family Friendly Policies

A host of programs and policies have emerged and evolved over time that influence the well-being of individuals and their families. This chapter begins where Chapter 9 left off, by discussing government policies to alleviate poverty, especially those that affect mother-only families since they often face the greatest difficulties. Next, we review some major features of the U.S. federal income tax and Social Security systems and point to some of their potential effects on paid work and family formation decisions. The remainder of the chapter discusses the competing demands of paid work and family faced by more and more individuals as single-parent and dual-earner families swiftly replace the traditional family of a breadwinner husband and homemaker wife. We discuss the potential role for government and employers in alleviating these conflicts. In examining family friendly policies, we consider not only those that are generally available in the United States, but also others that are only beginning to be introduced.

POLICIES TO ALLEVIATE POVERTY

This section examines several policies designed to help raise the incomes of people living in poverty in the United States, with emphasis on policies to assist mother-only families. We begin by describing Aid to Families with Dependent Children (AFDC), the federal program that, for over 60 years, guaranteed cash assistance to poor children and their families, with special attention paid to the concerns raised in the debate over changing welfare in the 1990s.[1] This provides a context for understanding recent policy changes, particularly the bill signed by President Clinton in August 1996 that replaced AFDC with a new program called Temporary Assistance for Needy Families (TANF). Next, we consider the major features of the 1996 legislation and early evidence concerning its potential for success. We also examine the Earned Income Tax Credit (EITC), intended to raise the incomes of welfare recipients in transition to work as well as the incomes of the working poor who are ineligible for welfare. Finally, we turn to policies designed to increase child support paid by noncustodial parents.

AFDC: OUR FORMER WELFARE PROGRAM

AFDC, initiated in 1935 as part of the Social Security Act, was an entitlement program, in which the federal government provided all eligible families, principally those headed by single parents, with cash assistance.[2] As the program evolved, AFDC recipients also generally qualified for in-kind benefits including food stamps and Medicaid, which is effectively government-provided health insurance. Many were eligible for housing subsidies as well.

AFDC came to be one of the most hotly debated government transfer programs, despite the fact that it made up only around 1 percent of the federal budget. This can be seen in Table 10.1, which provides expenditure figures on AFDC for 1970, 1993 (when caseloads were around their peak level), and 1998 (once TANF replaced AFDC). One concern was that since AFDC mainly provided benefits to single parents, it created an incentive for couples not to get married or to break up, in order for the mother and her children to be eligible for welfare. Public concern was heightened when it became clear that the program, originally intended to help families of poor widows, in fact mainly served divorced women and, more recently, increasing numbers of never-married mothers. As shown in Table 10.1, from 1970 to 1993, the percentage of families on AFDC with never-married mothers increased from 28 to 53 percent. It was, therefore, argued that this program discouraged marriage and encouraged unmarried women to have children. Recent evidence suggests, however, that while AFDC appears to have had an effect on these decisions, it cannot explain the dramatic rise in female headship or in births to unmarried women since the 1970s.[3]

While AFDC largely targeted single-parent families, it is less well known that, by the late 1980s, in nearly half of the states, some poor two-parent families with an unemployed parent were eligible for AFDC benefits under the Unemployed Parent Program. Congress extended this program to eligible two-parent families in all states as part of the

---

[1] For an excellent overview, see Rebecca M. Blank, "Fighting Poverty: Lessons from Recent U.S. History," *Journal of Economic Perspectives* 14, no. 2 (spring 2000): 3–19.

[2] For a description of the personal experiences of welfare recipients, see Mark Rank, *Living on the Edge: The Realities of Welfare in America* (New York: Columbia University Press, 1994); and Kathryn Edin and Laura Lein, *Making Ends Meet: How Single Mothers Survive Welfare and Low-Wage Work* (New York: Russell Sage Foundation, 1997).

[3] Robert A. Moffitt, "The Effect of Welfare on Marriage and Fertility," in *Welfare, the Family, and Reproductive Behavior: Research Perspectives,* ed. Robert A. Moffitt (Washington, DC: National Research Council, 1998), pp. 50–97; and Daniel T. Lichter, Diane K. McLaughlin, and David C. Ribar, "Welfare and the Rise in Female-Headed Families," *American Journal of Sociology* 103, no. 1 (July 1997): 112–43. For evidence that AFDC also may have encouraged cohabitation, see Robert A. Moffitt, Robert Reville, and Anne E. Winkler, "Beyond Single Mothers: Cohabitation, Marriage and the U.S. Welfare System," *Demography* 35, no. 3 (August 1998): 359–78.

TABLE 10.1 Selected Statistics on the AFDC/TANF Program, 1970, 1993, and 1998			
	1970	*1993*	*1998*
Benefits			
AFDC/TANF guarantee for three-person family[a]			
In current dollars	$194	$414	$431
In 1998 dollars	$781	$469	$431
Federal AFDC/TANF expenditures as % of federal expenditures	1.4%	1.0%	0.5%
AFDC/TANF tax rate (rate at which benefits are reduced)	67.0%	100.0%	varies
Recipient Characteristics			
Average monthly number of recipients (in thousands)	8,466	14,143	8,770
AFDC/TANF recipients as % of population	4.1%	5.5%	3.2%
AFDC/TANF families with earnings[b]	n.a.	7.4%	20.6%
AFDC/TANF families with never-married parent[c]	27.9%	53.1%	58.6%
AFDC/TANF families with teen parent[d]	6.6%	8.1%	4.2%
Average AFDC/TANF family size	3.9	2.8	2.8

[a] Weighted average monthly benefit computed as the benefit for each state weighted by that state's share of total AFDC/TANF families.

[b] Figure reported for 1993 is from 1992.

[c] Figures are from 1969, 1992 and 1996, respectively.

[d] Figures are from 1969, 1991, and 1998, respectively.

n.a. Not available.

Source: U.S. Department of Health and Human Services, *Indicators of Welfare Dependence,* Annual Report to Congress (March 2000); U.S. Department of Health and Human Services, Administration for Children and Families, *Characteristics and Financial Circumstances of TANF Recipients, FY 1998* (1999); U.S. Department of Health and Human Services, Administration for Children and Families, "Recipients and Families 1936–1999" and "Percentage of the U.S. Population on Welfare by Year Since 1960," www.acf.dhhs.gov.

Family Support Act of 1988 in the hope that access to this program would reduce the incentive for families to break up in order to receive AFDC benefits. Research, however, has not found that this policy change encouraged individuals to get or stay married.[4]

AFDC also created potential disincentives for work because it provided the maximum benefit, termed the "AFDC guarantee," for recipients who did not work. In 1993, an average family of three received $469 per month in cash (measured in 1998 dollars), along with food stamp benefits. As we saw in Chapter 4, an increase in nonlabor income increases the reservation wage, thereby reducing the probability of labor force participation. Furthermore, if a recipient entered the labor force, the AFDC guarantee was reduced by a dollar for each dollar earned on the job. In other words, recipients faced a 100 percent tax rate on their earnings.[5] Needless to say, for any individual, on welfare

---

[4] Anne E. Winkler, "Does AFDC-UP Encourage Two-Parent Families?" *Journal of Policy Analysis and Management* 14, no. 1 (winter 1995): 1–24.

[5] Actually, starting in 1981, the AFDC tax rate was set at 67 percent for four months and then rose to 100 percent thereafter. The rate on earnings differs slightly when the AFDC and food stamps programs are considered together.

or not, a 100 percent tax rate provides a considerable disincentive to work. Empirical evidence does show that AFDC reduced labor supply, but again the effects found were relatively small. Further, altering the tax rate has not been found to have much impact on recipients' propensity to work.[6]

AFDC further discouraged work because, by keeping their hours low, recipients could retain access to Medicaid, which would be lost once they were no longer receiving AFDC benefits.[7] In the late 1980s, legislation was passed to reduce this problem. First, the Family Support Act required states to provide temporary Medicaid benefits for at least 12 months to individuals who left AFDC for employment. Second, Congress expanded Medicaid to cover all children in poor families, regardless of AFDC eligibility. This latter reform has been found to have the desired effect of encouraging more people to work.[8]

There was also concern that AFDC promoted welfare dependency. It has been found that most *new* AFDC families actually stayed in the program for a relatively short time; 42 percent remained on welfare for two years or less. On the other hand, it has also been estimated that 75 percent of all AFDC families receiving benefits *at any point in time* would eventually receive AFDC for more than five years.[9] The apparent contradiction arises from the fact that the probability of being on welfare at any given point in time is higher for long-term as compared with short-term recipients. To sum up the evidence, most recipients used AFDC for transitory assistance, but others did rely on it for long periods of time.

Finally, AFDC and other transfer programs were the subject of a great deal of criticism because they had only modest success in alleviating poverty. Part of the reason that AFDC and other programs were not more successful is that the amount of money available grew to be increasingly inadequate. As the figures in Table 10.1 show, the value of the AFDC guarantee provided by states fell by 45 percent between 1970 and 1993 in inflation-adjusted terms. Although the impact of this decline was cushioned somewhat by an increase in the real value of food stamps, as of 1993, the combined value of the two benefits for a family of three still provided only two-thirds of the amount needed to reach the poverty threshold. The stagnation of real wages for less educated individuals

---

[6]   Robert A. Moffitt, "The Incentive Effects of the U.S. Welfare System: A Review," *Journal of Economic Literature* 30, no. 1 (March 1992): 1–61; and Rebecca M. Blank, "The Employment Strategy: Public Policies to Increase Work and Earnings," in *Confronting Poverty: Prescriptions for Change,* ed. Sheldon H. Danziger, Gary D. Sandefur, and Daniel H. Weinberg (New York: Russell Sage Foundation, 1994), pp. 168–204.

[7]   Anne E. Winkler, "The Incentive Effects of Medicaid on Women's Labor Supply," *Journal of Human Resources* 26, no. 2 (spring 1991): 308–37; and Robert A. Moffitt and Barbara Wolfe, "The Effect of the Medicaid Program on Welfare Participation and Labor Supply," *Review of Economics and Statistics* 74, no. 4 (November 1992): 615–26.

[8]   Aaron S. Yelowitz, "The Medicaid Notch, Labor Supply, and Welfare Participation: Evidence from Eligibility Expansions," *Quarterly Journal of Economics* 110, no. 4 (November 1995): 909–39. There is also evidence that the expansions in Medicaid encouraged marriage. See Aaron S. Yelowitz, "Will Extending Medicaid to Two Parent Families Encourage Marriage?" *Journal of Human Resources* 33, no. 4 (fall 1998): 833–65.

[9]   Estimates are from LaDonna A. Pavetti, "Who Is Affected by Time Limits?" in *Welfare Reform: An Analysis of the Issues,* ed. Isabel V. Sawhill (Washington, DC: Urban Institute, 1996), chap. 7. See also Peter Gottschalk, Sara McLanahan, and Gary Sandefur, "Dynamics of Poverty and Welfare Participation," in *Confronting Poverty: Prescriptions for Change,* ed. Sheldon H. Danziger, Gary D. Sandefur, and Daniel H. Weinberg (New York: Russell Sage Foundation, 1994), pp. 85–108.

since the early 1970s served to further compound the difficulty of raising low-income households out of poverty.

THE IRON TRIANGLE OF WELFARE

Redesigning welfare is made particularly difficult by the fact that three often-sought policy goals are in conflict: alleviating poverty, providing incentives to work, and limiting costs by keeping down the number of recipients. This conflict is sometimes referred to as the "iron triangle of welfare." It is impossible to simultaneously have a low tax rate on additional earnings of welfare recipients to encourage work, a high welfare guarantee to raise families out of poverty, and still maintain a low break-even level of income—the maximum income level at which benefits are available—in order to limit the number of eligible individuals and thus program costs.

Table 10.2 illustrates this dilemma. Consider a hypothetical case in which benefits under the program are computed as the guarantee minus taxable earnings. If the annual welfare guarantee is set at $10,000[10] and the tax rate on welfare benefits is 100 percent, families are eligible for assistance provided their earnings are below $10,000.[11] However, there is little incentive to work since benefits are reduced dollar for dollar with labor market earnings.

Next, suppose the government reduces the tax rate to 50 percent to encourage people to work. That is, benefits are now reduced by only $.50 for each dollar of labor market earnings. In this case, the earnings threshold for eligibility will increase from $10,000 to $20,000, meaning that a much larger percentage of the population will be eligible for the program. While work incentives for welfare recipients will increase, as will the number of individuals helped by the program, so will program costs. Finally, suppose the tax rate remains at 50 percent but the welfare guarantee is cut in half from $10,000 to $5,000. In this case, there will still be incentives to work, while the earnings threshold and the number of eligible individuals are reduced; however, many more families will be in poverty.

TABLE 10.2 Illustration of the Iron Triangle of Welfare		
Annual Welfare Guarantee	*Welfare Tax Rate (in percent)*	*Break-even Earnings*
$10,000	100	$10,000
$10,000	50	$20,000
$5,000	50	$10,000

Definitions:

Benefit formula: Benefits received = Guarantee − (tax rate × earnings).

Guarantee: Maximum welfare benefit (available if earnings are zero).

Break-even income: Maximum earnings level that qualifies for benefits.

---

[10] As a point of comparison, in 2000, the poverty threshold for a family of three was $13,737.

[11] This tax rate only applies to the earnings of *welfare recipients*; it differs from the federal income tax rates, which will be discussed shortly.

EMPLOYMENT STRATEGIES

Another problem is that employment, in and of itself, is quite often insufficient to lift families out of poverty. What is needed is a job that pays enough to live on and covers work-related expenses, including child care, transportation, and such additional clothing as may be needed.[12] In addition, it is crucial that health insurance be provided. To put this in perspective, in 2000, when the poverty line for a family of three was $13,737, full-time, full-year work at a minimum wage of $5.15 per hour provided earnings of only $10,300. As we shall see, the federal Earned Income Tax Credit does raise this figure to around the poverty line. Still, poor families with employed adults have to spend a larger share of their income on child care than higher-income families, and many jobs, particularly low-paying and part-time ones, fail to provide health insurance.[13]

The employment outlook for welfare recipients tends to be especially bleak because, as a rule, they have little education and few job skills. Many also face other barriers to employment, including discrimination or physical or mental health problems. In addition they may have problems getting to work due to lack of transportation.

Thus, while the government could simply assist people in finding jobs, which tends to be quite inexpensive to do, jobs alone are not likely to help many of them escape poverty. The alternative is to provide education and skills that raise the earnings of both welfare recipients and those who are poor but not on welfare. However, such investments involve considerable costs in the short run, as compared with merely maintaining welfare payments, and it takes some time for them to pay off.[14] Unfortunately, resources for this purpose from state and local governments have tended to be scarce, not only during times when obtaining additional funds would have required raising taxes, but even in the late 1990s and early 2000s, when many state governments, as well as the federal government, had budget surpluses.

The federal government has, however, been active in providing training and employment programs for at least some disadvantaged and unemployed workers since the 1960s. The most important initial program that was designed to help people prepare for better jobs was the Manpower Development and Training Act (MDTA) of 1962, which emphasized a rather centralized approach to these problems. It was replaced by the Comprehensive Employment and Training Act (CETA) of 1973, which gave a greater role in decision making and program implementation to local governments. Finally, the Job Training Partnership Act (JTPA), passed in 1982, placed greater reliance on the private sector.

Beginning in the 1980s, states initiated some education and training programs explicitly designed to move AFDC recipients from welfare to work. Subsequently, in 1988 Congress passed the Family Support Act, mentioned previously, which mandated that states expand the skills and training of AFDC recipients through JOBS—the Job Opportunities and Basic Skills program. This program required recipients, except those

---

[12] Gary Burtless, "Paychecks or Welfare Checks: Can AFDC Recipients Support Themselves?" *Brookings Review* 12, no. 4 (fall 1994): 33–37; and Blank, "The Employment Strategy."

[13] Health insurance coverage for children has been considerably expanded through the 1997 Child Health Insurance Program, but their parents are not covered under this program.

[14] Robert A. Moffitt further finds that training programs may even induce entry into welfare programs by those seeking to improve their qualifications, thereby expanding the welfare population and thus costs, in "The Effect of Employment and Training Programs on Entry and Exit from the Welfare Caseload," *Journal of Policy Analysis and Management* 15, no. 1 (winter 1996): 32–50.

with an infant or disability, to engage in activities such as job search, training, and education. To ease the transition to work, the Family Support Act also provided for child care and transitional Medicaid benefits. Analysis of a number of these welfare-to-work programs has indicated that such programs increased earnings, but most often not enough to lift individuals out of poverty.[15]

Most recently, following the passage of the 1996 welfare legislation, the federal government has largely shifted the emphasis of its employment strategy for welfare recipients away from job training and education as routes to self-sufficiency to an emphasis on employment. While the programs of individual states vary, one strategy that is being used, "work first," emphasizes job search and tries to get welfare recipients into paid employment as quickly as possible.[16] If this is unsuccessful, states may place welfare recipients in unpaid work or subsidized employment or offer them limited opportunities for education and training. The success of a "work first" approach depends on a number of factors, most notably a sustained healthy economy that creates sufficient jobs for lower-skilled workers.[17] Further, this strategy, without modification, may be insufficient not only for those who lack qualifications, but also for those who face the other types of employment barriers mentioned earlier. Finally, because even those who find employment are likely not to have adequate earnings, emphasis must also be placed on complementary policies that raise incomes, including the Earned Income Tax Credit.

TANF: OUR CURRENT WELFARE PROGRAM

The 1996 welfare legislation replaced AFDC with a new program called Temporary Assistance to Needy Families (TANF), which altered the federal provision of welfare transfers in a number of important ways. First, it shifted welfare from a federal entitlement program to a program of fixed dollar block grants administered by states and gave states much more discretion than in the past to set eligibility and program rules. The reason for this shift was the claim on the part of advocates of the new policy that states would be better able to tailor aid to their population, based on their own judgment of their needs. Second, it required large fractions of the adult welfare population to be employed in some capacity after two years, 25 percent by 1997, and 50 percent by 2002. Part of the argument for the work requirement was that most married women, including those with small children, are now employed, so it is not unreasonable to require women maintaining families to also be employed. Third, it attempted to reduce welfare dependency by mandating a five-year cumulative time limit on receiving federally funded welfare, albeit with exemptions possible for up to 20 percent of families. Fourth, it restricted eligibility for teen parents, so that only those who stay in school and live with their parents can receive benefits. Fifth, the legislation sought to promote responsibility among noncustodial parents, most often fathers, by stepping up child support enforcement.

---

[15]   Blank, "The Employment Strategy"; Demetra S. Nightingale and Robert Haveman, eds., *The Work Alternative* (Washington, DC: Urban Institute, 1994); and Edward Pauly and Judith M. Gueron, *From Welfare to Work* (New York: Russell Sage Foundation, 1991).

[16]   Pamela A. Holcomb, LaDonna Pavetti, Caroline Ratcliffe, and Susan Riedinger, *Building an Employment Focused Welfare System: Work First and Other Work-Oriented Strategies in Five States,* Executive Summary (Washington, DC: U.S. Department of Health and Human Services, Office of the Assistant Secretary for Planning and Evaluation, June 1998).

[17]   See David E. Card and Rebecca M. Blank, eds., *Finding Jobs: Work and Welfare Reform* (New York: Russell Sage Foundation, 2000).

Among the other major changes, it limited eligibility for food stamps for some adults, and cut the tie that had long-existed between Medicaid and AFDC.[18]

Pressure to restructure welfare had grown since the 1980s, as reflected in the emphasis on work in the 1988 Family Support Act, and President Clinton's promise during the 1992 campaign to "end welfare as we know it." In the early days of his presidency, he encouraged states to experiment with welfare reform. In response, over two-thirds of the states sought and received waivers from the federal government, which allowed them to try alternative approaches to welfare, including time limits for welfare receipt, requiring recipients to work after a certain period, limiting AFDC benefits for those who had additional children while receiving aid, providing sanctions or bonuses to encourage completion of high school, and cutting off benefits to teen mothers who did not live with their parents.[19] The 1996 welfare legislation embodies the main features of this earlier wave of reform. Nonetheless one fundamental difference is that the 1996 legislation ended the federal guarantee of assistance. Under TANF, states provide benefits to needy families only if they are willing and able to do so.

As might be expected, states (and the District of Columbia) have taken advantage of the greater latitude given to them by the federal government and are now essentially running 51 different welfare experiments.[20] For instance, in calculating welfare benefits, states now differ greatly as to how much of recipients' earnings they disregard, with some choosing to disregard a substantial fraction in an effort to increase work incentives.[21] States also have made different choices regarding eligibility for two-parent families, and whether or not benefits are reduced if recipients bear additional children. Since the policies generally include both "carrots" and "sticks" in an effort to encourage or discourage certain behaviors, it is virtually impossible to classify individual states as harsh or generous across the board. This fact also makes program evaluation rather difficult, since it is hard to isolate the influence of individual policies.

Though TANF was only fully implemented by 1997 and much remains to be learned, some conclusions about the initial success of welfare reform are possible. Most dramatic, as shown in Table 10.1, there has been nearly a 50 percent reduction in the national welfare caseload since 1993, when numbers were at or near their most recent peak. In fact, some states have even experienced budget windfalls because the block grants were tied to state spending when welfare caseloads were highest.[22] Overall, in 1998 just 3.2 percent of the U.S. population received welfare benefits, as compared with

---

[18] U.S. House of Representatives, *2000 Green Book.*

[19] For possible explanations behind states' experimentation with various welfare policies, see Robert A. Moffitt, "Explaining Welfare Reform: Public Choice and the Labor Market," *International Tax and Public Finance* 6, no. 3 (August 1999): 289–315; and Anne E. Winkler, "State Experimentation with Time-Limited AFDC Benefits: What Differentiates Reform-Minded States from Others?" *Public Finance Review* 26, no. 2 (March 1998): 155–83.

[20] State programs may also differ somewhat from federal rules because the 1996 legislation allows states that operated their welfare program under a welfare waiver to continue to do so until their programs expire. Details about state programs can be found at the State Policy Documentation Project web site, www.spdp.org; and at the Urban Institute web site, newfederalism.urban.org. See also U.S. Department of Health and Human Services, "Temporary Assistance for Needy Families (TANF) Program," Second Annual Report to Congress (August 1999).

[21] Barbara L. Wolfe, "Incentives, Challenges, and Dilemmas of TANF," unpublished working paper, University of Wisconsin-Madison (May 2000).

[22] Jason DeParle, "States Struggle to Use Windfall Born of Shifts in Welfare Law," *New York Times,* 28 August 1999.

5.5 percent in 1993. This dramatic decline is a result of three major factors: (1) changes in welfare, which began with the waivers in the early 1990s; (2) the expansion of the EITC (discussed shortly); and (3) the unprecedented U.S. economic expansion in the 1990s.[23] While these caseload reductions have lead to significant reductions in program costs, it is even more critical to determine whether they have been associated with increased employment and earnings and reductions in poverty rates of the target population. Beyond that, a full analysis should also consider the effects of welfare reform on a broader array of outcomes such as homelessness and children's well-being, including whether they are properly nourished and have adequate child care.[24] Another set of issues concerns what may happen when the economy turns down.

TANF and the other changes noted above do appear to have been successful at moving individuals from welfare to work and may have discouraged some from entering welfare to begin with. As noted in Chapter 4, since the mid-1990s employment among single mothers with children has increased considerably more rapidly than among married women with children. Further, the employment rate for single mothers receiving welfare, though still low, increased substantially, as was intended by a "work first" strategy. This can be seen in Table 10.1, which shows that nearly three times as many welfare recipients had earnings in 1998 as in 1993, prior to the new welfare legislation.

While many former recipients are employed, often full-time, there is considerable question as to the effects of welfare reform on earnings and poverty. One comprehensive study of the impact of recent welfare changes finds that they have lead to increases in family earnings and reductions in poverty. However, the 1996 changes alone do not appear to have benefited low-skilled workers in terms of earnings gains as much as the earlier welfare reforms under state waivers.[25] Other research has also raised some concerns,[26] and even the studies with the most favorable results caution that it is still too early to draw definitive conclusions. Among the qualifications is that it is the individuals who are most able to find acceptable jobs who have left welfare. Even for them, the question remains as to their long-term wage prospects, given the types of jobs they tend to find. And, by 2002, states must move a much greater fraction of welfare recipients to work, many of whom will likely face even greater employment barriers.[27] Furthermore,

---

[23] See, for instance, Council of Economic Advisers, "Economic Expansion, Welfare Reform, and the Decline in Welfare Caseloads: An Update (Technical Report)" (August 1999); Geoffrey Wallace and Rebecca M. Blank, "What Goes Up Must Come Down? Explaining Recent Changes in Public Assistance Caseloads," in *Economic Conditions and Welfare Reform,* ed. Sheldon Danziger (Kalamazoo, MI: W. E. Upjohn Institute, 1999); and Blank, "Fighting Poverty."

[24] Christina Paxson and Jane Waldfogel, "Work, Welfare, and Child Maltreatment," National Bureau of Economic Research Working Paper No. 7343 (September 1999).

[25] Robert F. Schoeni and Rebecca M. Blank, "What Has Welfare Reform Accomplished? Impacts on Welfare Participation, Employment, Income, Poverty, and Family Structure," unpublished working paper, RAND and University of Michigan (February 2000).

[26] See, for instance, Robert A. Moffitt and Jennifer Roff, "The Diversity of Welfare Leavers: Background Paper" (Baltimore: Johns Hopkins University, October 2000); Maria Cancian, Robert Haveman, Daniel R. Meyer, and Barbara Wolfe, "Before and After TANF: The Economic Well-Being of Women Leaving Welfare," Special Report No. 77 (University of Wisconsin-Madison, Institute for Research on Poverty, May 2000); and Pamela Loprest, "How Families That Left Welfare Are Doing: A National Picture," Policy Brief B-1 (Washington, DC: Urban Institute, August 1999).

[27] LaDonna Pavetti, "How Much More Can Welfare Mothers Work?" *Focus* 20, no. 2 (spring 1999): 16–19.

the gap in access to affordable, safe child care that already exists is likely to widen.[28] Finally, to the extent that welfare recipients flood the low-skilled labor market, this may depress wages and perhaps displace some workers who are already employed.[29]

Other concerns center on how states will respond and how individuals will fare in an economic downturn. This issue is particularly serious because in times of people's greatest economic need, states will have the least financial ability to provide economic assistance. A federal contingency fund has been established to provide some additional reserves, but there is reason to believe that these are not likely to be sufficient in the case of a serious recession.[30] There are also concerns that when budgets are stretched, there may be a "race to the bottom" as states tighten eligibility requirements and reduce benefits to the extent allowed by law in order to keep down the number of recipients and program costs.[31] Indeed, the greater autonomy given to states in the 1996 legislation increases the likelihood of such behavior. Moreover, once the economy moves into recession, it is going to be much more difficult for states to meet their work participation targets.[32]

One outcome of the 1996 welfare legislation that was not anticipated is that many fewer individuals are participating in Medicaid or using food stamps than would be expected. Part of the explanation is thought to be administrative; caseworkers may not be signing up all eligible individuals or states may be failing to process applications on a timely basis. At the same time, some eligible individuals may mistakenly believe they are ineligible.[33] Either way, this means that families struggling to make ends meet are losing out on potentially important benefits.

THE EARNED INCOME TAX CREDIT

The **Earned Income Tax Credit** (EITC) is a federal program that both raises income and encourages individuals with low potential wages to seek employment. The EITC is a refundable tax credit based on household earnings. In contrast to the usual tax credits, which benefit only households with an income high enough to pay taxes, the government provides a refund if the amount of the credit exceeds taxes owed, thereby particularly benefiting low-income households. Further, unlike the minimum wage, it targets only low-wage workers living in poor and near-poor households.[34]

The EITC was originally established in 1975 to offset the Social Security payroll tax for low-earner households with children, but has been expanded considerably since

---

[28] U.S. Department of Health and Human Services, "Only 10 Percent of Eligible Families Get Child Care Help, Report Shows," *HHS News,* 19 October 1999.

[29] Timothy J. Bartik, "Displacement and Wage Effects of Welfare Reform," in *Finding Jobs: Work and Welfare Reform,* ed. David E. Card and Rebecca M. Blank (New York: Russell Sage Foundation, 2000), pp. 72–122.

[30] David A. Super, Sharon Parrott, Susan Steinmetz, and Cindy Mann, "The Welfare Conference Bill" (Washington, DC: Center on Budget and Policy Priorities, 13 August 1996).

[31] Paul Peterson, "State Response to Welfare Reform: A Race to the Bottom?" in *Welfare Reform: An Analysis of the Issues,* ed. Isabel V. Sawhill (Washington, DC: Urban Institute, 1996), chap. 2.

[32] Daniel P. McMurrer and Isabel V. Sawhill, "Planning for the Best of Times," *Washington Post,* 18 August 1997, p. A19.

[33] Sheila R. Zedlewski and Sarah Brauner, "Declines in Food Stamp and Welfare Participation: Is There a Connection?" Assessing the New Federalism, 99–13 (Washington, DC: Urban Institute, October 1999); and Associated Press, "HHS Warns on Medicaid Applications," 22 March 1999.

[34] See, for instance, Saul D. Hoffman and Laurence S. Seidman, *The Earned Income Tax Credit* (Kalamazoo, MI: W. E. UpJohn Institute for Employment Research, 1990); Jeffrey B. Liebman, "The Impact of the

then. From 1991 to 2000, the inflation-adjusted value of the credit more than doubled. Further, beginning in 1994, low-income households without children also became eligible, though only for a very small credit. The amount of the credit varies according to presence of children and earnings. For example, in 2000, a family with two children and up to $9,720 in earnings was subsidized at a rate of 40 percent. A similar family with earnings between $9,720 and $12,690 received $3,888, the maximum credit available. Beyond $12,690, the credit was reduced by 21 cents for every additional dollar earned until it was fully phased out at $31,152.

The EITC has a substantial impact on raising families out of poverty. For instance, as shown in Table 10.3, the earnings of an employed single-parent with two children who works full-time, full-year at the minimum wage were increased from $10,300 to $14,188, just above the amount of the relevant poverty threshold. This family is also eligible for food stamps, which increases net income, but must pay federal payroll taxes on earnings. In addition, such a family may also receive some federal child care assistance, though not enough to fully cover child care costs. One study found that these factors, taken together, nearly offset one another, leaving income at about the level reported in Table 10.3 (for "Earnings plus EITC").[35] Another benefit not reflected in the simple calculation reported in Table 10.3 is that children under age 15 may also receive federally funded health care, either through Medicaid or via the Children's Health Insurance Program (CHIP) enacted in 1997, though their parents may or may not have health care coverage, depending on their employer.

In contrast to AFDC, which provided maximum payments to those not employed and imposed a very high marginal tax rate on earnings, the EITC encourages individuals to seek employment by subsidizing earnings.[36] For individuals in the low income

TABLE 10.3	Making Ends Meet for a Low-Earner Single-Parent Family with Two Children, 2000
Earnings (assume employed at minimum wage job full-time, full-year)[a]	$10,300
EITC (maximum credit)	$3,888
Earnings plus EITC	$14,188
Poverty threshold[b]	$13,737
Ratio of earnings plus EITC to poverty threshold	1.03

[a] Earnings are computed as $5.15 multiplied by 40 hours per week multiplied by 50 weeks per year.

[b] This figure is the Census Bureau's preliminary estimate of the poverty threshold for a three-person family for 2000.

Earned Income Tax Credit on Incentives and Income Distribution" in *Tax Policy and the Economy,* ed. James Poterba (Cambridge, MA: MIT Press, 1998), pp. 12:83–119; and Richard V. Burkhauser, Kenneth A. Couch, and Andrew J. Glenn, "Public Policies for the Working Poor: The Earned Income Tax Credit Versus Minimum Wage Legislation," in *Research in Labor Economics,* ed. Solomon Polachek (Greenwich, CT: JAI Press, 1996): 15:65–109.

[35]   David T. Ellwood, "The Plight of the Working Poor," Children's Roundtable Report #2 (Washington, DC: Brookings Institution, November 1999).

[36]   Most discussions on incentive effects, such as the one here, assume that the EITC is received on a regular basis throughout the year. However, virtually all recipients receive it as a lump sum, which may affect their response; see Timothy Smeeding, Katherine Ross Philips, and Michael O'Connor, "The EITC: Expectation, Knowledge, Use and Economic and Social Mobility," *National Tax Journal* (forthcoming).

range, the amount of the EITC increases with additional hours worked. At the same time, however, the EITC may cause some workers to reduce the number of hours worked. The provision of a fixed credit over the middle income range, for instance, provides these workers with a pure increase in income. As discussed in Chapter 4, with higher nonlabor income, individuals tend to work fewer hours.

For individuals in the highest income range among those eligible, the credit and thus the net wage are reduced as earnings increase. This tends to induce individuals to substitute toward nonmarket time and away from paid work because the opportunity cost of nonmarket time has fallen. At the same time, total income is still higher than it would otherwise be without the EITC program, also providing an incentive for individuals to work less. Hence, in this range, both the substitution and income effects operate to reduce hours worked.

The effect of the EITC program thus varies depending on which phase of the schedule individuals face. There is overwhelming evidence that the EITC provides a strong incentive for single mothers to enter the paid labor force. In fact, it has been estimated that nearly 60 percent of the increase in single mother's annual employment from 1984 to 1996 was due to the expansion of the EITC alone.[37] On the other hand, as would be expected, the design of the EITC also causes some secondary earners in married-couple families, typically wives, to leave the labor force. Wives' additional earnings often place the family's income in the phase-out range of the credit, thereby leading to receipt of a lower EITC or none at all. Indeed, one study finds that the expansions in the EITC caused labor force participation rates to rise slightly for married men, but to decline for married women by as much as one percentage point, leading to an overall decrease in family labor supply and pretax family earnings.[38] As will be discussed shortly, the EITC may also affect family structure if people take its earnings criteria into account in their decisions to marry or get divorced.

CHILD SUPPORT ENFORCEMENT

Child support enforcement is another strategy for aiding single-parent families. Over the last 25 years, child support enforcement in the United States has changed considerably, shifting from a "complaint-driven, court-enforced system" subject to considerable discretion to a system that is guided by state and federal laws and regulations.[39] The first major child support legislation was enacted in 1975 to enforce payments by noncustodial parents. Additional legislation in 1984 and 1988 considerably strengthened this law by requiring states to adopt numerical guidelines in setting child support awards and allowing them to collect income withheld from employers (garnish wages) or retain income tax refunds from

---

[37] Bruce D. Meyer and Dan T. Rosenbaum, "Welfare, the Earned Income Tax Credit, and the Labor Supply of Single Mothers," National Bureau of Economic Research Working Paper No. 7363 (September 1999). See also Nada Eissa and Jeffrey B. Liebman, "Labor Supply Response to the Earned Income Tax Credit," *Quarterly Journal of Economics* 111, no. 2 (May 1996): 606–37.

[38] Nada Eissa and Hilary Hoynes, "The Earned Income Tax Credit and the Labor Supply of Married Couples," unpublished working paper, University of California at Berkeley (1999).

[39] This characterization is from Elaine Sorensen and Ariel Halpern, "Child Support Reforms: Who Has Benefited?" *Focus* 21, no. 1 (spring 2000): 38–41. For a concise review of the major changes in federal laws and empirical evidence on the effects, see "Child Support Enforcement Policy and Low-Income Families," *Focus* 21, no. 1 (spring 2000): 3. See also Andrea H. Beller and John W. Graham, *Small Change: The Economics of Child Support* (New Haven, CT: Yale University Press, 1993), chap. 6.

noncustodial parents who do not make the required payments. The 1996 welfare legislation further instituted rules that make the establishment of paternity faster and easier, added a national registry system that makes tracking down delinquent parents across state lines possible, and set forth tough new penalties for nonpayment, including revoking professional licenses and seizing assets. Most recently, a law was passed in 1998 to toughen sanctions, including penalties of up to two years in prison, for "deadbeat" parents.

While mothers not receiving welfare can weigh the costs and benefits of pursuing child support through formal government channels before deciding whether to take this course, mothers on public assistance have been required to do so ever since 1975, as one of the conditions for receiving cash benefits.[40] Until the 1996 welfare legislation, all states allowed a small portion of child support monies received to directly "pass-through" to welfare recipients, while the rest was kept by the states to cover the costs of public assistance. The pass-through provided an incentive for noncustodial parents to make child support payments because they could assume that their children would get some of the benefits of their payments. The 1996 legislation changed this; it gave states new latitude in deciding the amount, if any, of the pass-through or disregard.[41] As many as two-thirds of states chose to eliminate it altogether. One notable exception is Wisconsin, where welfare families may keep all child support monies received.

Recent evidence indicates that the government policies outlined above (in the case of the pass-through, a policy that retains it) do lead to higher rates of child support receipt by families. Not surprisingly, these effects are found to be even stronger when combined with greater state expenditures on enforcement efforts. However, the success of recent enforcement efforts is not apparent in aggregate statistics on child support received, which show that the proportion of single-mother families who received child support (a full or partial payment) remained remarkably steady from the late 1970s to early 1990s, rising from 35 to just 40 percent. These aggregate figures have changed so little because at the same time that enforcement efforts increased, the composition of single-parent families changed as well.[42] Specifically, the proportion of never-married mothers increased and they are much less likely to get awards or actual payments as compared with divorced women. Nevertheless, there is evidence that child support award rates for never-married mothers, while still quite low, have been rising, in line with the fact that many of the new policies have been targeted at precisely this group.[43]

As new enforcement policies have proliferated, including additional sanctions on noncompliant parents, there has also been increasing concern that the current system is not sufficiently flexible to deal with the varied economic status of diverse noncustodial

---

[40] Tonya Brito, "The Welfarization of Family Law: The Case of Child Support," *Focus* 21, no. 1 (spring 2000): 67–71. For a discussion of the interaction between child support receipt and welfare participation, see Wei-Yin Hu, "Child Support, Welfare Dependency, and Women's Labor Supply," *Journal of Human Resources* 34, no. 1 (winter 1999): 71–103.

[41] A pass-through and a disregard differ somewhat, though they are used interchangeably in this brief discussion. See Judith Cassety, Maria Cancian, and Daniel R. Meyer, "Child Support Disregard and Pass-Through Policies," *Focus* 21, no. 1 (spring 2000): 64–66.

[42] Richard B. Freeman and Jane Waldfogel, "Dunning Delinquent Dads: Child Support Enforcement Policy and Never-Married Women," *Focus* 21, no. 1 (spring 2000): 27–30; and Sorensen and Halpern, "Child Support Reforms."

[43] Freeman and Waldfogel, "Dunning Delinquent Dads." See also Laura M. Argys and H. Elizabeth Peters, "Patterns of Non-Resident Father Involvement," unpublished working paper, University of Colorado, Denver and Cornell University (February 2000).

parents, typically fathers. The current guidelines are designed for those who have stable employment and adequate incomes. However, many face a different economic reality. They may have little education, lack stable employment, and consequently have very low earnings. These fathers, sometimes labeled "deadbroke" dads, may simply not be able to financially support their children, and, for them, existing policies may well promote counterproductive outcomes. For instance, such fathers may be induced to shift from legal employment to "under-the-table" work, with all its attendant disadvantages. In addition, these policies may lead some fathers to avoid social contact with their children.[44] In light of such concerns, in 2000 the federal government approved experimental programs in 10 states that will use federal funds to improve the economic opportunities for young unmarried fathers and encourage them to reconnect with their children.[45]

One alternative to the patchwork of child support policies that has evolved in the United States is to establish a Child Support Assurance System, similar to the one that already exists in Sweden.[46] Under this system, both parents and government would be responsible for the support of children. Awards from nonresident parents would be a percentage of their income, set by a court, and would be withheld from earnings, much as taxes are. If the parent cannot meet this obligation, the government would provide the minimum assured benefit. Experiments with modest versions of this program have been conducted in Wisconsin and New York and have shown signs of success. Such a program, however, has little chance of being adopted nationwide given the reluctance of many for the federal government's role to be expanded from one in which it sets guidelines and rules to encourage private child support payments, to one in which it would provide actual child support monies. Furthermore, thorny issues remain to be resolved, including whether eligibility for benefits should be means tested and whether establishment of paternity can be mandated.[47]

TAXES, SPECIALIZATION, AND MARRIAGE

Up to this point we have largely ignored the role of the federal income tax system, but it is in fact very important in this context. First, it helps to finance federal programs, including those discussed above. At the same time it means that individuals do not retain all their labor market earnings. Hence, the structure of the federal income tax system affects take-home pay and consequently decisions regarding whether and how much to

---

[44]   Maureen Waller and Robert Plotnick, "A Failed Relationship? Low-Income Families and the Child Support Enforcement System," *Focus* 21, no. 1 (spring 2000): 12–17; Anu Rangarajan and Philip Gleason, "Young Unwed Fathers of AFDC Children: Do They Provide Support?" *Demography* 35, no. 2 (May 1998): 175–86; and Irwin Garfinkel, Sara McLanahan, Daniel Meyer, and Judith Seltzer, eds. *Fathers Under Fire: The Revolution in Child Support Enforcement* (New York: Russell Sage Foundation, 1998).

[45]   U.S. Department of Health and Human Services, Administration for Children and Families, "HHS Awards Child Support Waivers to Help Promote Responsible Fatherhood," HHS Press Release, 29 March 2000.

[46]   For a discussion of child support systems elsewhere, see Anne Corden and Daniel R. Meyer, "Child Support Policy Regimes in the United States, United Kingdom, and Other Countries: Similar Issues, Different Approaches," *Focus* 21, no. 1 (spring 2000): 72–79.

[47]   Elaine Sorensen and Sandra Clark, "A Child-Support Assurance Program: How Much Will It Reduce Child Poverty and at What Cost?" *American Economic Review* 84, no. 2 (May 1994): 114–19; and Irwin Garfinkel, *Assuring Child Support: An Extension of Social Security* (New York: Russell Sage Foundation, 1992).

work, as well as decisions about family formation. Similarly, payroll taxes and the Social Security payments they fund also affect these decisions. Both federal income taxation and Social Security have been criticized for being biased in favor of the traditional, one-earner family.[48] Both these programs, which evolved when this type of family was the norm, in effect, subsidize married women who stay home. Therefore it can be argued that they need to be modified in light of the changing structure of American families.

One of the primary rules economists have proposed for fair taxation is **horizontal equity**, which simply means that those in similar circumstances should be treated the same.[49] We specifically consider the question of whether the current income tax and Social Security systems violate this rule in their treatment of one-earner and two-earner families.[50]

INCOME TAXATION POLICY

First and foremost, the present income tax system may be considered inequitable because the value of goods and services produced in the home is not taxed, whereas money income is subject to taxation. As a result, two couples with different levels of economic well-being may have the same taxable incomes. Suppose, for instance, that Ellen and Ed earn $25,000 each and produce $10,000 worth of goods and services in the household. Suppose too that Jim earns $50,000 and Jane, a full-time homemaker, produces $30,000 worth of goods and services in the home. Although Jim and Jane produce a total income of $80,000, including the value of home production, while Ellen and Ed only produce an income of $60,000, taxable income is $50,000 for both.

One of the concerns with such a policy is that it provides incentives for families to adopt the traditional division of labor and creates a disincentive for married women to participate in the labor force. The disincentive to work for pay additionally stems from the fact that the family is the unit of taxation and the tax structure is progressive, meaning that higher levels of family income are taxed at a higher *rate* than lower levels. As shown in panel a of Table 10.4, this means that if a married couple's earnings are $50,000, part of this amount is subject to a 15 percent tax rate and the remainder is subject to a 28 percent rate, assuming they file jointly. In general, progressive tax rates are considered to be desirable because they result in wealthier families paying a proportionately larger share of their incomes in taxes. The degree of progressivity in the tax system has varied considerably in recent years as rates have been changed. The Tax Reform Act of 1986 reduced the number of tax brackets from 15 brackets, with a top rate of 50 percent, to only two brackets, with stated rates of 15 and 28 percent. Subsequently, rates of 31, 36, and 39.6 percent were added under the administrations of Bush senior and Clinton.[51]

---

[48]   Here we focus on two major federal programs only, but it should be noted that most states have their own income tax, and there is an array of other taxes at the federal, state, and local levels.

[49]   The view that "there is a generally accepted standard of equity or fairness with respect to public finance measures: equal treatment of those equally circumstanced," was first expressed by Carl S. Shoup, *Public Finance* (Chicago: Aldine Publishing Company, 1969), p. 23 and has been widely shared ever since.

[50]   These topics have been discussed by economists for some time, from Nancy R. Gordon, "Institutional Responses: The Federal Income Tax System" and "Institutional Responses: The Social Security System," in *The Subtle Revolution,* ed. Ralph E. Smith (Washington, DC: Urban Institute, 1979), pp. 201–21, 223–55; to Edward J. McCaffery, *Taxing Women* (Chicago: University of Chicago Press, 1997).

[51]   Legislation in 1993 increased the *stated* top tax rate to 36 percent. However, it also introduced a surtax on taxes paid by couples with very high incomes, which actually created a higher *effective* top tax rate of 39.6 percent.

TABLE 10.4 Federal Individual Income Tax Rates and Calculation of Marriage Penalty/Bonus

(a) 2000 Federal Individual Income Tax Rate Schedules[a]

Single Schedule		Married Filing Jointly Schedule	
Taxable Income	Tax Rate	Taxable Income	Tax Rate
$0–$26,250	15.0%	$0–$43,850	15.0%
$26,250–$63,550	28.0%	$43,850–$105,950	28.0%
$63,550–$132,600	31.0%	$105,950–$161,450	31.0%
$132,600–$288,350	36.0%	$161,450–$288,350	36.0%
$288,350 +	39.6%	$288,350 +	39.6%

(b) Calculation of Marriage Penalty/Bonus Using 2000 Tax Rate Schedules[b]

Couple	Value of Home Production (not taxable)	Husband's Income (taxable)	Wife's Income (taxable)	Combined Income (taxable)	Tax liability if: Married Couple	Both Single	Marriage Penalty or Bonus
Ellen and Ed	$10,000	$25,000	$25,000	$50,000	$8,300	$7,500	$800 penalty
Jane and Jim	$30,000	$50,000	$0	$50,000	$8,300	$10,588	$2,288 bonus

[a] There are two other schedules not shown here, the head of household schedule for single individuals with a dependent child and a married filing separately schedule for couples who are separated.

[b] This table makes several simplifying assumptions. It assumes that there are no children and that taxable income equals gross income. In actual practice, taxable income is calculated as gross income less personal exemptions and less the standard deduction (which is less than twice as large for married couples as compared with single individuals).

The current tax structure results in a married woman, still generally considered to be the secondary earner by most families, facing a relatively high marginal tax rate on her potential income, should she decide to enter the labor market. The first dollar of her earnings is taxed at her husband's top marginal tax rate. This has the effect of reducing the incentive for her to enter the labor market. For instance, if Jane, a full-time home-maker, decides to work for pay, the first dollar she receives is taxed at a 28 percent rate, no matter how little she earns. This is because her income will be added on to Jim's and their tax liability will be determined using the married filing jointly tax schedule. As noted earlier, the EITC, which is part of the federal tax code, also discourages partici-pation by a secondary earner in low-earning families, because the value of the EITC eventually declines as family earnings rise.

In addition to these potential disincentives to participate in the paid labor force, there is the so-called marriage penalty, which has received considerable attention. A marriage penalty refers to the additional taxes a couple must pay if they are married as compared to the taxes they would have paid if they had remained single, while a mar-riage subsidy refers to possible tax savings due to marriage. The penalty arises because the brackets for married couples are less than twice the brackets for singles, and the standard deduction for married couples is less than twice that for singles (although the latter point cannot be seen in the simplified computations shown in Table 10.4).

Our current tax structure imposes penalties on being married for some couples and subsidies for others. For instance, consider again Jim and Jane and Ellen and Ed, but now suppose that they are unmarried, as shown in panel b of Table 10.4, which provides an illustrative example using the 2000 tax rates. If Jim earns $50,000 and marries Jane, who has no earnings, their combined tax liability declines by $2,288. Conversely, if Ellen and Ed each earn $25,000, their joint tax burden will rise by $800 if they get married. The reason for this difference is that the tax system essentially "splits" joint income between two married individuals and treats them as if they were two individuals with equal in-come. This lowers the tax liability for Jim and Jane because, as a result of the progres-sive tax system, part of Jim's income would have been subject to a higher rate if he had been single. Ellen and Ed do not benefit from this provision. On the contrary, when the wife is employed, couples often end up paying more in taxes than they would if they were single. This is the result of a policy change in 1969 that was undertaken to provide some relief to single taxpayers relative to their married-couple counterparts. However, in the process of reducing the relative tax liability of single taxpayers, this inevitably in-creased the relative tax liability for some married couples. In general, the tax system fa-vors single-earner married couples over two-earner married couples; those couples with fairly equal incomes tend to pay larger penalties.[52]

Overall, it has been estimated that, in 1999, as many as 40 percent of married cou-ples paid a marriage penalty averaging about $1,480 and 50 percent received a marriage subsidy averaging about $1,600.[53] The penalty tends to be larger for two-earner couples with very low or very high incomes. However, as a percent of income, low-income cou-

---

[52] Couples cannot get around this by filing separate returns. The tax rates for married filing separately are higher than the rates for single individuals.

[53] Congressional Budget Office, "Cutting Taxes," *Budget Options* (March 2000). The figures do not add up to 100 percent because some couples' tax liability is virtually unchanged. See also Stacy Dickert-Conlin and Scot Houser, "Taxes and Transfers: A New Look at the Marriage Penalty," *National Tax Journal* 51, no. 2 (June 1998): 175–217.

ples face the most severe penalty, and thus, the greatest disincentive to marry. One study found that the marriage penalty could be nearly 20 percent of combined earnings for some low-earner couples.[54] The reason that the penalty is so severe for these couples is that the EITC, for which low-earner couples are eligible, is based on family income. For instance, if a low-earner single mother with children currently receiving the EITC marries a low-earning man, this may well push family earnings high enough to make them ineligible for any credit. On the other hand, if a nonemployed woman with children who is ineligible for the EITC marries a low-earner male, the amount of their total credit will rise. Perhaps not surprisingly, given the magnitude of these subsidies and penalties, income tax policy has been found to affect the rate and timing of marriage, as well as the probability of divorce, although the effect on the latter appears to be small.[55]

The policy debate has centered almost exclusively around reducing or eliminating the marriage penalty, without regard to other biases in the tax system.[56] Concerning the marriage penalty, one way to eliminate it would be to make the width of the married couple brackets and the standard deduction twice as large as those for singles. However, while this solution would eliminate the marriage penalty, it would also reduce tax liabilities for couples already receiving a bonus, and substantially decrease federal tax revenues. A more modest proposal for tax relief would be to restore the two-earner deduction that was in place in the early 1980s. To reduce marriage penalties in the EITC, it would be necessary to address the high tax rate applied to the credit in the phase-out range. One possibility is to make the phase-out vary, depending on whether one or both spouses work for pay, so that the penalty associated with a secondary earner in the family is reduced.

An alternative proposal that would eliminate the work disincentives faced by a secondary earner would be to tax each person as an individual, as Canada, Sweden, and the United Kingdom do, and as the United States did prior to 1948. This approach, which would equalize tax rates for individuals with equal income, regardless of their marital status, has not received much support in this country. Such a policy would clearly be to the advantage of two-earner couples but would increase the tax liability of one-earner families, even though these families would still benefit because in-kind income is not taxed. Whether or not it is viewed as more equitable in its treatment of money income than the current arrangement (in the sense of establishing horizontal equity) depends on whether the individual or the family is viewed as the appropriate tax unit.[57] A flat tax, which imposes the same rate on all incomes, would also meet these goals, but even with a large personal exemption such a tax would be much less progressive than the current system.[58]

---

[54] Daniel R. Feenberg and Harvey S. Rosen, "Recent Developments in the Marriage Tax," *National Tax Journal* 48, no. 1 (March 1995): 91–101.

[55] James Alm, Stacy Dickert-Conlin, and Leslie A. Whittington provide a useful summary of recent research findings in "Policy Watch: The Marriage Penalty," *Journal of Economic Perspectives* 13, no. 3 (summer 1999): 193–204.

[56] Alternative policies are summarized in U.S. Congressional Budget Office, *For Better or for Worse: Marriage and the Federal Income Tax* (June 1997), www.cbo.gov.

[57] For instance, it has been argued by some that the family should be the unit of taxation because it is a basic economic unit in society and because husbands and wives pool income. However, recent empirical evidence has served to weaken the latter argument. See McCaffery, *Taxing Women*, chap. 1.

[58] The flat tax received a good deal of attention during the presidential primaries in 1995 and 1999, especially by Republican candidate Steve Forbes.

Finally, the possibility of taxing household production has received almost no attention. It is doubtful that such a proposal would command much popular support. Moreover, it would be extremely difficult to implement because of the great difficulties involved in obtaining reliable estimates of the value of household production, as discussed in Chapter 4.

THE SOCIAL SECURITY SYSTEM

The Social Security system also poses problems of equity between one-earner married-couple families, on the one hand, and two-earner married-couple families, unmarried couples, and single people, on the other hand.[59] The problem arises because payroll taxes are based on each individual's employment history, while Social Security benefits received are family based. As of 2000, individuals in jobs covered by Social Security (and Medicare) faced a 15.3 percent tax rate on earnings up to a maximum level, half to be paid by the employer, half by the worker. To receive benefits, individuals must obtain a threshold level of pay from jobs covered by Social Security for 40 calendar quarters. Spouses of covered workers are entitled to receive Social Security benefits equal to 50 percent of the amount received by the covered worker, and survivor benefits of 100 percent if the covered worker dies.[60] Alternatively, the spouse may receive a benefit based on his or her own earnings record, whichever amount is greater. Among married-couple families, it is almost invariably the husband who is either the sole wage earner or has the greater earnings, if both are employed. These cases are considered in turn.

The current Social Security system clearly favors traditional families with a full-time homemaker over all others; in such a family, only the husband pays payroll taxes while the family receives 150 percent of his Social Security benefit.

Next, consider the case of the wife who is employed, but who has substantially lower wages and a shorter worklife than her husband. In this case, the wife pays payroll taxes into the system too but the family still receives precisely the same benefits as they would if she were not employed and had paid no payroll taxes. Nevertheless, the husband and wife together receive more benefits than they would if they were single.

Finally, consider the case of the wife who earns enough to receive larger benefits in her own right than she would receive as a spouse.[61] The family will now receive somewhat larger benefits than they would in the other cases. However, unlike the wives in the prior two cases, this one gets no benefit from being a spouse; she and her husband receive exactly the same amount in benefits as if they were single.

The inconsistencies described above obviously violate the cardinal rule of horizontal equity, namely that equal contributions should secure equal returns. Each employed wife pays in as much as she would if she were single, but only the one who earns considerably less than her husband receives additional benefits as a spouse, and a wife who

---

[59]   Useful overviews of these issues are provided in McCaffery, *Taxing Women;* and Marianne A. Ferber, "Women's Employment and the Social Security System," *Social Security Bulletin* 56, no. 3 (fall 1993): 33–55.

[60]   Since 1977, spouses divorced after at least 10 years of marriage are entitled to the same benefit as current spouses.

[61]   Phillip B. Levine, Olivia S. Mitchell, and John W. Phillips find that two-thirds of wives who have 40 calendar quarters of employment receive benefits based on their own work history in "A Benefit of One's Own: Older Women's Retirement Entitlements Under Social Security," unpublished working paper, Wellesley College (August 1999).

is not employed receives benefits as a spouse without making any tax payments at all. Clearly this system provides secondary earners, typically wives, with yet another disincentive to work for pay. Not only do they pay income taxes on their earnings, while the value of home production is not taxed, but they get a much lower return on the payroll taxes they are required to pay as compared with full-time homemakers.

One way to bring about equity among couples is through "earnings sharing."[62] This proposal, which assigns an equal share of total household earnings to each spouse, recognizes that the division of labor in the home represents a joint decision and that both spouses contribute to family welfare through their market or nonmarket work. Unlike the present system, earnings sharing would not penalize dual-earner couples. In addition, the Social Security system would move in the direction of greater horizontal equity, in that equal contributions would yield equal benefits.[63] No couple would have an advantage as compared to any other couple or unmarried individual. Such a change would, however, create problems for traditional couples who, it might be argued, made their labor supply decisions under the existing rules. This could, however, be remedied by giving couples who married before a certain date the option of remaining under the current system. A change to earnings sharing might also raise concerns about the adequacy of benefit levels for single-earner families.[64] While such issues remain to be addressed, continued growth of the two-earner family is likely to increase support for policies that eliminate the existing advantages of one earner families, whether for individual taxation in the federal income tax system or earnings sharing in the Social Security system.

It is also worthwhile to consider the implications of recent Social Security reform proposals.[65] Most of them involve a "two-tier" system in which there would be a guaranteed safety net, similar to the present one, coupled with an upper tier of private investments. In such a system, women who spend time out of the labor market to rear children will be disadvantaged in that they will not accumulate retirement monies in the investment program. Even women in paid employment would likely accrue smaller amounts because of their lower earnings levels. On the other hand, if women did make individual contributions into their investment funds, they would presumably be able to keep them. It might also be possible to combine this reform with earnings sharing as well.

THE COMPETING DEMANDS OF WORK AND FAMILY

As described in Chapter 9, today a growing share of the work force has family responsibilities. There are greater numbers of two-earner families, including those with small children, and more single-parent families than in earlier days. While the burden of bal-

---

[62] For further discussion, see Ferber, "Women's Employment and the Social Security System."

[63] No Social Security taxes are paid on the value of what is produced in the household, but neither does the family accumulate benefits.

[64] Even under the current system, concerns have been raised about the adequacy of benefits for divorced, never-married, and widowed women, who tend to have the highest poverty rates among the elderly; see Timothy J. Smeeding, "Social Security Reform: Improving Benefit Adequacy and Economic Security for Women," Policy Brief No. 16 (Syracuse University: Aging Studies Program, 1999); and Steven H. Sandell and Howard M. Iams, "Reducing Women's Poverty by Shifting Social Security Benefits from Retired Couples to Widows," *Journal of Policy Analysis and Management* 16, no. 2 (spring 1997): 279–97.

[65] This discussion is based on Kathleen Feldstein, "Social Security's Gender Gap," *New York Times*, 13 April 1998, p. A27. See also U.S. General Accounting Office, "Social Security Reform: Implications for Women," Report T-HEHS-99–52 (Washington, DC: U.S. General Accounting Office, 3 February 1999).

ancing the competing demands of work and family is still largely borne by individuals, this section considers new and expanding programs provided by government and employers to help individuals in such families better balance the demands of their dual responsibilities.

Problems of balancing family demands and paid work tend to occur throughout the life cycle. Young workers often need to care for small children. As workers grow older, some may need to assist their teenage children in solving behavioral problems or to help grown children establish themselves. Frequently, they also have to meet the needs of aging relatives and perhaps close friends as well.

Because individuals have a limited amount of time and energy, they confront a trade-off between doing full justice to their job and fully meeting family responsibilities. Balancing these demands is generally most difficult for employed women with families because they typically do most of the housework, as well as child and elder care, thus in effect facing a "second shift."[66] As seen in Chapter 3, employed wives do over two and a half times as much housework as their husbands. It has been argued that time spent in housework may reduce the effort workers are able to expend for market work, thereby reducing wages. This negative effect would be expected to be greatest for women, and there is at least some evidence to support this.[67] It is also the case that many women provide care for their elderly parents, who at times have significant health needs.[68] Demands are especially great on women whose age places them in what has been called the "sandwich generation," those responsible for both the care of their parents and their children at the same time.

Some women respond to these competing demands by taking part-time rather than full-time jobs, in many cases putting their careers on hold. Indeed, as Table 10.5 shows, in 1999 less than one-half of all married mothers with children under 18 years of age were employed full-time; this was true of only 39 percent of married mothers with a child under age 3.[69] Those who do work full-time are more securely attached to the labor force and have higher incomes, but they are also likely to face the greatest time squeeze.

In the absence of adequate provisions for maternity leave, women in the paid labor force also face unique challenges since they are the bearers of children. For instance, as

[66]   Arlie Hochschild, *The Second Shift* (New York: Viking Press, 1989). See also Glenna Spitze and Karyn Loscocco, "Women's Position in the Household," *Quarterly Review of Economics and Finance* 39, no. 0 (Special Issue 1999): 647–61.

[67]   Gary S. Becker makes this theoretical argument in "Human Capital, Effort and the Sexual Division of Labor," *Journal of Labor Economics* 3, no. 1, pt. 2 (January 1985): 33–58. For empirical evidence, see Joni Hersch and Leslie S. Stratton, "Housework, Effort and Wages of Married Workers," *Journal of Human Resources* 32, no. 2 (spring 1997): 285–307.

[68]   Regarding elder care responsibilities, see Liliana E. Pezzin and Barbara S. Schone, "Intergenerational Transfers and the Distribution of Filial Responsibility for Parental Care: The Roles of Gender, Family, and Individual Effects," Johns Hopkins University School of Medicine and Agency for Healthcare Research and Quality (March 2000); Susan L. Ettner, "The Impact of 'Parent Care' on Female Labor Supply Decisions," *Demography* 32, no. 1 (February 1995): 63–108; and Douglas A. Wolf and Beth J. Soldo, "Married Women's Allocation of Time to Employment and Care of Elderly Parents," *Journal of Human Resources* 29, no. 4 (fall 1994): 1259–76.

[69]   Philip N. Cohen and Suzanne M. Bianchi obtain similar findings in "Marriage, Children and Women's Employment: What Do We Know?" *Monthly Labor Review* 122, no. 12 (December 1999): 22–31.

TABLE 10.5 Work Experience of Mothers, by Age of Youngest Child, 1999		
	All Mothers	*Married Mothers*
With child under age 18		
% employed	69.0	67.7
% employed full-time[a]	51.5	48.5
With child under age three		
% employed	57.7	57.5
% employed full-time[a]	39.5	38.7
With child under age one		
% employed	52.7	53.7
% employed full-time[a]	35.9	36.9

[a] Full-time refers to usually works 35 hours or more per week at all jobs.

Source: Bureau of Labor Statistics, "Employment Characteristics of Families in 1999," *News Release* USDL 00-172, 15 June 2000, Tables 5 and 6.

a general rule, pregnant women must be careful to avoid heavy lifting and excessive physical exertion. At the same time, in recent years larger fractions of women are engaged in occupations that require such activities. If firms do not accommodate the needs of pregnant women in such jobs by assigning them to alternative duties, the women may have to leave their jobs or may be terminated.[70] Also, breastfeeding, a practice strongly encouraged by the American Academy of Pediatrics, poses yet another potential work–family conflict, with women often choosing feeding practices that best accommodate their situation in the workplace.[71]

Given women's primary role as caregivers, they would be the main beneficiaries of more family friendly policies. Adoption of such policies would make it easier for them to remain attached to the labor force and to succeed on the job, while also meeting what many still regard as their family obligations.[72] This would in turn increase the incentives both for women themselves and for their employers to invest in women's human capital. Of course, those men who already shoulder sizable housework and child care responsibilities would benefit as well,[73] and others would find it easier to do a larger share. Thus family friendly policies would also be expected to promote a more equal division of labor in the household.

[70] Sue Shellenbarger, "Pregnant Workers Clash with Employers Over Job Inflexibility," *Wall Street Journal,* 10 February 1999, p. B1.

[71] Brian Roe, Leslie A. Whittington, Sara Beck Fein, and Mario F. Teisl, "Is There Competition Between Breast-Feeding and Maternal Employment?" *Demography* 36, no. 2 (May 1999): 157–71. While these authors find that mothers who have leaves of longer duration breastfeed their infants for a longer period of time, they also find that many mothers who return to the workplace manage to do both, with key factors being access to a private area and break time.

[72] As indicated in Chapter 9, it has generally been found that family responsibilities reduce women's earnings, though one recent study does not find evidence of this trade-off. See Peter Cappelli, Jill Constantine, and Clint Chadwick, "It Pays to Value Family: Work and Family Tradeoffs Reconsidered," *Industrial Relations* 39, no. 2 (April 2000): 175–98.

[73] For a discussion of men's difficulties in balancing work and family, see Joseph H. Pleck, "Balancing Work and Family," *Scientific American Presents* 10, no. 2 (summer 1999): 38–43.

College-Educated Women over the Last 100 Years:
Work, Family, or Both?

A recent study by economic historian Claudia Goldin finds that the ability of college-educated women to combine work and family has changed dramatically over the twentieth century.[*] College women are particularly interesting to study because, as a relatively career-oriented group, their experiences highlight the difficulties women have faced in balancing work and family.

Goldin begins with a cohort of women who graduated from college around 1910. She finds that they were expected to make a stark choice between a career (most often teaching) and having a family. Indeed, fully 50 percent did not marry or, if married, did not have children compared to only 22 percent of their contemporaries who did not attend college. Their experience suggests that prevailing social norms strongly discouraged married women from working outside the home.

The cohort of women who graduated from college around 1955 was more demographically similar to other women in the general population. During a time when Americans were generally marrying younger and having more children, college women were part of the trend, with only 17.5 percent not married or, if married, childless. Moreover, in contrast to their predecessors, many were able to have both a family *and* a job, though for the most part they did this in stages. Like many other women at that time, they first had a family and took a job later. However, the economic rewards to college for this group did not revolve solely around their own market work. They were much more likely to marry college men (who outnumbered them 2 to 1) and enjoyed a large financial gain by doing so. While the experience of this cohort suggests that it was becoming more acceptable for married women to work for pay, even the college-educated generally had "jobs" rather than "careers," which require substantial human capital investment and more continuous labor force participation.

Among the cohort of women graduating college around 1972, a larger share sought to have careers, rather than simply jobs. Because of the investment required in undertaking a career, many women in this cohort delayed childbearing and pursued the route of career first, family later. Still, Goldin's data suggest that the proportion of them who have been able to "have it all," that is, family and career, is surprisingly small. Only 13 to 22 percent of women in this cohort achieved both goals by about age 40, when family is defined as having given birth to at least one child and career as having earnings over a certain amount[†] or working full-time during the three preceding years. Of course, career is a difficult concept to define and the proportion found to have careers will undoubtedly vary with the definition. Moreover, the estimates of career may be low among the age group surveyed (35–44) because of the presence of young children among a substantial proportion of the women who had families.[‡] Yet even this qualification suggests that women face the need to make decisions and trade-offs seldom confronted by their male counterparts. Goldin's findings re-

[*] Claudia Goldin, "Career and Family: College Women Look to the Past," in *Gender and Family Issues in the Workplace,* ed. Francine D. Blau and Ronald G. Ehrenberg (New York: Russell Sage Foundation, 1997), pp. 20–59. Evidence below on the impact of children and maternity leave on women's earnings is from Jane Waldfogel, "Understanding the 'Family Gap' in Pay for Women with Children," *Journal of Economic Perspectives* 12, no. 1 (winter 1998): 157–70.
[†] Specifically, having income or average hourly earnings at least as high as a man at the 25th percentile of the college-educated male earnings distribution.
[‡] Using a sample of women predominantly in their fifties, Marianne A. Ferber and Carole Green found a larger share meeting this definition of career and family; see "Career and/or Family: What Choices Do Women Have?" Working Paper, University of Illinois (1999).

garding the difficulty of combining family and career are reinforced by considerable evidence suggesting that, among women as a group, children have a negative effect on earnings and employment.

While Goldin's results demonstrate the persistent difficulties for women of juggling a family and career, there is also reason to be more optimistic about the future. Access to family leave has been found to substantially mitigate the negative effect of children on women's wages. Thus, the difficulties that women have faced in achieving career and family are likely to decrease as more firms adopt such policies. Moreover, as discrimination in the labor market continues to decline, marriages gradually become more egalitarian, and various other family friendly policies are offered on a more widespread basis in the workplace, more women are likely to be able to successfully pursue careers and also have families.

WHO IS RESPONSIBLE FOR CHILDREN?

In all economically advanced countries, though with considerable variation, government plays some role in child care through such policies as mandated parental leave, public provision of day care, or financing of day care. However, in contrast to most other economically advanced countries, the government's role in the United States has been quite limited.[74] The U.S. government did not mandate that firms provide unpaid family leave to workers until the Family and Medical Leave Act (FMLA) was passed in 1993, while all other economically advanced nations provide *paid* leave, and most have been doing so for a considerable period of time. The U.S. government does to some extent subsidize child care for poor families and offers tax deductions to others, but does not generally provide day care itself. Consequently, families must make their own private arrangements or take advantage of benefits offered voluntarily by some firms such as on-site child care or help in finding child care. In comparison, France, Sweden, and Denmark, among others, provide free or heavily subsidized day care through the government sector.

The question of how the costs of raising children should be shared between parents, the government, and employers is quite complex.[75] One economic argument for government to play a role is that there are externalities associated with bearing and raising children. For instance, while children's parents undoubtedly receive a direct benefit from their own children and thus bear a special responsibility for their care, the nation also benefits when children grow up to be healthier, better-educated, and better-trained adults. This is because they will be more productive, will contribute more both as workers and as taxpayers, and are less likely to be a burden on the public. In other words, there are significant positive externalities when children are better cared for that benefit not only their parents, but the whole community. Employers also benefit when their employees have dependable child care arrangements in that it should reduce workers' absenteeism and increase the likelihood that they will not leave their current position. This suggests that government and employers, to some extent, should help finance the costs of raising children.

---

[74] Council of Economic Advisers, "The First Three Years: Investments That Pay" (Washington, DC: Council of Economic Advisers, 17 April 1997).

[75] For an excellent discussion of these issues, see Arleen Leibowitz, "Child Care: Private Cost or Public Responsibility?" in *Individual and Social Responsibility: Child Care, Education, Medical Care, and Long-Term Care in America,* ed. Victor R. Fuchs (Chicago: University of Chicago Press, 1996), pp. 33–57.

Issues of equity and redistribution provide another rationale for government to play a role. Government support for young children through such policies as subsidies for day care, parental leave, and infant nutrition serve to ensure that all children have a more equal chance at life, regardless of the economic status of the family into which they are born. Currently, various levels of government in the United States subsidize primary, secondary, and, to some extent, higher education. Arguably, it makes little sense to help educate youngsters from age five or six on, but not to help ensure that they will be ready to benefit from that education. Family leave, when taken by fathers as well as mothers, and subsidized day care also serve to enhance equity because they place female and male workers on a more equal footing, by reducing the potentially negative employment consequences associated with having to take time out for raising children.

An argument for government rather than employers playing a major role in providing benefits such as family leave and health insurance relates to a phenomenon called **adverse selection.** Adverse selection occurs if only some but not all firms offer such policies as family leave or health insurance coverage. It arises as a result of the fact that those workers who expect to benefit most from these policies are most likely to seek employment with firms that provide them. To understand the problem adverse selection poses, consider the following example. Suppose there was no federal family leave policy and instead only one firm offered it, basing its estimate of costs on the percentage of the total work force that might use it. It could then provide the benefit and offer its workers a somewhat lower wage that would cover its costs. Given the scarcity of this benefit, however, this firm would be prone to attract workers with a higher probability of using family leave than the work force at large. Hence, it would face higher costs than anticipated, and would be expected to try, to the extent it could, to pass along the cost increase in the form of still lower wages. This would further aggravate the adverse selection problem because those willing to work for these lower wages would increasingly consist of those who were most likely to take advantage of leaves, further increasing costs and thereby placing additional downward pressure on wages. In the end, the firm might well stop offering this benefit because it was too costly. More generally, adverse selection is likely to result in too few firms offering family leave relative to the optimal number, given workers' preferences. This suggests that a government mandate requiring all firms to offer such leave, thereby eliminating the adverse selection problem, might be very useful.[76]

The preceding discussion provides important efficiency and equity reasons as to why the government should play a role in raising children. However, in fully assessing the issue, potential costs should be considered too. For instance, government financing of any program, including subsidized day care and paid family leave, requires tax collection. Some research suggests that taxes cause individuals to work and save somewhat less than they would otherwise, thus reducing output.[77] It has been argued

---

[76] This example is drawn from Christopher J. Ruhm and Jackqueline L. Teague, "Parental Leave Policies in Europe and North America," in *Gender and Family Issues in the Workplace,* ed. Francine D. Blau and Ronald G. Ehrenberg (New York: Russell Sage Foundation, 1997), pp. 133–56. For a discussion of the adverse selection problem in general, see Harvey Rosen, *Public Finance,* 4th ed. (Chicago: Irwin, 1995).

[77] For evidence of the negative effect of taxes on labor supply, see, for instance, Jerry A. Hausman, "The Effect of Taxes on Labor Supply," in *How Taxes Affect Economic Behavior,* ed. Henry Aaron and Joseph Pechman (Washington, DC: Brookings, 1981), pp. 27–84.

that for this reason employer-mandated leave may be more efficient than leave paid for by the government, especially if the group that potentially benefits from the mandate bears the cost of the leave benefit in the form of lower wages. At least one study provides some evidence that wages do adjust and, thus, the policy is efficient.[78] Mandates would also boost economic efficiency to the extent that they encourage women to stay in the labor force, thereby raising the firm-specific human capital of the labor force.[79] On the other hand, mandates for unpaid leave, financed through wage reductions of the affected groups, eliminate any subsidy for parents. It may be recalled that such subsidies are advocated by some because of the benefits that society as a whole derives from children who become the next generation of productive citizens and workers. In addition, the lower wages, by reducing the incentive of these women to stay in the labor force, might even serve to counter the effects such policies would otherwise have on increasing women's labor force attachment. And finally, such a policy is particularly burdensome for low-income workers whose wages would be reduced further.

This discussion shows that the issues regarding family leave and subsidized day care are complex. It is therefore not surprising that there are considerable differences across countries in the extent of government's involvement, the manner in which policies are instituted, and the generosity of these policies.

FAMILY FRIENDLY POLICIES

While U.S. families bear much of the burden of balancing work and family, they do, as already noted, receive some voluntary assistance from firms. Employers may institute family friendly benefits in lieu of wage increases and other benefits. Alternatively, they may introduce them because they expect the gains to outweigh the costs. Possible benefits for employers include improved recruitment and retention of workers and greater productivity as a result of better morale and reductions in tardiness and absenteeism. It is often much less costly to provide workers with such benefits than to train new employees. Popular programs may also improve public relations. On the other hand, firms are likely to have additional costs because they may have to hire replacements and also may have to deal with scheduling problems. In addition, costs of such policies will tend to rise to the extent that more workers take advantage of them. On balance, however, we would expect that employers' incentives to adopt policies of this type will increase as a larger portion of the work force, both men and women, must cope with the difficulties of combining market work with home responsibilities.

It is becoming increasingly clear that family friendly policies have positive results for employees. A number of recent surveys of workers at large firms including, for in-

---

[78] Jonathan Gruber, "Incidence of Mandated Maternity Benefits," *American Economic Review* 84, no. 3 (June 1994): 622–41. Note, however, that if mandates are efficient, then they are not effective from a redistributive or equity standpoint because the group who benefits from the policy also bears the cost of the policy. For further discussion, see Susan N. Houseman, "The Effects of Employer Mandates," in *Generating Jobs: How to Increase Demand for Less-Skilled Workers,* ed. Richard B. Freeman and Peter Gottschalk (New York: Russell Sage Foundation, 1998), pp. 154–91.

[79] Christopher J. Ruhm, "The Economic Consequences of Parental Leave Mandates: Lessons from Europe," *Quarterly Journal of Economics* 113, no. 1 (February 1998): 285–318.

stance, Du Pont, indicate that such policies dramatically increased workers' satisfaction with the firm. Such benefits may also reduce work–family conflict by lowering stress.[80]

There are a number of reasons why family friendly policies are, nonetheless, being introduced only at a rather slow pace. First, their adoption requires a change in corporate "culture." Currently, family issues are seen as separate from the work sphere. For example, workers may be deemed unprofessional if they say they are delayed due to child care problems rather than car problems. Second, in many firms, workers are evaluated on the basis of "face time" (that is, the number of hours spent at the office or plant) rather than on output per se. There is concern that with more flexible policies, including family leave, job sharing, home-based work, and flextime, it may be harder to monitor employees. Thus, work may have to be organized differently.[81]

Large firms have generally been those at the forefront of implementing family friendly policies. Perhaps the main reason for this is that they can reap the advantages of economies of scale in setting up programs because the absolute number of workers who can potentially take advantage of them is so great. Needless to say, this is particularly true of firms with a high proportion of women, and hence, these firms are the ones that have been most likely to adopt such policies. Small firms have lagged behind, not only because they cannot take advantage of economies of scale in benefit provision, but also because even the short-term loss of a single highly trained individual may have a substantial impact on the operation of a small business. Further, training temporary workers is costly. Some analysts suggest "overstaffing a bit" to avoid a crisis if an employee is absent, developing floaters who can do several jobs, or instituting job sharing and developing contingency plans to deal with the absence of critical workers.[82]

Some of the most common policies to assist individuals in juggling their family and paid work are examined in detail next: family leave, alternative work schedules, flexible benefit plans, policies for couples, and child care.

FAMILY LEAVE

Family leave allows workers to take time off from their job for such reasons as pregnancy if there are complications or the nature of the work creates a hazard for the mother or fetus, childbirth, infant care, and tending to ill family members. Without such a policy, workers may have to deal with these problems by giving up their jobs, with loss not only of earnings, but of accrued benefits and seniority. The availability of family leave, even a relatively short and unpaid one, with provisions for job security and some other entitlements, is often helpful in enabling workers, particularly women workers, to avoid these high costs. It also increases incentives for women to invest in firm-specific training and for employers to provide them with opportunities to do so.

---

[80]   For a detailed discussion of family friendly policies, see James T. Bond, Ellen Galinsky, and Jennifer E. Swanberg, *The 1997 National Study of the Changing Workforce,* no. 2 (New York: Families and Work Institute, 1997). See also Tamar Lewin, "Workers of Both Sexes Make Trade-Offs for Family, Study Shows," *New York Times,* 29 October 1995, p. 25.

[81]   Charlene Marmer Solomon, "Work/Family's Failing Grade: Why Today's Initiatives Aren't Enough," *Personnel Journal* 73, no. 5 (May 1994): 72–87; and Olivia Mitchell, "Work and Family Benefits," in *Gender and Family Issues in the Workplace,* ed. Francine D. Blau and Ronald G. Ehrenberg (New York: Russell Sage Foundation, 1997), pp. 269–76.

[82]   "Family or Work: A Matter of Priorities," *USA Today* 123, no. 2600 (May 1995): 28–30.

The government has mandated two specific policies regarding leave.[83] The Pregnancy Discrimination Act of 1978 (an amendment to Title VII of the Civil Rights Act of 1964) prohibits employers from discriminating against workers on the basis of pregnancy. An employer may not, for example, terminate or deny a job to a woman because she is pregnant. Employers who have a medical disability program must provide paid disability leave for pregnancy and childbirth on the same basis as for other medical disabilities.[84]

More recently, President Clinton signed the Family and Medical Leave Act of 1993 (FMLA), which allows eligible workers to take up to 12 weeks of unpaid leave for birth or adoption; acquiring a foster child; illness of a child, spouse, or parent; or their own illness.[85] The worker may also take shorter leaves intermittently, pending the firm's approval. During the leave, the firm must continue health insurance coverage and, afterwards, the employee must be given the same or an equivalent position, with the same benefits, pay, and other conditions of employment. The FMLA applies to public- and private-sector workers who have been with the same employer for at least one year and worked at least 1,250 hours. However, the act only applies to firms with at least 50 workers. To the extent that some states mandate more generous benefits, these supersede the federal law.

The Family and Medical Leave Act was hotly debated. Opponents of the measure tended to ignore or minimize the potential benefits of leaves for employers and were particularly concerned about the costs imposed on them, since they must continue to pay for health insurance for workers on leave and also bear the costs of training replacement workers. (Pay for replacement workers, however, is not an added cost because workers on leave do not draw a paycheck.) Moreover, there are also benefits to employers in providing family leave, as we have already pointed out. Family leave reduces the costs of turnover, which can be quite substantial when training expenses are considered. Also, it may enhance workers' commitment to the firm and hence their productivity. In fact, a recent study by a bipartisan Commission on Leave found that for most employers, compliance with the FMLA has entailed few if any costs. The conclusion of the Commission's report was that providing short, unpaid leaves has not been unduly onerous for business.[86] International evidence also indicates that parental leave has not caused the severe problems for firms that had been anticipated by some critics.[87]

---

[83] For a review, see Eileen Trzcinski and William T. Alpert, "Pregnancy and Parental Leave Benefits in the United States and Canada," *Journal of Human Resources* 29, no. 2 (spring 1994): 535–54.

[84] Employers who do not have a medical disability program, however, are not required to provide paid disability for pregnancy and childbirth.

[85] From the late 1980s to the time the legislation had passed, approximately one-half of states had adopted some form of their own legislation. See Jacob Klerman and Arleen Leibowitz, "Labor Supply Effects of State Maternity Leave Legislation," in *Gender and Family Issues in the Workplace,* ed. Francine D. Blau and Ronald G. Ehrenberg (New York: Russell Sage Foundation, 1997), pp. 65–85. The debate over federal family leave is described in Andrew E. Scharlach and Blanche Grosswald, "The Family and Medical Leave Act of 1993," *Social Service Review* 71, no. 3 (September 1997): 335–59.

[86] Commission on Leave, *A Workable Balance: Report to Congress on Family and Medical Leave Policies* (Washington, DC: U.S. Department of Labor, 1996). Eileen Trzcinski and Matia Finn-Stevenson also reach the same conclusion in "A Response to Arguments Against Mandated Parental Leave: Findings from the Connecticut Survey of Parental Leave Policies," *Journal of Marriage and the Family* 53 (May 1991): 445–60.

[87] Organisation for Economic and Cultural Development (OECD), "Long-Term Leave for Parents in OECD Countries," *OECD Employment Outlook,* (July 1995): 171–202.

The overall effect of family leave on women's labor force attachment and wages is ambiguous a priori. On the one hand, availability of leave is likely to increase labor force attachment by enabling workers to return to the same employer following an absence, and thus to maintain job continuity. This would be expected to have a positive effect on wages because it will allow for longer job tenure, the maintenance of a good "job match," and provide the opportunity to continue climbing the firm's career ladder. On the other hand, to the extent that leave allows women to stay out of the labor market longer than they would have without such a policy, leave or the extension of leave time might have a negative effect due to the depreciation of human capital. This would be of particular concern in some other countries where leave time is considerably longer, often as much as 12 months or more, rather than in the United States where mandated leave is quite short. Even so, as previously suggested, widespread use of paid leave might reduce women's relative wages to finance the benefit, although this negative effect will be considerably mitigated to the extent that men as well as women avail themselves of leave. Finally, it is possible that employers might respond to increased costs by cutting back on employment.

Empirical evidence thus far indicates that the FMLA has had, if anything, a modest positive effect on employment, and no effect on wages.[88] Other work, which has looked at the availability of employer-provided leave, has found it to have a positive effect on both the wages and employment of women who become mothers.[89] These findings may reflect that leave in the United States is generally unpaid and of short duration. Where leave is paid and of medium or long duration, as in many other countries, there is some evidence of negative effects on employment and earnings.[90]

From a broader perspective, family leave, if taken by both fathers and mothers, likely promotes greater gender equality by encouraging both parents to share the job of caring for infants and meeting family emergencies. Another benefit of family leave is that it provides children with increased parental time, especially during infancy. At the same time, the FMLA has the advantage that parents can return to their previous job after taking it. Thus, some women who would have remained with their employers in any case may stretch their leave time a bit longer, and others who would have quit their jobs rather than return to work immediately postbirth will now stay with their employer.[91]

---

[88] Jane Waldfogel, "The Impact of the Family and Medical Leave Act," *Journal of Policy Analysis and Management* 18, no. 2 (spring 1999): 281–302. On the other hand, Katherin E. Ross found the FMLA had no effect on employment (she did not look at wages) in "Labor Pains: The Effect of the Family and Medical Leave Act on the Return to Paid Work After Childbirth," *Focus* 20, no. 1 (winter 1998–99): 34–36. For discussions of the effects of this and other leave policies, see Christopher J. Ruhm, "Policy Watch: The Family and Medical Leave Act," *Journal of Economic Perspectives* 11, no. 3 (summer 1997): 175–86.

[89] For evidence of positive effects of leave, see Jane Waldfogel, "The Family Gap for Young Women in the U.S. and Britain: Can Maternity Leave Make a Difference?" *Journal of Labor Economics* 16, no. 3 (July 1998): 505–45. For a summary of the issues, see Francine D. Blau and Ronald G. Ehrenberg, "Gender and Family Issues in the Workplace," in *Gender and Family Issues in the Workplace,* ed. Francine D. Blau and Ronald G. Ehrenberg (New York: Russell Sage Foundation, 1997).

[90] Ruhm and Teague, "Parental Leave Policies"; and Ruhm, "The Economic Consequences."

[91] Jacob Alex Klerman and Arleen Leibowitz find that the FMLA appears to have had only a small effect, at most, on job continuity in "Job Continuity Among New Mothers," *Demography* 36, no. 2 (May 1999): 145–55.

From the point of view of workers, a major problem with the FMLA is that it provides limited coverage. It does not cover workers in establishments with less than 50 employees, workers who fail to meet the 1,250 hours per year requirement, or workers who have been employed for less than one year. Hence, it is estimated that the FMLA covers just 46 percent of all women workers. For the remainder, coverage is much more sporadic, depending on state and firm-specific parental leave policies. Nevertheless, there is evidence that since the passage of FMLA in 1993, coverage has increased dramatically for many workers, though certainly not all. In 1997, fully 95 percent of full-time employees in medium and large establishments were entitled to such leaves, while this had been true for only 39 percent of female employees and 27 percent of male employees in 1991. On the other hand, even by 1997, only around 54 percent of part-time workers in medium and large establishments and 48 percent of full-time employees in small establishments had leave coverage, though these figures too reflect a considerable increase from 1991.[92]

Another problem with the present Family and Medical Leave Act for many families, along with the leave being very short, is that it is unpaid, which limits the ability of some covered workers, particularly those with low incomes, to take advantage of its provisions. In 1997, for instance, only 2 percent of establishments voluntarily offered paid family leave to full-time employees.[93] These figures are likely to understate the amount of time individuals can take off from work with pay because, as noted earlier, some workers may be covered by employers' short-term disability plans or may be able to use their sick leave or vacation time. However, since mandated leave is unpaid, it is not all that surprising that the utilization of leave specifically designated as "FMLA leave" has been found to be fairly low. The primary reason offered by workers who expressed a need for leave but did not take it was that they could not afford to lose pay.[94]

Given concerns that many individuals are still not covered by FMLA, or, if covered, cannot take advantage of it for financial reasons, several changes have been proposed or already undertaken to expand coverage to more workers and to make benefits more generous. For instance, former President Clinton recommended offering leave to workers in firms with 25 workers or more. In addition, he proposed expanding family leave to include 24 hours of unpaid time for essential family matters such as participating in a child's school activities and accompanying children and elderly relatives to medical appointments.[95] As of the end of 2000, neither change had been made at the federal

---

[92]   Figures are from Jane Waldfogel, "Family Leave Coverage in the 1990s," *Monthly Labor Review* 122, no. 12 (October 1999): 13–21.

[93]   U.S. Bureau of Labor Statistics, "Employee Benefits in Medium and Large Private Establishments, 1997," USDL 99–02, 7 January 1999; and U.S. Bureau of Labor Statistics, "Employee Benefits in Small Private Industry Establishments, 1996," USDL 98–240, 15 June 1998.

[94]   Commission on Leave, "Executive Summary," *A Workable Balance;* and Naomi Gerstel and Katherine McGonagle, "Job Leaves and the Limits of the Family and Medical Leave Act," *Work and Occupations* 26, no. 4 (November 1999): 510–34. There is, however, some evidence that the FMLA has affected utilization of leave for some women with infants, in particular those in medium-size firms who were less likely to have coverage before the legislation was passed. See Waldfogel, "The Impact of the Family and Medical Leave Act."

[95]   The White House, "President Clinton: Helping Parents Meet Their Responsibilities at Home and at Work," 23 May 1999; and "President Clinton Announces New Funds Enabling States to Provide Leave to America's Working Parents," 12 February 2000.

level, though Massachusetts did put into effect its own quite similar "Small Necessities Leave Act" in 1998.[96] In June 2000, President Clinton put regulations in place that allow states to use funds from their Unemployment Insurance (UI) programs to provide paid leave to families at the time of a birth or adoption. The UI system, established in 1935, currently provides payments to those who are involuntarily unemployed and are actively seeking work. Opponents argue that using these funds for the purpose of providing paid family leave goes against the fundamental principle of the program and might well jeopardize its financial solvency. Proponents, on the other hand, estimate that costs will be far lower than predicted by opponents of the program. Further, they note that some states already provide unemployment benefits to a broader constituency, including those who are training for jobs, so that this is merely a further extension of the program.[97]

ALTERNATIVE WORK SCHEDULES

A decrease in the standard workweek of full-time workers would clearly be advantageous to those with time-consuming household responsibilities. As noted in Chapter 4, there was a sizable decline in weekly work hours between the 1900s and the 1940s.[98] Since then, average weekly hours appear to have changed fairly little, although there have been important changes in hours among specific groups of workers.[99] The length of the workweek has generally declined for employees with less than a high school education, while it has risen for those with more than 12 years of schooling and particularly for those in professional, managerial, and technical occupations.[100] This increase in work hours for some individuals, combined with the fact that many Americans are single parents with responsibility for children or are members of a dual-earner family, has led to many more families facing an increasing "time squeeze." Alternative work schedules provide greater flexibility for workers to take care of family responsibilities and to arrange their personal lives more conveniently. They include flextime, nonstandard work schedules, part-time employment, job sharing, and home-based work.

Flextime   Flextime permits some degree of variation in work schedules at the discretion of the employee, ranging from modest changes in starting and quitting times to variation in the number of hours worked per day, week, or pay period. Such flexibility can

---

[96]   "State Law Grants Leave for Families' 'Small Necessities'," *Boston Herald*, 7 May 1998, p. 20.

[97]   Robert Pear, "Dispute Over Plan to Use Jobless Aid for Parental Leave," *New York Times,* 8 November 1999, p. A1.

[98]   Thomas J. Knieser, "The Full-Time Workweek in the United States: 1900–1970,"*Industrial and Labor Relations Review* 30, no. 1 (October 1976): 3–15.

[99]   Those finding a negligible effect overall include Mary T. Coleman and John Pencavel, "Trends in Market Work Behavior of Women Since 1940," *Industrial and Labor Relations Review* 46, no. 4 (July 1993): 653–76; Mary T. Coleman and John Pencavel, "Changes in Work Hours of Male Employees: 1940–1988," *Industrial and Labor Relations Review* 46, no. 2 (January 1993): 262–83; and Jerry A. Jacobs and Kathleen Gerson, "Who Are the Overworked Americans?" *Review of Social Economy* 54, no. 4 (winter 1998): 442–59. Others have found very modest positive or negative trends. For a review, see Deborah M. Figart and Lonnie Golden, "The Social Economics of Work Time: Introduction," *Review of Social Economy* 54, no. 4 (winter 1998): 411–24.

[100]   In sharp contrast, in 1890, workers in the top wage decile worked a shorter day than other workers. See Dora L. Costa, "The Wage and the Length of the Work Day: From the 1890s to 1991," *Journal of Labor Economics* 18, no. 1 (January 2000): 156–81.

be quite advantageous for many workers, especially for those with young children or other family members who depend on their care.[101] Another potential advantage of flextime is a reduction in commuting time. In fact, if enough workers are on flextime, this tends to reduce rush-hour traffic and benefits even those who are not on flextime. The degree of flexibility that can be offered depends on the nature of the enterprise and the type of work. Some employers will be reluctant to offer this benefit because they need key employees to be present during standard hours, perhaps to be available to handle customers or to meet work flow demands. They may also be concerned about the potential for abuse. It is estimated that in the United States, 29 percent of male workers and 26 percent of female workers had flexible schedules in 1997, up from 13 and 11 percent, respectively, in 1991. The availability of flextime, however, differs greatly by occupation, with as many as 42 percent of those in executive, administrative, and managerial positions receiving this benefit, in contrast to only 23 percent of administrative support (including clerical) workers and less than 20 percent of workers in most blue-collar occupations.[102] Also, at least one study has found that flextime is uncommon in small to medium-size establishments.[103]

Nonstandard Work Schedules Nonstandard work schedules,[104] where employees work rotating shifts, weekends, or nights, have been growing increasingly common, as many plants, factories and service firms have moved to 24-hour operation. Technological advances, including the fax machine, cell phone, and computer, have made much of this possible. In addition, women's increased labor force participation as well as the rise in single-parent and dual-earner families has fueled the demand for a 24-hour economy, as increasing numbers of individuals must shop for groceries, prescription drugs, and clothing for themselves and their family in the evening or on weekends. It is estimated that in 1997, only 60 percent of full-time workers over age 18 regularly worked a fixed schedule, say 9 to 5, Monday through Friday, with the rest working a nonstandard schedule.[105] Those with less education are much more likely to be working nonstandard schedules and this disparity has increased since the 1970s. Women are disproportionately affected because many of the top growth occupations that tend to have nonstandard work schedules are female-dominated, including cashier, nurse, retail salesperson, and home health aid.[106]

---

[101] It is interesting to note that some professionals, for instance university faculty, have always had a great degree of flexibility. They are responsible for teaching classes and attending committee meetings at specified times but have considerable discretion about when to prepare for classes, grade papers, and do their research.

[102] U.S. Bureau of Labor Statistics, "Workers on Flexible and Shift Schedules in 1997," *News,* USDL 98–119, 26 March 1998.

[103] Linda K. Stroh and Karen S. Kush, "Flextime: The Imaginary Innovation," *New York Times,* 27 November 1994, p. 11.

[104] The term *nonstandard* used here refers to work schedules, rather than to the type of worker or employment, as in Chapter 8. This section is drawn from Harriet B. Presser, "Toward a 24-Hour Economy," *Science* 284 (11 June 1999): 1778–79; and Harriet B. Presser, "Job, Family, and Gender: Determinants of Nonstandard Work Schedules Among Employed Americans in 1991," *Demography* 32, no. 4 (November 1995): 577–95.

[105] Figures are from Presser, "Toward a 24-Hour Economy." See also U.S. Bureau of Labor Statistics, "Workers on Flexible and Shift Schedules in 1997."

[106] See Daniel S. Hamermesh, "Changing Inequality in Markets for Workplace Amenities," *Quarterly Journal of Economics* 114, no. 4 (November 1999): 1085–123; and Harriet B. Presser, "The Work Schedules of Low-Educated American Women and Welfare Reform," *Monthly Labor Review* 120, no. 4 (April 1997): 25–34.

Unlike flextime, these schedules are typically set by employers rather than at the discretion of employees. Even so, there can be advantages of nonstandard schedules for employees because they potentially provide some flexibility in juggling child care, schooling, and the need to earn a living. On the other hand, to the extent that workers are not able to choose their schedules, those with young children may face tremendous difficulties finding child care on weekends and at night. In addition, in two-parent families with such schedules, adults tend to have less time to spend together, potentially leading to negative consequences, including divorce. There may also be biological difficulties for workers in adjusting to night work.

Part-Time Employment   Part-time employment is especially common among women (as well as young people going to school) and does offer flexibility as compared to a strict 9 to 5, five days a week schedule. As many as 25 percent of employed women and nearly 11 percent of employed men worked less than full-time (defined as at least 35 hours per week) in 1999.[107] As discussed earlier in Chapter 8, the main problems with much of part-time work as a solution to difficulties in combining job and family responsibilities are few fringe benefits (such as health care), frequently poor compensation, and few opportunities for promotion.

Job Sharing   Two individuals sharing one position is an innovative approach to opening up more challenging positions to part-time workers. It can be advantageous to employers who have large investments in their employees and would lose the benefits of these investments if these employees left. In fact, a 1998 survey of large corporations indicated that nearly one-third of them offered employees this option, up from around 10 percent in 1990. Actual utilization is far lower, perhaps either because employees do not know of the possibility or because it is discouraged by some managers. For those who do job share, one potential disadvantage is that they may receive only partial benefits or none at all.[108]

Home-Based Employment   Another potential solution is home-based employment,[109] which enables men and women to do paid work at home. Estimates of the extent of home-based work vary widely depending on the definition used. For example, it has been estimated that in 1997 as many as 18 percent of workers did at least some work at home for their primary job.[110] On the other hand, less than 3 percent were classified as working entirely at home in 1990, the most recent year for which such data are available.[111] Regardless of the definition used, however, the percentage of home-based work-

---

[107] U.S. Department of Labor, *Employment and Earnings,* January 2000, p. 175.

[108] Penny Singer, "For Some, Job Sharing Offers a Solution," *New York Times,* 13 June 1993, p. 12; and "Fair Shares," *Working Woman,* November 1999.

[109] The discussion that follows is drawn from William G. Deming, "Work at Home: Data from the Current Population Survey," *Monthly Labor Review* 117, no. 2 (February 1994): 14–20; Linda N. Edwards and Elizabeth Field-Hendry, "Home-Based Workers? Data from the 1990 Census of Population," *Monthly Labor Review* 119, no. 11 (November 1996): 26–34; and Linda N. Edwards and Elizabeth Field-Hendry, "Home-Based Work and Women's Labor Force Decisions," *Journal of Labor Economics* (forthcoming).

[110] U.S. Bureau of Labor Statistics, "Work at Home in 1997," *News,* USDL 98–93, 11 March 1998.

[111] U.S. Census Bureau, "Increase in At-Home Workers Reverses Earlier Trends," *Census Brief,* 98–2, March 1998.

ers increased since the 1980s. This increase is partly the result of improvements in computers and communications, but also due to the rise in women's labor force participation, the growing number of small individually and family owned businesses, and the competing demands of home and family. Home-based employment likely encourages paid work, especially by women, since the fixed costs associated with this type of employment tend to be lower: there are few, if any, additional costs of transportation, clothing, child care, or elder care. Parents may be able to keep a closer eye on teens as well. Further, the many home-based workers who are self-employed have the advantage of setting their own schedules and do not have to answer to an employer about the way they allocate their time. For those telecommuting with an employer based elsewhere, there are, however, significant issues related to how the firm measures workers' productivity and how often the employees need to keep in touch. Some companies, including, for instance, Merrill Lynch, have found that telecommuting is most successful if a formal agreement between employee and employer is set up so that expectations regarding the arrangement are clear on both sides.[112] Of course, in evaluating this alternative it is important to be realistic about its drawbacks as well as its benefits. Whether the home-based worker is self-employed or works for someone else, one issue is how much work can really be accomplished if there is an infant, toddler, school-age child, or infirm parent present who requires attention during work time. Another is the isolation the individual may experience when working at home.

The "Mommy Track"

In considering the problems employed women have when juggling job and family, substantial attention has focused on the relatively small number of women managers. This is probably in part because they tend to be prominent and potentially influential, but also because combining such a position with family responsibilities often does present substantial challenges. It is widely believed that the resulting strains cause high turnover among women executives, and that this in turn creates problems for their employers.

One suggested solution to these difficulties is for women to choose either, on the one hand, to devote themselves fully to their career and forgo having children or at least active involvement in rearing them or, on the other hand, to settle for a lesser job. In return, employers would be expected to offer adequate flexibility to the latter group, enabling them to do justice to their dual responsibilities to family and paid work. Proponents of such a policy,* the so-called "mommy track," begin from the premise that the basic characteristic that differentiates women from men is their role as mothers. They further hold that bringing this issue into the open is most useful and will permit appropriate adjustments both for the women concerned and their employers.

In this view, maternity involves a continuum that begins with an awareness of the ticking of the biological clock; proceeds to the anticipation of motherhood; includes pregnancy, childbirth, recuperation, and psychological adjustment; and continues to nursing, bonding, and childrearing. Such a commitment is not considered to make a woman unfit for employment. On the contrary, she may make a valuable and much-needed contribution. But

* See, for example, Felice N. Schwartz, "Management Women and the New Facts of Life," *Harvard Business Review* 67, no. 2 (January–February 1989): 65–76.

---

[112] Susan J. Wells, "For Stay-Home Workers, Speed Bumps on the Telecommute," *New York Times,* 17 August 1997, pp. 1 and 14.

only a woman who makes an early decision to devote herself exclusively to her career should expect to join the inner circle of top management.

Among the arguments on the other side[†] is the lack of hard data showing that businesses at present find it more expensive to employ women managers, or that most of these women are unable to successfully combine career and family. Moreover, making an irreversible decision for a lifetime at a relatively early age is not necessarily desirable. Perhaps most seriously, however, opponents of the mommy track are troubled by the stereotyping of women and men, making motherhood categorically different from fatherhood. No one questions that only women bear and nurse children. But for women who currently have a life expectancy of nearly 70 years and who have one, two, or even three children, these biological functions absorb only a very small share of their time and energy. It is rather the preparation for parenthood, the psychological adjustment to becoming a parent, and certainly bonding and childrearing that constitute a major commitment. There is no convincing evidence that fathers are not equally capable of such dedication. Hence, a more plausible solution is for employers to make adjustments that will enable men and women alike to bear their share of family responsibilities, including needed care not only for children but for other adults in cases of illness, disability, or infirmity.

[†] See, for example, letters to the editor in response to Schwartz, *Harvard Business Review* 67, no. 3 (May–June 1989): 182–214.

FLEXIBLE BENEFIT PLANS

As the work force becomes more diverse, with some workers who are members of traditional families, some who have employed spouses, some who are single, and others who live with partners they are not married to, flexible benefit plans are increasingly important as an alternative to standard or fixed benefit packages. This is because workers can tailor them to their particular needs. Flexible plans increase the value of fringe benefits to workers and may also provide a further inducement to individuals to enter or to remain attached to the firm and to the labor market.[113] For example, two-earner couples would be best served by avoiding double health insurance coverage (which occurs when one or both are covered under their own employer's health insurance program and under their spouse's), or parents of young children may prefer to receive child care benefits in exchange for smaller payments into a pension fund.

There are a number of types of flexible benefit plans. **Cafeteria plans** involve the allocation of an amount predetermined by the employer for employee benefits and permit covered employees to select from among a specified assortment of benefits worth up to that amount. Most often, any monies not used by the end of the year revert to the employer. **Flexible spending accounts,** on the other hand, involve the use of money taken out of paychecks on a pretax basis, which may be used by employees for particular job-related expenses, such as care of children and other dependents. In 1997, 13 percent of workers in medium and large firms were offered cafeteria plans, and 32 percent had access to flexible spending accounts. In small firms, the figures were only 4 and 12 percent,

---

[113] Federal and state tax policy has encouraged the growth of many employer-paid benefits in general by excluding them from taxable employee income, while permitting businesses to treat them as a normal business expense. See Marianne A. Ferber and Brigid O'Farrell, with La Rue Allen, eds., *Work and Family: Policies for a Changing Workforce* (Washington, DC: National Academy Press, 1991).

respectively.[114] The reason why small firms are less likely to offer flexible benefit plans is that it is costly to develop and administer such policies, and they are not able to achieve economies of scale as large firms can.

POLICIES FOR COUPLES

Dual-earner couples, married as well as unmarried, whether same or opposite sex, face particular problems in the workplace. Such couples, especially those with two professionals, must deal with the often daunting task of finding two jobs commensurate with their respective skills in the same location, or having a "commuting relationship," if both are to successfully pursue their careers. As discussed in Chapter 9, heterosexual couples are still considerably more likely to give priority to the husband's career, often leading the wife's career to suffer. Still, there is evidence that increasingly husbands are making sacrifices too.

Employers can assist two-career couples and, in particular, reduce the negative consequences for the "trailing partner" in a number of ways. For example, firms, either acting alone or with others, can actively help partners find employment. A recent survey by the Employee Relocation Council in Washington, DC, found that half of the employers surveyed in 1998 provided some assistance of this type.[115] This might include sending out the spouse's resume to an employer network or to a number of specific employers, or making use of personal contacts.

Many universities as well as some other establishments have set up programs for hiring couples, or offer jobs to partners of employees, whenever suitable positions can be found.[116] Businesses can also reduce difficulties for such couples by not penalizing employees who decline a promotion because they have family responsibilities or decline a transfer to an office or plant in a different location because their partner might find it difficult to locate a satisfactory job there. Indeed, a recent study finds that a substantial fraction of husbands and wives want the option to slow down the pace of their career at times, perhaps by turning down a promotion or refusing to move, but still retain the opportunity for upward mobility in the future.[117]

Antinepotism rules, once widely used to restrict the hiring or retention of relatives of employees, have virtually disappeared in academia and have become less common elsewhere as well. These rules not only prevented couples from being hired, but if two employees married, one—usually the wife—would have to go. The most common forms of restriction today are less severe; some employers restrict two family members, un-

---

[114] U.S. Bureau of Labor Statistics, "Employee Benefits in Medium and Large Private Establishments, 1997;" and U.S. Bureau of Labor Statistics, "Employee Benefits in Small Private Industry Establishments, 1996." Terminology used here differs somewhat from that employed by the BLS.

[115] This figure is cited in Eve Tahmincioglu, "Job Seekers are Looking Out for No. 2," *New York Times,* 25 October 2000.

[116] Eleanor Byrnes, "Dual Career Couples: How the Company Can Help," in *The Woman in Management: Career and Family Issues,* ed. Jennie Farley (Ithaca, NY: ILR Press, 1983), pp. 49–53; and Jane W. Loeb, "Programs for Academic Partners: How Well Can They Work?" in *Academic Couples: Problems and Promises,* ed. Marianne A. Ferber and Jane W. Loeb (Champaign: University of Illinois Press, 1997), pp. 270–98.

[117] "Catalyst Study Finds Dual-Career Couples Want Freedom and Control, Would Leave Their Companies if They Don't Find It," Press Release (New York: Catalyst Corporation, 20 January 1998); Kirstin Downey Grimsley, "The Roots of Their Reluctance; More Workers Spurn Transfers, Posing a Dilemma for Employers," *Washington Post,* 3 March 1996, p. H1; and Jeanne Peck, "Following Your Spouse Along the Career Path: Trailing Partners Face a Special Set of Challenges When They Move and Start Search for New Job," *Toronto Star,* 9 July 1998, p. C7.

married partners, or even couples with romantic attachments from working in the same department, or at least avoid having one partner directly supervising the other. In these cases, there is concern that a powerful partner may exert influence to have the other hired or promoted or that the couple would form a working alliance that may be resented by their coworkers.

Such abuses undoubtedly take place, but there is no evidence that they are any greater than when people simply are or become close friends. In fact, one might expect couples to be somewhat more circumspect because favoritism would be so obvious. In any case, the risk that such problems may occur must be weighed against the disadvantage of not being able to hire and retain the best-qualified people regardless of their relationship. One problem with even these remnants of antinepotism rules is that as long as husbands are senior to their wives and in higher positions, it is the woman who will be viewed as more expendable. Further, employment of the partner by a competitor may well create its own set of problems. For instance, the employee may inadvertently share confidential business information with the partner, putting the firm at risk.

Emerging policies for married couples, with and without children, have raised questions about fairness to those who are single or childless.[118] For instance, singles are at a disadvantage to the extent that employers pay lower wages as a result of providing benefits such as family leave, on-site day care, and free or subsidized spousal health care and pensions. Also, singles may be far less interested in flexible schedules and may regret the reduction in "face time" with coworkers. In addition, some single individuals claim that they are often called upon to shoulder extra responsibilities at work when a coworker's child becomes sick, or that they are expected to work weekends, nights, or holidays so that others can spend time with their families. Regarding benefits, one solution would be for firms to offer cafeteria plans, so that workers can choose the benefits they want. A more radical alternative would be to level the playing field by scaling back all such benefits. At the same time, if it is recognized that people's status changes— singles marry, children grow up, married people divorce or become widowed—most people might be willing to settle for existing policies.

Unmarried couples, whether opposite sex or same sex, are also at a disadvantage relative to married couples because they are generally not eligible for the substantial fringe benefits that are usually available to spouses. These frequently include dental and medical insurance, parental leave, life insurance, and leave in the case of a family member's illness. Since the early 1980s, the domestic partnership movement has been attempting to have these rules changed for employees of private organizations and especially for government employees, but so far with only modest success. Employers have tended to argue against extending such benefits to unmarried, opposite-sex couples on the grounds that they could have these privileges if they got married. This argument does not, however, apply to same-sex couples. Accordingly, some firms, including Lotus, IBM, Disney, and Microsoft, extend benefits such as health insurance and pensions to these couples.[119] Still,

---

[118] See Barbara Bergmann, "Work–Family Policies and Equality Between Women and Men," in *Gender and Family Issues in the Workplace,* ed. Francine D. Blau and Ronald G. Ehrenberg (New York: Russell Sage Foundation, 1997), pp. 277–79; and Daniel Akst, "In Defense of the Single and Childless," *New York Times,* 6 June 1999, p. 5.

[119] Patricia Horn, "Fringe Benefits for Gay Spouses," *Dollars and Sense,* December 1991, pp. 10–11 and 22; and "To Love and To Cherish," *Dollars and Sense,* June 1990, pp. 9–22. See also "Domestic Partners," *Congressional Quarterly Researcher* 2, no. 33 (September 1992): 761–84.

in the vast majority of cases, family continues to be defined for these as well as other purposes as a unit that consists of individuals related by blood, marriage, or adoption. Furthermore, the idea of marriage among same-sex couples has created a firestorm of opposition. One recent exception is Vermont, which, effective July 2000, has extended around 300 spousal rights available under state law to same-sex couples who obtain a "Civil Union" license.[120]

How to Handle a Job Interview

How much should you tell a potential employer during a job interview about your family responsibilities in order to learn about the employer's willingness to accommodate your family concerns?[*] This is not an easy question to answer. On the one hand, if you mention that you have young children or perhaps other family members who need care, or that you have a spouse who would also need to relocate, it may reduce your chances of being offered a position for which you are fully qualified. On the other hand, in order for you to be sure that you and the firm will be a good "match," you may need to get sufficient information about items like whether the potential employer will make it easier for you to handle possible family emergencies, or whether your progress would be impeded if you were reluctant to move. The question may even arise as to whether or not you would want to work for an organization that looks askance at anyone who has a life outside the workplace.

At the same time it is likely that because of the high costs of hiring and training workers, employers who interview you are also interested in making a good long-term match and therefore want to learn as much as possible about you. They too, however, face challenges and constraints. On the one hand, employers need to learn about your degree of commitment to the job. On the other hand, they are not allowed by law to ask directly about your family situation, including current or intended pregnancies, whether any family members have disabilities, or even your marital status.[†] One problem is that some employers may nevertheless ask questions that are illegal, fall into a gray area, or are at the very least "unwise," depending on how they are asked. This confronts you with the difficult decision of how to handle such a situation.

While it is impossible to offer suggestions on precisely what to say and do under all circumstances that may arise, there are some general recommendations that can be made that should help you to elicit the information that you need and send the message that you want, while avoiding a discussion about your family responsibilities, per se. For instance, you might ask your potential employer to describe a "typical day" or a "typical week" for a person who would hold your job or for your coworkers, more generally. This would give you a sense of whether you will likely be expected to work late hours during the week or on weekends, without asking the question directly and thus perhaps giving the appearance

---

[*] This inset is drawn from Sue Shellenbarger, "What You Should Say About Family Duties in a Job Interview," *Wall Street Journal,* 10 April 1996, sec. B1, p. 1; "Advice to Help You Get Ahead from the Experts: Business Newsletters, Magazines and Books; Job Seekers Should Beware," *Atlanta Constitution,* 20 June 1999; Kirsten Downey Grimsley, "Awkward Queries in Interviews," *San Francisco Chronicle,* 25 February 2000, p. B3; and Michael Barrier, "Hire Without Fear," *Nation's Business* (U.S. Chamber of Commerce), May 1999, p. 16.
[†] "Advice to Help You Get Ahead from the Experts," p. 1R.

---

[120] Ross Sneyd, "Vermont Senate Gives Final Approval to Gay Unions Legislation," CNN.com, 19 April 2000.

that you are not willing to work hard. Also, at a later stage in the interview process, you could ask for materials regarding conditions of employment, which may include information about options for flextime and various paid and unpaid fringe benefits, such as on-site child care. In addition, discrete conversations with potential coworkers may serve to answer questions you would be reluctant to raise with the employer directly. You might even "mount an offensive" concerning family responsibilities, by stating what kind of employee you expect to be, and emphasizing your reliability and commitment to work.‡

The types of issues discussed here will remain especially problematic for women as long as housework as well as child and elder care continue to be very unequally divided in the household. Under these circumstances, employers have the option of hiring men who may have few if any family responsibilities that will interfere with their devotion to their jobs. While public policies may facilitate change to some extent, only the determination of individual women and men to achieve more egalitarian marriages, and to encourage their children to move further in that direction, may be expected to bring about fundamental change.

‡ Shellenbarger, "What You Should Say."

CHILD CARE

Finding affordable, quality day care[121] is crucial for most single parents and dual-earner couples if their children are not to be penalized. In fact, a substantial fraction of such families face this problem very shortly after their child's birth, given that 59 percent of all women with infants (and presumably virtually all fathers) were in the labor force as of 1998.[122] In making their decision to continue working or go back to their job, parents must decide how much they value the earnings compared to the value of the forgone time at home. This includes the loss of leisure as well as goods and services they would have produced themselves if they had remained at home; among these, child care is generally foremost.

Although in the United States most of the costs of raising children are borne by parents, the federal government subsidizes purchased day care for employed parents through a number of channels including both the tax system and block grants—grants of a fixed dollar amount provided to states to be used for child care or given directly to child care providers. The government presumably does so because, as discussed earlier, children provide benefits not only for their parents but for society at large as the citizens and productive workers of tomorrow. In addition, subsidies help to make the playing field more equal for all children at an early age, regardless of their families' income.

---

[121] A thorough discussion of these issues is found in Myra H. Strober, "Formal Extrafamily Child Care— Some Economic Observations," in *Sex, Discrimination and the Division of Labor*, ed. Cynthia B. Lloyd (New York: Columbia University Press, 1975); Cheryl D. Hayes, John L. Palmer, and Martha J. Zaslow, eds., *Who Cares for America's Children? Child Care Policy for the 1990s* (Washington, DC: National Academy Press, 1990); Leibowitz, "Child Care"; Council of Economic Advisers, "The Economics of Child Care," (Washington, DC, December 1997); and William Gentry and Allison P. Hagy, "The Distributional Effects of the Tax Treatment of Child Care Expenses," in *Empirical Foundations of Household Taxation*, ed. Martin Feldstein and James M. Poterba (Chicago: University of Chicago Press, 1996), pp. 99–128.

[122] This figure is from U.S. Census Bureau, "Women 15 to 44 Years Old Who Have Had a Child in the Last Year and Their Percentage in the Labor Force," Historical Time Series Tables, www.census.gov. The percentage of mothers with an infant who were *employed*, as reported by the Bureau of Labor Statistics, was somewhat lower, 54 percent (see Table 10.5). See also Jacob A. Klerman and Arleen Leibowitz, "The Work–Employment Distinction Among New Mothers," *Journal of Human Resources* 29, no. 2 (spring 1994): 277–303.

Given that higher-income families tend to purchase better-quality care, this suggests that the highest priority for government should be to provide subsidies for low-income families in order that they may obtain such care.[123] This might be accomplished, for instance, by furnishing subsidies on a sliding scale, based on ability to pay.

As long as women are the primary caregivers, child care subsidies especially benefit mothers as compared to fathers. Such subsidies make it easier for mothers to take jobs that offer valuable experience and on-the-job training opportunities so that instead of permitting their human capital to deteriorate, they can stay on the job and add to it. Child care benefits also enable some mothers to leave welfare for employment. Beyond all that, as long as child care remains one of the most female-dominated occupations, greatly expanded day care facilities would help to provide jobs for many women, not only for trained teachers, but also for relatively unskilled women, including those in transition from welfare to work, who would often make excellent teacher's aides and day care workers.[124]

Still, despite the substantial potential benefits to children and families, there is some concern about government subsidies. One common argument against public subsidies for day care is that they benefit families with employed mothers at the expense of those with stay-at-home mothers. In evaluating this argument it is useful to recall from the earlier discussion on taxes that without such subsidies, the federal tax system heavily favors traditional families because home production is untaxed, and because income splitting favors one-earner couples. Thus, the subsidies may be seen as a way to offset this imbalance. Furthermore, while these subsidies may have the effect of encouraging some mothers to work outside the home who might not otherwise do so,[125] many are already employed and will remain employed in any case. In fact, as noted earlier, recent changes in welfare rules require that recipients take a job; child care subsidies are essential to enable them to do so.[126]

There is also some concern that subsidies, by reducing parents' costs of raising children, will encourage people to have more of them. However, as we have seen, providing subsidized day care will also encourage mothers to enter the labor market. To the extent that women acquire more—and more market-oriented—education in anticipation of this and accumulate more work experience as a consequence, they will have higher earnings. Hence, the opportunity cost of additional children will also increase. Further, it may be that women who work develop stronger preferences for market goods, and perhaps for having their own income, which gives them a greater feeling of independence. Therefore, it is not possible to determine a priori which set of forces is likely to be stronger.

Finally, a concern frequently voiced by opponents of publicly subsidized day care involves children's well-being. As discussed in Chapter 9, the evidence indicates that ad-

---

[123] For a discussion of the issues, see Leibowitz, "Child Care."

[124] While these are among the lowest-paid occupations, increased demand for their services would be expected to raise wages.

[125] See, for instance, Patricia M. Anderson and Philip B. Levine, "Child Care and Mothers' Employment Decisions," in *Finding Good Jobs: Work and Welfare Reform,* ed. David E. Card and Rebecca M. Blank (New York: Russell Sage Foundation, 2000), pp. 420–62; and Jean Kimmel, "Child Care Costs as a Barrier to Employment for Single and Married Mothers," *Review of Economics and Statistics* 80, no. 2 (May 1998): 287–99.

[126] Robert J. Lemke, Ann Dryden Witte, Magaly Queralt, and Robert Witt, "Child Care and the Welfare to Work Transition," National Bureau of Economic Research Working Paper No. 7583 (March 2000).

equate purchased care is not likely to be harmful to children, even during their first years of life. Nonetheless, the topic of public subsidies for day care remains highly charged and has generated much opposition.

Because of this opposition, it took several years of debate before the government expanded its role in child care and created two new block grants targeted at low-income and "at-risk" children in 1990. In the 1996 welfare legislation, these child care block grants, along with those created a couple of years earlier to provide child care for welfare recipients and those making the transition off welfare, were consolidated into the Child Care and Development Block Grant. The grant provides states with funds to expand day care services for low-income families as well as to improve the overall quality and supply of day care. For instance, states might provide grants to child care providers, who can then allow families to pay for child care on a sliding-scale basis, depending on their income. Alternatively states might give vouchers to low-income families, which would allow them to buy child care from an eligible provider or even from a friend or relative living outside of their home. Other federal support provided to lower-income children includes Head Start, the well-regarded preschool program, which is now available for children starting at age one.[127]

In addition to grants and direct expenditures, as of 2000, the federal government provides four types of tax subsidies for child care. Through the Dependent Care Tax Credit, employed parents receive a tax credit of 30 percent of expenses up to $2,400 for the care of one child, and $4,800 for the care of two or more children, provided their adjusted income is below $10,000. The credit falls to 20 percent of actual expenses for families with adjusted incomes above $28,000. However, this credit is nonrefundable, so low-income families who do not pay taxes do not benefit. The primary beneficiaries are thus members of the middle class.

Second is the Child Tax Credit introduced in 1998, which provides a $500 nonrefundable tax credit to families for each child under age 17. For married couples, this credit is phased out when their income reaches $110,000. This credit differs substantially from the Dependent Care Tax Credit in that families may receive it whether child care is purchased or not.[128]

Third is the Earned Income Tax Credit (EITC), discussed earlier, which does provide a refundable tax credit to low-income families. Like the child tax credit it need not be used for day care, although it will help many families purchase care. The maximum value for a family with two children was $3,888 in 2000.

The fourth tax subsidy, which was also discussed previously, consists of flexible spending accounts, which reduce tax liabilities for employees who have access to such accounts and use them.

Beyond the programs and tax subsidies provided by the government, a small but growing number of firms are offering child care benefits, either through employer-

---

[127] Other federal child care programs include the Child and Adult Care Food Program, which provides school lunches, and Title XX Social Service Block Grants. Estimates of the number of federal child care programs range between 20 and 40, depending on what is counted. See U.S. House of Representatives, *1998 Green Book*, Section 7.

[128] C. Eugene Steuerle points out that it may make sense to have both policies, since the child credit adjusts for differences in family size, while the child care credit adjusts for the costs of employment in "Systematic Thinking About Subsidies for Child Care, Part Three: Application of Principles" (Washington, DC: Urban Institute, February 1998). For another useful discussion, see Barbara R. Bergmann, "Subsidizing Child Care by Mothers at Home," *Feminist Economics* 6, no. 1 (March 2000): 77–88.

managed day care, on- or off-site, or by providing vouchers. In 1995–1996, overall 4 percent of employees working full-time for private establishments were eligible for these types of benefits, though this figure was as low as 2 percent for full-time employees in small establishments as compared to 8 percent for those in medium and large ones. Notably, such benefits were available to as many as 15 percent of professional and technical employees working full-time in medium and large establishments.[129] Other firms may offer referral services to assist workers in finding good day care.

On- and near-site day care has both advantages and drawbacks for employees, who must typically pay for at least part of the costs. On the one hand, parents do not have to make a separate trip to take children elsewhere, they are nearby in case of emergencies, and the children receive care during whatever hours the parent works.[130] On the other hand, children often have to be taken out of their own neighborhood, perhaps travel long distances, and must change caregivers when parents change jobs. Employers, for their part, have been slow to open centers because they are usually costly. Opening a center may require the construction of a new building or at least the redesign of currently available space to meet required safety standards, as well as obtaining licenses and costly insurance. In addition, smaller firms may not have enough employees with preschool-age children to warrant opening their own center, and there may not be other establishments in the neighborhood that would make combined centers a viable alternative.

In recent years, the use of purchased day care has boomed in part due to increases in the percentage of employed mothers with children and, no doubt, also as a result of the federal subsidies discussed earlier.[131] As Table 10.6 shows, the proportion of families with employed mothers using organized day care also rose, from 13 percent in 1977 to 30 percent in 1994. Still, the largest percentage of families, nearly 44 percent, continued to use child care by the child's father or other relatives, either in their own home or in a relative's home. An additional 21 percent used the services of a nonrelative, either in their own home or at the home of the day care provider. The remainder cared for their children at work. Often, parents find it necessary to use multiple arrangements, depending on their work schedules and available care.

The type of child care utilized differs depending on, among other factors, the financial situation of the family and the children's ages. Poor families are much less likely to use center care and more likely to have their children cared for by relatives.[132] Among those families that purchase day care, poor families pay less because of the type of care they use, whether it be provided at low cost by relatives or via subsidized programs targeted at the low-income population like Head Start. Nonetheless, because of their low incomes, poor families with employed mothers spend as much as 21 per-

[129] U.S. Bureau of Labor Statistics, "Employer-Sponsored Childcare Benefits," *Issues in Labor Statistics* (Washington, DC: U.S. Bureau of Labor Statistics, August 1998), Summary 98–9.

[130] Many such day care centers are at hospitals, where large numbers of women of childbearing age who have to work nonstandard hours are employed. There are also a very few innovative employers who are combining care for children and for the elderly, such as the Stride Rite Intergenerational Center. See Ferber, O'Farrell, and Allen, *Work and Family*.

[131] William Goodman, "Boom in Day Care Industry the Result of Many Social Changes," *Monthly Labor Review* 118, no. 8 (August 1995): 3–12.

[132] Jeffrey Capizzano, Gina Adams, and Freya Sonenstein, "Child Care Arrangements for Children Under Five: Variation Across States," Assessing the New Federalism, Series B, No. B-7 (Washington, DC: Urban Institute, March 2000).

TABLE 10.6   Child Care Arrangements Used by Employed Mothers in the United States for Children Under Five, Selected Years (Percent Distribution)

	1977	*1988*	*1994*
Care in child's home	33.9	28.2	33.0
By father	14.4	15.1	18.5
By other relative	12.6	7.9	9.4
By nonrelative	7.0	5.3	5.1
Care in another home	40.7	36.8	31.3
By relative	18.3	13.2	15.9
By nonrelative	22.4	23.6	15.4
Organized child care facilities	13.0	25.8	29.4
Mother cares for child at work	11.4	7.6	5.5
Other[a]	1.0	1.6	1.1

[a] Other includes school-based activity, child cares for self, and children in kindergarten/grade school.

Source: U.S. Census Bureau, Historical Time Series Tables, "Primary Child Care Arrangements Used for Preschoolers by Families with Employed Mothers: Selected Years, 1977 to 1994," www.census.gov.

cent of their income on day care on average, as compared with only 7 percent for non-poor families.[133]

Regarding the type of care, a much smaller percentage of infants are in organized group day care as compared with preschool children.[134] Parents of infants who can afford to do so may hire a nanny or find some other way to have their children cared for in their own home because the children generally receive more one-on-one attention and their exposure to infectious diseases is limited. For preschool-age children, group care has the advantage of contact with other children and teaches them to share and cooperate. For those who can afford to pay the price, adequate care is now generally available for this age group, but considerable problems remain not only for infants, but for preteen school-age children. It has been reported that as many as 9 percent of children ages 5 to 11 and just over 41 percent of children ages 12 to 14 were regularly left unsupervised.[135] While "self-care" can build self-esteem and independence in children in the latter age range, it is generally a poor and even a dangerous alternative for younger children. One solution, which is being adopted in many areas of the country and has received some federal support, is the creation of after-school programs. They allow students to engage in supervised recreational and educational activities, often right in their school building.[136]

Quality of care varies considerably across different kinds of settings—center-based care, family day care (in the home of a nonrelative), and relative care, as well as within

[133] U.S. Census Bureau, "Weekly Child Care Costs Paid by Families with Employed Mothers: Selected Years, 1985–1993," Historical Time Series Tables, www.census.gov; and U.S. Census Bureau, "What Does It Cost to Mind Our Preschoolers?" *Current Population Reports*, P70–52.

[134] Capizzano, Adams, and Sonenstein, "Child Care Arrangements for Children Under Five."

[135] U.S. Census Bureau, "Census Bureau Says 7 Million Grade-School Children Home Alone," Press Release CB00–181, 31 October 2000.

[136] John M. Broder, "Clinton Seeks $400 Million for After-School and Summer School Programs," *New York Times*, 7 January 1999, p. 28.

settings. Quality has typically been measured in terms of structural characteristics of the child care arrangement, and also in terms of children's experiences in that setting. Structural characteristics include level of teachers' education and training, group size, and the child–teacher ratio. The recommended ratios are 3 to 4 infants per adult, 5 to 7 two- to three-year olds per adult, and 8 to 10 four- to five-year olds per adult, though many states allow child care providers to greatly exceed these guidelines.[137] Measures of children's experiences in child care include the way caregivers relate to children, such as the child's exposure to language, and the continuity of care with the same caregiver. While there is some high-quality child care available, especially for those who can afford it, much of what is currently available tends to be of poor quality, suggesting that there is considerable room for improvement.[138]

In recent years, child care has become an especially high priority issue for families and society at large as a greater fraction of women are employed full-time, full-year, and as more low-income women have been moving from welfare to work. Among the concerns is that federal child care funds are insufficient to cover all eligible children; a recent government report indicates that only 10 percent of children eligible for federal child care assistance received it.[139] Further, until the supply of child care facilities increases sufficiently, a growing number of low-income mothers who are eligible for government-subsidized child care are competing for a limited number of spots.[140] Finally, as economic activity continues to shift to 24 hours per day, seven days per week, there is increasing need for child care that is available in the evenings, on weekends, and in the early morning. Solutions to this problem may well require a partnership of employers, workers, and community groups so that resources can be pooled to provide safe, affordable, quality care.[141]

CONCLUSION

This chapter began by examining the major changes we have seen in the last few years in the U.S. welfare system. At present, it remains difficult to provide a firm assessment of the success of these changes because the policy is still relatively new, and it was implemented at a time of unprecedented economic prosperity. There is clear evidence that welfare caseloads have fallen and the employment of single mothers has risen. There is also some indication that changes in welfare have led to increased earnings and reduced poverty for many, though not all families. It is still far too early to draw definitive conclusions, however, because it remains to be seen how families will fare under the new policy during an economic downturn.

While the effects of welfare changes remain to be sorted out, it is clear that the expansion of the Earned Income Tax Credit has been an important factor in reducing

---

[137] This figure is from the National Association of Education for Young Children (NAEYC), the largest organization of early childhood professionals, www.naeyc.org.

[138] Council of Economic Advisers, "The Economics of Child Care."

[139] Department of Health and Human Services, "Only 10 Percent of Eligible Families Get Child Care Help, New Report Shows," News Release, 19 October 1999.

[140] Peter Passell, "Day Care: Quality vs. Equality," *New York Times*, 25 December 1996, p. A1.

[141] U.S. Department of Labor, "Care Around the Clock: Developing Child Care Resources Before Nine and After Five," Women's Bureau Special Reports, 1995. For an example of the difficulties faced in providing such care, see Ellen Graham, "Marriott's Bid to Patch the Child-Care Gap Gets a Reality Check," *Wall Street Journal*, 2 February 2000, p. B1.

poverty. In addition, child support awards have increased for many single-parent families, particularly never-married mothers, as a direct result of recent changes in federal child support rules. Nevertheless, even these programs have limitations. For instance, the EITC reduces some women's incentive to seek employment and it may discourage some unmarried couples from marrying or encourage some married couples to get divorced. And, stepping up child support enforcement without sufficient recognition that many noncustodial parents have very low incomes themselves may further increase the distance, both geographic and emotional, between them and their children.

This chapter also identified some important ways in which both federal income taxes and Social Security affect the work and family decisions of individuals. Our review clearly shows that tax policies often favor families with full-time homemakers as compared to those with two earners, despite the fact that the latter are now the norm among married-couple families. We noted that it is critical for policy makers to consider the effects of policies on incentives for secondary earners to work for pay, especially when evaluating proposals to restructure Social Security or revamp the income tax system.

We have also seen that government and some employers have implemented new policies in recent years to help families meet the dual demands of paid work and family. These policies have become increasingly important as women have joined the paid labor force in record numbers in response to better opportunities in the labor market, as well as to help make ends meet, and in response to changes in welfare. At the same time, men have begun to take on more household responsibilities, including child care and elder care. Nevertheless, there are several points of concern. First, there continue to be large groups that are gaining little from the new programs. Part-time workers and workers in small establishments receive far fewer benefits than full-time workers in medium and large establishments. It is also likely that the growing fraction of non-standard workers, discussed in Chapter 8, have limited, if any, access to the types of family friendly benefits discussed here.

In addition, there continues to be a serious shortage of affordable quality child care, not just for infants, but for school-age children as well as poor children of all ages. These problems have increased, particularly as more low-income women leave welfare for work and as a greater fraction of businesses operate 24 hours per day, seven days per week. It is in the interest of firms that want a focused, committed work force now and in the future as well as society at large to find solutions to these problems. Before- and after-school programs, increased flextime, and additional child care subsidies would be useful steps in that direction.

A further issue of growing importance is that *family* is rather narrowly defined as it pertains to various policies. This problem must be addressed because living arrangements other than the traditional family of a husband, wife, and their own biological children residing in the same home are increasingly common. Often members of the same family live in different homes, as parents split up, remarry, or live with other partners, perhaps more than once. In such cases, the question arises as to whose policy covers a given child.[142] The growing number of unmarried couples also places increasing pressure on governments and employers to adjust their policies in this respect as well.

---

[142] Mitchell, "Work and Family Benefits."

QUESTIONS FOR REVIEW AND DISCUSSION

1. In what fundamental ways does TANF differ from the former AFDC program?

2. The Earned Income Tax Credit has received bipartisan support, while AFDC was far less widely accepted. What are the key differences in these programs that lead one to be popular and the other (now defunct and replaced by TANF) to have received so much less support?

3. Consider a married couple in which the wife has $45,000 in taxable earnings and the husband has $60,000 in taxable earnings. Assume there are no children and all income is from earnings. Using the information in Table 10.4:
   a. Compute their tax liability as a married couple.
   b. Compute their tax liability if they live together but are not married.
   c. Assuming they are married, compute their marriage bonus or penalty. Is this what you would have expected based on the discussion in the text? Explain.
   d. Answer the prior questions again, but this time assume that the husband has $110,000 in taxable earnings and the wife has no earnings. Does your finding differ? If so, explain why.
   e. Suppose the wife in d. is deciding whether or not to enter the labor force. What income tax rate affects this decision? Explain your answer.

4. In recent years, child support enforcement has been considerably stepped up. What are the pros and cons of this policy change?

5. When the Family and Medical Leave Act was passed in the United States in 1993, it was attacked as overly generous by some and as inadequate by others. Discuss the pros and cons of the FMLA.

6. Suppose you work for a "singles" lobby group. Point to the various policies that "work against singles." What sort of policies might be put together that would be more neutral with respect to family structure?

7. Discuss the pros and cons of taxing each spouse as an individual without regard to marital status.

8. Make the best case you can for:
   a. Parents being entirely responsible for the care of their children.
   b. Employer-financed day care.
   c. Government-financed day care.

9. Discuss the pros and cons of mandating that employers provide relatively long paid maternity leaves of, say, one year.

Suggested Readings

Beller, Andrea H., and John W. Graham. *Small Change: The Economics of Child Support.* New Haven, CT: Yale University Press, 1993.

Blank, Rebecca M. "Fighting Poverty: Lessons from Recent U.S. History." *Journal of Economic Perspectives* 14, no. 2 (spring 2000): 3–19.

———. *It Takes a Nation: A New Agenda for Fighting Poverty.* Princeton, NJ: Princeton University Press, 1996.

Blau, David M. *The Economics of Child Care.* New York: Russell Sage Foundation, 1991.

Blau, Francine D., and Ronald G. Ehrenberg, eds. *Gender and Family Issues in the Workplace.* New York: Russell Sage Foundation, 1997.

Card, David E., and Rebecca M. Blank, eds. *Finding Jobs: Work and Welfare Reform.* New York: Russell Sage Foundation, 2000.

Danziger, Sheldon H., ed. *Economic Conditions and Welfare Reform.* Kalamazoo, MI: W. E. Upjohn Institute for Employment Research, 1999.

Danziger, Sheldon H., Gary D. Sandefur, and Daniel H. Weinberg, eds. *Confronting Poverty: Prescriptions for Change.* New York: Russell Sage Foundation, 1994.

Edin, Kathryn, and Laura Lein. *Making Ends Meet: How Single Mothers Survive Welfare and Low-Wage Work.* New York: Russell Sage Foundation, 1997.

Garfinkel, Irwin, Sara McLanahan, Daniel Meyer, and Judith Seltzer, eds. *Fathers Under Fire: The Revolution in Child Support Enforcement.* New York: Russell Sage Foundation, 1998.

Hochschild, Arlie. *The Second Shift.* New York: Viking Press, 1989.

Hoffman, Saul D., and Laurence S. Seidman. *The Earned Income Tax Credit.* Kalamazoo, MI: W. E. UpJohn Institute for Employment Research, 1990.

Leibowitz, Arleen. "Child Care: Private Cost or Public Responsibility?" In *Individual and Social Responsibility: Child Care, Education, Medical Care, and Long-Term Care in America.* Edited by Victor R. Fuchs, pp. 33–57. Chicago: University of Chicago Press.

McCaffery, Edward J. *Taxing Women.* Chicago: University of Chicago Press, 1997.

Moffitt, Robert A. "The Incentive Effects of the U.S. Welfare System: A Review." *Journal of Economic Literature,* 30, no. 1 (March 1992): 1–61.

———, ed. *Welfare, the Family, and Reproductive Behavior: Research Perspectives.* Washington, DC: National Research Council, 1998.

CHAPTER 11

GENDER DIFFERENCES IN OTHER COUNTRIES

Chapter Highlights

- The Economic Status of the World's Women
- A Comparison of the United States to Other Economically Advanced Countries
- Developing Countries
- Countries of the Former Soviet Bloc

Up to this point we have focused almost entirely on the situation in the United States. Throughout, we emphasized the influence of economic factors in determining the status of women. This is not to suggest that nothing else matters, but rather that, everything being the same, economic considerations play an important role. Of course, in the real world, everything else is generally not the same. Societies differ in their political systems, economic and social policies, cultures, and religions. In this chapter, we turn to a consideration of women in other countries both to shed light on the causes of the substantial diversity in their status and to see what we can learn about institutions and policies elsewhere that have retarded or enhanced improvements in the position of women.

We begin with a broad description of the economic status of women as compared to men throughout the world, with special attention paid to women's labor market activity and the forces that influence it. Next, we turn to a more detailed consideration of the economically advanced countries that, in many ways, are most similar to the United States, focusing particularly on Sweden and Japan, the former because women have made great progress there and the latter because in that country women have made relatively little headway toward equality. Last, we briefly examine some of the issues of special concern in developing countries and in the countries of the former Soviet bloc, with their history of more than four decades of regimes that officially subscribed to Marxist ideology.

THE ECONOMIC STATUS OF THE WORLD'S WOMEN

There are a number of measures that, by general agreement, are regarded as useful indicators of women's economic status: women's labor force participation, the degree of occupational segregation by sex, the female–male earnings ratio, women's educational attainment, the fertility rate, the allocation of housework, and women's role in government as well as their standing before the law. These factors not only are themselves direct indicators of women's economic status but also are causally intertwined with one another.

LABOR FORCE PARTICIPATION

Labor force participation is arguably the most important indicator of women's economic status. While it is true that women perform a great deal of work in all economies, the total amount and the allocation between household and paid work differ substantially. Paid work is deemed to be particularly important because it provides women with status in their own right, allows for greater power and influence in decision making within the family, and raises the family's standard of living overall.[1] This is true not only in economically advanced countries but also in many developing countries, even though the burden of women's work in the household is particularly onerous there; water and fuel are often carried for long distances, clothes have to be washed in the river, food must be procured and prepared on a daily basis for lack of refrigeration, and many other goods and services that are generally purchased in economically advanced countries are produced at home.[2]

Table 11.1 provides figures on women's labor force participation and women's share of the labor force by broad regional grouping and for selected countries in these regions, while Table 11.2 provides information on labor force participation in a large number of economically advanced countries. The labor force participation rate is the more familiar concept to us since in previous chapters we have emphasized its trends and determinants in the United States. However, each measure has its advantages and disadvantages in international comparisons. Labor force participation is influenced not only by the age range of the population that is included, but also by the age distribution of the population, the typical school leaving and retirement ages, and the prevalence of market work itself versus family based activities, for example, which may not be counted. Using share of the labor force that is female largely mitigates these problems. However, it may be influenced by the sex ratio in the general population and also gives less direct information about the extent that women are involved in work outside the home. Note that in Table 11.1 we also present the ratio of women's to men's participation where available; this also addresses the problems of comparing the female participation rate across countries and is not affected by the sex ratio.

---

[1] Ester Boserup, *Women's Role in Economic Development* (New York: St. Martin's Press, 1970). For discussions on women's work in the world economy, see Susan P. Joekes, *Women in the World Economy, an INSTRAW Study* (New York: Oxford University Press, 1987); and Allen Tuovi, "Economic Development and the Feminization of Poverty," in *Women's Work in the World Economy,* ed. Nancy Folbre, Barbara Bergmann, Bina Agarwal, and Maria Floro (New York: New York University Press, 1992), pp. 107–19.

[2] Debra Ann Donahoe, "Measuring Women's Work in Developing Countries," *Population and Development Review* 25, no. 3 (September 1999): 543–76.

TABLE 11.1 Indicators of Women's Economic Status, by World Regions and Selected Countries[a]

	GNP per Capita 1998	Female Labor Force Participation Rate (15+) Late 1990s	Ratio of Female-to-Male Labor Force Participation Late 1990s
Low-income economies	$520	n.a.	n.a.
Excluding China and India	370	n.a.	n.a.
Middle-income economies	2,990	n.a.	n.a.
Low- and middle-income economies	1,250	n.a.	n.a.
Sub-Saharan Africa	510	62.0	72.1
Côte d'Ivoire	700	42.0[d]	47.4[d]
Ethiopia	100	66.5[d]	74.2[d]
South Africa	3,310	n.a.	n.a.
East Asia and Pacific	990	60.0	75.0
China	750	73.0[d]	85.9[d]
Korea	8,600	47.0	62.5
Thailand	2,160	65.8	80.7
South Asia	430	45.0[b]	53.6[b]
India	440	33.7[d]	41.9[d]
Pakistan	470	15.0	18.1
Europe and Central Asia	2,200	59.0	78.7
Russia	2,260	54.2	77.7
Middle East and North Africa	2,030	29.0	37.7
Egypt	1,290	23.0[d]	31.1[d]
Saudi Arabia	6,910	n.a.	n.a.
Latin America and Caribbean	3,860	45.0[c]	57.7[c]
Mexico	3,840	39.4	46.6
High-income economies	25,480	n.a.	n.a.
Japan	32,350	50.1	64.8
Sweden	25,580	n.a.	n.a.
United States	29,240	59.8	79.8

[a] All figures are from *World Development*, except columns 2 and 3; country data are from ILO and regional figures are from UN, *The World's Women 2000*. Regional definitions used by United Nations do not perfectly match definitions used by World Bank.

[b] Figure is for Southern Asia. For Southeastern Asia, women's participation rate is 62 and ratio to men's is 73.8.

[c] Figure excludes Caribbean. For Caribbean, women's participation rate is 53 and ratio to men's is 70.7.

[d] Côte d'Ivoire figure is for late 1980s. Remainder are for early to mid-1990s.

[e] Illiteracy is less than 5 percent.

The data in Tables 11.1 and 11.2 indicate that there is considerable variation in both measures, across regions and by selected country. Table 11.1 shows that among developing countries, women's labor force participation rates ranged from around 60 percent in Sub-Saharan Africa and East Asia to 29 percent in the Middle East and North Africa. Similarly the data for the economically advanced countries in Table 11.2 show considerable variation across countries, ranging from 44 percent in Italy, to just over 70 percent in the United States, and 75 percent in Denmark and Sweden. (Note that Tables 11.1 and 11.2 are based on different age ranges—15 and over and 15 to 64, respectively—so that levels of participation are not fully comparable across tables.) Table 11.2 also in-

Female Share of Labor Force (%) 1998	Adult Illiteracy Rate (%)				Total Fertility Rate [f]	
	Female		Male			
	1980	1998	1980	1998	1970	1998
40.6	60	41	35	22	6.0	3.1
41.2	65	46	43	29	6.3	4.3
38.6	22	15	15	10	4.6	2.5
40.1	48	33	29	18	5.6	2.9
42.2	72	49	51	32	6.5	5.4
33.1	87	64	66	47	7.4	5.0
40.9	89	70	72	58	5.8	6.4
37.6	25	16	22	15	5.7	2.8
44.5	43	22	20	9	5.7	2.1
45.2	48	25	22	9	5.8	1.9
41.0	11	4	3	1	4.3	1.6
46.3	17	7	8	3	5.5	1.9
33.1	75	59	48	35	6.0	3.4
32.1	74	57	45	33	5.8	3.2
27.7	86	71	59	42	7.0	4.9
46.1	8	5	3	2	2.5	1.6
48.9	2	1	1	0	2.0	1.2
26.9	72	48	44	26	6.8	3.5
29.7	75	58	47	35	5.9	3.2
14.8	67	36	33	17	7.3	5.7
34.4	23	13	18	11	5.2	2.7
32.6	22	11	14	7	6.5	2.8
42.9	e	e	e	e	2.4	1.7
41.2	e	e	e	e	2.1	1.4
47.9	e	e	e	e	1.9	1.5
45.7	e	e	e	e	2.5	2.1

[f]The total fertility rate is defined as the number of births that a cohort of 1,000 women would have if they experienced the age-specific birthrates occurring in the current year, throughout their childbearing years (see Table 9.2). Here it is divided by 1,000 to measure births per woman.

n.a. Not available.

For definitions of regions see *World Development Indicators 2000*.

Source: World Bank, *World Development Indicators 2000*; International Labour Organization, *Yearbook of Labour Statistics* (1997, 1998, 1999); and United Nations, *The World's Women 2000*.

cludes Russia for comparison purposes. While Russia has historically had very high female participation rates, well in excess of those in economically advanced countries, the current rate shown in Table 11.2 is estimated to be only 66.3 percent, down from 75.6 percent in the 1970s. While it is widely believed that the rates in this and other countries of the former Soviet bloc have fallen since the transition, survey methods may have changed, raising some question as to the reliability of the current figure as well as making it difficult to draw meaningful inferences about recent trends.[3]

---

[3] UNICEF, "Women in Transition," Regional Monitoring Reports No. 6 (Florence, Italy: UNICEF International Child Development Centre, 1999), chap. 2.

TABLE 11.2 **Labor Force Participation Rates for Selected Economically Advanced Countries, 1977 and 1997 (ages 15–64)**

	Women		Men	
	1977	*1997*	*1977*	*1997*
Australia	51.1	64.7	88.9	84.7
Austria	47.8	61.9	81.4	80.8
Belgium	44.5	56.5	80.4	71.8
Canada	52.6	67.8	85.4	82.0
Denmark	64.7	75.1	90.9	85.7
Finland	68.2	71.3	82.5	78.1
France	53.0	59.8	83.8	74.4
Germany	51.2	61.8	85.6	80.0
Greece	33.3	47.5	79.6	74.6
Ireland	34.1	50.4	89.4	77.8
Italy	37.6	44.1	83.5	75.4
Japan	53.0	63.7	89.2	92.1
Luxembourg	39.3	60.9	89.2	101.5[b]
Netherlands	31.9	62.2	80.6	82.8
New Zealand	42.8	64.9	87.8	82.5
Norway	58.5	75.8	89.4	85.9
Portugal	n.a.	65.1	n.a.	82.2
Russia[a]	75.6	66.3	84.1	77.7
Spain	33.0	47.1	85.8	74.6
Sweden	70.0	74.5	88.1	79.1
Switzerland	51.7	69.4	95.5	96.7
United Kingdom	56.3	67.5	91.6	84.2
United States	55.1	71.3	85.4	85.7

n. a. Not available.

[a] Russia is included for comparison purposes (ages 15–59 only for both years). Figure for earlier period is for Soviet Union, 1970; figure for later period is for Russia for 1996.

[b] Rate can exceed 100 percent because labor force includes foreign seasonal workers but population does not.

Sources: OECD, *Labour Force Statistics*, 1977–1997 (all figures but Russia/Soviet Union); ILO, *Economically Active Population*, Vol. IV (Geneva: ILO, 1986); and ILO, *Yearbook of Labour Statistics, 1997*.

In addition we can see from Table 11.1 that women's labor force participation rates and share of the labor force are strongly and positively related; in countries in which women's participation rates were 50 percent or higher, women typically comprised 40 percent or more of the labor force, while in the area with the lowest participation rates, the Middle East and North Africa, women comprised less than 30 percent of the total labor force.

Part of the explanation for differences in labor force activity by gender is that countries and, more generally, regions, are in various stages of economic development, ranging from agricultural to industrial and postindustrial. As discussed in Chapter 2, one hypothesis that receives some support from the evidence is that the relationship between economic development and women's labor force participation rates tends to be U-shaped. That is, female labor force participation is high in the stage of subsistence agriculture, when women tend to be heavily involved as family workers, but then declines during the early stages of economic development as the nature of agricultural work changes and the locus of much production moves out of the household and into factories and offices. One argument for much lower labor force participation at this stage, which is effectively the "bottom" of the U, is that there are often societal norms that work against women performing manual, factory-type work. Then, as countries become more developed and women's education and opportunities in white-collar employment rise, their labor force participation once again increases.[4] Consistent with this, we see in Table 11.1 relatively high rates of participation in countries that have only recently moved from the horticultural to the agricultural stage, such as those in Sub-Saharan Africa, but lower rates at the next stage of development, as is true for the countries of Latin America (excluding the Caribbean countries), most of them largely agricultural, but also experiencing the early stages of urbanization. Higher rates are found once again in more economically advanced countries.

Apart from stage of development, women's labor market activity is also determined by demand and supply factors that vary from place to place, as well as over time. The demand for women workers is influenced by such factors as the industrial mix of the economy, which helps to determine the nature of the jobs available in the labor market, and the preferences of employers for male versus female workers. Factors that influence the supply of female labor include the relative value of market earnings as compared to time spent in household production, which is itself strongly influenced by fertility rates, the availability of goods and services for purchase, perceptions of what type of work is appropriate for each sex, general attitudes toward the appropriate roles for women and men, and tastes for market goods as compared to commodities mainly produced at home.

Social forces such as religion, ideology, and culture also influence women's status, especially through their effect on women's labor market activity. For instance, women's labor force participation is considerably lower in countries dominated by religious faiths that particularly emphasize women's traditional roles as wives and mothers, such as in Latin America with its predominantly Catholic population and in the Middle East, which is largely Moslem. Marxist ideology, which strongly advocates women's entry into the work force, surely helps to explain why women's participation came to be extremely high in many of the former Soviet bloc countries. Similarly, concern for gender equality in the Scandinavian countries was one of the reasons for the introduction of policies that encouraged female labor force participation such as tax schedules favorable to two-earner couples, family leave, and subsidized day care. Apart from their direct effect, these policies may in turn have influenced attitudes about women's role in the economy. Women's economic role may also be related to other aspects of society, such as the practice of polygamy. While polygamy is rare elsewhere, it is practiced in at least 26 Sub-Saharan African countries, and in seven of these countries, more than 40 percent of women have husbands with one or more other wives.[5] It has been argued that one reason men take on several wives in these countries is because these wives perform an important economic function in traditional agricultural production, beyond the usual

---

[4] For a discussion and evidence, see Claudia Goldin, "The U-Shaped Female Labor Force Function in Economic Development and Economic History," in *Investment in Women's Human Capital,* ed. T. Paul Schultz (Chicago: University of Chicago Press, 1995), pp. 61–90; Kristin Mammen and Christina Paxson, "Women's Work and Economic Development," *Journal of Economic Perspectives* 14, no. 4 (fall 2000): 141–64; and Louise A. Tilly and Joan W. Scott, *Women, Work and Family,* 2nd ed. (New York: Routledge, 1987).

[5] United Nations, *The World's Women 2000: Trends and Statistics* (New York: United Nations, 2000). Polygamy is legal in some Moslem countries as well but is now rarely practiced.

household responsibilities.[6] This would suggest that as economic development proceeds and modern methods of production are introduced, polygamy should decline. It is also likely that polygamy is related to the sex ratio in the population, as well as to women's own education and labor market opportunities.[7]

OCCUPATIONS

In considering women's economic status, it is interesting to go beyond examining to what extent women participate in the labor market, and also consider what jobs they have. When making comparisons with other countries, there are two serious problems. First, many do not provide detailed data on the occupational distribution of men and women, and those that do tend to use various classification schemes. Second, the degree of segregation is affected by the distribution of all workers across the occupational structure. Thus, if, at the extreme, the majority of people in the labor force in one country were employed in a single occupation like agriculture, while in another they are distributed among a considerably larger number of occupations, the indexes of segregation would surely differ. One recent study largely overcame the first of these limitations and examined occupational sex segregation for over 40 countries from around the world using data on 75 consistent occupations. Table 11.3 shows the index of occupational segregation for each of these countries, which, as discussed in Chapter 5, is defined as the percentage of women (or men) that would have to change jobs in order for the occupational distribution of men and women to be the same. These figures indicate that occupational segregation by sex remains "very extensive in each and every country,"[8] but the extent of segregation varies, particularly across regions. For instance, the index tends to be substantially higher in countries in the Middle East and North Africa, and in "Other Developing Countries," as compared with elsewhere.

It appears that across all cultures and at all times, occupations have been sex segregated to a greater or lesser extent. One study, which looked at more than 200 cultures over time, found that metal working and hunting were, with few exceptions, exclusively male activities, while activities such as cooking, laundering, and spinning have been predominately female. However, with the exception of certain occupations such as these, the more general pattern is that while occupations tend to be sex segregated, they vary as to whether they are dominated by men or women.[9] For instance, while a sizable frac-

---

[6] For instance, see Hanan G. Jacoby, "The Economics of Polygyny in Sub-Saharan Africa: Female Productivity and the Demand for Wives in Cote d'Ivoire," *Journal of Political Economy* 103, no. 5 (October 1995): 938–71.

[7] Shoshana Grossbard-Shectman, *On the Economics of Marriage* (Boulder, CO: Westview Press, 1993), chap. 11.

[8] The study cited is Richard Anker, *Gender and Jobs: Sex Segregation of Occupations in the World* (Geneva: International Labour Office, 1998). The quote is from p. 407. See, especially, chap. 9 (main evidence) and chap. 16 (summary and conclusion).

[9] This conclusion is from Joyce P. Jacobsen, "Sex Segregation at Work: Trends and Predictions," *Social Science Journal* 31, no. 2 (1994): 153–69, based on data from George P. Murdock and Caterina Provost, "Factors in the Division of Labor by Sex: A Cross-Cultural Analysis," in *Ethnology* 12, no. 2 (April 1973): 203–25. See also William Rau and Robert Wazienski, "Industrialization, Female Labor Force Participation, and the Modern Division of Labor by Sex," *Industrial Relations* 38, no. 4 (October 1999): 504–21; and Anker, *Gender and Jobs,* chap. 16.

TABLE 11.3 Occupational Segregation by Sex, Selected Countries, 1980s/1990s[a]

Region/Country/Area	Occupational Segregation Index	Region/Country/Area	Occupational Segregation Index
Economically Advanced		**Other Developing**	
Australia	58.1	Angola	65.6
Canada	54.1	Costa Rica	59.8
Finland	61.6	Ghana	71.0
France	55.6	Haiti	66.9
Germany (West)	52.3	Senegal	57.3
Italy	44.9		
Netherlands	56.7	**Transition Economies**	
New Zealand	58.2	Bulgaria	54.1
Norway	57.3	Hungary	55.8
Spain	56.9	Poland	59.2
Sweden	63.0	Former Yugoslavia	54.0
Switzerland	58.1		
United Kingdom	56.7		
United States	46.3		
		Middle East	
Asia/Pacific		**and North Africa**	
China	36.3	Bahrain	62.7
Hong Kong	49.3	Egypt	58.7
India	44.6	Iran	68.1
Japan	50.2	Jordan	77.6
Korea	43.2	Kuwait	73.3
Malaysia	48.9	Tunisia	69.5

[a] Index is computed using 75 similar occupations. Years of data vary, but the majority are from 1985 to 1991.

Source: Richard Anker, *Gender and Jobs: Sex Segregation of Occupations in the World*, 1998, Table 9.1, column 3. Copyright © International Labour Organization 1998. Reprinted by Permission of the International Labour Organization.

tion of women in the United States is in the clerical sector, we shall see that this is not the case in Japan, nor is it the case in many other countries. This suggests that occupational differences cannot be explained simply by inherent differences between women and men or by differences in their human capital investment decisions alone. Factors such as social norms, traditions, and religious beliefs also appear to play an important part in the varied patterns of the distribution of men and women by occupation. Despite this variation, one common feature of women's employment is that it tends to be in lower-paying jobs.

There is also evidence that occupational segregation has declined in recent decades, albeit not in all countries or all regions. For instance, China actually experienced an increase in occupational segregation by sex from the early 1980s to 1990, and in Japan, there was virtually no change.[10]

---

[10] Anker, *Gender and Jobs*, chap. 13.

EARNINGS

The available evidence indicates that women everywhere earn less than men, although there are large variations in the extent to which this is the case. For instance, in 1998, the female–male earnings ratio in economically advanced countries ranged from a low of .64 in Japan to a high of .90 in Sweden.[11] We cannot be as specific about developing countries because of problems with data availability and reliability, but there appears to be considerable variability among these countries as well. A number of factors explain the observed variation, including differences among countries in the extent of occupational segregation, gender differences in educational attainment and labor force attachment, labor market discrimination, and government policies. In addition, general rewards for skills, such as education or labor market experience, or for employment in male-dominated occupations and industries are also a factor.

EDUCATIONAL ATTAINMENT

Women's educational attainment is also important as an indicator of women's economic status, in that it influences women's occupations and earnings, which, as we have seen, are themselves indicators of women's status. Also, it allows women to make better-informed decisions about affairs in their own household, their community, and their nation. Gender differences in educational attainment are fairly small among economically advanced countries, but vary considerably across all countries, as a result of, and related to, differences in levels of affluence, as well as differences in fertility, social customs, and government policy.

   One recent study estimated years of schooling for the average woman and man (age 15 and over) in various world regions for the years 1960 to 2000.[12] For 2000, they found that these two figures were close to parity for economically advanced countries and those of the former Soviet bloc. The average woman in South Asia, Sub-Saharan Africa, and the Middle East and North Africa, however, had only 60 to 76 percent as much schooling as the average man in the same region, though even these figures are considerably higher than they were in 1960. As might be expected, they also found that both women and men in these regions had the lowest average levels of schooling.

   Illiteracy rates provide another useful measure of educational attainment. As shown in Table 11.1 and Figure 11.1, female illiteracy rates in 1998 were still nearly 60 percent in South Asia, and close to 50 percent in Sub-Saharan Africa as well as in the Middle East and North Africa. The rates were considerably lower for men in each region. For example, in South Asia the male illiteracy rate was 35 percent, and in Sub-Saharan Africa and in the Middle East and North Africa, the male rates were 32 and 26 percent, respectively.

   An important factor that contributes to low levels of educational attainment for both men and women in the poorest countries is that large numbers of children do not even attend school because many of them, especially girls, are helping out at home, while others are employed (see the section on child labor). Hence, there is little reason to expect much progress in this respect unless parents are able to earn enough to support their families without assistance from their children.

---

[11] Data are presented later in Table 11.4.

[12] Robert J. Barro and Jong-Wha Lee, "International Data on Educational Attainment: Updates and Implications," National Bureau of Economic Research Working Paper No. 7911 (September 2000).

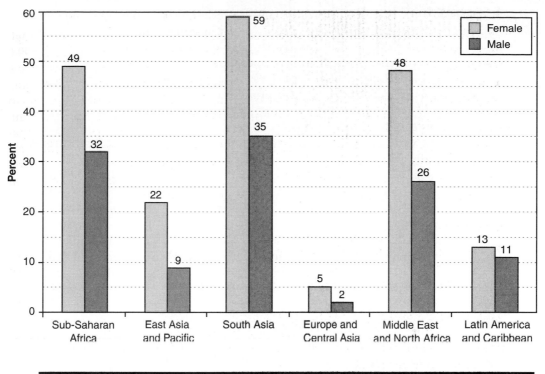

FIGURE 11.1   Illiteracy Rates, World Regions, 1998

While illiteracy rates for both women and men remain high in some regions, Table 11.1 also shows that they have declined quite a bit since 1980. The relatively high rates of female illiteracy that persist reflect, in part, the lower average levels of schooling in these regions as well as disparities in the treatment of girls and boys. They are, however, very likely to decrease further in the coming years because enrollment of girls in primary and secondary schools has increased substantially over the last couple of decades in many of the countries in these regions. Hence, while there will continue to be a sizable gender difference in average levels of schooling and illiteracy rates for the foreseeable future, the situation is expected to gradually improve.

FERTILITY

There is also a strong relationship between fertility, educational attainment, and labor market activity. Fertility rates are an important indicator of women's economic status because with fewer children, women have greater opportunities to engage in production for pay. Conversely, if birthrates are high, women have more incentive to remain full-time homemakers. As noted in earlier chapters, however, causation runs in the other direction as well. As women invest more in education and increase their participation in market work, particularly when it is away from the household, the opportunity cost of bearing children rises, thereby providing an incentive to reduce the number of children. In addition, fertility is at times related to explicit government policy, as well as religion and ideology. For instance, in recent history, some governments have implemented pro-natalist policies or policies that have pro-natalist effects, such as relatively generous child allowances, paid parental leaves, and subsidized day care. Some have also introduced laws prohibiting various types of family planning, often justifying them on the grounds of religious strictures. Other countries, however, have sought to control population growth; many have done so by making birth control information available, but China, for example, has gone so far as to impose severe economic penalties for having more than one child.

Given the various factors mentioned here, it is not surprising that fertility rates differ dramatically across regions. As shown in Table 11.1 and Figure 11.2, in 1998, fertility rates were as high as 5.4 births per woman in Sub-Saharan Africa, followed by the Middle East and North Africa and South Asia, with rates of around 3.5 births per woman. In sharp contrast, the U.S. rate was 2.1, just at replacement level, and the average rate among all high-income economies was 1.7. Figure 11.2, indicates, however, that even in regions where rates remain very high, they have fallen somewhat,[13] with quite substantial declines in a number of instances, including South and East Asia, as well as the Middle East and North Africa. Sub-Saharan Africa remains the one developing region where fertility declines have thus far been modest.

HOUSEWORK

As was discussed at some length in earlier chapters, the roles of women and men in the labor market are interrelated with their roles in the household. Nonetheless, we found that in the United States, although women's participation in the labor market has been increasing rapidly for some time, participation of men in housework began to increase only more recently and that the continued unequal division of household responsibilities potentially influences both the amount of leisure time men and women have and their achievements on the job. This unequal division of housework is also true across the other economically advanced countries and countries of the former Soviet bloc. The amount of time men spend on housework as compared to women ranges from 11.3 percent in Japan to 56.9 percent in Sweden, while the figure for the United States is 45.2 percent. These patterns are discussed in greater detail later. It is also important to recall that women in developing countries, especially in poor rural areas, often do an especially large amount of unpaid work needed for their families' subsistence, including carrying water and wood and growing agricultural products, in addition to the usual housework.

WOMEN'S ROLE IN GOVERNMENT AND THEIR STANDING BEFORE THE LAW

Finally, women's roles in government and their standing before the law also serve as important indicators of their status. Greater representation of women among public officials is widely thought to increase the extent to which women's issues receive attention from the government, and greater equality before the law affects, among other things, women's right to inherit and own property, as well as their rights within the family and

---

[13] In Ethiopia, while the fertility rate of 6.8 in 1998 exceeds the 1970 rate of 5.8, the rate has fallen since 1992, when it stood at 7.5 births per woman.

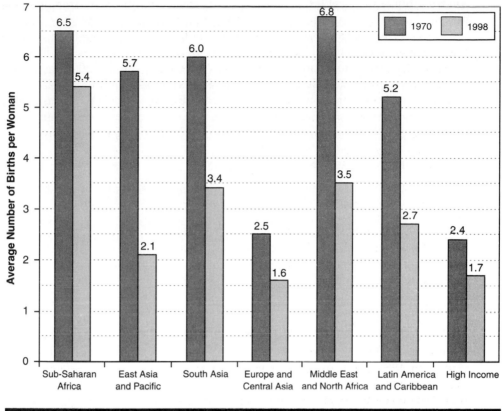

FIGURE 11.2 ₀Total Fertility Rates, World Regions, 1970 and 1998

in case of divorce. Although women today have the right to vote in virtually all countries that have representative institutions, they continue to be substantially underrepresented in public positions. For instance, as of 2000, only 17 women had ever been elected heads of state[14] and only 25 women had served as prime minister. There are, however, once again, considerable differences between countries and regions. Of the six female heads of state who were in office in 2000, four were in Europe and none were in North America. Also, women occupied one-third or more of all parliamentary seats in the Scandinavian countries and 13 percent in East Asia, but 5 percent or less in South Asia and in the Arab countries.[15] The distribution of ministerial positions followed a similar pattern. Women remain underrepresented in U.S. government as well. In 2000, only 13 percent of representatives and 9 percent of senators in Congress were women. Furthermore, then-President Clinton's cabinets included just a handful of women, though a much higher percentage than in the past. More encouraging is the fact that in the majority of countries that provide such information, women's representation has increased

---

[14] This figure excludes the tiny Republic of San Marino, where a number of women have served as head of state.

[15] United Nations, *The World's Women 2000,* chap. 6.

considerably at the local level. To the extent that such positions are stepping-stones to higher offices, this portends well for the future.

Similarly, women's progress toward equality before the law has been slow and uneven. In some countries it is still the case that only men can inherit and in some, husbands have the right to dispose of their wives' earnings.[16] Also, in 2000, there were still as many as 26 countries, including the United States and 17 countries in Asia and the Pacific, that had not ratified the Convention for the Elimination of All Forms of Discrimination Against Women (CEDAW). Further, "even when legal discrimination is removed, it can take generations for practice to catch up with the revised law."[17]

INTERPRETATIONS AND IMPLICATIONS

The evidence presented here and later in this chapter shows that there is substantial variation in the status of women among different regions and even across countries within the same region, as measured by any of the indicators discussed, whether it be labor force participation, female–male earnings ratios, educational attainment, distribution of housework, or their role in government. This suggests that while economic factors influence the status of women as compared to men, the situation is very complex, and that noneconomic influences play an important role as well. The picture is further complicated by the fact that women may be doing well in a country in terms of some criteria but not in terms of others.[18]

Women's economic status as it pertains to their position within the family and the economy is important not only for women themselves, but for their children as well. There is mounting evidence from both developed and developing countries that women who have their own income tend to allocate it differently than men. Most notably, they spend a larger share of it on their children, suggesting that both young boys and girls fare better in this respect when their mothers work for pay. In many developing countries, it has also been found that mothers tend to allocate their resources more heavily toward daughters than fathers would.[19] Such a reallocation promotes gender equality between boys and girls because fathers, who typically have control over most, if not all, of the family resources, tend to favor sons. One implication is that as greater numbers

---

[16] Ester Boserup, "Obstacles to Advancement of Women During Development," in *Investments in Women's Human Capital,* ed. T. Paul Schultz (Chicago: University of Chicago Press, 1995), pp. 51–60; and United Nations, *Human Development Report 1995.*

[17] United Nations, *Human Development Report 1995,* pp. 42–43. In addition, as Diane Elson points out, legal equality often means little for poor rural women as long as they are concentrated in the informal sector, or in female ghettoes of the formal sector, and intrahousehold distribution is not necessarily affected by these changes. See her "Introduction" in *Male Bias in the Development Process,* ed. Diane Elson (Manchester: Manchester University Press, 1991), pp. 1–28.

[18] A similar conclusion that the relation of economic development and women's status is at least to a degree erratic and not readily explainable was reached by Shirley Nuss and Larraine Majka, "The Economic Integration of Women: A Cross National Investigation," *Work and Occupations* 10, no. 1 (February 1983): 29–48.

[19] For evidence on developing countries, see Duncan Thomas, "Intra-Household Resource Allocation: An Inferential Approach," *Journal of Human Resources* 25, no. 4 (fall 1990): 635–64; Duncan Thomas, "Like Father, Like Son: Like Mother, Like Daughter: Parental Resources and Child Height," *Journal of Human Resources* 29, no. 4 (fall 1994): 950–88; and Bina Agarwal, " 'Bargaining' and Gender Relations: Within and Beyond the Household," *Feminist Economics* 3, no. 1 (March 1997): 1–51. For evidence from the United Kingdom, see Shelly J. Lundberg, Robert A. Pollak, and Terence J. Wales, "Do Husbands and Wives Pool Their Resources?: Evidence From the U.K. Child Benefit," *Journal of Human Resources* 32, no. 3 (summer 1997): 463–80.

of women work for pay, this should reduce the difference in the allocation of resources to girls and boys in countries where boys have traditionally been favored.[20]

As it stands, the current allocation of resources has resulted in serious neglect of girls in some cases. This has been found to affect girls' survival probabilities and, hence, the sex ratio—the ratio of men to women—in many developing countries, including China and India. Indeed, some evidence indicates that there is an inverse relationship between women's economic activity in a region and the sex ratio, suggesting that girls are more highly valued and better treated when women are working for pay, perhaps in part because women are better able to channel at least some resources to girls when they have their own income. For example, in Sub-Saharan Africa the ratio of women's economic activity to men's is high and the ratio of men to women in the population is low while in southern Asia (including India), just the opposite is observed.[21] China, however, does not appear to fit this pattern since it has a high female activity ratio *and* a high sex ratio. This suggests that cultural and historical influences likely play an important role in determining the sex ratio as well.

Taken together, the evidence points toward the conclusion that advances in women's economic status, as measured by higher rates of labor force participation, better jobs, and greater educational attainment, should have the long-term effect of providing a better start for children of both sexes and quite possibly enhancing girls' status relative to boys', thereby also lessening, at least to some degree, the gender disadvantage that girls and women currently face.

In recent decades, women from around the world, in spite of their wide cultural differences, have joined in efforts to improve women's status. A prime example of this is that, in 1995, women from nearly 190 nations attended the United Nations Fourth World Conference on Women in Beijing and put together a "Plan For Action" that focused on education as a key to women's progress, in addition to addressing a wide range of other issues, from violence against women to economic development. There is evidence that this platform, though not legally binding, has resulted in improvements in women's status in some countries. For instance, a growing number of African countries have since passed laws to limit or ban altogether the practice of ritual genital mutilation of girls, though it has by no means been eliminated (see inset), and a large number of governments have drawn up plans to increase women's rights.[22]

At the same time, as we have seen, women's status continues to remain low in many countries, and in addition, women face some new and growing difficulties. In Jordan, Pakistan, and India, women have continued to be victims of "honor killings," in retaliation for being suspected of having had an extramarital affair or having had premarital sex. Though illegal, girls continue to be forced into child marriages in India. In addition,

---

[20] It may also be the case that girls are more highly valued when women are more economically active, in part because they are viewed as potential providers of financial assistance to parents in old age. In addition, they may be seen as a source of a "bride-price," rather than as a financial drain on the family, that is, as requiring a dowry in order to get married.

[21] Jean Dreze and Amartya Sen, *Hunger and Public Action* (Oxford: Clarendon Press, 1989), chap. 4. See also Mammen and Paxson, "Women's Work and Economic Development"; and Marianne A. Ferber and Helen M. Berg, "Labor Force Participation of Women and the Sex Ratio: A Cross-Country Analysis," *Review of Social Economy* 48, no. 1 (spring 1991): 2–19.

[22] See "A World of Rights for Women," *Boston Globe,* 7 June 2000, p. A18; and Barbara Crossette, "Women See Key Gains Since Talks in Beijing," *New York Times,* 8 March 1998.

in civil wars in Bosnia and more recently in Sierra Leone, women have been systematically raped as a part of "warfare."[23]

Perhaps the most serious threat to the populations of many developing countries, men and women alike, is the HIV/AIDS epidemic. This is especially true in the countries of Sub-Saharan Africa, which have among the highest rates of infection in the world; in Botswana, for example, it is estimated that one-third of the adult population has the HIV infection. Moreover, while HIV infection rates are fairly similar for adult women and men in Africa, they are more than five times as high among teenage girls as for teenage boys.[24]

At a follow-up conference at the United Nations called "Beijing Plus Five," held in 2000, women representatives from around the world came together again to take stock of the progress that had been made since 1995, to press for additional rights, and to reaffirm each government's commitment to change. Apart from preserving the rights originally decided upon in 1995, after some heated debate, the final document went beyond earlier ones and declared that women have the right to decide freely all matters related to their sexuality and childbearing.[25] The document also added strong wording against "honor killings," trafficking in girls, genital mutilation, and other forms of violence against girls and women. These declarations should place increased pressure on countries to outlaw these types of violence and should serve to improve women's position.

The Taliban: Women Under a Fundamentalist Regime

While there has been progress in the status of women in most countries of the world, albeit often slow and uncertain, there have been some important exceptions. Recently, the most notable among these has been Afghanistan under the Taliban government.* Its repressive policies stand out even among the male-dominated societies of its neighbors in what has been termed "the patriarchal belt." As has been the case in some other instances, this rigid regime took over in reaction to a government that, under the influence of a foreign power (in this case the USSR after the 1978 revolution), sought to extend women's rights along with other secular reforms. To understand the situation in that country, it is necessary to have some grasp of its history.

Traditionally, the basic social unit has been the extended patriarchal family. Men owned all property, including women, who were viewed as part of the resources to be exchanged within "the community," which consisted only of men. Men acquired their wives in return for goods given by the groom's family to the family of the bride. Men controlled women

*This inset draws heavily on Valentine M. Moghadam, "Revolution, Religion, and Gender Politics: Iran and Afghanistan Compared," *Journal of Women's History* 10, no. 4 (winter 1999): 172–95; in addition to Elizabeth Drevillon, "Kabul: Women in the Shadows," *Unesco Courier* 51, no. 10 (October 1998): 3–8; and Bob Herbert, "Half a Nation, Condemned," *New York Times,* 8 October 1998, www.nytimes.com.

---

23 Minh T. Vo, "World's Women Get A Bit Safer," *Christian Science Monitor,* 8 June 2000, p. 1; John F. Burns, "Child Marriages, Though Illegal, Persist in India," *New York Times,* 11 May 1998; and Colum Lynch, "Sierra Leone Seeks Aid on Tribunal; U.N. Weighs Requests on War Crime Trials," *Washington Post,* 16 June 2000, p. A24.

24 Lawrence K. Altman," "U.N. Warning AIDS Imperils Africa's Youth," *New York Times,* 28 June 2000, p. A1; and United Nations, *The World's Women 2000,* chap. 3.

25 Barbara Crossette, "Rights Gains are Preserved at U.N. Forum on Women," *New York Times,* 11 June 2000, p. A4.

and enforced an unyielding code of behavior, including "modest dress" and strict segrega-tion. Any deviation from this was severely punished because it was viewed as bringing dis-honor not only on a woman's husband, but also on all his kin. Because there was also a hi-erarchy based on age among both men and women, the oldest man in the family had authority over everyone, and older women could coerce younger women to conform.

After the April 1978 revolution, the Democratic Republic of Afghanistan introduced radical reforms in the old system. One of the first steps was to introduce compulsory school-ing for girls as well as boys. Women's employment in many sectors of the economy began to increase. Also, the government outlawed the practice of financial compensation to the bride's parents at the time of her marriage by payment of what is termed a "bride-price," so that the young woman would no longer be seen as "bought and paid for." In addition, women were to be free to choose their partners.

Not surprisingly, this generated much resentment, particularly on the part of fathers of unmarried women who resented losing the bride-price they had been counting on, and fuelled resistance to the leftist government. Therefore, plans for further reforms, such as permitting women to sue for divorce and introducing family courts where women could sue to obtain their rights, never materialized. Instead, a rebellion by the fundamentalist Muslamic Mujahidin broke out, supported by Pakistan, Saudi Arabia, and Iran. Because the USSR intervened on the side of the government, the rebels even received U.S. backing. The rebellion was eventually successful but was followed by a disastrous civil war until the Pakistan-backed Taliban fighters, mainly religious students recruited from the refugee camps in that country, restored their brand of law and order, which amounted to the harsh-est Islamic dictatorship in the Muslim world today.

The laws and regulations imposed during the Taliban regime in the 1990s included prohibiting girls and women to attend formal schools, to seek jobs, to walk on the streets alone, to talk to strangers, or to go shopping unaccompanied by a male relative. They also were not permitted to wear clothes made of soft or rustling material, or to appear in pub-lic without a proper veil. Residents were even required to paint the windows of their homes black, or to put up screens, so that no female could be seen from the outside. These restrictions are all the more serious because the Taliban is considerably more efficient in enforcing their restrictive rules than the Mujahidin had been. There have been reports of women being beaten and threatened with hanging if they did not conform to these reg-ulations.

Among the most egregious consequences of these restrictions is that girls are unable to obtain the education they would need to become doctors or nurses and that, with rare ex-ceptions, women who are already qualified are not allowed to practice, and certainly not in hospitals. At the same time, male doctors are not permitted to touch or even see the bodies of female patients. Further, women are forbidden to seek care in public hospitals, and most cannot afford the cost of the few private clinics that are available. As a result, health care for women and girls has effectively vanished and so their medical needs frequently go un-attended.[†]

The conditions under which these people live today can perhaps be best expressed by those who live there. A 20-year-old woman is quoted as saying: "Before the Taliban came, I was a medical student. I wore jeans, I listened to music, I went to the movies and I went out with my friends. All that was prohibited overnight. Whenever I go out I have to wear the chadri, which gives me a headache. And my brother or my father must come with me. It's un-bearable."[†] Not as common, but far more horrifying, is a report that a medical doctor had to

---

[†] Drevillon, "Kabul."

watch his cousin die without being able to help her. He described the enforcers of current rules as "savages who do not consider women human beings," and explained why he had no children: "If by some misfortune I had a daughter, what kind of future would she have?"[†]

The situation in Afghanistan has led to widespread condemnations, including those by the United Nations and by the Nobel Peace Prize–winning organization Physicians for Human Rights. Such organizations have reported that Muslims throughout the world have been appalled by the actions of the Taliban and that Afghan women expatriates are at the forefront of international campaigns for the restoration of women's rights. Even Iran, which had itself experienced a fundamentalist revolution some years earlier, condemned their extreme repression of women. Nonetheless, these policies continue, and there is no guarantee that it could not happen elsewhere.

[†] Drevillon, "Kabul."

A COMPARISON OF THE UNITED STATES TO OTHER ECONOMICALLY ADVANCED COUNTRIES

The same trends that have occurred in the United States since the 1970s—women's rising labor force participation; improvements in the female–male wage ratio; a modest reallocation of housework among men and women; declining marriage rates; rising rates of divorce, cohabitation, and births to unmarried mothers—have occurred in other economically advanced countries, although in some, particularly Japan, to a more limited extent. For the most part, the explanations for these trends are similar to those offered for the United States in earlier chapters, such as changes in fertility, educational attainment, labor market opportunities, and social attitudes. However, other factors, including differences in government policies (for instance the availability and amount of family leave and whether or not it is with pay, the availability of publicly funded day care, the design of tax policy, and variations in wage structures), are particularly important in explaining cross-country differences in outcomes.[26]

This section provides some comparisons of policies relevant to the status of women and the well-being of their families among economically advanced countries, then goes on to examine labor market outcomes and changes in the division of housework, as well as some demographic trends, in greater detail. As previously noted, special attention is paid to Sweden and Japan because Sweden has made notable progress toward greater equality between men and women in the home as well as in the labor market, while Japan has been much slower to change.

The goal of Swedish policy has been to treat women and men, as far as possible, in the same way. Efforts have been made to discourage gender-based stereotypes at all levels of the educational system. All gender differences in public aid have been removed. Legislation has been introduced to make marriage an equal partnership; a husband is no longer required to support his wife. Full participation of women and men

---

[26] Constance Sorrentino, "The Changing Family in International Perspective," *Monthly Labor Review* 113, no. 3 (March 1990): 41–58; Siv Gustafsson, "Public Policies and Women's Labor Force Participation: A Comparison of Sweden, West Germany and the Netherlands," in *Investment in Women's Human Capital,* ed. T. Paul Schultz (Chicago: University of Chicago Press, 1995), pp. 91–112; and Francine D. Blau and Lawrence M. Kahn, "Wage Structure and Gender Earnings Differentials: An International Comparison," *Economica* 63 (supplement 1996): 29–62.

in the labor market has been established as a goal. To encourage married women to enter the labor force, the joint income tax for spouses has been eliminated (except for nonwage income) and replaced by a system of individual taxation. As discussed in Chapter 10, a joint income tax can have a considerable negative impact on work incentives, especially for wives, who are often perceived to be secondary workers. This is less true of individual taxation because the applicable marginal tax rate a married woman faces upon entering the labor market is lower than the rate she would have to pay as the second earner.[27]

As discussed in Chapter 7, antidiscrimination legislation is also expected to affect labor market outcomes. Since the 1970s, legislation has been enacted throughout the OECD countries, including Sweden in 1980 and 1992, and Japan in 1985, to ensure women's rights to equal opportunity in employment.[28] It is interesting to note, however, that in this respect all the OECD countries lagged considerably behind the United States, which adopted similar measures in the early 1960s.[29]

On the other hand, all economically advanced countries, with the exception of the United States, have mandated paid leave for mothers or for both parents, though most are less generous than in Sweden. It may be recalled that it was only in 1993 that the United States mandated that firms provide workers with unpaid family leave of 12 weeks and that the mandate is restricted to firms with more than 50 employees. The Swedish government provides 12 months of paid leave, which may be taken by either parent at 80 to 90 percent replacement pay, and an additional three months with a flat-rate payment. Workers are guaranteed their jobs when they return, and may work part-time (six hours per day) until the youngest child is eight. Similarly, in other industrialized countries, the duration of leave is often 10 to 12 months and wage replacement is often in excess of 80 percent. In addition, employers in these countries frequently go beyond compliance with government mandates in accommodating workers with dual responsibilities; many not only provide opportunities for part-time work, but also the option of flexible schedules and alternative work arrangements. Even Japan's policy is somewhat more generous than that of the United States. Mothers are entitled to 14 weeks leave at 60 percent replacement pay and either parent may take unpaid leave (including time spent on maternity leave) for up to a year;[30] part-time work has expanded considerably in Japan as well.[31]

As we noted in Chapter 10, the opportunity to take parental leave can be quite important to women in maintaining their attachment to the labor force and to the firm.

---

[27] In fact, in Sweden, any amount a wife earns by entering the labor market actually leaves the couple with more disposable income than the same amount of *additional* earnings her husband would be able to make by working harder or working longer hours. See Diane Sainsbury, "Taxation, Family Responsibilities, and Employment," in *Gender and Welfare State Regimes,* ed. Diane Sainsbury (Oxford: Oxford University Press, 1999), pp. 185–210.

[28] Sweden's 1992 Equal Opportunity Act superseded the 1980 Act. Among its provisions, employers must try to obtain a well-balanced sex distribution in various jobs and must make it easier for workers to combine work and family. For a brief overview, see Helina Melkas and Richard Anker, *Gender Equality and Occupational Segregation in Nordic Labour Markets* (Geneva: ILO, 1998), chap. 4.

[29] For a list of the laws passed, see OECD, *Women and Structural Change: New Perspectives* (1994).

[30] OECD, "Long-Term Leave for Parents in OECD Countries," *Employment Outlook* (July 1995): 171–202; and OECD, *Women and Structural Change.*

[31] Susan Houseman and Machiko Osawa, "Part-Time and Temporary Employment in Japan," *Monthly Labor Review* 118, no. 10 (October 1995): 10–18.

Indeed, relatively short leaves have been found to increase women's labor force attachment and wages. However, the situation may be more ambiguous for longer leaves. Such leaves (over 3 months in one study) have been found to have a modest negative effect on women's wages.[32] Moreover, since leaves tend to be disproportionately taken by mothers, even when available to both parents, they may reinforce traditional gender roles in the family and thus help to perpetuate differences in labor market outcomes between men and women. Also, as noted earlier, part-time work frequently provides less opportunity for upward mobility than full-time work. Thus, the generous provision for extended leaves and part-time employment may raise issues similar to those discussed in the debate about the "mommy track" in the United States.[33]

Only a few countries provide subsidized child care, but some of these have committed a large amount of resources for this purpose. For instance, in Sweden, heavily subsidized day care is available for more than half of preschool children. Still, quantity demanded exceeds quantity supplied at existing prices, so spaces must be rationed.[34] France subsidizes child care even more generously. There, all children ages three to five are eligible for free preschool, and virtually all of them do attend whether or not the mother is employed. In addition, one-half of two-year-olds and one-fourth of children under two are in day care centers. By way of contrast, in the Netherlands, public policies do not encourage women with young children to work for pay, and there is hardly any organized day care; in Germany full-day, out-of-home care is also rare.[35]

Wage-setting institutions also differ considerably by country. This has implications for wage structures and, hence, workers' standard of living, wage inequality, and the gender earnings ratio. The manner in which wages are determined may be highly centralized, as is true in many European countries, including Sweden. These countries have very strong unions; and wages are largely determined by a collective bargaining process.[36] On the other hand, the process can be quite decentralized, as in the United States, where only a very small proportion of the labor force belongs to labor unions and wages are largely determined by employers. Only 18 percent of workers in the United States are covered by collective bargaining agreements as compared with rates of 69 to 89 percent

---

[32] Christopher J. Ruhm, "The Economic Consequences of Parental Leave Mandates: Lessons from Europe," *Quarterly Journal of Economics* 113, no. 1 (1998): 285–317.

[33] See, for instance, Elena Bardasi and Janet C. Gornick, "Women and Part-Time Employment: Workers' 'Choices' and Wage Penalties in Five Industrialized Countries," Luxembourg Income Study Working Paper No. 223 (March 2000); and Maria Hemstrom, "Gender Differences in Pay Among Young Professionals in Sweden," in *Women's Work and Wages,* ed. Inga Persson and Christina Jonung (London: Routledge, 1998), pp. 145–72.

[34] For a historical perspective, see Anita Nyberg, "From Foster Mothers to Child Care Centers: A History of Working Mothers and Child Care in Sweden," *Feminist Economics* 6, no. 1 (March 2000): 5–20.

[35] Siv Gustafsson and Frank P. Stafford, "Three Regimes of Child Care: The United States, the Netherlands, and Sweden," in *Social Protection Versus Economic Flexibility,* ed. Rebecca M. Blank (Chicago: University of Chicago Press, 1994), pp. 333–61; Sheila B. Kamerman and Alfred J. Kahn, *Child Care, Parental Leave and the Under 3's* (New York: Auburn House, 1991); and Eileen Trzcinski, "Family Policy in Germany: A Feminist Dilemma?" *Feminist Economics* 6, no. 1 (March 2000): 21–44.

[36] Where unions are strong, collective bargaining agreements are often extended to nonunion workers and may also cause nonunion firms to voluntarily imitate union pay structures. See, for instance, Francine D. Blau and Lawrence M. Kahn, "International Differences in Male Wage Inequality: Institutions Versus Market Forces," *Journal of Political Economy* 104, no. 4 (August 1996): 791–837.

in the Scandinavian countries and 47 percent in Britain.[37] Wage structure refers to the relative wages paid for various labor market qualifications, such as the proficiency of a qualified crafts worker compared to an untrained laborer, or a college graduate compared to someone who only finished high school. In the United States today, less-skilled workers tend to receive lower relative pay than in most other economically advanced countries, at least in part because they are less likely to have their pay boosted by union wage scales. As a relatively low wage group in all countries, women disproportionately benefit from wage policies to "bring up the bottom" of the wage distribution.

Finally, most of these countries, with the exception of the United States, provide child benefits or a child allowance to families based on the number of children, without regard to income. In the United States, the tax system provides child exemptions but this serves to reduce taxes for higher-income families more than for those in lower tax brackets, and is of no help to families whose income is so low that they pay no income tax. While a child tax credit was introduced in 1997, this measure also provides no benefit to low-income families who have no federal tax liability. Further, most of these countries, unlike the United States, offer either national health insurance or a national health care system. Such programs reduce the cost of rearing children and potentially improve the health and, thus, the productivity of the present as well as future work force.

LABOR FORCE PARTICIPATION

Table 11.2 shows that between 1977 and 1997 women's labor force participation increased appreciably, while men's participation decreased somewhat in all of the economically advanced countries included in the table. Nevertheless, there were substantial cross-country differences, especially in women's participation rates. In 1997, participation rates were highest in Sweden and the other Scandinavian countries, with rates around 75 percent, followed closely by the United States at 71 percent.[38] A recent estimate for Russia, which is included in Table 11.2 for comparison purposes, suggests that its female labor force participation rate was only around 66 percent, though as noted earlier, there is some question about the reliability of this figure. Labor force participation rates were somewhat lower in countries such as Japan, Germany, and Austria, and considerably lower in southern Europe, including Greece, Spain, and especially Italy, where the rate was only 44 percent. Part of the reason for the particularly low rates in these latter countries may be their emphasis on the traditional family, related to their religious orientation, which would be expected to reduce labor force participation.[39]

---

[37] Francine D. Blau and Lawrence M. Kahn, *U.S. Labor Market Performance in International Perspective: The Role of Labor Market Institutions* (New York: Russell Sage Foundation, forthcoming,); and Blau and Kahn, "International Differences in Male Wage Inequality."

[38] Surprisingly, Sweden was hardly a leader in this respect in earlier days; married women there were not granted the legal right to enter into work contracts and to control their own earnings until 1920, as discussed in Christina Jonung and Inga Persson, "Combining Market Work and Family," in *Population, Economy and Welfare in Sweden,* ed. Tommy Bengtsson (New York: Springer-Verlag, 1994), pp. 37–64. For further discussion of cross-country trends, see Dora L. Costa, "From Mill Town to Board Room: The Rise of Women's Paid Labor," *Journal of Economic Perspectives* 14, no. 4 (fall 2000): 101–22.

[39] For Italy, Daniela Del Boca also points to a "mismatch" between the type of jobs married women with children would prefer and those that are available in "Environmental Effects on the Participation and Fertility Decisions of Married Women," unpublished working paper, University of Turin (September 1998).

The high labor force participation rate in Sweden is not surprising in view of all their policies intended to encourage women to enter and remain in the labor force.[40] At the same time, it should be noted that women at home caring for their young children, who are covered by Sweden's generous parental leave policy, are considered to be in the labor force. If these women were excluded, the female participation rate would be more in line with that of the United States. Further, a larger proportion of women in Sweden work part-time.[41] Nonetheless, the official labor force participation rate does provide a useful measure of women's attachment to the labor force because the leave policy gives mothers the right to return to their former job and to retain their seniority.

As noted earlier, Japan's female participation rate lies in the middle of the OECD countries included in Table 11.2. However, the nature of women's employment is different there in important respects from other economically advanced countries, including the United States. For instance, as of 1998, in the United States only 6 percent of women in the labor force were self-employed and less than 1 percent were unpaid family workers. In Japan, approximately 8 percent of employed women were self-employed and as many as 11 percent were unpaid workers in a family enterprise. Self-employed women earn less than others even in the United States and this is all the more true in Japan, where a good many do piece-rate work at home, which is generally both low-paying and dead-end work.[42] As for unpaid family workers, these women have no independent income over which they have control.

Lifetime participation patterns of women in Japan differ as well. As can be seen in Figure 11.3, in Japan there is an M-shaped pattern; labor force participation decreases during the childbearing years but increases to a second peak later. As we have seen, this pattern also prevailed in the United States between World War II and the early 1970s. Today, however, there is an inverted U pattern in the United States and especially in Sweden; labor force participation rises during the early years, reaches a plateau, and eventually declines as retirement age approaches. It has been argued that Japan is merely lagging behind these other countries and will eventually "catch up." It may be, however, that for historical and cultural reasons, the same factors that were operative in the United States and in Sweden are not operative in Japan, so that extrapolation based on their experience may be inappropriate.[43]

---

[40] Finland and Denmark have similar policies, with correspondingly high rates of labor force participation. For international comparisons, see Gustafsson and Stafford, "Three Regimes of Child Care"; Gustafsson, "Public Policies and Women's Labor Force Participation"; and Janet C. Gornick, Marcia K. Meyers, and Katherin E. Ross, "Public Policies and the Employment of Mothers: A Cross National Study," *Social Science Quarterly* 79, no. 1 (March 1998): 35–54.

[41] Christina Jonung and Inga Persson, "The Misleading Tale of Participation Rates in International Comparisons," *Work, Employment and Society* 7, no. 2 (1993): 259–74; Marit Ronsen and Marianne Sundstrom, "The Choice Between Full-Time Work for Norwegian and Swedish Mothers," in *Economics of the Family and Family Policies,* ed. Inga Persson and Christina Jonung (London: Routledge, 1997), pp. 159–77; and Janet C. Gornick, "Gender Equality in the Labor Market," in *Gender and Welfare State Regimes,* ed. Diane Sainsbury (Oxford: Oxford University Press, 1999), pp. 210–42.

[42] Data are computed from the International Labour Organization, *Yearbook of Labour Statistics,* 1987 and 1999. For a discussion of this issue, see Mary Brinton, *Women and the Economic Miracle: Gender and Work in Postwar Japan* (Berkeley: University of California Press, 1993).

[43] Brinton, *Women and the Economic Miracle,* p. 43.

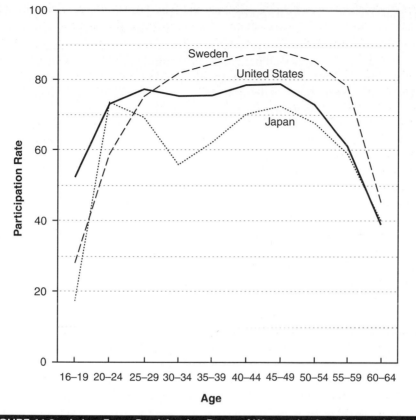

FIGURE 11.3 Labor Force Participation Rates of Women by Age, Selected Countries, 1998

Source: International Labour Organization *Yearbook of Labour Statistics,* 1999.

OCCUPATIONS

As previously noted, Table 11.3 shows that there is considerable sex segregation by occupation in the more economically advanced countries. Because Sweden's policies have been quite successful not only in raising women's labor force participation, but also in increasing their attachment to the labor force, one might have expected the index of segregation to be relatively low there. In fact, it is the highest of the economically advanced countries included in the table and quite a bit higher than that for the United States.[44] Women in Sweden continue to be disproportionately employed in traditionally female clerical and white-collar jobs, most notably in the government sector, and in health care, education, and child care. Moreover, while women are well represented in medicine as well as in diplomacy, few have degrees in other traditionally male fields such as engineering, the natural sciences, and mathematics.[45] Evidence on the trend in occupational segregation in Sweden is mixed, with one study finding a modest decline, and another

---

[44] Melkas and Anker, *Gender Equality and Occupational Segregation,* chap. 5–8.

[45] Sherwin Rosen, "Public Employment and the Welfare State in Sweden," *Journal of Economic Literature* 34, no. 2 (June 1996): 729–40; and "Strindberg's Nightmare," *Economist,* 8 June 1996, p. 55.

finding that it has not changed appreciably since the 1960s.[46] This stands in marked contrast to the United States, where the index decreased substantially over the same period.

Part of the explanation for so little change in occupational segregation in Sweden is that women are relatively well paid in predominantly female occupations. In addition, for a long time Sweden put far more emphasis on policies that encourage women to enter the labor market than on opening up new careers for them.[47] Since the first anti-discrimination legislation was not passed until 1980, it will likely take some time before its impact is fully realized. It has also been suggested that because of laws that permit long stretches of part-time work after childbirth, a high percentage of women are in jobs where that is acceptable, and these often tend to be "women's jobs." However, others argue that working part-time is likely to be less disruptive to maintaining and accumulating market skills than dropping out entirely.

Equally surprising as the high index of occupational segregation in Sweden is the low index for Japan. Part of the explanation for this is that a considerably larger share of the labor force in Japan is still employed in agriculture and blue-collar jobs and these happen to be occupations that employ a relatively large percentage of women in that country. It should also be noted that the low representation of women in white-collar positions in Japan is a disadvantage for them because many of these jobs are among the most prestigious and well paid, and are also most likely to be associated with permanent employment.[48]

Japan's lack of concern with gender equality is well illustrated by the fact that the government did not promulgate an equal opportunity employment law until 1985, when it became more acceptable to business as a consequence of internal labor shortages that made the hiring of women advantageous, and when external forces, including pressure from the United Nations, became difficult to ignore. Even then, employers were only asked to comply voluntarily and the government was not given the right to impose sanctions or financial penalties. Therefore it is not surprising that segregation *within* broad occupational categories remains very high in Japan. This may be a result of the weak enforcement mechanisms associated with the legislation, and may change as a result of some modifications that were made in 1999. In the meantime, while more university-educated women are now being hired as clerical and technical workers, they are largely assigned to lower status, mommy-track type positions and are rarely offered "core employment," which not only provides job security but also is typically associated with regular wage increases and steady promotions. This is in sharp contrast to their male counterparts, even those who perform the same work.[49] There is also evidence that Japanese

---

[46] Britta Hoem finds virtually no change in "The Way to the Gender-Segregated Swedish Labour Market," in *Gender and Family Change in Industrialized Countries,* ed. Karen O. Mason and An-Magritt Jensen (Oxford: Clarendon Press, 1995), pp. 279–96, while Anker finds a modest decline for the 1970s and 1980s in *Gender and Jobs,* chap. 13.

[47] Jane Lewis and Gertrude Astrom, "Equality, Difference, and State Welfare: Labor Market and Family Policies in Sweden," *Feminist Studies* 18, no. 1 (spring 1992): 59–87; and Jonung and Persson, "Combining Market Work and Family."

[48] Brinton, *Women and the Economic Miracle*; and Anker, *Gender and Jobs,* chap. 9.

[49] Kathleen Cannings and William Lazonick, "Equal Employment Opportunity and the 'Managerial Woman' in Japan," *Industrial Relations* 33, no. 1 (January 1994): 44–69; Helen A. Goff, "Glass Ceilings in the Land of the Rising Sons: The Failure of Workplace Gender Discrimination Law and Policy in Japan," *Law and Policy in International Business* 26, no. 4 (summer 1995): 1147–68; and Linda N. Edwards, "The Status of Women in Japan: Has the Equal Employment Opportunity Law Made a Difference?" *Journal of Asian Studies* 5, no. 2 (summer 1994): 217–40.

women employed in the manufacturing sector, who are more likely than men to be temporary workers or day laborers, bear a disproportionate burden of employment declines during economic downturns.[50]

Some part of the gender inequality in Japan's multiple-track system may be caused by the decision of many women themselves to remain in the less demanding tracks, in anticipation of having a family. This would be understandable because in Japan, core employment positions have been tailored for men in traditional families, who do extremely little housework. These positions require a degree of commitment that would be hard for women with families to manage. This system makes it difficult for women to take maternity leave and maintain their status in the firm, so that they are, in effect, faced with the choice of family or career. Moreover, husbands' employment in these positions means that they would find it difficult to share in household tasks and child care, even if they wanted to do so.

Furthermore, Japan permits employment practices that would be labeled as discriminatory in the United States. For instance, Japanese women may be explicitly evaluated in terms of highly subjective and personal criteria, including appearance, and may even be questioned regarding their virginity. Once employed, even women with substantial seniority may be asked to serve tea.[51] It is likely a reflection of Japanese culture that despite these practices, few lawsuits have been filed. Conditions may, nevertheless, be changing. Decisions such as a recent landmark case in which a local court found in favor of a young woman who was fired for refusing her boss's sexual advances may encourage more women to take legal action.[52]

THE GENDER WAGE GAP

Table 11.4 compares the ratio of women's to men's earnings in nonagricultural employment for the period from 1967 to 1998 in a number of economically advanced countries. It offers a useful overview, although a number of qualifications must be borne in mind. The data used are for hourly earnings, with the exception of Japan and the United States, for which only monthly and weekly earnings are available, respectively. Because weekly and monthly earnings are influenced by the number of hours and days worked, the earnings differential is likely to be larger than if hourly wages were compared. Also, data for the United States are reported for full-time workers, which is not the case for all countries, and the data are not precisely comparable in other respects either. In some cases they are for subgroups of workers, such as employees in manufacturing in Sweden and nonsupervisory workers in Australia. There are also differences in the definition of wages among various countries; they may or may not include income in kind, family allowances, and so on. In addition, in the 1990s, there were some substantial changes made to several earnings series. For this reason, both old and new earnings series are provided for Japan and the United Kingdom. In interpreting these data, it is important to keep in mind that one can only be confident about trends *within* each given series.

---

[50] Susan N. Houseman and Katharine G. Abraham, "Female Workers as a Buffer in the Japanese Economy," *American Economic Review* 83, no. 2 (May 1993): 45–51.

[51] Goff, "Glass Ceilings in the Land of the Rising Sons." See also Nicole Gaouette, "When a College Degree Means a Job Serving Tea," *Christian Science Monitor,* March 1998, p. B4.

[52] Victor Fic, "Sexual Harassment Still a Fixture in the Japanese Office," *Tokyo Business Today,* December 1994, p. 24.

| TABLE 11.4 | Ratio of Women's to Men's Hourly Earnings, Nonagricultural Workers, Selected Years, 1967–1998 | | | | | | | |

	1967	1970	1975	1980	1985	1990	1994	1998
Australia	n.a.	0.65	0.84	0.86	0.87	0.88	0.91	0.89
France	n.a.	n.a.	0.79	0.79	0.81	0.81	0.81	0.82[a]
Japan, Series I[b]	n.a.	0.52	0.56	0.54	0.52	0.50	n.a.	n.a.
Japan, Series II[b]	n.a.	n.a.	n.a.	n.a.	n.a.	n.a.	0.62	0.64
Germany (West)[c]	0.69	0.69	0.72	0.72	0.73	0.73	0.74	0.74
Norway[d]	0.74	0.75	0.78	0.82	0.84	0.86	0.87	0.88
Sweden[d]	0.78	0.80	0.85	0.90	0.90	0.89	0.90	0.90[a]
Switzerland	0.61	0.66	0.67	0.68	0.67	0.68	0.67[a]	n.a.
United Kingdom, Series I[e]	0.60	0.60	0.68	0.70	0.69	0.70	0.72	n.a.
United Kingdom, Series II[e]	n.a.	n.a.	n.a.	n.a.	0.74[a]	0.76	0.79	0.80
United States	0.62	0.62	0.62	0.64	0.68	0.72	0.76	0.77[a]

[a] Most recent year available.

[b] Japan Series I includes family allowances and midyear bonuses. Series II is regular scheduled cash earnings, private sector.

[c] Manufacturing sector 1994 and onwards.

[d] Manufacturing sector.

[e] Among the differences, U.K. Series I includes agricultural workers, while Series II does not.

n. a. Not available.

Source: Francine D. Blau and Lawrence M. Kahn, "The Gender Earnings Gap: Some International Evidence," in *Differences and Change in Wage Structure*, ed. Richard B. Freeman and Lawrence F. Katz (Chicago: University of Chicago Press, 1995) with updated data from Heather Joshi and Jane Waldfogel. Based on data from various issues of ILO, *Yearbook of Labour Statistics*; and U.S. Bureau of Labor Statistics, *Handbook of Labor Statistics*.

As shown in the table, in all these countries women are paid less than men, but also the ratio of women's to men's earnings has risen at least since the mid-1960s in all of them. Interestingly, however, the most rapid increases did not occur at the same time, nor did the ratios reach the same level in each of these countries. This is best shown in Figure 11.4, which highlights trends for a subgroup of countries: the United States, Sweden, Japan, the United Kingdom, and Australia. As discussed in Chapter 5, the ratio of usual median weekly earnings of full-time workers in the United States increased fairly steadily between 1975 and 1993 to a high of .77. For several years afterwards the ratio fell, but by 1999 it had rebounded to its earlier high.

In the case of Sweden, on the other hand, most of the gains had occurred by the early 1980s and the ratio has remained virtually unchanged since then at about .90, still the highest for any country for which data are available. In a number of other countries, including the United Kingdom, the ratio also increased substantially early on, then stagnated for some time, only to show recent evidence of a renewed increase.[53] As seen in Table 11.4, a new earnings series for the United Kingdom (UK

---

[53] For evidence on the pay gap in the United Kingdom, see, for instance, Peter Dolton, Donal O'Neill, and Olive Sweetman, "Gender Differences in the Changing Labor Market," *Journal of Human Resources* 31,

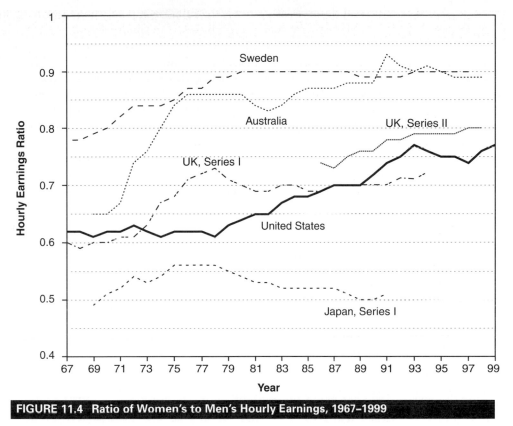

FIGURE 11.4 Ratio of Women's to Men's Hourly Earnings, 1967–1999

Source: See Table 11.4.

Series II), indicates a steady rise from .74 in 1986, when the new series began, to .80 in 1998.

In Australia, the ratio increased sharply from 1970 to 1976, as a result of the introduction of comparable worth (see the inset on Australia), and has risen somewhat further since. The earnings ratio in Japan has historically been lower than in other economically advanced countries and declined from .56 in 1975 to .50 in 1990. However, a newly available series, which cannot be directly compared with the earlier one, indicates that the gender wage ratio in Japan increased from .62 in 1994 to .64 in 1998, offering at least some preliminary evidence of a recent upward trend.

In sum, the overall trend for the selected countries provides some indication of relative wage gains for women in all countries, although the period of rapid increases of women's wages relative to those of men appears to have ended for the time being. It is difficult to sort out the reasons why this is the case, and they need not be the same for all countries. It is, however, likely that changing wage structures within countries, the degree of enforcement of antidiscrimination laws, and changes in the relative qualifications of women workers play a greater or lesser role.

no. 3 (summer 1996): 549–65; and Gerald Makepeace, Pierella Paci, Heather Joshi, and Peter Dolton, "How Unequally Has Equal Pay Progressed Since the 1970s? A Study of Two British Cohorts," *Journal of Human Resources* 34, no. 3 (summer 1999): 534–56.

Another issue that deserves attention is the relationship between the female–male earnings ratio and occupational segregation by sex. On the one hand, for the reasons discussed in Chapter 7, one might expect a negative relationship; the higher the degree of segregation the lower the female–male earnings ratio. On the other hand, if earnings for women are relatively high in women's fields, they may have less incentive to enter men's occupations so that one could observe both a high degree of segregation and a relatively high earnings ratio.[54] This might occur in countries with strong union policies that serve to compress the overall wage structure, as has been the experience in Sweden, or where "comparable worth" policies have been adopted.

It is also worthy of note that the earnings ratio in the United States falls in the middle of the selected countries, rather than closer to the top. This is surprising because the United States was among the first to promulgate antidiscrimination laws, beginning in the early 1960s, and U.S. women tend to have similar, if not higher, levels of human capital relative to men as compared to women in these other countries. The answer to this puzzle lies in the fact that the size of the gender gap is determined not only by differences across countries in women's qualifications and in the extent of discrimination against them but also by international differences in wage structure or the returns that the labor market sets for skills and employment in higher-wage occupations and industries.[55] Since women tend to have less experience than men, on average, and to be concentrated in low-wage sectors, the gender wage gap will be greater when the return to experience or the reward to employment in higher-wage occupations and industries is especially large.

A comparison with Sweden is particularly instructive. As we have seen, the gender wage ratio is much higher in Sweden than in the United States. One recent study suggests this is due to differences between the two countries in wage structure, with Sweden's reward structure being considerably more compressed than that in the United States.[56] This is largely caused by the role unions play in Sweden in determining wages. Since women tend to be disproportionately represented among lower-paid workers, wage compression in Sweden raises women's wages relative to men's. In contrast, U.S. wage setting is highly decentralized and characterized by considerable wage differences between lower-skilled and higher-skilled workers. This study suggests that the United States would have as high a gender wage ratio as Sweden if it had the same compressed wage structure. In fact, the high level of U.S. wage inequality raises the gender gap in the United States compared to many other economically advanced countries. In contrast, the even larger gender gap in Japan (which was not included in this study) likely reflects

---

[54] This is consistent with findings by Donald J. Treiman and Patricia A. Roos, "Sex and Earnings in Industrial Society: A Nine-Nation Comparison," *American Journal of Sociology* 89, no. 3 (April 1984): 612–46. They found that there was almost no effect of occupational distribution on earnings but quite substantial and complicated effects of rates of return for men and women within major occupational groups.

[55] For a more detailed discussion, see Francine D. Blau and Lawrence M. Kahn, "Gender Differences in Pay," *Journal of Economic Perspectives* 14, no. 4 (fall 2000): 75–100; and Blau and Kahn, "Wage Structure and Gender Earnings Differentials." For additional recent evidence, see Francine D. Blau and Lawrence M. Kahn, "Understanding International Differences in the Gender Pay Gap" unpublished working paper, Cornell University (March 2001).

[56] Blau and Kahn, "Wage Structure and Gender Earnings Differentials"; Francine D. Blau, "Where Are We in the Economics of Gender? The Gender Pay Gap," in *Women's Work and Wages,* ed. Christina Jonung and Inga Persson (New York: Routledge, 1998), pp. 15–35; and Francine D. Blau and Lawrence M. Kahn, "The Gender Earnings Gap: Some International Evidence," in *Differences and Changes in Wage Structures,* ed. Richard B. Freeman and Lawrence F. Katz (Chicago: University of Chicago Press, 1995), pp. 105–43.

factors specifically related to gender, including the high degree of segregation of women within broad occupational categories there.

Thus, the international evidence suggests that wage structure is an important factor influencing differences across countries in the size of the gender pay gap. This implies that changes over time in the extent of wage inequality are likely to have an impact on trends in the gender gap within countries as well. As you will recall from Chapter 8, the U.S. labor market experienced a dramatic increase in wage inequality over the 1970s and 1980s, driven to a great extent by rising returns to labor market skills and rewards for employment in predominantly male occupations and industries. This poses a question as to how the sizable reduction in the gender pay gap during that time was achieved since women remain less skilled than men, on average, and concentrated in female sectors. As we have seen, women were able to counter the unfavorable effects of the changes in overall wage structure by improvements in "gender-specific" factors: women's qualifications increased relative to men's and the unexplained portion of the pay difference between men and women with similar qualifications declined.[57]

The U.S. experience raises the question of to what extent wage gains for women in other countries were influenced by shifts in overall wage inequality versus changes in their qualifications and labor market treatment. Studies of this issue for Sweden and the United Kingdom provide an interesting comparison. Notably, in both cases, gender-specific factors were found to be of most importance in explaining the trends in the gender wage gap over time within each country. This is true even in the case of Sweden, where that country's solidarity wage policy did result in a dramatic narrowing of wage inequality. Although it was found that wage compression was an important factor in explaining the reduction in the gender wage gap between 1968 and 1974 (a period of particularly large reductions in wage inequality), taking the 1968 to 1981 period as a whole, gender-specific factors were nonetheless found to be of paramount importance.[58]

In sum, it appears that international differences in wage structure are an important factor in explaining differences across countries in the gender pay gap and, especially, for explaining the surprisingly large pay gap in the United States. However, within given countries for which this question has been considered, gender-specific factors have been found to be the primary determinant of changes in the pay gap over time. The reason wage inequality is so important in explaining international differences in the gender gap but not in explaining changes over time within a country may be because differences in the extent of wage inequality across countries are considerably larger than any changes in wage inequality that have occurred within countries. It is also the case that, as noted in Chapter 8, rising wage inequality has been associated with demand shifts that favored white-collar workers in general. Given the traditional male predominance in blue-collar jobs, this shift likely benefited women relative to men, as did increased computer use, both because women are more likely than men to use computers at work and because computers restructure work in ways that de-emphasize physical strength.

[57] Francine D. Blau and Lawrence M. Kahn, "Rising Wage Inequality and the U.S. Gender Gap," *American Economic Review* 84, no. 2 (May 1994): 23–28; and Francine D. Blau and Lawrence M. Kahn, "Swimming Upstream: Trends in the Gender Wage Differential in the 1980s," *Journal of Labor Economics* 15, no. 1, pt. 1 (January 1997): 1–42.

[58] For Sweden, see Per-Anders Edin and Katarina Richardson, "Swimming with the Tide: Solidarity Wage Policy and the Gender Earnings Gap," Office of Labour Market Policy Evaluation Working Paper 1999:3 (Uppsala, Sweden, June 1999); and for the United Kingdom, see Dolton, O'Neill, and Sweetman, "Gender Differences in the Changing Labor Market."

Comparable Worth in Australia

Australia has the distinction among economically advanced countries of having one of the highest female-to-male earnings ratios. As described here, the implementation of equal pay and, particularly, of comparable worth in Australia in the 1970s largely explains why.[*]

Australia has an unusual wage determination system, markedly different from that in the United States. In Australia, minimum-wage rates for occupations are determined by government wage tribunals. Up to 1969, the Australian pay structure explicitly discriminated against women. Until 1950, female award rates were set at 54 percent of male rates; that year they were raised to 75 percent. In 1969, the concept of equal pay for equal work was implemented, and the award rate was raised to 100 percent. In 1972, the federal tribunal moved toward "comparable worth" by deciding that the "equal pay for equal work" concept should be expanded to "equal pay for work of equal value" in order to cover employees in predominantly female jobs.

As can be seen in Table 11.4 and Figure 11.4, the result of the implementation of these policies, particularly of comparable worth, was a 19 percentage point increase in the gender earnings ratio among nonsupervisory workers, from 65 percent in 1970 to 84 percent by 1975. Moreover, during these years, the unemployment rate of women in Australia continued to fall relative to that of men, and employment continued to grow faster for women than for men. Critics have nevertheless suggested that implementation of comparable worth caused women's employment to increase less rapidly than would have been expected if their wages had not risen.[†] One explanation for the fairly small negative impact of comparable worth on women's employment is thought to be that the persistent high degree of occupational segregation constituted a substantial barrier to the replacement of women by men as the wage gap declined.

Clearly, the Australian institutional structure, with its reliance on wage tribunals to determine occupational pay rates, facilitated implementation of pay equity. As we have seen, this policy substantially reduced the gender wage gap, while apparently having little effect on women's employment. Nevertheless, an overall gender gap in Australian pay remains. Among the possible explanations, it has been suggested that it may be difficult to properly value women's work in female-dominated occupations such as health professionals, clerical workers, and entry sales workers, because no other occupations offer "obvious" comparison groups. Also, women are concentrated in part-time jobs and the pay in these jobs is often lower than in full-time employment. Other explanations have focused on the possibility that institutional features in the wage-setting process may hamper further improvements in women's relative pay.[‡]

---

[*] This account of comparable worth is based on Robert G. Gregory and Vivian Ho, "Equal Pay and Comparable Worth: What Can the U.S. Learn from the Australian Experience?" (The Australian National University, Centre for Economic Policy Research, Discussion Paper No. 123, July 1985); R. G. Gregory and A. E. Daily, "Can Economic Theory Explain Why Australian Women Are So Well Paid Relative to Their United States Counterparts?" in *Women's Wages: Stability and Change in Six Industrialized Countries, International Review of Comparative Public Policy, Research Annual*, ed. Steven L. Willborn (Greenwich, CT: JAI Press, 1991), pp. 3:81–125; and Mark Killingsworth, *The Economics of Comparable Worth* (Kalamazoo, MI: W. E. Upjohn Institute for Employment Research, 1990). See also Francine D. Blau and Lawrence M. Kahn, "The Gender Earnings Gap: Some International Evidence," in *Differences and Changes in Wage Structures*, ed. Richard B. Freeman and Lawrence F. Katz (Chicago: University of Chicago Press, 1995), pp. 105–43; Bob Gregory, "Labour Market Institutions and the Gender Pay Ratio," *Australian Economic Review* 32, no. 3 (September 1999): 273–78; and Jeff Borland, "The Equal Pay Case—Thirty Years On," *Australian Economic Review* 32, no. 3 (September 1999): 265–72.

[†] See Killingsworth, *The Economics of Comparable Worth.*

[‡] Borland, "The Equal Pay Case."

DEMOGRAPHIC TRENDS

Table 11.5 provides data on trends in fertility, births to unwed mothers, marriage, and divorce for selected economically advanced countries. As would be expected in view of the increasing labor force participation rate of women in all these countries, presumably at least in part in response to increased economic opportunities outside the home, the table shows that fertility rates have declined in most of them, and are now at or, in many cases, well below the replacement rate of 2.1 births per woman.[59] Sweden was a notable exception when it early on experienced both a rising fertility rate and a rising labor force participation rate, most likely as a result of its generous policies of paid family leave and subsidized day care, which encouraged women to enter the labor force and reduced the private cost of having children.[60] However, more recently, Sweden's fertility rate has fallen to 1.5, in line with those of other economically advanced countries.

Marriage rates have declined in all countries since the 1970s, but as of 1992, the most recent year for which comparable data across countries are available, they were still very high in the United States at 14 per 1,000 population aged 15 to 64. In Japan, on the other hand, the marriage rate fell considerably during the period, from 14 to 9. Among the explanations for the trend in Japan is not only the growing economic independence of women, but also the especially low status of married women; husbands spend con-

TABLE 11.5   Demographic Trends, 1970 to 1990s

	Total Fertility Rate[a]			Births to Unmarried Women (%)		Marriage Rate per 1,000 Population Age 15–64		Divorce Rate per 1,000 Married Women	
	1970	*1992*	*1998*	*1970*	*1992*	*1970*	*1992*	*1970*	*1992*
Canada	2.3	1.9	1.6	10	24[b]	14	10[b]	6	11
Denmark	1.9	1.8	1.8	11	46	12	9	8	13
France	2.5	1.8	1.8	7	33	12	7	3	9[b]
Germany	2.0	1.3	1.4	6	15	12	8	5	7
Italy	2.4	1.3	1.2	2	7	11	8	1	2
Japan	2.1	1.5	1.4	1	1	14	9[b]	4	6[b]
Netherlands	2.6	1.6	1.6	2	12	15	9	3	9
Sweden	1.9	2.1	1.5	18	50	8	6	7	12
United Kingdom	2.4	1.8	1.7	8	31	14	8[b]	5	12
United States	2.5	2.1	2.1	11	30	17	14	15	21

[a] Total fertility rate has same definition as in Table 9.2, but is divided by 1,000 here.

[b] Figures are for 1991.

Source: World Bank, *World Development Report*, 1994; World Bank, *World Development Indicators*, 2000; U.S. Bureau of the Census, *Statistical Abstract of the United States*, 1995 and 2000.

[59] It has, however, been argued that the present total fertility rate may understate the actual rate of childbearing of women in the United States and other industrialized countries because it does not adequately account for the continuing rise in the age of childbearing. See John Bongaarts, "Fertility Decline in the Developed World: Where Will It End?" *American Economic Review* 89, no. 2 (May 1999): 256–60.

[60] Family leave in Sweden and some other Western European nations was intended to encourage fertility. See Gustaffson and Stafford, "Three Regimes of Child Care."

siderable time working for their employer and do very little housework. Further, wives in Japan, as compared to those elsewhere, have a particularly strong cultural obligation to care for both their own and their husbands' elderly parents.[61] Interestingly, Sweden's marriage rate was only about one-half the U.S. rate in 1970 and has remained at a very low level, perhaps because getting married there continues to offer few tax or other advantages in this highly secular society.

In many economically advanced countries, while marriage rates have declined, rates of cohabitation have risen. The increase in cohabitation is a major factor in explaining the dramatic rise in births to unmarried mothers, although the degree to which these factors are associated varies considerably across countries.[62] For the mid-1990s, it is estimated that around 30 percent of Swedish women ages 25 to 29 were cohabiting as compared with about 10 percent of U.S. women of the same age, and 7 percent of U.S. women overall.[63] As shown in Figure 11.5, the proportion of births to unwed mothers in 1992 was as high as 50 percent in Sweden and 30 percent in the United States, and both these figures rose somewhat more by the latter part of the 1990s. It has been estimated that in Sweden virtually all of the babies born to unmarried mothers were actually brought home to live with cohabiting fathers. For the United States, a recent study found that the comparable figure was 40 percent.[64] The high rates of cohabitation in Sweden, in the rest of the Nordic countries, and increasingly elsewhere, suggest that most men and women continue to choose to live with partners, even as marriage rates decline, albeit without long-term legal (or religious) commitments. Undoubtedly such couples, much like those who do marry, are seeking companionship, but they probably also want to reap gains from economies of scale, and, to an extent, specialization and exchange. Rates of cohabitation for Japan are not known, but are likely to be very low, given the fact that births to unwed mothers, which tend to increase with cohabitation, are negligible.

Family structure has also changed since the 1970s because of rising divorce rates, though the extent to which they have risen varies considerably by country. In 1992, for instance, the United States had the highest divorce rate at 21 per 1,000 marriages. Rates in Canada, the United Kingdom, and Sweden were lower, ranging from 11 to 13 per 1,000, although they had risen during the preceding years. Divorce rates had also increased in Italy and Japan but at 6 per 1,000 or less were considerably below the rates in these other countries. The low divorce rate in Italy is widely believed to be the result of the strong influence of the Vatican. In Japan, it is most likely due to the adherence of married couples to traditional family patterns.

---

[61] T. R. Reid, "Male, Mid 20's Desperately Seeks Mate," *Washington Post Weekly Edition,* 27 September–3 October 1993, p. 19.

[62] For instance, Kathleen Kiernan observes that in the Netherlands and Germany, the rate of unwed births is lower than would be expected based on cohabitation rates, while the reverse is true for the United Kingdom and Ireland in "Cohabitation in Western Europe: Trends, Issues and Implications," unpublished working paper, London School of Economics (October 2000).

[63] Figures discussed but not reported in Table 11.5 are from Kiernan, "Cohabitation in Western Europe"; U.S. Census Bureau, *U.S. Statistical Abstract: 1999,* table 66; and Table 9.3. See also Sorrentino, "The Changing Family in International Perspective."

[64] The figures for Sweden and the United States, respectively, are from Sorrentino, "The Changing Family in International Perspective"; and Larry Bumpass and H.-H. Lu, "Trends in Cohabitation and Implications for Children's Family Context in the United States," *Population Studies* 54, no. 1 (March 2000): 29–41.

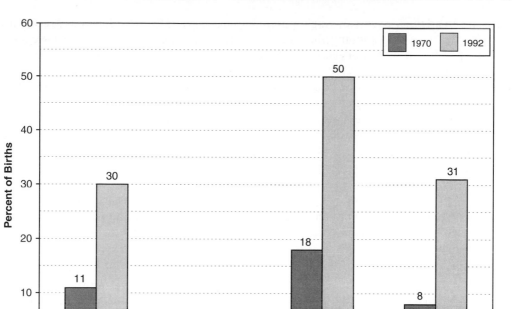

FIGURE 11.5   Births to Unmarried Women, 1970 and 1992

Families headed by single parents, most often mothers, also appear to be most common in the United States, but can be found in growing numbers in other economically advanced countries, with Japan once again the exception. Regrettably, statistics for different countries are not entirely comparable because some include cohabitors with children among married couples while others do not, and age limits for children differ. In the United States and most of these other countries, women most often become single mothers as a result of divorce or marital separation, but the proportion of never-married mothers has been growing. In the early to mid-1990s, women maintained 25 percent of families with dependent children in the United States and 22 percent in the United Kingdom, as compared with rates of 14 to 16 percent in Sweden, Canada, the Netherlands, and Germany. Consistent with what we have already seen, the figure for Japan was only 10 percent.[65]

---

[65] Figures are from Majella Kilkey and Jonathan Bradshaw, "Lone Mothers, Economic Well-Being and Policies," in *Gender and Welfare State Regimes,* ed. Diane Sainsbury (Oxford: Oxford University Press, 1999), pp. 147–84. Notably, the relatively high rate of single parenthood in Sweden is not due to high rates of cohabitation because cohabitors are counted as married couples, not single-parent families. On the other hand, in the United States, some "single-parent" families may be cohabitors with children. See Sorrentino, "The Changing Family in International Perspective."

In all these countries, single-parent families, especially those headed by women, are among the most economically vulnerable. Social policies to assist them vary considerably.[66] In Great Britain, single mothers are provided benefits on the assumption that they will stay home until their children reach age 16. There is no pressure on them to obtain a job or even job training. In Sweden, on the other hand, single mothers, like all adults, are encouraged to work for pay and are given sufficient support to do so, including parental leave and day care. In addition, Sweden has a child support "advance" system, which provides awards to custodial parents when the other parent fails to pay the agreed upon amount of support. In fact, in Sweden the overall poverty rate for women is slightly lower than that for men, in stark contrast to the United States, where women's poverty rates are well in excess of men's. Among the explanations for this is that Sweden has a lower proportion of single mothers, as discussed earlier, along with a more generous transfer system for single-parent families. In addition, Sweden has a more highly compressed wage structure, leading to a smaller proportion of single women earning below-poverty wages.[67]

HOUSEWORK

Data on housework presented in Table 11.6 provide further evidence on the relative position of women in various countries. In all countries, men do considerably less housework than women. However, with the exception of Japan, men are increasingly spending more time in housework and fewer hours in market work, while the trend has been the opposite for women.[68] As would be expected in view of women's high rates of labor force participation and the egalitarian policies in Sweden, men spend 56.9 percent as much time on housework as women, a higher percentage than in any of the other countries. Nonetheless, even in Sweden, women still do most of the housework.[69] Part of the reason may be that subsidized day care is in short supply. In the United States men spend only 45.2 percent as much time on housework as women, which is less than in Sweden, but in the same range.

In sharp contrast, men spend only 11.3 percent as much time on housework as women in Japan, substantially less than men in any of the other countries in Table 11.6. Indeed, it has been found that only 10 percent of Japanese husbands even feel an obligation to share in housework.[70] These findings are consistent with women's more traditional role in Japanese society. There is evidence that even among young Japanese fam-

---

[66] For a discussion of these issues, see Siv Gustafsson, "Single Mothers in Sweden: Why Is Poverty Less Severe?" in *Poverty, Inequality, and the Future of Social Policy,* ed. Katherine McFate, Robert Lawson, and Julius Wilson (New York: Russell Sage Foundation, 1995), pp. 291–325; and Sheila B. Kamerman and Alfred J. Kahn, "What Europe Does for Single-Parent Families," *Public Interest* no. 93 (fall 1988): 70–80.

[67] Karen Christopher, Paula England, Katherin Ross, Timothy Smeeding, and Sara McLanahan, "The Sex Gap in Poverty in Modern Nations: Single Motherhood, the Market, and the State," Joint Center for Poverty Research Working Paper No. 107 (November 1999).

[68] Francine D. Blau and Marianne A. Ferber, "Women's Work, Women's Lives: A Comparative Economic Perspective," in *Women's Work and Women's Lives: Continuing Struggle Worldwide,* ed. Hilda Kahne and Janet Z. Giele (Boulder, CO: Westview Press, 1992), pp. 28–46.

[69] Janeen Baxter reaches the same conclusion in "Gender Equality and Participation in Housework: A Cross-National Perspective," *Journal of Comparative Family Studies* 28 (autumn 1997): 220–47.

[70] Reid, "Male, Mid-20s."

TABLE 11.6   Time Spent on Housework and Market Work (hours per week)

		Total Work		Housework		Market Work	
		Men	Women	Men	Women	Men	Women
Denmark	1964	45.4	43.4	3.7	30.1	41.7	13.3
	1987	46.2	43.9	12.8	23.1	33.4	20.8
Finland	1979	57.8	61.1	13.8	28.6	44.0	32.5
Hungary	1977	63.7	68.9	12.9	33.8	50.8	35.1
Japan	1965	60.5	64.7	2.8	31.5	57.7	33.2
	1985	55.5	55.6	3.5	31.0	52.0	24.6
Norway	1971	53.2	54.6	15.4	41.3	37.8	13.3
	1980	51.0	50.6	16.8	33.0	34.2	17.6
Sweden	1984	57.9	55.5	18.1	31.8	39.8	23.7
United States	1965	63.1	60.9	11.5	41.8	51.6	18.9
	1981	57.8	54.4	13.8	30.5	44.0	23.9
Soviet Union[a]	1965	64.4	75.3	9.8	31.5	54.6	43.8
	1985	65.7	66.3	11.9	27.0	53.8	39.3

[a] The sample is from the city of Pskov.

Source: Adapted from F. Thomas Juster and Frank P. Stafford, "The Allocation of Time: Empirical Findings, Behavioral Models, and Problems of Measurement," *Journal of Economic Literature* 29, no. 2 (June 1991): 477. Adapted by permission.

ilies in which the wife is well-educated, holds a full-time job, and has children, three-fourths of the wives do most, and often virtually all, of the housework. On the other hand, there is more equal sharing of household responsibilities in such families in the United States, with only one-third of wives doing most of the household tasks. [71] Thus, there has been little progress toward more egalitarian marriages in Japan.

SUMMARY ON ECONOMICALLY ADVANCED COUNTRIES

This discussion indicates that real progress toward economic equality has been made by women in economically advanced countries over the last several decades but also that the gains have been somewhat uneven and that the rate of advance may be slowing. For instance, in Sweden, with its very high rate of labor force participation and high female-to-male earnings ratio, women still hold very different jobs than men. In Japan, women have been entering the labor market, but have not fared well in most other respects, and the earnings gap has not declined appreciably. And, in the United States, large numbers of single mothers continue to live in poverty. Government policies, along with distinctive cultural and historical differences, no doubt help to explain the considerable differences among countries. We still have much to learn about this, and also about ways to ensure the continuation of progress.

---

[71] Myra H. Strober and Agnes Miling Kaneko Chan, *The Road Winds Uphill All the Way: Gender, Work, and Family in the United States and Japan* (Cambridge, MA: MIT Press, 1999), p. 108

DEVELOPING COUNTRIES

Women in developing countries merit special attention because they face major challenges and difficulties as a result of the extremely low income level of these countries.[72] More than three-fourths of the world's population lives in these countries, but they receive only 15 percent of the income, while the wealthiest 20 percent receives 85 percent of the income.[73] Not surprisingly, therefore, developing countries are generally characterized by an extremely low standard of living, high rates of infant mortality, short life expectancy, and high rates of illiteracy. In many instances, they also have very high fertility rates that tend to exacerbate some of the other problems. Thus, most individuals in developing countries live in extremely difficult circumstances. In addition, there is evidence that most often women bear a disproportionate share of the burdens of economic and social deprivation.[74]

It is not possible here to fully cover women's situation in the Third World. To do so would require a book considerably larger than this one because there is great variation in many respects among the different countries, as shown by Table 11.1 and the accompanying discussion. Some can only euphemistically be called "developing," while others are soon likely to be reclassified as "economically advanced." There are also great differences in religion, customs, geographic location, and economic resource base, among other factors.[75]

In this section we take a fairly modest approach and focus on four issues of great importance to women in developing countries. The first is education, which potentially offers the promise of raising women's economic status, as well as enhancing prospects for development. Second is the very controversial question of public policies intended to influence the birthrate. These can be extremely problematic, whether they restrict access to information about means for controlling family size or attempt to force women to limit the number of children they have. Third is the issue of child labor, which has received considerable attention in the United States and internationally. Finally, we consider the potential role of microcredit in improving women's economic status.

EDUCATION AS THE PATHWAY TO EMPOWERMENT

The days when it was widely accepted that it was unnecessary to send daughters to school are long behind us. In affluent countries, and in a growing number of developing countries, virtually all girls and boys attend primary schools and, increasingly, secondary schools as well. Nonetheless, in many of the poorest countries, where even primary education is still far from universal, it is generally girls who are least likely to obtain even a minimal

---

[72] A number of very useful books and many interesting articles on women in developing countries have been written since the 1970s. The pioneering work among these was Ester Boserup, *Women's Role in Economic Development*. More recently, see, for instance, Ester Boserup, *Economic and Demographic Relationships in Development* (Baltimore: Johns Hopkins University Press, 1990); T. Paul Schultz, ed., *Investment in Women's Human Capital* (Chicago: University of Chicago Press, 1995); and papers in *World Development* 20, no. 11 (November 1992).

[73] United Nations, *Human Development Report 1995*.

[74] Tuovi, "Economic Development and the Feminization of Poverty."

[75] Boserup, "Obstacles to Advancement of Women."

amount of education, and illiteracy rates among women in these countries continue to be substantially higher than among men. It is estimated that of the approximately 876 million illiterate adults in the world, two-thirds are women.[76] More specifically, as Figure 11.1 shows, the illiteracy rate for adult women in South Asia is nearly 60 percent, and rates in Sub-Saharan Africa and the Middle East and North Africa are close to 50 percent.

Women's educational attainment has been historically lower than men's for several reasons. From a purely economic standpoint, the opportunity cost of sending daughters to school is often greater in terms of productive output forgone because, in many cases, girls do more household work and market work than boys. Even more important, sons will become the breadwinners and in most cultures are expected to support their parents in their old age, while girls marry into another family and have no independent means to support their parents. In addition, customs and religion have played an important role. In some cultures, education, beyond a minimal level, may actually reduce a woman's chance of marrying. In any case, education is likely to postpone marriage, which could defer and possibly reduce the bride-price (still common in many countries) when she does marry.[77] Finally, as we have noted in the case of economically advanced countries, to the extent that girls receive a smaller return on their educational investments than boys due to a shorter expected work life, it may be that they opt for less of it.

The low level of women's education in the developing countries, and particularly in the poorest among them, is most unfortunate. For education, more than anything else, is the key to improving the well-being of women, their families, and the country as a whole. There is, however, reason to believe that this situation is changing. There is growing awareness that education is not only the key to independence and empowerment for women, but that it gives them both the incentive and ability to reduce their fertility, as well as the opportunity to better contribute to their families. Hence, there is also increasing recognition that there are substantial links between women's education and a country's standard of living and general well-being. Indeed, as noted earlier, world conferences, including the 1995 conference in Beijing, have made women's education the centerpiece of policy.[78]

In terms of private benefits, education enhances women's potential for entry into the labor force, raises their potential earnings, and also increases women's productivity in the home. For one, they will be able to read labels and instructions, and are thus likely to be better informed about nutrition, proper hygiene, and health care, including birth control. Indeed, one recent study finds that mother's numeracy and literacy skills learned in school improve their children's health outcomes.[79] In addition, parental education has a significant influence on children's schooling, with some evidence that mother's schooling has a particularly important impact on daughters.[80] Finally, because the education of

---

[76] United Nations, *The World's Women 2000,* chap. 4.

[77] M. Anne Hill and Elizabeth M. King, "Women's Education and Economic Well-Being," *Feminist Economics* 1, no. 2 (summer 1995): 21–46.

[78] Seth Faison, "Women of the World Disperse: To What?" *New York Times,* 17 September 1995, sec. 4, p. 3.

[79] Paul Glewwe, "Why Does Mother's Schooling Raise Child Health in Developing Countries?" *Journal of Human Resources* 34, no. 1 (winter 1999): 124–59.

[80] Hill and King, "Women's Education and Economic Well-Being"; and Thomas, "Like Father, Like Son." See also T. Paul Schultz, "Investments in the Schooling and Health of Women and Men: Quantities and Returns," in *Investments in Women's Human Capital,* ed. T. Paul Schultz (Chicago: University of Chicago Press, 1995), pp. 15–50.

women increases the opportunity cost of raising children, they are likely to have fewer of them, allowing parents to devote more of their limited resources to each child.

From a societal perspective, education of women is an effective means of encouraging voluntary family planning that is vastly preferable to government coercion such as that pursued in China. Furthermore, as already suggested, it makes for a healthier, better-trained, and hence a more productive work force. One study offers evidence that countries in which the percentage of female-to-male enrollment is less than 75 percent can expect to have levels of GDP that are approximately 25 percent lower than in countries that are similar except for the gender difference in education.[81] Greater literacy among women in developing countries may also be one way to stem the rapid spread of the HIV/AIDS virus, which has already infected millions of teens and adults there, because it enables them to learn more about the vital importance of practicing safe sex, information they can pass on to the rest of their family. Even so, education is certainly not a panacea for this epidemic, for HIV/AIDS is a problem among educated people in industrialized countries as well. Last but not least, education is necessary for a better informed citizenry, so crucial to the achievement and functioning of a healthy democracy.

As also discussed earlier, women's education and economic empowerment not only shifts more resources toward children but reduces the considerable imbalance between resources devoted to boys as compared to girls. Women's education might even change the nature of societies themselves, where substantial gender inequality has stubbornly persisted. For instance, following the 1995 conference in Beijing, the emerging Islamic women's rights movement set forth access to education in basic religious writings and laws of Islam as one of its major goals. Currently only men read and interpret the religious texts. To the extent that women's interpretations differ and have some influence, this might lead to changes in women's roles.[82]

Governments throughout the developing world, as well as women's organizations, are beginning to take note of the larger societal benefits of women's education.[83] For instance, in Thailand, successive governments have emphasized the importance of women's health and education, with the result that female illiteracy in that country was 7 percent in 1998, well below the rate for its region (East Asia and the Pacific) of 22 percent. In addition, Thailand's fertility rate fell from 5.5 births per woman in 1970 to 1.9 in 1998.

FERTILITY AND POPULATION CONTROL

As already noted, fertility and population control[84] in developing countries are critically linked not only to women's economic status but to the economic viability of these countries, especially the poorest among them. The methods developing countries use to control fertility range from encouraging the voluntary use of contraceptives and other methods of family planning to coercive population control enforced by the government. China, for instance, has combined policies encouraging contraception and sex educa-

---

[81] Hill and King, "Women's Education and Economic Well-Being."

[82] Barbara Crossette, "Women's Rights Gaining Attention Within Islam," *New York Times,* 12 May 1996, sec. 1, p. 3.

[83] Ihsan Bouabid, "Women-Education: Nothing Less than a Human Right," Inter Press Service, 8 September 1995.

[84] For a more theoretical treatment, see T. Paul Schultz, "Demand for Children in Low-Income Countries," in *Handbook of Population and Family Economics,* ed. Mark R. Rosenzweig and Oded Stark (Amsterdam: Elsevier, 1997), pp. 1A:349–430.

tion, with strict limits on the number of children couples are permitted to have. The policies adopted by India have been less coercive but at times the government's tactics have not been far from compulsion.[85] In many other developing countries, family planning is entirely voluntary and increasingly common, while in yet others, family planning, including contraceptive use, is quite rare. Among the reasons: there may be a lack of adequate information about contraceptives; they may not be readily available or too costly; there may be concern about side effects; or, in some cases, there may be religious strictures that specifically discourage their use.

Expanding women's education is an exceptionally promising solution to controlling population growth because it enhances women's economic status while also reducing fertility, without using any form of compulsion. As already discussed, this is true in large part because the opportunity cost of raising children is greater for more highly educated women, and also because it gives women greater access to information about methods of birth control, at least where there is not strong resistance from an established religion or government policy.

As we have seen, the data in Table 11.1 and Figure 11.2 provide evidence that considerable strides have been made in much of the developing world over the last 20 years in reducing fertility. Only in Sub-Saharan Africa and in some Middle Eastern and North African countries do rates remain at five to six children per woman. Clearly, these high rates are a major point of concern.

A second concern is that in a handful of countries efforts to control fertility, whether voluntary or coercive, appear to have substantially increased the ratio of men to women in the population. This has especially been the case in countries in East and South Asia where there is a strong preference for boys over girls. This preference is evident in the historically lopsided sex ratio, particularly in China and India, which indicates the presence of considerably more men than women, as compared to what would be expected based on normal rates of infant mortality and subsequent survival rates.[86] In some cases, this has been the result of outright infanticide and, in other cases, of girls being given less food and medical care than boys, the latter amounting to what has been termed *passive infanticide*, so that the family would have more resources for present or future sons. With the advent of new technology, sex-selective abortion has become an increasingly common part of birth control in these countries as well as in South Korea and Taiwan. This practice likely explains why the sex ratio at birth has become so lopsided in all four of these nations. While around 104 to 107 boys would normally be expected to be born for every 100 girls, in the early 1990s this figure was estimated to be 119 in China, 112 in India, 114 in South Korea, and 110 in Taiwan.[87] The impact has been especially pronounced in second and higher-order births, suggesting that if a couple already has a girl, they are much less willing to accept another.

---

[85] Regarding China, see Ansley J. Coale and Judith Bannister, "Five Decades of Missing Females in China," *Demography* 31, no. 3 (August 1994): 459–79; and on India, see Amartya Sen, "Fertility and Coercion," *University of Chicago Law Review* 63, no. 3 (summer 1996): 1035–61.

[86] See, for instance, Fred Arnold, Minja Kim Choe, and T. K. Roy, "Son Preference, the Family-Building Process and Child Mortality in India," *Population Studies* 52 (November 1998): 301–15.

[87] Figures are from Sheila Tefft, "A Rush to Rob the Cradle—of Girls," *Christian Science Monitor,* 2 August 1995. See also Coale and Bannister, "Five Decades of Missing Females in China"; Rick Weiss, "Anti-Girl Bias Rises in Asia, Studies Show; Abortion Augmenting Infanticide, Neglect," *Washington Post,* 11 May 1996, p. A1; "Ultrasound Effects," *Economist,* 5 August 1995, p. 34; and "6.3 Brides for Seven Brothers," *Economist,* 19 December 1998, pp. 56–58.

Fewer baby girls translates into a shortage of marriageable women; a phenomenon that has already been observed in China, for example.[88] For this reason, among others, by the early 1990s a number of countries, including China, South Korea, and India, officially banned the practice of sex-selective abortion, though it is not clear that this ban has been effective. Ironically, the declining supply of women, which has resulted from a bias against women, may eventually increase their value in the "marriage market."[89]

It is particularly interesting to take a closer look at China, which has just over 20 percent of the world's population, and thus the distinction of being the most populous country in the world. Around 1980, it instituted a particularly rigid policy of "one couple, one child" for urban residents unless the first child was incapacitated or died. In rural areas, couples were allowed to try again if their first child was a daughter. The one-child policy was pursued through political and social pressure, as well as by creating powerful economic incentives. Couples with a single child were entitled to such perks as cash bonuses, longer maternity leave, better child care, and preferential housing. However, couples who had more than the number allowed, particularly in the city, could face steep fines or the loss of their jobs or other benefits.

This policy was rigorously administered until 1983, when it became clear that it was not accepted by the public and was thus eased somewhat. Greater emphasis was placed on other ways of reducing fertility such as later marriage and education about contraception. Also, more control was given to autonomous regions and provinces in setting their own policies, with exemptions for minority groups.[90] By the late 1990s, while residents of the largest cities were still restricted to one child with potentially large sanctions for doing otherwise, the rule was less aggressively enforced and lower monetary penalties were imposed in smaller cities, leading some residents to pay fines in exchange for permission to have additional children.[91]

As Table 11.1 shows, family planning policies in China, initially introduced in the 1970s, reduced fertility substantially from 5.8 children per woman in 1970 to 1.9 in 1998.[92] The decline has been greatest in urban areas, where about one-third of the population lives, presumably because of tighter government control and greater penalties.[93] Fertility declined much less in rural areas, where the majority of the population lives, in part because families there are more economically dependent on their children, particularly their sons, as is the case in many traditional societies. In addition, un-

---

[88] "China's Mania for Baby Boys Creates Surplus of Bachelors," *New York Times,* 16 August 1994, pp. A1, A8.

[89] It has been argued that another possible effect of parents' preference for sons, along with a preference for children who eventually marry, is that it may lead to a society in which upper-class families have boys because they have a good chance in life and a good chance to marry, while lower-income parents tend to choose daughters, who would have a good chance to marry men who are as well or better off than they are. See Lena Edlund, "Son Preference, Sex Ratios, and Marriage Patterns," *Journal of Political Economy* 107, no. 6, pt. 1 (December 1999): 1275–304. See also Arnold, Choe, and Roy, "Son Preference."

[90] Christina Wu Harbaugh, "Geographic and Demographic Setting," in *China: A Country Study,* ed. Robert L. Worden and Andrea Matles Savada (Washington, DC: GPO, forthcoming). For a more general discussion on China, see Ray Bowen, "China: A Nation in Transition," *Congressional Quarterly, Inc.* (Washington, DC: Congressional Quarterly, Inc., 1995), pp. 155–86.

[91] Seth Faison, "Chinese Happily Break the 'One-Child' Rule," *New York Times,* 17 August 1997, pp. 1 and 6.

[92] For a quantitative analysis, see Marjorie McElroy and Dennis Tao Yang, "Carrots and Sticks: Fertility Effects of China's Population Policies," *American Economic Review* 90, no. 2 (May 2000): 389–92.

[93] Harbaugh, "Geographic and Demographic Setting"; and Rosemary Santana Cooney and Jiali Li, "Household Registration Type and Compliance with the 'One Child' Policy in China, 1979–1988," *Demography* 31, no. 1 (February 1994): 21–32.

like most urban residents, they are not entitled to old-age pensions or heavily subsidized housing.

Recently, the Chinese government has been phasing out the one-child policy for urban residents, even those living in the largest cities, though it remains the official policy. In spring 2000, a new exemption was put in place that allows for married men and women who were both "only" children to have two children. In addition to social pressure, this change was prompted by the fact that the current fertility rate in China, as is the case in many economically advanced countries, is now below replacement level.[94]

While the one-child policy in China may well have increased discrimination against girls in the short run, and women are far from achieving equality either in the household or the public sphere, there has been some progress toward gender equality there. Women's labor force participation is very high as compared with other countries in the region such as India and Japan. Moreover, the existing gender imbalances in higher education and in the occupational distribution, although substantial, appear to be an improvement over the rather lowly position of women in the past.[95] On the other hand, the evidence concerning the earnings gap between women and men is mixed, with some studies finding only a minor gap and others finding a substantial difference.[96] Another cautionary note is that in China, as in other Asian countries, women are often the first to be let go from their jobs in economic downturns.[97]

CHILD LABOR

As discussed earlier, girls often face particular challenges in developing countries because of gender bias in parental investments in education and, in some cases, even bias in the basic nutrition they receive. Compounding this, many girls as well as boys in developing countries are engaged in economic activity, defined as doing work on a regular basis for which they receive pay or that results in output the family sells in the market. The International Labour Organization (ILO) estimates that in 1996, no less than 250 million boys and girls ages 5 to 14 engaged in such economic activity worldwide, and almost one-half of these children worked full-time. A greater fraction of child laborers who are officially counted are boys. Female child laborers tend to be undercounted because many are employed as domestic workers in other people's homes, outside the realm of the official statistics, and hence "invisible."[98] If they were counted, the total child labor force would be even higher. Child labor is not considered a problem to the extent that it involves performing light tasks after school such as helping with

---

[94] Seth Faison, "China Moves Quietly to Ease Its Strict One-Child-Per-Family Rule," *St. Louis Post-Dispatch*, 3 May 2000, p. A10.

[95] C. Montgomery Broaded and Chongshun Liu, "Family Background, Gender and Educational Attainment in Urban China," *China Quarterly* 145 (March 1996): 53–86.

[96] For a review of the evidence on both sides, see Margaret Murer-Fazio, Thomas G. Rawski, and Wei Zhang, "Inequality in the Rewards for Holding Up Half the Sky: Gender Wage Gaps in China's Urban Labour Market, 1988–1994," *China Quarterly* no. 41 (January 1999): 55–88.

[97] Elisabeth Rosenthal, "In China, 35+ and Female = Unemployable," *New York Times*, 13 October 1998; and Nicholas D. Kristof, "As Asian Economies Shrink, Women Are Squeezed Out," *New York Times*, 11 June 1998, p. A12.

[98] International Labour Organization, "The Girl Child Labourer: ILO-IPEC's Response," Unit 2: Gender Issues in the World of Work, ILO/SEAPAT's OnLine Gender Learning & Information Module, www.ilo.org; and International Labour Organization, *IPEC Action Against Child Labour: Achievements, Lessons Learned and Indications for the Future 1998–1999* (Geneva: ILO, 1999).

the farm or family business or doing household chores. Rather, international attention is focusing on labor that prevents children from going to school or that involves potential physical or mental harm.

The ILO classifies cases in which children work under forced labor conditions or in bondage, face hazardous working conditions, and where children are "vulnerable," such as those under age 12, as the worst forms of child labor.[99] More often than not, children end up in these situations because their families are in a dire economic situation, not because their parents are indifferent or seek to exploit them.[100]

Estimates of girls employed as domestic workers, many starting as young as six years old, are very high. The ILO estimates that 20 percent of all Brazilian, Colombian, and Ecuadorian girls between ages 10 to 14 in urban areas are domestic workers, with much higher figures in rural areas. In many cases, these arrangements are "akin to slavery;" the girls often work very long hours, are at the mercy of the family for whom they work, and may receive no compensation apart from room and board. The labels given them are indicative of their situation: in Bangladesh they are called "bandha," which means "tied down," and in the Dominican Republic they are termed "puerta cerrada" servants, which means "closed door."[101]

Helping girl domestic workers is one of the goals of the ILO's efforts. This has proven to be a difficult task, however, because the prevailing norm is that domestic work is women's work, regardless of the working conditions or the individual's age. Nevertheless, programs sponsored by the ILO have been instituted in a number of countries, including Brazil, Kenya, and Pakistan, to inform these girls of their rights and raise awareness about abuse. In addition, these programs typically provide assistance in the form of education, skills training, and counseling services.[102]

With regard to the larger issue of child labor, suggested policy solutions abound, but in order for them to be successful alternative ways to solve the problem of dire poverty must be found and each country's specific cultural and economic conditions must be considered. For instance, proposals to ban imports to the United States that were produced in developing countries using child labor may merely cause children's employment to shift from export-related industries to other sectors where conditions may be even more harmful. In one instance, just the anticipation of such policies caused many girls in Bangladesh to be forced out of work stitching carpets and into prostitution.[103] Another possibility is for developing countries, themselves, to ban child labor of any form in all sectors and seriously enforce the policy. However, any one country may well be reluctant to adopt such a policy if others do not take similar actions, because doing so unilaterally would likely make its producers less competitive and lead to a decline in employment. Further, such a policy ignores the harsh reality that, more often than not, children are employed out of economic necessity.

---

[99] U.S. Department of Labor, *By the Sweat & Toil of Children Volume V: Efforts to Eliminate Child Labor* (Bureau of International Labor Affairs, 1998), chap. 1.

[100] Allesandro Cigno and Furio C. Rosati, "Why Do Indian Children Work and Is It Bad for Them?" Institute for the Study of Labor (Bonn, Germany), Discussion Paper No. 115 (February 2000).

[101] UNICEF, "Child Domestic Work," *Innocenti Digests* 5 (1999): 1–20; and International Labour Organization, "The Girl Child Labourer."

[102] International Labour Organization, "The Girl Child Labourer."

[103] Kaushik Basu, "International Labor Standards and Child Labor," *Challenge* 42, no. 5 (September/October 1999): 80–93.

Under former President Clinton's administration, the United States proposed the establishment of a set of minimal labor standards, such as protection for workers and the right to organize, that would be universally adopted by all countries.[104] However, this policy faces considerable opposition in many developing countries, partly due to concern that it is strongly favored by protectionist lobbies in the United States whose goal is to limit competition from abroad. There is also concern as to who would enforce such standards, what sort of punitive measures would be taken if they were violated, and, as mentioned above, fear that their adoption might leave children and their families in developing countries worse off.[105] Another strategy is to make schooling compulsory, though in the poorest countries, an intermediate policy that encourages a combination of school and work may be more realistic. Such a policy would help the family to survive and also help to end the cycle of poverty because the children would at least get some education. Finally, government policies that increase families' incomes would be expected to reduce their dependence on child labor.[106] Thus, there is no simple solution, but there are ongoing international efforts lead by the ILO to at least eliminate the worst forms of child labor.[107]

MICROCREDIT FOR WOMEN: LIFELINE OR MIRAGE?

Most people are well aware that in a modern economy, businesses, large and small, are heavily dependent on credit. Funds are needed to keep an enterprise going, and even more so to expand it or to start a new one. In developing countries the amounts needed are often rather small, but have nonetheless been beyond the reach of millions of poor people, and particularly poor women, who frequently lack any contacts with potential lenders, have no collateral, and are generally regarded as poor credit risks. At the same time, demand for labor in large-scale agriculture has been declining as a result of mechanization, and demand in the emerging modern sectors is frequently entirely inadequate to absorb the rapidly growing populations. It is not surprising, therefore, that there has been growing interest in self-employment as one solution to this problem, and in the role credit can play in facilitating it. In recent years, both governments and nongovernmental organizations have begun to recognize the contribution that the extension of even very small loans could make toward increasing the earnings and raising the standard of living of the poor.[108]

Beginning with the Grameen Banks in Bangladesh, followed by the founding of similar institutions in other developing countries, including Indonesia, India, and Peru, and eventually also in depressed areas of economically advanced countries, there has been an enormous expansion of such establishments. By June 1998, the world Micro-

---

[104] International Labour Organization, "President Clinton Addresses International Labour Conference," Press Release, 16 June 1999.

[105] For a discussion of the issues, see Kaushik Basu, "Child Labor: Cause, Consequence, and Cure, with Remarks on International Labor Standards," *Journal of Economic Literature* 37, no. 3 (September 1999): 1083–119.

[106] Basu, "Child Labor."

[107] The White House, "Helping to Eliminate Child Labor and Improve the Lives of Working People in Bangladesh," Fact Sheet (20 March 2000).

[108] Interestingly, there are historic precedents in nineteenth-century Europe of similar organizations that lasted for many decades. Aidan Hollis and Arthur Sweetman found that organizations that obtained funds from depositors, especially if they were also able to adjust interest rates, were more long lasting than those that relied on charity in "Microcredit: What Can We Learn from the Past?" *World Development* 26, no. 10 (1999): 1875–89.

credit Summit reported that there were 15 million borrowers, a figure which is expected to continue to increase at an accelerating rate.[109]

One of the distinctive features of the microcredit institutions that make small loans to the poor is that they mainly extend credit to women. While the proportion of women among those obtaining loans from commercial banks is rarely above 20 percent, it is about 70 percent among those who borrow from the poverty-centered development banks, and some of them make loans only to women. This has been made possible by borrowers in local groups guaranteeing one another's loans, so that no one receives a second loan till all the first loans have been repaid. This has led to high repayment rates, often an astonishing 90 percent, which has enabled these banks not only to continue, but to expand.[110] Furthermore, because they lend at regular market rates, there is little pressure from affluent members of the community to extend loans to them, resulting in the largest share of the loans going to the poorest and most needy, many of them illiterate and unskilled women.

In addition to the loans, the microcredit institutions provide other useful services. These include sending agents to villages to collect payments and assist customers with necessary paperwork, or helping villagers organize and choose a representative who can make the trip to the bank to take care of these matters for everyone. Many microcredit institutions provide initial advice on what kind of business to start and how to run it, although they do not continue to do so once the businesses are established. The activities of the recipients of these loans range from the processing and sale of food, brewing of beer, and production of a variety of crafts, to petty trade in other items and the provision of services to affluent households as well as larger businesses.

Advocates of microcredit point to substantial evidence that the income of the women who were able to borrow these meager amounts rose perceptibly. Not only does this provide needed resources to their families, the fact that it is the wives' income that is increased should help to increase their decision-making power in the family, thus helping to improve their lives.[111] There is also evidence that other family members did a larger share of housework. Most important, perhaps, aspirations for children's education increased considerably.[112]

Even so, it would be a mistake to exaggerate the favorable effects or to ignore the reservations of critics. One critic points out that "most studies of microfinance programs have drawn their conclusions exclusively from successful borrowers in large, mature, and successful programs."[113] It has also been noted that a surprisingly large proportion

---

[109] Rosintan D. M. Panjaitan-Driodisuryo and Kathleen Cloud, "Gender, Self-Employment and Microcredit Programs: An Indonesian Case Study," *Quarterly Review of Economics and Finance* (Special Issue 1999): 769–79.

[110] Panjaitan-Driodisuryo and Cloud, "Gender, Self-Employment and Microcredit Programs," pp. 770–71.

[111] Myra Buvinic, Myra Valenzuela, and J. P. Valenzuela, "Investing in Women" (Washington, DC: International Center for Research on Women, Policy Series, 1992); Daisy Dwyer and Judith Bruce, "Introduction," in *Home Divided: Women and Income in the Third World,* ed. Daisy Dwyer and Judith Bruce (Stanford: Stanford University Press, 1988), pp. 1–19; and B. Elavia, "Women and Rural Credit," in *Capturing Complexity: An Interdisciplinary Look at Women, Households, and Development,* ed. Romy Borooah, Kathleen Cloud, Subadra Seshadri, T. S. Saraswathi, Jean T. Peterson, and Amitra Verma (New Delhi, India: Sage, 1994), pp. 151–62.

[112] Panjaitan-Driodisuryo and Cloud, "Gender, Self-Employment and Microcredit Programs."

[113] Michael J. V. Woolcock, "What Unsuccessful Cases Tell Us About How Group-Based Programs Work," *American Journal of Economics and Sociology* 58, no. 1 (January 1999): 17–42. Quote is from p. 36.

of eligible women do not choose to participate in such programs,[114] and that those who do participate rarely achieve more than a modest rise in their standard of living. Finally, the very group pressures that have been so successful in assuring high repayment rates can create serious hardships for the women who are subjected to them, especially so when in some instances husbands or other family members exploit women's success for their own purposes.[115] Therefore, microcredit should not be viewed as a panacea for either poverty or for women's inferior status. At the same time, any program that succeeds in mitigating the dire destitution and powerlessness of many women and helps to give their children a start toward a better life should not be heedlessly discarded, but should rather be seen as a useful first step toward solving these serious problems.

Genital Mutilation and Patriarchal Traditions

For some years, there has been a rising tide of condemnation of the age-old practice of genital cutting, voiced from the podiums of United Nations assemblies in Vienna, Cairo, and Beijing. Recently the United States has joined the chorus. This practice, frequently referred to as *female circumcision,* but in fact far more drastic than that term implies, dates back about 2,000 years, and continues to be widespread. It is, undoubtedly, one more indication of the strength of patriarchal tradition and of women's subservient status in the 28 countries where it is practiced.* It is most prevalent among Muslims but is also common among Christians and followers of traditional African religions; it is most general among the illiterate, but by no means unknown among those with some education, nor is it unknown among emigrants from countries where cutting has been traditionally practiced. The proportion of women who have been cut ranges from 5 in 100 in Niger to 9 out of 10 in Somalia and Mali. In these countries the practice is deeply entrenched and even accepted by a substantial number of women.

At the same time, there appears to be increasing awareness that women who are cut suffer excruciating pain, because the operation is usually performed without any kind of anesthetic and that they are deprived of normal sexual pleasure for the remainder of their lives. There are also reports that they frequently have very complicated deliveries, and that some die as a result of this cruel procedure.

Public interest in the United States was aroused by the story of Fauzija Kassindja, who arrived on these shores December 17, 1994.† She had fled her native Togo in order to avoid forced genital cutting and sought asylum in the United States. As it turned out, she spent more than a year in prison before a precedent-setting decision by the highest administra-

*The figures in this inset are from United Nations, *The World's Women 2000: Trends and Statistics* (New York: United Nations, 2000), chap. 6; and "Press Conference by United National Population Fund" (New York: United Nations, 29 June 2000). For more details regarding this practice see, Angela Neustatter, "It Cuts So Deep," *Independent* (London), 22 March 1998; and Waris Dirie and Catherine Miller, *Desert Flower: The Extraordinary Journey of a Desert Nomad* (New York: William Morrow & Co, 1998).
† Celia W. Dugger, "A Refugee's Body Is Intact but Her Family Is Torn," *New York Times,* 11 September 1996, pp. A1, B6–B7; and Celia W. Dugger, "Woman Betrayed by Loved Ones Mourns a Double Loss," *New York Times,* 11 September 1996, p. B7.

---

[114] Timothy G. Evans, Alayne M. Adams, Rafi Mohammed, and Alison H. Norris, "Demystifying Nonparticipation in Microcredit: A Population-Based Analysis," *World Development* 27, no. 12 (1999): 419–30.

[115] Aminur Rahman, "Micro-credit Initiatives for Equitable and Sustainable Development: Who Pays?" *World Development* 27, no. 1 (1999): 67–82.

tive tribunal in the immigration system reversed the decision of an immigration judge who had dismissed her story because he did not believe it and considered it irrational. As a result of publicity about this case and growing social awareness of the problem, support built for action on this matter, and in 1995 the Immigration and Naturalization Service (INS) introduced guidelines that advise asylum officers that gender-based persecution is an additional ground for asylum. Further, in 1996 Congress outlawed the practice of genital cutting in the United States. Still, this issue is not fully resolved. Advocates for refugees and some members of Congress have been adamant that current INS guidelines for those seeking asylum in the United States are insufficient because judges still have discretion over whether or not to grant asylum. Recent attention has focused on the case of Adelaide Abankwah, a refugee from Ghana, who was denied asylum by the INS in 1997 on the grounds that genital cutting was criminalized in Ghana in 1994, and is imposed now as a matter of "individual punishment," rather than as a general practice.‡ In 1999, after Ms. Abankwah had been detained for two years, the U.S. Court of Appeals overturned the earlier decision and granted her request; they agreed with her that she did have a well-grounded fear of persecution given the customs of her tribe.

One particularly vocal opponent of genital cutting has been supermodel, Waris Dirie, who spent her early life as a nomad in Somalia and was herself subjected to genital mutilation. In 1997, she was named Special Ambassador for the Elimination of Female Genital Mutilation for the United Nations Population Fund (UNFPA) and has since coauthored a book on her horrifying experience. Indeed, a growing awareness that genital mutilation is a form of violence against women has lead 10 African countries to take legislative action to address it, along with a ban by one country, though it is yet to be seen whether these governmental actions will substantially reduce the practice itself.

‡ Ginger Thompson, "No Asylum for a Woman Threatened with Genital Cutting," *New York Times*, 25 April 1999, p. B35; and *Adelaide Abankwah v. Immigration and Naturalization Service*, United States Court of Appeals for the Second Circuit, August Term 1998, Decided July 9, 1999, Docket No. 98–4304.

SUMMARY ON WOMEN IN DEVELOPING COUNTRIES

Given all their serious problems, the near-term outlook for women in developing countries may not seem overly bright. At the same time, it would be a mistake to overlook the progress that is being made. As a United Nations report notes, "the developing world has witnessed unprecedented improvement in human development in the past 30 years. It has covered as much distance during those 30 years as the industrial world did in a century."[116] The same report also states that "every country has made progress in developing women's capabilities."[117] As we emphasized, the gender gap in schooling has been declining with the growing recognition, both by individual governments and international organizations, that resources devoted to the advancement of women have a greater payoff than many other types of investments, and that growth is more rapid when gender inequality is reduced. Therefore, the emphasis of development policies may be expected to shift in this direction. Further, by and large, women have greater control over their own fertility. However, it is important to keep

[116] United Nations, *Human Development Report 1995*, p. 13.
[117] United Nations, *Human Development Report 1995*, p. 3.

in mind that women's empowerment will avail them little unless there is overall economic development. Everyone tends to benefit when governments invest more in infrastructure and transportation systems and encourage the development of business and industry. If, however, women are to share fully in the benefits of economic progress, it is also important to remove any existing barriers to their participation in the labor force.

COUNTRIES OF THE FORMER SOVIET BLOC

More than 10 years after the Soviet Union fell, women in countries that were part of the Soviet bloc for almost half a century after World War II face some problems that are more or less unique to them, much as women in developing countries do many years after colonialism ended. During the time of its dominance, the governments of the Union of Soviet Socialist Republics and its satellites in Central and Eastern Europe subscribed to Marxist ideology, including the relevant views about the role of women. The leaders who successfully carried out the revolution in Russia at the end of World War I and shaped the ideas that dominated that country during the early years viewed the relationship between men and women as inextricably entwined with the revolutionary reconstruction of society. They essentially espoused the notion that the abolition of private property and class structure is both necessary and sufficient for achieving equality between women and men. They struck down all legal discrimination against women. Equal treatment in the educational system and in the labor market was mandated. Liberal family laws were introduced, making the marriage contract egalitarian and legalized abortion readily available, though some of this legislation was later modified.[118] This was the dominant ideology of the Soviet bloc as long as it lasted.

Because there was, generally, not only full employment but often a labor shortage, doctrinal belief in labor force participation of women was reinforced by the need for them to help with the rapid industrialization that was the main goal of the regime. But for the very same reason, little progress was made in "socializing housework," the Soviet solution for women's "double burden."

Housework was to be made unnecessary by the provision of public services, from communal dining rooms to day care centers. In practice, however, much housework still needed to be done. Although there was substantial progress in providing child care in many of these countries, there were frequently long lines in stores where necessities had to be purchased and the appliances middle-class households take for granted in the economically advanced countries were often absent. Women were told that all these services would be made available as soon as higher-priority goals had been achieved. In the meantime, housekeeping continued to be a major burden and responsibility that rested squarely on the shoulders of women. For, while women were now expected to be workers as well as homemakers, there was no equivalent recognition that men could be homemakers as well as workers. Such sharing of household responsibilities was never part of the official ideology. Table 11.6, which provides figures on housework, illustrates

---

[118] This was particularly true during the Stalinist period when, for instance, abortions were made illegal, and again during later years when, in response to the very low birthrates, pro-natalist policies were introduced.

the considerable inequality in time spent on household tasks among men and women. Despite women's high rates of labor market activity, men spent only 44.1 percent as much time on housework as women, slightly less than the figure for the United States of 45.2 percent.

The results of this mixed situation were, inevitably, also mixed. On the one hand, the status of women was clearly better than it had been in earlier days, and in some respects it compared favorably with that of women in the economically advanced countries in the West. Women's labor force participation increased substantially, and stood at nearly 80 percent for a considerable period of time, well in excess of the rates in many economically advanced countries.[119] Also, occupational segregation declined, and both the amount and the kind of education women received more nearly approximated that of men. On the other hand, women continued to be concentrated in low-status, low-paying occupations, as well as in lower levels of the hierarchies within occupations. Moreover, the earnings gap appeared to be within the same range as that in market economies.[120] Nor did women succeed in penetrating the top echelons of the powerful government hierarchy.

Thus, the Marxist solution to "the woman question" left something to be desired, even in principle, and was far from satisfactory in practice. Consequently, most women in the Soviet orbit came to see their greater participation in paid work not as a right but rather as an obligation dictated by an oppressive regime and, in the satellite countries, one that was imposed by a foreign power. By the same token, women came to have an idealized view of the family as a refuge from the harsh realities of a world that was not of their own making. After "the turning point," as it was called in East Germany, or "the velvet revolution," as it was called in Czechoslovakia, it was widely assumed that many were ready to retreat to their more traditional roles as homemakers, and that women's labor force participation would decline substantially. This retreat was expected, all the more so, because of the diminution of labor market opportunities as reflected in most instances by higher unemployment rates,[121] the closing of child care centers, and in many of these countries the failure to enforce women's right to have their jobs held open during maternity and child care leaves. However, data from the late 1990s for these countries indicate that in most instances while women's labor force participation rates have declined more than men's since the economic transition, as can be seen for Russia in Table 11.2, there has not been a "tectonic shift" in the gender ratio in participation rates. Further, the proportion of women who work part-time remains very low compared to

---

[119] The figure in Table 11.2 for 1970 is 75.6 percent, but estimates have often been even higher, as noted by Elizabeth Brainerd, "Women in Transition: Changes in Gender Wage Differentials in Eastern Europe and the Former Soviet Union," *Industrial and Labor Relations Review* 54, no. 1 (October 2000): 138–62.

[120] For a comparison of women's earnings and labor market activity before and after the economic transition, see UNICEF, "Women in Transition," chap. 2 and 3. For earlier evidence, see Jacob Mincer, "Inter-Country Comparisons of Labor Force Trends and of Related Developments: An Overview," in *Trends in Women's Work, Education, and Family Building,* ed. Richard Layard and Jacob Mincer, *Journal of Labor Economics* 3, no. 1, pt. 2 (January 1985).

[121] One exception is Czechoslovakia, where the unemployment rate never reached 8 percent, and the subsequent Czech Republic, where it remained below 5 percent until 1998, though it increased subsequently. See OECD, *Employment Outlook,* 1999. For further discussion, see Robert J. Gitter and Markus Scheuer, "Low Unemployment in the Czech Republic: 'Miracle' or 'Mirage'?" *Monthly Labor Review* 121, no. 8 (August 1998): 31–37.

rates elsewhere, although it is not clear to what extent this is because women prefer working full-time or because there are few part-time jobs available. [122]

The effects of economic restructuring on the gender wage ratio in Russia and Eastern Europe have been quite varied. There is evidence that women in Russia and Ukraine have experienced a decline in their wages relative to men's, largely as a result of widening wage inequality in these countries. At the same time, women in Eastern Europe (e.g., Hungary, Poland, Czech Republic) have fared much better. While wage inequality also widened in these countries, it appears that this negative effect has been more than offset by the increase in women's return to labor market skills, resulting in an overall increase in the gender wage ratio.[123]

The fact that equality for women in the labor market, one of the main goals of feminist movements, was officially advocated by the Communist regimes also helps to explain why the numerous women's movements that have emerged in these countries are generally very small, single-issue organizations that, for the most part, are explicitly nonfeminist. In fact, "feminism, which got short shrift under communism (supposedly because it weakened the class struggle), is also under attack in post-communist Eastern Europe. Distaste for feminism is about the only thing on which there is great continuity between communism and capitalism."[124] Even so, women in these countries are pursuing a number of the same goals sought by feminist movements elsewhere.

Notably, many women's groups are agitating against abolishing the right to abortions and are putting up stiff resistance against the abolition of such family friendly policies as child care and generous paid maternity leave. Therefore it is not surprising that at least one well-informed scholar has suggested the possibility that "women's consciousness was affected by their experience of the identity of working woman as the norm: that they have greater self-esteem as a result, and are more outspoken. Such a view implies that it will be only a matter of time before they defend or attempt to regain the right to work, the right to reproductive choice, the right to political representation, the right to be heard."[125]

CONCLUSION

In this chapter, we found that women generally have lower educational attainment than men, though these differentials are smallest in the economically advanced countries and many of the countries of the former Soviet bloc and largest in developing countries. Women also tend to earn less, be segregated into different occupations, and hold fewer

---

[122] UNICEF, "Women in Transition," chap. 2 and 3. Quoted material is from p. 26.

[123] Brainerd, "Women in Transition: Changes in Gender Wage Differentials."

[124] Lynn Turgeon, "Afterword" in *Democratic Reform and the Position of Women in Transitional Economies,* ed. Valentine M. Moghadam (Oxford: Clarendon Press, 1993), pp. 353–57. See also Marianne A. Ferber and Phyllis Hutton Raabe, "Women in the Czech Republic: Feminism, Czech Style," in *Women in the Age of Transformation: Gender Impact of Reforms in Post-Socialist and Developing Countries,* 2nd ed., ed. Nahid Aslanbeigui, Steven Pressman, and Gale Summerfield (London: Routledge, forthcoming).

[125] Barbara Einhorn, *Cinderella Goes to Market: Citizenship, Gender and Women's Movements in East Central Europe* (London: Verso, 1993), p. 15.

government positions. International differences in these outcomes are the result of government policies, social custom, ideology, and religion, as well as a variety of economic factors. Women's status is particularly precarious in many of the developing countries, but almost everywhere there has been some degree of improvement.

We have also seen that government can play a crucial role in promoting education and women's participation in the labor market. In most of the developing countries, governments are making efforts to expand educational opportunity. In a number of economically advanced countries, notably the Scandinavian countries and particularly Sweden, governments have, with considerable success, used a variety of policies to encourage women's labor force participation, while also making it possible for them to take care of their families. Even there, the situation is far from perfect, mainly because occupational segregation remains high and housework continues to be divided quite unequally. Nonetheless, our review leads us to be cautiously optimistic about the outlook for women throughout the world, and also specifically about the possibility of government playing a constructive role in advancing their status.

QUESTIONS FOR REVIEW AND DISCUSSION

1. To what extent are comparisons of women's labor force participation among various countries a reliable indicator of women's contributions to the standard of living in those countries?

2. As seen in Table 11.2, women's labor force participation rates in economically advanced countries vary considerably. What economic and noneconomic factors might help to explain this?

3. What are some specific policies that might improve women's well-being in the poorest countries? What are the difficulties and challenges entailed in undertaking them?

4. How does the experience of women living in the United States, Sweden, and Japan compare in terms of the following?

    a. labor force participation

    b. occupational segregation

    c. gender wage ratio

    d. housework

4. Occupational segregation in Sweden is very high and yet it has the smallest gender earnings gap of any economically advanced country in the world. "This proves that occupational segregation does not reduce women's earnings relative to the earnings of men." Evaluate the validity of this statement.

5. A number of countries have policies intended to encourage people to have larger families, while others provide inducements to reduce family size. Would you favor either policy for the United States? Why or why not?

6. It is widely believed that government investments in women's education have societal, in addition to private, benefits. Discuss each. This is particularly important in developing countries. Why?

7. Some occupations are predominantly female in some countries and predominantly male in others. What factors might help to explain this?

Suggested Readings

Aslanbeigui, Nahind, Steven Pressman, and Gale Summerfield, eds. *Women in the Age of Transformation: Gender Impacts of Reforms in Post-Socialist & Developing Countries.* London: Routledge, 1994.

Blau, Francine D. "Gender and Economic Outcomes: The Role of Wage Structure." *Labour* 7, no. 1 (1993): 73–92.

Blau, Francine D., and Lawrence M. Kahn, "Gender Differences in Pay." *Journal of Economic Perspectives* 14, no. 4 (fall 2000): 75–100.

———. "Wage Structure and Gender Earnings Differentials: An International Comparison." *Economica* 63 (supplement 1996): 29–62.

Boserup, Ester. *Women's Role in Economic Development.* New York: St. Martin's Press, 1970.

Brainerd, Elizabeth. "Women in Transition: Changes in Gender Wage Differentials in Eastern Europe and the Former Soviet Union." *Industrial and Labor Relations Review* 54, no. 1 (October 2000): 138–62.

Brinton, Mary. *Women and the Economic Miracle: Gender and Work in Postwar Japan.* Berkeley: University of California Press, 1993.

Hill, M. Anne, and Elizabeth M. King. "Women's Education and Economic Well-Being." *Feminist Economics* 1, no. 2 (summer 1995): 21–46.

Mason, Karen Oppenheim, and An-Magritt Jensen. *Gender and Family Change in Industrialized Countries.* Oxford: Clarendon Press, 1995.

McFate, Katherine, Robert Lawson, and William Julius Wilson, eds. *Poverty, Inequality, and the Future of Social Policy: Western States in the New World Order.* New York: Russell Sage Foundation, 1995.

Melkas, Helina, and Richard Anker. *Gender Equality and Occupational Segregation in Nordic Labour Markets.* Geneva: International Labour Organization, 1998.

Mammen, Kristin, and Christina Paxson. "Women's Work and Economic Development." *Journal of Economic Perspectives* 14, no. 4 (fall 2000): 141–64.

Persson, Inga, and Christina Jonung, eds. *Economics of the Family and Family Policies.* London: Routledge, 1997.

———, eds. *Women's Work and Wages.* London: Routledge, 1998.

Sainsbury, Diane, ed. *Gender and Welfare State Regimes.* Oxford: Oxford University Press, 1999.

Schultz, T. Paul, ed. *Investment in Women's Human Capital.* Chicago: University of Chicago Press, 1995.

Strober, Myra H., and Agnes Miling Kaneko Chan. *The Road Winds Uphill All the Way: Gender, Work, and Family in the United States and Japan.* Cambridge, MA: MIT Press, 1999.

UNICEF. "Women in Transition." *Regional Monitoring Reports,* No. 6. Florence, Italy: UNICEF International Child Development Centre, 1999.

AUTHOR INDEX

SUBJECT INDEX